Praise for the Reformation Commentary on Scripture

"Protestant reformers were fundamentally exegetes as much as theologians, yet (except for figures like Luther and Calvin) their commentaries and sermons have been neglected because these writings are not available in modern editions or languages. That makes this new series of Reformation Commentary on Scripture most welcome as a way to provide access to some of the wealth of biblical exposition of the sixteenth and seventeenth centuries. The editor's introduction explains the nature of the sources and the selection process; the intended audience of modern pastors and students of the Bible has led to a focus on theological and practical comments. Although it will be of use to students of the Reformation, this series is far from being an esoteric study of largely forgotten voices; this collection of reforming comments, comprehending every verse and provided with topical headings, will serve contemporary pastors and preachers very well."

Elsie Anne McKee, *Archibald Alexander Professor of Reformation Studies and the History of Worship, Princeton Theological Seminary*

"This series provides an excellent introduction to the history of biblical exegesis in the Reformation period. The introductions are accurate, clear and informative, and the passages intelligently chosen to give the reader a good idea of methods deployed and issues at stake. It puts precritical exegesis in its context and so presents it in its correct light. Highly recommended as reference book, course book and general reading for students and all interested lay and clerical readers."

Irena Backus, *Professeur ordinaire, Institut d'histoire de la Réformation, Université de Genève*

"The Reformation Commentary on Scripture is a major publishing event—for those with historical interest in the founding convictions of Protestantism, but even more for those who care about understanding the Bible. As with IVP Academic's earlier Ancient Christian Commentary on Scripture, this effort brings flesh and blood to 'the communion of saints' by letting believers of our day look over the shoulders of giants from the past. By connecting the past with the present, and by doing so with the Bible at the center, the editors of this series perform a great service for the church. The series deserves the widest possible support."

Mark A. Noll, *Francis A. McAnaney Professor of History, University of Notre Dame*

"For those who preach and teach Scripture in the church, the Reformation Commentary on Scripture is a significant publishing event. Pastors and other church leaders will find delightful surprises, challenging enigmas and edifying insights in this series, as many Reformational voices are newly translated into English. The lively conversation in these pages can ignite today's pastoral imagination for fresh and faithful expositions of Scripture."

J. Todd Billings, *Associate Professor of Reformed Theology, Western Theological Seminary*

"The Reformers discerned rightly what the church desperately needed in the sixteenth century—the bold proclamation of the Word based on careful study of the sacred Scriptures. We need not only to hear that same call again for our own day but also to learn from the Reformation how to do it. This commentary series is a godsend!"

Richard J. Mouw, *President, Fuller Theological Seminary*

"Like the Ancient Christian Commentary on Scripture, the Reformation Commentary on Scripture does a masterful job of offering excellent selections from well-known and not-so-well-known exegetes. The editor's introductory survey is, by itself, worth the price of the book. It is easy to forget that there were more hands, hearts and minds involved in the Reformation than Luther and Calvin. Furthermore, encounters even with these figures are often limited to familiar quotes on familiar topics. However, the Reformation Commentary helps us to recognize the breadth and depth of exegetical interests and skill that fueled and continue to fuel faithful meditation on God's Word. I heartily recommend this series as a tremendous resource not only for ministry but for personal edification."

Michael S. Horton, *J. G. Machen Professor of Systematic Theology and Apologetics, Westminster Seminary, California*

"The Reformation was ignited by a fresh reading of Scripture. In this series of commentaries, we contemporary interpreters are allowed to feel some of the excitement, surprise and wonder of our spiritual forebears. Luther, Calvin and their fellow revolutionaries were masterful interpreters of the Word. Now, in this remarkable series, some of our very best Reformation scholars open up the riches of the Reformation's reading of the Scripture."

William H. Willimon, *Bishop of the North Alabama Conference of the United Methodist Church*

"The Reformation Scripture principle set the entirety of Christian life and thought under the governance of the divine Word, and pressed the church to renew its exegetical labors. This series promises to place before the contemporary church the fruit of those labors, and so to exemplify life under the Word."

John Webster, *Chair of Systematic Theology, University of Aberdeen*

"Since Gerhard Ebeling's pioneering work on Luther's exegesis seventy years ago, the history of biblical interpretation has occupied many Reformation scholars and become a vital part of study of the period. The Reformation Commentary on Scripture provides fresh materials for students of Reformation-era biblical interpretation and for twenty-first-century preachers to mine the rich stores of insights from leading Reformers of the sixteenth century into both the text of Scripture itself and its application in sixteenth-century contexts. This series will strengthen our understanding of the period of the Reformation and enable us to apply its insights to our own days and its challenges to the church."

Robert Kolb, *Mission Professor of Systematic Theology and Director of the Institute for Mission Studies, Concordia Theological Seminary*

"The multivolume Ancient Christian Commentary on Scripture is a valuable resource for those who wish to know how the Fathers interpreted a passage of Scripture but who lack the time or the opportunity to search through the many individual works. This new Reformation Commentary on Scripture will do the same for the Reformers and is to be warmly welcomed. It will provide much easier access to the exegetical treasures of the Reformation and will hopefully encourage readers to go back to some of the original works themselves."

Anthony N. S. Lane, *Professor of Historical Theology and Director of Research, London School of Theology*

"This volume of the RCS project is an invaluable source for pastors and the historically/biblically interested that provides unparalleled access not only to commentaries of the leading Protestant reformers but also to a host of nowadays unknown commentaters on Galatians and Ephesians. The RCS is sure to enhance and enliven contemporary exegesis. With its wide scope, the collection will enrich our understanding of the variety of Reformation thought and biblical exegesis."

Sigrun Haude, *Associate Professor of Reformation and Early Modern European History, University of Cincinnati*

"The Reformation Commentary on Scripture series promises to be an 'open sesame' to the biblical exegesis, exposition and application of the Bible that was the hallmark of the Reformation. While comparisons can be odious, the difference between Reformation commentary and exposition and much that both preceded and followed it is laid bare in these pages: whereas others write about the Bible from the outside, Reformation exposition carries with it the atmosphere of men who spoke and wrote from inside the Bible, experiencing the power of biblical teaching even as they expounded it. . . . This grand project sets before scholars, pastors, teachers, students and growing Christians an experience that can only be likened to stumbling into a group Bible study only to discover that your fellow participants include some of the most significant Christians of the Reformation and post-Reformation (for that matter, of any) era. Here the Word of God is explained in a variety of accents: German, Swiss, French, Dutch, English, Scottish and more. Each one vibrates with a thrilling sense of the living nature of God's Word and its power to transform individuals, churches and even whole communities. Here is a series to anticipate, enjoy and treasure."

Sinclair Ferguson, *Senior Minister, First Presbyterian Church, Columbia, South Carolina*

"I strongly endorse the Reformation Commentary on Scripture. Introducing how the Bible was interpreted during the age of the Reformation, these volumes will not only renew contemporary preaching, but they will also help us understand more fully how reading and meditating on Scripture can, in fact, change our lives!"

Lois Malcolm, *Associate Professor of Systematic Theology, Luther Seminary*

"Discerning the true significance of movements in theology requires acquaintance with their biblical exegesis. This is supremely so with the Reformation, which was essentially a biblical revival. The Reformation Commentary on Scripture will fill a yawning gap, just as the Ancient Christian Commentary did before it, and the first volume gets the series off to a fine start, whetting the appetite for more. Most heartily do I welcome and commend this long overdue project."

J. I. Packer, *Board of Governors Professor of Theology, Regent College*

"There is no telling the benefits to emerge from the publication of this magnificent Reformation Commentary on Scripture series! Now exegetical and theological treasures from Reformation era commentators will be at our fingertips, providing new insights from old sources to give light for the present and future. This series is a gift to scholars and to the church; a wonderful resource to enhance our study of the written Word of God for generations to come!"

Donald K. McKim, *Executive Editor of Theology and Reference, Westminster John Knox Press*

"Why was this not done before? The publication of the Reformation Commentary on Scripture should be greeted with enthusiasm by every believing Christian—but especially by those who will preach and teach the Word of God. This commentary series brings the very best of the Reformation heritage to the task of exegesis and exposition, and each volume in this series represents a veritable feast that takes us back to the sixteenth century to enrich the preaching and teaching of God's Word in our own time."

R. Albert Mohler Jr., *President, The Southern Baptist Theological Seminary*

"Today more than ever, the Christian past is the church's future. InterVarsity Press has already brought the voice of the ancients to our ears. Now, in the Reformation Commentary on Scripture, we hear a timely word from the first Protestants as well."

Bryan Litfin, *Associate Professor of Theology, Moody Bible Institute*

"I am delighted to see the Reformation Commentary on Scripture. The editors of this series have done us all a service by gleaning from these rich fields of biblical reflection. May God use this new life for these old words to give him glory and to build his church."

Mark Dever, *Senior Pastor, Capitol Hill Baptist Church, and Director of 9Marks.org Ministries*

"Monumental and magisterial, the Reformation Commentary on Scripture, edited by Timothy George, is a remarkably bold and visionary undertaking. Bringing together a wealth of resources, these volumes will provide historians, theologians, biblical scholars, pastors and students with a fresh look at the exegetical insights of those who shaped and influenced the sixteenth-century Reformation. With this marvelous publication, InterVarsity Press has reached yet another plateau of excellence. We pray that this superb series will be used of God to strengthen both church and academy."

David S. Dockery, *President, Union University*

REFORMATION COMMENTARY ON SCRIPTURE

OLD TESTAMENT

I

GENESIS 1–11

EDITED BY

JOHN L. THOMPSON

GENERAL EDITOR

TIMOTHY GEORGE

ASSOCIATE GENERAL EDITOR

SCOTT M. MANETSCH

IVP Academic

An imprint of InterVarsity Press
Downers Grove, Illinois

InterVarsity Press
P.O. Box 1400, Downers Grove, IL 60515-1426
World Wide Web: www.ivpress.com
E-mail: email@ivpress.com

InterVarsity Press® is the book-publishing division of InterVarsity Christian Fellowship/USA®, a movement of students and faculty active on campus at hundreds of universities, colleges and schools of nursing in the United States of America, and a member movement of the International Fellowship of Evangelical Students. For information about local and regional activities, write Public Relations Dept., InterVarsity Christian Fellowship/USA, 6400 Schroeder Rd., P.O. Box 7895, Madison, WI 53707-7895, or visit the IVCF website at <www.intervarsity.org>.

Excerpts from Balthasar Hubmaier: Theologian of Anabaptism, *edited and translated by H. Wayne Pipkin and John H. Yoder, are copyright © 1989 by Herald Press, Scottdale, PA 15683. Used by permission.*

Excerpts from The Essential Carlstadt, *edited and translated by E. J. Furcha, are copyright © 1995 by Herald Press, Scottdale, PA 15683. Used by permission.*

Excerpts from The Writings of Pilgram Marpeck, *edited and translated by William Klassen and Walter Klaassen, are copyright © 1978 by Herald Press, Scottdale, PA 15683. Used by permission.*

Excerpts from The Writings of Dirk Philips, 1504-1568, *edited and translated by Cornelius J. Dyck, are copyright © 1992 by Herald Press, Scottdale, PA 15683. Used by permission.*

Excerpts from Peter Riedemann's Hutterite Confession of Faith, *edited and translated by John J. Friesen, are copyright © 1999 by Herald Press, Scottdale, PA 15683. Used by permission.*

Excerpts from Lectures on Genesis, *chapters 1–5 and 6-14 in* Luther's Works 1-8, *edited by Jaroslav Pelikan and translated by George V. Schick et al., are © Concordia Publishing House, www.cph.org. Used by permission. All rights reserved.*

Design: Cindy Kiple
Images: Wooden cross: iStockphoto
> *The Protestant Church in Lyon: The Protestant Church in Lyon, called "The Paradise" at Bibliotheque Publique et Universitaire, Geneva, Switzerland, Erich Lessing/Art Resource, NY.*

ISBN 978-0-8308-2951-4

Printed in the United States of America ∞

Library of Congress Cataloging-in-Publication Data

Genesis 1-11 / edited by John L. Thompson.
   pages cm—(Reformation commentary on Scripture. Old
Testament; 1)
  Includes bibliographical references and index.
  ISBN 978-0-8308-2951-4 (hardcover : alk. paper)
  1. Bible. O.T. Genesis I-XI—Commentaries. I. Thompson, John Lee.
  BS1235.53.G455 2012
  222'.11077—dc23

2012009670

P	24	23	22	21	20	19	18	17	16	15	14	13	12	11	10	9	8	7	6	5	4	3	2	1
Y	33	32	31	30	29	28	27	26	25	24	23	22	21	20	19	18	17	16	15	14	13	12		

Reformation Commentary on Scripture
Project Staff

Project Editors
Brannon Ellis
Michael D. Gibson

Managing Editor
Allison Rieck

Copyeditor
Linda Triemstra

Editorial and Research Assistants
Todd Hains
Benjamin M. McCoy

Assistants to the General Editors
Gail Barton
B. Coyne
Le-Ann Little

Administrative Support
Nathan Baker-Lutz

Design
Cindy Kiple

Design Assistant
Beth Hagenberg

Typesetters
Gail Munroe
Maureen Tobey

Proofreader
Derek Lehr

Print Coordinator
Jim Erhart

InterVarsity Press

Publisher
Robert A. Fryling

Associate Publisher, Editorial
Andrew T. Le Peau

Associate Editorial Director
James Hoover

Production Manager
Anne Gerth

CONTENTS

ABBREVIATIONS

ACCS	Ancient Christian Commentary on Scripture. 29 vols. Edited by Thomas C. Oden. Downers Grove, IL: InterVarsity Press, 1998-2009.
ACW	Ancient Christian Writers: The Works of the Fathers in Translation. Mahwah, NJ: Paulist Press, 1946-.
ANF	The Ante-Nicene Fathers. 10 vols. Edited by Alexander Roberts and James Donaldson. Buffalo, NY: Christian Literature, 1885-1896. Several reprints; also available online.
bk.	book
CHB	*Cambridge History of the Bible.* 3 vols. Cambridge: Cambridge University Press, 1963-1970.
CO	Ioannis Calvini Opera quae supersunt omnia. 59 vols. Corpus Reformatorum 29-88. Edited by G. Baum, E. Cunitz and E. Reuss. Brunswick and Berlin, 1863-1900.
CRR	Classics of the Radical Reformation. 12 vols. Waterloo, ON, and Scottdale, PA: Herald Press, 1973-.
CTJ	*Calvin Theological Journal.* Grand Rapids: Calvin Theological Seminary, 1966-.
CTS	Calvin Translation Society edition of Calvin's commentaries. 46 vols. Edinburgh, 1843-1855. Several reprints, but variously bound; volume numbers (when cited) are relative to specific commentaries and not to the entire set.
CWE	Collected Works of Erasmus. 86 vols. planned. Toronto: University of Toronto Press, 1969-.
DLCPT	Digital Library of Classic Protestant Texts. Subscription database: http://alexanderstreet.com.
DMBI	*Dictionary of Major Biblical Interpreters.* Edited by Donald K. McKim. Downers Grove, IL: InterVarsity Press, 2007.
EEBO	Early English Books Online. Subscription database: http://eebo.chadwyck.com.
ET	English translation
FC	Fathers of the Church: A New Translation. 124 vols. Washington, DC: Catholic University of America Press, 1947-.
HTR	*Harvard Theological Review.* Cambridge, MA: Harvard Divinity School Press, 1908-.
LCC	The Library of Christian Classics. 26 vols. Edited by John Baillie et al. Philadelphia: Westminster, 1953-1966.
LW	Luther's Works [American edition]. 55 vols. St. Louis: Concordia; Philadelphia: Fortress, 1955-1986.

MO	Philippi Melanthonis Opera quae supersunt omnia. 28 vols. Corpus Reformatorum 1-28. Edited by C. G. Bretschneider. Halle: C. A. Schwetschke and Sons, 1834-1860.
NPNF	A Select Library of the Nicene and Post-Nicene Fathers of the Christian Church. 28 vols. in two series, denoted as NPNF and NPNF[2]. Edited by Philip Schaff et al. Buffalo, NY: Christian Literature, 1887-1894. Several reprints; also available online.
OER	Oxford Encyclopedia of the Reformation. 4 vols. Edited by Hans J. Hillerbrand. New York: Oxford University Press, 1996.
OS	Joannis Calvini Opera selecta. 5 vols. Edited by Peter Barth and Wilhelm Niesel. Munich: Christian Kaiser Verlag, 1970-1974.
PG	Patrologia cursus completus. Series Graeca. 161 vols. Edited by J.-P. Migne. Paris, 1857-1866.
PL	Patrologia cursus completus. Series Latina. 221 vols. Edited by J.-P. Migne. Paris, 1844-1864.
PML	The Peter Martyr [Vermigli] Library. 12 vols. projected. Kirksville, MO: Truman State University Press, 1994-.
q.	question
RCS	The Reformation Commentary on Scripture. 28 vols. projected. Downers Grove, IL: InterVarsity Press, 2011-.
r, v	Some early books are numbered not by page but by folio (leaf). Front and back sides (pages) of a numbered folio are indicated by recto and verso.
STC	A Short-Title Catalogue of Books Printed in England, Scotland, and Ireland and of English Books Printed Abroad, 1475-1640. 3 vols. Edited by A. W. Pollard, G. R. Redgrave et al. London: Bibliographical Society, 1976-1991.
WA	D. Martin Luthers Werke: Kritische Gesamtausgabe. 66 vols. Weimar: Hermann Böhlaus Nachfolger, 1883-1987.
WATr	D. Martin Luthers Werke: Kritische Gesamtausgabe: Tischreden. 6 vols. Weimar: Hermann Böhlaus Nachfolger, 1912-1921.
Wing	Short-title Catalogue of Books Printed in England, Scotland, Ireland, Wales, and British America, and of English Books Printed in Other Countries, 1641-1700. 3 vols. Edited by Donald Goddard Wing et al. New York: Index Society, 1945-1951.
WSA	The Works of St. Augustine. 50 vols. projected in three series. Hyde Park, NY: New City Press, 1990-.
ZSW	Huldreich Zwinglis Sämtliche Werke. 14 vols. Corpus Reformatorum 88-101. Edited by Emil Egli et al. Berlin: C. A. Schwetschke and Son; Zurich: Theologischer Verlag, 1905-1956.

GENERAL INTRODUCTION

The Reformation Commentary on Scripture (RCS) is a twenty-eight-volume series of exegetical comment covering the entire Bible and gathered from the writings of sixteenth-century preachers, scholars and reformers. The RCS is intended as a sequel to the highly acclaimed Ancient Christian Commentary on Scripture (ACCS), and as such its overall concept, method, format and audience are similar to the earlier series. Both series are committed to the renewal of the church through careful study and meditative reflection on the Old and New Testaments, the charter documents of Christianity, read in the context of the worshiping, believing community of faith across the centuries. However, the patristic and Reformation eras are separated by nearly a millennium, and the challenges of reading Scripture with the reformers require special attention to their context, resources and assumptions. The purpose of this general introduction is to present an overview of the context and process of biblical interpretation in the age of the Reformation.

Goals

The Reformation Commentary on Scripture seeks to introduce its readers to the depth and richness of exegetical ferment that defined the Reformation era. The RCS has four goals: the enrichment of contemporary biblical interpretation through exposure to Reformation-era biblical exegesis; the renewal of contemporary preaching through exposure to the biblical insights of the Reformation writers; a deeper understanding of the Reformation itself and the breadth of perspectives represented within it; and the recovery of the robust spiritual theology and devotional treasures of the Reformation's engagement with the Bible. Each of these goals requires a brief comment.

Biblical interpretation. During the past half-century, biblical hermeneutics has become a major growth industry in the academic world. One of the consequences of the historical-critical hegemony of biblical studies has been the privileging of contemporary philosophies and ideologies at the expense of a commitment to the Christian church as the primary reading community within which and for which biblical exegesis is done. Reading Scripture with the church fathers and the reformers is a corrective to all such imperialism of the present. One of the greatest skills required for a fruitful interpretation of the Bible is the ability to listen. We rightly emphasize the importance of listening to the voices of contextual theologies today, but in doing so we often marginalize or ignore another crucial context—the community of believing Christians through the centuries. The serious study of Scripture requires more than the latest Bible translation in one hand and the latest commentary (or niche study Bible) in the other. John L. Thompson has called on Christians today to practice the art of "reading the Bible with the dead."[1] The RCS presents carefully selected comments from the extant commentaries of the Reformation as an encouragement to more in-depth study of this important epoch in the history of biblical interpretation.

Preaching. The Protestant reformers identified the public preaching of the Word of God as an indispensible means of grace and a sure sign of the true church. Through the words of the preacher, the living voice of the gospel (*viva vox evangelii*) is heard. Luther famously said that the church is not a "pen house" but a "mouth house." The Reformation in Switzerland began when Huldrych Zwingli entered the pulpit of the Grossmünster in Zurich on January 1, 1519, and began to preach a series of expositional sermons chapter by chapter from the Gospel of Matthew. In the following years he extended this homiletical approach to other books of the Old and New Testaments. Calvin followed a similar pattern in Geneva. Many of the commentaries represented in this series were either originally presented as sermons or were written to support the regular preaching ministry of local church pastors. Luther said that the preacher should be a *bonus textualis*—a good one with a text—well-versed in the Scriptures. Preachers in the Reformation traditions preached not only about the Bible but also from it, and this required more than a passing acquaintance with its contents. Those who have been charged with the office of preaching in the church today can find wisdom and insight—and fresh perspectives—in the sermons of the Reformation and the biblical commentaries read and studied by preachers of the sixteenth century.

Reformation. Some scholars of the sixteenth century prefer to speak of the period they study in the plural, the European Reformations, to indicate that many diverse impulses for reform were at work in this turbulent age of transition from medieval to modern times. While this point is well taken, the RCS follows the time-honored tradition of using Reformation in the singular form to indicate not only a major moment in the history of Christianity in the West but also, as Hans J. Hillerbrand has put it, "an essential cohesiveness in the heterogeneous pursuits of religious reform in the sixteenth century."[2] At the same time, in developing guidelines to assist the volume editors in making judicious selections from the vast amount of commentary material available in this period,

---

[1]John L. Thompson, *Reading the Bible with the Dead* (Grand Rapids: Eerdmans, 2007).
[2]Hans J. Hillerbrand, *The Division of Christendom* (Louisville, KY: Westminster John Knox, 2007), x. Hillerbrand has also edited the standard reference work in Reformation studies, *OER*. See also Diarmaid MacCulloch, *The Reformation* (New York: Viking, 2003), and Patrick Collinson, *The Reformation: A History* (New York: Random House, 2004).

we have stressed the multifaceted character of the Reformation across many confessions, theological orientations and political settings.

Spiritual theology. The post-Enlightenment split between the study of the Bible as an academic discipline and the reading of the Bible as spiritual nurture was foreign to the reformers. For them the study of the Bible was transformative at the most basic level of the human person: *coram deo.* Luther's famous Reformation breakthrough triggered by his laborious study of the Psalms and Paul's letter to the Romans is well known, but the experience of Cambridge scholar Thomas Bilney was perhaps more typical. When Erasmus's critical edition of the Greek New Testament was published in 1516, it was accompanied by a new translation in elegant Latin. Attracted by the classical beauty of Erasmus's Latin, Bilney came across this statement in 1 Timothy 1:15: "Christ Jesus came into the world to save sinners." In the Greek this sentence is described as *pistos ho logos,* which the Vulgate had rendered *fidelis sermo,* "a faithful saying." Erasmus chose a different word for the Greek *pistos—certus,* "sure, certain." When Bilney grasped the meaning of this word applied to the announcement of salvation in Christ, he tells us that "immediately I felt a marvelous comfort and quietness, insomuch that my bruised bones leaped for joy."[3] The reformers all repudiated the idea that the Bible could be studied and understood with dispassionate objectivity, as a cold artifact from antiquity. Luther described the way the Bible was meant to function in the life of believers when he reproached himself and others for reacting to the nativity narrative with such cool unconcern. "I hate myself because when I see Christ laid in the manger or in the lap of his mother and hear the angels sing, my heart does not leap into flame. With what good reason should we all despise ourselves that we remain so cold when this word is spoken to us, over which everyone should dance and leap and burn for joy! We act as though it were a frigid historical fact that does not smite our hearts, as if someone were merely relating that the sultan has a crown of gold."[4] It was a core conviction of the Reformation that the careful study and meditative listening to the Scriptures, what the monks called *lectio divina,* could yield life-changing results. The RCS wishes to commend the exegetical work of the Reformation era as a program of retrieval for the sake of renewal—spiritual réssourcement for believers committed to the life of faith today.

Perspectives

In setting forth the perspectives and perimeters of the RCS, the following considerations have proved helpful.

Chronology. When did the Reformation begin, and how long did it last? In some traditional accounts, the answer was clear: the Reformation began with the posting of Luther's Ninety-five Theses at Wittenberg in 1517 and ended with the death of Calvin in

---

[3]See A. G. Dickens, *The English Reformation* (New York: Schocken, 1974), 79.
[4]WA 49:176-77, quoted in Roland Bainton, "The Bible in the Reformation," in *CHB,* 3:23.

Geneva in 1564. Apart from reducing the Reformation to a largely German event with a side trip to Switzerland, this perspective fails to do justice to the important events that led up to Luther's break with Rome and its many reverberations throughout Europe and beyond. In choosing commentary selections for the RCS, we have adopted the concept of the long sixteenth century, say, from the late 1400s to the mid-seventeenth century. Thus we have included commentary selections from early or pre-Reformation writers such as John Colet and Jacques Lefèvre d'Étaples to seventeenth-century figures such as Henry Ainsworth and Johann Gerhard.

Confession. The RCS concentrates primarily, though not exclusively, on the exegetical writings of the Protestant reformers. While the ACCS provided a compendium of key consensual exegetes of the early Christian centuries, the Catholic/Protestant confessional divide in the sixteenth century tested the very idea of consensus, especially with reference to ecclesiology and soteriology. While many able and worthy exegetes faithful to the Roman Catholic Church were active during this period, this project has chosen to include primarily those figures that represent perspectives within the Protestant Reformation. For this reason we have not included comments on the apocryphal or deuterocanonical writings.

We recognize that "Protestant" and "Catholic" as contradistinctive labels are anachronistic terms for the early decades of the sixteenth century before the hardening of confessional identities surrounding the Council of Trent. Protestant figures such as Philipp Melanchthon, Johannes Oecolampadius and John Calvin were all products of the revival of sacred letters known as biblical humanism. They shared an approach to biblical interpretation that owed much to Desiderius Erasmus and other scholars who remained loyal to the Church of Rome. Careful comparative studies of Protestant and Catholic exegesis in the sixteenth century have shown surprising areas of agreement when the focus was the study of a particular biblical text rather than the standard confessional debates.

At the same time, exegetical differences among the various Protestant groups could become strident and church-dividing. The most famous example of this is the interpretive impasse between Luther and Zwingli over the meaning of "This is my body" (Mt 26:26) in the words of institution. Their disagreement at the Colloquy of Marburg in 1529 had important christological and pastoral implications, as well as social and political consequences. Luther refused fellowship with Zwingli and his party at the end of the colloquy; in no small measure this bitter division led to the separate trajectories pursued by Lutheran and Reformed Protestantism to this day. In Elizabethan England, Puritans and Anglicans agreed that "Holy Scripture containeth all things necessary to salvation: so that whatsoever is not read therein, nor may be proved thereby, is not to be required of any man" (article 6 of the Thirty-nine Articles of Religion), yet on the basis of their differing interpretations of the Bible they fought bitterly over the structures of the church, the clothing of the clergy and the ways of worship. On the matter of infant baptism,

Catholics and Protestants alike agreed on its propriety, though there were various theories as to how a practice not mentioned in the Bible could be justified biblically. The Anabaptists were outliers on this subject. They rejected infant baptism altogether. They appealed to the example of the baptism of Jesus and to his final words as recorded in the Gospel of Matthew (Mt 28:19-20), "Go therefore, and make disciples of all nations, baptizing them in the name of the Father, and of the Son, and of the Holy Spirit, teaching them to observe all that I have commanded you." New Testament Christians, they argued, are to follow not only the commands of Jesus in the Great Commission, but also the exact order in which they were given: evangelize, baptize, catechize.

These and many other differences of interpretation among the various Protestant groups are reflected in their many sermons, commentaries and public disputations. In the RCS, the volume editor's introduction to each volume is intended to help the reader understand the nature and significance of doctrinal conversations and disputes that resulted in particular, and frequently clashing, interpretations. Footnotes throughout the text will be provided to explain obscure references, unusual expressions and other matters that require special comment. Volume editors have chosen comments on the Bible across a wide range of sixteenth-century confessions and schools of interpretation: biblical humanists, Lutheran, Reformed, Anglican, Puritan and Anabaptist. We have not pursued passages from post-Tridentine Catholic authors or from radical spiritualists and antitrinitarian writers, though sufficient material is available from these sources to justify another series.

The availability of digital resources has given access to a huge residual database of sixteenth-century exegetical comment hitherto available only in major research universities and rare book collections. The RCS has formed a partnership with the Alexander Street Press Digital Library of Classical Protestant Texts (DLCPT) to make available to our volume editors numerous imprints of sixteenth-century works in an online format. Through the help of RCS editorial advisor Herman Selderhuis, we have also had access to the special Reformation collections of the Johannes a Lasco Bibliothek in Emden, Germany. In addition, modern critical editions and translations of Reformation sources have been published over the past generation.

The design of the RCS is intended to offer reader-friendly access to these classic texts. Each volume in the RCS will include an introduction by the volume editor placing that portion of the canon within the historical context of the Protestant Reformation and presenting a summary of the theological themes, interpretive issues and reception of the particular book(s). The commentary itself consists of particular pericopes identified by a pericope heading; the biblical text in the English Standard Version (ESV), with significant textual variants registered in the footnotes; an overview of the pericope in which principal exegetical and theological concerns of the Reformation writers are succinctly noted; and excerpts from the Reformation writers identified by name according to the conventions of the *Oxford Encyclopedia of the Reformation*. Original translations of Reformation sources are given unless an acceptable translation already exists. Each volume will also include a bibliography of sources cited, as well as an appendix of authors and source works.

The Reformation era was a time of verbal as well as physical violence, and this fact has presented a challenge for this project. Without unduly sanitizing the texts, where they contain anti-Semitic, sexist or inordinately polemical rhetoric, we have not felt obliged to parade such comments either. We have noted the abridgement of texts with ellipses and an explanatory footnote. While this procedure would not be valid in the critical edition of such a text, we have deemed it appropriate in a series whose primary purpose is pastoral and devotional. When translating *homo* or similar terms that refer to the human race as a whole, we have used alternative English expressions to the word *man* (or derivative constructions used generically to signify humanity at large), whenever such substitutions can be made without producing an awkward or artificial construction.

As is true in the ACCS, we have made a special effort where possible to include the voices of women, though we acknowledge the difficulty of doing so for the early modern period when for a variety of social and cultural reasons few theological and biblical works were published by women. However, recent scholarship has focused on a number of female leaders whose literary remains show us how they understood and interpreted the Bible. Women who made significant contributions to the Reformation include Marguerite d'Angoulême, sister of King Francis I, who supported French reformist evangelicals including Calvin and who published a religious poem influenced by Luther's theology, *The Mirror of the Sinful Soul*; Argula von Grumbach, a Bavarian noblewoman who defended the teachings of Luther and Melanchthon before the theologians of the University of Ingolstadt; Katharina Schütz Zell, the wife of a former priest, Matthias Zell, and a remarkable reformer in her own right—she conducted funerals, compiled hymnbooks, defended the downtrodden and published a defense of clerical marriage as well as composing works of consolation on divine comfort and pleas for the toleration of Anabaptists and Catholics alike; and Anne Askew, a Protestant martyr put to death in 1546 after demonstrating remarkable biblical prowess in her examinations by church officials. Other echoes of faithful women in the age of the Reformation are found in their letters, translations, poems, hymns, court depositions and martyr records.

Lay culture, learned culture. In recent decades, much attention has been given to what is called "reforming from below," that is, the expressions of religious beliefs and churchly life that characterized the popular culture of the majority of the population in the era of the Reformation. Social historians have taught us to examine the diverse pieties of townspeople and city folk, of rural religion and village life, the emergence of lay theologies and the experiences of women in the religious tumults of Reformation Europe.[5] Formal commentaries by their nature are artifacts of learned culture. Almost all of them were writ-

---

[5]See Peter Matheson, ed., *Reformation Christianity* (Minneapolis: Fortress, 2007).

ten in Latin, the lingua franca of learned discourse well past the age of the Reformation. Biblical commentaries were certainly not the primary means by which the Protestant Reformation spread so rapidly across wide sectors of sixteenth-century society. Small pamphlets and broadsheets, later called *Flugschriften* ("flying writings"), with their graphic woodcuts and cartoon-like depictions of Reformation personalities and events, became the means of choice for mass communication in the early age of printing. Sermons and works of devotion were also printed with appealing visual aids. Luther's early writings were often accompanied by drawings and sketches from Lucas Cranach and other artists. This was done "above all for the sake of children and simple folk," as Luther put it, "who are more easily moved by pictures and images to recall divine history than through mere words or doctrines."[6]

We should be cautious, however, in drawing too sharp a distinction between learned and lay culture in this period. The phenomenon of preaching was a kind of verbal bridge between scholars at their desks and the thousands of illiterate or semi-literate listeners whose views were shaped by the results of Reformation exegesis. According to contemporary witness, more than one thousand people were crowding into Geneva to hear Calvin expound the Scriptures every day.[7] An example of how learned theological works by Reformation scholars were received across divisions of class and social status comes from Lazare Drilhon, an apothecary of Toulon. He was accused of heresy in May 1545 when a cache of prohibited books was found hidden in his garden shed. In addition to devotional works, the French New Testament and a copy of Calvin's Genevan liturgy, there was found a series of biblical commentaries, translated from the Latin into French: Martin Bucer's on Matthew, François Lambert's on the Apocalypse and one by Oecolampadius on 1 John.[8] Biblical exegesis in the sixteenth century was not limited to the kind of full-length commentaries found in Drilhon's shed. Citations from the Bible and expositions of its meaning permeate the extant literature of sermons, letters, court depositions, doctrinal treatises, records of public disputations and even last wills and testaments. While most of the selections in the RCS will be drawn from formal commentary literature, other sources of biblical reflection will also be considered.

Historical Context

The medieval legacy. On October 18, 1512, the degree *Doctor in Biblia* was conferred on Martin Luther, and he began his career as a professor in the University of Wittenberg. As is well known, Luther was also a monk who had taken solemn vows in the Augustinian Order

---

[6]Martin Luther, *Passional* (1522). See R. W. Scribner, *For the Sake of Simple Folk: Popular Propaganda for the German Reformation* (Cambridge: Cambridge University Press, 1981), xi.

[7]Letter of De Beaulieu to Guillaume Farel (1561) in J. W. Baum, ed., *Theodor Beza nach handschriftlichen und anderen gleichzeitigen Quellen* (Leipzig: Weidmann, 1851) 2:92.

[8]Francis Higman, "A Heretic's Library: The Drilhon Inventory" (1545), in Francis Higman, *Lire et Découvrir: la circulation des idées au temps de la Réforme* (Geneva: Droz, 1998), 65-85.

of Hermits at Erfurt. These two settings—the university and the monastery—both deeply rooted in the Middle Ages, form the background not only for Luther's personal vocation as a reformer but also for the history of the biblical commentary in the age of the Reformation. Since the time of the Venerable Bede (d. 735), sometimes called "the last of the Fathers," serious study of the Bible had taken place primarily in the context of cloistered monasteries. The Rule of St. Benedict brought together *lectio* and *meditatio*, the knowledge of letters and the life of prayer. The liturgy was the medium through which the daily reading of the Bible, especially the Psalms, and the sayings of the church fathers came together in the spiritual formation of the monks.[9] Essential to this understanding was a belief in the unity of the people of God throughout time as well as space, and an awareness that life in this world was a preparation for the beatific vision in the next.

The source of theology was the study of the sacred page *(sacra pagina)*; its object was the accumulation of knowledge not for its own sake but for the obtaining of eternal life. For these monks, the Bible had God for its author, salvation for its end and unadulterated truth for its matter, though they would not have expressed it in such an Aristotelian way. The medieval method of interpreting the Bible owed much to Augustine's *On Christian Doctrine*. In addition to setting forth a series of rules (drawn from an earlier work by Tyconius), Augustine stressed the importance of distinguishing the literal and spiritual or allegorical senses of Scripture. While the literal sense was not disparaged, the allegorical was valued because it enabled the believer to obtain spiritual benefit from the obscure places in the Bible, especially in the Old Testament. For Augustine, as for the monks who followed him, the goal of scriptural exegesis was freighted with eschatological meaning; its purpose was to induce faith, hope and love and so to advance in one's pilgrimage toward that city with foundations (see Heb 11:10).

Building on the work of Augustine and other church fathers going back to Origen, medieval exegetes came to understand Scripture as possessed of four possible meanings, the famous *quadriga*. The literal meaning was retained, of course, but the spiritual meaning was now subdivided into three senses: the allegorical, the moral and the anagogical. Medieval exegetes often referred to the four meanings of Scripture in a popular rhyme:

> The letter shows us what God and our fathers did;
> The allegory shows us where our faith is hid;
> The moral meaning gives us rules of daily life;
> The anagogy shows us where we end our strife.[10]

In this schema, the three spiritual meanings of the text correspond to the three theological virtues: faith (allegory), hope (anagogy) and love (the moral meaning). It should

---

[9]See the classic study by Jean Leclercq, *The Love of Learning and the Desire for God* (New York: Fordham University Press, 1961).
[10]A translation of the well-known Latin quatrain: *Littera gesta docet/Quid credas allegoria/Moralis quid agas/Quo tendas anagogia.* See Robert M. Grant, *A Short History of the Interpretation of the Bible* (New York: Macmillan, 1963), 119.

be noted that this way of approaching the Bible assumed a high doctrine of scriptural inspiration: the multiple meanings inherent in the text had been placed there by the Holy Spirit for the benefit of the people of God. The biblical justification for this method went back to the apostle Paul, who had used the words *allegory* and *type* when applying Old Testament events to believers in Christ (Gal 4:21-31; 1 Cor 10:1-11). The problem with this approach was knowing how to relate each of the four senses to one another and how to prevent Scripture from becoming a nose of wax turned this way and that by various interpreters. As G. R. Evans explains, "Any interpretation which could be put upon the text and was in keeping with the faith and edifying, had the warrant of God himself, for no human reader had the ingenuity to find more than God had put there."[11]

With the rise of the universities in the eleventh century, theology and the study of Scripture moved from the cloister into the classroom. Scripture and the Fathers were still important, but they came to function more as footnotes to the theological questions debated in the schools and brought together in an impressive systematic way in works such as Peter Lombard's *Books of Sentences* (the standard theology textbook of the Middle Ages) and the great scholastic *summae* of the thirteenth century. Indispensible to the study of the Bible in the later Middle Ages was the *Glossa ordinaria*, a collection of exegetical opinions by the church fathers and other commentators. Heiko Oberman summarized the transition from devotion to dialectic this way: "When, due to the scientific revolution of the twelfth century, Scripture became the *object* of study rather than the *subject* through which God speaks to the student, the difference between the two modes of speaking was investigated in terms of the texts themselves rather than in their relation to the recipients."[12] It was possible, of course, to be both a scholastic theologian and a master of the spiritual life. Meister Eckhart, for example, wrote commentaries on the Old Testament in Latin and works of mystical theology in German, reflecting what had come to be seen as a division of labor between the two.

An increasing focus on the text of Scripture led to a revival of interest in its literal sense. The two key figures in this development were Thomas Aquinas (d. 1274) and Nicholas of Lyra (d. 1340). Thomas is best remembered for his *Summa Theologiae*, but he was also a prolific commentator on the Bible. Thomas did not abandon the multiple senses of Scripture but declared that all the senses were founded on one—the literal— and this sense eclipsed allegory as the basis of sacred doctrine. Nicholas of Lyra was a Franciscan scholar who made use of the Hebrew text of the Old Testament and quoted liberally from works of Jewish scholars, especially the learned French rabbi Salomon Rashi (d. 1105). After Aquinas, Lyra was the strongest defender of the literal, historical meaning of Scripture as the primary basis of theological disputation. His *Postils*, as his

---

[11]G. R. Evans, *The Language and Logic of the Bible: The Road to Reformation* (Cambridge: Cambridge University Press, 1985), 42.

[12]Heiko Oberman, *Forerunners of the Reformation* (Philadelphia: Fortress, 1966), 284.

notes were called, were widely circulated in the late Middle Ages and became the first biblical commentary to be printed in the fifteenth century. More than any other commentator from the period of high scholasticism, Lyra and his work were greatly valued by the early reformers. According to an old Latin pun, *Nisi Lyra lyrasset, Lutherus non saltasset*, "If Lyra had not played his lyre, Luther would not have danced." While Luther was never an uncritical disciple of any teacher, he did praise Lyra as a good Hebraist and quoted him more than one hundred times in his lectures on Genesis, where he declared, "I prefer him to almost all other interpreters of Scripture."[13]

Sacred philology. The sixteenth century has been called a golden age of biblical interpretation, and it is a fact that the age of the Reformation witnessed an explosion of commentary writing unparalleled in the history of the Christian church. Kenneth Hagen has cataloged forty-five commentaries on Hebrews between 1516 (Erasmus) and 1598 (Beza).[14] During the sixteenth century, more than seventy new commentaries on Romans were published, five of them by Melanchthon alone, and nearly one hundred commentaries on the Bible's prayer book, the Psalms.[15] There were two developments in the fifteenth century that presaged this development and without which it could not have taken place: the invention of printing and the rediscovery of a vast store of ancient learning hitherto unknown or unavailable to scholars in the West.

It is now commonplace to say that what the computer has become in our generation, the printing press was to the world of Erasmus, Luther and other leaders of the Reformation. Johannes Gutenberg, a goldsmith by trade, developed a metal alloy suitable for type and a machine that would allow printed characters to be cast with relative ease, placed in even lines of composition and then manipulated again and again making possible the mass production of an unbelievable number of texts. In 1455, the Gutenberg Bible, the masterpiece of the typographical revolution, was published at Mainz in double columns in gothic type. Forty-seven copies of the beautiful Gutenberg Bible are still extant, each consisting of more than one thousand colorfully illuminated and impeccably printed pages. What began at Gutenberg's print shop in Mainz on the Rhine River soon spread, like McDonald's or Starbucks in our day, into every nook and cranny of the known world. Printing presses sprang up in Rome (1464), Venice (1469), Paris (1470), the Netherlands (1471), Switzerland (1472), Spain (1474), England (1476), Sweden (1483) and Constantinople (1490). By 1500, these and other presses across Europe had published some twenty-seven thousand titles, most of them in Latin. Erasmus once compared himself with an obscure preacher whose sermons were heard by only a few people in one or two churches while his books were read in every country

---

[13]LW 2:164.

[14]Kenneth Hagen, *Hebrews Commenting from Erasmus to Bèze, 1516-1598* (Tübingen: Mohr, 1981).

[15]See David C. Steinmetz, ed., *The Bible in the Sixteenth Century* (Durham: Duke University Press, 1990), and R. Gerald Hobbs, "Biblical Commentaries," *OER* 1:167-71.

in the world. Erasmus was not known for his humility, but in this case he was simply telling the truth.[16]

The Italian humanist Lorenzo Valla (d. 1457) died in the early dawn of the age of printing, but his critical and philological studies would be taken up by others who believed that genuine reform in church and society could come about only by returning to the wellsprings of ancient learning and wisdom—*ad fontes*, "back to the sources!" Valla is best remembered for undermining a major claim made by defenders of the papacy when he proved by philological research that the so-called Donation of Constantine, which had bolstered papal assertions of temporal sovereignty, was a forgery. But it was Valla's *Collatio Novi Testamenti* of 1444 that would have such a great effect on the renewal of biblical studies in the next century. Erasmus discovered the manuscript of this work while rummaging through an old library in Belgium and published it at Paris in 1505. In the preface to his edition of Valla, Erasmus gave the rationale that would guide his own labors in textual criticism. Just as Jerome had translated the Latin Vulgate from older versions and copies of the Scriptures in his day, so now Jerome's own text must be subjected to careful scrutiny and correction. Erasmus would be *Hieronymus redivivus*, a new Jerome come back to life to advance the cause of sacred philology. The restoration of the Scriptures and the writings of the church fathers would usher in what Erasmus believed would be a golden age of peace and learning. In 1516, the Basel publisher Froben brought out Erasmus's *Novum Instrumentum*, the first published edition of the Greek New Testament. Erasmus's Greek New Testament would go through five editions in his lifetime, each one with new emendations to the text and a growing section of annotations that expanded to include not only technical notes about the text but also theological comment. The influence of Erasmus's Greek New Testament was enormous. It formed the basis for Robert Estienne's *Novum Testamentum Graece* of 1550, which in turn was used to establish the Greek *Textus Receptus* for a number of late Reformation translations including the King James Version of 1611.

For all his expertise in Greek, Erasmus was a poor student of Hebrew and only published commentaries on several of the psalms. However, the renaissance of Hebrew letters was part of the wider program of biblical humanism as reflected in the establishment of trilingual colleges devoted to the study of Hebrew, Greek and Latin (the three languages written on the *titulus* of Jesus' cross [Jn 19:20]) at Alcalá in Spain, Wittenberg in Germany, Louvain in Belgium and Paris in France. While it is true that some medieval commentators, especially Nicholas of Lyra, had been informed by the study of Hebrew and rabbinics in their biblical work, it was the publication of Johannes Reuchlin's *De rudimentis hebraicis* (1506), a combined grammar and dictionary, that led to the recovery of *veritas Hebraica*, as Jerome had referred to the true voice of the Hebrew Scriptures. The

---

[16]See E. Harris Harbison, *The Christian Scholar in the Age of the Reformation* (New York: Charles Scribner's Sons, 1956), 80.

pursuit of Hebrew studies was carried forward in the Reformation by two great scholars, Konrad Pellikan and Sebastian Münster. Pellikan was a former Franciscan friar who embraced the Protestant cause and played a major role in the Zurich reformation. He had published a Hebrew grammar even prior to Reuchlin and produced a commentary on nearly the entire Bible that appeared in seven volumes between 1532 and 1539. Münster was Pellikan's student and taught Hebrew at the University of Heidelberg before taking up a similar position in Basel. Like his mentor, Münster was a great collector of Hebraica and published a series of excellent grammars, dictionaries and rabbinic texts. Münster did for the Hebrew Old Testament what Erasmus had done for the Greek New Testament. His *Hebraica Biblia* offered a fresh Latin translation of the Old Testament with annotations from medieval rabbinic exegesis.

Luther first learned Hebrew with Reuchlin's grammar in hand but took advantage of other published resources, such as the four-volume Hebrew Bible published at Venice by Daniel Bomberg in 1516 to 1517. He also gathered his own circle of Hebrew experts, his *sanhedrin* he called it, who helped him with his German translation of the Old Testament. We do not know where William Tyndale learned Hebrew, though perhaps it was in Worms, where there was a thriving rabbinical school during his stay there. In any event, he had sufficiently mastered the language to bring out a freshly translated Pentateuch that was published at Antwerp in 1530. By the time the English separatist scholar Henry Ainsworth published his prolix commentaries on the Pentateuch in 1616, the knowledge of Hebrew, as well as Greek, was taken for granted by every serious scholar of the Bible. In the preface to his commentary on Genesis, Ainsworth explained that "the literal sense of Moses's Hebrew (which is the tongue wherein he wrote the law), is the ground of all interpretation, and that language hath figures and properties of speech, different from ours: These therefore in the first place are to be opened that the natural meaning of the Scripture, being known, the mysteries of godliness therein implied, may be better discerned."[17]

The restoration of the biblical text in the original languages made possible the revival of scriptural exposition reflected in the floodtide of sermon literature and commentary work. Of even more far-reaching import was the steady stream of vernacular Bibles in the sixteenth century. In the introduction to his 1516 edition of the New Testament, Erasmus had expressed his desire that the Scriptures be translated into all languages so that "the lowliest women" could read the Gospels and the Pauline epistles and "the farmer sing some portion of them at the plow, the weaver hum some parts of them to the movement of his shuttle, the traveler lighten the weariness of the journey with stories of this kind."[18] Like Erasmus, Tyndale wanted the Bible to be available in the language of the common people. He once said to a learned divine that if God spared his life he would cause the

---

[17]Henry Ainsworth, *Annotations Upon the First Book of Moses Called Genesis* (Amsterdam, 1616), preface.
[18]John C. Olin, *Christian Humanism and the Reformation* (New York: Fordham University Press, 1987), 101.

boy who drives the plow to know more of the Scriptures than he did![19] The project of allowing the Bible to speak in the language of the mother in the house, the children in the street and the cheesemonger in the marketplace was met with stiff opposition by certain Catholic polemists such as Johann Eck, Luther's antagonist at the Leipzig Debate of 1519. In his *Enchiridion* (1525), Eck derided the "inky theologians" whose translations paraded the Bible before "the untutored crowd" and subjected it to the judgment of "laymen and crazy old women."[20] In fact, some fourteen German Bibles had already been published prior to Luther's September Testament of 1522, which he translated from Erasmus's Greek New Testament in less than three months' time while sequestered in the Wartburg. Luther's German New Testament became the first bestseller in the world, appearing in forty-three distinct editions between 1522 and 1525 with upwards of one hundred thousand copies issued in these three years. It is estimated that five percent of the German population may have been literate at this time, but this rate increased as the century wore on due in no small part to the unmitigated success of vernacular Bibles.[21]

Luther's German Bible (inclusive of the Old Testament from 1534) was the most successful venture of its kind, but it was not alone in the field. Hans Denck and Ludwig Hätzer, leaders in the early Anabaptist movement, translated the prophetic books of the Old Testament from Hebrew into German in 1527. This work influenced the Swiss-German Bible of 1531 published by Leo Jud and other pastors in Zurich. Tyndale's influence on the English language rivaled that of Luther on German. At a time when English was regarded as "that obscure and remote dialect of German spoken in an off-shore island," Tyndale, with his remarkable linguistic ability (he was fluent in eight languages), "made a language for England," as his modern editor David Daniell has put it.[22] Tyndale was imprisoned and executed near Brussels in 1536, but the influence of his biblical work among the common people of England was already being felt. There is no reason to doubt the authenticity of John Foxe's recollection of how Tyndale's New Testament was received in England during the 1520s and 1530s: "The fervent zeal of Christians in those days seemed much superior to these our days and times, as manifestly may appear by their sitting up all night and reading and hearing: also by their expenses and charges in buying of books in English, by whom some gave five marks, some more, some less, for a book; some gave a load of hay for a few chapters of St. James or of St. Paul in English."[23]

---

[19]This famous statement of Tyndale was quoted by John Foxe in his *Acts and Monuments of Matters Happening in the Church* (London, 1563). See Henry Wansbrough, "Tyndale," in Richard Griffith, ed., *The Bible in the Renaissance* (Aldershot, VT.: Ashgate, 2001), 124.

[20]John Eck, *Enchiridion of Commonplaces*, trans. Ford Lewis Battles (Grand Rapids: Baker, 1979), 47-49.

[21]The effect of printing on the spread of the Reformation has been much debated. See the classic study by Elizabeth L. Eisenstein, *The Printing Press as an Agent of Change* (Cambridge: Cambridge University Press, 1979). More recent studies include Mark U. Edwards Jr., *Printing, Propaganda and Martin Luther* (Minneapolis: Fortress, 1994), and Andrew Pettegree and Matthew Hall, "The Reformation and the Book: A Reconsideration," *Historical Journal* 47 (2004): 1-24.

[22]David Daniell, *William Tyndale: A Biography* (New Haven: Yale University Press, 1994), 3.

[23]John Foxe, *Acts and Monuments*, 4:212.

Calvin helped to revise and contributed three prefaces to the French Bible translated by his cousin Pierre Robert Olivétan and originally published at Neuchâtel in 1535. Clément Marot and Beza provided a fresh translation of the Psalms with each psalm rendered in poetic form and accompanied by monophonic musical settings for congregational singing. The Bay Psalter, the first book printed in America, was an English adaptation of this work. Geneva also provided the provenance of the most influential Italian Bible published by Giovanni Diodati in 1607. The flowering of biblical humanism in vernacular Bibles resulted in new translations in all of the major language groups of Europe: Spanish (1569), Portuguese (1681), Dutch (New Testament, 1523; Old Testament, 1527), Danish (1550), Czech (1579-1593/94), Hungarian (New Testament, 1541; complete Bible, 1590), Polish (1563), Swedish (1541) and even Arabic (1591).[24]

Patterns of Reformation

Once the text of the Bible had been placed in the hands of the people, in cheap and easily available editions, what further need was there of published expositions such as commentaries? Given the Protestant doctrine of the priesthood of all believers, was there any longer a need for learned clergy and their bookish religion? Some radical reformers thought not. Sebastian Franck searched for the true church of the Spirit "scattered among the heathen and the weeds" but could not find it in any of the institutional structures of his time. *Veritas non potest scribi, aut exprimi*, he said, "truth can neither be spoken nor written."[25] Kaspar von Schwenckfeld so emphasized religious inwardness that he suspended external observance of the Lord's Supper and downplayed the readable, audible Scriptures in favor of the word within. This trajectory would lead to the rise of the Quakers in the next century, but it was pursued neither by the mainline reformers nor by most of the Anabaptists. Article 7 of the Augsburg Confession (1530) declared the one holy Christian church to be "the assembly of all believers among whom the Gospel is preached in its purity and the holy sacraments are administered according to the Gospel."[26]

Historians of the nineteenth century referred to the material and formal principles of the Reformation. In this construal, the matter at stake was the meaning of the Christian gospel: the liberating insight that helpless sinners are graciously justified by the gift of faith alone, apart from any works or merits of their own, entirely on the basis of Christ's atoning work on the cross. For Luther especially, justification by faith alone became the criterion by which all other doctrines and practices of the church were to be judged. The cross proves everything, he said at the Heidelberg disputation in 1518. The distinction between law and gospel thus became the primary hermeneutical key

---

[24]On vernacular translations of the Bible, see *CHB* 3:94-140 and Jaroslav Pelikan, *The Reformation of the Bible/The Bible of the Reformation* (New Haven: Yale University Press, 1996), 41-62.

[25]Sebastian Franck, *280 Paradoxes or Wondrous Sayings*, trans. E. J. Furcha (Lewiston, NY: Edwin Mellen Press, 1986), 10, 212.

[26]John H. Leith, ed., *Creeds of the Churches* (Atlanta: John Knox, 1963), 70.

that unlocked the true meaning of Scripture.

The formal principle of the Reformation, *sola Scriptura*, was closely bound up with proper distinctions between Scripture and tradition. "Scripture alone," said Luther, "is the true lord and master of all writings and doctrine on earth. If that is not granted, what is Scripture good for? The more we reject it, the more we become satisfied with men's books and human teachers."[27] On the basis of this principle, the reformers challenged the structures and institutions of the medieval Catholic Church. Even a simple layperson, they asserted, armed with Scripture should be believed above a pope or a council without it. But, however boldly asserted, the doctrine of the primacy of Scripture did not absolve the reformers from dealing with a host of hermeneutical issues that became matters of contention both between Rome and the Reformation and within each of these two communities: the extent of the biblical canon, the validity of critical study of the Bible, the perspicuity of Scripture and its relation to preaching and the retention of devotional and liturgical practices such as holy days, incense, the burning of candles, the sprinkling of holy water, church art and musical instruments. Zwingli, the Puritans and the radicals dismissed such things as a rubbish heap of ceremonials that amounted to nothing but tomfoolery, while Lutherans and Anglicans retained most of them as consonant with Scripture and valuable aids to worship.

It is important to note that while the mainline reformers differed among themselves on many matters, overwhelmingly they saw themselves as part of the ongoing Catholic tradition, indeed as the legitimate bearers of it. This was seen in numerous ways including their sense of continuity with the church of the preceding centuries; their embrace of the ecumenical orthodoxy of the early church; and their desire to read the Bible in dialogue with the exegetical tradition of the church.

In their biblical commentaries, the reformers of the sixteenth century revealed a close familiarity with the preceding exegetical tradition, and they used it respectfully as well as critically in their own expositions of the sacred text. For them, *sola Scriptura* was not *nuda Scriptura*. Rather, the Scriptures were seen as the book given to the church, gathered and guided by the Holy Spirit. In his restatement of the Vincentian canon, Calvin defined the church as "a society of all the saints, a society which, spread over the whole world, and existing in all ages, and bound together by the one doctrine and the one spirit of Christ, cultivates and observes unity of faith and brotherly concord. With this church we deny that we have any disagreement. Nay, rather, as we revere her as our mother, so we desire to remain in her bosom." Defined thus, the church has a real, albeit relative and circumscribed, authority since, as Calvin admits, "We cannot fly without wings."[28] While the reformers could not agree with the Council of Trent (though some

---

[27]Martin Luther, "Defense and Explanation of All the Articles Which Were Rejected by the Roman Bull" (1521), WA 7:317.1-9; LW 32:11-12.

[28]John C. Olin, ed., *John Calvin and Jacopo Sadoleto: A Reformation Debate* (New York: Harper Torchbooks, 1966), 61-62, 77.

recent Catholic theologians have challenged this interpretation) that Scripture and tradition were two separate and equable sources of divine revelation, they did believe in the coinherence of Scripture and tradition. This conviction shaped the way they read and interpreted the Bible.[29]

Schools of Exegesis

The reformers were passionate about biblical exegesis, but they showed little concern for hermeneutics as a separate field of inquiry. Niels Hemmingsen, a Lutheran theologian in Denmark, did write a treatise, *De methodis* (1555), in which he offered a philosophical and theological framework for the interpretation of Scripture. This was followed by the *Clavis Scripturae Sacrae* (1567) of Matthias Flacius Illyricus, which contains some fifty rules for studying the Bible drawn from Scripture itself.[30] However, hermeneutics as we know it came of age only in the Enlightenment and should not be backloaded into the Reformation. It is also true that the word *commentary* did not mean in the sixteenth century what it means for us today. Erasmus provided both annotations and paraphrases on the New Testament, the former a series of critical notes on the text but also containing points of doctrinal substance, the latter a theological overview and brief exposition. Most of Calvin's commentaries began as sermons or lectures presented in the course of his pastoral ministry. In the dedication to his 1519 study of Galatians, Luther declared that his work was "not so much a commentary as a testimony (*ennaratio*) of my faith in Christ."[31] The exegetical work of the reformers was embodied in a wide variety of forms and genres, and the RCS has worked with this broader concept in setting the guidelines for this compendium.

The Protestant reformers shared in common a number of key interpretive principles such as the priority of the grammatical-historical sense of Scripture and the christological centeredness of the entire Bible, but they also developed a number of distinct approaches and schools of exegesis.[32] For the purposes of the RCS, we note the following key figures and families of interpretation in this period.

Biblical humanism. The key figure is Erasmus, whose importance is hard to exaggerate for Catholic and Protestant exegetes alike. His annotated Greek New Testament and fresh Latin translation challenged the hegemony of the Vulgate tradition and was doubtless a factor in the decision of the Council of Trent to establish the Vulgate edition as

---

[29]See Timothy George, "An Evangelical Reflection on Scripture and Tradition," *Pro Ecclesia* 9 (2000): 184-207.

[30]See Kenneth G. Hagen, "'*De Exegetica Methodo*': Niels Hemmingsen's *De Methodis* (1555)," in *The Bible in the Sixteenth Century*, ed. David C. Steinmetz (Durham: Duke University Press, 1990), 181-96.

[31]See Kenneth Hagen, "What Did the Term *Commentarius* Mean to Sixteenth-Century Theologians?" in Irena Backus and Francis M. Higman, eds., *Théorie et pratique de l'exégèse* (Geneva: Droz, 1990), 13-38.

[32]I follow here the sketch of Irena Backus, "Biblical Hermeneutics and Exegesis," *OER* 1:152-58. In this work, Backus confines herself to Continental developments, whereas we have noted the exegetical contribution of the English Reformation as well. For more comprehensive listings of sixteenth-century commentators, see Gerald Bray, *Biblical Interpretation* (Downers Grove, IL: InterVarsity Press, 1996), 165-212; and Richard A. Muller, "Biblical Interpretation in the Sixteenth and Seventeenth Centuries," *DMBI*, 22-44.

authentic and normative. Erasmus believed that the wide distribution of the Scriptures would contribute to personal spiritual renewal and the reform of society. In 1547, the English translation of Erasmus's *Paraphrases* was ordered to be placed in every parish church in England. John Colet first encouraged Erasmus to learn Greek, though he never took up the language himself. Colet's lectures on Paul's epistles at Oxford are reflected in his commentaries on Romans and 1 Corinthians.

Jacques Lefèvre d'Étaples has been called the "French Erasmus" because of his great learning and support for early reform movements in his native land. He published a major edition of the Psalter, as well as commentaries on the Pauline Epistles (1512), the Gospels (1522) and the General Epistles (1527). Guillaume Farel, the early reformer of Geneva, was a disciple of Lefèvre, and the young Calvin also came within his sphere of influence.

Among pre-Tridentine Catholic reformers, special attention should be given to Thomas de Vio, better known as Cajetan. He is best remembered for confronting Martin Luther on behalf of the pope in 1518, but his biblical commentaries (on nearly every book of the Bible) are virtually free of polemic. Like Erasmus, he dared to criticize the Vulgate on linguistic grounds. His commentary on Romans supported the doctrine of justification by grace applied by faith based on the "alien righteousness" of God in Christ. Jared Wicks sums up Cajetan's significance in this way: "Cajetan's combination of passion for pristine biblical meaning with his fully developed theological horizon of understanding indicates, in an intriguing manner, something of the breadth of possibilities open to Roman Catholics before a more restrictive settlement came to exercise its hold on many Catholic interpreters in the wake of the Council of Trent (1545-1563)."[33] Girolamo Seripando, like Cajetan, was a cardinal in the Catholic Church, though he belonged to the Augustinian rather than the Dominican order. He was an outstanding classical scholar and published commentaries on Romans and Galatians. Also important is Jacopo Sadoleto, another cardinal, best known for his 1539 letter to the people of Geneva beseeching them to return to the church of Rome, to which Calvin replied with a manifesto of his own. Sadoleto published a commentary on Romans in 1535. Bucer once commended Sadoleto's teaching on justification as approximating that of the reformers, while others saw him tilting away from the Augustinian tradition toward Pelagianism.[34]

Luther and the Wittenberg School. It was in the name of the Word of God, and specifically as a doctor of Scripture, that Luther challenged the church of his day and inaugurated the Reformation. Though Luther renounced his monastic vows, he never lost that sense of intimacy with *sacra pagina* he first acquired as a young monk. Luther provided three rules for reading the Bible: prayer, meditation and struggle (*tentatio*). His exegetical

---

[33]Jared Wicks, "Tommaso de Vio Cajetan (1469-1534)," *DMBI*, 283-87.
[34]See the discussion by Bernard Roussel, "Martin Bucer et Jacques Sadolet: la concorde possible," *Bulletin de la Société de l'histoire de protestantisme français* (1976): 525-50, and T. H. L. Parker, *Commentaries on the Epistle to the Romans, 1532-1542* (Edinburgh: T&T Clark, 1986), 25-34.

output was enormous. In the American edition of Luther's works, thirty out of the fifty-five volumes are devoted to his biblical studies, and additional translations are planned. Many of his commentaries originated as sermons or lecture notes presented to his students at the university and to his parishioners at Wittenberg's parish church of St. Mary. Luther referred to Galatians as his bride, "my own epistle, to which I have plighted my troth; my Katie von Bora." He considered his 1535 commentary on Galatians his greatest exegetical work, although his massive commentary on Genesis (eight volumes in LW), which he worked on for ten years (1535-1545), must be considered his crowning work. Luther's principles of biblical interpretation are found in his *Open Letter on Translating* and in the prefaces he wrote to all the books of the Bible.

Philipp Melanchthon was brought to Wittenberg to teach Greek in 1518 and proved to be an able associate to Luther in the reform of the church. A set of his lecture notes on Romans was published without his knowledge in 1522. This was revised and expanded many times until his large commentary of 1556. Melanchthon also commented on other New Testament books including Matthew, John, Galatians and the Petrine Epistles, as well as Proverbs, Daniel and Ecclesiastes. Though he was well trained in the humanist disciplines, Melanchthon devoted little attention to critical and textual matters in his commentaries. Rather, he followed the primary argument of the biblical writer and gathered from this exposition a series of doctrinal topics for special consideration. This method lay behind Melanchthon's *Loci communes* (1521), the first Protestant theology textbook to be published. Another Wittenberger was Johannes Bugenhagen of Pomerania, a prolific commentator on both the Old and New Testaments. His commentary on the Psalms (1524), translated into German by Bucer, applied Luther's teaching on justification to the Psalter. He also wrote a commentary on Job and annotations on many of the books in the Bible. The Lutheran exegetical tradition was shaped by many other scholar-reformers including Andreas Osiander, Johannes Brenz, Caspar Cruciger, Erasmus Sarcerius, Georg Maior, Jacob Andreae, Nikolaus Selnecker and Johann Gerhard.

The Strasbourg-Basel tradition. Bucer, the son of a shoemaker in Alsace, became the leader of the Reformation in Strasbourg. A former Dominican, he was early on influenced by Erasmus and continued to share his passion for Christian unity. Bucer was the most ecumenical of the Protestant reformers seeking rapprochement with Catholics on justification and an armistice between Luther and Zwingli in their strife over the Lord's Supper. Bucer also had a decisive influence on Calvin, though the latter characterized his biblical commentaries as longwinded and repetitious. In his exegetical work, Bucer made ample use of patristic and medieval sources, though he criticized the abuse and overuse of allegory as a "blatant insult to the Holy Spirit." He declared that the purpose of his commentaries was "to help inexperienced brethren [perhaps like the apothecary Drilhon, who owned a French translation of Bucer's *Commentary on Matthew*] to understand each of the words and actions of Christ, and in their proper order as far as possible, and to retain an explanation of them in their natural meaning, so that they will not distort God's Word through age-old aberrations or by inept interpretation, but rather with a faithful comprehension of everything as written by the Spirit of God, they may expound to all the churches in their firm upbuilding in faith and love."[35] In addition to writing commentaries on all four Gospels, Bucer published commentaries on Judges, the Psalms, Zephaniah, Romans and Ephesians. In the early years of the Reformation, there was a great deal of back and forth between Strasbourg and Basel, and both were centers of a lively publishing trade. Wolfgang Capito, Bucer's associate at Strasbourg, was a notable Hebraist and composed commentaries on Hosea (1529) and Habakkuk (1527).

At Basel, the great Sebastian Münster defended the use of Jewish sources in the Christian study of the Old Testament and published, in addition to his famous Hebrew grammar, an annotated version of the Gospel of Matthew translated from Greek into Hebrew. Oecolampadius, Basel's chief reformer, had been a proofreader in Froben's publishing house and worked with Erasmus on his Greek New Testament and his critical edition of Jerome. From 1523 he was both a preacher and professor of Holy Scripture at Basel. He defended Zwingli's eucharistic theology at the Colloquy of Marburg and published commentaries on 1 John (1524), Romans (1525) and Haggai-Malachi (1525). Oecolampadius was succeeded by Simon Grynaeus, a classical scholar who taught Greek and supported Bucer's efforts to bring Lutherans and Zwinglians together. More in line with Erasmus was Sebastian Castellio, who came to Basel after his expulsion from Geneva in 1545. He is best remembered for questioning the canonicity of the Song of Songs and for his annotations and French translation of the Bible.

The Zurich group. Biblical exegesis in Zurich was centered on the distinctive institution of the *Prophezei*, which began on June 19, 1525. On five days a week, at seven o'clock in the morning, all of the ministers and theological students in Zurich gathered into the choir of the Grossmünster to engage in a period of intense exegesis and interpretation of Scripture. After Zwingli had opened the meeting with prayer, the text of the day was read in Latin, Greek and Hebrew, followed by appropriate textual or exegetical comments. One of the ministers then delivered a sermon on the passage in German that was heard by many of Zurich's citizens who stopped by the cathedral on their way to work. This institute for advanced biblical studies had an enormous influence as a model for Reformed academies and seminaries throughout Europe. It was also the seedbed for sermon series in Zurich's churches and the extensive exegetical publications of Zwingli, Leo Jud, Konrad Pellikan, Heinrich Bullinger, Oswald Myconius and Rudolf Gwalther. Zwingli had memorized in Greek all of the Pauline epistles, and this bore fruit in his powerful expository preaching and biblical exegesis. He took seriously the role of grammar, rhetoric and historical research in explaining the biblical text. For example, he disagreed with Bucer

---

[35]Quoted in D. F. Wright, "Martin Bucer," *DMBI*, 290.

on the value of the Septuagint, regarding it as a trustworthy witness to a proto-Hebrew version earlier than the Masoretic text.

Zwingli's work was carried forward by his successor Bullinger, one of the most formidable scholars and networkers among the reformers. He composed commentaries on Daniel (1565), the Gospels (1542-1546), the Epistles (1537), Acts (1533) and Revelation (1557). He collaborated with Calvin to produce the *Consensus Tigurinus* (1549), a Reformed accord on the nature of the Lord's Supper, and produced a series of fifty sermons on Christian doctrine, known as *Decades*, which became required reading in Elizabethan England. As the *Antistes* ("overseer") of the Zurich church for forty-four years, Bullinger faced opposition from nascent Anabaptism on the one hand and resurgent Catholicism on the other. The need for a well-trained clergy and scholarly resources, including Scripture commentaries, arose from the fact that the Bible was "difficult or obscure to the unlearned, unskillful, unexercised, and malicious or corrupted wills." While forswearing papal claims to infallibility, Bullinger and other leaders of the magisterial Reformation saw the need for a kind of Protestant magisterium as a check against the tendency to read the Bible in "such sense as everyone shall be persuaded in himself to be most convenient."[36]

Two other commentators can be treated in connection with the Zurich group, though each of them had a wide-ranging ministry across the Reformation fronts. A former Benedictine monk, Wolfgang Musculus, embraced the Reformation in the 1520s and served briefly as the secretary to Bucer in Strasbourg. He shared Bucer's desire for Protestant unity and served for seventeen years (1531-1548) as a pastor and reformer in Augsburg. After a brief time in Zurich, where he came under the influence of Bullinger, Musculus was called to Bern, where he taught the Scriptures and published commentaries on the Psalms, the Decalogue, Genesis, Romans, Isaiah, 1 and 2 Corinthians, Galatians and Ephesians, Philippians, Colossians, 1 and 2 Thessalonians and 1 Timothy. Drawing on his exegetical writings, Musculus also produced a compendium of Protestant theology that was translated into English in 1563 as *Commonplaces of Christian Religion*.

Peter Martyr Vermigli was a Florentine-born scholar and Augustinian friar who embraced the Reformation and fled to Switzerland in 1542. Over the next twenty years, he would gain an international reputation as a prolific scholar and leading theologian within the Reformed community. He lectured on the Old Testament at Strasbourg, was made regius professor at Oxford, corresponded with the Italian refugee church in Geneva and spent the last years of his life as professor of Hebrew at Zurich. Vermigli published commentaries on 1 Corinthians, Romans and Judges during his lifetime. His biblical lectures on Genesis, Lamentations, 1 and 2 Samuel and 1 and 2 Kings were published posthumously. The most influential of his writings was the *Loci communes* (*Commonplaces*), a

---

[36]Euan Cameron, *The European Reformation* (Oxford: Oxford University Press, 1991), 120.

theological compendium drawn from his exegetical writings.

The Genevan Reformers. What Zwingli and Bullinger were to Zurich, Calvin and Beza were to Geneva. Calvin has been called "the father of modern biblical scholarship," and his exegetical work is without parallel in the Reformation. Because of the success of his *Institutes of the Christian Religion* Calvin has sometimes been thought of as a man of one book, but he always intended the *Institutes,* which went through eight editions in Latin and five in French during his lifetime, to serve as a guide to the study of the Bible, to show the reader "what he ought especially to seek in Scripture and to what end he ought to relate its contents." Jacob Arminius, who modified several principles of Calvin's theology, recommended his commentaries next to the Bible, for, as he said, Calvin "is incomparable in the interpretation of Scripture."[37] Drawing on his superb knowledge of Greek and Hebrew and his thorough training in humanist rhetoric, Calvin produced commentaries on all of the New Testament books except 2 and 3 John and Revelation. Calvin's Old Testament commentaries originated as sermon and lecture series and include Genesis, Psalms, Hosea, Isaiah, minor prophets, Daniel, Jeremiah and Lamentations, a harmony of the last four books of Moses, Ezekiel 1-20 and Joshua. Calvin sought for brevity and clarity in all of his exegetical work. He emphasized the illumination of the Holy Spirit as essential to a proper understanding of the text. Calvin underscored the continuity between the two Testaments (one covenant in two dispensations) and sought to apply the plain or natural sense of the text to the church of his day. In the preface to his own influential commentary on Romans, Karl Barth described how Calvin worked to recover the mind of Paul and make the apostle's message relevant to his day: "How energetically Calvin goes to work, first scientifically establishing the text ('what stands there?'), then following along the footsteps of its thought; that is to say, he conducts a discussion with it until the wall between the first and the sixteenth centuries becomes transparent, and until there in the first century Paul speaks and here the man of the sixteenth century hears, until indeed the conversation between document and reader becomes concentrated upon the substance (which must be the same now as then)."[38]

Beza was elected moderator of Geneva's Company of Pastors after Calvin's death in 1564 and guided the Genevan Reformation over the next four decades. His annotated Latin translation of the Greek New Testament (1556) and his further revisions of the Greek text established his reputation as the leading textual critic of the sixteenth century after Erasmus. Beza completed the translation of Marot's metrical Psalter, which became a centerpiece of Huguenot piety and Reformed church life. Though known for his polemical writings on grace, free will and predestination, Beza's work is marked by a strong pastoral orientation and concern for a Scripture-based spirituality.

---

[37]Quoted in A. M. Hunter, *The Teaching of Calvin* (London: James Clarke, 1950), 20.

[38]Karl Barth, *Die Römerbrief* (Zurich: TVZ, 1940), 11, translated by T. H. L. Parker as the epigraph to *Calvin's New Testament Commentaries,* 2nd ed. (Louisville, KY: Westminster John Knox, 1993).

Robert Estienne (Stephanus) was a printer-scholar who had served the royal household in Paris. After his conversion to Protestantism, in 1550 he moved to Geneva, where he published a series of notable editions and translations of the Bible. He also produced sermons and commentaries on Job, Ecclesiastes, the Song of Songs, Romans and Hebrews, as well as dictionaries, concordances and a thesaurus of biblical terms. He also published the first editions of the Bible with chapters divided into verses, an innovation that quickly became universally accepted.

The British Reformation. Commentary writing in England and Scotland lagged behind the continental Reformation for several reasons. In 1500, there were only three publishing houses in England compared with more than two hundred on the Continent. A 1408 statute against publishing or reading the Bible in English, stemming from the days of Lollardy, stifled the free flow of ideas, as was seen in the fate of Tyndale. Moreover, the nature of the English Reformation from Henry through Elizabeth provided little stability for the flourishing of biblical scholarship. In the sixteenth century, many "hot-gospel" Protestants in England were edified by the English translations of commentaries and theological writings by the Continental reformers. The influence of Calvin and Beza was felt especially in the Geneva Bible with its "Protestant glosses" of theological notes and references.

During the later Elizabethan and Stuart church, however, the indigenous English commentary came into its own. Both Anglicans and Puritans contributed to this outpouring of biblical studies. The sermons of Lancelot Andrewes and John Donne are replete with exegetical insights based on a close study of the Greek and Hebrew texts. Among the Reformed authors in England, none was more influential than William Perkins, the greatest of the early Puritan theologians, who published commentaries on Galatians, Jude, Revelation and the Sermon on the Mount (Mt 5-7). John Cotton, one of his students, wrote commentaries on the Song of Songs, Ecclesiastes and Revelation before departing for New England in 1633. The separatist pastor Henry Ainsworth was an outstanding scholar of Hebrew and wrote major commentaries on the Pentateuch, the Psalms and the Song of Songs. In Scotland, Robert Rollock, the first principal of Edinburgh University (1585), wrote numerous commentaries including those on the Psalms, Ephesians, Daniel, Romans, 1 and 2 Thessalonians, John, Colossians and Hebrews. Joseph Mede and Thomas Brightman were leading authorities on Revelation and contributed to the apocalyptic thought of the seventeenth century. Mention should also be made of Archbishop James Ussher, whose *Annals of the Old Testament* was published in 1650. Ussher developed a keen interest in biblical chronology and calculated that the creation of the world had taken place on October 26, 4004 B.C. As late as 1945, the Scofield Reference Bible still retained this date next to Genesis 1:1, but later editions omitted it because of the lack of evidence on which to fix such dates.[39]

---

[39]*The New Scofield Reference Bible* (New York: Oxford University Press, 1967), vi.

Anabaptism. Irena Backus has noted that there was no school of "dissident" exegesis during the Reformation, and the reasons are not hard to find. The radical Reformation was an ill-defined movement that existed on the margins of official church life in the sixteenth century. The denial of infant baptism and the refusal to swear an oath marked radicals as a seditious element in society, and they were persecuted by Protestants and Catholics alike. However, in the RCS we have made an attempt to include some voices of the radical Reformation, especially among the Anabaptists. While the Anabaptists published few commentaries in the sixteenth century, they were avid readers and quoters of the Bible. Numerous exegetical gems can be found in their letters, treatises, martyr acts (especially *The Martyrs' Mirror*), hymns and histories. They placed a strong emphasis on the memorizing of Scripture and quoted liberally from vernacular translations of the Bible. George H. Williams has noted that "many an Anabaptist theological tract was really a beautiful mosaic of Scripture texts."[40] In general, most Anabaptists accepted the apocryphal books as canonical, contrasted outer word and inner spirit with relative degrees of strictness and saw the New Testament as normative for church life and social ethics (witness their pacifism, nonswearing, emphasis on believers' baptism and congregational discipline).

We have noted the Old Testament translation of Ludwig Hätzer, who became an antitrinitarian, and Hans Denck that they published at Worms in 1527. Denck also wrote a notable commentary on Micah. Conrad Grebel belonged to a Greek reading circle in Zurich and came to his Anabaptist convictions while poring over the text of Erasmus's New Testament. The only Anabaptist leader with university credentials was Balthasar Hubmaier, who was made a doctor of theology (Ingolstadt, 1512) in the same year as Luther. His reflections on the Bible are found in his numerous writings, which include the first catechism of the Reformation (1526), a two-part treatise on the freedom of the will and a major work (*On the Sword*) setting forth positive attitudes toward the role of government and the Christian's place in society. Melchior Hoffman was an apocalyptic seer who wrote commentaries on Romans, Revelation and Daniel 12. He predicted that Christ would return in 1533. More temperate was Pilgram Marpeck, a mining engineer who embraced Anabaptism and traveled widely throughout Switzerland and south Germany, from Strasbourg to Augsburg. His "Admonition of 1542" is the longest published defense of Anabaptist views on baptism and the Lord's Supper. He also wrote many letters that functioned as theological tracts for the congregations he had founded dealing with topics such as the fruits of repentance, the lowliness of Christ and the unity of the church. Menno Simons, a former Catholic priest, became the most outstanding leader of the Dutch Anabaptist movement. His masterpiece was the *Foundation of Christian Doctrine* published in 1540. His other writings include *Meditation on the Twenty-fifth Psalm*

---

[40]George H. Williams, *The Radical Reformation*, 3rd ed. (Kirksville, MO: Sixteenth Century Journal Publishers, 1992), 1247.

(1537); *A Personal Exegesis of Psalm Twenty-five* modeled on the style of Augustine's *Confessions*; *Confession of the Triune God* (1550), directed against Adam Pastor, a former disciple of Menno who came to doubt the divinity of Christ; *Meditations and Prayers for Mealtime* (1557); and the *Cross of the Saints* (1554), an exhortation to faithfulness in the face of persecution. Like many other Anabaptists, Menno emphasized the centrality of discipleship *(Nachfolge)* as a deliberate repudiation of the old life and a radical commitment to follow Jesus as Lord.

Reading Scripture with the Reformers

In 1947, Gerhard Ebeling set forth his thesis that the history of the Christian church is the history of the interpretation of Scripture. Since that time, the place of the Bible in the story of the church has been investigated from many angles. A better understanding of the history of exegesis has been aided by new critical editions and scholarly discussions of the primary sources. The *Cambridge History of the Bible*, published in three volumes (1963-1970), remains a standard reference work in the field. The ACCS built on, and itself contributed to, the recovery of patristic biblical wisdom of both East and West. Beryl Smalley's *The Study of the Bible in the Middle Ages* (1940) and Henri de Lubac's *Medieval Exegesis: The Four Senses of Scripture* (1959) are essential reading for understanding the monastic and scholastic settings of commentary work between Augustine and Luther. The Reformation took place during what has been called "le grand siècle de la Bible."[41] Aided by the tools of Renaissance humanism and the dynamic impetus of Reformation theology (including permutations and reactions against it), the sixteenth century produced an unprecedented number of commentaries on every book in the Bible. Drawing from this vast storehouse of exegetical treasures, the RCS allows us to read Scripture along with the reformers. In doing so, it serves as a practical homiletic and devotional guide to some of the greatest masters of biblical interpretation in the history of the church.

The RCS gladly acknowledges its affinity with and dependence on recent scholarly investigations of Reformation-era exegesis. Between 1976 and 1990, three international colloquia on the history of biblical exegesis in the sixteenth century took place in Geneva and in Durham, North Carolina.[42] Among those participating in these three gatherings were a number of scholars who have produced groundbreaking works in the study of biblical interpretation in the Reformation. These include Elsie McKee, Irena Backus, Kenneth Hagen, Scott H. Hendrix, Richard A. Muller, Guy Bedouelle, Gerald Hobbs, John

---

[41]J-R. Aarmogathe, ed., *Bible de tous les temps*, 8 vols.; vol. 6, *Le grand siècle de la Bible* (Paris: Beauchesne, 1989).

[42]Olivier Fatio and Pierre Fraenkel, eds., *Histoire de l'exégèse au XVIe siècle: texts du colloque international tenu à Genève en 1976* (Geneva: Droz, 1978); David C. Steinmetz, ed., *The Bible in the Sixteenth Century* [Second International Colloquy on the History of Biblical Exegesis in the Sixteenth Century] (Durham: Duke University Press, 1990); Irena Backus and Francis M. Higman, eds., *Théorie et pratique de l'exégèse. Actes du troisième colloque international sur l'histoire de l'exégèse biblique au XVIe siècle, Genève, 31 août-2 septembre 1988* (Geneva: Droz, 1990); see also Guy Bedouelle and Bernard Roussel, eds., *Bible de tous les temps*, 8 vols.; vol. 5, *Le temps des Réformes et la Bible* (Paris: Beauchesne, 1989).

B. Payne, Bernard Roussel, Pierre Fraenkel and David C. Steinmetz. Among other scholars whose works are indispensible for the study of this field are Heinrich Bornkamm, Jaroslav Pelikan, Heiko A. Oberman, James S. Preus, T. H. L. Parker, David F. Wright, Tony Lane, John L. Thompson, Frank A. James and Timothy J. Wengert.[43] Among these scholars no one has had a greater influence on the study of Reformation exegesis than David C. Steinmetz. A student of Oberman, he has emphasized the importance of understanding the Reformation in medieval perspective. In addition to important studies on Luther and Staupitz, he has pioneered the method of comparative exegesis showing both continuity and discontinuity between major Reformation figures and the preceding exegetical traditions (see his *Luther in Context* and *Calvin in Context*). From his base at Duke University, he has spawned what might be called a Steinmetz school, a cadre of students and scholars whose work on the Bible in the Reformation era continues to shape the field. Steinmetz serves on the RCS Board of Editorial Advisors, and a number of our volume editors have pursued doctoral studies under his supervision.

In 1980, Steinmetz published "The Superiority of Pre-critical Exegesis," a seminal essay that not only placed Reformation exegesis in the context of the preceding fifteen centuries of the church's study of the Bible but also challenged certain assumptions underlying the hegemony of historical-critical exegesis of the post-Enlightenment academy.[44] Steinmetz helps us to approach the reformers and other precritical interpreters of the Bible on their own terms as faithful witnesses to the church's apostolic tradition. For them, a specific book or pericope had to be understood within the scope of the consensus of the canon. Thus the reformers, no less than the Fathers and the schoolmen, interpreted the hymn of the Johannine prologue about the preexistent Christ in consonance with the creation narrative of Genesis 1. In the same way, Psalm 22, Isaiah 53 and Daniel 7 are seen as part of an overarching storyline that finds ultimate fulfillment in Jesus Christ. Reading the Bible with the resources of the new learning, the reformers challenged the exegetical conclusions of their medieval predecessors at many points. However, unlike Alexander Campbell in the nineteenth century, their aim was not to "open the New Testament as if mortal man had never seen it before." Rather, they wanted to do their biblical work as part of an interpretive conversation within the family of the people of God. In the reformers' emphatic turn to the literal sense, which prompted their many blasts against the unrestrained use of allegory, their work was an extension of a similar impulse made by Thomas Aquinas and Nicholas of Lyra.

This is not to discount the radically new insights gained by the reformers in their dynamic engagement with the text of Scripture; nor should we dismiss in a reactionary way

---

[43]For bibliographical references and evaluation of these and other contributors to the scholarly study of Reformation-era exegesis, see Richard A. Muller, "Biblical Interpretation in the Era of the Reformation: The View From the Middle Ages," in *Biblical Interpretation in the Era of the Reformation: Essays Presented to David C. Steinmetz in Honor of His Sixtieth Birthday*, ed. Richard A. Muller and John L. Thompson (Grand Rapids: Eerdmans, 1996), 3-22.

[44]David C. Steinmetz, "The Superiority of Pre-Critical Exegesis," *Theology Today* 37 (1980): 27-38.

the light shed on the meaning of the Bible by the scholarly accomplishments of the past two centuries. However, it is to acknowledge that the church's exegetical tradition is an indispensible aid for the proper interpretation of Scripture. And this means, as Richard Muller has said, that "while it is often appropriate to recognize that traditionary readings of the text are erroneous on the grounds offered by the historical-critical method, we ought also to recognize that the conclusions offered by historical-critical exegesis may themselves be quite erroneous on the grounds provided by the exegesis of the patristic, medieval, and reformation periods."[45]

George Herbert was an English pastor and poet who reaped the benefits of the renewal of biblical studies in the age of the Reformation. He referred to the Scriptures as a book of infinite sweetness, "a mass of strange delights," a book with secrets to make the life of anyone good. In describing the various means pastors require to be fully furnished in the work of their calling, Herbert provided a rationale for the history of exegesis and for the Reformation Commentary on Scripture:

> The fourth means are commenters and Fathers, who have handled the places controverted, which the parson by no means refuseth. As he doth not so study others as to neglect the grace of God in himself and what the Holy Spirit teacheth him, so doth he assure himself that God in all ages hath had his servants to whom he hath revealed his Truth, as well as to him; and that as one country doth not bear all things that there may be a commerce, so neither hath God opened or will open all to one, that there may be a traffic in knowledge between the servants of God for the planting both of love and humility. Wherefore he hath one comment[ary] at least upon every book of Scripture, and ploughing with this, and his own meditations, he enters into the secrets of God treasured in the holy Scripture.[46]

Timothy George
General Editor

---

[45]Richard A. Muller and John L. Thompson, "The Significance of Precritical Exegesis: Retrospect and Prospect," in *Biblical Interpretation in the Era of the Reformation: Essays Presented to David C. Steinmetz in Honor of His Sixtieth Birthday*, ed. Richard A. Muller and John L. Thompson (Grand Rapids: Eerdmans, 1996), 342.
[46]George Herbert, *The Complete English Poems* (London: Penguin, 1991), 205.

A GUIDE TO USING THIS COMMENTARY

Several features have been incorporated into the design of this commentary. The following comments are intended to assist readers in making full use of this volume.

Pericopes of Scripture

The scriptural text has been divided into pericopes, or passages, usually several verses in length. Each of these pericopes is given a heading, which appears at the beginning of the pericope. For example, the first pericope in the commentary on Ezekiel is "1:1-28 The Living Creatures and the Glory of the Lord." This heading is followed by the Scripture passage quoted in the English Standard Version (ESV) across the full width of the page. The Scripture passage is provided for the convenience of readers, but it is also in keeping with Reformation-era commentaries, which often followed the patristic and medieval commentary tradition, in which the citations of the reformers were arranged according to the text of Scripture.

Overviews

Following each pericope of text is an overview of the Reformation authors' comments on that pericope. The format of this overview varies among the volumes of this series, depending on the requirements of the specific book of Scripture. The function of the overview is to provide a brief summary of all the comments to follow. It tracks a reasonably cohesive thread of argument among reformers' comments, even though they are derived from diverse sources and generations. Thus, the summaries do not proceed chronologically or by verse sequence. Rather, they seek to rehearse the overall course of the reformers' comments on that pericope.

We do not assume that the commentators themselves anticipated or expressed a formally received cohesive argument but rather that the various arguments tend to flow in a plausible, recognizable pattern. Modern readers can thus glimpse aspects of continuity in the flow of diverse exegetical traditions representing various generations and geographical locations.

Topical Headings

An abundance of varied Reformation-era comment is available for each pericope. For this reason we have broken the pericopes into two levels. First is the verse with its topical heading. The reformers' comments are then focused on aspects of each verse, with topical headings summarizing the essence of the individual comment by evoking a key phrase, metaphor or idea. This feature provides a bridge by which modern readers can enter into the heart of the Reformation-era comment.

Identifying the Reformation Texts

Following the topical heading of each section of comment, the name of the Reformation commentator is given. An English translation (where needed) of the reformer's comment is then provided. This is immediately followed by the title of the original work rendered in English.

Readers who wish to pursue a deeper investigation of the reformers' works cited in this commentary will find full bibliographic detail for each reformation title provided in the bibliography at the back of the volume. Comments translated from original-language Reformation-era commentaries and sermon collections can be readily located in the source texts by Scripture reference. Information on English translations (where available) and standard original-language editions and critical editions of the works cited is found in the bibliography.

The Footnotes

To aid the reader in exploring the background and texts in further detail, this commentary utilizes footnotes. The use and content of footnotes may vary among the volumes in this series. Where footnotes appear, a footnote number directs the reader to a note at the bottom of the right-hand column, where one will find annotations (clarifications or biblical cross references), information on English translations (where available) or standard original-language editions of the work cited.

Where original-language texts have remained untranslated into English, we provide new translations. Where there is any serious ambiguity or textual problem in the selection, we have tried to reflect the best available textual tradition. Wherever current English translations are already well rendered, they are utilized, but where necessary they are stylistically updated. A single asterisk (*) indicates that a previous English translation has been updated to modern English or amended for easier reading. We have standardized spellings and made grammatical variables uniform so that our English references will not reflect the linguistic oddities of the older English translations. For ease of reading we have in some cases edited out superfluous conjunctions.

INTRODUCTION TO
GENESIS 1–11

In 1598, Christophor Pelargus published a 694-page commentary with an unusual title: *A Commentary on the Ocean of All the Prophets, or*—as the title went on to explain—*on Genesis, the Sacred [Book of] Moses.*[1] However much we might wonder at finding Genesis apparently categorized among the prophetic books of the Old Testament (though readers of sixteenth-century commentaries would have quickly learned that the category was not so inappropriate), Pelargus's depiction of Genesis as an ocean is especially arresting: with a single word, he unabashedly claims for the Bible's first book a vastness of scope and inexhaustible depth as a source for prophecy and teaching. Yet one might fairly wonder, then, what was *not* to be found in Genesis?

What Is This Book Good For? The Encyclopedic Allure of Genesis

Genesis has always been both blessed and burdened by the exceedingly high expectations of its readers and interpreters. Its historical value is obvious, for this first book of Moses is virtually the only source for the early history of the people of Israel. Anyone reckoned among the physical or spiritual descendants of Abraham would naturally be interested in the patriarchs Abraham, Isaac and Jacob—especially given the colorful (if not audacious) details of their stories—and also, in turn, in the twelve sons of Jacob from whom the tribes of Israel would trace their descent.

The earlier chapters of Genesis, however, were also uniquely instructive for a more general human self-understanding. The catastrophe of the flood, which destroyed the entirety of the world as it was originally created (including, some speculated, the original Garden of Eden), and the debacle of the tower "reaching to the heavens" that people began to build at Babel, which ultimately accounted for the diversity and disparity of human

---

[1] Christophor Pelargus, *In prophetarum omnium oceanum, sive Genesin sacram Mosaicam ex antiquitate puriore magna parte erutus Commentarius* (Leipzig, 1598). Highly regarded in his own day but largely forgotten in ours, Pelargus was a superintendent general of the (Lutheran) church in Brandenburg who provoked great controversy when he supported the new elector of Brandenburg, John Sigismund, when he publicly converted to Calvinism on Christmas Day, 1613. See Bodo Nischan, "The 'Fractio Panis:' A Reformed Communion Practice in Late Reformation Germany," *Church History* 53 (1984): 17-29, esp. 22-23.

language—these stories shined a light on the character of the nations and peoples of the earth, so painfully divided into those who sought to follow God and those who sought to rebel. That stark division was traced back much further, of course—to that first homicide, the murder of Abel by his brother, Cain. Indeed, of greater interest still were the three opening chapters of Genesis, which not only described the origins of the first man and woman but also disclosed the enduring character of women and men, particularly in light of their temptation and fall in Genesis 3.

But readers were just as captivated by the opening chapters of Genesis for what they told of prehistory—not just human prehistory, but prehuman history. These chapters spoke of many things for which there were no eyewitnesses and no other written records. Long before Darwin, Genesis furnished an authoritative account of "the origin of species," of plants and animals and "creeping things." Here too were enigmatic but fascinating hints about the fashioning of the heavens and the earth, and of the creation of the universe itself. And what better place to stand than "in the beginning" in order to try to learn something of what God was like or what God was doing before the Deity became the Creator, indeed, before there was time?

The historical narrative and the more immediate theological message of Genesis 1–11 were therefore constantly at risk of being upstaged or even discarded by those who sought to mine this book for other information—for cosmology, astronomy, geography, natural history (including properties of plants and animals), human biology, psychology and political science, not to mention possible mystical and metaphysical meanings. But not all interested parties were friendly readers. Genesis attracted attention from many who wanted to ridicule it or discredit its adherents, and the history of the Bible's interpretation was shaped early on by the need of Christians and Jews to marshal a defense of the Bible's credibility—including many contested details found in the book of Genesis.

Given the potential of Genesis to function as an encyclopedia, it becomes less surprising that older commentaries often filled so many hundreds of pages, or that some of these commentators did not live to complete their task![2] Yet all of this intense scholarly activity, particularly on the part of the commentators of the Reformation era, would seem to beg an important question. Granting for the moment that the Bible is a book of great significance to Christians and Jews, and that Genesis is itself of special interest on account of all the factors already mentioned, isn't there some sort of self-contradiction in the propensity of Protestants to write commentaries at all? Shouldn't the impulse to free God's Word from the encumbrance and overlay of human traditions and return to "Scripture alone" have led to a profound demotion, if not dismissal, of all such merely human voices and writings, as biblical commentaries necessarily are?

---

[2]See the inventory of sixteenth-century commentaries on Genesis in Mickey Leland Mattox, *"Defender of the Most Holy Matriarchs": Martin Luther's Interpretation of the Women of Genesis in the "Enarrationes in Genesin," 1535-1545* (Leiden: Brill, 2003), 277-99, which often indicates page counts and whether the work was completed.

What Are *Commentaries* on Genesis Good For? And Why Read *Old* Ones?

Commentaries are a peculiar kind of writing. In theory, at least, they come into existence not for their own sake but for the sake of some other book that invariably commands greater recognition than the commentary does on its own. Indeed, a commentary succeeds only to the extent that, like John the Baptist, it calls attention to the significance of that to which it points—in this case, the Bible. Commentaries are never supposed to have anything like the authority of Scripture itself, but they are supposed to be helpful.

Accordingly, however much early Protestants are remembered and lauded for espousing the principle of *sola Scriptura*, "Scripture alone" as their authority, the Latin slogan is frequently understood far more shallowly than befits actual Protestant practices.[3] Early reformers reacted viscerally wherever they saw human traditions, especially ecclesiastical traditions, rivaling or subverting the clear teachings of Christ and the apostles as found in the Bible, particularly when those traditions imposed laws or requirements that had no biblical foundation but terrified the consciences of Christians, who feared that any breach of these spurious laws and traditions might result in the loss of salvation. Yet, at the same time, these Protestants knew very well (better than their Catholic contemporaries, they would have claimed) that sound theological writings, including biblical commentaries, could serve Christians very well precisely by explaining Scripture and cultivating the life of discipleship. So when they affirmed the principle of *sola Scriptura* and thereby looked to the Bible as the unique and preeminent authority in faith and life, they never meant to discard useful human traditions or edifying Christian writings. Neither did they mean to ignore or deny the historical embeddedness of both church and Bible: for just as the Bible is to be read in light of its original context, so should the church present the Bible's message—whether expressed in songs, sermons or service—in ways suited to the church's context today.

Accordingly, if we ourselves wonder about the utility of commentaries, particularly old commentaries such as those excerpted in this volume, we are not really raising any question that the reformers themselves did not ask. If the Reformation advocated a return to the Bible, that return was not meant as a rejection of all prior theology or theological writing—far from it! A fine example of a critical appreciation and appropriation of the Christian past, typical of early Protestantism, can be found in one of the lesser-known episodes in the career of John Calvin.

One of the more enigmatic fragments Calvin left behind was the undated draft of an introduction to a proposed translation of the sermons of John Chrysostom, the highly regarded preacher of Antioch and bishop of Constantinople at the end of the fourth century.[4] Chrysostom's sermons on Genesis had been translated into Latin by Johannes

---

[3]See Anthony N. S. Lane, "*Sola Scriptura?* Making Sense of a Post-Reformation Slogan," in *A Pathway into the Holy Scripture*, ed. Philip E. Satterthwaite and David F. Wright (Grand Rapids: Eerdmans, 1994), 297-327.

[4]W. Ian P. Hazlett, "Calvin's Latin Preface to His Proposed French Edition of Chrysostom's Homilies: Translation and Com-

Oecolampadius as recently as 1523; Calvin's project, however, envisioned translating them into French. But why? It is obvious that Calvin's appreciation for Chrysostom not only matched that of Oecolampadius, who valued Chrysostom's literal exegesis as a model for Reformation interpreters, but even surpassed it, insofar as Calvin commended Chrysostom not just for pastors but for the laity as well—for in a day when it was controversial, even dangerous, to produce vernacular translations of the Bible, a vernacular edition of Chrysostom would be an even greater oddity.

Calvin's introduction, however, offers not just an endorsement of Chrysostom but also a sustained argument that the propagation of commentaries and homilies was viewed by the church fathers themselves as a pastoral duty on behalf of "ordinary Christians." Calvin wanted to replicate this service to the laity and even extend it to pastors in his own day, who were often insufficiently versed in Greek and Latin "to understand these ancient writers in the original."[5] Such writings are useful not only as resources for a "true understanding" of the Word of God; they are also important to teach pastors about the church in its ancient and purer form, including its orderly government, its sanctity and discipline, its use of ceremonies, and so on.[6] But Calvin's most provocative remark emerges from how he characterizes these exegetical works:

> Since, however, the Lord, with the same consideration by which he illuminates us through his Spirit, has, in addition, granted us aids, which he intends to be of assistance in our labor of investigating his truth, there is no reason for us either to neglect them as superfluous, or even to care less about them as if irrelevant. For what Paul said ought to be borne in mind, that *though everything belongs to us, we however belong to Christ*. Therefore, let those things which the Lord has provided for our use be of service to us.[7]

Calvin's argument is not surprising to him, but perhaps it is to us. The exegetical assistance that these "ancient writers" offer is by no means superfluous or unnecessary, he insists. Rather, it is *provided by God* for our use, alongside the Holy Spirit, and, as he later adds, "the people themselves would be lacking in gratitude, were they not eager to take up the gift of God offered to them."[8] In other words, Calvin does not think we should try to get along without the exegetical writings of the early church (received not uncritically, of course), and it takes only a small inference to conclude that he would have commended his own commentaries and those of his colleagues with equal seriousness.

Calvin's translation project never went beyond his rough draft of the introduction, but his essay amply attests the profound connection with the church fathers that was

---

mentary," in *Humanism and Reform: The Church in Europe, England, and Scotland*, ed. James Kirk (Oxford: Blackwell, 1991), 129-50.

[5]Hazlett, "Calvin's Latin Preface," 141-43.

[6]Hazlett, "Calvin's Latin Preface," 150.

[7]Hazlett, "Calvin's Latin Preface," 141 (italics in original).

[8]Hazlett, "Calvin's Latin Preface," 143.

recognized and cultivated among early Protestants. Any contemporary invocation of *sola Scriptura* has to reckon with the reformers' own assertion of their necessary continuity with the Fathers and with the first five centuries of Christianity, despite the fact that (as the reformers knew well, and as Calvin's essay acknowledged) the Fathers by no means agreed on everything.

Calvin's goals in reading the church fathers' commentaries and sermons stand in full accord with the four goals of the Reformation Commentary on Scripture (as explained by Timothy George[9]), but it is worth underscoring Calvin's distinctive perspective. First, he says, *we need help* in reading and appropriating the Scriptures; and, second, in the person of the church fathers and other godly predecessors, *we have been furnished with such help*. Indeed, this help is God-given, and we are obliged to be grateful to the Holy Spirit for such gifts. But a third part of Calvin's perspective is less explicit, though it may be even more important for us today. To take seriously—that is, to *read*—the biblical exegesis of generations long past is also an expression of something Calvin may have taken for granted, yet something he was also quick to defend: the continuity of the newly-reforming church with the church founded by Christ and the apostles, indeed, the church that flourished in the patristic era.

For Calvin and his colleagues, the continuity of the church, past and present, was a crucial tenet—whether he considered the continuity of the people of God from the Old Testament to the New, or the people of God from the first century to the sixteenth. Like many Christian writers throughout the ages, Calvin was acutely aware of the cloud of witnesses that surrounded him. His writings—his footnotes, so to speak—tell of that awareness, that debt to the past that formed him and fitted him for his own day. We need this too. We need to absorb the legacy of both the Fathers and the reformers—not to parrot them, but to be formed by their witness and spirit as part of one continuous body of Christ that flourishes also in our own day. It is, in brief, a matter of forming Christian identity and a Christian authenticity rooted fully in the whole Christ and his whole church. Granted that what is offered here does not intend to represent the whole history of the Christian exegesis of Genesis, it is nonetheless a significant supplement, especially healthful for those whose Christian roots run through the Reformation and who need to be shaped by a concentrated sampling and encounter with the legacy of the Reformation and its encounter with God's Word.

What Do We Need to Know to Read Reformation Commentaries on Genesis?

A book such as this one can be a mixed blessing. Inevitably, many will park this volume

---

[9]See above, p. xiii: "The RCS has four goals: the enrichment of contemporary biblical interpretation through exposure to Reformation-era biblical exegesis; the renewal of contemporary preaching through exposure to the biblical insights of the Reformation writers; a deeper understanding of the Reformation itself and the breadth of perspectives represented within it; and the recovery of the robust spiritual theology and devotional treasures of the Reformation's engagement with the Bible."

on a shelf until some exegetical question arises (provoked, no doubt, by late-night preparations for a sermon, a Bible study or some seminary assignment), then turn directly to chapter and verse, hoping for an instant insight or blessing. A treasury of excerpts can hardly avoid being so used, but a cold plunge into the sixteenth century with no preparation or background is not recommended.

There are, in fact, some spectacularly bad ways to read these excerpts, just as there are bad ways to read the past in general. Sometimes readers venture into the theological past in order to recruit allies or to find and vilify opponents. In this way, historical figures are pressed into service as proxies for present-day conflicts that may or may not genuinely pertain to the distant past. All too often, Christian writers of bygone days are valued only for the sake of some supposedly clever quotation or sound bite, which is then hauled back to the present, stripped of its original context. But there are other, more subtle ways in which many are keen to find anticipations of the theological or ecclesiastical present among writers of the past. Protestants are understandably proud of what they regard as the recovery of the literal reading of the Bible in the wake of the Reformation, including the discarding of spurious allegorical readings and the prizing of "Scripture alone." Some would even argue that the great advance of historical-critical exegesis ought to be traced directly to the reformers. However, these are partial truths, at best—and, as we will see, the alleged rejection of allegory was by no means universally practiced or agreed on, and even disfavored figural readings of the church fathers often found ways to re-enter the conversation.

How, then, can we read these writers—these excerpts—well? The most important factor is simply this: *context*. Visiting the past, like visiting any foreign country, is best preceded by some serious study of the local history, geography and cultural distinctives—as well as by some feel for how the local realities fit into the bigger picture of history and culture. All these ingredients, of course, can amount to a fairly tall order for a short vacation, but for our purposes here, there are two kinds of context for Reformation exegesis that will prove helpful to most readers. First, it is worth reviewing the complex and diverse theological discussions and practical changes that were precipitated by the Protestant Reformation—sometimes by design, but sometimes following the law of unintended consequences—because an awareness of the range of sixteenth-century pastoral and social issues can only sharpen our appreciation for some of the practical dimensions of sixteenth-century exegesis. Second, it is also worth surveying the exegetical context, including some of the changes in exegetical method, but also some of the specific exegetical trajectories in Genesis that the reformers inherited, reshaped more or less, and passed on to their descendants.

The Exegesis of Genesis in Its Reformation Context

The great slogans of the Reformation are undeniably stirring, to Protestants at least, particularly Luther's radical assertion that we are saved *sola fide*, by faith alone, which we receive *sola gratia*, solely by God's grace and not by our works of merit, and which is a teaching that will be clear to anyone who submits to *sola Scriptura*, to the Bible alone as the authority above all others. Yet it is all too easy to content ourselves with the casual conclusion that the Reformation was all about justification by faith, freedom of conscience and a straightforward movement back to the Bible. Who would guess, looking back, that the Reformation would also promote a deliberate secularization of marriage, or that immigration and poor relief would become hot topics or that Protestant exegesis would begin the process of dismantling the divine right of kings in favor of a social-contract theory that fostered the right to resist tyranny?

In this part of our introduction, we will explore the rich and intricate context of the Reformation exegesis of Genesis by tracing some of the many doctrines, practices and social or political implications that were connected with Luther's insights about justification and his concomitant displacement of the authority of the papal church by the authority of Scripture. While an overview of this sort runs its own risk of oversimplification, we will still be able to get a glimpse of how great a social revolution the Reformation (and not just Luther's part of it) came to embody and precipitate—and how these social and theological changes were intertwined with the book of Genesis.

It would be a vast oversimplification to think that the Reformation began promptly on October 31, 1517, right after Luther posted his Ninety-five Theses against the papacy's practice of granting indulgences.[10] Rather, it was only through a more gradual process over the next two years, through his teaching and disputations, that Luther's doctrine of justification attained full clarity of definition, even as his writings spread through much of Europe during this time, stirring controversy in their wake. Yet even if we give pride of place to justification by faith alone or to the distinctive Protestant understanding of Scripture's authority, to treat the Reformation as if it were concerned with nothing but these one or two doctrines would leave us with less than even a half-truth.

The doctrine of *justification by faith alone* that early Protestants embraced was not an isolated element of piety, deeply spiritual but divorced from life: rather, just as Luther's insight emerged from a complex late medieval context, so too was this doctrine the bellwether of theological and social changes already underway. But justification by faith alone was also tightly joined with the Protestant doctrine of *sola Scriptura*. It had to be, of course, because salvation by faith alone as proclaimed by the reformers was a direct contradiction of Catholic doctrine, which insisted that faith became saving only if infused with a "habit" of love or charity, and that such love would need to be manifested in one's deeds and good works in order for one to receive salvation, eventually, when one's original purity had been fully restored by love and good works. The reformers' dissent was anchored in the conviction that Scripture taught no such doctrine and that Scripture's

---

[10]An *indulgence* was often bestowed in the form of a certificate or writ, most famously issued by the pope, that claimed to shorten someone's time in purgatory by applying the extra merits of Christ and the saints in exchange for monetary donations.

authority trumped that of the church and its tradition, no matter how "apostolic" that tradition purported to be. Not surprisingly, Reformation commentators were also quick to find their views attested in Genesis, in the persons of Abel, Enoch, Noah and others—each of whom demonstrated in one way or another that he too was justified by precisely such "faith alone," not by works.

Yoked to a high doctrine of Scripture, justification was quickly recognized as part of a matrix of doctrines and practices that brought this theological insight into contact with virtually all spheres of daily life among all classes and for both men and women. Implications led off in every direction, as the reformers were quick to see. One of the better known is Luther's doctrine of the universal priesthood, commonly known as *the priesthood of all believers*. As Luther would explain it, one benefit of faith is to quiet the conscience against the accusations of sin and the law (and Genesis pays ample attention to law and gospel, as well as to sin and conscience). But an additional benefit of faith is that it unites us, spiritually and mystically, with our bridegroom, Christ, who makes us to be not only his brothers and sisters, not only co-heirs with him, but also to be priests: "worthy to appear before God to pray for others and to teach one another divine things."[11]

The doctrine of the universal priesthood, however, is itself also densely matrixed: it builds on the unique and sole adequacy of faith to please God and thus is a reflex of *the denial of merits* as significant to our salvation; and it has radical implications for one's *doctrine of ministry*, insofar as it repudiates any special or sacramental priesthood in favor of a pastoral office that intends to represent the people of God and to be merely representative, in that a pastor performs a public service or function that any Christian might fill, were he duly called and qualified. Or, for that matter, *she*: Luther's Catholic opponents mocked him for the implications of this universal priesthood, because it implied that even women might preach—and, on that occasion at least, Luther granted that they might, except for their lack of education and proper speaking voice.[12]

Regardless of Luther's inconsistent remarks about women in leadership,[13] the doctrine of the universal priesthood gradually came to necessitate support for *catechism and primary education*—for girls as well as boys, and not just in Germany but in many Protestant lands. Indeed, because the Reformation was deeply invested in the Bible, it was necessarily also invested not just in *vernacular translations* of the Bible but also in a *vernacular literacy* that could read it with understanding. The faith that alone now justified Christians was not the "implicit faith" described by medieval theologians, which consisted more in submitting to the teachings of the church than in actively understand-

---

[11]Luther, *On the Freedom of a Christian* (1520), LW 31:355.

[12]Luther, *On the Misuse of the Mass* (1521), LW 36:151-52; discussed with other Luther texts in John L. Thompson, *John Calvin and the Daughters of Sarah: Women in Regular and Exceptional Roles in the Exegesis of Calvin, His Predecessors, and His Contemporaries* (Geneva: Droz, 1992), 198-202.

[13]See *Luther on Women: A Sourcebook*, trans. Susan C. Karant-Nunn and Merry E. Wiesner-Hanks (New York: Cambridge University Press, 2003), 15-31, 58-87.

ing the Bible's saving doctrines. The quest for literacy in service of personally knowing the gospel thus led to the writing and adopting of catechisms. It also led to *accountability for knowing one's catechism*, along with the Apostles' Creed and the Lord's Prayer—a knowledge that one might be asked to demonstrate during the visits regularly conducted by Lutheran and Reformed clergy, who stressed the importance of the family in catechism and in forming Christian character and who would find evidence in Genesis that the heads of households were diligent in teaching and training their children in godly beliefs and ways of life. However much justification by faith was celebrated for freeing the conscience from works of the law, Protestantism also established an early reputation for *moral seriousness and discipline* in lay and clergy alike and for various mechanisms of social control to encourage it.

These *mechanisms of social control*, such as the Genevan consistory (a panel of pastors and elders that could not only mandate attendance at sermons but also advise civil authorities to undertake severer measures), brought the "Bible alone" to bear on all kinds of issues. The separation of *church and state* that we so often take for granted was, in the sixteenth century, neither so very clear nor so very much desired by most Protestants—with the notable exception of the Anabaptists and other radical reformers, who locked horns with both Protestants and Catholics on a number of theological issues and practices. But in Lutheran and Reformed cities and territories, civil magistrates filled a venerable office, indeed, one established in Genesis 2 when God assigned Adam to cultivate the garden and rule the animals. Magistrates were also God's servants, and they commonly enforced the instructions of their local reformers—except when they balked. The illusion that John Calvin was a despot in Geneva is belied by his struggle for almost two decades to see the city council adopt some of his priorities, such as the frequency of the Lord's Supper, or *the suppression of "popular" immorality* such as gaming or dancing or other lewd conduct at inns or taverns, or the adoption of *sumptuary legislation* that would prohibit excessive and wasteful consumption of scarce goods on the part of a few wealthy citizens. Calvin's commitment to the last of these points should be of special interest to us: by mid-century, Geneva had become a safe haven for *religious refugees*, many of whom arrived destitute and thereby strained the city's resources, good will and patience with these foreign-born immigrants. In his own exegesis of Genesis, Calvin was not slow to find analogies with the homelessness of Abraham or the losses suffered by Noah and his family.

One point on which reformers and Protestant magistrates tended to agree, however, was on the need to reform what the Roman Catholic Church had come to teach about the *indissolubility of marriage*—despite what Jesus said in Matthew 5:32 and 19:9 or what Paul suggested in 1 Corinthians 7, that at least some marriages could be honorably dissolved. Catholic theology had long since committed to marriage as a sacramental bond that could be broken only by the death of one of the spouses, but Protestants did not find this an adequate account of Scripture. Genesis 2 proved to them that monogamous marriage was not a Christian invention, much less a sacrament, but rather a universal human institution that should be regulated as such, however much it might also depict the union of Christ and the church. In practice, Protestant marriages continued to be celebrated in churches but with a new involvement on the part of civil authorities. Such involvement was especially conspicuous in cases where one or both spouses petitioned for a dissolution of the marriage *and* for the right to remarry. Protestant reformers and cities were highly reluctant to grant divorces, but they did so consistently if sparingly, citing both biblical grounds and a few others (such as desertion or undisclosed impotence) that they judged to be of analogous validity.

Alongside the question of divorce, Protestants found themselves deeply tangled in other debates stemming from *the theology and practice of marriage* almost at the outset of the Reformation. Indeed, while some of Luther's most influential theological treatises stem from 1520,[14] it was barely a year after that, in 1522, that he felt compelled to publish *On the Estate of Marriage*. There were many reasons for addressing marriage at that particular moment, some of which were perennial issues (lust and misbehavior) while others were directly provoked by the Reformation. The treatise makes a strong case not just for the goodness of marriage, but more specifically that *marital sexuality and procreation* are normally God's mandate for every man and woman. Luther thus argues partly against clerical celibacy and the notion that celibacy was more virtuous than marriage (as based on the old patristic distinction between Jesus' commands and his "counsels of perfection" that led to greater merit), but also partly for the dignity of a woman's particular *calling or vocation* as wife and mother, and even for a degree of mutuality in marriage. Like many of the other reformers, Luther had concluded from Scripture that not only was there no special merit before God in being a priest or monk, there was also no warrant for the church to require a vow of celibacy in order to pursue an ordained calling. All these ingredients—ordination as a sacrament, mandated celibacy and involuntary vows—were unbiblical and spiritually hazardous. So, far from being second best, marriage and procreation were good things—*very* good, even for clergy, as Luther and others argued not only from the first account of marriage in Genesis 2 but also from the marriages of the earliest patriarchs of Genesis.

That the reformers put marriage back in the control of the state and demoted it from sacramental status was not an indication of their indifference to marriage and family, then, but just the opposite. Protestants were defenders of marriage and the married, and these possibly surprising changes were largely motivated by the Protestant reading of Scripture. The authority they ascribed to the Bible led to a multitude of other *changes in worship and sacraments*, too. The sacramental controversies over baptism and the Lord's Supper are well-known disputes that not only divided Protestants from Roman Catholics

---

[14]Including treatises *On the Freedom of a Christian* and *On Good Works*, his address *To the Christian Nobility of the German Nation Concerning the Reform of the Christian Estate*, and *The Babylonian Captivity of the Church*.

but also Lutherans from Calvinists and Zwinglians, and all of them from Anabaptists. One might think that Genesis would be free from such controversies, but commentators found many types, analogies and adumbrations of the sacraments in general (and for baptism and the Eucharist in particular) whenever they reflected on such things as the sacramental function of the tree of the knowledge of good and evil or the significance of the sacrifices offered by Cain and Abel. And the still larger issue of what God requires of human beings by way of worship would prove to be a major theme in the earliest strands of this book (beginning with the question of the sabbath on the seventh day), just as it was a major controversy throughout the Reformation.

The Protestant insistence on *sola Scriptura* changed worship in other ways, too, but at a more fundamental level it changed the definition of the church itself. The Roman Catholic Church ratified its authority by looking to its demonstrable *apostolic succession*—the unbroken line of authority that began with Christ and the apostles, was handed down to bishops as their successors and continues to the present day, with the bishop of Rome preeminent among the other bishops. Protestants also claimed apostolicity but grounded it in their fidelity to the apostles' writings—the New Testament—rather than a succession of bishops. Some Protestant churches did away with the traditional office of bishop (again, on the grounds that the Bible did not distinguish between elders and overseers), but all Protestant churches experienced both the freedom and the potential chaos of appealing only to Scripture and the Holy Spirit to govern and unite (or not) the diverse Reformation movements. And all Protestant commentators were happy to point out that the authority of the patriarchs in Genesis rested directly on their responsiveness to God's word.

The point of this condensed survey of the theological and practical implications and effects of the shift in Protestant thinking about Scripture and about the doctrine of justification is not that it should substitute for a more nuanced and extensive account. For that, there are many worthy histories of the Reformation, its context and its theology. But this survey does try to indicate how connected everything was in the sixteenth century—doctrine, exegesis, church practices, political decisions, family life—just as these things are today. Even more to the point, readers should not expect that a sixteenth-century commentary will somehow float along in isolation from the lives and concerns that are the very substance of any serious theology, as well as any exegesis worth reading. Inevitably, all of these issues show up somewhere in Genesis, and they lurk also in the wings of virtually every Reformation commentary, if not onstage, front and center.

The Reformers' Place in the History of the Interpretation of Genesis

In addition to the work as reformers of the church that forced them to deal with the myriad of issues presented above, Reformation commentators also participated in a world of intellectual discourse that transcended their place and time. That is to say, as commentators, they carried on a constant conversation with the exegetes of past centuries—particularly the fathers of the early church, who were so largely respected by them, but also medieval commentators and glossators, rabbis, classical writers of Greece and Rome, and anyone else who might help them elucidate the inspired text of the Bible. In this section, we will place these Reformation commentators in the context of their work more precisely as Scripture scholars by examining the new climate for reading the Bible that emerged in the sixteenth century. In the next section, we will survey some of the specific conversations about the book of Genesis into which commentators routinely entered.

The sixteenth century was an exciting time to be a Scripture scholar. Protestant reformers were in a position to take advantage of several major changes in the ways that scholars thought about texts in general and the Bible in particular. The most obvious change was the dissemination of the printing press throughout the cities of Europe. As the cost of printing fell, books ceased to be the exclusive possession of scholars or the wealthy. Cheap print, including single-sheet pamphlets, enabled messages and movements to spread through society at virtually all levels. Cheap print also raised academic standards, as it became more feasible and more desirable to produce critical editions of important writers rather than having to depend on manuscripts of unequal and uncertain reliability. Indeed, the passion for authentic original sources was embodied in the motto of Renaissance scholars: *ad fontes*, "back to the sources." In the realm of biblical studies, the growth of the printing industry coincided with a growing interest on the part of Christian scholars in learning Hebrew as well as in learning about Hebrew biblical scholarship, including all kinds of rabbinic commentaries and texts, as a way of further probing the meaning of obscure Old Testament passages. As a consequence, the authority of the Septuagint fell deeply into eclipse behind the Hebrew Bible, even as Erasmus's text-critical edition of the Greek New Testament in 1516 sparked ongoing controversy for having challenged the authority of the Latin Vulgate.

Christian commentators on Genesis typically displayed a love-hate relationship toward Jewish sources, as we will see: they are often found to admire rabbinic insights and to find corroboration of their own views in the Targums, but the excesses of midrash, with its penchant for creative storytelling, is almost always heavily criticized. But Protestant commentators also had a love-hate relationship with a good deal of patristic and medieval exegesis, too. One must first acknowledge their indebtedness to the Fathers, particularly Jerome (for his general biblical scholarship and knowledge of Hebrew) and Augustine (who wrote multiple commentaries on Genesis but whose retelling of the history of the Old Testament in *The City of God* made it possibly the longest patristic work on the book of Genesis). Nonetheless, both Jerome and Augustine are also targets of criticism for their unchecked theological speculation as well as for what is usually described as allegorical excess.

The Reformation rejection of allegorical exegesis is often seen as a direct corollary of the doctrine of *sola Scriptura*, and it is true that Protestant writers never tire of expressing how awful it is to subvert the true, plain, simple, genuine, literal sense of Scripture by foisting some farfetched allegory onto it. Origen almost always comes in for a drubbing on this point, and Protestants, beginning with Luther, mark it as a point of pride that they follow neither "Jewish fables" nor the vanity of Origen's allegories. Contempt for allegory, of course, was not all that new in the Reformation. Some credit for the reemergence of interest in "literal" exegesis (as well as in the use of the rabbis in service of literal exegesis) must be given to the fourteenth-century *Postils* of Nicholas of Lyra, who was an important source for Luther in particular, but who also reserved a place for "mystical" or figurative readings of the Bible. (Indeed, we will see that even Protestants found some allegories in Genesis irresistible.)

What is more truly a new development in the Reformation era is the growth of interest in rhetorical analysis as a tool for better exegesis. Prevailing models of exegesis might classify biblical books according to Aristotle's categories of causation, or impose scholastic distinctions, or force the text to conform to a supposed patristic consensus, or merely append isolated glosses or comments.[15] But commentators who were trained in rhetoric (including Melanchthon, Bucer, Bullinger, Calvin, and others) now sought instead to expound the biblical text in terms of the "scope" or purpose of the author and to use the principles of classical rhetoric to analyze each part of the text in accord with its genre and the author's general and specific intentions. This procedure will sound simple and natural to us, and it ought to, but even modern historical-critical commentaries can run onto sidetracks and fail to consider what a biblical author intended his text to *do*. In the Reformation, rhetorical exegesis was never interested in detached analysis, because the Bible's inspired texts were originally meant to do something, namely, to move readers to respond, confess, believe, pray and live a new life in Christ. When these mostly Protestant commentators turned their eyes to what Moses wrote in Genesis, they knew that however many curious questions one might ask, the truly important questions are those that convey divine lessons and that both demand and elicit a response of faith and discipleship.

Ironically, however, the Protestant commitment to "practical" exegesis often meant that the moral or figurative lessons formerly conveyed by the traditional allegorical readings were not so much discarded as recycled and repackaged, albeit perhaps in a more rhetorically acceptable form as "analogies" or "applications." Medieval exegesis is often described in terms of the *quadriga* or "fourfold rule" that looked to find in the Bible not just a historical narrative but also lessons about morality, doctrine and the life to come— elegantly expressed in Latin as *agenda, credenda* and *speranda*: what we should do, what we should believe and where we should place our hope. Reformation exegesis was quick to

---

[15]For a detailed account of rhetorical criticism in the earliest Reformation exegesis, see Timothy J. Wengert, "Philip Melanchthon's 1522 Annotations on Romans and the Lutheran Origins of Rhetorical Criticism," in *Biblical Interpretation in the Era of the Reformation*, ed. Richard A. Muller and John L. Thompson (Grand Rapids: Eerdmans, 1996), 118-40.

repudiate fanciful allegories, but what Christian commentator could rightly ignore these other dimensions? Indeed, the chief point of rhetorical criticism was that people write texts to make things happen, and what God's Word seeks to make happen is to shape the people of God in each generation so that they may know what to do, what to believe and where to place their hope. Much of what we will find in the pages to follow was written with this implicit agenda.

Reformation Exegesis and the Major Themes of Genesis 1–11

The book of Genesis could be read as a stage drama with four or five acts. The last of these acts begins at the end of Genesis 11 and continues through the end of the book, telling the story of God's call and promise to Abraham and how Abraham's descendants survived to find themselves a great multitude living in Egypt—not quite yet the promised land. The earlier acts, however, focus first on creation (Gen 1–2), then on the catastrophe of human sin (Gen 3), and then on two more "new beginning" stories. One tells the story of how two lines of humans descended from Adam and Eve, represented by the murderer Cain and the righteous Abel (replaced, more or less, by Seth). These two families live at odds with one another in Genesis 4–5 until the crisis in Noah's day, when the extremes of corruption described in Genesis 6 lead to a new catastrophe: the universal flood. A second "new beginning" takes up after the flood, but little seems to have changed. There is an ever more isolated godly line running from Noah and Shem to Abram, but they live in a world that is hostile to the righteous, as the story of the tower of Babel once again proves.

A historian of Renaissance art wrote not so long ago of "the fallacy that art copies life, whereas in fact more often than not it copies earlier art."[16] There is a parallel observation to make about commentary literature, for commentaries, too, are often shaped more by other commentaries on a text than by the text itself. To be sure, there is a virtue in knowing what one's predecessors and contemporaries say about a text of Scripture, for there is little sense in "rediscovering" known dead ends or in repeating old mistakes. Accordingly, one of the final elements of these introductory remarks will consist in presenting here a map of sorts, that is, a survey of where the reformers stand in the history of the interpretation of the major sections of Genesis 1–11—creation, fall, Cain and Abel, Noah and the line leading to Abraham—so that we can more clearly see their exegetical debts and the influences that may have shaped them.[17]

Genesis 1–2: Creation. The first two chapters of Genesis touch on a number of themes in which Reformation commentaries scarcely differ from their patristic and medieval predecessors, often because their theological interests or priorities have not changed dramat-

---

[16]A. Richard Turner, *Inventing Leonardo* (New York: Alfred A. Knopf, 1993), 145.
[17]For a truly detailed survey, see Arnold Williams, *The Common Expositor: An Account of the Commentaries on Genesis, 1527-1633* (Chapel Hill: University of North Carolina Press, 1948).

ically—or, in some cases, because the texts trigger more curiosity or speculation than any issue of theological weight. In the former group would be the texts that speak of God's rest on the seventh day (a favorite source for exhortations about Sabbath practices, but not yet especially controversial), or the dominion originally enjoyed by men and women over creation, or the sacramental nature of the two trees in paradise. In the latter group one might place quite a number of other texts, including many of the merely interesting details of the six days of creation, such as the nature of the firmament or how there was light without the sun, as well as similar details about the nature and location of paradise (often an occasion for rhapsodic nostalgia), the difficult problem of matching the four rivers of paradise with known rivers today, and so on.

On many of these topics, even the supposedly restrained writers of Protestantism could speculate at length and thereby showcase their knowledge of past exegesis or their other scholarly gifts—including, only rarely, the ability to write concisely and with discipline. Notably, the Fathers and medievals more commonly expressed a special interest in the work of creation by writing commentaries with the title *Hexaemeron* or "the six days." Such works often engaged an amazing if daunting miscellany of tangents. Among Christian writers, the classics were the contributions of Basil the Great and Ambrose, though they were preceded by Philo, the first-century Jewish writer, who wrote a similar work, *On the Creation of the World*.[18] The genre endured in the Reformation but was not widespread: Wolfgang Capito published his *Hexemeron* in 1539, a rather disparate work, while Jerome Zanchi's *On the Works of God Created in the Space of Six Days* appeared in 1591.[19]

For many modern commentators, the contrasting accounts of creation found in Genesis 1:1–2:1 and Genesis 2:2-5 are often explained by attributing them to two different authors and source traditions—the Elohist and Yahwist strands of the Pentateuch, according to the so-called documentary hypothesis—and there is no necessary commitment to any harmonization of the two. Ancient commentators, however, working with confidence in the unity of Moses' authorship, were more intrigued than troubled by the two accounts, for it was obvious to them that the second was an elaboration of the first. Accordingly, the shift in the name for God that occurs at Genesis 2:4, where Yahweh is first named, is mined for its implications for theology but not authorship. But this observation depended on an awareness of the Hebrew text, of course, because neither the Greek nor the Latin versions of Genesis have any change here—and such observations of the shift in divine names tended to be registered only from the sixteenth century on, when the new Christian Hebraism had taken root and it came to be more the rule than the exception for Christian commentators to read Hebrew.[20]

---

[18]All these works were inventoried and described a century ago by Frank Egelston Robbins, *The Hexaemeral Literature: A Study of the Greek and Latin Commentaries on Genesis* (Chicago: University of Chicago Press, 1912).

[19]Wolfgang Capito, *Hexemeron Dei opus* (Strasbourg, 1539); *Hieronymus Zanchi, De operibus Dei intra spacium sex dierum creatis opus* (Neustadt, 1591).

[20]Thus even Nicholas of Lyra's rabbinically informed commentary, composed in the 1320s, ignored the new name for God at

Of greater interest than the unity of the Pentateuch was the question of the material nature of the world—a question that, one way or another, could invoke the ghosts of Plato and Aristotle. On the one hand, Origen had provoked great controversy by describing a kind of spiritual creation that was prior to any of the elements described in the opening verses of Genesis, and Augustine seemed only to renew the controversy in the later chapters of his *Confessions*. Both of these Fathers were more than a little sympathetic to the principles of later Platonism, particularly the tendency to identify the troublesome Pauline flesh with the physical body as a clog to the soul's progress toward God. Medieval theologians, on the other hand, were more alarmed by the revival of the Aristotelian assertion that the physical world was eternal: for if the heavens and the earth were not "created," God cannot be identified as the Creator and Genesis 1 is wrong. Both controversies seem less urgent in the sixteenth century. Indeed, while Reformation exegetes were regularly willing to discount Augustine's speculations on many points, his views on the spiritual "pre-creation" were simply ignored. And if greater attention was paid to claims about the eternity of the world, in the sixteenth century the controversy seems more staged than real—more an occasion to observe the failings to which secular pagan philosophy is liable on account of its ignorance or neglect of the revelation possessed by Christians in the Bible.

Another traditional focus at the outset of Genesis arose from Christian eagerness to find evidence for the triune nature of God wherever possible, particularly for use against Jewish counterclaims. Some Christian commentators argued that "in the beginning" really meant "in Christ," while others sought evidence for the Trinity in the text's mention of God, God's speaking (implying his Word) and the spirit that hovered over the waters. Arguments for the Trinity are common among Fathers, medievals and reformers, and if not all Christian interpreters felt justified in finding Father, Son and Holy Spirit in Genesis 1:1, there was more agreement that the plural "let us make" in Genesis 1:26 signals a plurality of persons in God. By the time of the Reformation, the argument was a familiar tool for dismissing Jewish claims that God was speaking instead to the angels or perhaps with a plurality of majesty.

The divine "image and likeness" in which both "male and female" were made (Gen 1:26-27) provoked some of the lengthiest discussions—partly because Reformation commentators often disagreed with their predecessors, partly because they disagreed somewhat among themselves, but most of all because they felt that something central to the Reformation was at stake here. The patristic consensus favored identifying the image of God with human reason as that which distinguishes men and women from lesser ani-

---

Genesis 2:4, whereas Cardinal Cajetan, writing two centuries later, felt compelled to find an exegetical implication each and every time the Hebrew text of Genesis shifted from one divine name to another. To be sure, if some Reformation writers saw the juxtaposition (in Gen 2:4) of the singular *Yahweh* with the plural *Elohim* as a lesson about the Trinity or distinctive divine attributes, many others, including Luther and Calvin, offered no comment.

mals. Once again, Augustine set an influential precedent by discovering a triune structure within human reason: even as God is Father, Son and Holy Spirit, so also does God's image (our mind or reason) manifest itself in three aspects, as memory, intellect and will. A notable exception to Augustine's view, however, was found in John Chrysostom, who read these verses in light of Genesis 1:28, so that *dominion* would be the chief sign of bearing God's image. But in the medieval West, Augustine's clever exegesis dominated and was coordinated with the struggle to differentiate *image* from *likeness*: the former lay in the faculty of reason, which was damaged in the fall but not wholly lost, while the latter was identified with our moral rectitude, which was obliterated by sin. Protestant exegetes knew and often admired these traditional readings, but they could not let them go uncontested: Augustine's account of the "vestiges" of the Trinity in the image of God was dismissed as too clever by half, even as the medieval distinction of image and likeness betrayed a complete failure to grasp the workings and significance of Hebrew parallelism.

With their knowledge of Hebrew, then, Reformation commentators could not divorce image from likeness in Genesis 1, nor could they embrace Augustine's triad in good conscience. But Protestant theology also nudged these exegetes to read the loss of the image through sin with a strong note of pessimism: the image and likeness are now sufficiently damaged so as to be nearly unrecognizable in us. Certainly, that image was not to be found in human reason, which the reformers tended to speak about distrustfully, reacting in no small part against scholastic assertions that they saw as exalting reason at the expense of faith. The reformers also seem more aware of the difficulty of harmonizing Genesis 1:27 with the other biblical texts that speak of the image of God, including those identifying Christ as that image, as well as 1 Corinthians 11:7, which a minority of readers saw (following Ambrosiaster in the fourth century) as denying that women possess God's image at all. However, the general Reformation synthesis preferred to explain the image of God in terms of human *righteousness*, which may be possessed equally by men and women, lost equally through sin, perfectly modeled in Christ alone and restored only by him. In this way, Protestants could avoid defining the image in any way that would seem to survive sin (as reason seemed to do) and most of them could then invoke *dominion* as a lesser part of the image that need not be shared equally by all men, much less women.

Before moving on, it is worth returning to the nature and relationship of men and women, looking this time at Genesis 2. There are obvious details added to the bare mention in Genesis 1:26-28 of men and women as created in the image of God and granted dominion. Those details elicited a string of curious questions, many derived from rabbinic commentaries and patristic literature. Examples are too numerous to list, but they included such concerns as the meaning of the name *Adam*; why the man was created outside paradise and of earth (in contrast to woman, made in paradise from the man's rib); whether the man was originally defective (having an extra rib) or became so afterwards (having lost a rib to Eve); and so on. Such questions are far more entertaining than edifying, to be sure, though they also had the unfortunate effect of provoking Christian outbursts against the "frivolous" character of Jewish exegesis, even though one suspects that many Christian writers enjoyed presenting these rabbinic speculations for their own sake and sometimes even agreed with them.

But the account of woman's creation was also an occasion for displaying traditional Christian patriarchy—not at all surprising, given the stated reason for her creation, to be "a helper fit for the man." The Reformation brought in its train many social changes, as noted earlier, including renewed recognition of the equal dignity of men and women with respect to salvation, the dignity of marriage as God's original and enduring design, an incremental increase in women's literacy, and the occasional roles of leadership and influence exercised by women in the Reformation. It would seem unlikely for these changes to have no effect on exegesis—and such is indeed the case. Reformation commentators by no means set aside their commitments to the traditional male-centered hierarchy, but they do seem more aware that women are actively listening to sermons and possibly even reading commentaries. There is an attempt to soften some harsher expressions of Christian patriarchy, even if not enough for modern readers. Such ameliorations include repeating the old allegory (found in Lombard's *Sentences* and elsewhere) that woman was made of Adam's rib so that she would neither rule him as head nor be crushed by his feet, but Protestant commentators had still more to say. They stressed the complementarity, the mutuality and companionability and occasionally even the equality of the first man and woman as a regular theme in Genesis 2. Augustine had bluntly asserted that when God designed to make a helper for the man, God must have been thinking of woman as a helper only in procreation, because for every other task—whether labor or conversation—another *man* would surely have been better suited.[21] Few Reformation commentators would have been comfortable to express that view, despite their residual patriarchy: Luther defends woman against defamation and the stereotype of being "a necessary evil," Brenz urges that "helping" be seen as a mutual obligation of spouses, and Calvin lauds the woman as "another self" to the man. Such words indicate the changing shape of home, family, marriage and church in the Reformation. They also indicate the other role most Protestant commentators filled: that of the *pastor*, with a flock in constant need of attention and guidance in matters domestic and otherwise.

Genesis 3: Fall. For many traditional commentators, one of the most provocative aspects of the first chapter of Genesis is something that is unexpectedly *not* mentioned: angels. One should mark with care that while Protestant theology was clear and deliberate about jettisoning the devotion to saints that marks Roman Catholicism and Eastern Orthodoxy to this day, there was no wholesale rejection of *angelology*—rare as the topic has become in modern theologies. There was, to be sure, a call for restraint on the topic,

---

[21]Augustine, *The Literal Meaning of Genesis* 9.5.9 (ACW 42:75).

but Genesis 1 was a nonstarter, and commentators often felt constrained to explain the silence, given the prominence of angels later on. So when the serpent appears at the outset of this chapter as the woman's tempter—and Satan is nowhere named—commentators were traditionally quick to make the connection for their readers, just as the New Testament does in Revelation 12 and 20. Reformation commentators do not differ much from their predecessors here, except that they generally eschew elaborate speculation on angels and demons and are concerned that readers understand that there is a real distinction between Satan and the serpent, which was merely Satan's instrument.

The overwhelming trajectory pursued in Genesis 3, though, revolves around blame and praise: the blame is levied by turns on the serpent, Satan, the woman and the man; the praise is reserved almost exclusively for God, though some commentators will assume that Adam and Eve are to be credited with repentance and a recovery of their faith in God. The narrative of the chapter is dissected with great interest in each detail, but few Reformation commentators can resist one of the oldest questions addressed to the text, namely, *who sinned more*, the man or the woman? The same question is implicit in the assertion made in 1 Timothy 2:14, that while the woman was deceived, the man was not, and that is why women may not teach or have authority over men. Yet the canonical answer of 1 Timothy only exacerbated the problem, because if Adam was not deceived, he must have sinned deliberately, and wouldn't that have been a worse deed? So, far from ending the discussion, 1 Timothy only made it more interesting, as commentators cast about for the missing solution. In the Reformation, the venerable solution of Augustine—that Adam sinned not from deception or ignorance but out of misplaced loyalty to his wife—falls from favor, but no single alternative emerged to take its place. Chrysostom had solved the problem by glossing "Adam was not deceived" in 1 Timothy 2:14 with "by an equal," implying that it is somehow more shameful to be deceived by a talking serpent than by another human. There are variations on Chrysostom's approach among the reformers, but more interesting still are some of their passing remarks, such as Calvin's speculation that under other circumstances, Adam too might well have been deceived. Likewise, given that Genesis 2 is usually taken as an account not only of an arguably historical Eve but also of Everywoman, with Eve's failings read as universals of women everywhere, it is hugely surprising to hear Wolfgang Musculus assert that this generalization is not always true, particularly of godly Christian women who have often faithfully resisted the devil. What needs to be borne in mind is that the sixteenth century inherited a centuries-old double standard that placed greater suspicion on women in law and society, so that any departure or challenge or even awareness of the double standard represents something of a novelty.

For Christian commentators, possibly the most important point to be gleaned from Genesis 3 arises in verse 15, where God says to the serpent, "I will put enmity between you and the woman, and between your seed and her seed; he shall bruise your head, and you shall bruise his heel." This verse was commonly understood by traditional commentators as the *protoevangelion*, the first proclamation of the gospel of Christ's triumph over Satan. The woman's seed was usually understood, then, to be Jesus Christ, and the verse served to anchor the parallels drawn by early Christians not only between the first Adam and the second, but also between Eve and Mary. The notion that God had promised to the descendants of Adam and Eve a "seed" who would deliver them from sin and Satan was traditionally invoked as a hermeneutical key to explain many of the patriarchs' stranger deeds—particularly the obsession with offspring that drove some of them to polygamous unions or to concubinage. In other words, they were understood as longing for children not only for the usual reasons but also because they hoped to see this promised seed and deliverer born in their own lifetimes. The argument can be traced back at least to Augustine,[22] but it becomes a major topic throughout the lectures of Luther and later Lutheran commentators. It is also important for Reformed exegetes, not least in order to rebut a medieval view that *seed* refers not to Christ but to Mary, but the theme is a bit more muted among the Reformed, and Calvin dilutes the specific link to Christ here. However, later Reformed writers, such as William Perkins, will be equally interested in this verse for its resemblance to a formal covenant.

Genesis 4–6 and 9–11: Two lines of descent. Just as it was typical for commentators to read the story of Adam and Eve in order to generalize about what all men and women are like, and how and why they got that way, so too were the later chapters in Genesis read as a taxonomy of two kinds of people: the ungodly, who have always been prosperous and numerous; and the godly, whose numbers are small and their circumstances reduced. This motif of two families covers all the chapters that extend from the expulsion from paradise in Genesis 3 to the calling of Abraham in Genesis 12. In a sense, the flood simply interrupts and resets the pattern, replacing the line of the godly that led from Seth to Noah with a new line leading from Shem to Abraham.

The pattern for discussing the flourishing of the ungodly and the sufferings of the godly—besides being canonized by the Psalms—was given a decisive stamp by Augustine in *The City of God*. Indeed, Augustine's sprawling narrative is a favorite among patristic works cited in Reformation commentaries. Clearly, they appreciated anew the typology Augustine drew from Cain and Abel in order to explain all of human history and politics as a conflict between those who build cities on earth and those who are pilgrims here, on a journey to a heavenly and better city. Along the way, however, the reformers will attach lessons of their own, including distinctive Protestant concerns for purity of worship as illumined by the offerings of Cain and Abel; or a careful exegesis of God's warning to Cain to master his sin as either proof of free will (for Anabaptists) or not at all a proof of the same (for Luther); or Calvin's use of Abel as a textbook instance of "double justification," which teaches that not only are *we* accepted only by God's grace, the same holds for our works, too.

---

[22]Augustine, *On the Good of Marriage* 9.9; 26.35 (NPNF 13:403, 413; PL 40:380, 396).

A good deal of the reformers' exegesis of these passages breaks no new ground but retraces the basic moral lesson that the godly can expect to be persecuted in this life, yet God sees and cares. To be sure, the narrative flow of these chapters is regularly interrupted by long genealogical lists and chronologies that seem tedious, as the reformers themselves admit. Yet there are a few cameos of interest: Lamech the vengeful polygamist, Enoch who walked with God, the long-lived Methuselah. All of these laconic references are mined for as much doctrine as possible, most or all of it leading to moral exhortations and lessons. A slightly distinctive Reformation line appears with respect to the ambiguous references to the "sons of God" and "giants" in Genesis 6. As Augustine had noted, the Septuagint (in a variant reading) has "angels of God," giving rise to the provocative but farfetched idea that angels were having intercourse with the daughters of men—an idea that Augustine earnestly dismisses in favor of identifying "sons of God" here as, in effect, godly sons.[23] The story's point, then, is that an awakened lust drew the men of Seth's godly line to pursue women from the line of Cain. The reformers agree, and if anything they amplify this more naturalistic explanation—the one without actual angels. And they do likewise with respect to the *Nephilim* or giants in Genesis 6:4, who (according to Luther, for instance, among others) may have been gigantic only in their reputation or arrogance, not their actual stature. Many Reformation commentators thus take the reference as depicting a tyrannical abuse of power, not a physiological or supernatural prodigy.

Genesis 6–9: Noah, the flood and its aftermath. The account of the destruction of all life on earth by a great deluge, with the divine preservation of Noah's family and the earth's animals on a fragile ark, is an amazingly long and detailed narrative in a context that has mostly consisted of actuarial entries and one-sentence biographies. Exegetes in all ages clearly welcomed the inrush of narrative detail and made the most of it.

One of the major concerns for commentators, however, was the question of the plausibility of the entire account. The story was ridiculed in the patristic era by the opponents of Christians and Jews (including pagans, Manichaeans and others), who doubted that the ark as described could hold all the land animals of the earth, along with sufficient food for so many months. They also doubted that the flood could reach so high as to cover the tops of the highest mountains. So from an early time, exegetes labored in defense of the account, with each generation of commentators enlisting the arguments of all their forebears. Protestant exegesis thus tends to shun only allegorical explanations for details clearly intended as historical, not figurative, and Origen's novel argument that the cubits of Genesis 6 are "geometric" cubits marks a rare case in which Origen is lauded by at least some Protestants for a point of literal interpretation. But Protestants by no means refuse to acknowledge that the workings and practicality of the ark are also a matter of

---

[23]Augustine, *City of God* 15.22-23.

mystery, though they are also skilled in adorning most details with plausible solutions.

One of the more poignant considerations raised by commentators of the Reformation era may strike us as unexpected. That they should see the severity of the flood's destruction as a parallel to the last judgment is understandable, but several of these writers reflect at length and with feeling on the question of the final destiny of those who drowned. More than one commentator refuses to conclude that God's judgment by water precluded either *repentance* on the part of those outside the ark or *mercy*, subsequently, on the part of God. But even more attention is given to the plight of Noah and his family, for whom this divine rescue was itself a long trial—and even an experience of abandonment, despite escaping the flood waters. Noah is thus extolled as a saint, a man of great faith, but also a man of great sorrows.

Predictably, there is great fascination with the rainbow and the promise or covenant attached to it. The perennial question was whether there had ever been a rainbow before the ark came to rest on dry land. Here, Reformation writers argue both sides and come to no consensus. It was also a perennial move to offer allegorical readings of the ark and the rainbow, drawing parallels between the ark and Christ or the ark and the church, and finding significance in the colors of the rainbow, which itself was seen as the covenant's sacramental sign. However much Protestants complained about the abuses of allegory elsewhere, Noah's story frequently seemed to uncork their pent-up allegorical skills. Luther's excursus fills fifteen pages of the American edition of his lectures on Genesis, but he is by no means alone among Protestants in probing the allegorical implications of the text—warranted, to be sure, by 1 Peter 3, which draws an analogy between the ark and baptism.

The valorization of Noah as a man of faith and obedience exacerbated another traditional crux of interpretation: his drunkenness and exposure subsequent to the ark's safe landing and his family's disembarkation. How could such a holy man commit such an obscene lapse? For some of the Fathers and medievals, he didn't: the tale is an allegory of something far more edifying. With this episode, we encounter the first of a long series of patriarchal immoralities—deeds that would be self-evidently evil were it not for the fact that they are perpetrated by the supposed heroes of the Old Testament. In such cases, many Jewish and Christian commentators labor to find excuses and ameliorations, whether for their polygamy, their lies or their double-dealing.[24] In the case of Noah's drunkenness, many were fond of the reading proposed by Augustine, who drew parallels from Noah to Christ. After all, Christ too took a chalice of wine, only to hang naked on the cross. Heretics view Christ with mockery as Ham viewed Noah, but others—Shem and Japheth, progenitors of (believing) Jews and Gentiles, respectively—respond with

---

[24]The classic study on this topic is Roland H. Bainton, "The Immoralities of the Patriarchs According to the Exegesis of the Late Middle Ages and of the Reformation," *HTR* 23 (1930): 39-49; updated by John L. Thompson, "The Immoralities of the Patriarchs in the History of Exegesis: A Reassessment of Calvin's Position," *CTJ* 26 (1991): 9-46.

reverence.[25] Augustine thus allows the "prophetic significance" of Noah's inebriation to upstage and silence the question of whether he also did wrong. Later writers will elaborate on Augustine's allegory and find new applications—including the lesson, particularly odious to many Protestants, that clerical sins should be covered up, not exposed.[26]

Some Protestants appreciated the typological relationship between Noah and Christ, even in this passage, but no Protestant wanted to excuse Noah's drunkenness without further qualification. Some grant that he may have been traumatized by the destruction of the world and its inhabitants and sought some comfort in drink, but it is more common for Protestants simply to acknowledge that even the greatest of saints can still fall prey to serious sin and moral failure—and, of course, they will have looked ahead in Genesis to see that the pattern of failure will recur in Abraham, Isaac and Jacob. However, all these Old Testament saints were, according to Protestant theology, justified by grace through faith, not by their works. So the principal pattern to emerge from all these tales of patriarchal misdeeds is a pattern thoroughly familiar to reformers and their readers: sin, followed by repentance.

Noah's drunkenness, however, leads to family strife and to further "prophetic significance." Once sober, Noah proclaims a curse on the offending party—sort of. In fact, as is well known, he curses not Ham, who mocked him, but Ham's son Canaan, who is destined to be his brothers' slave. This is another thorny text. Why curse the grandson rather than the offending party? Modern commentators will understand the story as an aetiological tale, meant to provide a retrospective understanding or justification for the conflict between Israel and the Canaanites later on, at the time of the conquest (an insight approximated by Musculus as well). But traditional commentators wanted a clearer rationale for cursing the otherwise innocent Canaan, and they found it by imagining unrecorded misdeeds of his own or by allegorizing Canaan as the "fruit" of Ham's actions (so Augustine). Yet the allegorical explanation had no appeal for Reformation writers, who appealed more generally to the justness of using a son's servitude to chastise his father, indeed, to indicate that the father was all the more reprehensible—as if God so despised Ham that his name could not be uttered.

Later interpretations of the curse on Canaan will skew this tale in tragic ways, extending Canaan's curse to Ham, identifying Ham's descendants as principally African and asserting that one effect of this curse was a darkening of the skin.[27] These are the ingredients that were concocted in the eighteenth and nineteenth centuries as a supposedly biblical rationale for enslaving Africans in the Americas, and no one can study this episode in the history of exegesis without grief. But with respect to this develop-

---

[25]Augustine, *City of God* 16.1-2.

[26]On this point, see David C. Steinmetz, "Luther and the Drunkenness of Noah," in *Luther in Context* (Bloomington: Indiana University, 1986), esp. 104, 106.

[27]My account here is indebted to the recent study by David M. Whitford, *The Curse of Ham in the Early Modern Era: The Bible and the Justifications for Slavery* (Burlington, VT: Ashgate, 2009).

ment, Reformation writers stand between the times, so to speak. Earlier centuries, in the Middle Ages, also saw the curse on Canaan exemplified in their own day but applied it to European serfs in their midst, not to foreigners and not to those with dark skin. By the time of the Reformation, feudalism and serfdom had faded, and the most that can be said is that the reformers contributed to a blurring of matters by speaking not only of Canaan as cursed but Ham as well, though Scripture does not make the point explicit. Most other ingredients would come later, at the ends of the sixteenth and seventeenth centuries, except for some fantastic claims about the long life, travels and influence of Noah after the flood—claims circulated under the name of the ancient historian Berosus, who was mentioned by Josephus but whose writings were regarded as lost until Annius of Viterbo published a forgery purporting to be Berosus, now recovered. This pseudo-Berosus was known to some of our Reformation commentators, but the forgery's effect on the exegesis of this passage in the sixteenth century was essentially nil. Of greater interest to Reformation writers was the identification of Japheth as the precursor of the Gentiles, and the blessing on Japheth was therefore taken by most as finding its fulfillment when the gospel came to the Gentiles—an event that Luther is happy to see culminating even in the Reformation itself.

Genesis 10–11: From the dispersion at Babel to the calling of Abraham. If the misdeeds of the "sons of God" and the giants in Genesis 6 were the final straw that led to divine intervention and signaled the end of God's (and Scripture's) interest in the ungodly descendants of Cain, the episode that opens Genesis 11 tells a similar tale. There, Nimrod—Cush's son, Ham's grandson and Noah's great-grandson—built a city and a tower called Babel; and there, merely three generations after the flood, arrogance, defiance and depravity had returned to the human race at a pitch comparable to the opening of Genesis 6. Once again, God intervenes, this time not to destroy but merely to confuse and scatter. And once again, Reformation commentators had no serious reason to leave the patterns of exegesis they inherited, which were partly explanatory but mostly moral: the vanity and insecurity of worldly people is stressed, and the traditional parallel is drawn between Babel and Pentecost as proof of what Christ can do for human unity that human agency alone cannot.

As the text of Genesis 11 then turns to the genealogy of Shem, it is clear that the story of the descendants of Ham and of Japheth will be abandoned as Shem's line is traced another eight generations to Terah, and then to his son Abraham. Reformation commentators, not all that differently from their predecessors, delighted to see God call Abraham from obscurity and even, it seems, from idolatry, and to see God on the verge of delivering Sarah from barrenness—for these early Protestants similarly felt that they, too, had been delivered from idolatry and barrenness to be a small band of faithful pilgrims, despite the many odds against them.

Some Remarks on Commentators and Translations

Although many readers will be fairly uninterested in the details of translating (and understandably so), there are a few reasons to add a few notes on authors and sources. First, one of the goals of the Reformation Commentary on Scripture is to draw readers from the excerpts below to the complete original works wherever possible, so it will be useful to call attention to any published translations of these works that are available.[28] Second, readers who consult other English editions will discover that their wording may differ from what appears here, so a brief account of the translations here will explain what otherwise might seem like errors or arbitrary discrepancies. Finally, this is also a good place to say a few words about which commentaries were *not* chosen, and why.

Fifty or more commentaries on Genesis appeared in the sixteenth century, as noted earlier, but not all were good candidates for inclusion here. Some works were bypassed because their comments on verses or words were too brief, or too much an inventory of other authors' views, or too focused on technical matters of grammar or philology or (at another extreme) too disconnected from the text. Among these works, one represents a forerunner of sorts to this RCS volume: the compilation of exegesis prepared by Augustine Marlorat in which he stitched together rather short excerpts on Genesis from eleven contemporary commentators—Lutheran, Reformed, and Catholic.[29] Another remarkable work not easily rendered by excerpted paragraphs are Cyriacus Spangenberg's sixty tables on Genesis, which resemble nothing so much as flow charts incorporating the biblical text, brief explanations, precepts and applications.[30] Clearly, sixteenth-century commentaries could be as varied in format and quality as anything we find printed in our own day!

Among *Lutheran commentators* selected for this volume, Philipp Melanchthon contributes the earliest work by way of his rather spare annotations on Genesis 1–6, published in 1523. Later in the 1520s, Luther himself preached through Genesis, but his *magnum opus* is unquestionably the set of lectures he gave on Genesis from 1535 until late in 1545. By arrangement with Concordia Publishing House, Luther's lectures appear here in the fine translation produced fifty years ago as part of the American edition of Luther's works; I have only rarely altered that translation. Other Lutheran commentaries in this volume are those of Johannes Brenz (1553), David Chytraeus (1557), Nikolaus Selnecker (1569) and Christophor Pelargus (1598); these works are translated for the first time here.

Commentaries on Genesis from *moderate or "reformist" Catholic writers* are not exactly

---

[28]For a regularly updated list of commentary literature available in English, see the appendix to John L. Thompson, *Reading the Bible with the Dead: What You Can Learn from the History of Exegesis That You Can't Learn from Exegesis Alone* (Grand Rapids: Eerdmans, 2007), and http://purl.oclc.org/net/jlt/exegesis.

[29]Augustin Marlorat, *Genesis cum catholica expositione ecclesiastica* (Morges: Jean Le Preux and Eustache Vignon, 1584), digital copy online at http://dx.doi.org/10.3931/e-rara-2581.

[30]Cyriacus Spangenberg, *In sacri Mosis Pentatevchvm, sive quinque libros, Genesim, Exodum, Leuiticum, Numeros, Deuteronomium, tabvlae CCVI* (Basel: Johannes Oporinus, 1563). In this first volume, Spangenberg published 206 tables on the Pentateuch; in 1567, he offered another 267 tables on Joshua through Job. Three of Spangenberg's tables—on Genesis 3, 6, and 9—are reproduced in translation below.

abundant. The most notable Catholic commentator of the early decades of the Reformation, however, is surely Thomas de Vio, Cardinal Cajetan, the papal legate who confronted Luther at the Diet of Augsburg in 1518. During what could be described as his semi-retirement, from 1527 until his death in 1534, Cajetan undertook a commentary on the entire Bible, and his unexpected interest in literal exegesis and willingness to challenge traditional readings in the Latin (Vulgate) Bible led Luther to remark that "Cajetan, in later days, has become a Lutheran."[31] Cajetan's exegesis is supplemented by a few extracts from Desiderius Erasmus, who was hugely influential on New Testament and patristic scholarship in the sixteenth century. Although not formally a commentator on Genesis, Erasmus contributes some pertinent excerpts from his *Paraphrases on the New Testament*. The *Paraphrases* began to appear in Latin in 1517 and were fully translated into English by mid-century; they are also appearing, gradually, in a new English version, though the translation here is my own, as is the translation of Cajetan's commentary.

Of all those involved in sixteenth-century reform, *Anabaptists and other radical reformers* are the least likely to have written commentaries at all, much less on the Old Testament. There were a few exceptions, but none leading to a dedicated commentary on Genesis. Nevertheless, these Christians and their leaders were much interested in certain themes rooted in Genesis, particularly questions bearing on the image of God, the dynamics of sin and disobedience and the contrast between the first and the second Adam. They were also eager to find precedents or exemplars for their vision of the people of God and of true Christian discipleship. For this project, I have consulted the works of Menno Simons as well as most of the volumes in the Classics of the Radical Reformation (Herald Press), a series that features influential figures from the 1520s (Andreas Karlstadt, Balthasar Hubmaier) and the 1530s (Hans Denck, Pilgram Marpeck, David Joris), as well as from the two or three decades beyond that (Peter Riedemann, Dirk Philips). The CRR translations appear here mostly unchanged.

Continental *Reformed Protestants* were avid commentators, and Genesis was by no means neglected. Zwingli's self-deprecatingly titled *Farrago* or "mishmash" of annotations appeared in 1527, and the next decade greeted in succession the commentaries of Konrad Pellikan (1532), Johannes Oecolampadius (1536) and Wolfgang Capito (1539). Though Vermigli's commentary was not published until 1569, seven years after his death, his original lectures were delivered in the early 1540s. Commentaries from John Calvin and Wolfgang Musculus appeared almost simultaneously in 1554. The translations of Zwingli, Pellikan and Musculus are wholly my own, but excerpts from Oecolampadius were translated primarily by my RCS colleague Mickey Mattox and are forthcoming in the series Reformation Texts with Translation (Marquette University Press). Vermigli's commentary will soon appear in The Peter Martyr Library (Truman State University

---

[31]The remark, from Luther's "table talk" (WATr 2:596.14, #2668), is cited by Jared Wicks, in *Cajetan Responds: A Reader in Reformation Controversy* (Washington, DC: Catholic University of America Press, 1978), 37.

Press), and my own translation here was greatly helped along by Daniel Shute and John Patrick Donnelly, S.J., who allowed me to consult an early draft of their PML translation. Calvin's lectures were translated by John King for the Calvin Translation Society in 1847, and they are widely available in print and in digital format. King's work is commendably accurate, but he too often renders Calvin's elegant but convoluted Latin prose into equally difficult English. I have significantly updated the CTS edition in light of the original Latin, departing from King's wording wherever I felt clarity could be better served.

Two other Reformed Protestants require special mention: Katharina Schütz Zell and Anna Maria van Schurman. Zell was one of many remarkable women of the Reformation era. Married to the early reformer and Strasbourg pastor Matthias Zell, she left a remarkably varied written legacy, ranging from a defense of clergy marriage, through letters of consolation, to informal works of exegesis. Though she did not comment on Genesis, some topical excerpts from her writings have been included here from Elsie McKee's recent published translations. Anna Maria van Schurman falls at the far end of the RCS's definition of the Reformation era and was much more a part of the so-called Dutch Second Reformation than the first. Excerpts from her paraphrase or "expansion" of Genesis 1–3 are presented here, however, as part of what might be regarded as the first formal commentary on Genesis by a woman. These excerpts are drawn from a full translation of her work currently in preparation by Albert Gootjes and John L. Thompson; readers should note that the format here forces a line break in the midst of each of the Dutch original's rhymed couplets.

Finally, *English Protestants and Puritans* are represented here by Andrew Willet, a loyal Anglican priest and controversialist, as well as a prolific commentator; and by William Perkins, a fellow of Christ's College (Cambridge), also a controversialist, and an extremely influential Puritan theologian. Although Perkins did not comment on Genesis, several topical excerpts from his works have been included here. Willet is represented here by his massive *Hexapla* or "sixfold commentary" on Genesis, in which he not only presented his own views but also credited (on the title page) three other important commentators of the sixteenth century: Johannes Mercerus (Jean Mercier), noted Hebraist and translator of rabbinic writings who became a Huguenot sympathizer and whose commentary on Genesis was posthumously published by Theodore Beza; Benedict Pererius, Jesuit author of a sprawling multivolume commentary used by many Protestants; and Augustin Marlorat, noted earlier, who had himself excerpted what he regarded as the best of contemporary commentaries on Genesis. These works of Willet and Perkins originally appeared in English, but while their prose may have been polished and eloquent in their own day, readers today will be distracted by obsolete vocabulary, irregular spelling and punctuation, and inverted syntax. In order to give them an equal hearing among the Latin sources translated here into contemporary prose, I have modernized their vocabulary, spelling, punctuation and syntax, trying at all times to make as few changes as possible.

With the exception of Luther, Calvin and the various radical reformers, most writers are translated into English for the first time here. Given that so many of these works began as spoken lectures, I have felt free to use idioms appropriate to spoken English. I should also add a word about gender. Latin has the advantage of a clear distinction between *homo* and *vir*, and while each of these can be translated into English as *man*, the Latin *homo* more precisely denotes humanity, human beings, humankind, or men and women considered collectively. Accordingly, I have translated *homo* in all of these ways and have given a similar treatment to the related masculine pronouns.[32] To translate *homo* inclusively, of course, is not to assert that a writer necessarily meant to be inclusive or egalitarian, but it is at least a way of signaling something of the original vocabulary that lies beneath the English presented here.

Acknowledgments

One of the most important lessons embedded in the Heidelberg Catechism is that a life lived toward God is meant to be characterized by gratitude, above all. Indeed, gratitude is a spiritual discipline, for by giving thanks, we acknowledge not only how much we have received but also that our lives are never really lived alone. It is especially fitting to give thanks at the culmination of a long project such as this one, because I have a lot to be thankful for, and I have neither lived nor worked alone.

First, I'm grateful to InterVarsity Press and Timothy George, general editor, for inviting me in 2005 to join the Reformation Commentary on Scripture project and to dedicate my efforts to this volume in particular. I have long loved Genesis, but I have also long loved the biblical commentators of the ancient, medieval, and Reformation church, who wrestled with these divine Scriptures so that they might illumine their own lives and those of their contemporaries. It has been a deeply moving experience, therefore, to spend time with the people, words and teachings of the Bible alongside the words and teachings of these sixteenth- and seventeenth-century writers in the hope of bringing forth a similar kind of illumination. In brief, I have loved working on this project, and I shall miss it.

Trolling through long out-of-print commentaries has its special challenges, so I'm also grateful to have had the help of able student assistants. Early on, a good deal of my labor entailed straining my eyes over photocopies made from microfiche images of these old books, a task facilitated by Rachel Grassley Young. An initial uncertainty about the availability of the American edition of Luther on Genesis had me enlist Young-Chun Kim to work with Lenker's earlier translation. David Cannon compiled Luther's Latin texts and helped inventory the hundreds of excerpts that appear here. The final draft was proofread by David Chao and Steven Tyra, the latter of whom also assembled a complete Latin source file from my many scattered fragments.

---

[32]The exception to this rule is the translation of Luther, which is that of the American edition. However, readers are reasonably safe in assuming that generic instances of "man" (etc.) in Luther represent *homo*, not *vir*.

Sometimes my progress in translating was stopped cold by the inscrutable Latin of my sixteenth-century sources. I'm especially grateful to Beth Kreitzer and Mickey Mattox, longstanding friends and volume editors in this series, for allowing me to pester them with emails carrying such pathos-laden subject lines as "Five words, two friends, need help!" Others to thank for linguistic aid include Albert Gootjes, whom I initially recruited to translate Anna Maria van Schurman from the Dutch but who has since become my collaborator in further work on her; Dan Shute and Pat Donnelly, who shared an early draft of their translation of Peter Martyr Vermigli; Stephen Burnett, who never seems to mind my questions about late medieval rabbinic sources; and Mickey Mattox (again), who let me use his nearly-finished translation of Oecolampadius.

If one benefit of this project has been the opportunity to read new texts and make new friends from among these old commentators, another benefit has been to make new friends also among the living—the blessed byproduct of our close working relationships. I'd certainly number among such friends Joel Scandrett, Michael Gibson, and Brannon Ellis, RCS project editors at IVP, who proved to be not only superb diplomats but also deeply devoted to the highest aims of this series. And I have especially enjoyed building a friendship with Scott Manetsch, associate general editor, truly a kindred spirit in pursuing the study of the Reformation for the sake of building up Christ's church today.

Closer to home, it should not need to be said that most writers write with the hope, however vain, that someone will read what they have written. In my case, that hope has been fed by two close friends, Skip Barber and Dale Irvine, whose continued expressions of interest and whose demonstrated appetites for reading about the Bible give me some confidence that they will also be among the keenest readers of this volume—and not just because I promised them free copies. That same hope of a readership has also been nourished by my indefatigable father-in-law, Bob Meye, who enthusiastically read an earlier draft of this volume in its entirety.

A special word is due to my wife and New Testament colleague, Marianne Meye Thompson. After more than three decades of marriage and theological pillow-talk (sorry, no details), there are of course many reasons to thank her and to be thankful for her, ranging from our shared family life and ministry through numerous travels and travails. But let me also credit her quite specifically for prodding me to focus my introduction to this volume on an eminently practical matter, namely, what do we need to know in order to use this volume well? When I raise this question on page xlvi, let readers remember that it was originally posed to me by Marianne: pastor to her students, mentor and mother to our daughters, my dearest friend and companion.

This volume is dedicated to James E. Bradley, my colleague in church history for as long as I've been a professor and a loyal friend for even longer. For more than a decade, Jim and I have team-taught the graduate course in historiography here at Fuller and found ourselves in a dialectic comprised, by turns, of mutual intimidation and mutual admiration. Nonetheless, this is my book, so I get the last word for now: I never cease to be amazed and inspired by how much Jim knows and how well he has integrated his knowledge of history and theology with his sure sense for the character and identity of the church and its ministry. Theologically, ecclesiastically, pedagogically, and pastorally, I have been deeply formed by his intellect and faith as well as by his gentleness and generosity. I hope this book mirrors something of Jim's life and loves, as a token of what I have received from him.

What solace do we have in this human society,
so filled with delusions and distress, except
the unfeigned loyalty and mutual love
of good and true friends?

Augustine, *The City of God*

John L. Thompson
Volume Editor

1:1-23 THE FIRST FIVE DAYS OF CREATION

¹*In the beginning, God created the heavens and the earth.* ²*The earth was without form and void, and darkness was over the face of the deep. And the Spirit of God was hovering over the face of the waters.*

³*And God said, "Let there be light," and there was light.* ⁴*And God saw that the light was good. And God separated the light from the darkness.* ⁵*God called the light Day, and the darkness he called Night. And there was evening and there was morning, the first day.*

⁶*And God said, "Let there be an expanse*ᵃ *in the midst of the waters, and let it separate the waters from the waters."* ⁷*And God made*ᵇ *the expanse and separated the waters that were under the expanse from the waters that were above the expanse. And it was so.* ⁸*And God called the expanse Heaven.*ᶜ *And there was evening and there was morning, the second day.*

⁹*And God said, "Let the waters under the heavens be gathered together into one place, and let the dry land appear." And it was so.* ¹⁰*God called the dry land Earth,*ᵈ *and the waters that were gathered together he called Seas. And God saw that it was good.*

¹¹*And God said, "Let the earth sprout vegetation, plants*ᵉ *yielding seed, and fruit trees bearing fruit in which is their seed, each according to its kind, on the earth." And it was so.* ¹²*The earth brought forth vegetation, plants yielding seed according to their own kinds, and trees bearing fruit in which is their seed, each according to its kind. And God saw that it was good.* ¹³*And there was evening and there was morning, the third day.*

¹⁴*And God said, "Let there be lights in the expanse of the heavens to separate the day from the night. And let them be for signs and for seasons,*ᶠ *and for days and years,* ¹⁵*and let them be lights in the expanse of the heavens to give light upon the earth." And it was so.* ¹⁶*And God made the two great lights—the greater light to rule the day and the lesser light to rule the night—and the stars.* ¹⁷*And God set them in the expanse of the heavens to give light on the earth,* ¹⁸*to rule over the day and over the night, and to separate the light from the darkness. And God saw that it was good.* ¹⁹*And there was evening and there was morning, the fourth day.*

²⁰*And God said, "Let the waters swarm with swarms of living creatures, and let birds*ᵍ *fly above the earth across the expanse of the heavens."* ²¹*So God created the great sea creatures and every living creature that moves, with which the waters swarm, according to their kinds, and every winged bird according to its kind. And God saw that it was good.* ²²*And God blessed them, saying, "Be fruitful and multiply and fill the waters in the*

seas, and let birds multiply on the earth." [23]*And there was evening and there was morning, the fifth day.*

a Or *a canopy*; also verses 7, 8, 14, 15, 17, 20   b Or *fashioned*; also verse 16   c Or *Sky*; also verses 9, 14, 15, 17, 20, 26, 28, 30; 2:1   d Or *Land*; also verses 11, 12, 22, 24, 25, 26, 28, 30; 2:1   e Or *small plants*; also verses 12, 29   f Or *appointed times*   g Or *flying things*; see Leviticus 11:19-20

Overview: The first chapter of the book of Genesis is, obviously, without parallel in the entire canon of Scripture, largely because it purports to recount what we call prehistory—that period before there were any human observers, much less historians or human scribes. For that reason, this comparatively brief chapter was routinely probed with all kinds of questions about the nature and intentions of God the Creator and, in turn, about the nature and design of all that was created.

With respect to God, in addition to the traditional but fruitless inquiry about what God was doing before creation, commentators tended to wonder more seriously about God's means of creation (whether God created directly or by means of agents, including angels), and this question often provoked Christian writers to find hints of the Trinity by highlighting the presence in this chapter of God's Word and God's Spirit—though not always with a consensus of opinion. Naturally, this line of questioning often led to polemical interaction with Jewish commentators as well as with heretics from the Christian past.

With respect to creation itself, among the first problems commonly raised were the twin issues of the relationship of eternity to time and the relationship of spirit to matter. Famously, Origen and Augustine had argued for a first creation that was wholly spiritual—a view rejected out of hand by Reformation commentators. But these same commentators were also led into controversy with non-Christian philosophers such as Aristotle, who had insisted on the eternity of the world, contradicting the received notion that creation took

place *ex nihilo* or "out of nothing." Yet despite their rejection of Aristotle on this point, there were other philosophical issues to address, because the early verses of Genesis seemed to provoke more questions than answers, especially given the incongruity of God apparently having created something at the very first that was chaotic, that is, "without form and void." So, then, what sort of creation or matter might such formlessness have been? Indeed, when did the eternal God create time—and how could that time have been marked or distinguished without the means that we take for granted, such as the movement of planets and stars, which were created only on the fourth day? Even setting aside the problem of time and eternity, there still loomed the question of why an omnipotent creator needed or wanted to extend the act of creation over six days.

It is easy to see, then, that Genesis 1 could look very much like an archaeological site where commentators could dig at will into such fields as cosmology, the calendar and the almanac, philosophy, geology, natural history and anthropology—as well as theology, of course. The temptation to speculate, to second-guess the text or to read behind it, or to lose oneself in the minutiae of Hebrew, Greek or Latin was a constant danger that many of the Reformation commentators recognized. Consequently, their best exegetical work represents a dialectic between their desire to stick with the plain and literal sense of the text, and their concern to do so without failing to appreciate even the smallest details of what God meant to reveal in those plain and literal words, and particularly what God intended both ancient and contemporary readers to derive from these words that would contribute to their genuine edification. The attentiveness of Reformation exegetes to the use or utility of *all* Scripture is frequently manifested in the way their commentaries begin, namely, with a separate preface (often called the book's "argument") that furnished the reader with an overview of the aims and outline of the sacred text.

Prolegomena: *What Is This Book Good For?*

GENESIS IDENTIFIES GOD AS HE WHO CARES FOR HIS OWN. PETER MARTYR VERMIGLI: The aim of the book of [Genesis] is to form in one's mind a worthy conception of God and the church. God is a beneficent father, a merciful guardian and a defender of that particular part of his church that belongs to him not only in name but also in fact. COMMENTARY ON GENESIS, INTRODUCTION.[1]

CREATED TO SHARE ALL OF GOD'S GOODNESS. DAVID CHYTRAEUS: God created human beings for this reason, so that there might be a creature to be seen in this world with whom he could share himself—his goodness, wisdom, righteousness and happiness for all eternity—and by whom he might in turn be acknowledged and celebrated. Indeed, God does not impart himself or his blessings except to those who acknowledge him and who knowingly delight in his wisdom and goodness. God therefore wishes to be known by us human beings: and in order that he might be known, not only did he disperse rays of his light and wisdom into human minds, but he also disclosed himself to our first parents right away, speaking with a clear voice, and revealed the hidden promise of his Son, the mediator. Later, he also committed to writing the trustworthy teaching handed on through the prophets, Christ, and the apostles, which he wishes to be read by us, heard, pondered,

set forth and explained to others. By our reading and reflecting on these writings, he kindles in our minds the true and eternal light, righteousness and life. COMMENTARY ON GENESIS, PROLEGOMENA.[2]

GENESIS SETS FORTH THE MASTER PATTERN OF SIN AND GRACE. PHILIPP MELANCHTHON: Besides showing the fashioning of things, Genesis is especially useful for this, that you may learn the origin of sin, and the first promise of grace, two topics (*loci*) from which the whole of Scripture subsequently hangs. There are also examples presented in which both the children of wrath and the children of grace are foreshadowed: the former examples teach the fear of God; the latter, faith. Truly, what sadder example can you find than the flood, or the destruction of Sodom? And how could faith be established with greater assurance than if you consider how gently, how sweetly, he protects the children of grace—even on the cross? COMMENTARY ON GENESIS, PREFACE.[3]

THE BOOK OF DIVINE MANIFESTATIONS. WOLFGANG MUSCULUS: In this book God is manifested to be the creator, propagator, governor and sustainer of all things, especially of the human race, which he created for the indescribable glory of his name and by his wondrous counsel. The corruption and sin of the human race is manifested, and then the first promise of heavenly grace. The difference between the elect and the reprobate is manifested in the sons of Adam, Noah, Abraham, Isaac and Jacob, who stood as the heads and fathers of the people of God. In the reprobate, their impiety toward God is manifested, along with their cruelty toward the elect; in the elect, their piety toward the Creator and their humanity toward all. Also manifested is the

---

[1]*In Primum Librum Mosis* (1569), 1v. [2]*In Genesin* (1576), 1-2. [3]MO 13:761.

lot and hardship of the pious, living in this world under the cross and its afflictions. Likewise, the justice of God, who guards the pious but condemns and destroys the impious. In short, manifested here is that providence of God that first of all guards everything he created, then especially those whom he has loved as a special possession and a people for his own, never leaving them unguarded in time of need and encircling his own with love. So it is not without reason that you could call this book the Book of the Manifestations of God. Wherefore it is beyond all dispute that the use of this book is of the greatest necessity. It embraces the foundations of our faith, without which no one can move on to the rest. . . . COMMENTARY ON GENESIS, PREFACE.[4]

GENESIS REVEALS WHAT IS NECESSARY TO BE KNOWN. JOHN CALVIN: This book of Moses deserves to be regarded as an incomparable treasure, since, at the very least, it instills in us a sure confidence that the world was created, and if that were taken away, we would not deserve to be sustained by the earth. For the moment, I will pass over the account of the flood, which comprises a mirror not only of God's terrifying vengeance in the destruction of the human race but also of his gratifying favor in their restoration. This one consideration establishes the book's inestimable value: that it alone reveals those things that are utterly necessary to know, [namely,] how God adopted a church unto himself after the destructive fall of humankind; what constituted the true worship of himself and what duties of piety the holy fathers practiced; how pure religion, having collapsed for a time on account of human indolence, returned to a state of integrity as if back from exile. [It also tells us] when God entrusted to a particular people his gratuitous covenant of eternal salvation; how a small progeny gradually proceeded from one man—himself barren and tottering, nearly half-dead, and (as Isaiah

[51:2] calls him) *solitary*—yet suddenly grew to an immense multitude; and how, by unexpected means, God both raised up and defended a household chosen by himself, however poor and destitute of protection they were, as well as exposed to all kinds of storms when countless enemies surrounded them on all sides. Each of us, then, may judge from our own use and experience just how needful the knowledge of these things may be. LETTER TO HENRI OF NAVARRE.[5]

GENESIS IS A MIRROR OR THEATER OF LIFE. CHRISTOPHOR PELARGUS: Genesis itself, explained methodically, encompasses a mirror of all of life, or rather is rightly called a theater of life, whether one wishes to consider divine matters, or politics, or household affairs. For the instruction of a godly prince in all matters, one cannot propose any examples more distinguished than those of the patriarchs, who were the monarchs of the first world. . . . In this extremely abundant and unexhausted sea of Scriptures, you will always succeed in finding something either that no one has discovered before you, or something that you find after others have seen it, or something that has been diligently sought not only on one's own but also thanks to others. COMMENTARY ON GENESIS, DEDICATION.[6]

ON THE UTILITY OF THE HISTORY OF CREATION. WOLFGANG CAPITO: If a reader who has any sort of confidence in the Scriptures should contemplate the ordering of God's work as explained by Moses, it will quickly be recognized that God's strength and power are infinite. Then one will also understand that this universe and all its parts depend on his

---

[4]*In Mosis Genesim* (1554), 1. [5]CTS 1:50* (CO 20:119). Calvin's letter dedicated the 1563 edition of his *Commentary on Genesis* to the future king of France. [6]Dedication Letter to Joachim Frederick, Elector of Brandenburg in 1598, *In prophetarum oceanum* (1612), sig. (:)4v–(:)(:)1r; Pelargus is invoking the traditional advice genre known as the "mirror of princes."

will and word. Once persuaded that everything was created *ex nihilo* solely by the Father's coeternal word, we will conclude that this one and the same [Father] keeps all things in existence as far as he wishes.

But whether we are pious or ungodly—or, rather, if we are [at all] moved by this awareness—we will realize at once that power does not give rise to itself, nor does the hand of change move itself. We will simultaneously begin to perceive that we are part of the universe that in its entirety arises and abides through the power of the one word of God, and until it should pass away, he acts and rests by turns. We will recognize that all things that have been made are the prerogative of him who created [them], just as God is also as generous when he uses his power as he wishes to be and withholds generosity whenever he sees fit. In this way, God governs everything by a nod or shake of his head, just as he created all things by his word, and there is no one who would hinder him. Indeed, who resists the will of the Lord? Who, out of the very weakness of nothing, establishes such great energy and efficacy in things by his word alone? Thus those who are pious will credit all their actions, whosesoever they either are or seem to be, to God as their author, just as those who are impious are warned thereby.

But the benefits that arise here are evident from what is written. Regarding ourselves, insofar as we are left without God's remarkable resources, we know in our hearts that we are nothing. Likewise, by paying attention to the order of things before us, we discern that we are unable to avoid despair. Once we have recognized this, we will conclude that whatever we are and whatever we do, it is nothing other than the power of the divine word that has securely consigned us and all we own for safekeeping. In this way, zeal for being restored to a better life and entrusting oneself to the Lord God by faith will guard one inwardly and destroy that deadly *philautia* or self-love.

Indeed, this is the first step and, as it were, the foundation for building up the full assurance of faith.

If the creation of things is understood, it directly supplies what we need and what we all lack by nature, namely, a knowledge of God that is pure, abundant and complete. For from such knowledge, one may discern who God is and what God wishes to be in himself. Through such knowledge the benevolence of the unimaginable God shines clearly in the mind of an attentive person, namely, that God is in himself father, patron, chief executive, a refuge in danger, a helper in our undertakings, and all in all. Such life-giving knowledge therefore equally dispels the opposite tendencies in the same human being, so that whoever truly believes and begins to perceive the *weakness* of humanity, also inwardly experiences God's unlimited, life-giving *power*. When these two things are joined together, someone who is by nature an abject sinner, afflicted by a guilty verdict and by all its punishments, at the same time dares to profess that he or she is a blessed child of God. ON GOD'S WORK OF THE SIX DAYS.[7]

A PRIMER ON REPENTANCE. JOHANNES BRENZ: Nothing is more necessary for us than that we should take up the pursuit of repentance, by which we might escape the wrath that is coming upon the world. For this purpose, then, I have chosen the first book of Moses, . . . because scarcely any book in all of the sacred Scriptures seems more suited for this theme. Indeed, it contains not only the beginnings and progress of this world, so freshly made, but also distinguished examples of repentance, by which the difference between the pious and the impious is clearly revealed: the former are saved by repentance in an amazing way, but the latter perish most miserably on account of their impenitence.

---

[7]*Hexemeron* (1539), 17v-19r.

When Adam had sinned, and by his sin come to deserve both a bodily and an eternal death, he was yet saved by repentance. If God had been marking sins, Noah should have perished in the flood with the others; but because he repented, he himself was marvelously saved while others were miserably lost. Abraham worshiped with others devoted to idolatry in Chaldaea and he deserved eternal destruction, but after he repented and followed God's calling, he became the father of many nations and was chosen to be the greatest of the patriarchs, from whose race descended Christ, the savior of the world. Lot was indeed accepted by God and freed from the conflagration of Sodom by repentance; but his impenitent fellow citizens were deemed worthy to be consumed by fire dropped from heaven. These and other things of this kind are written in Genesis for our instruction, so that by the examples of the patriarchs we may be incited to repentance. . . . Indeed, in this book we read about how we may be made truly just and holy before God, even as the Scriptures say of Abraham, "Abraham believed God and it was reckoned to him as righteousness." Therefore this book ought to be highly commended among us, because it teaches us the true way to pursue righteousness and holiness. COMMENTARY ON GENESIS 1.[8]

GENESIS CONTAINS THE WHOLE GOSPEL OF JESUS CHRIST. JOHN CALVIN: This is the argument of the book: After the world had been created, the first humans were placed in it as in a theater, so that by beholding God's wonderful works above and below, they might reverently adore their Author. Secondly, that all things were ordained for their use, so that by being more deeply obliged to God, they might be wholly devoted and dedicated to his service. Thirdly, that being endowed with understanding and reason, they might be distinguished from brute animals by meditating on a better life, indeed, that they might

direct their course straight towards God, whose image was engraved upon them. Afterwards followed the fall of Adam, whereby they alienated themselves from God and were deprived of all rectitude. Moses thus represents humankind as devoid of all good, blinded in understanding, perverse in heart, vitiated in every part, and under sentence of eternal death; but he soon adds an account of the restoration, in which Christ shines forth with the benefit of redemption. From there, he not only describes an unbroken narrative of God's remarkable providence in governing and preserving the church, but he also points us to the true worship of God, [in that] he teaches us where salvation is to be found and urges us, by the example of the patriarchs, to bear the cross with meekness. Accordingly, those who desire to make good progress in this book should keep these main topics in mind. But they should especially observe that, after Adam had ruined himself and all his posterity by his deadly fall, *this* is the basis of our salvation, *this* the origin of the church: that we have been uprooted from the deepest darkness and have obtained a new life sheerly by the grace of God; that the patriarchs have by faith been made partakers of this life (just as it was offered to them by God's word); that this word, in turn, was founded upon Christ; and that all the pious who have lived since then have, in fact, been sustained by the very same promise of salvation by which Adam was revived in the beginning. COMMENTARY ON GENESIS, ARGUMENT.[9]

GENESIS COVERS THE SWEEP OF CHRISTIAN DOCTRINE. DAVID CHYTRAEUS: It is extremely useful in the interpretation of Scripture to refer the main parts of the text to the common topics that comprise the substance of Christian doctrine, and then to show the sequence of its members, explaining the

---

[8]*Opera* 1:1-2. [9]CTS 1:64-65* (CO 23:11-12).

words, phrases, and figures of divine discourse by consulting the roots of the language, considering the arts of speech, and comparing similar testimonies of Scripture. Therefore, with God as my help, I will try to attend to these duties of the interpreter with a modicum of faith and diligence.

And since the whole body of Christian doctrine may be gathered into ten main topics or members, as it were, I will strive to bring the main sayings and stories of Genesis and the following books under the headings of these ten topics, as a pyramid of sorts. For in learning and teaching, it is quite beneficial to have the substance of doctrine arrayed in a learned and methodical order and carefully distributed into specific topics. Thus, those who are studious in their reading of Genesis should refer its teachings and stories to these ten members of Christian doctrine:

I. GOD and the three divine persons, of which testimonies appear in Genesis 1, 3, 18, 19, 48, and 35; of the two natures in Christ, in chaps. 3, 12, 22, and 49.

II. CREATION AND PROVIDENCE, chaps. 1 and 2; of good and evil angels, chap. 3; of the image of God, according to which humanity was fashioned, chap. 1.

III. SIN and the cause of sin, and the fall of angels and human beings, chap. 3; of original sin, chaps. 3, 5, 6, 8, 12; of venial and mortal sin, and of the lapses of the saints, chaps. 4, 9, 19, 38, 20.

IV. The LAW of God, chap. 3.

V. The GOSPEL, or the promise of the remission of sin for Christ's sake and the benefits of Christ, chaps. 3, 12, 14, 22, 26, 28, 48, 49; of predestination, which is God's eternal decree concerning those who were to be received into eternal life for Christ's sake, chap. 25; on justification by faith, chaps. 4, 15, 12.

VI. GOOD WORKS, chap. 4; on the fear of

God, chaps. 6, 7, 19; on faith, chaps. 12, 15, 32, 3; on the true invocation of God, chap. 32; on chastity, chaps. 2, 39, 34, 19; on clemency, chap. 50 etc.

VII. SACRAMENTS, chaps. 4, 17, 9; on circumcision, chap. 17; on sacrifices, chaps. 4, 8, 22; on the priesthood of Christ, chap. 14.

VIII. REPENTANCE, chap. 3.

IX. The CHURCH, chaps. 4, 5, 27, 17, 18; on the miraculous preservation of the church and the godly, chaps. 6, 7, 41, 19; on the cross and the calamities of the church, and on true consolations, chaps. 3, 37; on the kingdom of Christ, chap. 49.

X. The LAST JUDGMENT, bodily resurrection and eternal life, chaps. 4, 25; on civil magistrates and the dignity of political affairs, chaps. 9, 11, 13; on marriage and household life, chaps. 2, 24, 29.

These headings contain nearly the whole substance of Christian doctrine that everyone needs to recognize for the knowledge of God and the salvation of their souls. COMMENTARY ON GENESIS, PROLEGOMENA.[10]

ALL THE LAWS AND PROMISES BEGIN HERE. PETER MARTYR VERMIGLI: How does it happen that, wishing to treat the laws and promises, [Moses] does not inaugurate the account from there but rather from the crafting of the world and the history of the fathers? This is easily answered: before the Law may be issued, or certain people enticed by the promises, two matters must be expounded beforehand. First, one must expound what may be the authority of him who issues the law, on the basis of which emperors and kings add or append an epigraph where they honor themselves by their titles and assert the

---

[10]*In Genesin* (1576), 4-7.

majesty of their name. So too in this case is it written that, before everything, God must be heard by right and merit when he gives orders or makes promises to what he has fashioned, because he is the Lord of all things: thus authority is joined to him. As far as promises are concerned, in the history of events in the time of the fathers it is declared how constantly he always stood by the promises and covenants. Secondly, one must then state what sort of people is this to whom such great things were promised and to whom, moreover, such useful things were commanded: it is God's church, whose dawning is traced back to the first parents. COMMENTARY ON GENESIS, INTRODUCTION.[11]

WHETHER DERIVED FROM CREATION OR REDEMPTION, KNOWLEDGE OF GOD IS PRACTICAL. WOLFGANG CAPITO: The knowledge of God is twofold: natural and divine. The former is handed down in the writings of the philosophers and also gleaned by reading things written without the Spirit's illumination by human reason as it thoughtfully contemplates God's eternal power. We may label this as watchtower knowledge, for it amounts to nothing more than watching God when God is known but not for the purpose of glorifying him; nor does such knowledge incline a person toward the doing of good.

The latter knowledge, however, is divine or revealed, gathered only from divine oracles, provided that the Spirit accommodates one's hearing of them as a teacher would, because otherwise such things surpass the capacity of our nature and the mind is neither profitably persuaded nor genuinely moved. This knowledge comes into play not so much in one's thoughts as in one's practices and activities, where it is tireless and unceasingly concerned about our entrusting ourselves to God, for our calling upon him, for accepting all things from him, and for giving thanks to him alone. For it is a trustworthy conviction that God is

both willing and able to guard and protect us by his word.

Moreover, knowledge of this kind, which arises from Scripture, is [itself] twofold, because when we know God through his works, those things are also set forth in two ways by the divine writings, as the works of creation and the works of restoration. This knowledge is distinguished in two ways, according to the nature of the works: for knowledge of the creator is one thing and knowledge of the restorer is another, and both persons are called by names that suit them. For at the beginning of creation, it names that infinite creative power as distributed into three persons: God, Word and the Spirit of God. But from the restoration set forth in the covenant with the patriarchs and procured through Christ, the same three persons of a single divinity are called Father, Son and Holy Spirit. Indeed, creation declares God's infinite power and might; but in addition to his omnipotence, restoration declares his kindness and mercy. Therefore he is called *God* on account of his virtue and vitality, while the *Spirit* of God is named because he is energetic; these are names that correspond to the nature of things. But for redemption, the title of *Father* is appropriate because it is he who pursues us sinners with unparalleled benevolence, while *Son* [fits] the one who, having been brought forth from a woman without an earthly father, atoned for our sins; and *Holy Spirit* is the one through whom we are made holy, strengthened, and brought back to life. ON GOD'S WORK OF THE SIX DAYS.[12]

IN CREATION, GOD BECOMES VISIBLE IN HIS WORKS. JOHN CALVIN: The intention of Moses in beginning his book with the creation of the world is to render God, as it were, visible to us in his appearance. . . . We know God,

---

[11]*In Primum Librum Mosis* (1569), 1v. [12]*Hexemeron* (1539), 100v-101v.

who is himself invisible, only through his works. . . . This is why the Lord, in order to invite us to the knowledge of himself, places before our eyes the crafting of heaven and earth and therein renders himself visible in a certain sense. COMMENTARY ON GENESIS, ARGUMENT.[13]

1:1 *In the Beginning, God Created the Heavens and the Earth*

THE SIX DAYS ARE A SEA OF WISDOM, A COMPLETE CATECHISM. CHRISTOPHOR PELARGUS: Among the most ancient writers, Theophilus speaks most truly of the *hexaemeron*, that is, the works of the six days, in his second book to Autolycus: If someone had a hundred tongues and a hundred mouths, it would not suffice for fathoming this sea of wisdom, not even if one lived to be a hundred years old. . . .[†] Truly, you may see many things contained in this first chapter, just as in the following two as well. Together, these are a catechism of the teachings of the Old and New Testaments, for in their narratives they exhaustively deal with all the speeches of the prophets and apostles. Thus, each one of us ought to revere and admire the majesty of Scripture here. But because things are remembered that possess good order, we will especially keep in mind the orderly way in which these things are staged. First, *who* is the creator of all things, namely, God, he who is before all things and therefore eternal. Second, *what* he created, heaven and earth and all that is in them (v. 1). Third, *how*: by his word and his spirit, moving across the waters (vv. 2-3). Fourth, *how many days*: six . . . COMMENTARY ON GENESIS 1.[14]

"IN THE BEGINNING" HAS NO SECRET MEANING. MARTIN LUTHER: Even if we should engage in endless speculation and debate, these matters nevertheless remain outside our comprehension. And if we do not

fully understand even the things which we see and do, how much less shall we grasp those? What will you assume to have been outside time or before time? Or what will you imagine that God was doing before there was any time? Let us, therefore, rid ourselves of such ideas and realize that God was incomprehensible in His essential rest before the creation of the world, but that now, after the creation, He is within, without, and above all creatures; that is, He is still incomprehensible. Nothing else can be said, because our mind cannot grasp what lies outside time. . . . It is folly to argue much about God outside and before time, because this is an effort to understand the Godhead without a covering, or the uncovered divine essence. Because this is impossible, God envelops Himself in His works in certain forms, as today He wraps Himself up in Baptism, in absolution, etc. If you should depart from these, you will get into an area where there is no measure, no space, no time, and into the merest nothing, concerning which, according to the philosopher, there can be no knowledge. Therefore we justly pass over this question and are satisfied with the simple explanation of the phrase "in the beginning." LECTURES ON GENESIS 1:2.[15]

GOD WAS NOT LONELY OR BORED. WOLFGANG MUSCULUS: It is frivolous when [the Manichaeans] say, "Is it possible that, in that beginning, it bored God to be alone?" God was not alone before he made the world: all the things to come were present to him, and the things that did not yet exist were no less in his sight than if the things themselves had been there. Nor is solace to be sought for him from those things that he made, for all life and happiness finds its source in his very self, from whom whatever is of solace pours forth to

---

[13]CTS 1:58, 59* (CO 23:5-6, 7-8). [14]*In prophetarum oceanum* (1612), 10; [†]Pelargus mimics the first sentence of Theophilus, *To Autolycus* 2.12 (ANF 2:99), then quotes it in Greek (omitted here). [15]LW 1:11 (WA 42:9-10).

everything he has made. . . . The Son of God is not alone, because he is conjoined with the Father. And was God alone before the world was created, when Father, Son, and Spirit were conjoined in incomprehensible divinity? Commentary on Genesis 1:1-2.[16]

Where Was God Before Creation? Johannes Brenz: In thinking about the creation of the world, another thing comes to mind that provokes some to doubt. Indeed, they think, if God created the world some thousands of years ago, where was he before the world was created, when the prophet says, "Heaven is my throne, and the earth is my footstool." Or what was he doing before there was a world here? He wasn't idle, was he? And because that seems absurd, they regard it as equally absurd that the world did not exist from eternity, just like God himself. Augustine tells of someone in his own day who was asked what God was doing before he made heaven and earth and who jokingly replied, "He was preparing hell for those who pry into things." And that is a good response to those who are merely curious, but there is a different response for those who are pious and earnestly seeking to learn. For so far as concerns God himself, he does not need the world for his throne and footstool: rather, the world needs him as its creator and conservator. Indeed, content in himself, filled with all goodness and self-sufficient, God lives from eternity in the highest blessedness. And the Father with the Son and the Holy Spirit, existing from eternity, needed neither the service of angels nor that of earthly ministers, but from the greatness of his own self he initiates every kind of blessedness. And he ordained from eternity to fashion this world with its seasons and to create the human race, from which he would choose for himself a church with which he might share his beatitude. . . . So when it is asked where God was before creating the world, one should reply that because they are

three persons, Father, Son and Holy Spirit, the Father was then present with the Son, and the Son with the Holy Spirit was present with the Father, in the highest blessedness and in no need of ministers, of course, because God is sufficient unto himself. Commentary on Genesis 1:1.[17]

Our Hope Is in a God Who Is above Time, Change and Matter. Johannes Oecolampadius: Scripture clearly shows that God made the heavens without causing change to himself. Even if creation commenced with the beginning of the world, still the creation itself caused no change in God. Because God decreed at some point within himself, the creation began at some time to be completed, not because God himself experienced a new operation, but because the things he had previously decreed within himself began to exist by his own will. . . . He who is the author of heaven and of earth is also the author of motion and time. And we do not make God liable to time or createdness, for he is incorporeal and therefore above all things. It is suitable for Christians to think worthily about God. Among ourselves, moreover, we draw great hope and faith when we learn that God made heaven and earth from nothing, and we are immediately prepared to believe other miracles of God, "who calls things that are not as though they were." Whoever rightly believes this knows that God himself is able to deliver him from the greatest dangers. He also believes that the body, dead and gone to ashes, may easily be revived. But if anyone wishes instead to comply with the demands of reason, he will afterwards forever be the prisoner of his own reason, unable to believe anything that reason has not determined beforehand. Lectures on Genesis 1:1-2.[18]

---

[16]*In Mosis Genesim* (1554), 4. [17]*Opera* 1:4-5; citing Is 66:1 (=Acts 7:49) and Augustine, *Confessions* 11.12. [18]*In Genesim* (1536), 8v-9r, citing Rom 4:17.

"In the Beginning" Is Not a Reference to Christ or Wisdom. Wolfgang Musculus: In this verse, *beginning*† is a word for *inception*, and it corresponds to things that begin to happen. But in amazing ways, human meticulosity twists in upon itself in order to contrive some abstruse meaning for the word *beginning*, as is plain not only in Jewish writings but also in some of our own. They anxiously seek what might be that beginning in which or through which God fashioned heaven and earth. Some interpret this beginning as Christ, the word of God; others understand it as God's wisdom. Certain writers think it was said about the beginning of time, which many then deny. . . . While we embrace the simplicity of Moses' words, we do not deny that God created heaven and earth by his wisdom; yet we do not read with the Jerusalem Targum, "In wisdom God created the heaven and earth." For Moses was not ignorant of the fact that God created everything by the counsel of his wisdom, but he makes no mention of this in the present context. There are enough clear testimonies found in other places in the Holy Scriptures that it is not necessary to abandon the simple sense of the words that Moses uses here. Likewise, we do not deny that Christ, the word of God, fashioned all things; yet we do not follow the exposition of those who understand Christ by the word *beginning*. We know and confess with John, that "through him all things were made, and nothing was made without him." But at the same time we also confess with John what he says, that "In the beginning was the word, and the word was with God, etc." He does not say, "The beginning *was* the word"— even though he is the alpha and omega, the beginning and the end—but "*In* the beginning was the word," that is, at the very beginning of all things, when God made the heaven and the earth. Commentary on Genesis 1:1.[19]

"In the Beginning" Refutes Arius. Martin Luther: Arius was unable to deny that Christ existed before the creation of the world, because Christ also says (Jn 8:58): "Before Abraham was, I am." And it is written in Proverbs (8:27): "Before the heavens were, I am." Therefore he shifted to the position that Christ, or the Word, was created before all things and later on created all things and was the most perfect creature, but that He had not always been in existence. This insane and wicked opinion must be countered with the fact that Moses briefly says "in the beginning" and does not assert that anything else was in existence before the beginning except God, to whom he gives a name in the plural number. The minds of men arrive at these foolish conclusions when they are determined to do their thinking about such lofty matters without the Word. Lectures on Genesis 1:2.[20]

God as Creator Is Foundational to Faith. Peter Martyr Vermigli: The invisible things that we here perceive are innumerable but are all rounded up into three categories: power, wisdom and goodness. The greatness of the things brought forth, their sudden coming into being from nothing, solely by order of the word, argue for the greatest power. Moreover, the craftsmanship, beautiful appearance, adornment and exceptional arrangement attest to the artificer's wisdom. The usefulness that we on our part gather from here teaches how great is his goodness. It is of great importance for us to embrace this making of the world with faith, so that the Creed may take its starting point from here. Should this be taken away, the first sin will not stand out, the promises about Christ will collapse, and all the power of religion is sunk to the bottom. And since all the articles of our faith are more or less propositions or principles of our piety, among all of them this one is

---

[19]*In Mosis Genesim* (1554), 2-3; †the Latin here is *principium*, which, like the Greek *archē*, connotes not only "beginning" but also "cause, power, ruler," etc. [20]LW 1:13 (WA 42:11).

considered first in order. COMMENTARY ON GENESIS, *INTRODUCTION*.[21]

TRUSTING GOD AS CREATOR INSTILLS CONTENTMENT AND COMPASSION.

WOLFGANG MUSCULUS: The knowledge that we all have the same creator and maker admonishes us not to harbor contempt for God's work, whether in ourselves or in another, by asking "Why did he make it like this?" Thus we read in Isaiah, "Woe to anyone who, like an earthen potsherd, argues with its maker. Shall the clay say to the potter, 'What are you making?'" And in Proverbs, "Whoever disregards the needy insults their maker." And so this faith, wherein we believe that we have been created by God, brings about these three things in our hearts: First, that with all our hearts we depend in all things upon God our creator. Second, that each of us be contented with our circumstances—indeed, that we embrace them with thanksgiving, given that God our creator has placed us in them. Third, that none of us view our neighbor's circumstances with contempt, however vile and miserable they be, lest we thereby cast aspersions upon our common creator. COMMON PLACES.[22]

CREATION IS MEANT TO GLORIFY GOD.

WILLIAM PERKINS: The end of creation is the glory of God. As Solomon says, God made all things for his own sake, yea, even the wicked for the day of evil. And God propounds this principal end to himself, not as though he lacked glory and would purchase it for himself by the creation; for he is most glorious in himself and his honor and praise, being infinite, can neither be increased nor decreased: but rather that he might communicate and make manifest his glory to his creatures, and give them occasion to magnify the same. For the reasonable creatures of God, beholding his glory in the creation, are moved to testify and declare the same to others. EXPOSITION OF THE APOSTLES' CREED.[23]

THE BOOK OF NATURE POINTS TO GOD.

PETER RIEDEMANN: Creation, from which we all can learn, is the first book written by God's own hand and given to us. It is a book that all people without exception can read: poor or rich, powerful or humble, noble or common, educated or uneducated. All created things point to obedience to God, for they all obey him and bear their fruit in season according to his bidding. . . . Therefore, we fully believe that everything was made and created by God for his honor, but used by humans to dishonor and shame him, will be a witness against those selfsame people at the last judgment. God's judgment will surely come upon them, and they will receive what they deserve. CONFESSION OF FAITH.[24]

HEAVEN AND EARTH POINT AWAY FROM THEMSELVES TO GOD.

KONRAD PELLIKAN: It is as if [Moses] wished to say, "Whatever you see or do not see in the whole world, whether on high or below, had a beginning—at one time did not exist, was made out of nothing—by the one and only God, whom alone a man or woman [*homo*] ought to worship and adore, whom all these things serve and are God's creatures, and they absolutely cannot be worshiped in place of God." [This is] the first statement of the law. . . . COMMENTARY ON GENESIS 1:1.[25]

GOD'S VISIBLE WORKS SHOULD LEAD US TO TRUST GOD'S PROVIDENCE.

WOLFGANG MUSCULUS: Note that he speaks with specificity, saying, "In the beginning God created *this* heaven and *this* earth." We are here reminded that the Holy Spirit acted through Moses with special care so that he might instruct a simple and untutored people not about invisible things created by God, such as the highest

---

[21]*In Primum Librum Mosis* (1569), 1v-2r. [22]Musculus, *Loci communes* (1560), 18; *Common Places* (1578), 26-27; citing Is 45:9; Prov 14:31. [23]*Works* (1608) 1:143, citing Prov 16:4. [24]CRR 9:63. [25]*Commentaria Bibliorum* (1532) 1:1r.

heaven, . . . angels or angelic hierarchies, principalities and powers, but about visible things—about that heaven which we daily see with our eyes, and this earth, which we inhabit as long as we are in the flesh. This is why, in the whole course of six days, he mentions not a single invisible creature, but he does relate how God made those that are familiar and visible, which everywhere pass before the eyes of mortals. . . . If only all individuals, or as many as label themselves as Christians, had been instructed in these beliefs about creation, so that those who gaze at this heaven, in which the sun and the moon shine forth, might not doubt but that they behold the work of God himself, their heavenly father and the creator of all; and that those who dwell in this earth might discern that it, too, was made by God the Father and given to humans to inhabit for their own use! In this way, they would more easily have been led from beliefs about creation to a trust in divine providence and benevolence toward all other things. COMMENTARY ON GENESIS 1:1.[26]

THE ART OF MOSES' NARRATIVE. HULD-RYCH ZWINGLI: Moses wished to depict God's vast undertaking quite clearly to everyone, so he used the clearest and most familiar words: earth, water, air, etc. He depicts God for us as a sort of master craftsman, who produces a work that is rough and indistinct at first, then adds light, shadows and outlines, and adorns each thing with its colors. ANNOTATIONS ON GENESIS 1:1.[27]

WE SEE GOD'S REFLECTION IN CREATION ONLY WITH THE SPECTACLES OF SCRIPTURE. JOHN CALVIN: Now in describing the world as a mirror in which we ought to behold God, I would not be understood to assert either that our eyes are sufficiently clear-sighted to discern what the fabric of heaven and earth represents, or that the knowledge we thereby derive suffices for salvation. As a

matter of fact, because the Lord invites us to himself by means of created things but with no effect except thereby to render us inexcusable, he has added (as was necessary) a new remedy, or at any rate mitigated the coarseness of our disposition by means of other assistance. For with Scripture as our guide and teacher, not only does he make plain those things that would otherwise escape our notice, he virtually forces us to behold them, as if he had assisted our dull sight with eyeglasses.[†] On this point (as we have already observed) Moses insists. For if the mute instruction of heaven and earth were sufficient, Moses' own teaching would have been superfluous. This herald therefore approaches, who stirs our attention so that we may understand that we have been placed in this theater in order to behold the glory of God: and not just as witnesses, but also so that we might enjoy all the riches that are set forth here, just as the Lord has ordained and subjected them to our use. And he not only declares generally that God is the architect of the world, but he also shows through the whole course of this history how admirable is his power, his wisdom, his goodness, and especially his deepest solicitude for the human race. Besides, since the eternal Word of God is the lively and express image of himself, he recalls us to this point. What the apostle teaches is thus verified, that through no other means than faith can it be understood that the world was formed by the word of God (Heb 11:3). For faith is properly destined for this end: that having been taught by the ministry of Moses, we no longer wander in foolish and trifling speculations, but contemplate the true and only God in his genuine image. COMMENTARY ON GENESIS, ARGUMENT.[28]

---

[26]*In Mosis Genesim* (1554), 7. Musculus goes on to cite Ps 8:3-4 as an example of how the heavens can teach faith in God's providence. [27]ZSW 13:6. [28]CTS 1:62-63* (CO 23:9-10). [†]Calvin's comparison of Scripture to eyeglasses was developed more famously in 1559, in the final Latin edition of his *Institutes* (at 1.6.1).

CREATION IS A REVELATION ONLY TO THOSE HUMBLED BY FAITH AND TUTORED BY CHRIST.

JOHN CALVIN: Truly, it is pointless to reason as philosophers do on the workmanship of the world unless we are among those who, having first been humbled by the preaching of the gospel, have learned to submit the whole of their mind's discernment to the "foolishness" of the cross (as Paul calls it). We will find nothing above or below that will raise us up to God, I say, until Christ has instructed us in his own school. Yet this cannot be done unless, having emerged from the depths of hell, we are borne up above all heavens by the chariot of his cross, so that by faith we may there apprehend things that no eye has ever seen nor ear ever heard, things that far surpass our hearts and minds. Truly, it is not the earth that is set before us there, as if to supply us with its fruits as daily nourishment; rather, Christ offers himself to us unto life eternal. Nor is it heaven, by the shining of its sun and stars, that enlightens our bodily eyes, but the same Christ himself, the Light of the World and the Sun of Righteousness, shines into our souls. Neither does the air stretch out its empty space for us to breathe, but the very Spirit of God quickens us and causes us to live. There, in short, the invisible kingdom of Christ fills all things, and his spiritual grace is diffused through all. Yet this does not prevent us from applying our senses to the contemplation of heaven and earth, which is also where we should seek the things that will confirm us in the true knowledge of God. For Christ is that image in which God sets forth for our view not only his heart, but also his hands and his feet. I give the name *heart* to that secret love with which he has embraced us in Christ; by *hands* and *feet* I understand those works of his that are displayed before our eyes. But the moment we have departed from Christ, there is nothing, however gross or insignifi-cant in itself, in which we are not inevitably delusional. COMMENTARY ON GENESIS, ARGUMENT.[29]

GOD'S UNITY AND TRINITY.

WOLFGANG MUSCULUS: *Elohim* is plural in number, *bara* is singular, so that it could be read, "Gods created." Thus the Holy Triad is beautifully inscribed in the word *Elohim*, and the mystery of [God's] unity in the word *created*. COMMENTARY ON GENESIS 1:1.[30]

CREATION IS THE WORK OF THE TRINITY.

ANNA MARIA VAN SCHURMAN:
But who may be the Creator
    of all these wonders so blessed,
and how all these things took place,
    must be here more clearly confessed:
God the Father, God the Son,
    and God the Spirit Holy,
He was the beginning
    of this great work, and he only.
This the creature does not teach,
    but one finds it proclaimed
from the depths of the divine Word,
    where it is contained.
For however much a work of art
    displays its Maker's skill,
how many its Makers are,
    it never has revealed nor will,
especially when those who adorn
    a work with art are many
and differ not among themselves
    in the smallest degree, if any:
much less in this mystery,
    since these Three are One indeed
and all the works they do for us
    are common to all Three.
How the Father still preserves his works,
    and guides and controls,
one can understand
    from reason's Creator, and the soul's.

---

[29] CTS 1:63-64* (CO 23:9-12), alluding to 1 Cor 1:18 and 2:9.
[30] *In Mosis Genesim* (1554), 7.

But that the Father created all
by his living Word,
and these Two, through the Spirit,
is from the Scripture to be heard.
Paraphrase of Genesis 1–3.[31]

God the Father Is Also Indicated in the Act of Creation. Wolfgang Capito: The Father is creating in the beginning, which is truly shown in these words, "In the beginning God created." For God [here is] *Elohim*, because it is the name of his whole nature or substance. The mention that is made of the Son and Spirit in the same context of the speech—the former, in the phrase "in the beginning," and the latter, in the words "and the spirit of God was hovering"—is necessary lest the primary name appear to be listed to no purpose, as it were, so that a third person in the Godhead, which is the Father, should be made manifest to the believer. In this way you now have the God who creates: the Father, I say; the Word through whom he creates, who is the Son; and the one in whom he creates, the Spirit of God, who is also the same as the Holy Spirit. On God's Work of the Six Days.[32]

A Plural Word for God Is No Proof of the Trinity. John Calvin: Moses has *Elohim*, a plural noun, from which some are accustomed to infer that in God three persons are here indicated. But since it seems to me too insubstantial a proof for so great a matter, I would not make my stand on this word; in fact, readers should be urged to guard themselves against forced interpretations of this kind. They think they have a testimony against the Arians, to prove the deity of the Son and of the Spirit, but they meanwhile involve themselves in the error of Sabellius, because Moses afterwards adds that the Elohim had spoken, and that the Spirit of the Elohim rested upon the waters. Yet if we suppose three persons to be indicated here, there will be no distinction between them. Indeed, it will follow that the

Son is begotten by himself, and that the Spirit is not of the Father but of himself. For me, it's enough that the plural number expresses the powers that God displayed in creating the world. I do admit, of course, that even if Scripture enumerates many powers of God, it nonetheless always recalls us to the Father, and his Son, and the Spirit, as we will see a bit later on. Commentary on Genesis 1:1.[33]

The Trinity Is Not Proved Here but Is Strongly Implied. Johannes Oecolampadius: Many seek [to establish] the mystery of the Trinity from this beginning, an effort which, to be sure, should by no means be condemned. But that is not established suitably here in this text. When, for instance, they infer the Son and God the Father and the Holy Spirit through "the beginning," they seem to seek the sense violently, although they could do so in other more appropriate ways. We know the world was formed by the word, as it says in the letter to the Hebrews. But here we gladly uncover a threefold reference even on the first day. For next it follows: "God said, and immediately it appeared," [an assertion] to which John the Evangelist surely alluded, and cited most gladly. Likewise, "And God saw that the light was good," that is, he approved it. The will of God implies a third person. Thus, happily enough, those deepest mysteries are [here] commended to us. Lectures on Genesis 1:1-2.[34]

Why Angels Are Not Mentioned Here. Peter Martyr Vermigli: It seems a puzzle why the creation of the angels should be so covered by silence that in all the writings of the Old Testament no mention of it is made. . . .

---

[31]*Uitbreiding*, 2.11-26. [32]*Hexemeron* (1539), 72v-73r. [33]CTS 1:70-72* (CO 23:15). In the third century, Sabellius argued that the Father and Son were merely modes of the Godhead, not distinct persons; in the fourth century, Arius asserted that the Son was not eternal but was created by the Father. [34]*In Genesim* (1536), 10r, alluding to Heb 1:10 and presumably to Jn 1:1-14.

One reason is that if they were described as brought forth at the beginning, God might have seemed afterwards to have used their work in the fashioning of other things. But in order that we might attribute to him alone all power of bringing things forth, Moses therefore passed over it in silence, lest we imagine that we ourselves, perhaps, might be a thing of their devising. Just as our redemption is regarded as received only from Christ the Son of God and not from angels, so with equal cause was this true regarding creation. A second reason is on account of the human fondness for idolatry. For if they worshiped heaven, stars, beasts of burden, serpents and birds, what if Moses had described that spiritual creature in all its colors? What if he said that they were made to serve us, to be placed in charge of regions, to attend to individual human beings? What wouldn't people have done then? They would have gone insane in worshiping them! COMMENTARY ON GENESIS 1:1.[35]

WHAT ABOUT THE ANGELS? MARTIN LUTHER: Here Moses seems to be forgetting himself, because he does not deal at all with two very important matters, namely, the creation and the fall of the angels, and relates only the state of affairs of physical things, although there is no doubt that the angels were created. . . . It is surprising that Moses should remain silent about these weighty matters. Since men were without definite information, the result was that they invented something, namely, that there were nine choirs of angels and that they fell for nine entire days. They also invented an account of a very great battle and how the good angels withstood the evil ones. . . . So it happens that where there are no clear statements on the subject, rash people usually consider themselves free to come up with imaginary ideas. . . . Let these ideas be worth what they may. I for my part would not compel anybody to agree with such opinions.

But this much is certain: the angels fell and the devil was transformed from an angel of light into an angel of darkness. Perhaps there may also have been a conflict between the good and the evil angels. Because Moses was writing for a people without learning or experience, he wanted to write what was necessary and useful to know. Other, unnecessary information about the nature of the angels and the like he passed over. Therefore we should not be expected to say more about this whole business either, especially since the New Testament, too, deals in a rather limited way with this doctrine; it adds nothing beyond the fact that they have been condemned and are held bound in prison, as it were, until the Day of Judgment. So it is sufficient for us to know that there are good and evil angels and that God created all of them alike, as good. From this it follows necessarily that the evil angels fell and did not stand in the truth. How this came about is unknown; nevertheless, it is likely that they fell as the result of pride, because they despised the Word or the Son of God and wanted to place themselves above Him. More than this I do not have. LECTURES ON GENESIS 1:6.[36]

1:2a *The Earth Was Without Form and Void*

"CREATING" IS BY DEFINITION *EX NIHILO*. WOLFGANG MUSCULUS: Moses does not simply say, "God made," but "God created heaven and earth." To create is different than to make . . . for to create is to build something out of nothing, a sense that the word "to make" does not have. COMMENTARY ON GENESIS 1:1.[37]

THE SON OF GOD BRINGS ORDER TO CHAOS. MARTIN LUTHER: Water and abyss

---

[35]*In Primum Librum Mosis* (1569), 2r. [36]LW 1:22-23 (WA 42:17-18), citing Rev 20:2, 7. [37]*In Mosis Genesim* (1554), 2.

and heaven are used in this passage for the same thing, namely, for that dark and unformed mass which later on was provided with life and separated by the Word. Now these are functions of the Second Person, that is, of Christ, the Son of God: to adorn and separate the crude mass which was brought forth out of nothing. Lectures on Genesis 1:2.[38]

God Cannot Be Known Outside His Word. Martin Luther: It is therefore insane to argue about God and the divine nature without the Word or any covering, as all the heretics are accustomed to do. They do their thinking about God with the same sureness with which they argue about a pig or cow. Therefore they also receive a reward worthy of their rashness in that they arrive at so dangerous a view. Whoever desires to be saved and to be safe when he deals with such great matters, let him simply hold to the form, the signs, and the coverings of the Godhead, such as His Word and His works. For in His Word and in His works He shows Himself to us. . . . But those who want to reach God apart from these coverings exert themselves to ascend to heaven without ladders (that is, without the Word). Overwhelmed by His majesty, which they seek to comprehend without a covering, they fall to their destruction. This is what happened to Arius. He thought that there was some intermediate being between the Creator and the creature and that all things were created by that intermediate being. It was inevitable that he should hit upon this idea after he had denied, contrary to Scripture, the plurality of the Persons in the Godhead. Since he argues his position apart from and without the Word of God and relies on his thinking alone, he cannot avoid falling into error. Lectures on Genesis 1:2.[39]

From Formlessness to Beauty by the Power of God's Word. Johannes Brenz:

Heaven and earth were one huge mass, partly water or moisture, partly earth or hardness. This whole mass was covered in darkness, because light had not yet been created but everything seemed to be an abyss—a huge mass having neither beginning nor end nor shape. Indeed, it was adorned with neither heaven nor stars, nor was the firmament in its place. The land was not improved with plants or buildings, nor with fields or roads. This is what *tohu* and *bohu* mean: empty and hollow. Yet just as this mass was created by God, so also was it tended by the Spirit of God. . . . God himself nurtured it, as if his Holy Spirit were incubating this watery mass, which then became so decorated, arranged and adorned that nothing can be imagined that would be more beautiful or more ornate in its physical appearance. It seems amazing to us how the utterly beautiful bodies of the heavens and the earth and all that is in them lay as if jumbled together in an indistinct heap. But if we rise up from considering the minuscule parts of the world to contemplate the world's entire mass or bulk, we may sketch what that mass was like without any obscurity. Look at a grain, or at an apple or pear seed. A grain seems truly tiny, but in it are contained and comprehended roots, its timber or trunk, branches, leaves and fruits, all at the same time. . . . [Yet] if by his word God can create out of nothing this mass, like a grain or seed of the entire world, and afterwards by his word alone arrange it with loveliness and adorn it with all of the beauty that is set before our eyes; then by his word he surely can also do what he revealed to us in his promise, to cause us to flourish before our enemies, and to keep us free from harm not only in death itself but also to grant us eternal life. God is not to be shut in by the limits of our reason or power. Instead, we should realize that God can do what he wills and wishes, whatever he

---

[38]LW 1:9 (WA 42:8). [39]LW 1:13-14 (WA 42:11).

signifies and promises by his word. COMMEN-TARY ON GENESIS 1:2.[40]

GOD'S POWER CREATES NOT ONLY FROM NOTHING, BUT EVEN FROM CONTRARIES. WOLFGANG CAPITO: Originally, the forms of the works of the [six] days were not virtually or formally present in matter at the beginning. For because God made all things for the revelation of his glory, it was fitting that he should protect the series of things to be created (by which his eternal power would be made known) by paying attention to individual works. That [power] truly is [made known], so that not only would nothing of the forms to come have been observed either in the emerging matter or in the later works, but even the opposite of those forms would have been seen instead. Regarding that fact, as Elias Orientalis would say, once matter has been established, God designates himself as the cause that creates all later things. Indeed, what is the reason for him to create light except darkness, that is, scarcity, nature's need to make use of light as a thing required? Likewise, in regeneration, the Savior God looks at nothing except what ruined sinners think, [namely,] that they are grateful for the work of the one who is freely forgiving their sins. And so, in order that his infinite power might be more vividly manifested before our eyes, an opposite points directly to the work to come. Hence, in the beginning he creates from nothing heaven and earth, but not such as they now appear. In fact, he describes them so as to show that there is no power in these things, neither to bring forth a form from themselves nor to receive one offered from elsewhere: for he brands them with three names and epithets. The names are *heaven and earth*, *abyss* and *waters*, but the epithets *desolate*, *void* and *darkness* are set forth as unformed matter, so to speak, that clears a path for the omnipotence of the Creator, so that he might declare that he is omnipotent through the works that follow. . . .

Let us look, then, at the beginning from darkness. What was present there, really, either of some power or of an anticipation of the light that was going to spring from the darkness? Surely, nothing whatsoever! Nay, the opposite of light is what is noticeable in darkness, and yet God said, "Let there be light," and there was light where previously there had been nothing but the deepest darkness. He thus opposes light to darkness. From this it appears how great the power of the Creator is! For he commands the light to arise from darkness and it arises when he speaks, and darkness has not impeded the fabrication of light. ON GOD'S WORK OF THE SIX DAYS.[41]

1:2b Darkness Was over the Face of the Deep

THE DARKNESS AND ABYSS SHOW HOW WE NEED GOD'S LIGHT. WOLFGANG MUSCU-LUS: In the works of God there are deeps and darkness. That manifestation warns us that God's works are unsearchable in themselves unless they are revealed when light breaks in. Without it we will ponder them in vain. Indeed, the human intellect cannot penetrate the depth and darkness of the divine works by its own understanding. Wherefore one should pray that he who works wondrous things may illuminate and reveal his works by bringing light. COMMENTARY ON GENESIS 1:2.[42]

DARKNESS IS NOT EVIL. WOLFGANG CAP-ITO: Because God made it, darkness is a good thing. For all God's works are good, wherefore God's act in [creating darkness] is just as appropriate as in the case of any good thing, and the action of the word that pertains to God also comes to completion in it. Indeed, it reads "And God called the darkness night."

---

[40]*Opera* 1:6.   [41]*Hexemeron* (1539), 109r-10r. Elias Orientalis was a rabbi of the late fifteenth century.   [42]*In Mosis Genesim* (1554), 8.

Likewise, God is clearly the author of darkness for Isaiah [45:7]: "I have fashioned light and I have created darkness," he says, "I have made peace and I have created evil." But Rabbi Eleazar contends otherwise, that darkness is an evil thing and God's name is therefore not to be associated with it. However, that man was deceived by the fact that [darkness] is frequently used in metaphors and allegories for an evil and harsh thing. But changing the context of a thing so that it signifies something evil does not prove that the thing is evil in itself. ON GOD'S WORK OF THE SIX DAYS.[43]

1:2c *The Spirit of God Was Hovering over the Face of the Waters*

THE SPIRIT HOVERED OVER CREATION LIKE A MOTHER HEN. KONRAD PELLIKAN: The good pleasure of the creator of all things distributed the power of germination over the earth and the abyss just as an egg is warmed by a bird: while the chick is developing, the heat of the mother's body is supplemented by natural feelings of love, that is, by the operation of the divine spirit diligently caring for all things, directing and distributing power through each thing to be created here below according to the command and will of the Creator. COMMENTARY ON GENESIS 1:2.[44]

THE SPIRIT WHO MOVES OVER THE WATERS ALSO MOVES IN THE HEARTS OF THE ELECT. WOLFGANG MUSCULUS: Here there is an image of God's working to be considered. Accordingly, in the midst of tribulations and the shadow of death, however they may appear, God refreshes and revives the hearts of the elect by his spirit and preserves them for the happiness of the light that will follow. This passage offers a great consolation. No matter what our impression is of the works by which God undertakes to benefit mortals, they never lack that spiritual and life-giving operation by which they are not only pre-

served in their primitive state but also carried along to their final perfection. COMMENTARY ON GENESIS 1:2.[45]

GOD'S SPIRIT VIVIFIES. MARTIN LUTHER: Some explain that "the Spirit of the Lord" simply means "wind." . . . But it is more to my liking that we understand Spirit to mean the Holy Spirit. Wind is a creature which at that time did not yet exist, since so far those masses of heaven and earth lay mixed together. Indeed, it is the great consensus of the church that the mystery of the Trinity is set forth here. The Father creates heaven and earth out of nothing through the Son, whom Moses calls the Word. Over these the Holy Spirit broods. As a hen broods her eggs, keeping them warm in order to hatch her chicks, and, as it were, to bring them to life through heat, so Scripture says that the Holy Spirit brooded, as it were, on the waters to bring to life those substances which were to be quickened and adorned. For it is the office of the Holy Spirit to make alive. LECTURES ON GENESIS 1:2.[46]

"SPIRIT" HERE MAY MERELY BE WIND. WOLFGANG MUSCULUS: What the text has here . . . can also be translated, "And the wind, breeze or breath of God was brooding or stirring or blowing over the face of the waters." In my judgment, Moses is not speaking in these words of some secret and hidden operation of the Holy Spirit; rather, he is describing the disposition of the waters, how they should be considered. . . . I know that the more recent as well as many of the older writers refer these things not to the movement of the wind but to the Holy Spirit, and in this place I allow their

---

[43]*Hexemeron* (1539), 145r-v. Eleazar was one of several rabbis with this name in the Middle Ages. [44]*Commentaria Bibliorum* (1532) 1:1v, echoing Jerome, *Hebrew Questions* 1:2, and Basil of Caesarea, *Hexaemeron* 2.6 (NPNF² 8:63). [45]*In Mosis Genesim* (1554), 8. In the margin, Musculus identifies this "image" of the Holy Spirit's operation as an *anagoge*. [46]LW 1:9 (WA 42:8); note Pellikan's use of the same image of the brooding hen, above.

opinion: follow it if you like. But I am typically more satisfied by explanations that seem simpler. COMMENTARY ON GENESIS 1:2.[47]

1:3 *"Let There Be Light"*

GOD SPEAKS REALITIES, NOT BARE WORDS. MARTIN LUTHER: Here attention must also be called to this, that the words "Let there be light" are the words of God, not of Moses; this means that they are realities. For God calls into existence the things which do not exist (Rom 4:17). He does not speak grammatical words; He speaks true and existent realities. Accordingly, that which among us has the sound of a word is a reality with God. Thus sun, moon, heaven, earth, Peter, Paul, I, you, etc.—we are all words of God, in fact only one single syllable or letter by comparison with the entire creation. We, too, speak, but only according to the rules of language; that is, we assign names to objects which have already been created. But the divine rule of language is different, namely: when He says: "Sun, shine," the sun is there at once and shines. Thus the words of God are realities, not bare words. LECTURES ON GENESIS 1:5.[48]

GOD ADDED LIGHT THAT WE MIGHT SEE HIS WORKS. HULDRYCH ZWINGLI: By *light* he means here neither sun nor moon but is speaking so far according to human custom. Indeed, those who have to work at night or in darkness are accustomed to light a lamp before doing anything else. Not that God needs light, but by this way of speaking Moses wishes to explain the difference between these works. Earlier, he had said that the unformed mass was indistinct and in darkness. So now he points to the arrangement of the works and their adornment, lest they have been created in vain—and vain they would have been, if they remained unseen. ANNOTATIONS ON GENESIS 1:3.[49]

WHEN LIGHT IS CREATED, THE ETERNAL WORD IS REVEALED—NOT MADE. JOHN CALVIN: Moses now, for the first time, introduces God in the act of speaking, as if he had created the mass of heaven and earth without the Word. Yet John testifies that "without him nothing was made of the things which were made" (Jn 1:3). And it is certain that the world had been begun by the same efficacy of the Word by which it was completed. God, however, did not manifest his Word until light came into existence, because his Wisdom begins to be conspicuous as things are differentiated. That alone is enough to refute the blasphemy of Servetus[†] here, that foul dog who barks that this was the first beginning of the Word, when God commanded that there be light—as if a cause, truly, were not prior to its effect! Indeed, if things that were not in existence should suddenly arise by God's Word, we should instead conclude that [the Word's] essence is eternal. The apostles therefore rightly prove the divinity of Christ from this, that since he is the Word of God, all things have been created by him. Servetus imagines a new quality in God when he begins to speak. But we should think about the Word of God far differently, for truly, he is the Wisdom that indwells God and without which God could never exist—even though its effect appeared only when light was created. COMMENTARY ON GENESIS 1:3.[50]

WORDS ARE CREATED BY THE UNCREATED WORD. MARTIN LUTHER: Here men have differentiated between the uncreated Word and the created word. The created word is brought into being by the uncreated Word. What else is the entire creation than the Word of God uttered by God, or extended to the outside? But the uncreated Word is a divine

---

[47]*In Mosis Genesim* (1554), 3. [48]LW 1:21-22 (WA 42:17). [49]ZSW 13:8. [50]CTS 1:74-75* (CO 23:16); [†]Michael Servetus, Calvin's longtime adversary, was well-known for his opposition to the doctrine of the Trinity.

thought, an inner command which abides in God, the same as God and yet a distinct Person. Thus God reveals Himself to us as the Speaker who has with Him the uncreated Word, through whom He created the world and all things with the greatest ease, namely, by speaking. Accordingly, there is no more effort for God in His creation than there is for us in the mention of it. LECTURES ON GENESIS 1:5.[51]

GOD'S SPEECH IS VASTLY DIFFERENT FROM OUR OWN. WOLFGANG MUSCULUS: "God said, 'Let there be light.'" Moses is speaking about God in human fashion. Since darkness was obscuring everything, right away he commands that there be light, which was missing there at the beginning. It was just as if a householder, when dusk creeps up at nightfall and obscures everything, should order a light to be lit by which the house might be delivered from the inconvenience of darkness. God, however, did *not* speak in human fashion. The power and efficacy of his will issued forth his word. Given that whatever we want to be understood or believed or done we express by the utterance of a word, so also when God's will is expressed, it is called a word. That is how Moses would explain why God said, "Let there be light." And so that he might express the efficacy of God's will, he appends, "And there *was* light." He did not say, "Light was brought, or a light was lit," but "Let there be light, and there was light," so that we might understand at the outset that light was made from nothing. COMMENTARY ON GENESIS 1:3.[52]

LIGHT WAS CALLED OUT OF DARKNESS ITSELF. MARTIN LUTHER: This Word is God; it is the omnipotent Word, uttered in the divine essence. No one heard it spoken except God Himself, that is, God the Father, God the Son, and God the Holy Spirit. And when it was spoken, light was brought into existence,

not out of the matter of the Word or from the nature of Him who spoke but out of the darkness itself. Thus the Father spoke inwardly, and outwardly light was made and came into existence immediately. In this manner other creatures, too, were made later. This, I say, is sufficient knowledge for us concerning the manner of the creation. LECTURES ON GENESIS 1:3.[53]

GOD DID NOT NEED THE SUN OR MOON TO FURNISH LIGHT. JOHN CALVIN: It did not, however, happen by chance or accident that light preceded the sun and the moon. To nothing are we more prone than to bind God's power to those instruments whose agency he employs. The sun and moon supply us with light and, according to our notions, we so restrict this power to them that if they were taken away from the world, we would regard it as impossible for any light to remain. Therefore the Lord bears witness by the very order of creation that he holds the light in his hand and, without sun or moon, can lavish it upon us. COMMENTARY ON GENESIS 1:3.[54]

GOD DID NOT NEED THE SUN TO NOURISH THE EARTH. KONRAD PELLIKAN: By the will and command of God, not by its natural properties or by powers seemingly its own, does the earth bring forth seed—when, how and as much as God wills. The production of seed is a miraculous work of sorts, by which God restores that which human use has depleted. Trees, too, bring forth their fruits as nourishment for animals and people—and all these things were produced before the sun was ordained. Not without reason were people taught by the Law that so many blessings were brought forth for our sake, lest they should suppose that the sun is God. But we should attribute all things to God himself, "who

---

[51]LW 1:22 (WA 42:17). [52]*In Mosis Genesim* (1554), 8. [53]LW 1:19 (WA 42:15). [54]CTS 1:76* (CO 23:16-17).

works all in all." COMMENTARY ON GENESIS 1:9-10.[55]

THIS FIRST LIGHT WAS DIMMER THAN THE SUN . . . MARTIN LUTHER: This was true light . . . [but] it was not such a clear and brilliant light as it was later on when it was increased, adorned, and perfected by the light of the sun. Similarly, the Holy Scriptures also bear witness that on the Last Day God will make more brilliant and glorious the present daylight of the sun, as though it were a weak light in comparison with the future glory (Is 30:26). As, therefore, the present daylight is, so to speak, a crude and coarse mass of light if it is compared with the future light, so that first light was crude when compared with this present light. LECTURES ON GENESIS 1:3.[56]

. . . DESPITE WHAT THE ANCIENTS BELIEVED. WOLFGANG CAPITO: Would the light of the first day have been more perfect than the light of the sun? To this question ancient writers responded with considerable consensus, that the smallest little portion of the first light was assigned to the luminaries and the stars, while the rest of it was reserved for the use of the righteous, so that they might thoroughly enjoy it in the age to come. But there is nothing about this in the passage above, and the sequence of creation is incompatible with thoughts of this kind. Indeed, in that respect, the steadfastness of an infallible providence is accustomed to proceed from a work just begun and not yet complete to one that is nearer to perfection—not to go backwards, as if worn out from too much effort. . . . Add that the Fathers regarded it as certain that Scripture conveyed no suspicion of this to them. Without a doubt, that first light would have been in many respects clearer than daylight as it now is. Yet, on the other hand, it would seem evident from the order and nature of creation that the light that was begun on that first day would have been brought to a

high point on the fourth, when, at last, the luminaries had been created and the stars were shining over the earth. That may be the reason why the clause "and it was so" is not joined to the making of light on the first day. Indeed, light was not like it is now until the fourth day, when it would have been raised up in this manner and to this peak. ON GOD'S WORK OF THE SIX DAYS.[57]

1:4 *The Light Was Good*

THE MOST IMPORTANT CHARACTERISTIC OF LIGHT IS THAT IT IS GOOD. WOLFGANG MUSCULUS: Notice that he does not say, "And God saw that the light was of pleasing appearance, that it was wonderful," but rather "that it was good." Thus God does not so much seek in his works the splendor and glory of his own name as the utility and advantage of those for whom he created all things. His works are indeed splendid, pleasant and glorious, and therefore well-suited for glorifying his name: yet he did not so much create them for these purposes, but so that they might be *good* and useful. With this in mind, what will we conclude except that the character of the true God is just like that of a good person, who delights in good works? Christ calls us to imitate this goodness in Matthew 5[:16] when he says, "Let your light shine before others, so that they may see your good works and glorify your Father in heaven." COMMENTARY ON GENESIS 1:4.[58]

GOD PRAISES HIS WORKS TO INSTRUCT US. KONRAD PELLIKAN: We are accustomed to praise whatever we see done with meticulous care. Thus Scripture, unable to speak about God in an unworthy manner, speaks as if to the weak and accommodates our

---

[55]*Commentaria Bibliorum* (1532) 1:2r, quoting 1 Cor 12:6b. [56]LW 1:19-20 (WA 42:16). [57]*Hexemeron* (1539), 246v-47r. [58]*In Mosis Genesim* (1554), 12.

childishness; as if God would praise light, his own work in which he himself took pleasure and approved. And so it is said to be *good* because approved by the Lord, from whom every good thing comes. COMMENTARY ON GENESIS 1:4.[59]

LIGHT IS NOT ONLY GOD'S FIRST WORK, IT IS ALSO HIS NATURE. WOLFGANG MUSCULUS: John says that God is light. Therefore see how fitting it was that he produced light right away, at the beginning of his works, when everything was enveloped in darkness. He who is himself the true light thus loves light, and he consecrates light by his works. The prince of darkness loves darkness and hates the light: and therefore he wraps his works not in light but in darkness. . . . Let us also consider how fittingly an image has been sent ahead here of that light which through the gospel of Christ has illumined this dark world. Everything was covered in darkness. Then, at God's command, there is light. Likewise, when the world was utterly plunged into the darkness of ignorance, God gave the command that in the midst of darkness light should begin to shine, by which the hearts of mortals would be illumined by the knowledge of the glory of God in the face of Jesus Christ. COMMENTARY ON GENESIS 1:3.[60]

GOD PRONOUNCES HIS WORK "GOOD" TO COMMEND IT TO US. JOHN CALVIN: Here God is introduced by Moses as surveying his work, that he might take pleasure in it. But he does it for our sake, to teach us that God has made nothing without a certain reason and design. But Moses' words should not be read as if God did not know his work was good until it was finished. Rather, the true meaning is that the work was approved by God just as it now appears to us. Nothing remains for us to do, then, but to acquiesce in this judgment of God. COMMENTARY ON GENESIS 1:4.[61]

1:5a *Day and Night*

GOD'S "NAMING" OF THE LIGHT AS DAY IS MORE POTENT THAN ADAM'S NAMING OF THE ANIMALS. WOLFGANG MUSCULUS: Observe first of all how the word *called* is to be attributed to God. In the following chapter we read that Adam, when the animals of the earth had been brought to him, imposed names and called them all by their respective names. But this sort of naming conferred nothing on them except the bare names. Here, however, God calls the light "day" so that by that appellation he might *constitute* that light as day; and he calls the darkness "night" so that he might make it to *be* night. Therefore, for God to "call" is not only to impose a name on something but also to confer the very thing that is expressed in the meaning of the name. COMMENTARY ON GENESIS 1:5.[62]

1:5b *The First Day*

WHY GOD USED REAL DAYS. JOHANNES BRENZ: When the world was created by God, not everything in this world was created at once, but each thing in its place and over the course of six days. Indeed, there are some who have said that God did not create on distinct days but rather everything in a single moment and that Scripture speaks of the six days allegorically. . . . Certainly, God could have created all things in a single moment, but what is to be sought here is what God did, not what he could do. Thus, he completed the work of creation not in one instant but over six continuous days. First of all, Scripture itself clearly testifies that the days during which creation was completed are natural days, not mystical or allegorical. Indeed, if they weren't natural days, then the creatures made on those

---

[59]*Commentaria Bibliorum* (1532) 1:1v. [60]*In Mosis Genesim* (1554), 11, citing 2 Cor 4:6. [61]CTS 1:77* (CO 23:17). [62]*In Mosis Genesim* (1554), 12.

days wouldn't be natural creatures but only allegorical ones. But it is clear that they are truly external, real or natural creatures. So the days that are numbered in this chapter were also truly real or natural days. In the second place, God preferred to create the world and its parts in orderly succession rather than all at once in order to show that he is a God not of confusion but of order. We are exhorted by his example to undertake everything that needs doing or finishing in an orderly way. And because God is the author of order and not confusion, he pours out his blessing or increase upon order, not upon confusion. COMMENTARY ON GENESIS 1:2.[63]

WHY GOD DID NOT CREATE EVERYTHING AT ONCE. HULDRYCH ZWINGLI: By a single word of his strength—or, better, by the sheer power of his living will—he was able to create everything. But, accommodating himself to our senses so that we might perceive and understand his works more clearly and easily, he did things a day at a time, after the fashion of humans, who are used to doing one thing after another. ANNOTATIONS ON GENESIS 1:6.[64]

WHY GOD CREATED IN SIX DAYS RATHER THAN ALL AT ONCE. WILLIAM PERKINS: God could have made the world and all things in it in one moment: but he began and finished the whole work in six distinct days, . . . and that, especially for three causes. First, to teach us that we ought to have a distinct and serious consideration of every creature: for if God had made the world in a moment (some might have said), this work is so mystical that no one can speak of it. But for the preventing of this cavil, it was his pleasure to make the world and all things therein in six days: and the seventh day he commanded it to be sanctified by us, that we might distinctly and seriously meditate upon every day's work of the creation. Second, God made the world and everything therein in six

distinct days to teach us what wonderful power and liberty he had over all his creatures: for he made the light when there was neither sun nor moon nor stars, to show that in giving light to the world, he is not bound to the sun, to any creature, or to any means: for the light was made the first day: but the sun, the moon and the stars were not created before the fourth day. Again, trees and plants were created the third day: but yet the sun, moon, and the stars, and rain, which nourish and make herbs, trees, and plants to grow, were not created till after the third day: which shows plainly, that God can make trees, plants, and herbs to grow without the means of rain, and without the virtue and operation of the sun, the moon and the stars. Third, he made the world in six distinct days and framed all things in this order to teach us his wonderful providence over all his creatures: for before human beings were created he provided for them a dwelling place and all things necessary for their perpetual preservation and perfect happiness and felicity. So also he created beasts and cattle; but not before he had made herbs, plants and grass, and all means whereby they are preserved. And if God had this care over human beings when as yet they were not: much more will God have care over them now when they are. EXPOSITION OF THE APOSTLES' CREED.[65]

DIVINE WISDOM PERFECTS THINGS, BUT BY STAGES, FOR OUR SAKE. JOHANNES OECOLAMPADIUS: We learned above in the first verse about the highest power of God, who made heaven and earth from nothing; it remains that we might also learn about his highest wisdom and goodness. In order that the divine wisdom might be made known to us, however, understand that it is of wisdom to bring to completion that which is incomplete, and to adorn and embellish things that have been completed. God could have brought all

---

[63]*Opera* 1:5. [64]ZSW 13:8. [65]*Works* (1608) 1:143-44.

things to completion and made them most perfect all at once, in the first instant, but he did not wish to, for the reason that his wisdom should be more obvious and more intelligible to us. You have heard that the earth was empty and darkness was over the face of the waters. In that verse a certain incompleteness was signified, from which one may know that God made creatures voluntarily, not coerced by any other, either of the angels or mortals, since none was there to do that. For if he had at first produced completed creatures, then those who claim that God made all things by necessity might have persisted obstinately in their error. LECTURES ON GENESIS 1:6-8.[66]

GOD'S WORKS ALMOST ALWAYS BEGIN IN A HUMBLE MANNER. WOLFGANG MUSCULUS: In this place it is to be observed how God leads his works to consummation and perfection in succession, so that first they might be roughly formed, then rise as by degrees and be completed. In the beginning, then, he furnished the world with the bare basics, in a sense, and afterward applied the ornamentation. Thus . . . he did not immediately fill the day with the splendor of sunlight, nor did he instantly soften the night with the comfort of the moon. He did not mark the heavens right away with stars and constellations, nor did he immediately endow the earth with its manifold fruitfulness nor crowd it with beasts. By this example we are taught how God's works usually begin. Namely, not only is their initial appearance rough, but there is nothing of what is to come. They look just like rough lumber: secrets lurk in concealment and it appears as if darkness has been drawn across the surface. Nor did this happen only in the beginning of heaven and earth, but the same manner of working can frequently be discerned in other works of God, and in all of them one may see how the beginnings of God's works are often rude, unformed, humble and obscure. COMMENTARY ON GENESIS 1:2.[67]

THE VISIBLE WORKS OF THE SIX DAYS SHOULD LEAD US TO HIGHER THOUGHTS OF GOD. WOLFGANG CAPITO: It is to be conceded, I think, that we should first be stirred up by the visible works of the six days and by what ought to be familiar, so that we might imagine the invisible things of God and so that the mind might then raise itself up from those things observed in order to know God. Nonetheless, eternity is in God, and it is not observed by contemplating his works according to the Scriptures unless the mind's eye be directed to the beginning of creation, with diligent reflection upon those things that are higher than the beginning of time. Therefore the first stage of cognition begins from the senses, but that cognition is completed only by the mind, which is higher than sensible things and sees far beyond the beginning of things. Indeed, in the mind are these things discerned: what God was in the beginning, what the Word was, what the Spirit of God was, and thus that the one God existed before the beginning of time in his everlasting state of being. Mysteries, then, are best understood from the hidden beginnings of things. ON GOD'S WORK OF THE SIX DAYS.[68]

1:6-8 The Separation of the Waters by the Expanse of Heaven

THE UNIVERSE'S IMPROBABLE DESIGN IS PROOF OF GOD'S EXISTENCE. MARTIN LUTHER: The heaven, which cannot stand firm by means of its bounds (for it is watery), stands firm through the Word of God because we hear these words here: "Let there be a firmament." The more observant among the philosophers drew from this source what is in truth not an insignificant proof: that all things are

---

[66]*In Genesim* (1536), 12v-13r. [67]*In Mosis Genesim* (1554), 7. Musculus goes on to compare the unformed earth with how King David was but a boy when first anointed by Samuel. [68]*Hexemeron* (1539), 105v-6r.

done and guided, not planlessly but by divine providence, inasmuch as the movements of the masses on high and of the heaven are so definite and unique. Who would say that they are accidental or purely a matter of nature, when the objects fashioned by artisans—such as round or three-cornered or six-cornered columns—are not accidental but the result of a definite plan and skill? LECTURES ON GENESIS 1:6.[69]

THE WATERS ARE RESTRAINED BY THE POWER OF GOD. JOHN CALVIN: Truly, it is contrary to common sense and absolutely incredible that there are some waters that are above the heavens. Hence, some resort to allegory and philosophize concerning angels, but this is utterly out of place, for to my mind, it is a fixed premise that nothing is treated here except the form of the visible world. Whoever wants to learn astrology and the other occult arts should go somewhere else! Here, the Spirit of God wishes to teach everyone without exception, and therefore what Gregory falsely and mistakenly declares with respect to statues and pictures† is truly applicable to this account of creation, namely, that it is "the book of the illiterate." Thus, all the things he mentions pertain to the adornment of the theater that he places before our eyes, from which I conclude that the waters meant here are such as even the simple and unlearned may perceive. The assertion of some, that they have embraced by faith what they read about the waters above the heavens, no matter how little they may understand them, is not in accordance with the design of Moses; and truly, further inquiry into a matter that is clear and on display is superfluous. We see that the clouds suspended in the air threaten to fall upon our heads, yet they leave us space to breathe. Those who deny that this takes place by God's wonderful providence are vainly inflated with the folly of their own minds. We know indeed that rain is naturally

produced; but the deluge sufficiently shows how speedily we might be overwhelmed by the bursting of the clouds, unless the cataracts of heaven be shut in by the hand of God. Nor is it an accident that David numbers this among God's miracles, that he "lays the beams of his chambers on the waters" (Ps 104:3), and he elsewhere calls upon the celestial waters to praise God (Ps 148:4). Since, therefore, God has created the clouds and assigned them to a region above us, we should not forget that they are restrained by the power of God, lest they gush forth with sudden violence and swallow us up—especially since no other barrier is opposed to them than the clear and evanescent air, which would easily give way if this word were not to prevail: "Let there be an expanse between the waters." COMMENTARY ON GENESIS 1:6.[70]

THE MIRACLE OF THE ATMOSPHERE. MARTIN LUTHER: These are, therefore, wonders of God, in which the omnipotence of the Word is observed: that although the heaven is softer and more tenuous than water and yet is driven on by the swiftest motion among so great a variety of bodies and motions, no part of it has deteriorated or become weak in the course of so many thousands of years. This is what Job says: that the heavens are cast of bronze, as it were, although by nature they are extremely soft. We know how tenuous the air is in which we live; for it is not only impossible to touch it, but it cannot even be observed. But the heaven is even more tenuous and finer by nature than this air. Its blue color is proof, not of its compactness but of its remoteness and tenuousness. If you should compare it with the masses of clouds, the latter are like the smoke of moist wood that is being kindled. It is this tenuousness

---

[69]LW 1:25 (WA 42:20). [70]CTS 1:79-81* (CO 23:18-19), †alluding to Gregory the Great's letter to Serenus of Marseilles in 599 (text in PL 77:1027-28).

and yet unchanging permanence that Job notes. LECTURES ON GENESIS 1:6.[71]

THE SEPARATION OF THE WATERS UNLOCKS A DUAL BIBLICAL METAPHOR.

WOLFGANG CAPITO: On account of the firmament that has been placed between them, the waters are now twofold, upper and lower, each with its peculiar nature. Accordingly, metaphors drawn from the waters will work in two ways: comparisons to good things are drawn from the heavenly waters; but to adverse and evil things, from the lower waters. Indeed, the heavenly waters are first transferred to the Holy Spirit and to the blessing of minds; then, to the ministry of the gospel, by which minds are cleansed; and finally, to human beings who are washed by the word and the Spirit.

First, that the Holy Spirit and the heavenly blessing of souls should appear under the title of *waters* is hereby made clear. The Lord will relieve his parched church from its afflictions and fear, as Isaiah 44[:3] says, "I will pour out water on your thirsty land and streams on your dry ground." At the same time he adds how one should understand that water and those streams: "I will pour out my spirit on your seed," he says, "and my blessing on your sprouts." What does this mean, except that the descendants brought to spiritual Israel and increased by the Spirit would never want for blessings. In fact, there were always those who were taught the gospel of the kingdom. . . . Waters, therefore, represent the Holy Spirit, the renewal of what has grown old, the grace of adoption, the gift of faith, the continual and perpetual action of the heart by which we who embrace God through Christ might come to trust in the one God dutifully and with a debt of heartfelt gratitude. For just as the bubbling waters of a spring emerge secretly in a perpetual flow, so the Holy Spirit and the gifts of God (which are not without the Spirit) are urged on by perpetual movement. . . . These life-giving waters and this Spirit and grace are conferred by our Lord Christ, who gives to his disciples the Spirit, which no one can resist. . . .

In the second place, waters represent the ministry of the gospel, under which is contained teaching, the keys, baptism and the Eucharist. For the activities of the church as much as its sacraments are not without a word of promise, which is the same thing as the gospel, by which the grace of Christ (as well as Christ himself and God) is effectively given to the believer. For a minister speaks not his own word but that of the one who sent him. This heavenly water is a life-giving drink for a thirsty heart, without which it remains forever barren. It is the rain that waters the fields of the Lord and brings fertility to the tender shoots of Christ's true vine so that they might bear much fruit and that we might be equipped for every good work. . . .

It is also no great stretch to extend the metaphor, as when the jurisdiction of the church is represented by heavenly waters. For it not uncommonly happens that someone clearly guilty of sin is censured by a conscientious brother in private or by a pastor or by the authority of the church and is restored to the right path. Thus, through the keys, the soul recovered from death is counted to their own gain. . . . And to restrain a shameless person from evil—that is, to render him in some way pure—is to free the church from disgrace and to wash away the stain with the keys, that is, with the heavenly waters. The reasoning is no different for why baptism, repentance, the Lord's Supper, Christ himself and the elect are compared with the heavenly waters. . . .

The earthly waters, however, seeing that they are called seas and that certain of them taste of earth and are deceptive and brackish, are taken to represent an earthly spirit, which is sour, harsh and bitter, as is seen in hypocrites and in all worldly righteousness, which removes itself by the greatest distance from

---

[71]LW 1:24-25 (WA 42:19-20).

any feeling of piety. . . . In fact, human beings who have been carried away by a worldly spirit are not ineptly called a sea, or infernal and terrestrial waters, on account of the foul smell and harshness and the furious assault of the flesh. Truly, they are an evil and destructive sea, ignorant of innocence and simplicity. They are like water, inconstant in themselves, easily swayed by vices, and cast about by the waves of every disturbance and vice. On God's Work of the Six Days.[72]

1:9-10 Creation of the Dry Land and the Seas

Dry Land Is Protected by God's Power. Martin Luther: Thus it happens through divine power that the waters do not pass over us, and until today and until the end of the world God performs for us the well-known miracle which He performed in the Red Sea for the people of Israel. . . . For what is our entire life on this earth but a passage through the Red Sea, where on both sides the sea stood like high walls? Because it is very certain that the sea is far higher than the earth, God, up to the present time, commands the waters to remain in suspense and restrains them by His Word lest they burst upon us as they burst forth in the Deluge. But at times God gives providential signs, and entire islands perish by water, to show that the sea is in His hand and that He can either hold it in check or release it against the ungrateful and the evil. Lectures on Genesis 1:9.[73]

The Dry and Fruitful Earth Should Prompt Us to Praise. Konrad Pellikan: God approved all things by his holy will, so that they might be good: [that is,] so that we might learn to praise the Lord God on account of all he created, but especially for having granted the earth to us as dry and fruitful, suitable to nourish and console us. Commentary on Genesis 1:9-10.[74]

God's Special Care for Human Habitation. Martin Luther: Here Moses adds this favorable comment ["And God saw it was good"] in spite of the fact that nothing had been done beyond the separating of the waters and the bringing forth of the insignificant bit of earth. Above he did not add this brief statement to a most beautiful part of the works of God. Perhaps this is because God wanted to indicate to us that He was more concerned about our dwelling place than about His own, and thus to arouse our gratitude. We were not to live in the air or in the heaven but on the earth, where we were to support our life with food and drink. Lectures on Genesis 1:10.[75]

1:11-12 The Creation of Plants and Trees

God's Wondrous Gift of Plants. Johannes Brenz: Another miracle of the third day is that with a single word, God made the whole earth fertile with such abundance and such a variety of herbs, shrubs, trees and fruits that no human ingenuity could know or explain it adequately enough. For each of these kinds and varieties has its color, taste, powers and effects. Indeed, some are good for adornment, others for food, others for medicine. Many have scrutinized the kinds of plants and written about herbs and botanicals. Solomon himself, as 1 Kings 4:33 says, "described plant life, from the cedar of Lebanon to the hyssop that grows out of walls." And yet no one can explain this miracle of God sufficiently. Nor does this miracle consist only in its abundance and variety, but also in its persistence: just as the word of God from the beginning raised up herbs, shrubs and trees from the earth, so also

---

[72]Capito's treatment of the separation of the two waters in Gen 1:6 fills nearly eighty pages of his *Hexemeron*, 160r-99r. This excerpt is abridged from fol. 161v-64v, 188v-90r and 197r-v in order to give a sense of the whole. [73]LW 1:35 (WA 42:26). [74]*Commentaria Bibliorum* (1532) 1:2r. [75]LW 1:35 (WA 42:26-27).

to this day does this word sound throughout the earth, raising up all kinds of shrubs and fruits every year, each in its season as divinely ordained. This miracle reminds us of many things. First, of God's *omnipotence*, that by his word he created so many lovely, varied, and useful things. Then, of his *wisdom*: no human mind could devise such variety and diversity, or so many herbs, shrubs and trees. . . . In addition, we are reminded of God's *goodness*, that it is by his care that so much works not only on behalf of our utility and need, but also for our enjoyment, . . . delight and refreshment. Commentary on Genesis 1:11-12.[76]

Springtime and Harvest Were Simultaneous in Paradise. Martin Luther: It was a miracle of the first world that suddenly all these plants came into existence in such a way that the earth sprouted and the trees bloomed, and suddenly also fruits followed. This miracle came to an end at that time. For those kinds, as they were created at that time, are now reproduced through seeds. Therefore it is fallacious to argue from the natural working to the supernatural. It must be granted that in the first work of creation the Creator speeded up the functions of spring and fall so far as the herbs and the fruits of the trees were concerned. Lectures on Genesis 1:11.[77]

The Earth Produces Fruit by the Power of God's Word and Decree. John Calvin: God acts through creatures, not as if he needed external help, but because it was his pleasure. When he says, "Let the earth bring forth vegetation that produces seed and trees that bear their seed," he signifies not only that plants and trees were created then, but that each was also endowed at that same time with the power of propagation in order that their species might be perpetuated. Since, therefore, we daily see the earth pouring forth to us such riches from its lap, since we see plants produc-

ing seed, with that seed received and cherished in the bosom of the earth till it springs forth, and some trees sprouting up from other trees—all this flows from that same word. If we inquire, then, how it happens that the earth is fruitful, that a bud is produced from a seed, that fruits come to maturity, and that their various kinds reproduce each year, no other cause will be found but that God has once spoken: that is, he has issued his eternal decree, while the earth and all that comes from it offer their obedience to God's command, which they always hear. Commentary on Genesis 1:11.[78]

God's Attention to Detail in Caring for Plants Tells Us Much but Not All. Wolfgang Capito: From this word, "Let the earth bring forth the seed of plants" (which is a general statement), it is deduced that *this* rose in *this* flower bed turns red while another of the same stock is decorated with a different color, and that lilies and violets spring up nearby, and even that each seed-pod of each little flower is created by this word of God. For once we recognize that nothing, however small, sprouts from the earth without the word [God uttered] on this day, we will hold as beyond all doubt that no one is given light or protection except through Christ, the light and savior of all. Meanwhile, however, we do not know why some places are arid while others are fertile and well watered: because to know that is none of our business. Thus we do not know why one person should be adorned with a more abundant gift than someone else, nor even why of "two in one bed, one is taken and the other is left" [Lk 17:34]. For in both of these works of God, uncertainty is fitting for our human nature, which is incapable of knowing things that are infinite. Nor does revelation set forth anything except what

---

[76]*Opera* 1:11. [77]LW 1:37 (WA 42:28). [78]CTS 1:83* (CO 23:20).

builds us up in God through Christ. For now we know the creator of all things and that all things were created for our sake. But we do not know why he would have heaped upon us such a great and abundant plenitude of different things, nor yet why he would have brought forth a particular thing at some given place or time or circumstance and placed it before our eyes to contemplate. If we are seized by a greater admiration for the way that divine providence does nothing rashly, so that we come to regard the cause of individual works and of the disposition of all things as utterly sure and convincing, nonetheless we do not labor to know it or anything that the creator was not pleased to disclose. On God's Work of the Six Days.[79]

Were People Vegetarians Before the Flood? Andrew Willet: I think it more probable that both humans and beasts after the fall [but] before the flood did indifferently use both the fruits of the earth and the flesh of beasts for food. . . . First, that one beast did not devour another in the state of innocence, two principal reasons may be given: one, because as yet death had not entered into the world; the other, because the first humans, bearing perfect rule and dominion over the creatures, kept them in order. But after the fall, both of these causes were taken away, for not only did death enter upon humankind, but the other creatures were brought into the same bondage and were killed for sacrifice: as Abel offered of the fat of the sheep (Gen 4:4). If it were lawful then to slay beasts, why not to eat of their flesh? And again, humankind having lost sovereignty over the creatures, they then began one to rage upon another, as no longer standing in the same awe and fear of humans as before. . . . Second, seeing that in the old world two great sins abounded—carnal lust and concupiscence, and tyranny and oppression (Gen 6:2, 4)—and that tyranny and oppression brought forth bloodshed, which is

why the prohibition against shedding human blood is so directly forbidden after the flood, that God "will require it at the hands of every beast, and of a man's brother" (Gen 9:5), how likely is it that they would abstain from killing beasts that spilled human blood, or from eating flesh, which is more apt to provoke lust than the simple fruits of the earth? Third, if the flesh of beasts was not eaten before the flood, what then became of the increase of cattle? How was not the earth overrun with them? This was the reason given for why the Lord would not at once but little by little destroy the Canaanites before the Israelites, lest the beasts of the field increase excessively (Deut 7:22), because they not only helped to destroy the cruel beasts but also ate the unclean ones, as swine and the like, both of which by their multitudes otherwise might have been an annoyance to the Israelites. But before the flood, there was greater fear of overspreading the earth with increase of beasts if no such provision had been made to diminish their number. Finally, Genesis 7:2 most of all confirms our opinion, where mention is made of clean and unclean beasts. This distinction was observed before the flood and continued by tradition not only in regard to sacrifice but also eating, as it appears in the reviving of this law afterward in Leviticus 11:47, . . . [where] the law's definition of a clean beast [is] that which might be eaten; unclean, that which might not be eaten. So I conclude this question with this statement from Ambrose, that "he who prepares a feast first kills his oxen and fat cattle and then invites his guests: so the Lord first prepared the other beasts as food and then invited human beings, as friends, to the banquet." His opinion is that the cattle were provided by God to be food for humans. Mercerus judges otherwise, that the eating of flesh was generally avoided before the flood (which is also the

---

[79]*Hexemeron* (1539), 234v-35r.

opinion of the Hebrews) both because it was necessary in order to preserve the kinds of cattle and also because herbs, being then of greater virtue and strength before the flood and after, might suffice for human sustenance. But [Mercerus's] arguments are not conclusive. Just as after the flood, when liberty was granted to eat flesh as well as the green herb, they still abstained for a time, till the breed of cattle was increased; so also before the flood [and] immediately after the creation, they might have abstained for a time from the eating of flesh, but not altogether. And while the great virtue and strength of herbs suggests that the eating of flesh was not so general or necessary then as afterward, it does not prove a total abstinence from all eating of flesh. COMMENTARY ON GENESIS 1:29.[80]

VEGETARIANISM PREVAILED BEFORE THE FALL AND THE FLOOD. MARTIN LUTHER: You see also what sort of food He provides for us, namely, herbs and fruits of the trees. Hence I believe that our bodies would have been far more durable if the practice of eating all sorts of food—particularly, however, the consumption of meat—had not been introduced after the Deluge. Even though the earth was cursed after Adam's sin and later on, at the time of the Deluge, had also become very corrupt, nevertheless a diet of herbs rather than of meat would be far finer today. LECTURES ON GENESIS 1:11.[81]

OUR ORIGINAL DIET REMINDS US OF WHAT WE HAVE LOST. WOLFGANG MUSCULUS: Notice the quality of the nourishment that God prescribed for human beings at the beginning. He gave them plants and the fruits of trees for food, not flesh, except after the flood. This kind of food was undoubtedly wholesome and easily obtained, both suitable and healthful for our nature. Therefore, as often as we eat flesh, let us think back on the change from our innocent state and, along with

it, how the kind of food and nourishment we take have changed. COMMENTARY ON GENESIS 1:29-31.[82]

WHEN DID FRUITLESS TREES ARISE? MARTIN LUTHER: I think that in the beginning all trees were good and productive and that the beasts of the field, together with Adam, had a common table, as it were, and lived on rye, wheat, and other higher products of nature. There was also the greatest abundance of all creatures. But only after Adam's sin was it said to the earth that it should produce thorns and thistles (Gen 3:18). There is no doubt, therefore, that it is also a punishment for sin that we have so many trees and herbs which have no use as food. LECTURES ON GENESIS 1:11.[83]

1:14 Let There Be Lights in the Expanse of the Heavens . . . Let Them Be for Signs

GOD MADE US TO UNDERSTAND THE HEAVENS. MARTIN LUTHER: Now, therefore, from this fourth day our glory begins to be revealed: that God gives thought to making a creature which may understand the motion of the bodies created on the fourth day and may take delight in that knowledge as part of his nature. All these facts should stir us to an expression of thanks. By citizenship we belong to that homeland which we now look at, admire, and understand, yet like strangers and exiles; but after this life we shall look at these things more closely and understand them perfectly. LECTURES ON GENESIS 1:14.[84]

CONTEMPLATING THE HEAVENS AS PROOF OF THE SOUL'S IMMORTALITY. MARTIN LUTHER: But here the immortality of the soul

---

[80]*Hexapla* (1608), 19-20, citing Ambrose, *Epistle* 43.3 [corrected], and Mercerus, *In Genesin* 1:29. [81]LW 1:36 (WA 42:27). [82]*In Mosis Genesim* (1554), 48. [83]LW 1:38 (WA 42:29). [84]LW 1:46 (WA 42:35).

begins to unfold and reveal itself to us, inasmuch as no creature apart from man can either understand the motion of the heaven or measure the heavenly bodies. A pig, a cow, and a dog are unable to measure the water they drink; but man measures the heaven and all the heavenly bodies. And so here there gleams a spark of eternal life, in that the human being busies himself by nature with this knowledge of nature. This concern indicates that men were not created to live permanently in this lowest part of the universe but to take possession of heaven, because in this life they admire, and busy themselves with, the study of, and the concern about, heavenly things. LECTURES ON GENESIS 1:14.[85]

WHY DIDN'T MOSES WRITE LIKE AN ASTRONOMER? JOHN CALVIN: Here lies the difference: Moses used a popular style to write about things that all ordinary people perceive with their common sense, even if they lack instruction or literacy. Astronomers, however, painstakingly investigate whatever the acuity of the human mind can comprehend. Nevertheless, such study is not to be disapproved, nor is this science to be condemned in the way that some rash and frantic people tend to reject whatever is unknown to them. For astronomy is not only pleasant to know, but also extremely useful: and it cannot be denied that this art unfolds the admirable wisdom of God. Wherefore, just as ingenious people who have invested useful labor in this subject ought to be honored, so also those who have sufficient leisure and means should not neglect this kind of exercise. Certainly, Moses did not mean to discourage us from that pursuit when he omitted the details that pertain to this science, but because he was ordained to teach the simple and uneducated no less than the learned, he could not otherwise fulfill his office than by descending to this more rudimentary method of instruction. Had he spoken of things generally unknown, the

uneducated might have pleaded in excuse that such subjects were beyond their capacity. Lastly, since the Spirit of God here establishes a school that is open to everyone alike, it is not surprising if he should chiefly choose subjects that would be intelligible to all. If an astronomer searches for the actual dimensions of the stars, one will find that the moon is smaller than Saturn; but this is not obvious, for to the eyes it appears otherwise. Moses thus adapts his discourse to the more common usage. For, given that the Lord stretches forth his hand to us, so to speak, in enabling us to enjoy the brightness of the sun and moon, how great would our ingratitude be if we deliberately closed our eyes against our own experience? There is therefore no reason for know-it-alls to deride Moses as uneducated for depicting the moon as the second luminary, because he is not calling us up into heaven, but only setting forth things that lie open before our eyes. Let astronomers possess their more exalted knowledge, then. But meanwhile, all those who perceive the splendor of night by the light of the moon will be convicted of perverse ingratitude by their very use of it unless they acknowledge therein the beneficence of God. COMMENTARY ON GENESIS 1:16.[86]

THE BIBLE NEITHER SPEAKS NOR CONFLICTS WITH THE LANGUAGE OF SCIENCE. MARTIN LUTHER: One must accustom oneself to the Holy Spirit's way of expression. With the other sciences, too, no one is successful unless he has first duly learned their technical language. Thus lawyers have their terminology, which is unfamiliar to physicians and philosophers. On the other hand, these also have their own sort of language, which is unfamiliar to the other professions. Now no science should stand in the way of another science, but each should continue to have its own mode of procedure and its own terms.

---

[85]LW 1:45-46 (WA 42:34). [86]CTS 1:86-87* (CO 23:22-23).

Thus we see that the Holy Spirit also has His own language and way of expression, namely, that God, by speaking, created all things and worked through the Word, and that all His works are some words of God, created by the uncreated Word. Therefore just as a philosopher employs his own terms, so the Holy Spirit, too, employs His. An astronomer, therefore, does right when he uses the terms "spheres," "apsides," and "epicycles"; they belong to his profession and enable him to teach others with greater ease. By way of contrast, the Holy Spirit and Holy Scripture know nothing about those designations and call the entire area above us "heaven." Nor should an astronomer find fault with this; let each of the two speak in his own terminology. So also the word "time" must be understood in this passage. "Time" does not have the same meaning for the Hebrew and the philosopher; but for the Hebrew the word "time" denotes theologically fixed festivals, likewise intervals of days which make up a year. For this reason it is translated almost everywhere with the noun "feast" or "festival," except when the text deals with the tabernacle. I consider this warning to be in place before we proceed, and I believe that this maxim is useful: Every science should make use of its own terminology, and one should not for this reason condemn the other or ridicule it; but one should rather be of use to the other, and they should put their achievements at one another's disposal. LECTURES ON GENESIS 1:14.[87]

THE STARS ARE SIGNS, NOT GODS. PETER MARTYR VERMIGLI: When God said the stars were signs, he didn't want us to make more of them than was proper, did he? Indeed, even if we deny that God has endowed them with grand powers, nonetheless we should always regard God as the author of events, so that we ascribe them not to the constellations but to him, and name the stars as his instruments, his [heavenly] host, and (so far as they pertain to

our knowledge) his signs. Although they should not be dismissed by us in conducting matters that require certain kinds of weather patterns, still, we should not allow them to make up our minds or give them charge of running our affairs. For the things in nature that predict the outcomes of rain, say, or wind and weather, can be directed by God in ways other than these things may indicate. Jeremiah gave the order not to fear the signs in the sky as the nations were accustomed to do. The nations regarded these things as gods, so it's no wonder if they feared them. This doesn't invalidate nautical astronomy or the study of the stars' courses and movements, for those things are truly God's noble gifts. But the authority of horoscopes *is* disparaged, and the powers of the stars are subjugated to God, their source. COMMENTARY ON GENESIS 1:14.[88]

SEASONS AND STARS DO NOT RULE US BUT ARE THEMSELVES RULED BY GOD. JOHANNES OECOLAMPADIUS: From the course of the moon are measured years and months in order that human affairs might be better established. At the same time, [to think] that we ought to learn from these [signs] the art of hunting, so that we might state whatever sort of things will come to pass in the future, whether those born under Mercury or Mars will be fortunate or not—clearly, this is the greatest vanity and leads away from true faith in God. Even if we say that great power has been given to the stars, still, we understand that everything was *given* to the stars, so that all things may be ruled by God. For if we have become familiar with the sermons of the prophets, then we will hear that the Lord holds back the rains, and thus it is certain that nothing comes to pass without his nod. At the same time, those things carried out for human welfare are obstructed and are not noticed by

[87]LW 1:47-48 (WA 42:35-36). [88]*In Primum Librum Mosis* (1569), 5v, citing Jer 10:23.

people. Since we do not acknowledge things that are right there in front of our eyes and before our feet, how shall we consider the things that are above us? Neither are all things arranged by the number and course of the planets, as Rabbi Moses [Maimonides] teaches. Let us consider above all what is the will of God and how God wants his works to be used, so that we should neither worship nor abuse them. LECTURES ON GENESIS 1:14-19.[89]

No Basis for Astrology Here. MARTIN LUTHER: I shall never be convinced that astrology should be numbered among the sciences. . . . Even if there were something sure about these predictions, what stupidity it is to be much concerned about the future! For granted that the future can be known through the astrological predictions—if they are bad, ignorance of them is certainly better in many respects than knowledge of them, as Cicero also declares. An abiding fear of God and prayer are preferable to the fear of future events. LECTURES ON GENESIS 1:14.[90]

1:16-18 The Greater and Lesser Lights

The Light of the Trinity Lit the First Three Days. HULDRYCH ZWINGLI: Here arises a question that tormented the old theologians: Why would the sun and moon have been created only now, on the fourth day, when light was made on the first day and thus day and night, which depend upon the sun and moon? . . . By his nature, God is light and gives light to all things, for "he dwells in inaccessible light." Therefore by his own light he made daylight for the first three days and it shone without any other means (and no one who is pious doubts that the mystery of the Trinity lurks here). We thereby learn that he alone is the light that illumines all things, the one from whom all things have light, and we are warned lest we worship the sun and moon for their own

sake, as the pagans do. Nor should we suppose that light derives from them rather from God himself alone, the source of light, but recognize instead that the sun and moon are at most the instruments of his light. ANNOTATIONS ON GENESIS 1:14.[91]

How Sun and Moon Are—and Are Not—Legitimate Signs. ANDREW WILLET: By *signs* here we need not understand those extraordinary signs that it has pleased God at times to show, as with the sun in Joshua and afterward in Hezekiah's time, for in this place the ordinary use of these creatures is showed. Nor yet are we forced to refer it to the astronomical signs, though the Scripture also approves the lawful use of them (Job 9:9, "He makes Arcturus, Orion, Pleiades, and the climates of the south"), for this combining and conjunction of the stars was afterward found out by art and experience. But these celestial bodies do serve both for *political observations*, as the computation of months and years, and the celebration of festivals among the Jews; and also for *signs of natural things*, as for setting, sowing, planting and discerning the weather and seasons of the year—as Orion brings rain, the Pleiades the spring (Job 38:31). We acknowledge then four lawful uses of these celestial bodies: to distinguish the day and night, light and darkness; to be for signs of weather; to serve for times and seasons, as weeks, days and years; and to give influence by their heat, light and motion to these inferior parts.

But for *moral matters*, as to calculate [horoscopes] and to discern a person's disposition to good or evil; or for *supernatural* [*matters*], to foretell things to come, to discover secrets, find things that are lost, or such like, these celestial signs have no use at all, nor does the vain and superstitious invention of astrol-

---

[89]*In Genesim* (1536), 17r-v, alluding to such texts as Amos 4:7. [90]LW 1:45 (WA 42:33-34). [91]ZSW 13:10-11; cf. 1 Tim 6:16.

ogy have any ground at all out of this text, but is altogether repugnant to the Scripture, against reason, vain and impious. . . . The impiety of this science is evident, because they ascribe all to the influence and operation of the stars, and so bring in a fatal necessity and rob God of his honor and glory. Commentary on Genesis 1:14.[92]

The Future of Sun and Moon. Martin Luther: Here some raise a question concerning the future life: Will this service of the heavenly bodies come to an end? However, that future life will be without time; for the godly will have an eternal day; the wicked will have everlasting night and darkness. Lectures on Genesis 1:14.[93]

1:20-21 *Living Creatures in Sea and Sky*

The Details of Animals Matter to God. Peter Martyr Vermigli: When you hear that both fish and birds were created, bear in mind that all the wondrous things described here or perceived in them were bestowed on them by God. He teaches us here how it is appropriate for God's word to be concerned with the study of nature, undoubtedly so that we may give God credit as the author of the unique properties of each thing's nature. God neglected no detail in the things he made, but prepared for each its means of defense, its organs and useful tools. His skill in this is amply taught by treatises on anatomy and studies of animal behavior. Commentary on Genesis 1:21.[94]

God Cares for Sea Monsters and for Us. Martin Luther: The question can be raised here why he mentions only the sea monsters by name. . . . I believe the reason for this is that we should know that such large bodies are the works of God, lest we be frightened by their size and believe that they are apparitions. Then it is easy to conclude that since such large bodies were created by

God, the smaller fish (such as herring, trout, carp, and others) were also created by God. . . . Descriptions of this kind open our eyes and buoy up our faith that we may more readily believe that God can preserve us too, even though we are far smaller beings. Lectures on Genesis 1:21.[95]

Creation's Wonders Teach Us to Trust God. Martin Luther: These things are written down and must be carefully learned that we may learn to be filled with wonderment at the power of the Divine Majesty and from those wonderful deeds build up our faith. Nothing—even raising the dead—is comparable to the wonderful work of producing a bird out of water. We do not wonder at these things, because through our daily association with them we have lost our wonderment. But if anyone believes them and regards them more attentively, he is compelled to wonder at them, and his wonderment gradually strengthens his faith. Since God is able to bring forth from the water the heaven and the stars, the size of which either equals or surpasses that of the earth; likewise, since He is able out of a droplet of water to create sun and moon, could He not also defend my body against enemies and Satan or, after it has been placed in the grave, revive it for a new life? Therefore we must take note of God's power that we may be completely without doubt about the things which God promises in His Word. Here full assurance is given concerning all His promises; nothing is either so difficult or so impossible that He could not bring it about by His Word. The heaven, the earth, the sea, and whatever is in them prove that this is true. Lectures on Genesis 1:20.[96]

Nature Does Not Guide God, but God Guides Nature. John Calvin: It hardly

---

[92]*Hexapla* (1608), 11, crediting Johannes Mercerus and Franciscus Junius in part. [93]LW 1:44 (WA 42:33). [94]*In Primum Librum Mosis* (1569), 6r. [95]LW 1:51 (WA 42:38). [96]LW 1:49 (WA 42:37).

seems in accord with reason that he should report that the birds proceeded from the waters, and mockers seize upon this in order to quibble. But even if there should appear no other reason but that it so pleased God, wouldn't it be proper for us to acquiesce to his judgment? Why should it not be lawful for him who created the world out of nothing to bring forth the birds out of water? And how is the origin of birds from water more absurd, I pray, than that of the light from darkness? They who so shamelessly mock their creator should therefore expect a judge who will reduce them to nothing! Nonetheless, if we are going to argue over natural causes, we do know that water has greater affinity with air than the earth has. But it would be better to listen to Moses, our teacher, who wishes us to contemplate God's works and thus to be seized by admiration. And, truly, though the Lord is the author of nature, he has not followed nature in the slightest as a guide for creating the world, but has preferred to put forth proofs of his power that ought to reduce us to bewilderment. Commentary on Genesis 1:20.[97]

Birds and Fish Offer Not Omens, but Lessons. Johannes Brenz: Let us consider the purpose of the fish and the birds that God created here on the fifth day. Indeed, it is no secret that later on, in [Genesis] 9, fish and winged creatures are given to humans as food for the body, along with the rest of the animals. Nor is it unknown that in their appearance and song, birds bring great delight as much to the human eye as to the human ear. But just as human beings were not created chiefly to enjoy bodily pleasures, so also fish and birds were not created chiefly to be physical food for human beings and a visual delight, but rather so that they might feed and delight people spiritually, that is, so that they might incite people to know the true God and to pursue true and eternal salvation in God himself. The pagans of old misused the best birds for divination and omens. Having seen birds carried aloft and fly towards heaven (which they said was where the gods dwelt), they concluded that birds were privy to celestial secrets and were interpreters and emissaries of the gods. And so they made judgments about the outcome of future events based on the chattering, flight and feeding patterns of birds. . . . There were also those who deduced prophecies from fish. These are called *ichthyomancers*, but they are godless impostors, whom even the slightly smarter pagans ridiculed and dismissed. And in Moses [Deut 18:10] the commandment is utterly severe: "Let no one be found among you who interprets dreams and omens." For if it were at all licit to find omens in birds and fish, the sacred writings would instruct us to look above all to one bird in particular, namely, the dove, in whose guise the Holy Spirit appeared and testified that Jesus is the son of Mary, the true Messiah, the eternal Son of God, and he commands us to listen to him. There is also one fish that we are directed to attend to above all, namely, the one that contained the prophet Jonah in its stomach for three days. In fact, that fish is a prophecy that Christ the Son of God was going to remain in the heart of the earth until the third day after the resurrection. This is the best kind of *ornithomancy* and *ichthyomancy*, which leads us to the true knowledge of Christ the Son of God. But let us expound the purpose for which fish and birds were generally created: just like the creatures made on the previous days, fish and birds were created to make known the wondrous *power* of God . . . [and] the *wisdom* of God the creator. Commentary on Genesis 1:20-23.[98]

God Does Not Always Create from Nothing. John Calvin: A question arises here from the word *created*, because earlier we contended that the world was made out of nothing because it was created; but now Moses

---

[97]CTS 1:88-89* (CO 23:23). [98]*Opera* 1:15-16.

also describes things are formed from other matter as created. People who assert that fish really were created, strictly speaking, because the waters were in no way fit or suitable for their production, are only looking for a way out, because it would still have been the case that the material [from which they were made] existed previously, which the proper sense of the word [created] does not allow. However, I don't restrict "creation" here to the work of the fifth day, but rather suppose it to refer to that shapeless and confused mass that was like the spring from which the whole world gushed forth. It is therefore said that God created whales and the rest of the fishes, not because the beginning of their creation is to be reckoned from that moment in which they receive their form, but because they are contained in the entirety of that body which was made from nothing. COMMENTARY ON GENESIS 1:21.[99]

WERE FLIES AND WORMS AMONG THE "CREEPING THINGS"? ANDREW WILLET: If every kind of worm and creeping thing were created in the beginning, then we refuse Augustine's idea that such creatures as are generated of dead bodies were not then made. For just as other perfect beasts were at the first formed out of the earth, yet afterward left to their usual generation, so these creeping worms, flies, and such like, might then have been created as the rest were, though they are now engendered by corruption of other matter. Likewise we reject Pererius's idea that those creatures that spring from corruption and are noisome and offensive to us did not have their beginning then: for by this reason, neither should the serpent have been created, [and] these creatures, though hurtful now to human nature, should not have been so if humanity had not fallen. We therefore rather allow Basil's opinion, that even these small beasts, which spring from corruption now, were produced in the first creation, and this is more agreeable to the text, which says that every

creeping thing was made then. Yet we do not think that there may not be, or is not in the world, any other form or fashion of fly or worm, than there was in the first creation, but that the general kind was then formed of such several creeping things, and a general power and ability given to produce them out of such corruptible matter as is fit for their generation. COMMENTARY ON GENESIS 1:25.[100]

EVEN POISONOUS PLANTS AND ANIMALS HAD A PROPER PLACE. HULDRYCH ZWINGLI: "Everything was good," even venomous things, considered according to their own class. If you abuse wine, in a way you make wine into a poison for yourself that renders the body useless, corrupting and eventually destroying it. ANNOTATIONS ON GENESIS 1:25.[101]

MANY THINGS NOW IN NATURE RESULT FROM SIN, NOT FROM GOD'S FIRST INTENTION. JOHN CALVIN: One should also note that nothing is included in the works of the six days except those things that constitute the world's lawful and genuine adornment. Later on, God will say, "Let the earth bring forth thorns and briers," by which he indicates that the appearance of the earth would be different from what it was in the beginning. But the explanation is obvious: many things seen in the world today are rather corruptions of it than any part of its proper adornment. For ever since the human race degenerated from its original appearance, it has been likewise necessary that the world should continually decline from its own nature. The same sort of thing is to be held with respect to fleas, locusts, and other insects. In all of these things, I would say, there is some deformity of the world, which should by no means be regarded as in the order of nature, since it

---

[99]CTS 1:89* (CO 23:23-24). [100]*Hexapla* (1608), 13, citing Augustine, *De Genesi ad litteram* 3.14; and Basil, *Hexaemeron* 7. [101]ZSW 13:13.

proceeds more from human sin than from the hand of God. Truly, these things too are created by God, but by God as an avenger. COMMENTARY ON GENESIS 2:2.[102]

DANGEROUS ANIMALS SHOW THAT GOD IS BOTH OUR TUTOR AND OUR PROTECTOR.

JOHANNES OECOLAMPADIUS: One might react in amazement, as if those things were done to the detriment of the human race, the creation, that is, of lions and wolves, and all kinds of dangerous animals. But if humans had persisted in their own innocence, they also would have been lords over those animals and would better have recognized their own power and how much good they had received from the Lord, so that they should be able to stand before those unaggressive animals, even by the word alone. Later we will hear that those animals received their names from Adam himself. Also Noah afterwards commanded the animals to go into the ark without any difficulties. In truth, seeing that God foreknew that humans would sin, thence he also created these beasts so that human beings might be exercised and so that they might fear God. For the young, rods and threats are useful, by which they should be better educated. And yet God in his singular providence made those ferocious beasts depart more into the wilderness, so that they should be far off from humankind, and that they should better hunt out their food by night rather than by day. Let us consider well, moreover, how much greater harm there might have been than just savage animals had God not prohibited it. LECTURES ON GENESIS 1:24-25.[103]

1:22 And God Blessed Them

GOD'S BLESSING BRINGS FECUNDITY.

MARTIN LUTHER: Here one can observe what the blessing really is, namely, the increase. As for ourselves, when we bless, we do nothing else than express our good wishes; what we wish, we are unable to bestow. But God's blessing announces an increase and is effective immediately. Likewise, in contrast, His curse involves a decrease. This, too, is effective. LECTURES ON GENESIS 1:21-22.[104]

GOD'S BLESSINGS, UNLIKE OURS, ARE ALWAYS EFFICACIOUS.

JOHN CALVIN: God does not pray in human fashion, for with a single nod he brings about what humans try to obtain by making vows and promises. He therefore blesses his creatures when he commands them to increase and grow; that is, by his word, he pours out fruitfulness upon them. COMMENTARY ON GENESIS 1:22.[105]

CREATION'S WONDERS SHOULD EVOKE GRATITUDE, NOT IDOLATRY.

KONRAD PELLIKAN: "Let one beget another, and another beget many, so that the congregations of the waters might fill the sea and rivers according to the wondrous fullness of their kinds. And let the varieties of birds on the earth and in the air also be multiplied, and their kinds through countless individuals, to the glory of God, the author of all nature, but equally to the use of humankind." Whence from things of this kind, adorned with such variety, we ought to recognize the Lord as the creator of all things, including us—as well as admire, revere, worship and thank him, and be obedient to his will. But from these things we should *not* fashion stupid and impious gods for ourselves, including images, pictures or idols of people and beasts, as if by a sacred law we should honor, admire or adore, and invest them with the confidence of all our hope whatsoever, we who neglect and ignore, if not hold in contempt, how good to us is God, who does not suffer his honor to be given to another but wishes alone to be adored and worshiped. COMMENTARY ON GENESIS 1:22-23.[106]

---

[102]CTS 1:104* (CO 23:32). [103]*In Genesim* (1536), 19v-20r. [104]LW 1:53 (WA 42:40). [105]CTS 1:90* (CO 23:24). [106]*Commentaria Bibliorum* (1532) 1:2v.

1:24-31 THE SIXTH DAY OF CREATION

[24]And God said, "Let the earth bring forth living creatures according to their kinds—livestock and creeping things and beasts of the earth according to their kinds." And it was so. [25]And God made the beasts of the earth according to their kinds and the livestock according to their kinds, and everything that creeps on the ground according to its kind. And God saw that it was good.

[26]Then God said, "Let us make man[a] in our image, after our likeness. And let them have dominion over the fish of the sea and over the birds of the heavens and over the livestock and over all the earth and over every creeping thing that creeps on the earth."

[27]So God created man in his own image,
in the image of God he created him;
male and female he created them.

[28]And God blessed them. And God said to them, "Be fruitful and multiply and fill the earth and subdue it and have dominion over the fish of the sea and over the birds of the heavens and over every living thing that moves on the earth." [29]And God said, "Behold, I have given you every plant yielding seed that is on the face of all the earth, and every tree with seed in its fruit. You shall have them for food. [30]And to every beast of the earth and to every bird of the heavens and to everything that creeps on the earth, everything that has the breath of life, I have given every green plant for food." And it was so. [31]And God saw everything that he had made, and behold, it was very good. And there was evening and there was morning, the sixth day.

a The Hebrew word for *man* (*adam*) is the generic term for mankind and becomes the proper name *Adam*

OVERVIEW: All traditional commentators recognized that the first five days of creation move in a crescendo toward the sixth day—the day on which the first man and the first woman are created in God's image. The sixth day begins, however, with the creation of both domestic and wild animals. For many Reformation commentators, domestic animals are of interest here only insofar as they represent God's finishing touch in preparing a home for the first human couple. (They will show more interest in the animals for their own sake later on, when Noah is tasked with gathering the animals into the ark.)

Probably no element of the sixth day elicits more discussion than the question of the image of God. Western theology had long enjoyed a fairly polished account here. Taking the plural "let us make" in Genesis 1:26 as a sure sign of the Trinity, Augustine had concluded that the image, too, had to be trinitarian, and he developed the already traditional identification of God's image with human reason by discerning within reason itself a triune structure: memory, intellect and will. Embracing Augustine's popular exposition, medieval commentators further distinguished between God's *image* as our triune rational capacity and God's *likeness* as our moral rectitude, and they went on to explain that while the image (identified as our natural gifts) was damaged in the Fall, our graced moral likeness to God (identified as our supernatural gifts) was wholly lost.

Commentators of the Reformation era often admired these distinctions and sometimes even perpetuated them. But they were also aware, by virtue of their growing knowledge of Hebrew and the Old Testament's predilection for parallelism, that the distinction between image and likeness cannot be sustained and that Augustine's triune construct was completely speculative. Consequently, early Protestant writers were quick to critique their predecessors and to reopen the question of whether there are additional ingredients to the image of God and, indeed, whether God's image even admits of anything like a simple definition.

The character of that image is further complicated by Genesis 1:28, which introduces the dominion of humankind over all other creatures—a privilege that Chrysostom thought was definitive of the image itself. But the question of human dominion also raised problems for how the image was possessed by male and female, for if men generally seem to exercise a more obvious and more powerful lordship, some wondered if men also have a greater or even exclusive possession of God's image—as Augustine's contemporary Ambrosiaster had long ago argued from 1 Corinthians 11:7. Less controversial among the reformers was the mandate to be fruitful and fill the earth, a verse that ratified their rejection of clerical celibacy and their new vision for Christian marriage, all of which bore divine approval as being "very good."

1:24-25 Creation of the Beasts of the Earth

THE SIX DAYS PREPARE US TO RECOGNIZE GOD'S GENEROSITY. MARTIN LUTHER: I prefer that we reflect on the divine solicitude and benevolence toward us, because He provided such an attractive dwelling place for the future human being before the human being was created. Thus afterwards, when man is created, he finds a ready and equipped home into which he is brought by God and commanded to enjoy all the riches of so splendid a home. On the third day He provides kitchen and provisions. On the fourth, sun and moon are given to man for attendance and service. On the fifth the rule over the fish and the birds is turned over to him. On the sixth the rule over all the beasts is turned over to him, so that he might enjoy all this wealth free, in proportion to his need. And all this generosity is intended to make man recognize the goodness of God and live in the fear of God. This care and solicitude of God for us, even before we were created, may rightly and profitably be considered here; the rest of the ideas are without profit and even uncertain.

There is a similar beneficence of God toward us in His spiritual gifts. Before we were brought to faith, Christ, our Redeemer, is above in the Father's house; He prepares mansions so that when we arrive, we may find a heaven furnished with every kind of joy (Jn 14:2). Adam, therefore, when he was not yet created, was far less able to concern himself with his future welfare than we are; for he was not yet in existence. We, however, hear these promises given us by the Word of God. Therefore let us look upon the first state of this world as a type and figure of the future world; and so let us learn the kindness of God, who makes us rich and gives us wealth before we are able to concern ourselves with ourselves. It is far better to meditate and wonder at this concern, care, generosity, and benevolence of God, both in this life and in the one to come, than it is to speculate about why God began to equip the earth on the third day. LECTURES ON GENESIS 1:11.[1]

---

[1]LW 1:39 (WA 42:29-30).

GOD'S HOSPITALITY. JOHANNES BRENZ: Even if humans are the most eminent of all the animals, they were nonetheless created by God last of all. But this was not done apart from God's deliberate plan. Indeed, once God had decided to make heaven and earth and all that is in them for the sake of humankind, it was fitting that before humans were created, guest quarters should be readied for them and fitted with every kind of furnishing. We are accustomed, when we have invited a worthy guest to our home, to furnish the house in order to receive that guest in a worthy manner. It is a sluggish householder who only begins to decorate the house when an invited guest has already arrived. But the Lord our God is the best and most prudent head of his household. So when he was going to create humans in his image, whom he would cause to share in his own blessedness, he wished to prepare beforehand a lodging filled with all kinds of good things, so that humans would recognize the majesty, power, wisdom and goodness of the creator God, and by that recognition take hold of the highest delight and blessedness. The human mind cannot grasp nor can the human tongue explain how much joy, gladness and delight would have flooded over Adam when, fresh from being created, he suddenly saw heaven and earth, that is, his guest quarters, so lavishly decorated and adorned. Certainly, nothing could have kept him from admiring and loving his creator with his whole heart. COMMENTARY ON GENESIS 1:24-27.[2]

GOD'S SPECIAL CARE IN CREATING HUMANS. KONRAD PELLIKAN:

After a home had been fully prepared and the vast world fashioned and adorned with all things, only then—as if the Lord God needed to take special care and counsel in fashioning humankind, that smaller part of the world for whom God had previously created all things—does he say, "Let us make humankind in our image . . ." COMMENTARY ON GENESIS 1:26.[3]

1:26a *"Let Us Make . . ."*

THE DIVINE SENATE IN SESSION. JOHANNES BRENZ: When God says, "Let us make humankind," we should understand the Father to be speaking with the Son and the Holy Spirit. This is the holiest senate and the most sacred of councils that was ever convened. In this council of the Father, Son, and Holy Spirit, it was concluded and ordained that humankind would be created in the image and likeness of God, and that they would be partakers of the divine blessedness and preside over all the other creatures on earth, in the sea and in the sky, and thus be like God on earth. This is the final resolution, so to speak, of that divine and heavenly council. COMMENTARY ON GENESIS 1:26-27.[4]

GOD WAS NOT SPEAKING TO THE ANGELS WHEN MAKING HIS IMAGE. WOLFGANG MUSCULUS: Here it is asked, to whom God might have spoken these words, "Let us make humankind according to our image and likeness," and whether there were several makers in whose image humankind was made. . . . Some say that God spoke in this way to the angels, as if he would have wished to use their works to create humankind. Unthinkingly, they do not see how absurd it is to appoint as our creators those whom we regard as fellow servants under one God. If angels are the makers of our nature, how will we deny them the honor of worship and adoration due to our maker and creator? But if they are not our makers but rather our fellow servants, nor God's coworkers in the work of creation but rather his handiwork just as we are, then how is it to be understood that God said to *them*, "Let us make humankind"? Further support arises in that he does not say, "according to my image and likeness," but "according to our image and likeness." If he had spoken to the

---

[2]*Opera* 1:18. [3]*Commentaria Bibliorum* (1532) 1:3r. [4]*Opera* 1:19.

angels, we would now have angels not only as our creators but also our archetypes, so that we would be created according to the image not only of God but also of them. But if these things are deservedly rejected as absurd and incompatible with the Holy Scriptures, it follows that God was not speaking to the angels here. . . . This opinion is clearly detestable for the suspicion it raises, as if after making heaven, the sea, the earth, and all the things that now fill them, God were unable to create humankind by himself and instead found it unavoidable to summon help from his own creatures! Commentary on Genesis 1:26-27.[5]

"Let Us Make" Refers to the Trinity, Not to the Angels or the "'Royal' We." John Calvin: Given that the Lord needs no other advisor, there can be no doubt but that he consulted with himself. [Certain Jewish writers], however, are wholly ridiculous when they imagine that God conducted a conversation with the earth or the angels. Obviously, the earth was a most excellent advisor! But to ascribe the least portion of such an exquisite work to the angels is a sacrilege to be abhorred. Where, indeed, will they find that we were created according to the image of the earth or that of the angels? Does not Moses explicitly exclude *all* creatures the moment he declares that Adam was created after the image of God? Others, who deem themselves more acute (but are doubly benighted), say that God spoke of himself in the plural number, according to the custom of princes—as if that barbarous style of speaking that has grown into use within the past few centuries had even then prevailed in the world! . . . Christians properly contend from this testimony, then, that there exists in God a plurality of persons. Commentary on Genesis 1:26.[6]

"Let Us Make" Points to God's Unity and Trinity. Wolfgang Musculus: Let us

understand that by this locution . . . the mystery of the Holy Trinity is faithfully and truly expressed a bit more brightly than before, and that in this way God the Father expressed his consultation with the Word and the Spirit. We should also understand, next, that Moses narrated events with caution and care so as not to say, "And *they* created humankind," lest he seem to introduce a plurality of gods and confirm the impiety of the nations, but spoke in the singular, "And God created." Likewise, he also did not say, "And *they* said, 'Let us make humankind,' " but "And God said, 'Let us make humankind,' " so that he might thereby give a nod to the communion of the works of the Holy Trinity in a way that would at the same time not obscure the divine unity. Commentary on Genesis 1:26-27.[7]

God's Esteem for Us Should Bind Us to Him. Huldrych Zwingli: When he wished to create humankind, God employed much deliberation and great counsel. Indeed, he did not merely say, "Let it be done, let the earth emerge from the water," as with the earlier things, but descending into himself from on high, he fortifies his speech with weighty words, saying, "Let us make!" We are thus to discern, first of all, the divine nature in the special character of its persons; and, second, we should learn of our own nobility and dignity. For even if man (*homo*) was made from earth, God nonetheless made him with his own hand, so that we might see how highly God regarded humans, so that humans might serve their creator alone, worship only him, trust and cling to him alone—not to the earth, nor to the sun, nor to the water. Annotations on Genesis 1:26.[8]

---

[5]*In Mosis Genesim* (1554), 40-41; he goes on to refute that God was addressing the four elements or speaking in the plural merely to express royal dignity. [6]CTS 1:92-93* (CO 23:25). [7]*In Mosis Genesim* (1554), 41, distinctly echoing the ninth homily in Basil's *Hexaemeron*. [8]ZSW 13:13.

1:26b God's Image and Likeness

DISCOVERING AN IMAGE WE HAVE NEVER SEEN. JOHANNES BRENZ: Adam himself, who felt and experienced this image before he first sinned, was able to discuss the image of God much more explicitly than his descendants. The difference between Adam and us is like that between someone who was endowed with sight for a while but became blind, and someone blind from birth. The former can argue about colors because he saw them once upon a time; the latter, because he has never seen colors, how can he dispute about them? In the same way, because we were conceived and born in sin, we cannot understand or explain the true nature of this image except insofar as the Scriptures teach us about it and to the degree that we regain it in this life in Christ and by faith. God's image in us has been corrupted by sin, and the primary reason for the Holy Spirit to explain certain things about it is not to indulge our curiosity but rather, by pointing out the beauty of this image as it was in the beginning, to excite our interest in its restoration. But it cannot be regained except by being regenerated through faith in Christ. Truly, may it happen that we may be adopted as God's children, renewed by the Holy Spirit, and begin again to resemble God, until God's perfect image is finished and completed in us in the age to come. COMMENTARY ON GENESIS 1:26-27.[9]

GOD'S IMAGE MEASURED BY RIGHTEOUSNESS AND GENEROSITY. KONRAD PELLIKAN: Truly, even before humans were fashioned, God seems to have smothered them with his blessings, as it were, in all the things he had already created, the delightful joy and utility of which they would need to ponder and by which they might be provoked to love God more ardently as their beneficent father, to revere him more piously and to worship him more worthily. Nor is the reading to be disapproved, but rather embraced, that the image of God according to which humans were created is called the law (ius) of human nature, by which one ought to be absolutely eager to do good to all, just as God does. That [image] is possessed neither by brute beasts nor by the impious and the unjust, but rather by those who cultivate righteousness and bear the character of God the Father by imitating Christ the Son of God through their mercy and kindness, innocence of life and gracious generosity. These are the ones who truly bear God's image—that image according to which they were made, which was immediately corrupted by Adam, and which by Christ was truly cleansed and renewed. COMMENTARY ON GENESIS 1:26.[10]

GOD'S IMAGE CONSISTED OF WISDOM AND HOLINESS. WILLIAM PERKINS: This image of God has two principal parts: wisdom and holiness. Concerning wisdom, Paul says, "Put on the new self, which is created in knowledge after the image of him which created him." This wisdom consists in three points. First, he knew God his Creator perfectly, for Adam in his innocence knew God as far as it was fitting for a creature to know his Creator. Second, he knew God's will, as far as it was fitting for him, to show his obedience thereunto. Third, he knew the wisdom and will of his Creator touching the particular creatures: for after Adam was created, the Lord brought every creature unto him, presenting them unto him as being lord and king over them, that he might give names unto them. Whereby it appears that Adam in his innocence knew the nature of all creatures and the wisdom of God in creating them, else he could not have given them fit names; and when God brought Eve unto Adam, he knew her at the first and said, "This is now bone of my bone, and flesh of my flesh, she shall be called woman, etc." The

---

[9]*Opera* 1:22-23. [10]*Commentaria Bibliorum* (1532) 1:3r.

second part of God's image in us is holiness and righteousness, which is nothing else but a conformity of the will and affections and of a person's whole disposition both in body and soul to the will of God our Creator. EXPOSITION OF THE APOSTLES' CREED.[11]

HOW WE IMAGE GOD. PETER MARTYR VERMIGLI: The image of anyone is a *form* that calls him to mind. The likeness of anyone is a *quality* that calls him to mind. But it has to be explained in the simplest terms just what this image might be. Human beings not only possess powers of understanding, by which they are not unrelated to God, but they are also created with the most distinguished or, more precisely, divine characteristics, endowed with justice, wisdom, compassion, self-control, and charity. Paul urges us to be restored to this image, to that human being who, according to God, was created in holiness and truth. Christ is the fullness of God's *image* according to his divine nature, and in his human nature one finds as much of the divine *likeness* as is possible. . . . We have been made so that we might be like him, for we have the capacity for understanding and divine perfections. We were created with these attributes, but we cannot be restored to them without the help and example of Christ, who is the first and true image. How we may be God's image is clear from our happiness, which we hold in common with God, that is, with him whom we are called to love and know. COMMENTARY ON GENESIS 1:26-27.[12]

WE IMAGE GOD WHEN WE REMEMBER. JOHANNES BRENZ: Human beings were created not only to consider the present moment but also to remember the things of the past. A trace of this gift and ornament has remained in us after sin. Indeed, we remember and keep in mind not only things we saw or did yesterday or the day before, but also the things we did or witnessed as adolescents many

years ago. God's remembrance, however, is so great that he regards things done many thousands of years ago as if now present. . . . Thus, human beings were created in an image similar to God in that they are endowed with memory, by which they remember the past. COMMENTARY ON GENESIS 1:26-27.[13]

NATURAL LAW CONNECTS GOD'S IMAGE TO THE GOLDEN RULE. HULDRYCH ZWINGLI: Some refer [the image] to dominion over creatures, that humans should preside over all just as God does; others connect it to the mind. But I think this image and likeness is what we call the law (*ius*) of nature: "What you would have done to you, do to others!" This image is inscribed and impressed on our hearts. Brute beasts do not have this; rather, nature has assigned animals of every kind to protect themselves in life and body. Therefore, those who attend to justice, who seek God, who imitate God and Christ in innocence of life toward all as well as doing good to them in turn—these are the ones, in the final analysis, who bear that ancient image of God, which has been cleansed and restored by Christ. For just as in Adam we are all corrupted, so in Christ we are all renewed, when, having been endowed with the divine mind, we conduct ourselves according to the character of Christ. ANNOTATIONS ON GENESIS 1:27.[14]

CONSCIENCE, TOO, IMAGES GOD. ANNA MARIA VAN SCHURMAN:
In us, as in a temple,
    there is a member that abides
and, like a looking glass,
    reflects what in every soul resides.
I speak of that member
    that can its Maker praise
and teach its neighbors

---

[11]*Works* (1608) 1:150-51, conflating Eph 4:24 and Col 3:10.
[12]*In Primum Librum Mosis* (1569), 7r, citing Eph 4:24; Col 3:10; 2 Cor 3:18; Heb 1:3; Col 1:15-19; Rom 8:29; Mt 3:17. [13]*Opera* 1:21. [14]ZSW 13:13-14; cf. Mt 22:34; 1 Cor 15:22.

of its inner state and ways.
But see how conscience
    serves a purpose of a deeper sort;
this power works inside us
    and convenes the highest court.
As a power in our souls,
    it is crafted to amaze:
a light to us, a witness,
    and the judge of all our ways,
a tribunal where heaven's judgments
    cannot but unfold,
where all our deepest inner secrets
    cannot but be told.
It brings to us a peaceful life
    or else brings troubled weather;
it gladdens hearts with heaven's joy
    or makes them live forever.
As law and judge, it rules within
    to keep us on the path
and makes us know if we deserve
    God's favor or his wrath.
In it the blind see something,
    in it the deaf can hear
the voice of nature sounding
    in every human ear,
calling out, "There is a God,
    all-powerful, good and wise,
who made us that his highest praise
    might evermore arise."
PARAPHRASE OF GENESIS 1–3.[15]

GOD'S LIKENESS REMAINS IN US LIKE A SPARK COVERED WITH ASHES. BALTHASAR HUBMAIER: If before the Fall God's likeness was free and unbound in us, since the Fall it is held captive and the sin of the Fall is damning. After the restoration of the Fall through Christ, this likeness is made free again, although captive in the sinful and poisoned body; but the curse has been removed from the sin of the Fall insofar as we do not by our own wickedness make it damning again by rebelliously walking in it. . . . The image or inbreathing of God is still in us all, although captive and as a live spark covered with cold ashes is still alive and will steam if heavenly water is poured on it. It also lights up and burns if one blows on it. That is the source of the conscience in the Jews, pagans, and Christians, as Paul writes about it, Rom. 2:15. But Christ restored the quenched spark of flame on Easter Day when he breathed upon his disciples and said, "Receive the Holy Spirit." Now Christ has ordered his servants to inbreathe and blow by proclaiming his holy Word, that the wounded soul may be reawakened from sleep. A CHRISTIAN CATECHISM.[16]

GOD'S IMAGE MEANT FREEDOM FROM FEAR. MARTIN LUTHER: My understanding of the image of God is this: that Adam had it in his being and that he not only knew God and believed that He was good, but that he also lived in a life that was wholly godly; that is, he was without the fear of death or of any other danger, and was content with God's favor. In this form it reveals itself in the instance of Eve, who speaks with the serpent without any fear, as we do with a lamb or a dog. For this reason, too, if they should transgress His command, God announces the punishment: "On whatever day you eat from this tree, you will die by death," as though He said: "Adam and Eve, now you are living without fear; death you have not experienced, nor have you seen it. This is My image, by which you are living, just as God lives. But if you sin, you will lose this image, and you will die." So we see now what great dangers and how many varieties of death and chances of death this wretched nature is compelled to meet with and to endure in addition to the execrable lust and other sinful passions and inordinate emotions that arise in the hearts of all. We are never secure in God; apprehension and terror cause us concern even in sleep. These and similar evils are the image of the devil, who stamped them on us. LECTURES ON GENESIS 1:26.[17]

---

[15]*Uitbreiding*, 4.13–5.4. [16]CRR 5:360. [17]LW 1:62-63 (WA 42:47).

God's Image May Be Known from God's Own Character. Johannes Brenz: In the beginning, not just one part but the whole person was created to be an image or facsimile similar to God. To understand it aright, we should compare those things that were in us before sin (at least, so far as such things can be inferred from Scripture or from human misery) or that still remain in us, with those things that are in God or that *are* God himself (so far as the Holy Spirit wishes to reveal them through Scripture). And first, God created humans wise and industrious, and endowed with such intelligence that they might know not only how to administer the things of this earth, which had been given to them to rule, but also that God was their creator. . . . That Adam bestowed names on all the animals is proof of his wisdom as well as his dominion. And when, having been awakened from sleep, he beheld Eve, he spoke prophetically not only of her, but of Christ and his bride, the church, just as Paul explains. So Adam as created was the greatest philosopher and the greatest prophet, that is, the wisest of all bodily creatures. Yet there is no doubt but that God surpasses all things in his wisdom and that, truly, he is wisdom itself. . . . Thus, when God had made human beings wise, yet is himself wisest of all by far, it is clear that human beings are created in God's image in just this way, that they were made wise and intelligent. Commentary on Genesis 1:26-27.[18]

The Image of God Represented the Pinnacle of Integrity. Martin Luther: The image of God, according to which Adam was created, was something far more distinguished and excellent, since obviously no leprosy of sin adhered either to his reason or to his will. Both his inner and his outer sensations were all of the purest kind. His intellect was the clearest, his memory was the best, and his will was the most straightforward—all in the most beautiful tranquility of mind, without any fear of death and without any anxiety. To these inner qualities came also those most beautiful and superb qualities of body and of all the limbs, qualities in which he surpassed all the remaining living creatures. I am fully convinced that before Adam's sin his eyes were so sharp and clear that they surpassed those of the lynx and eagle. He was stronger than the lions and the bears, whose strength is very great; and he handled them the way we handle puppies. Both the loveliness and the quality of the fruits he used as food were also far superior to what they are now.

But after the Fall death crept like leprosy into all our perceptive powers, so that with our intellect we cannot even understand that image. Adam would not have known his Eve except in the most unembarrassed attitude toward God, with a will obedient to God, and without any evil thought. Now, after sin, we all know how great passion is in the flesh, which is not only passionate in its desire but also in its disgust after it has acquired what it wanted. Thus in both instances we see neither reason nor will unimpaired, but passion greater than that of cattle. Is this not a serious and pernicious leprosy, of which Adam was free before sin? Moreover, he had greater strength and keener senses than the rest of the living beings. To what extent is man today surpassed by the boars in their sense of hearing, by the eagles in their sense of sight, and by the lion in his strength? Therefore no one can picture in his thoughts how much better nature was then than it is now. Lectures on Genesis 1:26.[19]

Three Options for the Image of God, but Dominion Is Best. Wolfgang Musculus: The extent to which one is rendered similar to God matters greatly, since it cannot happen that we become like God in every way.

---

[18]*Opera* 1:21. [19]LW 1:62 (WA 42:46-47).

God has his *essence*, in which three divine persons uniquely share. He has his *natural quality*, by which he is just, good, wise, etc. And there is also *divine power*, by which the Lord and King of all governs everything that is in heaven and on earth. Therefore we must see according to which of these three we have been created to be the image. I cannot imagine that anyone has ever thought that the human race was created according to the image of God's essence, even if you consider a genius. Therefore it remains that we were created as the image and likeness either of his *quality* or of his *power* to rule all things. And here the views of Christians are divided. Some understand it of the rational soul, in which there is memory, intellect and volition, so that humans were created as God's image according to [the soul]; and thus they situate the image of God in the inner person as understanding, wisdom, thoughtfulness and upright living. . . . Others expound [it] of the power and dignity to rule all things, according to which man was created according to the image of God and constituted lord over the earth and all the things that are in it. . . . I prefer to follow this view rather than one that breathes philosophical subtlety and is, moreover, of such a kind that with equal reason the angels, too, could be seen as created according to God's image. Indeed, if it is fitting to consider reason, wisdom, volition, intellect, and other things of this kind in this matter and to lodge the image of God in those things, nothing prevents angels, who are in any case much more righteous than we, from also being named as created according to God's image. For they draw considerably nearer to divine wisdom and understanding than we do. Yet Scripture does not attribute to them as it does to us, that they were made according to God's image and likeness. Why? Namely, because they were not constituted lords of earth and of beasts, a dignity God expressly conferred on humankind. COMMENTARY ON GENESIS 1:26-27.[20]

THE IMAGE WAS DESIGNED WITH CHRIST IN MIND. KONRAD PELLIKAN: "Let us make humankind in our image, according to our resemblance or designs." Namely, let us form and produce humankind, the noblest creature of the world, according to that form, exemplar, model or effigy that has been predestined before the formation of all creatures to be united to the Son of God and taken up by him in Christ, who is called the firstborn of all creatures, in whom all things were made; and according to that appearance (*speciem*) preformed from eternity and assumed by the Word. COMMENTARY ON GENESIS 1:26.[21]

WHAT THE IMAGE IS AND IS NOT. ANDREW WILLET: We do not approve the opinion of Rupert, who by *image* here understands the second person of the Trinity [and] by *likeness* or *similitude* the third person, namely, the Holy Spirit: for when the Lord says "Let us make humankind in our image," the image of the whole Trinity is expressed, and not the image of the Father only. Neither are the words so to be taken, as though humanity was made according to the likeness of that human nature which Christ the Son of God was to assume: for the Scripture says that Christ took upon himself human likeness (Phil 2:7), not [that humanity took on] his likeness. We also reject the idea of Eugubinus and Oleaster, who think that *God* took upon himself a human shape when he created humanity, . . . for God the Father never appeared in any such shape, nor could it be said to be God's image, being assumed but for a time. Neither yet do we distinguish these words, as some of the Fathers (Origen, Basil, Ambrose), who refer "image" to the *natural gifts* of reason, understanding and memory; [and] "likeness" to the *supernatural gifts* of grace, as of holiness and righteousness:

---

[20]*In Mosis Genesim* (1554), 41-42, also citing Chrysostom and Gratian in support of his view. [21]*Commentaria Bibliorum* (1532) 1:3r.

for we see that the apostle applies the image to the work of grace in our renovation or regeneration (Col 3:10). . . . We therefore conclude that there is no difference in the sense and meaning of these words, but that one is the explication of the other. . . .

But to put all out of doubt, the apostle shows how we are to understand the image of God in humankind in Ephesians 4:24 ("Which after God is created in righteousness and true holiness") and Colossians 3:10 ("Put on the new man, which is renewed in knowledge, after the image of him that created him"). This image then consists not so much in the substance of the soul or in the natural faculties thereof, as of understanding, free will, memory, but in the knowledge and illumination, holiness and justice of the soul, which are now wrought in us by grace, [but] then were given by creation. Our reasons [include] that . . . the image after which people are naturally begotten is not the image of God: for it would be absurd, if not impious, to say that God's image may be naturally propagated. Rather, by nature we receive the image of the reasonable soul, as Adam begot Seth "in his own likeness after his image" (Gen 5:3), that is, like unto him both in soul and body, so that the image of God does not consist in the substance of the reasonable soul. [In addition,] that image of God according to which Adam was created is by his fall utterly lost and extinguished, for otherwise this image need not be renewed and revived in us, as it is by Christ, as the apostle shows [above]. But the substance of the reasonable soul with its natural faculties and powers are not lost; this image, therefore, is not expressed therein. Commentary on Genesis 1:26-27.[22]

Likeness Points to God's Covenant with Adam and with Us. Peter Riedemann: God's covenant is an everlasting covenant, existing from the beginning and continuing into eternity. It shows that it is his will to be our God and Father, that we should

be his people and beloved children. Through the covenant, God desires continually to pour into us through Christ every divine blessing and all good things. That such a covenant of God existed from the beginning is shown in that God created people in his own likeness. All was well with them, and there was no corrupting poison in them. Even when people were deceived and robbed of this likeness by the counsel of the serpent, God's purpose nevertheless endured. The covenant which he had previously made expresses this clearly, namely, that he should be our God and we his people. Out of this comes a promise to take away the devil's power through the woman's offspring. This makes it clear that it was God's intention to redeem us from the devil's power and restore us as his children. Thus, God made his covenant first with Adam, and then more clearly with Abraham and his descendants. Now he has made this covenant with us through Christ and has established and confirmed it through Christ's death. Just as a will is not valid until the death of the one making the will, in the same way God gave his Son up to death, so that we would be redeemed from death through him and be the children of his covenant forever. Confession of Faith.[23]

Image Does Not Differ from Likeness. John Calvin: Interpreters do not agree about the meaning of these words. Yet it suits most of them, if not all, to distinguish *image* from *likeness*. And this distinction is almost universal: that the image resides in the substance of a thing, while likeness is found in its accidents. Those who want to define things briefly say that the *image* includes the endowments that God conferred on human nature, while they explain *likeness* in terms of God's gratuitous gifts. But Augustine, more than anyone, specu-

---

[22]*Hexapla* (1608), 14-15, citing Rupert of Deutz, *De Trinitate* 2.2. [23]CRR 9:90-91, alluding to Wis 1.12-14; Heb 6:17-20; 9:11-16; 2 Cor 6:16; Acts 3:17-26; and many other texts.

lates far too cleverly in order to fabricate a Trinity within human beings. For he takes hold of the three faculties that Aristotle enumerates in the soul—intellect, memory and will—and from one Trinity subsequently derives many. If any readers have the leisure and wish to be amused by such speculations, let them read the tenth and fourteenth books of *On the Trinity* and the eleventh book of *The City of God*. To be sure, I confess that there is something in a human being that refers to the Father and the Son and the Spirit, nor do I have any difficulty in admitting as well that distinction of the faculties of the soul (although the simpler division into two parts, which is more usual in Scripture, is better suited to a sound doctrine of piety). But a definition of the image of God ought to rest on a firmer basis than such subtleties. As for myself, before I would define the image of God, I deny that it differs from his likeness. For, later on, when Moses repeats the same things, he disregards the likeness and is content to mention the image. If anyone should stipulate that he was merely trying to be concise, I answer that where he twice stresses the word *image*, he makes no mention of likeness. We also know that it was common among the Hebrews to repeat the same thing in different words; and besides, the phrase itself shows that the second term was added for the sake of explanation: "Let us make," he says, "in our image, according to our likeness," that is, so that they may be like God or represent God's effigy. COMMENTARY ON GENESIS 1:26.[24]

MANICHAEANS AND ANTHROPOMORPHITES BOTH ERR ABOUT THE IMAGE OF GOD.
WOLFGANG MUSCULUS: The Manichaeans seek in this text how what Moses writes could be true, that humankind was made according to the image of God. And since they understand [this image] as a figure of our *body*, they argue that surely God does not have a body

and members configured as our members, because he is a spirit. Next, the Anthropomorphites, because they see that certain bodily members are attributed to God in the Holy Scriptures, . . . understand humans to be created according to God's image and likeness so that God truly does have a body conformed to the human body. They do not reject the Scriptures of the Old Testament, but their misunderstanding leads them to swallow this error and so perceive God in unworthy ways. The Manichees, however, do not accept the Old Testament, and since they know God is a spirit and does not have a body and members, they raise a quibble against Moses in this place, as if what he wrote could in no sense be true, that humans were made according to God's image. We must therefore seek how to understand that what Moses says is true and, at the same time, that the Anthropomorphites are wrong, and that the Manichees have impiously raised a quibble against the truth. COMMENTARY ON GENESIS 1:26-27.[25]

THE GOSPEL BEGINS TO RESTORE THE IMAGE.
MARTIN LUTHER: Intellect and will indeed have remained, but both very much impaired. And so the Gospel brings it about that we are formed once more according to that familiar and indeed better image, because we are born again into eternal life or rather into the hope of eternal life by faith, that we may live in God and with God and be one with Him, as Christ says (Jn 17:21). And indeed, we are reborn not only for life but also for righteousness, because faith acquires Christ's merit and knows that through Christ's death we have been set free. From this source our other righteousness has its origin, namely, that newness of life through which we are zealous to obey God as we are taught by the Word and aided by the Holy Spirit. But this righteousness has merely its beginning in this life, and it

---

[24]CTS 1:93-94* (CO 23:25-26). [25]*In Mosis Genesim* (1554), 41.

cannot attain perfection in this flesh. Nevertheless, it pleases God, not as though it were a perfect righteousness or a payment for sin but because it comes from the heart and depends on its trust in the mercy of God through Christ. Moreover, this also is brought about by the Gospel, that the Holy Spirit is given to us, who offers resistance in us to unbelief, envy, and other vices that we may earnestly strive to glorify the name of the Lord and His Word, etc. In this manner this image of the new creature begins to be restored by the Gospel in this life, but it will not be finished in this life. But when it is finished in the kingdom of the Father, then the will will be truly free and good, the mind truly enlightened, and the memory persistent. Then it will also happen that all the other creatures will be under our rule to a greater degree than they were in Adam's Paradise. Until this is accomplished in us, we cannot have an adequate knowledge of what that image of God was which was lost through sin in Paradise. But what we are stating faith and the Word teach, which, as if from a distance, point out the glory of the divine image. Just as in the beginning the heaven and the earth were unfinished masses, so to speak, before the light had been added, so the godly have within themselves that unfinished image which God will on the Last Day bring to perfection in those who have believed His Word. Lectures on Genesis 1:26.[26]

The Image of God May Be Known from Its Restoration. John Calvin: Since the image of God has been destroyed in us by Adam's fall, what it was originally like must be deduced from its restoration. Paul says that we are transformed into the image of God by the gospel. And according to him, spiritual regeneration is nothing else than the restoration of the same image (Col 3:10; Eph 4:24). However, that he locates this image "in righteousness and true holiness" is a synecdoche,[†] for however much these are the chief part,

they are not the whole of God's image. By this word, therefore, the integrity of our whole nature is designated, for Adam would have been endowed with right understanding, with his affections in harmony with reason, all his senses sound and well-regulated, and he truly would have excelled in everything good. Accordingly, the chief seat of the divine image was in his mind and heart, where it would have been prominent, yet there was no part of him in which some sparks of it did not shine forth. Indeed, there was in each of the parts of the soul a moderation that corresponded with its rank: in the mind, the light of right understanding flourished and reigned, while rectitude stood by as the mind's companion, all the senses were designed and eager for due obedience to reason, and there was a suitable correspondence in the body with this internal order. But now, even if some obscure tracings of that image are found remaining in us, they are nonetheless so damaged and mutilated that they may truly be said to be destroyed. For besides the degradation that appears so hideously everywhere, this evil also is added, that no part is undefiled by the stain of sin. Commentary on Genesis 1:26.[27]

A Degree of Solidarity in Having Lost the Image of God. Wolfgang Capito: We are made from the same clay and we are all equally the dead offspring of the dead Adam. No one, therefore, is better by nature than anyone else, but there are some to be found who are more destructive than others with respect to their morals and pursuits, insofar as they conceal less than others the stinking corpse of their soul and the pus of their rotten heart. Their evil appearance is decorated with showy pretense and lies hidden in other things that are claimed

---

[26]LW 1:64-65 (WA 42:48). Luther's reference to will, mind and intellect alludes to Augustine's trinitarian speculations about the image of God. [27]CTS 1:95* (CO 23:26-27), echoing also Eph 4:24. [†]*Synecdoche* is a figure of speech in which only a part of something is used to designate the whole.

as superior to good sense and the virtues of the soul. But they alone are good who have received an alien goodness, that is, Christ the Lord.

From what has been said so far, it is clear (I think) what it means for us to be recreated in the image of God—we who are human beings born from other human beings in the image of Satan. The first human was created so that he would have progressed every day in that same image and according to that same likeness, just as he was corrupted according to the same image of Satan by his guilt, . . . from which we are now reformed into the image of God. For by repairing what had fallen into ruin, the plan is the same and the goal is the same as what was well founded in every way at the beginning. But who does not know from this revelation of the gospel that we are to regard that person as renewed who bears by faith a mind illumined by the mortification of the flesh? Therefore the life of the first human being and the disposition of one who is in the image and according to the likeness of God will be nothing other than the knowledge of God's benevolence toward us and the will and affection of the senses that our first parents had by means of the light of God. Adam's original nature was fully equal to the gift we receive by our faith, which is understood from its effects. ON GOD'S WORK OF THE SIX DAYS.[28]

THE POLISHED MIRROR IS NOW A FRIGHT MASK. DAVID CHYTRAEUS: The image's *deformation*, which resulted from our first parents' fall and was passed on to all of us through carnal propagation, ought to be contemplated and deplored. Indeed, all those now born from virile seed carry within their minds a darkness that is unaware of God, along with doubts about God's will and providential care. In our wills there is an abhorrence of God and an absence of the fear of God, of faith and love; there is a carnal security, mistrust, self-regard, concupiscence

and depraved tendencies. In our hearts, all our affections defy God's will and these evils render us liable to God's wrath and eternal death. So while human beings ought to be a polished mirror and the express image of God, through the fall of our first parents we've become the devil's fright mask. And yet just as a mirror spattered with mud still renders some image, however obscure, so too in us do some marks and traces of God remain even after the fall, and these are gradually given luster in this life by the Son of God, until the entire image of God in us is restored. COMMENTARY ON GENESIS 1:26-27.[29]

CHRIST RESTORES ADAM (AND US) TO THE PURITY OF GOD'S IMAGE. DAVID JORIS: The true restitution is the first, which has thus occurred in Christ. Put briefly, everything we have lost in the first Adam, by disobedience through the devil, is restored by and through the obedience of Jesus Christ. Also, that those who now believe in the name of Jesus, that he is Christ, and call upon him as his head and Lord and prove to be obedient, in these people all things will be restored and renewed; changed from flesh into spirit, from death into life, from the earthly into the heavenly beings, until they have become once again the likeness and true image of God through Christ Jesus, by grace. They will be just as God made Adam in the beginning as an image of God: immortal, pure, without spot or sin, simple and innocent, just like God. We must again put on these clean unspotted, white garments of simplicity and innocence, else we cannot enter into Eden, that is, into the life and kingdom of God. Pay attention. These are the pure wedding garments which few people upon the earth have known. Yes, these are the garments of faith, in which exist the union and incorporation. These were given first to Adam from the rising of the sun, and now

---

[28]*Hexemeron* (1539), 280v-81v. [29]*In Genesin* (1576), 68-69.

have been entrusted to me through grace, from the rising of the sun. THE WONDERFUL WORKING OF GOD.[30]

THE MINISTRY OF THE CHURCH IS INVOLVED IN RESTORING GOD'S IMAGE AND LIKENESS. WOLFGANG CAPITO: An *image* is an internal and holistic expression of the substance. But what do you find like this in the divine writings, except in the eternal Word of the Father, who is Jesus Christ? For of him it is written that "he is the image of the invisible God," and "the splendor of his glory, and the image of his substance, upholding all things by the word of his power." Indeed, he is begotten from eternity, and as the Father understands himself perfectly, he who is in that very same Word expresses himself wholly—just as an earthly image expresses its original in part. *Likeness*, however, is not an expression of substance, but more like a resemblance to qualities found in God. For even if God's wisdom and truth and goodness and similar kinds of virtue are, as we humans say, nothing in God but God's own essence, nonetheless let us wholly regard them as characteristics of God's qualities, as if they were attributes of things. Nor does human reason conceive of them otherwise than the way Scripture speaks, namely, that God accommodates the things of God to our capacity. Accordingly, we who have been corrupted by Adam's sin are then completed in God's image and according to his likeness by the grace of adoption, when we are initiated into the sacraments of Christ and when, the gospel having been heard, faith effects for us the remission of sins through Christ.

The whole ministry of the church—the word of proclamation, baptism and the Eucharist, and the exercise of the keys [discipline]—plays a part toward this end. For through [the church] we are renewed to the image of God that has been displayed, that is, according to the example of the eternal Son;

through it we are restored from death to life and we put on Christ, the eternal image of the Father; and through it we become the image and glory of God, in that, by the Holy Spirit working within us, we become one with Christ. It is thereby clear how we are reformed according to the image of God. But by this same ministry of the church we are [also] daily fashioned into God's likeness, if, having been enlightened by grace, "we put on a heart of compassion, kindness, humility, meekness and patience, and we bear with one another and forgive one another if anyone has a complaint against another: just as Christ forgave you, so also should you forgive." ON GOD'S WORK OF THE SIX DAYS.[31]

LIVING FROM THE IMAGE. PETER MARTYR VERMIGLI: This passage also reminds us of the obligation, intention and appearance of all our actions. Whenever we are about to do something, we should ask ourselves, "Does this reflect my Father? Is this what it means to live out his image?" COMMENTARY ON GENESIS 1:26-27.[32]

GOD'S IMAGE IS THE BASIS FOR LOVING EVEN ENEMIES. JOHN CALVIN: We are not to consider what people deserve on their own merits but should rather attend in everyone to the image of God, to whom we owe all honor and love. However, it is among those of the household of faith that this same image is more carefully to be observed, insofar as it has been renewed and restored through the Spirit of Christ. Therefore, whoever you may meet who needs your aid, you have no reason to refuse to help.

Say that these people are strangers: yet the Lord has impressed a mark upon them that ought to be familiar to you, and by that means

---

[30]CRR 7:122-23.   [31]*Hexemeron* (1539), 276v-77v, closely quoting Col 1:15; Heb 1:3; Col 3:12-13.   [32]*In Primum Librum Mosis* (1569), 7v.

he forbids you to despise your own flesh.

Say that they are contemptible and of no account: yet the Lord shows them to be those whom he has deemed worthy of the beauty of his image.

Say that you owe nothing for any service of theirs: yet they have been substituted, as it were, in the place of God, toward whom you ought to recognize the many and great benefits by which he has bound you to himself.

Say they are undeserving that you should exert yourself in the least for them: yet God's image, by which they are commended to you, is so worthy that you should offer to it yourself and all your possessions.

Now if someone has not only deserved nothing good from you but has also provoked you by unjust acts and injuries, not even this is just cause for you to desist from embracing them in love and pursuing the duties of love. You will say, "They have deserved something far different of me." Yet what has the Lord deserved? When he commands you to forgive them for whatever sins they have committed against you, truly he wishes them to be charged against himself. INSTITUTES 3.7.6.[33]

GOD'S IMAGE IS WORTHY OF HONOR ESPECIALLY IN OTHERS. WOLFGANG MUSCULUS: No one can sufficiently weigh just how great a dignity it is to be created according to the image and likeness of God, even if one should ponder it as greatly as possible. It is clearly worthy of the greatest admiration that Adam, having been taken from the earth (according to his name), is formed according to the image of God. Now if a beggar were elevated to be the image of a king, everyone would marvel at his unparalleled good fortune. It seems a great thing that a Hebrew boy taken out of chains was promoted to be the image and likeness of the king in Egypt. With how much greater wonder should it be celebrated in this case that dust and earth is

formed by God to be God's image and likeness? We are therefore admonished by this consideration that, first, mindful of our origins, we should respond to God's esteem for us with godly and pious lives, lest we profane the divine image in us by shameful living. Then, that we should honor this dignity in all mortals, especially in our brethren and other believers, lest we heedlessly injure another. . . . It is madness to come to the point that we honor God's image in ourselves yet pay it no respect in our neighbors. On this point, those who have neither guarded an angelic dignity in themselves nor paid respect to the divine image in others bear a resemblance less to God than to Satan. COMMENTARY ON GENESIS 1:26-27.[34]

1:27 Male and Female . . . in God's Image

THE PRIMAL UNITY OF ADAM AND EVE. MARTIN LUTHER: Thus even if this image has been almost completely lost, there is still a great difference between the human being and the rest of the animals. Before the coming of sin the difference was far greater and more evident, when Adam and Eve knew God and all the creatures and, as it were, were completely engulfed by the goodness and justice of God. As a result, there was between them a singular union of hearts and wills. LECTURES ON GENESIS 1:26.[35]

MAN ALONE IS BUT HALF A HUMAN BEING. JOHN CALVIN: It is not pointless repetition that the image of God is again mentioned here. In fact, it is a remarkable instance of the divine goodness, something that can never be sufficiently proclaimed. At the same time, he calls

---

[33]OS 4:156.32-157.15 (cf. LCC 20:696-67); citing Gal 6:10; Is 58:7; Mt 6:14; 18:35; Lk 17:3; Mt 5:44. [34]*In Mosis Genesim* (1554), 44. The "Hebrew boy" in question is Joseph. [35]LW 1:67 (WA 42:50).

our attention to the excellence we have lost, so as to kindle in us the desire for its recovery. When he shortly adds that "God created them male and female," he commends to us that conjugal bond by which the society of the human race is nurtured. For this form of speaking, "God created humankind, male and female created he them," is of the same force as if he had said that the man himself was but half a human being. COMMENTARY ON GENESIS 1:27.[36]

EVE SHARED GOD'S IMAGE AND DOMINION. MARTIN LUTHER: In order not to give the impression that He was excluding the woman from all the glory of the future life, Moses includes each of the two sexes; for the woman appears to be a somewhat different being from the man, having different members and a much weaker nature. Although Eve was a most extraordinary creature—similar to Adam so far as the image of God is concerned, that is, in justice, wisdom, and happiness—she was nevertheless a woman. For as the sun is more excellent than the moon (although the moon, too, is a very excellent body), so the woman, although she was a most beautiful work of God, nevertheless was not the equal of the male in glory and prestige. However, here Moses puts the two sexes together and says that God created male and female in order to indicate that Eve, too, was made by God as a partaker of the divine image and of the divine similitude, likewise of the rule over everything. LECTURES ON GENESIS 1:27.[37]

WHY ADD "AND FEMALE"? WOLFGANG CAPITO: There was a need for this phrase, lest someone should say that the man alone was created in the image of God. For he made the whole human in the image of God, and it is not just man who is included in the term *human* but also woman, which is proved by the following words: "For God created him, male and female he created them." Neither the plan

for the image nor the plan for this speech ends with the one man, but the force of each pertains also to the woman. And from this phrase stems that statement of the apostle: "Neither the man without the woman," he says, "nor the woman without the man in the Lord. For just as woman comes from man, so also man comes through woman. But all things are from God," therefore the man is said to be most like the image and glory of God, "but woman is the glory of the man," and through him as her head, if the matter is borne in orderly fashion, a pious woman is also the glory of God, no less than a faithful man. All things, indeed, are from God. Nonetheless, she is subjected to the man for the sake of order as well as from the sequence of creation: for she was taken out of the man, not only on account of sin and the deceptions of the serpent that were allowed in before the man's fall. Wherefore in a marriage that is pious and restored to its first state, you should understand that it ought to be the arrangement that a woman be underneath the man no less than in a common marriage. For Eve was blameless when taken from the man and given to him as a helper. Indeed, he created the man alone, then he built the woman from the rib taken from the side of the sleeping man, so that she would be a helper to the man and dutifully bear the authority of her husband, always nearby, assisting the man. ON GOD'S WORK OF THE SIX DAYS.[38]

EVE NOT A "DEFECTIVE MALE." MARTIN LUTHER: Lyra also relates a Jewish tale, of which Plato, too, makes mention somewhere, that in the beginning man was created bisexual and later on, by divine power, was, as it were, split or cut apart, as the form of the back and of the spine seems to prove. Others have expanded these ideas with more obscene details. But the second chapter refutes these

---

[36]CTS 1:97* (CO 23:27-28). [37]LW 1:68-69 (WA 42:51-52). [38]*Hexemeron* (1539), 287v-88r, citing 1 Cor 11:11-12; 1 Cor 11:7.

babblers. For if this is true, how can it be sure that God took one of the ribs of Adam and out of it built the woman? These are Talmudic tales, and yet they had to be mentioned so that we might see the malice of the devil, who suggests such absurd ideas to human beings. This tale fits Aristotle's designation of woman as a "maimed man"; others declare that she is a monster. But let them themselves be monsters and sons of monsters—these men who make malicious statements and ridicule a creature of God in which God Himself took delight as in a most excellent work, moreover, one which we see created by a special counsel of God. These pagan ideas show that reason cannot establish anything sure about God and the works of God but only thinks up reasons against reasons and teaches nothing in a perfect and sound manner. LECTURES ON GENESIS 1:27.[39]

1:28a *"Be Fruitful and Multiply"*

EVE IS INTRODUCED HERE TO SIGNAL THE PROMISED BLESSING OF PROCREATION. WOLFGANG MUSCULUS: That he says, "Male and female he created them," is not to be understood in such a way that Eve was created at the same time, one with Adam. Rather, he spoke of the female by way of anticipation; her fashioning will be specially explained in the following chapter. But he wanted to mention her in this place in order to herald both sexes, the male and the female, on account of the blessing of procreation, which he was about to mention. COMMENTARY ON GENESIS 1:27.[40]

GOD'S BLESSING GUARDS US BETTER THAN OUR NATURAL CLEVERNESS. WOLFGANG CAPITO: [Some] suppose that it is proof of this authority over all things, that even ferocious beasts should fear and tremble, more or less, when humans are present. Truly, that is the outstanding preeminence of human beings, but it should not be credited to human cleverness, much less to our strength, even if we are

intellectually superior to the other animals. In the fears that spring up within animals at the sight of humans, we call attention to the power of this divine benediction, which by itself prevailed on behalf of uncorrupted sinners, and to which we have consigned ourselves for protection. Nonetheless, after the flood a trace of this subjection would be renewed on behalf of those who would have lost it on account of their guilt. If the divine benevolence had not wished to make a plan for these ungrateful people, the whole human race would have perished. Indeed, he said in the benediction to Noah, "the fear and terror of you will be on every beast of the earth and on every bird." And so, the fear that animals have of human beings is proof of the divine benediction bestowed in paradise, which is renewed to Noah himself after the flood, and we respond by extolling the glory of God, who in this way looks out for our safety. Yet with the wisdom of an inflated age, some admire human dignity in and of itself, on the basis of that eminence, as if it had been acquired by our efforts: and while there are also some who pay lip service to God as [nature's] originator, they are in fact thoroughly pleased with themselves on account of their natural endowments, and I have no idea how they can marvel at nature rather than God! ON GOD'S WORK OF THE SIX DAYS.[41]

FAMILIES EXIST TO IMAGE GOD. PETER MARTYR VERMIGLI: Ancient Jewish writers said that if anyone reached the age of maturity but did not enter into marriage, they would be guilty of shedding human blood. Their view is not absurd if we consider what evils are caused by an unnatural and wandering lust. And when we are ordered to be fruitful, it is with the understanding that we should beget such images of God as we have been made to be, so that the church might have more citizens.

---

[39]LW 1:70 (WA 42:53). [40]*In Mosis Genesim* (1554), 40. [41]*Hexemeron* (1539), 294r-v, citing Gen 9:2.

Indeed, we do not bring forth children for ourselves, but for the Lord. Spouses ought to desire children and raise those they receive with this goal: that they reflect their creator. And if there are some who are bereft or are for some other reason childless, let them strive as much as they can, so that by their word, example and prayers they may not go on living without fruit—that is, without some gain for the sake of others, just as Paul did, who became all things to all people so that he might gain them all. Commentary on Genesis 1:28.[42]

Fruitfulness Was Given as a Blessing, Not as a Law. Wolfgang Capito: Some ancient writers made a law out of the benediction given to the first married pair. But from 1 Corinthians 7, it will be hidden to no one just how much truth that opinion has. Indeed, that first [statement], "Be fruitful and multiply," is not a precept, but as it reads, we consider it to be a benediction given by the word of the Lord that pertains to physical union in marriage. Nonetheless, we are not without a precept for contracting marriage, just as we are not by nature estranged from the desire to bring forth offspring. For when the law says, "You shall not allow adultery," in so many words it commands the same thing, that "each one should have his own wife in order to avoid fornication," and it likewise sums up the whole law of marriage, . . . just as that too has been explained by the apostle. This law regarding the taking of a wife is general [in its scope]. Indeed, it encircles the male and the female sex, yet it does not rule over a Christian simplistically, because "each has a particular gift from God, one after this manner, and another after that." For the apostolic spirit considers the precepts of the Second Table not as they are in nature, but as beyond nature and so that what exists in nature by God's gift might be done; and each individual is directed toward what is to be undertaken by that first precept, on which all the others depend. In

fact, against those who impose a requirement to beget offspring, the apostle admirably commends celibacy. On God's Work of the Six Days.[43]

Procreation Is Meant for Marriage. John Calvin: God does intend for the human race to be multiplied by procreation, but not by indiscriminate coupling, as in brute animals. For he has joined the man to his wife so that they might produce offspring that are godly, that is, legitimate. Let us then mark who in the world it is that is addressed by God here when he commands them to increase, and to whom he limits his benediction. Certainly, he does not slacken the reins upon men and women, lest they charge headlong into unbridled wantonness. Rather, beginning with the subject of holy and chaste marriage, he then proceeds to speak of procreation. . . . However, the question is proposed as to whether fornicators and adulterers become fruitful by the power of God, because if that is true, then God's blessing is likewise extended to them. My answer is that this is a corruption of the divine plan, but that because God raises up offspring also from a pond no less than from the pure fountain of marriage, this will tend to their greater destruction. Still, the pure and lawful method of increase that God ordained from the beginning remains firm as a law of nature that common sense declares to be inviolable. Commentary on Genesis 1:28.[44]

Procreation, Not Promiscuity. Johannes Brenz: When God would create male and female so that they might multiply, he did not intend human desire to be confused, promiscuous and wandering—as some have perverted the meaning of this text. Indeed, just

---

[42]*In Primum Librum Mosis* (1569), 7v, citing 1 Cor 9:22. [43]*Hexemeron* (1539), 292r-v, citing 1 Cor 7:2, 7; the passage continues as a pastiche of 1 Cor 7:8-9, 17; Mt 19:12, 11; 1 Cor 7:35; 1 Tim 4:1-3. [44]CTS 1:98* (CO 23:28-29).

as . . . when human beings were established as lords of the earth, they were first created in God's image (that is, wise, just and pious) and thus would have been so established in justice and piety that they would have properly wielded this dominion and not rashly hijacked the possessions of others; so too in this context, when it is said to the male and the female to increase and multiply, we should understand that this was said to those who had been created in God's image: that is, just, pious, chaste, modest. But justice, chastity and modesty are *virtues*: they do not permit wandering desires or the sharing of wives or women, but they limit us to a legitimate marriage bed, just as Adam (while he was still holy) proclaimed of the holy law of marriage. . . . Indeed, God abominates incest, promiscuity and sexual impurity, and he is accustomed to punish these things not just corporally but also with eternal penalties. COMMENTARY ON GENESIS 1:28.[45]

SATAN PERVERTS GOD'S DESIGNS FOR "MALE AND FEMALE." WOLFGANG MUSCULUS: Truly, who does not know that the whole human race is divided into male and female? But it seems that Moses expressed a thing quite well known to everyone to this end, that he might condemn the abuse of those who pervert the arrangement of the sexes: that which not only the Sodomites but also many pagans practiced and which was done long ago by the Romans, as Paul's epistle to them attests. Wherefore, so that he might warn about the order of the sexes that God arranged at the outset of the human race and condemn its perversion, he urges upon everyone that male and female were created by God so that the human race might be multiplied by their coming together. That is why he immediately appended the benediction dealing with procreation, signifying a clear curse upon however many who pervert the order of creation and human procreation. Satan

introduced their damnable impurity into the church of Christ and brought indelible shame upon the Christian name under the pretext of celibacy and monastic discipline. Having transformed himself into an angel of light, he brought it about that males by themselves and even females might come together separately as a result of a vow of celibacy and a prohibition of legitimate matrimony. God created and joined together male and female; his adversary Satan joined each sex separately, males with males and females with females. COMMENTARY ON GENESIS 1:26-27.[46]

GOD'S BLESSING WAS MEANT TO FOSTER CONCORD. JOHN CALVIN: Indeed, God himself could have covered the earth with a crowd of human beings, but it was his will that we should all proceed from a single fountain, so that our desire for mutual concord might be the greater and that each of us might more freely embrace one other as our own flesh. Besides, just as human beings were created to occupy the earth, so should we assuredly conclude that God has marked out the expanse of earth that would suffice to accommodate human beings and to provide them with a suitable abode. Any inequity that is contrary to this arrangement is nothing else than a corruption of nature that derives from sin. COMMENTARY ON GENESIS 1:28.[47]

1:28b Dominion over Every Living Thing

"DOMINION" DISPLAYS GOD'S CARE FOR THE WHOLE HUMAN RACE. JOHN CALVIN: From this we may deduce the purpose for which all things were created, namely, that human beings might lack none of the conveniences and necessities of life. Even in the very ordering of creation, God's fatherly care for

---

[45]*Opera* 1:25. [46]*In Mosis Genesim* (1554), 45. [47]CTS 1:97-98* (CO 23:28).

humanity is thoroughly evident, because even before they were formed, for their sake he furnished the world with everything they would need, indeed, with an immense profusion of resources. Thus, they were rich before they were born. But if God had such care for us before we existed, he will by no means leave us destitute of food and the other necessities of life now that we are placed in the world. Yet if he often seems to keep his hand closed to us, that is to be attributed to our sins. Commentary on Genesis 1:26.[48]

Dominion Is but a Secondary Part of God's Image.

Wolfgang Capito: The power to rule over animals of either kind is not the image of God, but an effect thereof. For external activity and interacting with other things that are outside oneself follow from one's substance and one's implanted character. As [Adam] could not have been made otherwise than in the image and according to the likeness of God, it is appropriate if he himself ought to be mastered by royal authority in other matters. . . . On the other hand, since Adam was made in the image and according to the likeness of God and was thereby made to obey God, it was fitting that by giving him authority, the fish of the sea, the birds of heaven and the animals of the earth were, for their part, obeying him in the same way as he himself obeyed God the Creator. Truly, just as he resembled God in goodness, wisdom and righteousness, it was also fitting for him to obtain the faculty of divine authority in governing the world. On God's Work of the Six Days.[49]

Dominion Is Not by Bodily Strength.

Peter Martyr Vermigli: If you ask by which of these powers they would exercise dominion, it's certainly not by their physical powers, for with respect to these, humans are surpassed by many animals. Therefore it is by reasoning, deliberation and skill, by which not only are these creatures defeated and captured, but vast numbers [of them] are both moved and changed. This power is restored primarily by faith: "You will tread upon the asp and the serpent" (Ps 91[:13]). Commentary on Genesis 1:28.[50]

Dominion Implies Stewardship.

Wolfgang Musculus: Dominion over the beasts is conceded to us so that we might use it not to gratify our willful desires but to provide for our needs. If they have done harm to our needs, we should exert our God-given authority over them. People therefore act like tyrants when they take such extensive pleasure in hunting wild beasts that they do not wish them to be confined in submission even when they lay waste to their crops, and whole herds take for themselves what with great effort had been prepared for the use of wives and children, indeed, for everyone. On the other hand, I would by no means approve allowing anyone whatsoever to hunt animals in any way they like without regard to order. For an unbounded and indiscriminate liberty is not advantageous to most people. There are limits, laws and boundaries by which the desire of mortals [to exploit] animals ought to be restrained, not only for the sake of the animals but also for the common benefit of humankind. Commentary on Genesis 1:28.[51]

Human Dominion Was Meant to Reveal God's Glory.

Peter Riedemann: God has created heaven and earth and everything in them out of nothing, for his honor and glory. Because God was one and alone, there was no one else to know him. This was not sufficient for his glory and divinity, since he could be praised by no one. In order, therefore, that God's glory, majesty, and divinity might be seen, known, and praised, he created

---

[48]CTS 1:96* (CO 23:27). [49]Hexemeron (1539), 280v-81v. [50]In Primum Librum Mosis (1569), 7r. [51]In Mosis Genesim (1554), 46.

heaven and earth and everything in them. He made heaven his throne but gave the earth with all that adorns it to people, making them rulers over it so that they might learn to know the Creator and Overseer. . . . Thus it is evident that all of God's creatures, whatever they may be, are given to teach and to lead people to God. As soon as people became perverse and turned away from God, the Creation also became perverted for them, so that what had formerly served for people's benefit now, on the contrary, served for their harm. . . . Thus, though Creation should lead the unbeliever to God, it does the opposite and leads the unbeliever away from God. Creation, however, reveals that it is not Creation itself but people's evil will and unjust acquisition and use of Creation by which they have become corrupted and made worthless. CONFESSION OF FAITH.[52]

OUR DISTORTED DOMINION. JOHANNES BRENZ: Because our God is the Lord of all things, he wished to represent this part of himself in human beings and to make them lords over things on earth and in the sea, so that God's majesty might be sketched, so to speak, by this human dominion. . . . The first thing to consider, however, is that what is recounted here about the dominion of human beings was said before humans sinned and, by that sin, defected from God. For if human beings had not sinned, their dominion would have remained secure and unimpaired. . . . But after that sin, this dominion is partly lost, partly disturbed and confused, and for the sake of preserving some tranquility in the land, it was necessary to institute new orders and laws by which human greed would be curbed and people would be constrained by a degree of external justice. From here derives the domination of women by men; from here, the distinction of lord and servant; from here, the authority of magistrate over subject. From here arise so many kinds of laws, rights and punish-

ments; from here flows the anxious and meticulous division of property, along with pacts, charters, signatures and seals, deeds, receipts, and other contracts. And yet neither public nor private tranquility can be preserved even by these means: such is the effect of sin! COMMENTARY ON GENESIS 1:28.[53]

DOMINION IS MOSTLY LOST NOW, BUT WE MAY LEARN FROM ITS VESTIGES. WOLFGANG MUSCULUS: Some ask of this text how could it be true that humans dominate the fish of the sea and the birds of the air, when they do not even dominate the beasts of the earth—not to mention fish, which are far removed from human activities, and birds, which fly off into the open air! Chrysostom responds to this question that, after sin, this dominion was abolished by divine mandate, so that now we have disobedient and hostile beasts where before sin they had been obedient. . . . Basil contends that glimmering traces of this dominion survive to this day, a great measure of which he then discerns in the ingenuity by which beasts, having been seized with terror at the sight of a man, scamper away from the herd, whereby they are either captured or forced into service. Consequently, I regard it as established that the fullness of this dominion has been lost to the human race through sin, so that the disobedience of beasts should prompt us to ponder the evil of having violated the divine precept. Moreover, some relics of it survive to this day, so that we might be led by them to a recollection of this lost authority, which is also safeguarded in our circumstances by God's benevolence. At the same time it is to be considered that this authority has been restored to us through Christ, so that not only the fish of the sea, the birds of the air and the beasts of the earth, but all things in the universe—the world, life, death, the present and the future, Paul,

---

[52]CRR 9:62-63, alluding to Is 66:1. [53]Opera 1:23.

Apollos, Cephas—are ours. COMMENTARY ON GENESIS 1:26-27.[54]

WERE WILD ANIMALS MEANT FOR DOMINION? PETER MARTYR VERMIGLI: A problem arises with respect to this domination over the animals: Why were those wild beasts that afflict human beings created? My answer is, so that wicked children might be castigated. After sin, there was need for a whip, because sin has armed our own servants against us. Accordingly, the attacks of beasts are inflicted by God, as Scripture attests in Ezekiel, "I will send famine and wild beasts against you." When human beings were righteousness, all the animals obeyed them as tame and domesticated. But now, although they may rebel, it is God's mercy that only a few die from it; and if some *are* killed by them, the benefit derived from it for us is twofold. First, it is an example of divine severity, as in the case of the Samaritans who were killed by lions, or the boys who mocked Elisha and were killed by bears, or the disobedient prophet whom a lion killed. It shows, moreover, how great God's majesty is, that wild beasts should avenge an insult to him or anything of this sort. Second, you should take note here of God's goodness to us, for he has removed these harmful animals to the wilderness and desert places and allows them to wander about to some extent only at night. A person may also see here our calamity after sin, that one so great and so large should die from the sting of a tiny scorpion or from the bite of a mad dog. Nonetheless, despite our sin, beasts have not entirely been able to shake off the yoke placed on them, and they are terrified and tremble when they see us. Not only that, you may well see a boy leading, striking or threatening the largest of brute beasts, yet they fear in him the image of that God. COMMENTARY ON GENESIS 1:28.[55]

DOMINION DID NOT EXTEND TO EVERY INDIVIDUAL ANIMAL. CARDINAL CAJETAN:

See what results from humankind having been made in the image of God—the results, I say, relative to other animals. Moses speaks in the plural number, "*they* will make subjects," in order to signify that not one person but a multitude of people will subjugate animals. And he speaks with no less care when he adds the preposition *among*, saying "among the fish of the air and among the birds, etc." Clearly, it is thereby signified that even a multitude of people will not subjugate *all* the fish of the sea, nor all the birds, nor thus the other creatures—always assuming that no animal is marked as exempt so that it couldn't be subjugated by somebody, just as no part of the earth is released from subjection to humankind. COMMENTARY ON GENESIS 1:28.[56]

OUR DOMINION OVER THE BEASTS SURVIVES IN FOUR WAYS. ANDREW WILLET: Human rule and dominion was absolute before the fall, for not only would humans then have been of more excellent government by reason of their excellent wisdom to keep the creatures in subjection, but the beasts, by God's providence, would also have had a natural inclination to obedience—of which we have a precedent in Genesis 2, when all the creatures presented themselves before Adam to receive their names from him. Since Adam's fall, this preeminence and dominion . . . over the beasts is greatly diminished and impaired, that as he first disobeyed his Creator, so they also have cast off our yoke. Yet, notwithstanding, though we now have not so absolute a command over the creatures, the lordship and authority which is exercised over the creatures still remains, by these four ways and means. First, there yet remains a natural instinct of obedience in those creatures which are for human use, as in the ox, ass, horse, wherein

---

[54]*In Mosis Genesim* (1554), 42, citing 1 Cor 3:22.   [55]*In Primum Librum Mosis* (1569), 7r, citing Ezek 5:17; 2 Kings 17:25; 2 Kings 2:24; 1 Kings 13:24.   [56]*Commentarii illustres* (1539), 13-14.

God's mercy appears, that though we by sin be deprived of authority over the wild and great beasts, as lions [and] bears, yet the more necessary and serviceable creatures are kept in subjection still. . . . Secondly, God by his extraordinary work and miracle subdues the fierce and cruel beasts unto human beings, as when they all came unto Noah in the ark, the lions' mouths were stopped against Daniel, [or when] the viper had no power to hurt Paul. Thirdly, this dominion lost by Adam is restored by Christ and the beasts are subdued to the faithful when the Lord sees fit. . . . Thus by God's providence many of his children have been preserved, as Jonah by his faithful prayer was preserved in the belly of the whale. . . . Fourthly, sometimes people subdue beasts by their strength, as Sampson slew a lion and David a bear; or, where strength fails, by intellect and cunning, as James 3:7 says. COMMENTARY ON GENESIS 1:28.[57]

SUBDUING THE EARTH DOES NOT WARRANT TYRANNY. WOLFGANG MUSCULUS: That we inhabit this earth and subject it to our authority is something we do by divine right, because it was subjected to us at the very outset of creation by our creator himself. We should not claim its use for ourselves either just because we can or because we are people endowed with reason, wisdom and what not; but rather because that authority was conceded to us at the very outset of our race. For this reason, those who are godly will claim nothing for themselves from the whole earth that does not conform to this divine concession. But the ungodly claim for themselves authority over ever so much of the earth based on what God said, "Subdue the earth," . . . as if that authority were clearly unrestricted and granted to human beings in such a way that God would retain no rights for himself over it but would possess authority only in heaven. Against this impious notion, one should bear in mind what the apostle proposed to the Athenians in Acts

17[:24-46]. . . . Therefore the earth is subjected to you in such a way that the places and times of its habitation are determined by God. We must detest the arrogance of those who try to subject any regions they desire to their tyranny and to extend their dominion beyond legitimate boundaries. Nonetheless, whatever they may undertake to do, they will not subject as much land as they desire nor control more riches on earth than divine majesty allows. COMMENTARY ON GENESIS 1:28.[58]

HUMAN DOMINION IS LIMITED BY GOD'S COMMAND. JOHN CALVIN: Humanity had already been created with this injunction, that they should subject the earth to themselves, but now they are finally given possession of this right when they hear what the Lord has given them. Moses expresses this still more fully in the next verse, when he introduces God as granting them the plants and fruits. For it is of great importance that we touch nothing of God's bounty but what we know he has permitted us, nor can we enjoy anything with a good conscience unless we receive it as if from the hand of God. COMMENTARY ON GENESIS 1:28.[59]

USE CREATURES, ENJOY GOD. KONRAD PELLIKAN: It is not a study of brambles but an impression carefully and faithfully derived, that we should *use* creatures but *enjoy* only God, that we might be his suppliants and obedient to him. COMMENTARY ON GENESIS 1:30.[60]

1:31 "God Saw Everything That He Had Made, and Behold, It Was Very Good"

---

[57]*Hexapla* (1608), 17. [58]*In Mosis Genesim* (1554), 46. Musculus goes on to cite Alexander the Great as a ruler still limited by God, despite his fortunate career. [59]CTS 1:98-99* (CO 23:29). [60]*Commentaria Bibliorum* (1532) 1:3v. This is Augustine's well-known distinction between *uti* and *frui*: only God is worthy of our highest love, and all lesser attachments should serve one's love of God.

The Creator's Wisdom Exceeds Our Understanding. Konrad Pellikan: God approved of everything he made and the ordering of these things, and therefore they were good, elegant and useful. Nothing in the whole world was made rashly or without an appropriate purpose, even if the reasons and causes of what he made are unknown to us on account of our fragility of understanding. Commentary on Genesis 1:31.[61]

God's Approval Is Not Passive. Peter Martyr Vermigli: For God, to see something is for him to approve it. Nor does God approve a thing because he discovers something of good in it, but it is rather the case that some good things are discerned in a thing because that thing pleases and is approved by God. The whole is deservedly said to be "very good," because common benefits are always preferred over private ones. It is said of each thing individually that it is *good*, but now it is said generally of the whole that it is *very good*. Commentary on Genesis 1:31.[62]

God's Approval Preceded the Goodness of Creatures Rather Than Followed It. William Perkins: God, in framing his creatures in the beginning, made them good—yea, very good. Now the goodness of the creature is nothing else but the perfect estate of the creature, whereby it was conformable to the will and mind of the Creator allowing and approving of it when he had made it. For a creature is not first good and then approved of God; but because it is approved of God, therefore it is good. But wherein, will some say, stands this goodness of the creature? *I answer*, in three things. First, in the comeliness, beauty and glory of every work. . . . Second, in the excellence of the virtue which God has given to it: for as he has appointed every creature for some special end, so he has fitted and furnished it with sufficient power and virtue for the accomplishing of the same

end. Third, in the exceeding benefit and profitableness that came by them to human beings. But since humanity's fall, this goodness of the creature is partly corrupted and partly diminished. Therefore when we see any want, defect or deformity in any of them, we must have recourse back again to the apostasy of our first parents, and remember our fall in them, and say with a sorrowful heart: this comes to pass by reason of our most wretched sin, which has defiled heaven and earth, and drawn a curse not only upon ourselves, but upon the rest of the creatures for our sake, whereby their goodness is much defaced. Exposition of the Apostles' Creed.[63]

Were Noxious Creatures Also "Very Good"? Andrew Willet: The Manichaeans here objected that God created many things hurtful and pernicious to humans, such as venomous and harmful herbs and beasts [and] many superfluous things for which humans have no use, so how were all things created good? Augustine answers this objection most fully, saying, first, that God has made nothing superfluous, even if we do not know a thing's use: just as in an artisan's workshop, we do not condemn those instruments and tools that we are ignorant of, even if we cut our hands with them. Second, we need not complain of those things that are profitable or superfluous, for the latter hurt not and the former are for our use; and by those which are pernicious, we are either punished, or exercised, or terrified. "Use the useful creatures, take heed of the dangerous, and leave the superfluous ones alone." To this answer of Augustine, it may be added that these noxious creatures, which now serve for our correction, would not have been hurtful if humanity had not fallen through transgression; and again, they are not now altogether unprofitable, for even those crea-

---

[61]*Commentaria Bibliorum* (1532) 1:3v. [62]*In Primum Librum Mosis* (1569), 8r. [63]*Works* (1608) 1:142-43.

tures that are venomous and not fit for food are yet profitable for medicine. COMMENTARY ON GENESIS 1:28.[64]

NOTHING WAS LACKING WHEN GOD FINISHED CREATING. JOHN CALVIN: Moses expresses more than he did previously, for he adds *meod*, that is, "very." Each of the other days was given a simple word of approval. But now, after the fabrication of the world was complete in all its parts, and had received, so to speak, the final and finishing touch, he declares it to be perfectly good, so that we may know that there is in the symmetry of God's works the highest perfection, to which nothing can be added. COMMENTARY ON GENESIS 1:31.[65]

---

[64]*Hexapla* (1608), 17, citing Augustine, *On Genesis against the Manichees* 1.16.26 [corrected]. [65]CTS 1:100* (CO 23:30).

2:1-3 GOD RESTS ON THE SEVENTH DAY

[1]*Thus the heavens and the earth were finished, and all the host of them.* [2]*And on the seventh day God finished his work that he had done, and he rested on the seventh day from all his work that he had done.* [3]*So God blessed the seventh day and made it holy, because on it God rested from all his work that he had done in creation.*

OVERVIEW: If the sixth day represents the crown of God's creative activity, it is nonetheless upstaged by the seventh, when God rested from his labors. All traditional commentators were well aware that God's rest was addressed by many other passages of Scripture—not just Exodus 20:11, where the Decalogue enjoins Sabbath-keeping on the grounds of God's own resting on the seventh day, but also such chapters as Hebrews 3–4, where God's rest or sabbath is the eschatological hope of the people of God. Thus, both the Old Testament and the New anchor the practice of Sabbath-keeping, both as a command and as a promise, an imperative and a blessing. All these themes emerge among Reformation commentators, who attempt to expound the wisdom of this divine arrangement for human beings and its rich implications.

2:1 *Finishing the Host of Heaven and Earth*

WE ARE GUARDED BY GOD'S EARTHLY HOST, TOO. MARTIN LUTHER: Moses . . . uses military terminology in this passage and calls the stars and the luminaries of heaven the army or host of heaven; but men, beasts, and trees he calls the host of the earth. Perhaps he does this in view of later usage, because later on God calls Himself the God of the armies or of the hosts, that is, not only of the angels or of the spirits but of the entire creation, which carries on warfare for Him and serves Him. After Satan had been cast away by God on account of his sin, he was filled with such hatred of God and of man that, if he were able, he would in one moment rob the sea of its fish, the air of its birds, the earth of its fruits of every kind, and would destroy everything. But God created all these creatures to be in active military service, to fight for us continually against the devil, as well as against men, and to serve us and be of use to us. LECTURES ON GENESIS 2:1.[1]

2:2 God Rested from All His Work

GOD'S RESTING IS ACTIVE AND VIGILANT. JOHANNES BRENZ: When it is said that God rested on the seventh day, one should not suppose that he would have deserted this world and led a life of leisure. Rather, it is said that he rested on the seventh day because he did not continue by building a new physical world but was satisfied with protecting, administering and governing this one. Indeed, when the Lord says of Zion, "This is my resting place for ever and ever," one should not think that he would remain idly encamped in Zion but that he would defend and guard Zion against its enemies, not desert it. Whence it is added, "Here I will dwell, for I have desired it." COMMENTARY ON GENESIS 2:1-3.[2]

GOD RESTED BECAUSE CREATION WAS PERFECT. MARTIN LUTHER: When Moses states that the Lord rested, he is speaking about the original state of the world. Because there was no sin, nothing new was created in it. There were neither thorns nor thistles, neither serpents nor toads; and if there were any, they were neither venomous nor vicious. Thus he is speaking about the creation of the world in its perfection. At that time the world was pure and innocent because man was pure and innocent. Now, when man is different on account of sin, the world, too, has begun to be different; that is, the fall of man was followed by the depravation and the curse of the creation. LECTURES ON GENESIS 2:2.[3]

DIVINE PROVIDENCE NEVER RESTS. JOHN CALVIN: With good reason, it is customary to ask what kind of rest this was. Given that God sustains the world by his power, governs it by his providence, nourishes all creatures and even propagates them, it is certain that he is constantly at work. Therefore that saying of Christ is true, that his Father and he himself had been working from the beginning until now, because if God were to withdraw his hand even a little, all things would immediately perish and dissolve into nothing, as is declared in Psalm 104:29. Truly, God is not properly acknowledged as the creator of heaven and earth unless we also ascribe to him that uninterrupted activity of invigorating all things. But the solution of the difficulty is well known: God ceased from all his work, in that he desisted from the creation of new kinds of things. COMMENTARY ON GENESIS 2:2.[4]

HOW COULD GOD REST IF, AS JESUS SAYS, HIS FATHER ALWAYS WORKS? WOLFGANG MUSCULUS: Here it is asked how Moses could write that God completed his works on the seventh day and rested from them, when it would more befit him never to cease from his works, just as Christ says in John 5, "My Father is working to this moment, and I am working." Daily he creates new souls, daily he fashions new individuals, ceaselessly he works, governing and conserving the universe with its parts: heaven, earth, sea, and all the kinds of creatures that are contained therein, none of which could endure without divine attention, not even for a moment, and still less on the seventh day. Nor indeed are God's works so constructed that after they have been made they would require no further work from their maker: just as the works of artisans, when finished, can endure on their own without extra work from the artisan. So when God never ceases from his works, it is asked, how can Moses say here that on the seventh day he

---

[1]LW 1:74 (WA 42:57). [2]*Opera* 1:29; citing Ps 132:14. [3]LW 1:77-78 (WA 42:59). [4]CTS 1:103-4* (CO 23:31-32).

completed his works and rested from them? And here the Manichaeans quibble that Moses contradicts the gospel of God.

The answer is that God rested not absolutely, from all his works, but only from those that he had created during the six days and had now completed. So Moses does not simply say, "And God completed his work on the seventh day," but he adds, "which he had made." And when he had said, "He rested on the seventh day from all his work," again he appends, "which he had accomplished," so that he might indicate not that God rested from paying close attention to things needing to be done, but from those works that he had created: not so that he would not govern and guide them, but so that he added nothing to them by way of creation that had not been there before. Thus let no one conclude from these words that God was utterly at leisure after the works of the six days and that the things that happen in heaven and on earth and in the sea come to pass by their own natural powers, but let us understand that Moses speaks about God's resting in this way, so that we do not contradict other passages of Scripture or the words of Christ. COMMENTARY ON GENESIS 2:1-3.[5]

THE SEVENTH DAY OF CREATION PERPETUALLY REPEATS. JOHANNES BRENZ: Nothing of the other six days recurs as it was in the beginning. Indeed, no new physical world is created in the way it happened on the other days: no earth, no heaven, no sun, no stars. Everything remains in its order, just as it was created on those six days. But the seventh day constantly repeats, according to his plan, and it perpetually returns, because God always remains in this world to govern it. . . . None of the days of this world repeat, except for the seventh day, for this purpose: that we might know God, serve God, and glorify God. That is why we have been put here. COMMENTARY ON GENESIS 2:1-3.[6]

2:3 God Made the Seventh Day Holy

THE PURPOSE OF THE SEVENTH DAY.
MARTIN LUTHER: It follows, therefore, from this passage that if Adam had remained in the state of innocence, he nevertheless would have held the seventh day sacred. That is, on this day he would have given his descendants instructions about the will and worship of God; he would have praised God; he would have given thanks; he would have sacrificed, etc. On the other days he would have tilled his fields and tended his cattle. Indeed, even after the Fall he kept this seventh day sacred; that is, on this day he instructed his family, of which the sacrifices of his sons Cain and Abel give the proof. Therefore from the beginning of the world the Sabbath was intended for the worship of God. LECTURES ON GENESIS 2:3.[7]

THE SABBATH WAS SANCTIFIED SO THAT WE MIGHT BE HOLY. HULDRYCH ZWINGLI: Here's what we say, lest someone suppose that God bestowed sanctity on this day beyond any of the others. Indeed, the Sabbath is in no way better or holier than the rest of the days if considered in itself. But it *is* holier when we ourselves are holier on that day. God sanctified the Sabbath, therefore, not to delight us with holidays or leisure time, but so that we might be freed from all our labors to assemble on that day and recall God's blessings with gratitude, attend to his law and his word, worship him, serve him, and then exercise care for our neighbors. ANNOTATIONS ON GENESIS 2:3.[8]

SABBATH-KEEPING IS PART OF IMAGING GOD. ANDREAS BODENSTEIN VON KARLSTADT: God laid out before us all commandments and prohibitions to make us aware of our inner image and likeness, and to under-

---

[5]*In Mosis Genesim* (1554), 50. [6]*Opera* 1:30. [7]LW 1:79-80 (WA 42:60). [8]ZSW 13:16.

stand how God created us in his image to become as God is, i.e., holy, tranquil, good, just, wise, strong, truthful, kind, merciful, etc. All commandments of God demand of us to be godlike; in fact, they have been given us so that we might be conformed to God. . . . Thus the Sabbath has been instituted by God that we might desire to become holy as God is holy and rest like him, letting go of our works as he did and yet perform God's work in a passive manner for eternity, so that God may do our work without ceasing. This is a spiritual reason for the Sabbath which was commanded to honor God and to benefit us. For God is honored when his children become like him who is our Father. We should regard this foundation alone and not our own benefit. Just as God is concerned about our benefit and holiness, so we, too, are to be concerned about and seek God's glory, honor, and the benefit of the neighbor, not of ourselves. Regarding the Sabbath and Holy Days.[9]

The Sabbath Is a Sign of Our Immortality. Martin Luther: It is also shown here that man was especially created for the knowledge and worship of God; for the Sabbath was not ordained for sheep and cows but for men, that in them the knowledge of God might be developed and might increase. Therefore although man lost his knowledge of God, nevertheless God wanted this command about sanctifying the Sabbath to remain in force. On the seventh day He wanted men to busy themselves both with His Word and with the other forms of worship established by Him, so that we might give first thought to the fact that this nature was created chiefly for acknowledging and glorifying God. Moreover, this is also written that we might preserve in our minds a sure hope of the future and eternal life. All the things God wants done on the Sabbath are clear signs of another life after this life. Why is it necessary for God to speak with us through His Word if we are not to live

in a future and eternal life? If we are not to hope for a future life, why do we not live like people with whom God does not speak and who do not know God? But because the Divine Majesty speaks to man alone and man alone knows and apprehends God, it necessarily follows that there is another life after this life; to attain it we need the Word and the knowledge of God. For this temporal and present life is a physical life, such as all the beasts live that do not know God and the Word. Lectures on Genesis 2:3.[10]

Holiness and Obedience, Not Idleness. Peter Martyr Vermigli: Here, to *sanctify* is to set something aside for divine worship. . . . And God sanctified the Sabbath by this very act, when he rested from his work. Later on, he not only replicated this sanctification [of the Sabbath day] in the Law, but he also observed it in his actions, when on that particular day he did not provide manna for the people in the wilderness. But should the people of God be idle on that day, or any other? By no means, but just as God did not cease from all activity . . . but only from the making of things in *nature*, so also should we abstain from the deeds of our *damaged* nature. We should not be deterred from obeying God's promptings— on the contrary, on holy days we ought to pursue this one work even more. Paul explains it like this in Hebrews 4:10: we should abstain not from all works whatsoever, but from *our own* works, which is something a Christian should do one's whole life long. Hence, we shouldn't be accused in Christianity of not observing the Sabbath, when we have consecrated every moment of our life as a sabbath. Commentary on Genesis 2:3.[11]

"Resting" on the Seventh Day Means Meditating on God. John Calvin: This

---

[9]CRR 8:319. [10]LW 1:80-81 (WA 42:60-61). [11]*In Primum Librum Mosis* (1569), 8r-9v.

benediction is nothing else than a solemn consecration, by which God claims for himself our devotion and activities on the seventh day. This is indeed a proper subject for lifelong meditation, one in which we should daily exercise ourselves in this magnificent theater of heaven and earth to consider God's unfathomable goodness, justice, power and wisdom. However, if people should happen to pay attention to this subject with less seriousness than it deserves, every seventh day has been specially chosen for the purpose of supplying what was lacking in their regular meditation. First, therefore, God rested; then he blessed this rest, so that people throughout the ages might hold it sacred. Or one might say that he dedicated every seventh day to rest, so that his own example might be a perpetual rule. But the design of the institution must be always kept in mind: for God did not command us simply to have a holiday every seventh day, as if he delighted in our indolence, but rather that, by releasing us from all other business, we might more readily apply our minds to the creator of the world. In short, it is a sacred calling that snatches people from the world's distractions in order to dedicate them entirely to God. COMMENTARY ON GENESIS 2:3.[12]

SABBATH REST IS THE SOUL'S BEST WORK.
ANNA MARIA VAN SCHURMAN:
> The world was now complete,
>   and God himself was said to rest,
> which teaches us to let our souls
>   delight in God as best.
> God blessed this day
>   in order to imply
> that God's first church
>   this day should sanctify.
> Even if its body was strong,
>   it was to save its strength
> by waxing stronger yet again
>   through quiet rest at length.
> To praise God's holy name—
>   this would be rest for the soul,

> which, like heaven, took
>   delight in never-ending toil.
> Thus God gave to each a day
>   by which both would be pleased:
> to one he gave more work,
>   while the other's work would cease.
> But human beings shall not
>   enjoy complete respite
> until both body and soul
>   in heaven's work delight.
> It was their duty, then,
>   that garden to cultivate,
> but this day of rest
>   to celebrate and consecrate
> as a sign that their toil must here
>   be laid aside, however blessed,
> and to signal that after such work
>   they would enter heaven's rest.
> The work of the spiritual life
>   thus here becomes our story:
> to go from virtue to virtue
>   and to give God his glory.
> Yet as this work and rest
>   could mean pain for us as well,
> that day could also be an image
>   of our grave, or hell.
> God rested from his very first works
>   on that holy day;
> yet another day of rest is seen
>   in what follows, I say,
> after God's works of grace:
>   in that everlasting repose
> when the church leaves the earth
>   and the old labors there imposed.
> PARAPHRASE OF GENESIS 1–3.[13]

IF WE FAIL TO REST IN GOD, WE ALSO MISUNDERSTAND GOD. JOHANNES OECOLAMPADIUS: Let us learn here that the Sabbath day was made for us, so that we might rest from our evil works and, truly, be restored in God. It is our highest dignity if we have come to God. On the seventh day God rested, but

---

[12]CTS 1:105-6* (CO 23:33). [13]*Uitbreiding*, 7.3-26.

we find no rest unless we leave off from all the works of this world. For he wishes to say that if we realize that everything was made on our account and that God wishes us well, we should seek true rest in him. So long as we delight in lesser things we cannot be satisfied, and the earth is not rightly perfected in us, and it seems to us that God has not completed his own work, because we are not at rest. Lectures on Genesis 2:2.[14]

Forced Rest and Boredom Also Serve God's Purposes. Andreas Bodenstein von Karlstadt: We must consider diligently that leisure brings forth boredom and was commanded [so] that we experience tedium and ennui when we rest in God and experience leisure like God. Through leisure, among other things, God commanded those who are tougher and stronger and well able to work (and who greatly delight in their work), to break their delight and fall into listlessness and dread of life and . . . think on how evil, fragile, foolish, weak, loveless, and without faith in God they are; how they pursue greed and are full of anxiety and do not seek God's honor uprightly nor take God's commandments to heart or do them when they work. Such reflection of their evil will is caused by idle ennui or boring idleness. Therefore, we must observe the Sabbath diligently and learn how ennui or listlessness is useful and why God urges us to be idle. But we must be careful not to turn leisure into pleasure for the simple reason that it is better to enter a house of mourning than to enter a house of pleasure, for God has imposed idleness on us to make the Sabbath also a day of renunciation, sadness, and tribulation. Regarding the Sabbath and Holy Days.[15]

We Should Admire God's Works in Creation, Especially on the Sabbath. William Perkins: Whereas God the Father is creator of all things and has given us reason, understanding and ability more than to other creatures, we are taught to consider and meditate on the work of God's creation. This the sage teaches us, saying, "Consider the work of God." And indeed it is a special duty of everyone who professes to be a member of God's church, as he or she acknowledges God to be the Creator, so to look upon his workmanship and view and consider all creatures. A skillful worker can have no greater disgrace than, after having done some famous thing, to have a friend pass by the work and not so much as look upon it. If it be demanded for what end we must look upon the work of God's creation, I answer that in it we may see and discern God's power, wisdom, love, mercy and providence, and all his attributes, and in all things his glory. This is a most necessary duty to be learned by everyone: we think nothing too much or too good to bestow on vain shows and plays, idle sports and pastimes, which are human vanities, and we do most willingly behold them, meanwhile utterly neglecting and holding in contempt the glorious work of God's creation. Well, the Lord has appointed his Sabbath to be sanctified not only by the public ministry of the word and by private prayer, but also by a special consideration of and meditation on God's creatures: and therefore the duty of everyone is this, distinctly and seriously to view and consider the creatures of God; and thereby take occasion to glorify his name by ascribing unto him the wisdom, glory, power and omnipotence that is due unto him. . . . Exposition of the Apostles' Creed.[16]

Sabbath Is an Antidote for the Curse of Labor and Sweat. Andreas Bodenstein von Karlstadt: God has shown us great mercy in relieving us from the serious and strict command to work daily. For . . . if

---

[14]*In Genesim* (1536), 27r-v. [15]CRR 8:338, alluding to Eccles 7:2.
[16]*Works* (1608) 1:144.

we are to eat our bread in the sweat of our brow, we have to work every day and make up for Adam's desire by our disinclination and labor, which would be rather too hard and unbearable. For not only is Adam's disobedience atoned by us, but the constant labor also means that in the long run we must die, for Scripture says that unbearable work ages us and leads to our death. It would not be unreasonable for God to do away with us and kill us through work. God is fully in the right to strangle us with work and reduce us to ashes. But God our Lord has shown paternal love and unmerited mercy toward us. He does not remain angry forever nor does he want to exterminate us. Therefore, God issued the commandment of the Sabbath by which we are to work for six days only. The seventh day he set aside for a Sabbath and a day of leisure for our benefit, so that we might revive and strengthen ourselves and restore our exhausted strength. For this we cannot sufficiently thank the merciful God. REGARDING THE SABBATH AND HOLY DAYS.[17]

"REST" BEFITS BOTH THE SEVENTH DAY AND THE LORD'S DAY. PETER MARTYR VERMIGLI: This verse reminds people that if they are directed by the church to keep themselves free for divine worship on some day of the week, this is by no means a human invention, nor does it only concern the law of Moses. Rather, it took its beginning from here, and it also contributes to our imitation of God. But if you ask why this day of observance has not been retained in our church, I answer that we certainly have retained it, in that we ought to regard all such days as a time to rest from our works. But if one day is chosen for the external worship of God over another, it is because through Christ the church was free to decide what it considered more appropriate. Nor did the church choose the worst course if, for observing the Lord's day, it preferred the memory of perfection's restoration (that is,

Christ's resurrection) to the memory of when the making of this world was completed. Yet there were also works that were not forbidden on the Sabbath, and they should have been particularly occupied by them. So, too, with our feast days, everything that pertains to the worship of God is to be recommended, such as hearing the word of God, praying, praising God's name, along with serving our neighbors. COMMENTARY ON GENESIS 2:3.[18]

HOLY SATURDAY WAS ALSO THE SABBATH. JOHANNES OECOLAMPADIUS: Another mystery ought to be brought up here, one that the saints often mention. The day when the human being was created was the same day, of course, that Christ suffered, the sixth day, and he rested in the tomb on the Sabbath. Thus when God at that time also rested from his own works, and when on the cross he cried out "It is finished!" doubtless both these things were brought together for the salvation of the human race, and it was fitting to portray it both as the grave and as rest. If we have been buried with Christ, with him also we rightly rest. We have to die to this world and thus rest with him in order for us to rise into glory and newness of life. This will be the Sabbath rest of all creatures, when we too rise in glory incorruptible. Therefore God blessed the seventh day on our account, that we might truly be blessed if we keep it. Therefore let no one bring this day into disrepute, as if it should be cursed and detestable. LECTURES ON GENESIS 2:3.[19]

THE MORAL SABBATH LOOKS TO AN ETERNAL SABBATH. ANDREW WILLET: There are three purposes for observing the Lord's day: *a religious and holy use*, for to this end by his own example and commandment did the Lord consecrate this day to be spent in holy exer-

---

[17]CRR 8:337. [18]*In Primum Librum Mosis* (1569), 9r. [19]*In Genesim* (1536), 28r-v.

cises; *the civil or political use* of the Lord's day is for the rest of ourselves, our servants and cattle; *the ceremonial or symbolical end* was to shadow forth our spiritual rest in Christ. In this last respect, I confess the ceremony of the Sabbath to be abolished in part: for it is a symbol still of our everlasting rest in heaven (Heb 4:9). But in the other two respects, the law of the Lord's day is perpetual. . . . As the Sabbath came in with the first man, so must it

not go out but with the last: for if keeping a day of rest holy unto the Lord be part of the moral law (as it cannot be denied), then it must continue as long as the Lord has his church on earth, and the moral sabbath must stand till the everlasting sabbath succeed in its place. COMMENTARY ON GENESIS 2.[20]

---

[20]*Hexapla* (1608), 40-41.

2:4-7 THE FORMATION OF THE FIRST MAN

⁴*These are the generations*
of the heavens and the earth when they were created,
in the day that the LORD *God made the earth and the heavens.*

⁵*When no bush of the field*ᵃ *was yet in the land*ᵇ *and no small plant of the field had yet sprung up—for the* LORD *God had not caused it to rain on the land, and there was no man to work the ground,* ⁶*and a mist*ᶜ *was going up from the land and was watering the whole face of the ground—*⁷*then the* LORD *God formed the man of dust from the ground and breathed into his nostrils the breath of life, and the man became a living creature.*

a Or *open country*   b Or *earth*; also verse 6   c Or *spring*

OVERVIEW: Just like its predecessor, the second chapter of Genesis was commonly treated by Jewish and Christian commentators as an encyclopedia, with each detail of the text often serving as a springboard for all kinds of questions—many of them unanswerable without recourse to massive speculation. For instance, traditional commentators wondered why the first man was created outside of paradise, why he was made from earth or clay, whether his formation gave him greater dignity than the woman, and so forth. Often, ques-

tions about the prehistory of the earth and anthropology were imported into Genesis without the presence of any actual textual prompt, as in the case of the commonplace observation that the upright stature of human beings is a testimony that we are uniquely designed to contemplate heaven while yet remaining on earth.

Once again, Reformation commentators were well aware of these questions and were not beyond considering many of them. At the same time, they often made it a point of pride to note how they were really setting such questions aside, along with various traditional allegories, in favor of a straightforward account of the literal sense of the text. Still, that same literal sense would not be functioning as Scripture if it did not also carry practical or moral implications for the reader, and the Reformation commentators excelled at bringing these applications to light. Two in particular emerge with respect to Adam's formation here: one is doxological and looks for ways that God's power and wisdom are attested by the various details; the other is more moralistic and focuses on the lessons we should absorb from Adam's (and our own) fashioning and the resulting perfection and original dignity of human beings.

2:4a *The Generations of Heaven and Earth*

MOSES DENIES THAT THE WORLD IS
ETERNAL. JOHN CALVIN: The design of Moses was to fix deeply in our minds the origin of heaven and earth, which he designates by the word *generation*. For there have always been ungrateful and malignant people who have tried to obscure God's glory, either by feigning that the world is eternal or by obliterating the memory of the creation. COMMENTARY ON GENESIS 2:4.[1]

2:4b *The LORD God Made . . .*

GOD'S NAME HERE COMBINES SINGULAR-
ITY WITH THE PLURAL. WOLFGANG MUSCULUS: In Hebrew, this is the place where Moses begins to use the Tetragrammaton (YHWH) as a name for God. For up to now he has used only the word *Elohim*, that is, "gods" or "powers." But now he calls God *Yahweh Elohim*, which they[†] translate as "Lord God." They offer this explanation, that after the entire scheme of the universe had been completed and both humans and animals created,

thus splendidly declaring that *this* God is the one and true BEING, only then would that word YHWH be suitably used, that is, "Being," which belongs to God alone and may be shared with no creature. Next, as often as we see these two words *Yahweh Elohim* conjoined, we will reflect also on the mystery of the Holy Trinity. For *Yahweh* is singular in number, but *Elohim* is plural, as if you were to say "Being-Gods." In *Yahweh* there is the mystery of one divine essence, for that word is derived from HWH, which signifies "to be." But in *Elohim* there is the mystery in the divine nature of three persons. Therefore in these two words one may observe a divine nature that is one in essence and three in persons. COMMENTARY ON GENESIS 2:1-3.[2]

GOD'S COMPLETE TITLE ACCOMPANIES THE
COMPLETION OF HIS WORK. ANDREW WILLET: "In the day that the Lord God" is the first place of Scripture where the Lord is called by his name *Jehovah*.[†] The Hebrews give as a reason that, as *Elohim* is a name of power and justice given unto God in the creation, so now *Jehovah*, a name of mercy, is attributed to God [when] the whole work is finished, because therein his mercy appeared. Or rather, now, after God had made his work full and complete, he is also set forth in his full and complete titles. The Hebrews very superstitiously avoid reading or naming this word *Jehovah* and use instead *Adonai*, which word we confess is soberly to be used, and that it cannot fittingly be pronounced because it borrows all the vowel points from *Adonai*. We also condemn the heathens' profanation of this name, who from [it] derive other grammatical forms of the noun *Jupiter*, [namely,] *Jovis* and *Jovi*. Some would argue that this name *Jehovah*

---

[1]CTS 1:108-9* (CO 23:34). [2]*In Mosis Genesim* (1554), 55; the Hebrew here is unpointed in the Latin text. [†]*They* probably indicates a rabbinic reading; though Musculus does not elaborate, something along these lines is reported at Exodus 3 by Sebastian Münster's *Hebraica Biblia* (1534), 54v.

expresses the Trinity, because it consists of three kinds of letters; others by the double *he* (ה) understand the two natures of Christ, but this is too curious. It is derived from *haiah*, which signifies God's being and essence, and therefore he is called *Jehovah*, as [the One] by whom humans and all other things have their being. COMMENTARY ON GENESIS 2:4.[3]

2:5-6 No Plant Had Yet Sprung Up

IN THE BEGINNING, PLANTS WERE DIRECTLY NOURISHED BY GOD. JOHN CALVIN: It is not without reason that plants are again mentioned here, so that we might know that they were then produced, preserved and propagated in a manner different from that which we perceive today. For plants and trees are produced from seed, or grafts are taken from another plant's roots, or they grow by putting forth shoots—and human industry lends a hand. But at that time, the method was different: God clothed the earth not in the same manner as now (for there was neither seed nor root, nor plants to germinate). Rather, they would spring into existence, all of a sudden, at God's command and by the power of his word. That vitality persisted in order that they might stand firm by its effects rather than by the natural vegetative power that we now perceive. They survived not by the help of rain or human irrigation or cultivation, but because God watered the earth with vapor. COMMENTARY ON GENESIS 2:5.[4]

2:7a Formed of Dust from the Ground

THE RELATION OF GENESIS 2 TO GENESIS 1. MARTIN LUTHER: Moses is still dealing with a description of the work of the sixth day. What he had briefly stated in the first chapter: "Let Us make a man," that he wants to develop more fully in this chapter in order to establish the difference between man and the rest of the animals by more than a single

proof. And so he devotes the entire second chapter to describing the creation of man. LECTURES ON GENESIS 2:20.[5]

GOD DELIGHTS TO USE CREATURELY MEANS. JOHANNES BRENZ: It is not a sign of God's weakness that he does not create human beings from nothing in the way he had previously created the mass of heaven and earth, but used the clay that he had created earlier. Indeed, if he was able to create heaven and earth from nothing, certainly he could have created the human body from nothing, too! Rather, this stems from God's plan. He wished to signify that he had created his creatures not to be lazy and useless, but to be the tools or instruments that he would use to make whatever he wished. Truly, while God isn't the prisoner of his creatures but rather utterly free, in his ordinary activities he is nonetheless in the habit of using their labors, not condemning them. He does this with regard for us, that we should be in the habit of using those instruments, which are set before us so that we might pursue true and eternal life. God calls us to a heavenly life and commands us to make use of the preaching and hearing of his Word, as well as his sacraments. But there are many who think that it is not only unfitting but even absurd that the Holy Spirit, which is obviously a thing from heaven, should be given through things that are physical and quite common in their outward appearance. But let us consider that God made and ordained his creatures for this use, so that by them he might accomplish his works. We, therefore, should follow not so much his example as his decree. COMMENTARY ON GENESIS 2:4-7.[6]

GOD'S USE OF CLAY REMINDS US OF HIS POWER AND OUR HUMILITY. HULDRYCH

---

[3]*Hexapla* (1608), 26, crediting Junius and Mercerus. †*Jehovah* is an older way of translating YHWH, usually rendered today as *Yahweh*. [4]CTS 1:110-11* (CO 23:34-35). [5]LW 1:120 (WA 42:91). [6]*Opera* 1:31.

ZWINGLI: A lovely metaphor drawn from potters, who mentally conceive the form of some kind of vessel and then, applying their hands to the clay on the wheel, shape the model and finish it. In the same way, whatever God conceives of in his mind instantly takes place if he should will it. . . . The Hebrew signifies both clay and dust, but *clay* fits better here. These things remind us of our fashioning and origination. First, so that we might learn how impure, how unclean, nay, how humans are nothing without the spirit of God. Truly, clay soils, contaminates and befouls all things. So also the flesh, if left to itself, thinks and does nothing except what is filthy. Then we learn from this passage how unseemly it is for anyone to prefer himself to another, to grow prideful and puff up his chest, because we have all been fashioned from the same clay. What reason can clay and ashes have for haughtiness? ANNOTATIONS ON GENESIS 2:7.[7]

OUR BODIES ATTEST TO GOD'S CARE—AND OUR COMMON ORIGINS. KONRAD PELLIKAN:

After the world was made, the omnipotent Lord God himself shaped and molded the human body: not merely with the word of his mouth as the other things he had already produced, but as a potter does, as if with the application of his hand, forming it from the humblest elements of all, from clay and dust, from the slime of the earth. Let us always bear in mind, we terrestrial people of clay, our humble fashioning and origin: whether rich or poor, great or small by human standards, all alike were produced from the same humble and impure mass, and with the same fate. COMMENTARY ON GENESIS 2:7.[8]

A MIXTURE OF NOBILITY AND CLAY. JOHN CALVIN: He now explains what he had previously omitted in the man's creation, that his body was taken from the earth. He had said that he was formed "according to the image of God," and this is incomparably the

highest nobility. However, lest people use this nobility as an excuse for showing their disdain, their first origin is set before them, so that they might learn that this blessing was not theirs as a natural inheritance, even as Moses recounts that the man, in the beginning, was dust of the earth. Let foolish people now go and boast of the excellency of their nature! Concerning other animals it was said, "Let the earth bring forth every living creature." Now, however, Adam's body is formed of clay, devoid of sense, lest anyone exult in the flesh beyond measure. Anyone who does not learn humility from this is more than dense! COMMENTARY ON GENESIS 2:7.[9]

THE HUMBLE DIGNITY OF DUST AND CLAY. CHRISTOPHOR PELARGUS: If anything at all among the works of creation ought to be given serious consideration, certainly it is what we read written about our own creation. Indeed, it is not in vain that Moses repeated what seems to have been said in the first chapter: for it ought to be clearly implanted in our minds that we are a representation not of the stars, not of heaven, not of the earth, but of God himself. This is why he once again points out that humankind was formed by the Lord God (using words that point to the entire Holy Trinity). After the efficient cause, he adds the "from which" or material cause, namely, *from dust*, or *from the earth's dirt*: so that if we are deservedly regarded as noble on account of our creation, on account of our dirt and clay (really, what else are we?) we should always conduct ourselves more humbly. Accordingly, we must be mindful of our origin. At the same time, we should also consider here how great our dignity, that for our sake God handles dust, and fashions and shapes it with his inspiration so that it constitutes for him a home or a sort of temple

---

[7]ZSW 13:17-18. [8]*Commentaria Bibliorum* (1532) 1:4r. [9]CTS 1:111* (CO 23:35).

that he might dwell in. It is surely a great thing that potter's clay became a human being. It is a greater thing that, after we too have returned to dust, Jehovah condescends to touch it, raising us up and joining us to heavenly things. But greatest of all is that the Logos assumes our lump of clay! "Nothing is more sublime than God" (these are the words of Bernard), "nothing more vile than clay. And nonetheless, God descends into clay with such great worthiness, and with such great esteem the clay ascends to God. Thus, whatsoever God has done in it, the clay may be credited as having done; and whatsoever the clay has endured, God may be said to have suffered in it—as ineffable [there] as in the incomprehensible sacrament." COMMENTARY ON GENESIS 2:7.[10]

MORE LESSONS FROM CLAY. JOHANNES BRENZ:

While God could have fashioned human beings from a particle of heaven or even from the sun, he wished instead to use clay or dust. This reminds us of many things. First, God is pleased to demonstrate his diligence in this wonderful work. How great a display of diligence is it, to make from common clay such an eminent creature, distinguished by so many and so varied inward and outward parts, and to make it immortal and in his very own image? Indeed, at the very beginning, humans were made immortal. There are some who call a human being a *microcosm* or a little world, because it is as if a compendium of everything in the universe is contained in human beings. Next is seen how this miracle instructs us about the resurrection from the dead. Indeed, after humans sinned and became mortal on account of sin, they were liable to decay into clay and dust, just as they were at the beginning—which is why it was later said, "Dust you are and to dust you will return." It seems impossible that someone who has decayed into dust should rise up again to life. Therefore let us draw

near to our first condition. Indeed, he who created humans from clay and dust can and will recall to life those who have decayed into clay. No human can see a person by looking at clay, but God sees, and his vision is not vain or empty; and what he sees, he necessarily brings forth in due time. Eusebius writes that the pagans pursued the teaching of God about the resurrection of the dead with such hatred that they burned the martyrs' bodies and spread their remains together with others nearby, hoping thereby to forestall the resurrection. "Now let's see," they said, "whether they will rise again and whether their God can cause their scattered and dried-up ashes to coalesce again into a body!" But what scheme could be crazier? Cannot he who made us from dust not also raise us again from dust? Third, God was pleased to make human beings from clay or from a lump of clay so that we might always recognize in ourselves the arrogance and pride before God and towards our neighbor that ought to be suppressed. He had earlier created angels and distinguished them with great gifts, but many of them were taken with their own beauty and were lifted up with prideful hearts against God and lost their blessedness. So when God undertook to make human beings in an image like himself, that is, to be by far the noblest of the creatures, he took a mass of clay, the commonest stuff, so that every day we might think about our origin, not to exalt ourselves in our own minds, either against God our maker or against our neighbor whose origin is like ours, but to lower our crests and acknowledge God, to whom we owe all obedience. COMMENTARY ON GENESIS 2:4-7.[11]

---

[10]*In prophetarum oceanum* (1612), 46-47, alluding to Aristotle's notion of four causes and quoting Bernard of Clairvaux's *Sermon for the Vigil of the Lord's Nativity* 3.8 (PL 183:98). See *St. Bernard's Sermons on the Nativity* (reprint ed.; Devon: Augustine, 1985), 82.   [11]*Opera* 1:31; citing Eusebius, *Ecclesiastical History* 5.1.

2:7b *The LORD God Breathed into His Nostrils the Breath of Life*

GOD'S BREATH INSTILLS HIS LIKENESS AND CHARACTER. PETER RIEDEMANN: No one should be so foolish as to think that the Godhead is like flesh and blood, or that flesh and blood is a resemblance of the Godhead. Flesh and blood is of the earth and therefore earthly; the likeness of God, however, is heavenly. So the whole of a person's life should be a reflection of God's likeness. . . . Now since people have been created after God's likeness and should make this likeness manifest, it is God's will that people should be spiritually minded, not carnally minded. For this reason God breathed on them with his own breath. He gave people the spirit of his truth and the image of his glory, to rule over the earthly body and to demonstrate and show God's character. In this way people bring glory to their Creator. For as God the Lord breathed upon the human race, it received a living soul. This wind or breath coming from God and given to the human race is a true picture and image of God. CONFESSION OF FAITH.[12]

GOD'S BREATH IN US IS NO REASON FOR PRIDE. WOLFGANG MUSCULUS: Note how Moses has framed these words, so that even in that part of us that is superior an occasion might be arranged for acknowledging our humility. He speaks of the infusion of the soul and calls this the breath of life and the soul of the living: which words pointedly do not express the excellence of human reason and are applied in the Scriptures even to the beasts. Then, when he could simply have said, "And he breathed into him the breath of life," he preferred to say, "And he breathed *into his nostrils* the breath of life." But as for how much one ought to make of man, whose spirit is in his nostrils, just as we see that breath is equally in the nostrils of all the other animals alike, Scripture is not silent. Moses does not deny that a human being is infused with a soul possessing reason and understanding: but . . . he preferred to speak of the human soul like this, so that we might be recalled by his considerations to a modest outlook. What is this insanity by which our hearts are puffed up, when the arguments for our humility are obvious not only in our flesh but also in our soul? And that, whether they are considered separately or together! To whom is it not a thing of dread, to observe a lifeless body? Indeed, such a sight, encountered but once, could have furnished anyone with an everlasting cause for modesty, had we not become entirely insensitive. And this animal breath, how many troubles is it liable to? Then, how much do we differ in it from the beasts? Indeed, on how many occasions are we even outlasted by them? COMMENTARY ON GENESIS 2:1-3.[13]

2:7c *This Living Human Creature*

HUMAN BEINGS ARE A MICROCOSM. ANNA MARIA VAN SCHURMAN:
> Last of all, with great care, God
>   gave that glorious creature birth:
> the image of its Creator,
>   as well as of heaven and earth.
> A creature of dust and ashes,
>   taken from earth's red clay,
> its finest part drawn from above
>   as heaven to portray.
> What a wondrous unity, this:
>   spirit and earthen vessel,
> where all that is, comes together,
>   joined as one and mutual. . . .
> We are thus, I say,
>   rightly to be appraised
> as an abstract of God's
>   wondrous works and ways:

---

[12]CRR 9:89-90, alluding to Rom 8:5-9. [13]*In Mosis Genesim* (1554), 56, referencing but not quoting Is 2:22, "Stop regarding man in whose nostrils is breath, for of what account is he?"

our souls bear the image
   of heaven's very crown,
and our bodies are an image
   of the earth's own renown.
I will not enter in upon
   the sea of wondrous art
that God poured forth into us,
   yea, in every human part:
a heathen who but once
   beholds the body's limbs
finds God's handiwork there
   and honors him with hymns.
PARAPHRASE OF GENESIS 1–3.[14]

ADAM'S FORMATION WAS A MARVEL, BUT SO IS OUR OWN. MARTIN LUTHER: It is a great miracle that a small seed is planted and that out of it grows a very tall oak. But because these are daily occurrences, they have become of little importance, like the very process of our procreation. . . . All these developments afford the fullest occasion for wonderment and are wholly beyond our understanding, but because of their continued recurrence they have come to be regarded as commonplace, and we have verily become deaf to this lovely music of nature. . . . If it had pleased the Lord to create us by the same method by which Adam was created from the clay, by now this, too, would have ceased to hold the position of a miracle for us; we would marvel more at the method of procreation through the semen of a man. LECTURES ON GENESIS 2:21.[15]

ADAM'S PERFECTION OF BODY AND AGE. ANDREW WILLET: It is without question that Adam was created as at a perfect age, because his body was in the first instant ready for procreation: for the Lord said to them, "increase and multiply," and immediately after their transgression Cain was begotten (Gen 4:1-2). But at what age and with what stature of body Adam was created is not so certain. Some think he was made about the years of Christ's age, between 30 and 40. But I rather approve the inference of those who think that, at creation, his body was of the same growth and perfection as those long-lived patriarchs were when they were ready to procreate, which was about 65 years, for at that age Kenan and Enoch begot children but no one younger did (Gen 5:12). It follows, then, that if Adam's body did appear to be 50 or 60 years old at his creation, he might well be thought to be longest-lived of all the patriarchs: for he lived 930 years after his creation, to which add 50 years for the time during which his body, if it had been born, would have been growing to that state in which he was created. He would thus exceed the age of Methuselah, who lived but 969 years. COMMENTARY ON GENESIS 2:7.[16]

HUMANITY WAS STILL EARTHLY AND IMPERFECT. JOHN CALVIN: In 1 Corinthians 15:45, an antithesis between this living soul and the life-giving spirit that Christ confers upon the faithful is posited by Paul, for no other purpose than to teach us that the state of humankind was not perfected in the person of Adam. Rather, that we should be renewed to a life that is celestial is a benefit uniquely conferred by Christ. Indeed, prior to the fall of Adam, their lives were only earthly, for they had no firm or settled constancy. COMMENTARY ON GENESIS 2:7.[17]

---

[14]*Uitbreiding*, 2.1-6; 3.5-12. [15]LW 1:126-27 (WA 42:95).
[16]*Hexapla* (1608), 31-32. [17]CTS 1:112-13* (CO 23:36).

2:8-14 THE GARDEN OF EDEN

⁸*And the* LORD *God planted a garden in Eden, in the east, and there he put the man whom he had formed.* ⁹*And out of the ground the* LORD *God made to spring up every tree that is pleasant to the sight and good for food. The tree of life was in the midst of the garden, and the tree of the knowledge of good and evil.*

¹⁰*A river flowed out of Eden to water the garden, and there it divided and became four rivers.* ¹¹*The name of the first is the Pishon. It is the one that flowed around the whole land of Havilah, where there is gold.* ¹²*And the gold of that land is good; bdellium and onyx stone are there.* ¹³*The name of the second river is the Gihon. It is the one that flowed around the whole land of Cush.* ¹⁴*And the name of the third river is the Tigris, which flows east of Assyria. And the fourth river is the Euphrates.*

OVERVIEW: The Garden of Eden has always held fascination for readers. Many regard it as a fabled and even magical land, and not a few wondered if this paradise still existed somewhere, like the lost island of Atlantis. Likewise, traditional commentaries had speculated at length about the properties of the two special trees planted in that garden. And, not surprisingly, other writers reacted against such fabulous speculations by dismissing the entire narrative in Genesis as allegorical or altogether fictional.

With their commitment to reading Genesis as a literal and historical narrative, the commentators of the Reformation attempted to resist speculation, but they also felt constrained to defend this narrative against those who treated it with skepticism or contempt. Consequently, they strongly insisted that this "garden of Paradise" was a real place, even if it no longer exists on account of the flood. That same insistence led them to consider with care what the text does and does not mean to say about those two remarkable trees. It is perhaps surprising that despite the skepticism that often greeted Augustine's more speculative insights, Protestant interpreters generally liked his notion that the two trees bore a sacramental function for our first parents, as well as

having other remarkable powers.

A defensive posture emerges even more distinctly in the way exegetes labored to make sense of Eden's four rivers, given that none of the known geographies of the world enabled them to locate *four* rivers that would correspond to the account in Genesis. Calvin was thus by no means the only writer so exercised by this problem as to add the expense of a map to his commentary to clarify matters, yet—like most of his contemporaries—he was forced to conclude that these rivers, like the garden itself, have been changed beyond recognition by the passage of time and the catastrophe of the flood.

So long as the matters at stake seemed to bear on the literal and historical meaning of the text, then, the reformers were liable to pay great attention to traditional background questions. Yet, at the same time, they were just as prone as their predecessors to rhapsodize about paradise as a golden age and to express a painful sense of nostalgia for what was lost—and in some cases used allegory to press this point home.

2:8 God Planted a Garden in Eden

"GOD PLANTED" IS AN ACCOMMODATION TO COMMON SPEECH. JOHN CALVIN: Moses says

"God planted," accommodating himself to the capacity of common people by using a simple and uncultivated manner of speech. For since the majesty of God cannot be expressed as it really is, Scripture is accustomed to describe it according to human conventions. Commentary on Genesis 2:8.[1]

Was Paradise an Earthly Place? Wolfgang Musculus: Are the things Moses writes about paradise to be understood in a historical sense, or mystically? Some have arisen—not only among the heretics, who deny a visible paradise, as did the Seleucians,[†] but also among Catholics—who have treated everything about it in the mystical sense. Ambrose writes about paradise in that way, so that if you should seek anything pertaining to the historical sense, you will find nothing at all. For he bends everything to the service of understanding mysteries, not things tangible. On the other hand, the things Moses writes are seen by some to be understood so historically that there is nothing in them that has any figure of spiritual things. Third, there are those who embrace both the historical sense and at the same time see in the bodily and visible matters shadows of spiritual things. There are three kinds of exposition that bear on the present text: first, an exclusively spiritual exposition; second, one that is only bodily; third, one by which the location of paradise and its trees and fountain are explained both bodily and spiritually. So far as concerns my opinion, I am by no means displeased by what Augustine wrote in book 8 of *On Genesis*, in his first chapter. For great care is to be taken lest the things Moses composed not as figurative expressions but clearly as historical narrative be appropriated in a way that loses the truth of the history. Rather, the historical sense is to be firmly accorded first rank; only then, if a fitting occasion should arise in something corporeal, should one consider whether some image of spiritual things may be shining through. No pious person will deny that the word *paradise*, when Christ told the thief "Today you will be with me in paradise," can be taken not of the earthly paradise in which Adam sinned, but should be understood of the heavenly and true happiness of the life to come. For all that, however, no necessity forces us to deny that an earthly paradise was created by God. Commentary on Genesis 2:8.[2]

Paradise Was Real, Not an Imaginary Place. Andrew Willet: To be rejected are the views of those who imagine that paradise is no earthly or physical place but is to be spiritually understood, as Philo and Origen, whom Epiphanius refutes by this reason, that where there are actual rivers, as the Euphrates, which is confessed by all to be one of the rivers of paradise, [and] where there were also actual trees and plants, there paradise must be an earthly place. Neither can the whole earth be taken for paradise, as some have thought, because it is said here to be planted in Eden, which was the name of a specific country (Ezek 27:23). Likewise for the location of paradise: it was neither in a remote place beyond the ocean (Ephrem); nor a place higher than all the earth (Damascene); nor next to heaven (Rupert); nor reaching up to the moon, as others have imagined; nor in the air, though not so high as the moon (Alexander of Hales, Tostatus); nor below the equator (Bonaventure). For the Tigris and Euphrates rivers, which flowed out of paradise, and the country Eden, where paradise was, were not near the equator; they are known to be in Asia, not in any remote and unknown country, on earth, not in the air or next to the moon. All these are ridiculous and

---

[1]CTS 1:113* (CO 23:36). [2]*In Mosis Genesim* (1554), 58. Musculus's account here is indebted throughout to Augustine's *Literal Commentary on Genesis* 8.1; [†]the Seleucians were a Gnostic group mentioned elsewhere by Augustine, in *On Heresies* 59 (PL 42:41-42; WSA I/18:49).

childish fancies and need no long refutation. COMMENTARY ON GENESIS 2:8.[3]

WHERE WAS PARADISE LOCATED? MARTIN LUTHER: My answer is briefly this: It is an idle question about something no longer in existence. Moses is writing the history of the time before sin and the Deluge, but we are compelled to speak of conditions as they are after sin and after the Deluge. . . . For time and the curse which sins deserve destroy everything. Thus when the world was obliterated by the Deluge, together with its people and cattle, this famous garden was also obliterated and became lost. LECTURES ON GENESIS 2:8.[4]

EDEN'S PLEASURES POINT TO THE INTEGRITY OF OUR FIRST PARENTS. HULDRYCH ZWINGLI: These things signify that God—who is "the sun of righteousness" and thus the dawn of all order, delight and beauty—formed humans with a sound and utterly innocent nature; that is what is most pleasing and the greatest delight. ANNOTATIONS ON GENESIS 2:7.[5]

GOD'S RICH PROVISION EXPOSES HUMAN INGRATITUDE. JOHN CALVIN: Moses expressly declares that every kind of fruit-bearing tree had wonderfully adorned that place, so that there might be a full and truly happy abundance of all things. Given that the Lord took such pains to do this, how much less an excuse is there for human cupidity if, instead of being content with such a splendid abundance, sweetness and variety of produce, they should hurl themselves against God's commandment—just as came to pass. The Holy Spirit deliberately recounts through Moses also how deeply happy Adam was, in order to reveal more clearly his disgraceful lack of self-control, which even such affluence was not enough to keep from bursting forth toward the forbidden fruit. And certainly it was shameful ingratitude that he could not

rest in a state so happy and desirable. Truly, that lust was more than beastly, which such great generosity was unable to satisfy. COMMENTARY ON GENESIS 2:9.[6]

2:9 The Two Trees

TO EAT FROM ONE, TO ABSTAIN FROM THE OTHER. JOHANNES BRENZ: Paradise, where Adam was placed, had . . . every kind of fruit-bearing tree, among which the most notable were the tree of life and the tree of the knowledge of good and evil. The former, they think, was so called not because it would have preserved those who ate of its fruit in this bodily and animal life forever, but because it would have kept them in sound and stable health, not allowing them to be affected either by death or by the inconveniences of old age until that time in their lives when they would have been transferred from this bodily life into one that was spiritual and heavenly. But the tree of the knowledge of good and evil was named from its outcome, that from eating its fruit, which was prohibited, human beings would come to learn in actual fact how much good they lost on account of disobedience and how much evil they brought upon themselves. We needn't bother here with whether there was only one tree of life and only one tree of the knowledge of good and evil, or whether there were several. Certainly, these were more notable than the others, having been made for this purpose: that by eating from one of them, we might enjoy the constant benefit of youth and vitality, while by abstaining from the other, we might declare our deference, obedience, and gratitude toward God. COMMENTARY ON GENESIS 2:8-9.[7]

---

[3]*Hexapla* (1608), 27, citing Philo, *On Creation*; Epiphanius, *Epistle to John of Jerusalem*; John of Damascus, *On the Orthodox Faith* 2.14.3; Bonaventure, *Commentary on the Sentences of Lombard* 2.17. [4]LW 1:88 (WA 42:67). [5]ZSW 13:19; cf. Mal 4:2. [6]CTS 1:115-16* (CO 23:38). [7]*Opera* 1:34.

THE TREE OF KNOWLEDGE WAS GOOD, BUT SIN MADE IT EVIL.

MARTIN LUTHER: This tree of the knowledge of good and evil was Adam's church, altar, and pulpit. Here he was to yield to God the obedience he owed, give recognition to the Word and will of God, give thanks to God, and call upon God for aid against temptation. . . . Therefore let us learn that some external form of worship and a definite work of obedience were necessary for man, who was created to have all the other living creatures under his control, to know his Creator, and to thank Him. If, therefore, Adam had not fallen, this tree would have been like a common temple and basilica to which people would have streamed. Similarly, later on, after our nature had become depraved, a definite place was set aside for divine worship: the temple at Jerusalem. Now, after this tree has become the occasion of so awful a fall, it is correctly called by Moses the tree of the knowledge of good and evil on account of the unfortunate and wretched outcome. LECTURES ON GENESIS 2:9.[8]

GOD ACCOMMODATED HIMSELF TO US IN THE SIGNS AND SACRAMENTS OF THE TWO TREES.

WOLFGANG MUSCULUS: It is worth considering why God did not say, "You shall not *desire* the knowledge of good and evil," but instead, "You shall not *eat of the tree* of the knowledge of good and evil." God was unwilling to issue a command about a matter that was utterly invisible and abstract except as clothed by its visible and tangible sign. He accommodated himself to human capacity, but he also wanted the story of humanity's fall to make sense to those who came after. But we have been so constituted that we should aspire to those things that are spiritual not only with our spirit but also with our external senses, as far as that can be done. So God displayed the prolongation of life externally, in a tree, and he visibly bound up the desire to know good and evil in another tree, which he wished to be a sign and figure of this knowledge. In a similar way, God displayed his presence to Israel, first in the pillar of cloud and fire and then in the ark—external and visible signs that contained, as it were, the sacrament of something invisible. Thus is God accustomed to accommodate himself to human capacity and to set up visible signs of invisible things. COMMENTARY ON GENESIS 2:15-17.[9]

THE TREE OF LIFE WAS A SACRAMENT FOR ADAM AND EVE.

JOHN CALVIN: The name of the tree of life arose not because it would impart to them that life with which they had already been endowed, but so that it might be a symbol and a reminder of the life they had received from God. As we know, it is hardly unusual for God to attest to his power by means of external symbols. To be sure, he does not transfer his power into outward signs but uses them to extend his hand to us, because we cannot ascend to him without assistance. He therefore intended that as often as human beings tasted the fruit of that tree, they would recall the source of their life and acknowledge that they lived not by their own power but by the kindness of God alone, and that life is not an "intrinsic good" (as they commonly say) but proceeds from God. Finally, this tree stood as a visible testimony to the declaration that "in God we live, and move, and have our being." But if Adam, while still in possession of his integrity and upright nature, needed signs to prompt him and lead him to the knowledge of divine grace, how much more are signs necessary today for the great weakness of our character, on account of which we have fallen away from the true light? However, I'm not displeased by what has been handed down by some of the fathers, such as Augustine and Eucherius, that the tree of life was a figure of Christ, inasmuch as he is God's eternal Word. Indeed, it could not really be a symbol of life

---

[8]LW 1:95 (WA 42:72). [9]*In Mosis Genesim* (1554), 67.

except by figuratively representing him. COMMENTARY ON GENESIS 2:9.[10]

OUR FIRST PARENTS HAD TWO SACRA-MENTS. WILLIAM PERKINS: Adam's sacraments were two: the tree of life and the tree of knowledge of good and evil: these served to exercise Adam in obedience unto God. The tree of life was to signify assurance of life forever, if he kept God's commencements. The tree of knowledge of good and evil was a sacrament to show him that if he transgressed God's commandments, he should die: and it was so called, because it signified that if he transgressed this law, he should have experience both of good and evil in himself. EXPOSITION OF THE APOSTLES' CREED.[11]

LIKE ALL SACRAMENTAL SIGNS, THE TREE HAD NO INTRINSIC POWER. JOHANNES OECOLAMPADIUS: The name for the tree was chosen from the event, not that the tree itself could provide the knowledge of good and evil. . . . It truly was a tree, but it did not have within itself that kind of power, even if its fruit was visible. Theodoret explains that with this text what is said here is like what is said concerning baptism, i.e., that we should be reborn: not that the water itself is somehow more efficacious than other water, but that within this water we are reborn by the giving of the Holy Spirit. The same manner of speech is used of the Lord's Supper, when we call it the body of the Lord. So also we understand the tree of life, not that the tree itself was able to vivify, for that ability belongs to the divine Spirit alone. For the flesh does not vivify—even the flesh of Christ apart from the divinity—but only the Spirit. How much less some tree? That tree was set up as a sign that if humankind had been found obedient and had refrained from the forbidden tree, on account of their obedience they would have been able to eat of the tree of life and thus by a divine gift to have become immortal. LECTURES ON GENESIS 2:9.[12]

THE TREES WERE TO BE SACRAMENTS, OR LIKE A TEMPLE. DAVID CHYTRAEUS: The tree of the knowledge of good and evil was named from the outcome that followed the transgression. For after Adam sinned by that tree, he saw not only what good he had lost but also how immense the evils were of body and soul into which he had been cast by his disobedience. For if Adam hadn't fallen, this tree would have been a temple in which he would have worshiped God, where he would have had occasion for speaking about God with others and declaring his obedience to God by means of an external work. Allegorically, the tree of the knowledge of good and evil is the law, separating good deeds from evil ones with a fixed barrier. The tree of life is the gospel, or the body of Christ received in the Lord's Supper. For just as the tree of life promised immortality of the body when received, so also is there divine power for immortality in this sacrament of communion, for it offers us a taste of wisdom and transforms our souls and bodies for eternal life. Older writers used this image for consolation and as a remedy for their sorrows and afflictions. The tree of the cross of Christ appears to be shriveled and sorrowful, but to those who eat of its fruit, it becomes the tree of eternal life; by contrast, the tree of the knowledge of good and evil which, once tasted, brought death to Adam and his offspring, appeared to be verdant and delightful. COMMENTARY ON GENESIS 2:16-17.[13]

GOOD AND EVIL WERE TO BE LEARNED FROM GOD, NOT ON OUR OWN. PETER MARTYR VERMIGLI: Different writers teach various things about why that name was imposed on the tree. Some want it named

---

[10]CTS 1:116-17* (CO 23:38), alluding to Augustine's *Literal Commentary on Genesis* 8.4.8 (ACW 42:38) and Eucherius of Lyons's *Commentarii in Genesim* 2:9 (cf. PL 50:907). [11]*Works* (1608) 1:152. [12]*In Genesim* (1536), 33r-v. [13]*In Genesin* (1576), 88-89.

from the outcome, because by eating what was forbidden, those first humans would have perceived by experience what evil was like, even as they would have experienced how much good was lost, something they previously would not have noticed in this way. . . . Others want it called this because a legal prohibition had been issued about the tree, and a characteristic of law is to indicate good and evil. Neither of these views is to be discounted. Here, however, in considering God's command, I would light upon the essence of all law: God prohibits this thing lest we prefer to know and decide which things are good and which are evil, based on our own sense and reasoning, but God wants us to depend only on him and his word. Whatever he judges to be good, we should consider as such; and what he judges as evil, we too should hold to be evil. This is what it means to trust God: to depose our own understanding and to prefer God's counsel to our own. This is worship of God, this is pure obedience: and the opposite of this is the prudence of the flesh, of which but a taste brings death. You may say this is an allegorical interpretation, but I say that I do want the history preserved here: that a certain forbidden fruit was eaten by Adam that he should not have eaten. But by the name of that tree, I say, we are taught what God requires of us above all else in his precepts, namely, that we reckon good and evil based on his authority. This is the first law given: that we take our stand on God's judgments. The natural law and the law written by Moses or by the prophets and saints, who were inspired by the divine Spirit, show us what things are good or evil according to God's intention, lest we fashion other rules for ourselves. COMMENTARY ON GENESIS 2:9.[14]

THE TREE OF LIFE. MARTIN LUTHER: This tree of life would have preserved perpetual youth. Man would never have experienced the inconveniences of old age; his forehead would never have developed wrinkles; and his feet, his hands, and any other part of his body would not have become weaker or more inactive. Thanks to this fruit, man's powers for procreation and for all tasks would have remained unimpaired until finally he would have been translated from the physical life to the spiritual. Therefore the remaining trees would have supplied delightful and most excellent food, but this one would have been like a medicine by which his life and his powers were forever maintained at their utmost vigor. LECTURES ON GENESIS 2:9.[15]

ONE TREE ATTESTED GOD'S GENEROSITY, THE OTHER TAUGHT A LESSON. KONRAD PELLIKAN: He had also planted one tree within that most beautiful garden that was called, and was, the tree of life: so that the one who would eat from it would live as long and as happily as possible: truly, a life-giving tree, the fruits of which would furnish powers of bodily health and, perhaps, renew our core moisture† for a long time. God thus was and wished at that time to be seen as merciful and generous toward the human race. The almighty and creator of all also provided another tree, which bore the knowledge of good and evil. Indeed, it was able to lavish upon the one eating of its fruits the power to distinguish between good and evil. Not that the tree was rational in its own nature or would have had knowledge of good and evil, but because disobedient human beings learned from it by experience how good it is to attend to God's commands, and how pernicious to disdain them. COMMENTARY ON GENESIS 2:9.[16]

---

[14]*In Primum Librum Mosis* (1569), 11r. [15]LW 1:92 (WA 42:70). [16]*Commentaria Bibliorum* (1532) 1:4v. †Some medieval authorities held that signs of aging indicated a gradual diminishment of one's *humidum radicale* or core moisture; see Michael McVaugh, "The 'Humidum Radicale' in Thirteenth-Century Medicine," *Traditio* 30 (1974): 259-83.

LIKE CHRIST, THE TREE SUSTAINED LIFE.
PETER MARTYR VERMIGLI: The fruit of the
tree of life possessed the power . . . to preserve
life. It restored the humidity of one's nature so
that it would have been what it was before it
had been used up. It also strengthened one's
natural heat so as to suffice for one's activities
forever. But for us, allegorically, this tree refers
to Christ, who is our life, as he himself
testifies when he says, "I am the way, the truth,
and the life." COMMENTARY ON GENESIS 2:9.[17]

HOW THE TREE OF LIFE WORKED. ANDREW
WILLET: This was a visible tree, planted in the
midst of paradise, in a visible place, not
spiritually or allegorically to be understood
(Origen); nor is it called the tree of life because
it was able to give immortality and to preserve
from death forever (Tostatus), or only because
it was able to preserve people from death till
such time as they should be translated to
immortality (Scotus, Thomas, et al.); neither
need it be disputed whether the tree of life had
this power to preserve from death by a supernatural gift (Bonaventure) or by a natural
faculty (Hugh, Thomas, Pererius). For it is
evident that this tree had no power to give
immortality at all by the taste of its fruit,
because no corruptible food can make the body
incorruptible. . . . Again, human beings had by
their creation been given power [not] to die, if
they had not sinned: so immortality was the
gift of their creation, not the effect of the
eating of the tree. And if it could have given
immortality, it must have had a power to
preserve from sin, for by sinning, human
beings became mortal: so that if it could not
defend them from sin, it was no more the tree
of life in regard to its effect than any other tree
of the garden. . . . So our opinion is that it was
called the tree of life not so much for its
workings (though we confess it might give
strength and virtue also to the body [Merce-
rus]) but chiefly for its signification, because it
was both a sign of life received from God and a

symbol of Christ, who is our true life. Herein
we approve the opinion of Steuchus, who
thinks it was called the tree of life, not *effectu-
ally* but *significatively*, as a sign of the true
immortality that they should receive of God if
they continued in obedience. So, first, it is the
tree of life as the other was of knowledge of
good and evil, which was so called not because
it gave knowledge but was a *seal* unto them of
the miserable knowledge that they would get
by experience in their transgression (Lombard); therefore the tree of life must be so
called, because it was a seal and pledge of life.
Secondly, Scripture significatively and sym-
bolically expounds the tree of life, as in
Proverbs 3:18 ("Wisdom [which is Christ] is a
tree of life") and Revelation 2:7 ("To the one
who overcomes I will give to eat of the tree of
life"). COMMENTARY ON GENESIS 2:9.[18]

**GOD BLESSED ADAM DESPITE FOREKNOW-
ING HIS SIN.** PETER MARTYR VERMIGLI: God
did not want Adam to be idle, but to occupy
himself with a sweet and pleasant activity like
agriculture—not the backbreaking kind, but
the sort that princes and noblemen delight in.
Nor should the fullness of God's goodness
here escape your notice: Adam piled up
blessings great and numerous from God, who
knew well ahead of time that Adam was going
to sin. By contrast, if *we* knew that someone
was going to rebel against us, we would never
give him or her any good thing of our own.
COMMENTARY ON GENESIS 2:16.[19]

**THE WHOLE WORLD WOULD HAVE BEEN
LIKE PARADISE IF NOT FOR SIN.** JOHN
CALVIN: There was a definite place assigned by
God to the first man, in which he would have
had his home. I say this with some urgency,

---

[17]*In Primum Librum Mosis* (1569), 11r, citing Jn 14:6. [18]*Hexapla* (1608), 27-28, citing Tostatus, *Commentaria in Genesim* 13
(q. 175); Scotus, *Commentary on the Sentences of Lombard* 2.19.1;
Augustino Steucho, *Cosmopeia*; Lombard, *Sentences* 3.17. [19]*In
Primum Librum Mosis* (1569), 11r.

because there have been some who would extend this garden throughout all regions of the world. Truly, I confess, if the earth had not been cursed on account of humanity's sin, the whole of it would have been the loveliest scene not only of abundance but also of delight, just as it had been blessed from the beginning. In brief, it would have been not unlike paradise when compared with the deformity we now behold. COMMENTARY ON GENESIS 2:8.[20]

2:10-14 *A River Flowed Out of Eden*

THE SPIRITUAL MEANING OF THE TREES AND RIVERS OF PARADISE. KONRAD PEL-LIKAN: If this passage about physical things were to be considered for its spiritual meaning, it is utterly clear that "spiritual" paradise is the state of innocence of life and righteousness of nature that was established, introduced and created by God (which could also be called *original sanctity*) and a certain propensity to obey God's will, yet without coercion and with freedom to act well or badly. As for the tree of life and the tree of salvation, what else could that be said to be except perfect wisdom, which is Christ, something to be grasped not immediately, of course, but in his own day later on. The tree of the knowledge of good and evil is fittingly said to be human wisdom and—apart from the prevenient grace of God—natural reason, self-concern and love of self. Truly, the command of God is extremely light: not to abound in self-concern but to think with sober judgment [Rom 12:3]; to trust one another, being quick to agree; to adhere firmly to the infallible truth; and to obey God.

But the rivers of paradise, irrigating the innocent and godly soul and rendering the field of the human heart fertile, are not unfittingly [understood as] the virtues or the graces of virtue: just as Pishon, which means *extension*, signifies faith, which extends itself to recognize and love the highest good. Gihon—that is to say, *sighing*—will denote

modesty of spirit and the virtue of humility. After that, the third, Tigris, . . . can also easily mean *acute*: it indicates that obedience to God is to be unsurpassed. Euphrates, that fourth river of paradise, will fittingly teach that love of neighbor is to increase.

All these things that some wish to bring to this passage will eventually be found to be more certain if readers of the Holy Scriptures consider them thoroughly. COMMENTARY ON GENESIS 2:17.[21]

MYSTICAL LESSONS FROM THE EARTHLY PARADISE. WOLFGANG MUSCULUS: We should see in passing what a mystical consideration of this text has to teach us. At the outset, we should not despise the Fathers for seeing in the earthly paradise an image of true and heavenly happiness. First, they found it beautifully fitting that the Lord planted a garden for humankind in Eden, that is, in the loveliest of all places and regions—and that, at the very beginning. Even so, before the world was constituted, he prepared for us a heavenly paradise, the most splendid mansion of all. Second, the trees in paradise are not only admirable but also useful. In the same way, in the heavenly paradise there are spiritual blessings (*charismata*) that are both delightful to contemplate and profitable to use. Third, in the earthly paradise there are two trees, the tree of life and of knowledge. Likewise in the heavenly kingdom, namely, the kingdom of Christ, there is true life and true knowledge. Fourth, a river arises in the earthly paradise and waters all of it. In the same manner, a river bubbles up in the heavenly paradise, not only making the hearts of all to be fruitful but also making them glad, according to that saying of the prophet, "The streams of the river make the cities of God joyful." That river is the grace of the spirit of Christ, which is mentioned in John 7:38. Fifth,

---

[20]CTS 1:113-14* (CO 23:36). [21]*Commentaria Bibliorum* (1532) 1:5r.

the river of the earthly paradise goes forth to the nearby nations in four headwaters. So also that grace of the spirit of Christ is diffused to all four parts of the world—north, south, east and west—through the advance of the gospel's proclamation, with Christ himself working alongside for the sake of the elect. In just this way, I think, the narrative about the earthly paradise could be fittingly accommodated to images of spiritual things. Nor do they go astray who see in the tree of life a figure of the gospel, and in the tree of the knowledge of good and evil a figure of the law, for just as from that tree, so also from the law has death come through sin and captured the human race. COMMENTARY ON GENESIS 2:8-14.[22]

THE FOUR RIVERS OF EDEN ARE UTTERLY CHANGED TODAY. MARTIN LUTHER: This is one of the greatest causes of offense in Moses. For anything that lies before the eyes cannot be denied. Now this description applies properly to India, which he calls Havilah, where there is the Pison or the Ganges. Regarding the other three rivers, the Gihon, the Hiddekel, and the Prath—that is, the Nile, the Tigris, and the Euphrates—it is known also that their sources are very far apart. And so the question is: Since it is established that these rivers, the best-known to the entire world, are very far removed from one another, how can it be true when Moses says that they flow from one single source, that is, that they rush forth in the Garden of Eden toward the east? For although the source of the Nile is unknown, there are certain evidences that it has its source in the south. But the Ganges, the Tigris, and the Euphrates flow from the north and thus have their source in the opposite direction. Moses, therefore, is most obviously contradicting reason. This has given many the opportunity to imagine that Eden was the entire earth. Even if this were not obviously wrong, it still would not safeguard Moses' statement that the source of these rivers is the

same. . . . What shall we say, then, about this passage of Moses? Because it opposes reason and experience, it has been a very abundant source of offense, giving Origen and others an opportunity for amazing twaddle. Some interpreters disregard this cause of offense and, as it were, walk through this sea with dry feet. But this attitude, too, should be far removed from an interpreter. Hence my opinion . . . is, first, that Paradise was closed to man by sin, and, secondly, that it was utterly destroyed and annihilated by the Flood, so that no trace of it is visible any longer. . . . For the entire surface of the earth was changed. LECTURES ON GENESIS 2:11.[23]

ALTHOUGH THE EARTH IS NOW DEFILED, IT IS STILL THE SAME EARTH GOD CREATED. JOHN CALVIN: Although I admit that from the time that the earth was cursed, it has been driven back from its original beauty to a state of miserable squalor, as if dressed in mourning, and that it was further devastated in many places by the flood later on, I still say that it was the same earth that was created in the beginning. Add to this, that Moses (in my judgment) accommodated his topography to the capacity of his age. COMMENTARY ON GENESIS 2:10.[24]

THE FOUR RIVERS ARE NOW LOST TO US. ANDREW WILLET: Seeing that not only the names but the channels and currents of rivers and streams may be altered and changed in time, it can hardly now be defined which are these four streams of the Euphrates. It suffices us to know that at some time this river was so divided by branches, where[ever] the location of paradise was. [But] the particular place whereof is not now known. COMMENTARY ON GENESIS 2:10.[25]

---

[22]*In Mosis Genesim* (1554), 62, quoting Ps 45:5 (Vulgate). [23]LW 1:97-98 (WA 42:74-75). [24]CTS 1:119* (CO 23:40). [25]*Hexapla* (1608), 30, citing Mercerus.

LET THE RIVERS SIMPLY BE RIVERS—AND BLESSINGS. JOHANNES OECOLAMPADIUS: There are some who try to bring in different allegories for these rivers. Some bring forth the four evangelists, others the four doctors† of the church. Avoid such trifles. It is much safer just to know that God wished humankind well, and that he gave all the resources of this world in order that we might enjoy them to his glory. LECTURES ON GENESIS 2:10-14.[26]

---

[26]*In Genesim* (1536), 34r-v, †referring to Ambrose, Jerome, Augustine and Gregory the Great.

2:15-17 AN EARTHLY TASK AND A DIVINE COMMANDMENT

[15]*The LORD God took the man and put him in the garden of Eden to work it and keep it.* [16]*And the LORD God commanded the man, saying, "You may surely eat of every tree of the garden,* [17]*but of the tree of the knowledge of good and evil you shall not eat, for in the day that you eat*[a] *of it you shall surely die."*

a Or *when you eat*

OVERVIEW: The short paragraph comprised by Genesis 2:15-17 was mined for some extremely important principles. The bare description of the first man having been placed in the garden "to work it and keep it" was thus emblematic not only of the entire vocation of humankind—namely, to worship and to work—but also of the basic institutions of human society, insofar as Genesis 2:15 could be read as setting the tone for our understanding of church, family and statecraft.

Naturally, the prohibition surrounding the tree of the knowledge of good and evil drew commentators back to further speculation on the nature and powers of this tree in particular, but also on the nature of law—and the need for it—both in the state of paradise or perfection and in the state of sin that was shortly to follow. Once again, commentators were keenly aware of how things were meant to be before sin and, consequently, what has been lost.

2:15 To Work and Keep the Garden

LESS TO GARDEN THAN JUST TO LIVE THERE. HULDRYCH ZWINGLI: "Cultivate" would be better [than "work" here], in the sense of "inhabit." There was no need for Adam to work the earth, which brought forth everything by divine urging, without labor or sweat. But "cultivate" in Latin indicates not only to till the land by plowing but also to inhabit it. So Adam was placed in a most delightful garden to inhabit it as the head of a household, and thus did God surround him with riches and delights on all sides. ANNOTATIONS ON GENESIS 2:15.[1]

---

[1]ZSW 13:19.

ADAM'S PLEASANT WORK BEFORE THE FALL. WOLFGANG MUSCULUS: Some ask here whether the condition of paradise was such that it needed human cultivation, and also how an obligation to labor could be imposed on the first man when he had not yet sinned. For the burden of working seems to have been imposed on him only after sin. . . . God could have kept paradise in its pristine state from the time when it was planted to the very end all by himself, without any human cultivation or labor. But he wanted the first man to add his own work and cultivation so that he might think about what he was doing and thereby discover again and again the providence and goodness of his maker. God did not want even the angels to be idle but made them ministering spirits. Is it any surprise, then, if he imposed on the first man some obligation to cultivate and care for paradise, so that he would pay attention to what went into God's own working? It's just as if some official duty were assigned to the son of a king, lest from his abundance of luxuries, wealth and privilege the sluggard should avoid it. . . . But the things imposed as punishment after sin differ greatly from the care and labor enjoined upon Adam in paradise, in which there was nothing of sorrow or affliction, nothing burdensome and nothing of sweat. Neither was the earth liable to any curse: having produced neither thistles nor thorns, it was obliging and generous in response to human cultivation. In a word, the cultivation imposed on Adam in paradise was of a sort that would have brought him the greatest pleasure and the fullest opportunity for knowing God's providence and benevolence. COMMENTARY ON GENESIS 2:15-17.[2]

ADAM WAS NOT WITHOUT A TWOFOLD VOCATION. WILLIAM PERKINS: [Adam's] *particular* calling was to come into the Garden of Eden, to keep it and to dress the trees and fruits thereof. This shows unto us a good lesson, that everyone must have a particular calling wherein he or she ought to walk: and therefore such as spend their time idly in gaming and vain delights have much to answer to God at the day of judgment. It will not excuse us, then, to say that we had land and a living to maintain and therefore could live as we wished; for even Adam in his innocence had all things at his will and wanted nothing, yet even then God employed him in a calling: therefore none must be exempted, but every person both high and low must walk in his or her proper calling. Adam's *general* calling was to worship his Creator, to which he was bound by the right [i.e., law] of creation, considering that the moral law was written in his heart by nature. EXPOSITION OF THE APOSTLES' CREED.[3]

HUMANS WERE MEANT TO FIND PLEASURE IN WORK, NOT INDOLENCE. JOHN CALVIN: Moses now adds that the earth was given with this condition, that they should occupy themselves in cultivating it. So it follows that people were created to be doing something, not to lie about in sloth and sluggishness. Truly, this labor was pleasant, filled with delight, and wholly devoid of annoyance or boredom. But because God wanted to train people in caring for the earth, he condemned all useless leisure on their part. For this reason, nothing is more contrary to the order of nature than to spend our lives eating, drinking and sleeping, all the while proposing nothing for ourselves to do. COMMENTARY ON GENESIS 2:15.[4]

GARDENING AND GRATITUDE. ANDREW WILLET: Though man should not have toiled or wearied himself with any labor in paradise (for that was laid upon him as a punishment afterward, to "eat his bread in the sweat of his brow," Gen 3:19), yet it is evident that he should have exercised himself in some honest

---

[2]*In Mosis Genesim* (1554), 63.　[3]*Works* (1608) 1:152.　[4]CTS 1:125* (CO 23:44).

labor, even in paradise. His charge was both to dress the garden by planting and nourishing its trees (in which kind of husbandry many even now do take delight and hold it rather to be recreation than any weariness unto them) and also to keep it from being spoiled by the beasts. This labor was enjoined upon Adam so that, being thus occupied in continually beholding the goodly plants in paradise, he might thereby be stirred up to acknowledge the goodness and bounty of the Creator. The Lord also thereby looked to our instruction, for if Adam was not to live idly in paradise, how much less should we now spend our days doing nothing? Commentary on Genesis 2:15.[5]

Three Things to Do in Paradise. Johannes Brenz: God put the newly-created humans in paradise not as a holiday for slackers but so that they might have both bodily and spiritual exercises and nourishment. There were three main kinds of activities: the first two are physical, the third is spiritual.

One was to "work it" (that is, paradise), to plant and cultivate it. Here was the beginning of *agriculture*. It would not have been right for people to be idly at leisure, even if sin had not entered into the world, but they would have been obliged to cultivate, sow and propagate the land. Nonetheless, this labor would have brought no annoyance but would have been a great pleasure, carried out with great enthusiasm. But now, after sin has entered into the world, agriculture hasn't been abolished, but a curse has been added. . . .

Another kind of exercise was to "keep it," that is, to keep it from the beasts, lest what people had cultivated be destroyed by animals. Even if the beasts had not been as ferocious as they are now, after humankind has sinned, because beasts aren't endowed with reason, they still would have randomly barged into pastures on impulse, destroying them so as no longer to be fit either for human use or their own. So even back then they needed to be restrained and kept away from cultivated fields. Here was the beginning of the *military*, which, when it was instituted at the beginning, was directed only against beasts who lack reason, but when sin had entered later on, was necessarily directed also against those human beings who were like beasts, to prevent them from inflicting poverty and to constrain them within their limits.

A third kind . . . was spiritual exercise and the institution of divine worship. God permitted Adam to eat of the fruits of all the trees in paradise. He excluded only one kind of tree and prohibited him from eating its fruit. God chose this kind of tree as if it were a temple where Adam might meet with his family and teach them there about God and God's mercy, and about his goodness and the blessedness that would come after this bodily life either by change or by transfer out of this life. Even if there had been the maximum of tranquility in this physical life, if sin had not entered into this world, the spiritual and heavenly blessedness of the life to come far outweighs all tranquility in this physical life. Accordingly, Adam would have taught his family about the magnitude of such blessedness; he would have exhorted them to demonstrate to God their deference and obedience by abstaining from the fruit of this tree, and to attest their gratitude towards such a benefactor. Here, then, was the beginning of *ecclesiastical ministry*, and so you now have three classes, whether of activities or of circumstances in life: agriculture, the military or political magistracy, and the ministry of the church. Commentary on Genesis 2:15-17.[6]

Gardening Retains Only a Trace of Its Original Pleasure. Martin Luther: Even now in this wretched state of nature we observe that for someone who has a delightful

---

[5]*Hexapla* (1608), 33. [6]*Opera* 1:34-35.

garden sowing, planting, or digging are not a hardship but are done with zeal and a certain pleasure. How much more perfect this would have been in that garden in the state of innocence! LECTURES ON GENESIS 2:15.[7]

THEY POSSESSED FOUR KINDS OF DIGNITY. WILLIAM PERKINS: [Another] point to be considered in the creation of humankind is the dignity of their person: for David says, "You have made them a little inferior to the angels, and crowned them with glory and worship." This dignity consists of four points. First, [there was] a *blessed communion* with the true God: for Paul, speaking of the Gentiles who were not called, says they were strangers from the life of God. By contrast, we may gather that our first parents in their innocence lived the life of God, which is nothing else but to lead a life here on earth as that the creature shall have a blessed and immediate fellowship with God; which stands in this, that before humanity's fall, God revealed himself in a special manner unto them, so that their very body and soul was a temple and dwelling place of the Creator. This fellowship between God and human beings in their innocence was made manifest in the familiar conference which God granted them; but since the fall, this communion is lost: for we cannot abide the presence of God. . . . The second point wherein their dignity consists is that they were made *lord and king over all creatures*, as David says, "You have made them to have dominion over the works of your hands." And therefore God, having created them in his image, bids them rule over the fishes of the sea, over the fowl of the heaven and over every beast that moves upon the earth: and afterward he brought them all to [Adam], as to a sovereign lord and king to be named by him: and answerably every creature in its kind gave reverence and subjection unto him, before his fall, as unto their lord and king. . . . The third part of

human dignity by creation is that before their fall they had a *wonderful beauty and majesty above all creatures in their bodies*: whereupon David says, "the Lord has crowned them with glory and worship." And in the renewing of the covenant with Noah, God says that the dread and fear of humans shall be upon all creatures: which now though it be but small, yet does it plainly show what was the glory and majesty of their person at the first. The fourth dignity of their estate in innocence is that *labor was without pain or weariness*: if they had never fallen, [Adam] would have labored in the garden, but such that he would never have been wearied thereby. For when Adam was fallen, God said, "In the sweat of your face shall you eat your bread." Now if the pain in labor comes afterward, as a curse upon them for their transgression, then before the fall they felt no pain in these affairs. And in these four things consisted the dignity which humankind had in the creation. EXPOSITION OF THE APOSTLES' CREED.[8]

2:16-17a *You Shall Not Eat of the Tree*

ADAM WAS GOD'S VASSAL, AND COVENANT HEAD. ANNA MARIA VAN SCHURMAN:
But God gave him this law:
    from one fruit to abstain,
or face God's holy wrath
    and death's eternal pain.
And as a servant granted such a fief
    is duly and justly paid
if he should lose his inheritance
    because his lord he has betrayed,
so had Adam to remain faithful
    and godly ways prefer,
to cling even more closely unto God,
    now that he could err.
The head he was of this covenant,
    and trunk of the human race,

---

[7]LW 1:103 (WA 42:78). [8]*Works* (1608) 1:151, citing Ps 8:5-6 (Heb 2:7); Lk 5:8.

whose branches' life depended on
whether he stood or met disgrace.
Paraphrase of Genesis 1–3.[9]

A Strange Commandment, Yet Strangely Easy. Johannes Brenz: Why would God prohibit the eating of the fruit of a tree rather than some other kind of sin? Surely the tree and its fruit weren't intrinsically evil or pernicious, were they? And why doesn't he rather read the Ten Commandments to Adam, which he later recited to the Israelites in the wilderness of Sinai? First, the tree wasn't evil per se, nor was its fruit harmful in itself. Indeed, "God saw everything that he made, and it was very good." Then, he did not recite the Decalogue because it had already been engraved on creation for Adam: he understood it well and intelligently, and he took pleasure especially in observing it. This is natural law: there would have been no need to repeat it later on in the wilderness if our understanding of it had not been obscured by sin. So when Adam was still uncorrupted in his nature, God saw no need to read the Ten Commandments to him, which were already known to human reason. Rather, he gave him special directions about worship that were not inscribed on human reason, but by which human reason might attest its obedience and reverence. In this way, even though he would not understand from his own nature what worship God wished for himself here, he would give God praise and glory for his wisdom and recognize that he owed obedience to God. Truly, God wished to impose on Adam nothing extraordinary or burdensome, but a thing seemingly laughable and easy to fulfill, so that he would become famous for his obedience and would have no excuse on account of its difficulty. Commentary on Genesis 2:15-17.[10]

The Tree of Knowledge Was Prohibited So That Adam and Eve Would Seek Wisdom from God. John Calvin:

Concerning the tree of the knowledge of good and evil, we ought to recognize that it was not prohibited because God wanted human beings to wander around like sheep, devoid of the ability to discern things or make judgments. Rather, it was so that they would aspire to be no wiser than was fitting for them, lest, having cast off God's yoke and trusting in their own understanding, they set themselves up as arbiters and judges of good and evil. Their sin proceeded from an evil conscience, so it must follow that they had been endowed with judgment, by which they might discriminate between virtues and vices. Otherwise, what Moses had said earlier—that they were created in the image of God—could not be true, seeing that the image of God comprises in itself the knowledge of that one who is the highest good. . . . We can now grasp what is meant by abstaining from the tree of the knowledge of good and evil, namely, that in attempting one thing or another, Adam would not rely on his own prudence but rather cleave to God alone and become wise only by his obedience. Accordingly, "knowledge" is to be taken in a bad sense here, as disparaging that wretched experience that humans began to acquire for themselves when they departed from the only fountain of perfect wisdom. And this is also the origin of free choice, that Adam wished to be independent and dared to try to find out what he was strong enough to do. Commentary on Genesis 2:9.[11]

Why Was One Tree Forbidden? How Did It Get Its Name? Wolfgang Musculus: Here arises a famous and highly troubled question: Why was God unwilling to allow Adam to use this tree, namely, the tree of the knowledge of good and evil? Were the fruits of this tree evil and harmful? Or did God envy him the knowledge of good and evil and wish

---

[9]*Uitbreiding*, 6.1-8. [10]*Opera* 1:35-36. [11]CTS 1:118* (CO 23:39).

him to remain destitute of this knowledge, like the beasts? The answers are hardly alike! But it is utterly necessary that this restriction would have been made for some reason. Some seek the answer in the *quality* of this knowledge of good and evil; others, in the good of *obedience*. The former say that the knowledge of good and evil mentioned here, while it might be good in itself, was nonetheless of such a sort that it was suitable only for God, not for humans. . . . But it is not to be supposed that God would have *attached* the divine knowledge of good and evil to the fruits of the tree but that he wished this tree to be a sort of *figure* of it. Thus, in order to forewarn Adam to be careful not to aspire to a state higher than was properly his and claim the glory of divine knowledge for himself, God expressly prohibited eating from that tree. . . . Otherwise, it would come to pass that when he thought he could acquire the glory of the divine knowledge for himself, he would lose immortal happiness by becoming mortal. And this is my own view. . . . Others, however, think God wished to prescribe this law so that Adam might be trained in the good of obedience. And the tree was called the tree of the knowledge of good and evil because from it, by transgressing this law, Adam came to know the difference between the good of obedience and the evil of disobedience, as well as between the good of innocence and immortality and the evil of a sinful and mortal nature. . . . They thus understand [the tree] in terms of the *experience* of good and evil that befalls those who transgress God's precept, and they distinguish between the knowledge that comes from wisdom and that which comes through experience. Commentary on Genesis 2:15-17.[12]

The Command Was Easy and Given to Both. Andrew Willet: Though Augustine thinks this precept of not eating was given only to Adam, and by him to Eve, we hold it

more probable that God gave this charge unto them both together. First, Eve confesses that God spoke unto both of them and said, "You shall not eat of it" (Gen 3:2). Secondly, the Lord said to both of them together, "Behold, I have given unto you every herb and every tree, etc." (Gen 1:29) at which time also it is likely that he gave them the other prohibition, of not eating from that one tree: for if God had made that exception before, he would not have given a general permission after, or if this general grant had gone before, the exception now should seem to abrogate the former grant. Thirdly, the Septuagint seem to be of this mind, that this precept was given both to Adam and Eve, reading thus in the plural number, "In the day you eat thereof, you shall die" (so also Gregory). But if the precept had originally been given in the name of Adam only, that would have been so because Adam was the more principal and he had charge of the woman; and because the greatest danger was in *his* transgression, which was the cause of his posterity's ruin. As Mercerus well notes, *Adam* was the common name both of the man and woman (Gen 5:2) and is thus taken in verse 15 and likewise here.

If it be asked *why* the Lord gave this precept to Adam, we answer (with Gregory) that it was fitting that, for the better trial of Adam's obedience, he should be prohibited to do that which of itself was not evil, so that in abstaining from that which was good, Adam might show his humility to his Creator. In that God gave Adam so easy a precept to keep—only to refrain from eating of one tree, having liberty to use all the rest beside it (not nearly as hard or difficult as the commandment given to Abraham, to sacrifice his only son)—herein Adam's transgression and disobedience [is plain]. Commentary on Genesis 2:16.[13]

---

[12]*In Mosis Genesim* (1554), 63-64; the second view is attributed to Augustine and those who follow him. [13]*Hexapla* (1608), 33, citing Augustine, *The Literal Meaning of Genesis* 8.17 (ACW 42:58); Gregory, *Morals in Job* 35.10.

God's Prohibition Establishes the Church—Before the Home or State.

Martin Luther: Here we have the establishment of the church before there was any government of the home and of the state; for Eve was not yet created. Moreover, the church is established without walls and without any pomp, in a very spacious and very delightful place. After the church has been established, the household government is also set up, when Eve is added to Adam as his companion. Thus the temple is earlier than the home, and it is also better this way. Moreover, there was no government of the state before sin, for there was no need of it. Civil government is a remedy required by our corrupted nature. It is necessary that lust be held in check by the bonds of the laws and by penalties. . . . Therefore if men had not become evil through sin, there would have been no need of civil government; but Adam, together with his descendants, would have lived in utmost serenity and would have achieved more by moving one finger than all the swords, instruments of torture, and axes can achieve now. At that time there would have been no robber, murderer, thief, envier, and liar. What need, therefore, would there have been of laws and of civil government, which is like a cauterizing iron and an awful remedy by which harmful limbs are cut off that the rest may be preserved? Therefore after the establishment of the church the government of the home is also assigned to Adam in Paradise. But the church was established first because God wants to show by this sign, as it were, that man was created for another purpose than the rest of the living beings. Lectures on Genesis 2:16-17.[14]

Obedience Is the Only Rule for Living Well.

John Calvin: Moses now teaches that humans had been put in charge of the earth, with this exception, that they should nevertheless be subject to God. As a sign of subjection, a law is imposed on them: for it would not have mattered to God if they had eaten freely of any fruit whatsoever, and so the prohibition of one tree was a test of obedience. In this way, God determined at the outset that the whole human race should become accustomed to show reverence to his deity. Given that they had been adorned and enriched with so many excellent gifts, it was undoubtedly necessary for them to be held under some restraint, lest they break forth into wanton behavior. To be sure, there was another special reason that we touched on earlier, namely, that Adam should not desire to be wise beyond measure. But this is to be kept in mind as God's general design, that he wants people to be subject to his authority. Abstinence from the fruit of the one tree was therefore a kind of elementary lesson in obedience, so that they might know that their lives had a guide and Lord on whose will they ought to depend and to whose commands they ought to assent. And truly, this is the only rule for living well and properly, that we should train ourselves in obeying God. Commentary on Genesis 2:16.[15]

Obedience Resides in the Details.

Peter Martyr Vermigli: You should also learn here that God's law is not to be evaluated by the things it regulates, for it often seems to circle around common sorts of things, as here, where it is concerned with the fruit of a tree, with eating and drinking, with sexual relations. The prudence of the flesh, when it considers such things in themselves, regards them as trivial. But pay attention to what the goal is, namely, *obedience*, so that God's wisdom may be preferred to our own. Commentary on Genesis 2:16.[16]

Why Give a Command If You Know It Will Be Ignored?

Andrew Willet: *Why [did] the Lord give this precept to Adam, which*

---

[14]LW 1:103-4 (WA 42:79). [15]CTS 1:125-26* (CO 23:44). [16]*In Primum Librum Mosis* (1569), 11r-v.

he knew he would not keep? For an answer, we first say that God gave him a precept that was possible to be kept, and Adam had power to keep it if he willed. It was not the fault of God who gave him free will, then, but his own, who abused that gift. Secondly, if it be replied, *Why did God not give him grace and keep him from transgression?* I answer that God could have given such grace, and to the angels as well, that they should not have fallen: but it was fitting that God should leave creatures to their free will and not hinder the course of nature that he had made. Thirdly, though God foresaw man's transgression, that was still no reason to withhold the precept: for then God should have made neither the angels nor human beings, because he saw that some of both should be reprobates; and for the same reason, God should not have given his written Word, because many heretics do pervert it to their destruction. Fourthly, as God foresaw our transgression, so he knew how to turn it to good, as in showing mercy to sinners and in sending Christ to restore what humans lost. Accordingly, notwithstanding his foresight of Adam's transgression, God was not to abstain from charging Adam with this commandment in view of the great good that God also foresaw would ensue. COMMENTARY ON GENESIS 2:16.[17]

THE TREES FORESHADOW ALSO OUR RESTORATION. HULDRYCH ZWINGLI: In all of God's doings it is especially to be observed that these corporeal and visible things by which the divine majesty acts among us have a similarity to the matters he teaches and signify them in some way. We see the same thing here in the two trees. They should not touch the tree of the knowledge of good and evil, they should not eat of its fruit; he prohibits it with a penalty of death. What else are we to think this indicates except that no human being should try to learn or under-stand what is good and what is evil on one's own, as is customary, but from God alone? For even though a person has been endowed with intellect, will and knowledge, an acquaintance with good and evil is to be had only when God reveals it—whence he rebukes through the prophet those "who call evil good and good evil." . . . Thus God, through these two trees, foreshadows the fall and restoration of humankind. Indeed, when one falls back upon oneself and forgets the voice of God, by death he dies; from there, he is restored by the tree of life, namely, by Christ. ANNOTATIONS ON GENESIS 2:16-17.[18]

2:17b *In That Day You Shall Die*

WHAT DID GOD MEAN BY DEATH? ANDREW WILLET: The first question here is, what death God threatened to Adam, whether the death only of the body, or the soul, or of both. We do not think that only the spiritual death of the soul is signified here, whereby the soul is separated by sin from God (Philo, Eucherius), for we see that the Lord himself threatened the death of the body to Adam in Genesis 3:19: "You are dust, and to dust you shall return." Neither is the death of only the body here implied, as some have thought, but the death of the soul by sin also, which brings forth the death of the body, as the apostle shows in Romans 5:12. . . . There was first sin in the soul, before there followed death in the body. We also do not think that everlasting death is here excluded (Pererius), for the apostle says, "We were by nature the children of death, as were others" (Eph 2:3); and if by Adam's transgression we were the children of wrath, how much more was he who made us so? And if by sinning Adam did not make himself guilty of eternal death, why was the promise made unto him immediately upon his fall of the Messiah (Gen 3:15), whose office is to redeem us from sin and everlasting damnation?

---

[17]*Hexapla* (1608), 34. [18]ZSW 13:19-20; cf. Is 5:20.

We therefore think with Augustine, that by *death* here is understood whatsoever death, whether of the soul or body, temporal or eternal. For Augustine defines four kinds of death: the temporal death of the soul, when it is for a time separated from God by sin; the eternal death of the soul, when it is separated from the body; the temporal death of the body, when it is separated from the soul; and the eternal death of the body in hell. So Adam first died in his soul, by losing his innocency; he died in body, returning to dust; and he was also subject to everlasting death both of body and soul—but from that he was redeemed by Christ. In addition, under the name of death are comprehended all other miseries, calamities and sorrows, which are the forerunners of death: so that we may aptly compare death with the center, and all other miseries with the circle or circumference around the center. Or, as Scripture likens it, death is the burning coal, while other sorrows and miseries are the sparks that rise from the coal (Job 5:7). Commentary on Genesis 2:17.[19]

"Death" Meant a Life of Misery under the Tyranny of Sin. John Calvin: What kind of *death* does God mean in this place? It seems to me that a definition is to be sought from its opposite, by which I mean that it is to be inferred from the kind of *life* that was lost. They were, in every respect, happy: their life therefore looked after body and soul alike, for right judgment flourished in their souls along with a proper moderation of the affections, for life also reigned there. In their bodies there was no defect, so that they were wholly immune to death. Their earthly life would have been temporary, of course, but they would have passed into heaven without dying and without injury. Death is therefore now a terror to us: first, because it is a kind of annihilation for the body; then, because the soul perceives the curse of God. We must also consider what the cause of death is, namely,

alienation from God. From this it follows that this word *death* includes all the miseries in which Adam involved himself by his defection. Indeed, as soon as he revolted from God, the fountain of life, he was cast down from his former state, in order that he might perceive that human life without God is wretched and lost, and is therefore no different than death. Thus, their condition after their sin is not improperly called both death and the absence of life. The miseries and evils of both body and soul, with which they will be beset so long as they remain on earth, are a kind of entry-way into death, till death itself entirely engulfs them. Indeed, Scripture everywhere names as "dead" all those who are oppressed by the tyranny of sin and Satan and who breathe nothing but their own destruction. So the question is superfluous as to how it was that God threatened Adam with death *on the day* when he touched the fruit, when the punishment was deferred for so long, for at that moment Adam was consigned to death and death began its reign in him, until grace should arrive and bring a cure. Commentary on Genesis 2:16.[20]

Did God Create Death? Andrew Willet: Seeing that by God's sentence death laid hold of Adam, the question is whether God made death, and whether this physical death is a punishment of sin. We answer, that death is a defect of nature, beside the first intention of the Creator, brought into the world by sin, so that God is not its author; it exists only as the fruit and effect of sin. But as death is a just punishment inflicted for sin, so it is of God, who though he originally did not make death, yet he now administers it, thereby showing his justice upon human transgression: so that, as

---

[19]*Hexapla* (1608), 34-35, citing Philo, *On the Allegories of Moses* 2; Eucherius, *Commentarii in Genesim* bk. 1 (at 2:16-17; cf. PL 50:908); Pererius, *Commentari[a] et disputation[es] in Genesim* bk. 4 q. 4; Augustine, *City of God* 1.12. [20]CTS 1:127-28* (CO 23:45-46).

Augustine said, speaking of the beginning of darkness, "God did not make darkness but regulated it." So may it be said of death. COMMENTARY ON GENESIS 2:17.[21]

DEATH IS BOTH NATURAL AND A PUNISHMENT. CARDINAL CAJETAN: Note well that we do not say that human beings, before they had sinned, were immortal (because death is natural to human beings as a necessary consequence of their materiality). Rather, we say that they would have been preserved from death as a divine gift—of which gift human beings were deprived on account of their sin of disobedience. For this reason, death, which was utterly natural to humankind, is also a punishment brought about by the sin of the first humans. COMMENTARY ON GENESIS 2:17.[22]

---

[21]*Hexapla* (1608), 35, paraphrasing Augustine, *On Genesis against the Manichees* 1.9.15 (PL 34:180). [22]*Commentarii illustres* (1539), 23.

2:18-25 THE FORMATION OF WOMAN AND THE FIRST MARRIAGE

[18]*Then the LORD God said, "It is not good that the man should be alone; I will make him a helper fit for[a] him." [19]Now out of the ground the LORD God had formed[b] every beast of the field and every bird of the heavens and brought them to the man to see what he would call them. And whatever the man called every living creature, that was its name. [20]The man gave names to all livestock and to the birds of the heavens and to every beast of the field. But for Adam[c] there was not found a helper fit for him. [21]So the LORD God caused a deep sleep to fall upon the man, and while he slept took one of his ribs and closed up its place with flesh. [22]And the rib that the LORD God had taken from the man he made[d] into a woman and brought her to the man. [23]Then the man said,*

"This at last is bone of my bones
and flesh of my flesh;
she shall be called Woman,
because she was taken out of Man."[e]

[24]*Therefore a man shall leave his father and his mother and hold fast to his wife, and they shall become one flesh. [25]And the man and his wife were both naked and were not ashamed.*

a Or *corresponding to; also verse 20* **b** Or *And out of the ground the LORD God formed* **c** Or *the man* **d** Hebrew *built* **e** The Hebrew words for *woman* (ishshah) and *man* (ish) sound alike

OVERVIEW: The climax of Genesis 2 is the completion of creation by the advent of the first human couple. That part of the narrative begins with God's declaration that the man should not be alone and with a seemingly trial-and-error approach to finding a companion and a helper fit for the man by passing all living creatures before the man to see what he would call them. In addition to wondering how all these animals were marshaled before Adam, commentators traditionally took this occasion to note Adam's dominion over these creatures as well as his wisdom. Indeed, unfallen Adam is usually credited with a perfect knowledge of nature, and some commentators also presumed that Adam had prophetic gifts so as to know not only what took place while he slept during the formation of Eve, but possibly even so as to know something about the mystery of the incarnation. Arguably, commentators of the Reformation era tended to speak somewhat more modestly about Adam, but only slightly more so.

The failure to find a helper or companion among the animals led God to make the woman from one of Adam's ribs. Earlier exegetes worried about whether Adam was created with an extra rib or, if not, whether he was therefore deformed by the loss of one. Reformation commentators were generally uninterested in questions of this sort, but other traditional exegetical moves—such as exploring the allegorical significance of the rib for Eve's role as helper or seeing an analogy between the creation of Eve and the formation of the church—were more often embraced. The actual content of Eve's help, however, did not change much among Reformation commentators: the first two of Augustine's three "goods" of marriage (mutual fidelity, offspring, sacramental significance) were retained by Protestant reformers, who also reiterated the utility of marriage as a remedy against fornication. All of these themes could easily lead to the reiteration of

gender stereotypes in the course of exegesis, but there were other instances where Protestant interpreters explicitly repudiated misogynistic commonplaces.

Eve's creation in Genesis 2 is unlike the account of the creation of male and female in Genesis 1: there is no possibility of seeing her creation here as simultaneous with the man's. The sequence of their creation thus invited questions about whether there was a hierarchy of dignity between man and woman—questions raised most influentially by the apostle Paul. The present passage thus constitutes yet another crucial text for our understanding of gender roles in which the text of Genesis is significantly affected if not dominated by canonical, New Testament interpretations. Earlier, we noted how woman's sharing in the image of God in Genesis 1:26 is challenged, to say the least, by 1 Corinthians 11:7. In similar fashion, the role of woman as the man's helper and her creation both from and after him are given hugely influential apostolic interpretations in 1 Corinthians 11:8-9 and 1 Timothy 2:13. It is important to recall that however much the Reformation began with concerns over justification or church authority, it quickly found itself defending not only the dignity of marriage but also women's participation in the Reformation itself as readers (and sometimes even as proclaimers) of the gospel. Consequently, traditional exegetical arguments about gender roles received increased scrutiny as well as newly nuanced expositions, as will be evident from the following mixture of the expected patriarchal views with less predictable egalitarian affirmations.

The dignity of marriage and the rejection of clerical celibacy went hand in hand for Protestant theologians, and both themes found a natural home toward the end of Genesis 2. The opportunity for moral exhortation was missed by no one here, but Protestants in particular were able to capitalize on the image of Adam and Eve as "naked and unashamed" in order to underscore also the goodness of procreation and family life—even though, as we have seen throughout this chapter, the pristine character of all aspects of human life before the fall is something to be known only from the narrative of Genesis and not, alas, from our own experience.

2:18-20 *Seeking a Helper from among the Beasts and Birds*

GOD MAY WELL HAVE APPEARED TO ADAM (AND EVE). WOLFGANG MUSCULUS: In my judgment, it is no aberration to believe that God, who in any case has no visible form, acted by means of visible forms with Adam and Eve. Indeed, why should we suppose that in the narrative of Adam and Eve there was no place for this manner of acting, when it frequently occurs in the Scriptures and was God's usual pattern? Thus it is believable that he acted in the same way also with Adam, so that God—whether in his own person, or through the ministry of angels, or in some visible form—spoke with Adam, presented the animals to him, introduced the woman and brought about all the rest of the things later on in a manner that was visible and perceivable by the external senses. This explains the fact that he heard the voice of the Lord in paradise and labored to hide himself from his face. For if Adam had previously seen no visible form of God but had known everything only by the secret and invisible impulse of the spirit, what reason would he have had for concealing himself in some obscure place for the sake of fleeing and hiding from the face of the Lord? COMMENTARY ON GENESIS 2:18-25.[1]

REVIEWING THE ANIMALS TAUGHT ADAM TO CHERISH EVE. PETER MARTYR VERMIGLI: The animals weren't brought before Adam as if *God* wanted to find out whether some suitable helper for the man might be found among them. The Lord perfectly well knew that one

would not be discovered, but he brought the animals so that his gift would be welcomed by *Adam* all the more, lest he happen to think that there was no need for the creation of woman, because something could have been discovered among the animals as suitable for him as the woman was. God wanted Adam to learn for himself that no such helper was to be found. COMMENTARY ON GENESIS 2:20.[2]

ADAM'S INNATE KNOWLEDGE OF ANIMALS. MARTIN LUTHER: Since we do not possess a knowledge even of the natures of the animals, what their abilities and activities are, it is not surprising that we have no knowledge of God. There are in existence various books with descriptions of the natures of plants and animals. But how much time and how much observation were necessary until these could be collected this way through experience! There was a different light in Adam, who, as soon as he viewed an animal, came into possession of a knowledge of its entire nature and abilities, and, moreover, a far better one than we can acquire even when we devote an entire life to research into these things. Just as this knowledge in Adam was an outstanding gift of God, so it also pleased God exceedingly and delighted Him. LECTURES ON GENESIS 2:19.[3]

HUMANS WERE DESIGNED AS SOCIAL ANIMALS, NOT FOR SOLITUDE. JOHN CALVIN: Moses now explains God's design in creating the woman, namely, that there should be human beings on the earth who would cultivate mutual society among themselves. Yet a doubt may arise whether this notion should also be extended to offspring, for the words simply mean that since it was not expedient for the man to be alone, a wife must be created to be his helper. However, I take the meaning to be that God does indeed begin at the first step

---

[1]*In Mosis Genesim* (1554), 72. [2]*In Primum Librum Mosis* (1569), 12r. [3]LW 1:120 (WA 42:90).

of human society, yet he also intends to include others, each in its proper place. It is a general principle, then, that human beings were made to be social animals. Now, the human race could not exist without the woman. Therefore, among all human connections, that sacred bond by which husband and wife come together in one body and one soul is especially preeminent—just as nature itself taught Plato and others of the sounder class of philosophers to affirm. Furthermore, even though God addressed this to Adam, that it would not be helpful for him to be alone, I do not restrict the declaration to him alone but rather regard it as a law that is common to the human condition. Thus, we all should receive this saying, that solitude is not good, as addressed to each of us, excepting only those whom God exempts as by a special privilege. COMMENTARY ON GENESIS 2:18.[4]

ADAM SEARCHED FOR A MATE IN GOD'S IMAGE. ANNA MARIA VAN SCHURMAN:
When at last to this lord
   all the animals came,
he knew their natures
   and he gave to each its name.
He saw with an eye that differs now
   from that by which we see,
for our gaze falls upon the skin
   and knows not what makes things be.
But he had clearer sight,
   an image of the inside, as it were,
by which at once he could comprehend
   their essence and their nature.
He saw the beasts in pairs,
   yet himself he found alone,
and though he sought his mate,
   none was with him to be known:
she neither was nor came until
   God willed a fitting wife to make him,
to adorn her with His image so that
   in marriage she could take him.
From one, God makes two, and
   from those two he again makes one;

when man sees her, he knows as well
   his very flesh and bone.
God therefore wills that every man
   should call his own wife a *wo-man*
and love her more than father and
   mother as his true companion.
PARAPHRASE OF GENESIS 1–3.[5]

ADAM AND EVE KNEW MANY THINGS, BUT NOT EVERYTHING. ANDREW WILLET: This imposing of names upon the creatures makes evident Adam's great knowledge and wisdom in natural things, for names were given at the first according to the special properties and nature of creatures. And if Solomon had such exact knowledge of beasts and fowls, of trees and plants, even from the cedar to the hyssop (1 Kings 4:33), no doubt Adam had greater knowledge, whom we may safely hold to have been far wiser than Solomon—notwithstanding 1 Kings 3:12, where Solomon is said to be the wisest of all before or after him, for that is spoken of the common generation of men, where both Adam is excepted, created after God's image, and Christ, that holy seed born without sin (*contra* Tostatus). . . . Adam also had knowledge of supernatural things, for he was not ignorant of the mystery of the Trinity, according to whose image he was made, part of which entails knowledge (Col 3:10). It may also be safely held that Adam had knowledge of Christ to come, though not as a redeemer (for that promise was first made after the fall, Gen 3:15) but as the author and fountain of life, whereof the tree of life in paradise was a symbol. However, whereas some think that Adam and the woman were not ignorant of the fall of the angels (Catharinus), it seems to be otherwise, as may appear by the conference of Satan in the serpent with the woman, wherein she is altogether without suspicion. A knowledge of the fall of the angels would have made her more careful not to commit the same sin of

[4]CTS 1:128* (CO 23:46). [5]*Uitbreiding*, 6.9-22.

pride by desiring to be like unto God, though not in the same measure or degree. COMMENTARY ON GENESIS 2:19.[6]

SIN DESTROYED HUMAN AUTHORITY TO COMMAND WILD BEASTS. JOHN CALVIN:

That "God brought" the animals signifies nothing else than that he instilled them with a disposition to obedience, so that they would voluntarily offer themselves to the man, to the end that, after they had been closely examined, he might distinguish them with individual names that suited the nature of each one. This gentleness toward humans would have remained even in wild beasts, if the authority Adam received had not been lost on account of his defection from God. Now, as soon as he began to defy God, he experienced the ferocity of brute animals against himself. Indeed, while some can be broken with great effort, others always remain untamed, and some inspire us with terror by their fierceness, even when unprovoked. COMMENTARY ON GENESIS 2:19.[7]

2:21-22 Making Woman from Adam's Rib

MARRIAGE'S CHARTER TEXT. DAVID CHYTRAEUS: The doctrine of matrimony is necessary for the whole church. The original establishment of marriage, as well as its true, complete and learned definition, is handed down in this text, which ought to be recited in these very words on a daily basis in our district schools. Marriage is the indissoluble joining of one man and one woman who are lawfully able to be joined. It is divinely instituted so that we might come to know that God is a pure and spotless[†] mind, and we should serve him in purity.[†] In this way, through the propagation of the human race, God's eternal church is gathered. COMMENTARY ON GENESIS 2:18-25.[8]

WOMAN'S CREATION FROM A RIB IS LIKE A FAIRY TALE. MARTIN LUTHER: But so far as

this account is concerned, what, I ask you, could sound more like a fairy tale if you were to follow your reason? Would anyone believe this account about the creation of Eve if it were not so clearly told? . . . Here the woman herself is created from the man by a creation no less wonderful than that of Adam, who was made out of a clod of earth into a living soul. This is extravagant fiction and the silliest kind of nonsense if you set aside the authority of Scripture and follow the judgment of reason. LECTURES ON GENESIS 2:21.[9]

WOMAN WAS NOT LITERALLY DERIVED FROM A RIB. CARDINAL CAJETAN: From the text itself and its context, I am constrained to understand this production of the woman so that it is taken not literally but as a mystery—though not allegorically, but like a parable. If the text is taken literally in the first things said here, "a rib was removed from Adam," it will inevitably run to absurdity: because either Adam was a monster before the rib was removed from him, or he was maimed after the rib was removed from him. Either of these is clearly absurd, but everyone recognizes that nothing absurd should be alleged in the first production of things. . . . The context also insinuates the same thing. For to bring the animals before Adam and not to find among them a fitting helper for him, if it is understood literally, it signifies a ridiculous line of questioning. Really, in whose mind could certainty be overturned as to whether a fitting helper for Adam might be found among the birds? Hence, this kind of divine inquisition (introduced by Moses when he says, "no helper was found") is introduced for this purpose: so

---

[6]*Hexapla* (1608), 37. Alonso Tostato was a fifteenth-century Franciscan commentator; Ambrosius Catharinus was a Dominican commentator and a vocal opponent of Luther, Cardinal Cajetan and Erasmus. [7]CTS 1:132* (CO 23:48). [8]*In Genesin* (1576), 99. [†]"Pure and spotless" and "purity" render *castam* and *castitate*, which could also be translated as "chaste" and "chastity." [9]LW 1:123 (WA 42:92).

that we may understand that the later formation of the woman from the man's rib was not
to be understood according to the literal sense
but as a similitude. . . . The same point is made
by Moses' text about the sixth day, in which it
is clearly written that "male and female he
created them." Truly, in this way—in that
Moses had written that the woman was
created on the sixth day, and then subsequently describes her as formed from the man's
rib after humanity had been transferred into
paradise—he gave an opening to understand
this kind of formation from a rib† not in the
strict sense but as a similitude. If indeed the
woman was brought forth on the sixth day, he
did not suppose we should understand that she
was brought forth a second time. Commentary on Genesis 2:21.[10]

What Adam Gained and Lost. Konrad
Pellikan: He cast him into a deep sleep lest
he be terrified that he would feel pain from the
opening of his side, the removal of a rib or
putting his flesh back into place. And so, from
the union of the woman with the man, it is as
if the man lost no small measure of his solidity,
constancy and manly fortitude when his rib
bone was removed, in the place of which he
acquired a certain softness of the flesh and
became smaller and more fragile, accustomed
to feminine charm and affection—however
reluctantly husbands may have the heart to
admit it. Even Christ, the new Adam, endured
the ultimate in suffering; and through his
death, as a sacred promise, the church of
Christ was made his beloved bride. Commentary on Genesis 2:21.[11]

**Rib and Flesh, Strength and Gentle-
ness.** Peter Martyr Vermigli: The
metaphor of God "building" can take account
of the shape of a woman's body, which is
thicker in the lower part and thinner in the
upper, so that it can support a womb. . . . The
woman was formed from a rib, so that you

might thereby consider the strength of a
human helper as compared with other
helpers. But if we consider the man from
whom the rib was taken, to the degree that a
thing is smaller, the part should yield to the
whole. A bone is taken from Adam in the
creation of the woman and replaced with
flesh, because she should not be governed by
rigid authority but with consideration and
mildness. Nor should men be harsh toward
their wives, though neither should they
thereby become utterly soft and effeminate,
since of their many ribs, only one was plucked
out. If you consider how God built the rib, it
might come to mind that, before this, the
human body was molded from dust. All these
things here are expressed in figurative speech
and they describe God in terms of human
emotions. But in these things we also ought
to notice that Christ would have deserved
some new mode of being born, for he himself
would prove to be the author of a new generation of humans. The body of Adam was
formed from dust; that of Eve, from the man's
rib; but Christ, from a woman without a man.
Commentary on Genesis 2:22.[12]

**Commending Intimacy, Friendship and
Love.** Johannes Oecolampadius: God
wished to form the woman, Eve, to be the
man's companion, so that there should be the
most intimate closeness and friendship
between the man and the woman. So he took
her out of Adam's side, sending sleep on Adam
beforehand. Of course, God could have with
all ease done so without putting him to sleep,
but he did not want to. Rather this was the
counsel of God, so that it might appear that
the woman was extracted from the man with
some effort, so to speak, and so that, for her
part, she would be commended to the man

---

[10]*Commentarii illustres* (1539), 14-15; †a marginal note alerts the
reader to the discomfort of Cardinal Cajetan's later editor with
these progressive views. [11]*Commentaria Bibliorum* (1532) 1:5v.
[12]*In Primum Librum Mosis* (1569), 12r.

even more. The Lord made use of such means lest any sort of consternation overwhelm the man at the beginning of [her] fashioning. It is necessary here that we bid farewell to our reason and let the story be the story. For the God who made all things, it was most easy to remove a rib and put flesh upon it. By that miracle God wanted to commend to us the highest love and friendship, which the married ought to preserve between them, and finally to teach each one to acknowledge one's spouse as one's own flesh. COMMENTARY ON GENESIS 2:21-22.[13]

ADAM'S SLEEP DEPICTS THE AWAKENING AFTER DEATH. MARTIN LUTHER: But the sleep of Adam—so sound that he was not aware of what was being done to him—is a picture, as it were, of the transformation which would have taken place in the state of innocence. The righteous nature would have experienced no death but would have lived in the utmost joy, in obedience to God, and in admiration of the works of God until the time of the change had arrived. Then Adam would have experienced something similar to this sleep which happened to him as something most delightful while he lay among roses and under the loveliest trees. During that sleep he would have been changed and transported into the spiritual life without experiencing any pain, just as he did not realize that his body was being opened and that a rib, with flesh, was being taken out. Now this corrupt nature suffers death. In the case of the godly a sweet sleep follows this disintegration of the body until we awake in a new and eternal life. Moreover, here Adam is impelled by admiration and says: "This is bone from my bones," and yet he had been so overcome by sweet sleep that he did not realize that it had been taken out of him. So on that Day we shall say: "Behold, into what great glory this body, consumed by worms, has suddenly risen!" LECTURES ON GENESIS 2:21.[14]

ADAM WAS CREATED MORE NOBLY. KONRAD PELLIKAN: Now in fact he did not say "let us make" as in the case of Adam, but the singular "I will make." From this more majestic way of speaking it further appears that the creation of the man was more noble than that of the woman. "Before him" or "belonging to him," he said, so that the woman would defer to man and stand by to assist him, not one who debates or heaps cares upon her husband. COMMENTARY ON GENESIS 2:18.[15]

ADAM TRADED A RIB FOR A COMPANION WHO COMPLETED HIM. JOHN CALVIN: Some object either that the rib removed from Adam was superfluous, or that his body would have been mutilated by losing that rib. To either of these one may reply that they are inventing a great absurdity. If, however, we should say that the rib from which he would form a second body had been already prepared by the world's creator, I find nothing in this answer that disagrees with divine providence. Yet I am more in favor of a different conjecture, namely, that something was removed from Adam in order that he might embrace with greater kindness a part of himself. Thus, he did lose a rib. But he was repaid for it with a far richer reward, since he obtained a faithful and lifelong companion. Even more, he now saw himself made whole in his wife, where previously he had been but half a self. And in this we see a true likeness of our union with the Son of God, for he became weak that the members of his body might be endowed with strength. COMMENTARY ON GENESIS 2:21.[16]

IGNORE THESE CURIOUS QUESTIONS ABOUT MAKING THE WOMAN. ANDREW WILLET: It is a superfluous question, out of which side of Adam Eve was taken, whether out of the right

---

[13]*In Genesim* (1536), 39r-v. [14]LW 1:130-31 (WA 42:97-98).
[15]*Commentaria Bibliorum* (1532) 1:5r. [16]CTS 1:133* (CO 23:49).

or left. It is resolved by most as out of the left, because Adam's heart lay there; but these are frivolous and needless matters. So also is the question unnecessary (and more curious than profitable) whether this rib was one of Adam's necessary and substantial parts, or one supernumerary and superfluous. A man now has twenty-four ribs, twelve per side, and some think that this rib was one of them and that God created a new rib to replace it. But this opinion seems contrary to the text, because it is said, "God closed up the flesh in its place." If flesh were in place of the rib, then another rib was not made instead thereof. Again, God had already finished with the creation of Adam, . . . but if Adam had a rib created afterward, then he was not perfectly created before. So it is more likely that this rib was above the usual number of ribs created on purpose by the Lord, not as a superfluous or monstrous part, but as necessary for the creation of the woman, as God intended. And therefore Cajetan need not have been so perplexed with this question that he left the truth of the story and flew to allegories, finding no other solution. Finally, though no mention is made here of the creation of the woman's soul, yet it may be gathered that she received her soul directly from God just as Adam had, because they were both created according to God's image. COMMENTARY ON GENESIS 2:22.[17]

TRIVIAL QUESTIONS ABOUT EVE'S CRE-ATION MISS THE POINT. MARTIN LUTHER: Why is it necessary to discuss where God found the remaining material, God, who is able to do anything by a single word and who creates all things? These questions have their origin in philosophy and in the science of medicine, which discuss the works of God without the Word. Moreover, the result of this procedure is that the glory of Holy Scripture and the majesty of the Creator are lost. LECTURES ON GENESIS 2:21.[18]

THE CREATION NARRATIVES DO NOT DEMAND A LITERAL INTERPRETATION. CARDINAL CAJETAN: It doesn't matter if it be objected that woman's production from the man's rib is narrated by Scripture in a historical manner, as if recounting things that happened. First, because the six natural days are narrated no less in a historical manner, with evening and morning, and yet it is nonetheless not appropriate to understand that those works happened through this kind of natural six days. Next, because the serpent's punishment is also described in a historical manner (further below), and yet it's obviously childish to understand it physically, as it sounds. Nor is that same understanding therefore opposed to the sober sense of Holy Scripture, just as a sober reading of the divine line of questioning mentioned above is that of inquiring according to a similitude and not of finding God [literally] as described. COMMENTARY ON GENESIS 2:21.[19]

2:23 "Bone of My Bone and Flesh of My Flesh"

GOD ACTS AS MATCHMAKER FOR ADAM AND EVE. WOLFGANG MUSCULUS: This may be considered the betrothal of Eve, who was so recently born. He who had just created her, now betroths her and at the same time acts as her matchmaker. . . . He does not say here, "And he brought her to Adam, so that he might see what he would call her," but so that she might be a helper to him in marriage. The manner of presentation was like this because she had already been announced by God's words, when he said, "It is not good for the man to be alone, let us make for him a helper similar to him," and it did not seem necessary to repeat this. So this presentation was nothing other than an act of true matchmak-

---

[17]*Hexapla* (1608), 38, crediting Mercerus and Calvin. [18]LW 1:130 (WA 42:97). [19]*Commentarii illustres* (1539), 25.

ing. And Adam rightly understood this, and when she had been presented to him, he recognized the woman and took her for his partner, saying, "This is now bone of my bones, and flesh of my flesh." COMMENTARY ON GENESIS 2:18.[20]

ADAM RECOGNIZED EVE AS "ANOTHER SELF."

JOHN CALVIN: In using the expression, "This at last," Adam indicates that until now, he had been missing something, as if he had said, "At last, now I have obtained a suitable companion, who shares the substance of my flesh and in whom I behold, as it were, another self." And he gives to his wife a name taken from that of man, that by this testimony and this mark he might attest God's wisdom with an everlasting remembrance. COMMENTARY ON GENESIS 2:23.[21]

ADAM'S PURE AND HOLY PASSION FOR EVE.

MARTIN LUTHER: The word [translated as] "now" or "this time" or "at last," is not superfluous, as it appears to be; it expresses most beautifully the affection of a husband who feels his need for a delightful and full relationship or cohabitation in both love and holiness. It is as if he were saying: "I have seen all the animals. I have carefully considered the females which were provided for the increase and the preservation of their kind, but they are of no concern to me. But this at last is flesh of my flesh and bones of my bones. I desire to live with her and to accede to God's will by procreating descendants." This little word indicates an overwhelmingly passionate love. Today that purity and innocence is lost; there still remains the bridegroom's delight and his love for the bride, but because of sin it is impure and imperfect. Adam's love was most pure and most holy and also pleasing to God. Impelled by this love, he says: "This now is bone from my bones, not from wood, not from stone, not from a clod of the earth. It concerns me more

closely, for it is made from my bones and my flesh." LECTURES ON GENESIS 2:23.[22]

WHAT IT MEANS FOR A WIFE TO BE HER HUSBAND'S RIB.

KONRAD PELLIKAN: Having been taught that she was taken from the body of the man, a wife should not be proud or disdainful but should look up to the source of her existence; she should honor and cherish and allow herself to be ruled and instructed by her husband; she should guard loyalty to him as to her very self, and work with him for the household needs without anger or argument. In turn, she should be loved by her husband as another self to him and, like a noble member of his own body, she should be constantly cherished as his heart's most loyal guardian. COMMENTARY ON GENESIS 2:23.[23]

HUSBANDS SHOULD REGARD A WIFE AS GOD'S WORKMANSHIP.

WOLFGANG MUSCULUS: Note here that the formation of woman was undertaken for the man's sake. . . . But it is also set forth for husbands' consideration that they ought to embrace their wives lovingly, for they were prepared and destined for them when they were conceived and fashioned in the maternal womb. For what befell Adam by God's plan, that Eve was formed for his sake, the same happens to every man as long as the world endures, that a wife is destined by God for each man before he is born. . . . For this reason a pious husband will constantly give thought to his wife. She is the one whom the Lord destined for you in her mother's womb, and he formed her to be such as she is. He will summon this thought above all, to the end that wives may be loved in the Lord and be treated piously and honorably. COMMENTARY ON GENESIS 2:18-25.[24]

---

[20]In Mosis Genesim (1554), 70. "Matchmaker" here translates the unusual word *nymphagogia*. [21]CTS 1:135* (CO 23:50). [22]LW 1:136-37 (WA 42:102-3). [23]Commentaria Bibliorum (1532) 1:5v. [24]In Mosis Genesim (1554), 73-74.

Eve Created from Adam to Bind Them Together. John Calvin: Although this method of forming woman may seem ridiculous to profane persons, some of whom may say that Moses is writing fables, to us the wonderful providence of God nonetheless shines forth here. Indeed, in order that the kinship of the human race might become more sacred, he wanted both males and females to spring from one and the same source. He therefore created human nature in the person of Adam and then formed Eve from him, so that the woman would be only a portion of the whole race. Moses' words in Genesis 1:28, above, intend the same thing: "God created humankind, he made them male and female." In this way Adam was taught to recognize himself in his wife, as in a mirror; and Eve, in her turn, to submit herself willingly to her husband, as being taken out of him. But if the two sexes had proceeded from different sources, there would have been occasion either for mutual contempt or for envy or strife. Commentary on Genesis 2:21.[25]

"Woman" in Hebrew Connotes Parity. Martin Luther: We are altogether unable to imitate the nicety of the Hebrew language. *Ish* denotes a man. But he says that Eve must be called *Isha*, as though for "wife" you would say "she-man" from man, a heroic woman who performs manly acts. Moreover, this designation carries with it a wonderful and pleasing description of marriage, in which, as the jurist also says, the wife shines by reason of her husband's rays. Whatever the husband has, this the wife has and possesses in its entirety. Their partnership involves not only their means but children, food, bed, and dwelling; their purposes, too, are the same. The result is that the husband differs from the wife in no other respect than in sex; otherwise the woman is altogether a man. Whatever the man has in the home and is, this the woman has and is; she differs only in sex. Lectures on Genesis 2:23.[26]

Woman's Equal Dignity. Johannes Brenz: Our forebears explained, not without insight, that woman was created not from the man's head or foot but from his side, to signify that woman should not lord it over the man or be a footstool for his feet, but be of equal right and dignity. At the same time, the order should be observed that the man be the head with the woman under him, so that together with the man she might enjoy his industry and dignity as members of a single body. Commentary on Genesis 2:21-22.[27]

2:23 [2:18] *"A Helper Fit for Him"*

The "Suitability" of the Woman's Help Suggests Lifelong Companionship. Wolfgang Musculus: This word *kenegdo* signifies that a woman is prepared for the man and placed alongside him so that the companionship and intimacy that they share living together may be undivided, not like that of animals who come together but once a year for procreation and afterwards wander off separately and unrestrained. A wife ought to be so yoked to her husband that she is inseparable from him. Commentary on Genesis 2:18.[28]

What Makes Eve a Fitting Helper? John Calvin: I take "fit" here in its natural sense, as if she were a kind of counterpart, like an antiphon.[†] Indeed, woman is said to be "directly across" from the man, because she ought to respond to him. . . . Certainly, Moses intended to indicate a measure of correspondence between them, which thereby refutes the error of some,[‡] who think the woman was formed only for the sake of propagation and who restrict the word *good*, which was just mentioned in this verse, to the production of offspring. They do not think that a wife was

---

[25]CTS 1:132-33* (CO 23:48-49). [26]LW 1:137 (WA 42:103). [27]*Opera* 1:39. [28]*In Mosis Genesim* (1554), 74.

personally necessary for Adam, because at that point he was free from lust—as if she had been given to him only to share his bed and not far more to be his inseparable companion in life! COMMENTARY ON GENESIS 2:18.[29]

MARRIAGE IS SAFER. KONRAD PELLIKAN: It is good for a man to be as Paul was, namely, an apostle and evangelist, without the burden of rearing children, a wife and family. . . . But it is safer to be as God said here, "I will make him a helper like unto him." COMMENTARY ON GENESIS 2:18.[30]

WOMAN OFFERS THE MAN THREE KINDS OF HELP. WOLFGANG MUSCULUS: Wives are given by God for this, or rather they are *formed* for this, that they may be helpers of their husbands. She who is unable to help her husband cannot duly fulfill the role of wife. But a woman's help is of three kinds.

First, *for procreating offspring*. The womanly sex was created for this above all, so that from the legitimate conjunction of a man and a woman the human race would be led to that fullness of its multiplication for which it was eternally predestined. In this matter, neither a man without a woman nor a woman without a man avails for anything. That is precisely why marriage was established by God, and it was for that very reason God created and blessed not men alone nor women alone, but male and female together, saying, "Increase and multiply, etc." The power of God overturns neither this common law nor the need for a spouse, even though he brought forth Adam from the dust of the earth without father or mother, Eve from Adam without a mother, and Christ from the virgin Mary without a father.

A woman's second kind of help is, as a wife, *to offer her husband a remedy against the temptations of fornication and illicit lust*. The apostle reminds us of this in 1 Corinthians 7, saying, "On account of fornication, each man should have his own wife, and each woman her

own husband," and "If they cannot control themselves, they should marry, for it is better to marry than to burn with passion." Therefore marriage is not only for procreating offspring but was also instituted by God for avoiding sins of every kind of impurity. That this is a greater reason for legitimate marriage ought to have been recognized, nominally at least, by those whose office should have given them a zealous interest, for the sake of sound doctrine, in cutting off every occasion of sin in the church of God with a two-edged sword—especially in these extraordinarily corrupt latter days which are so amazingly exposed to so many occasions for wrongdoing. . . .

The third kind of help prepared for men in the formation of the female sex is *economic*: namely, that a wife ought to accommodate her labor to her husband by administering the home, managing household affairs, educating children, and other things of this sort. The advantage of this womanly help in running the household is great and exceedingly necessary, something that men who are heads of a household can grievously miss, for it is vastly easier for a woman to manage her household without the works of a man than for a man to do so without the works of a woman. Indeed, the husband occupies first place, and the more important aspects of the household economy belong to his care; but those things that are secondary and referred to the care of the wife are more or less comparable, so that a husband labors in vain unless his wife faithfully fulfills her duties. Many things have to be managed by her in the absence of her husband, and a worthy matron illumines her home with the splendor of her diligence—just as the moon shines in the absence of the sun. COMMENTARY ON GENESIS 2:18-25.[31]

---

[29]CTS 1:130-31* (CO 23:47-48). †*Antistoikon* and *antistrophon* describe parallel constructions in Greek poetry. ‡Calvin is surely criticizing Augustine here. [30]*Commentaria Bibliorum* (1532) 1:5r, echoing 1 Cor 7:7. [31]*In Mosis Genesim* (1554), 74.

GOD'S SPEECH HERE IS FOR THE SAKE OF WIVES TODAY. HULDRYCH ZWINGLI: "It is not good for the man to be alone." Surely God was not unaware of this before he fashioned the man? Of course not, but all these things are said anthropopathically. Indeed, if architects see something missing from a building, they are accustomed to supply and provide for it. However, these things occur so that women might learn that they owe reverence and obedience to their husbands, since the wife was created by God for her husband and after him and in his image. ANNOTATIONS ON GENESIS 2:18.[32]

WOMAN WAS ALSO CREATED IN THE IMAGE OF GOD, BUT IN A SECONDARY WAY. JOHN CALVIN: When the human race was created in the person of the man, the common dignity of our whole nature was honored with one eulogy, without distinction, when it was said, "Let us make man." Nor was it necessary to be repeated in creating the woman, who was nothing else than an addition to the man. Certainly, it cannot be denied that woman too was created in God's image, though in the second degree. It therefore follows that what was said in the creation of the man belongs as well to the female sex. COMMENTARY ON GENESIS 2:18.[33]

THE SEQUENCE OF CREATION IS NOT THE SOLE BASIS FOR ADAM'S EMINENCE. PETER MARTYR VERMIGLI: [Paul says] the man was formed before the woman. He seems to draw his argument from sequence (*a tempore*), but because that was not in itself firm enough, it is therefore strengthened by an argument from purpose (*a fine*), and it is said that "woman was created for man"—not vice versa, that man was made for woman. As for sequence, there are many things that were created before man (*hominem*) that nonetheless do not excel him in dignity. Yet it is not the case that you should say that the woman and the man were equally

created for God, because even if we know that God has created all things for his own sake, we continually recognize that there is a certain order among the purposes of things. Certainly, the glory of God does occupy first place among everything, but that does not mean that the woman was not made for the man (as Scripture attests). COMMENTARY ON 1 CORINTHIANS 11:8-10.[34]

EVE'S SUBORDINATION WAS A FORM OF EQUALITY. ANDREAS BODENSTEIN VON KARLSTADT: God created a helpmeet for Adam who was his equal, yet different. He therefore created Adam first and Eve afterward and gave the man authority and the woman submissiveness. Just as he created Adam to the glory of God so that he might fully cling to God's will, praise, counsel, and help. Spouses retain their equality if they remain in the instituted unity, with the woman being obedient and submissive to her husband, holding him in honor and treating him well, always mindful that she has been taken from the man and is called *she-man*. A husband, on the other hand, must not forget that woman is his bone, flesh, and blood. He ought always to love her and never hate or envy her. He ought to refrain from anything that might separate him from his wife, as Adam says, "On this account a man shall leave his father and mother and cling to his wife." When married people pervert the instituted order so that she becomes man and he she-man, it is inevitable that conflicts and tensions arise. For wherever God does not govern, there unrest and the devil's play take over. Man is the head on the basis of the divine order. This order is perverted when the woman rules and the man is being ruled. I do not here speak of the ordering of the kitchen,

---

[32]ZSW 13:21, alluding to 1 Cor 11:7. [33]CTS 1:129* (CO 23:46). [34]*In priorem ad Corinth.* (1551), 287v; conflating elements of 1 Tim 2:13 ("For Adam was formed first, then Eve") with 1 Cor 11:8-9.

the barn, or such like. I speak of the governing of the will and of advice, of which this chapter speaks. Just as equality is found in the unity of both wills, so it is with giving assistance in physical service. . . . For this reason God made women (who are normally soft and gentle) especially tough. He hardened them so that they may serve their husbands. I doubt it not that many men would become tired of a woman's work. REGARDING VOWS.[35]

EVE WAS MEANT TO BE ADAM'S EQUAL.

MARTIN LUTHER: Moses wanted to point out in a special way that the other part of humanity, the woman, was created by a unique counsel of God in order to show that this sex, too, is suited for the kind of life which Adam was expecting and that this sex was to be useful for procreation. Hence it follows that if the woman had not been deceived by the serpent and had not sinned, she would have been the equal of Adam in all respects. For the punishment, that she is now subjected to the man, was imposed on her after sin and because of sin, just as the other hardships and dangers were: travail, pain, and countless other vexations. Therefore Eve was not like the woman of today; her state was far better and more excellent, and she was in no respect inferior to Adam, whether you count the qualities of the body or those of the mind. LECTURES ON GENESIS 2:18.[36]

WOMAN IS MAN'S PARTNER, NOT HIS POSSESSION OR SLAVE.

WOLFGANG MUSCULUS: God did not form woman from the dust of the earth as he formed Adam, but from Adam's own body: and even then, not from a lock of hair or a patch of skin, but from his flesh and bone. He took her from the innermost parts of the man because he formed her to be united to him. Who does not see that God wished the man and the woman to be bound together tightly and to embrace one another in mutual love? To be sure, he joined every kind of animal in pairs, but of none do we read that they take females that have sprung from their own flesh; rather, it was enough that they should have the same bodily form, similar in appearance but differing in sex. Here, however, there appears the unique relationship of having the same flesh, indeed, the very same, on account of which the apostle says, "He who loves his wife loves himself. After all, no one ever hated his own body, but he feeds and cares for it." Note also that when God wished to form the woman from Adam's own body, he took her to be formed not just from any part of Adam but from his side: not from Adam's head, lest the woman grow haughty on account of her origin; nor from his feet, lest she seem to be demoted to the worthlessness and insignificance of a slave; but rather from Adam's side, so that he would know she was made to be his partner and the inseparable companion of his life, and so that she might legitimately cleave to his side, whence she was taken. This consideration argues against the inhumanity of those who treat their wives no differently than as if they had been acquired for a price along with other possessions, so that you would regard them as scarcely differing at all from handmaids. Such is especially the case for the marriages of those who practice polygamy. COMMENTARY ON GENESIS 2:18-25.[37]

WOMAN WAS NOT A NECESSARY EVIL, BUT THE MAN'S COMPANION.

JOHN CALVIN: The order of nature implies that the woman should be a helper to the man. Truly, it is a vulgar proverb that "woman is a necessary evil," but far better that we should listen to the voice of God, which declares that she was added as the man's companion and partner, to

---

[35]CRR 8:97-98. [36]LW 1:115 (WA 42:87). [37]*In Mosis Genesim* (1554), 74, citing Eph 5:28-29. The homily about why Eve was made from Adam's rib rather than his head or feet is often credited to Peter Lombard, but there are earlier precedents, including rabbinic parallels.

assist him to live well. Commentary on Genesis 2:18.[38]

Helping Is a Mutual Calling. Johannes Brenz: He calls the woman a *helper*. She helps the man, first, in preserving the economy, that is, in propagating and preserving the citizens of this earth. She also helps the man in preserving the church of God, that is, in multiplying the citizens of the heavenly kingdom. Indeed, human beings are created and multiplied not merely to inhabit the earth, but above all to take hold of the heavenly kingdom. . . . The words then added, *like him*, ought to be read as "with him" or "in his presence." They signify that for human beings the marriage of a man and woman ought to be a life joined together indivisibly. . . . In these words the terms of an honest and godly marriage are set forth and spouses are instructed in their duties. First, marriage is not an impure way of life, but divinely ordained and holy. Therefore, in marriage, one is to lead an honorable, holy and chaste life. Second, each spouse is the helper of the other—a helper not in impiety or for wickedness, but rather for the sake of honesty and holiness. Wherefore spouses sin gravely who are hindrances to one another, either through quarreling or other wicked acts, so that they do not lead a pious and honorable life. Finally, given that a woman ought to be a helper alongside her husband, it is a horrible sin if spouses vent their wrath on each other, so that one forsakes the other on account of the other's faults and vices. Commentary on Genesis 2:18.[39]

On the Four Names Given to Eve. Wolfgang Musculus: The first two names are those imposed by God. One pertains to her first creation, which is from the earth from which Adam was taken, from whose flesh and bone afterwards Eve was formed, in order to signify that she too, like Adam, was born of the earth. And that is why she is called by the common name *Adam*, for earth is called *adamah*. Wherefore the first and shared name that pertains to woman is *Adam*, which I call the name of her first creation. The second name pertains to sex, expressing the mark of the feminine sex, namely, *neqebah*, a word derived from perforation or puncture that means "provided with an entrance." This word designates the womanly sex, just as *zakar* indicates masculinity. Both words occur in the preceding chapter, "Male and female he made them." The last two names were imposed on her by Adam by his right as a husband, and these pertain to her not so much as female or earthly but more as of his flesh and as his companion. One is *ishah*, already mentioned as [the feminine form of] *man*, to which an explanation is added, namely, that she was *me-ish*, that is, "taken out of man." The woman belonged to him to this extent, seeing that she was taken out of him. Thus, this name pertains not so much to her creation as to the law of matrimony; it signifies that the woman is no longer merely female but is also destined for marriage. The last name is *Havah*, that is, *Eve*. Adam imposed this name on her later, in chapter three, where again an explanation is added, that she would be "the mother of all the living." . . .

By considering these things, pious women may be advised about the nature of their creation. Let them first of all bear in mind that they too are *Adams*, that is, they are just as *earthly* as their husbands are, lest they make undue claims for their rights on the grounds that they were created from the flesh and bone of the first human. For they too were earth, even though it was displayed in a different form. Second, that they are *neqeboth*, that is, *females* by sex, and it is therefore by no means fitting for them to regard those things that safeguard the modesty of their sex as foreign to themselves. Third, that they are *ishoth*, that

---

[38]CTS 1:129-30* (CO 23:47).   [39]*Opera* 1:37-38.

is, *counterparts*, destined for marriage as partners and wives. . . . Fourth, they are *Havoth*, that is, *Eves* and mothers of the living. It is a great honor but at the same time a great burden to bear the office of motherhood. Wherefore mothers need faith, that they may rely on God's providence to regulate all things most faithfully. COMMENTARY ON GENESIS 2:18-25.[40]

2:24 The First Marriage

SPOUSES MUST BE DEARER THAN PARENTS. PETER MARTYR VERMIGLI: Not that he does not support them or honor them, but he will now be so closely glued to his wife that he who was previously called a part of his father has now been torn from him to become one flesh with his wife. These words are uttered ambiguously, so that you do not know whose they are, God's or Adam's. Nonetheless, uttered by Adam, they are to be regarded as God's. Here it is signified that one's father and mother have to be let go of, and that no future relationship will ever be more closely joined. Consequently, those paternal and maternal connections that appear to be so all-important would seem to be abandoned here. COMMENTARY ON GENESIS 2:24.[41]

MARRIAGE PREVAILS OVER THE COMMAND TO HONOR FATHER AND MOTHER. WOLFGANG MUSCULUS: The command to honor one's parents is not to be given such weight that it should dissolve or invalidate the prior command. Adam and Eve were spouses before they were parents. The law of marriage takes precedence over the law pertaining to parents. No one is a father before he is a husband; no one is a mother before she is a wife. Unless the marriage is solid, it will not proceed to parenthood. Therefore, so that there might be a place for that law about honoring parents, it is necessary that it be preceded by a stable marriage—and not just preceded, but such

stability should continue lifelong. For this reason, just as it is wrong for a mother to be a mother in such a way that she shirks her obligations as a wife to her husband (that is, sundering the marriage bond on account of the children and being devoted more to the children than to her husband), so also is it wrong for a husband to cling to his parents more than to his wife. COMMENTARY ON GENESIS 2:18-25.[42]

INFIDELITY IMPAIRS THE "ONE FLESH" OF A MARRIAGE. PETER MARTYR VERMIGLI: By the woman's formation from a rib, it is declared that in a marriage there ought to be a union of *the whole to the part* (and therefore a man pines for a wife) and of *the part to the whole*, so that the part may be preserved there (and therefore a woman seeks a husband). A husband therefore seeks a part of himself and gets back the member that was taken from him. It is also noted here that it is Christ's own teaching that marriage ought to be an indissoluble bond. You would recognize this so long as they are able to be one flesh, but it is destroyed by fornication, as well as by all those obstacles by which spouses are unable to be one flesh in such a way that they may both require and provide mutual kindness and service to one another. COMMENTARY ON GENESIS 2:24.[43]

NO POLYGAMY IN PARADISE. JOHANNES BRENZ: When Adam says . . . "The two shall be one flesh," and Christ thus explains, "They are no longer two, but one flesh," it signifies without obscurity that it is not licit according to the natural law of marriage for one man to have two or more wives at the same time. Indeed, when God was going to give a wife to Adam, he created from his rib not two women

---

[40]*In Mosis Genesim* (1554), 78. [41]*In Primum Librum Mosis* (1569), 12v. [42]*In Mosis Genesim* (1554), 79-80. [43]*In Primum Librum Mosis* (1569), 12v.

but only one. And he says that two, not three, shall be one flesh. This also agrees with what Paul says in 1 Corinthians 7:4, "A husband does not have authority over his own body, but his wife does." He clearly teaches that whoever takes one wife cannot, while she lives, pledge his troth to another spouse, because that is beyond his right. So what should we say about the patriarchs, who, though they were the holiest of men, still possessed more wives than one? My response is that this custom among the holy patriarchs was more tolerated by God than approved. Commentary on Genesis 2:24.[44]

Marriage Harmed by Sin, but Good Still Remains. John Calvin: I confess, indeed, that in this corrupt state of the human race, the blessing of God that is described here is neither perceived nor flourishes. However, the cause of this evil must be considered, namely, that the order of nature appointed by God has been inverted by us. For if our integrity had remained to this day such as it was from the beginning, that divine institution would be clearly discerned and the sweetest harmony would reign in marriage: because then the husband would look with reverence to God, the woman would likewise be a faithful assistant to him, and with one accord they would both cultivate a mutuality that was no less friendly and peaceful than it was holy. But now, by our own fault and by the corruption of our nature, it has come to pass that this happiness of marriage has in large part been lost, or at the least is now mingled and stained with many difficulties. Hence arise quarrels, troubles, bitterness, disagreements, and an enormous sea of evils; and hence it happens that men are often upset by their wives and feel hindered by them. But for all that, marriage was not capable of being so spoiled by human depravity that the blessing that the Lord once sanctioned by his word should be entirely abolished and extin-

guished. Therefore, amid the many difficulties of marriage that are the fruits of our degenerate nature, some remnants of divine good persist, just as in a fire apparently smothered, some sparks still glitter. Commentary on Genesis 2:18.[45]

Adam Saw the Mystery of Matrimony; We See Christ and the Church. Peter Martyr Vermigli: Some say that "the Lord caused a deep sleep to fall on Adam" . . . so that he would not feel the pain of a rib being removed and thus dread the woman. I don't think that is true, for even if he had suffered pain, he would have been able to love her afterwards, just as a mother loves a child whom she has delivered in pain. One should believe, moreover, that God would have removed the rib gently and without the feeling of suffering. I tend more to approve that the mystery of matrimony was shown to Adam while he was in that sleep or trance, and that's why he uttered the holy statement that "This is now bone of my bones. For this reason a man will leave his father and mother." The woman was taken from the man's side so that she might be perfectly joined to him by a bond of charity. From this text, we understand that by Christ's holy union with the church, we have partaken of his strength, while for our sake he clothed himself with our frail flesh. In this case, too, God filled the place of the rib with flesh. And Christ slept on the cross in the sleep of death, so that we who are his church might be able to be reborn in him and be made new creatures. You'll also note the force of the phrase, "to build a rib." Truly, it is the rib of Christ—the rib of the man, I say, who is the second Adam—whose strength is the foundation of the church, upon which it is *built*. It's no accident, therefore, that this metaphor was selected. Commentary on Genesis 2:21.[46]

---

[44]*Opera* 1:40. [45]CTS 1:129-30* (CO 23:47). [46]*In Primum Librum Mosis* (1569), 12r.

2:25 *Naked and Not Ashamed*

ORIGINAL SIN IS MORE THAN LUST.
MARTIN LUTHER: When the sophists speak of original sin, they are speaking only of wretched and hideous lust or concupiscence. But original sin really means that human nature has completely fallen; that the intellect has become darkened, so that we no longer know God and His will and no longer perceive the works of God; furthermore, that the will is extraordinarily depraved, so that we do not trust the mercy of God and do not fear God but are unconcerned, disregard the Word and will of God, and follow the desire and the impulses of the flesh; likewise, that our conscience is no longer quiet but, when it thinks of God's judgment, despairs and adopts illicit defenses and remedies. . . . In the case of the soul the outstanding fact is this: that the knowledge of God has been lost; that we do not everywhere and always give thanks to Him; that we do not delight in His works and deeds; that we do not trust Him; that when He inflicts deserved punishments, we begin to hate God and to blaspheme Him; that when we must deal with our neighbor, we yield to our desires and are robbers, thieves, adulterers, murderers, cruel, inhuman, merciless, etc. The passion of lust is indeed some part of original sin. But greater are the defects of the soul: unbelief, ignorance of God, despair, hate, blasphemy. Of these spiritual disasters Adam, in the state of innocence, had no knowledge. LECTURES ON GENESIS 2:17.[47]

OUR OWN NAKEDNESS SHOULD TEACH US TO LIVE IN PEACE, UNARMED.
WOLFGANG MUSCULUS: They were created not hairy or furry like most animals, but naked, and in that condition all of us, their offspring, are also born both naked and plainly defenseless. This should admonish us how repugnant to our nature is that malice by which we arm and disfigure this naked and defenseless body of ours, born for peace and not for slaughter, with so many kinds of weapons for slaughter and cruelty. Indeed, if some beast should be born with an appearance like our own armoring, it would be regarded not only as a kind of monster but also as liable to destroy both humans and animals—something either to flee from with horror or to destroy straightaway. Thus, anyone who is sensible is warned by our nature at birth and by the defenseless nakedness of the human body . . . that we should lead lives that are innocent and devoted to peace. That warlike armament, prepared not for the slaughter of beasts but for the blood of our own kin, was no human invention but is wholly of the devil. COMMENTARY ON GENESIS 2:18-25.[48]

THE MEANING OF NAKEDNESS.
ANDREW WILLET: Adam was not ashamed, but not (as some Hebrews say) because Eve was of his own flesh, for afterward they were ashamed to behold the nakedness of one another. Nor does Moses set them forth as impudent and shameless persons (as the Adamites† are, taking this example as a pretense), mingling together like brute beasts. Rather, this nakedness of their bodies shows the nakedness and simplicity of their minds: for shame is the fruit of sin, and thus they were not ashamed before sin entered. Some think that in children who are not ashamed of their nakedness, there yet remains some shadow of our first estate. But children are without shame because they lack reason, similar to what is seen in brute beasts. But in the kingdom of heaven, we shall be all naked and without shame as Adam was—and without fear or danger of sin, which Adam was not. COMMENTARY ON GENESIS 2:25.[49]

---

[47]LW 1:114 (WA 42:86). "Sophists" is Luther's contemptuous name for the scholastic theologians. [48]*In Mosis Genesim* (1554), 81. [49]*Hexapla* (1608), 39; †various heresies from the second century on were called Adamites, but their enduring and obvious characteristic seems to have been the practice of nudism.

Sin Brought Shame Even to Procreation. Martin Luther: But who can describe in words the glory of the innocence we have lost? There still remains in nature the longing of the male for the female, likewise the fruit of procreation; but these are combined with the awful hideousness of lust and the frightful pain of birth. Shame, ignominy, and embarrassment arise even among married people when they wish to enjoy their legitimate intercourse. So universal is the most oppressive evil of original sin! The creation indeed is good, and the blessing is good; but through sin they are so corrupted that married people cannot make use of them without shame. All these things would not have existed in Adam's state of innocence; but just as married people eat and drink together without shame, so there would have been a transcendent decency, not shame and embarrassment, in procreation and birth. Lectures on Genesis 2:16-17.[50]

Shame Is the Fruit of Sin. Peter Martyr Vermigli: Nothing was planted by God in the human body or soul that would have been indecent. Nor would they have felt in their members or affections "another law that waged war with the law of their minds" (as Romans 7 puts it). Not at all! Rather, all of their members would have seemed no less honorable than how we now regard a hand, a face or a foot. One cannot find here any praise that is merely lukewarm for their condition: for in them, no illicit impulse or affection was aroused by the sight of any of their members. They had been clothed with the most magnificent glory and honor, and therefore nakedness was not a matter of shame to them. Shame, bashfulness and embarrassment are reckoned as the fruits of sin. Commentary on Genesis 2:25.[51]

The Goodness of Sex Was Second Only to Preaching. Martin Luther: If Adam had persisted in the state of innocence, this intimate relationship of husband and wife would have been most delightful. The very work of procreation also would have been most sacred and would have been held in esteem. There would not have been that shame stemming from sin which there is now, when parents are compelled to hide in darkness to do this. No less respectability would have attached to cohabitation than there is to sleeping, eating, or drinking with one's wife. Therefore was this fall not a terrible thing? For truly in all nature there was no activity more excellent and more admirable than procreation. After the proclamation of the name of God it is the most important activity Adam and Eve in the state of innocence could carry on—as free from sin in doing this as they were in praising God. . . . When we look back to the state of innocence, procreation, too, was better, more delightful, and more sacred in countless ways. Lectures on Genesis 2:18.[52]

[2:25] *Summary Remarks on Adam and Eve*

Adam and Eve, the First Philosophers. Martin Luther: If, then, we are looking for an outstanding philosopher, let us not overlook our first parents while they were still free from sin. They had a most perfect knowledge of God, for how would they not know Him whose similitude they had and felt within themselves? Furthermore, they also had the most dependable knowledge of the stars and of the whole of astronomy. Eve had these mental gifts in the same degree as Adam, as Eve's utterance shows when she answered the serpent concerning the tree in the middle of Paradise. There it becomes clear enough that she knew to what end she had been created and pointed to the source from which she had this knowledge; for she said (Gen 3:3): "The Lord

---

[50]LW 1:104-5 (WA 42:79). [51]*In Primum Librum Mosis* (1569), 12v. [52]LW 1:117-18 (WA 42:88-89).

said." Thus she not only heard this from Adam, but her very nature was pure and full of the knowledge of God to such a degree that by herself she knew the Word of God and understood it. LECTURES ON GENESIS 1:26.[53]

LESSONS OF FAITH, HOPE AND LOVE. PETER MARTYR VERMIGLI: In this creation of all things, we are taught about *faith*, seeing that we believe all things were made not by chance or by some other unspecified power, but by the word of God, and we refer the one created in God's image, to whom all things are to be subjected, to Christ, as Hebrews 2:6-9 implies. We are also educated about *hope*, for when we hear that God has thus provided all things, we also have confidence that he will not abandon us. Anyone who would want us to be his images will not, in the end, rashly spurn us for hoping, because no one wants to see his own likeness, whether statues or images, come to ruin. The doctrine of *love* is also found here. If God has willed everything to be useful, then he has designed those things for some use. We ought to behave toward our brothers and sisters in a like manner. To this end, love is commended in wedlock not only between spouses but also for children and for all of those who are connected with us by any relationship whatsoever. And while God could have produced all human beings as he made the first pair (or likewise the first animals), he nonetheless wished them to be born by procreation, so that some specimen of God's love for us would be evident in us. COMMENTARY ON GENESIS 2:1.[54]

CHURCH, LAW, PROPHECY AND MARRIAGE IN THE GARDEN. PETER MARTYR VERMIGLI: See here already the privileges of the church! God is its author: he cares for it, nourishes and adorns it. Already the law is found there, in the tree of the knowledge of good and evil, while Christ is in the tree of life. Holy matrimony is male and female. Already Adam is a

prophet, so that a prophecy might be given to the church immediately, at the very outset. Marriage is instituted here, and Adam, the church's first ruler, dealt with this. Accordingly, rulers of the church were admonished by the divine Peter (as Clement attests in one of his epistles) to see that young men in the church be joined in matrimony, lest the church be rendered impure by their unclean desires. Here, however, Adam speaks about marriage in such a way that he might look also to the union of Christ and the church. If a man and a woman abide together in marriage in a pure and holy manner, God is among them. COMMENTARY ON GENESIS 2:24.[55]

EVERYTHING ABOUT ADAM AND EVE PREFIGURES CHRIST AND THE CHURCH. WOLFGANG MUSCULUS: The things that happened prior to the sin of Adam (who was, so to speak, the first head of the human race) should be considered by us not only historically but also mystically. For in them we may contemplate images of spiritual things, the truth of which is made known in Christ, the head of the elect and of those to be saved. . . . Thus, just as God did not wish Adam, whom he constituted to be the head of the human race, to remain alone, so also he did not suffer his son Christ to be alone, whom he predestined from eternity to be the head and prince of the multitude of the elect. . . . Then, God could have removed the rib even while Adam was awake, but instead a figure of things to come was outlined. . . . A certain figure and shadow of the death of Christ emerges from the sleep of Adam. Thus, just as Eve was taken from Adam the first man while he slept, so the church was formed and brought to life from Christ the second man while he was dead on the cross. . . . Then, that the woman was built from Adam's rib and the place where the rib

---

[53]LW 1:66-67 (WA 42:49-50). [54]*In Primum Librum Mosis* (1569), 8v. [55]*In Primum Librum Mosis* (1569), 12v.

was removed was filled and closed with flesh provides a lovely figure of how the *strength* of Christ's divinity, prefigured by Adam's rib, is communicated to the church of the faithful and the bride of Christ. Similarly, the flesh, that is, the *infirmity* of human nature, is transferred to Christ.... [In Genesis 2:22b,] Eve, just arisen, is betrothed to Adam from whom she was formed. The church, freshly arisen from the flesh and blood of Christ is betrothed to him from whom she was taken. ... [Finally, in Genesis 2:25,] our Adam hung naked on the cross, fell asleep naked, was resurrected naked and was translated naked to the heavenly paradise. We too are reborn naked by him, naked do we walk with him, naked are we translated to heaven. We are reborn naked when every pretense of worldly righteousness or a righteousness of our own has been stripped off and we have despoiled the old nature.... How truly happy are all those who dwell naked with the second Adam and are not ashamed of their nudity but bear the shame of the cross of Christ with brave hearts, "going to him outside the gates." COMMENTARY ON GENESIS 2:18-25.[56]

---

[56]*In Mosis Genesim* (1554), 81-83, citing Heb 13:13.

3:1-6 TEMPTATION AND FALL

[1]*Now the serpent was more crafty than any other beast of the field that the* LORD *God had made.*

He said to the woman, "Did God actually say, 'You[a] shall not eat of any tree in the garden'?" [2]*And the woman said to the serpent, "We may eat of the fruit of the trees in the garden,* [3]*but God said, 'You shall not eat of the fruit of the tree that is in the midst of the garden, neither shall you touch it, lest you die.'"* [4]*But the serpent said to the woman, "You will not surely die.* [5]*For God knows that when you eat of it your eyes will be opened, and you will be like God, knowing good and evil."* [6]*So when the woman saw that the tree was good for food, and that it was a delight to the eyes, and that the tree was to be desired to make one wise,[b] she took of its fruit and ate, and she also gave some to her husband who was with her, and he ate.*

a In Hebrew *you* is plural in verses 1-5 **b** Or *to give insight*

OVERVIEW: The premise for the disastrous events of Genesis 3 is furnished in the preceding chapter, in Genesis 2:17, where God forbids eating the fruit of the tree of the knowledge of good and evil and warns that death will follow disobedience. Accordingly, the curious questions of cosmology, natural history, geography and anthropology that were provoked in abundance by Genesis 1 and 2 give way here, to a large degree, to a line of inquiry more suited to a courtroom than a classroom. Indeed, Genesis 3 does unfold like a courtroom drama, so it is no surprise that commentators instinctively posed a jurist's questions of the narrative's four characters—Adam and Eve, the serpent, God—in order to search out basic facts that would enable them to weigh motives and excuses and to assign appropriate blame.

In considering the verses of this chapter, then, Reformation exegetes would have found an agenda already set by a host of traditional questions and answers, and even the more obscure of these usually drew at least some attention (sometimes, it seems, as a guilty pleasure). Yet distinctive contributions from Protestants do emerge: sometimes derived from the era's more sophisticated knowledge of Hebrew, or by way of restraining or rejecting mistakes in patristic, medieval or rabbinic exegesis; or else in the course of finding new exegetical supports for their views on justification or marriage and family over against their Catholic opponents.

At the same time, it is often difficult to discern a single Protestant party line. Not only is there frequently no consensus, there are also outright disputes. Anabaptists dissent from Reformed writers over the nature of free will after the Fall; Protestants analyze the first sin with different results; John Calvin regularly insinuates a tacit critique of Martin Luther, whom he read closely. Some even changed their minds from one commentary to another (as did Wolfgang Musculus, on Eve).

In this first section of the chapter, the high theological topics of sin and grace are considered from a distinctly pastoral perspective, namely, the mechanism of temptation and moral failure. At the same time, the failings of Adam and Eve are also of interest for what they tell us about gender, yet the search for blame inevitably adds fuel to the proverbial war between the sexes. However, as in the preceding chapter, any reading of Genesis 3 had to consider also what the New Testament said—including the assertion in 1 Timothy 2:14 that Adam was not deceived and other texts that built on Eve's character or punish-

ment. Despite their differences, (male) Jewish, Catholic and Protestant commentators were more often united in their patriarchy. Yet even here one may discern subtle shifts in Protestant exegesis that reflected their concern to restore the dignity of marriage as well as their advocacy for a priesthood of believers that looked also to women as Bible readers and lay leaders in their own sphere, if not usually in the public realm.

3:1 The Serpent's Crafty Lies

LAW AND GOSPEL IN GENESIS 3. NIKOLAUS SELNECKER: The historical narrative is about the fall of our first parents, who were lured away from God's word and command by the devil's schemes and flattery. From there, together with all their descendants (or the whole human race), they rushed headlong into the wrath of God and a multitude of punishments. They let the dignity of their original righteousness slip away along with their reputation. They were stripped and despoiled of all their original endowments, as well as all the integrity and purity of their powers, mind, will and affections. This first part of this chapter pertains to the law. The other part is consolation, and comprehensive instruction about the promise of the woman's seed who was going to crush the head of the serpent— that is, about the coming liberator who was going to overthrow the devil's kingdom and power, reconcile God's wrath, do away with sin and death and restore righteousness and eternal life to the church. This part belongs to the gospel. COMMENTARY ON GENESIS 3.[1]

PARADISE WAS NO SANCTUARY FROM TEMPTATION. WOLFGANG MUSCULUS: However unique and extraordinary, the special privileges of paradise did not protect the parents of our race against the temptations of

---

[1]*In Genesin* (1569), 152-53.

Satan. No one, therefore, no matter where on earth one may dwell, is promised any security by reason of the sanctity of their location. If anyplace on this earth deserves the privilege of sanctity, paradise, regarded in the state of innocence, could have claimed this glory for itself above all. Yet even in that place Satan the tempter, the serpent, Satan's tool, is found; humankind is led astray and transgresses God's command; and the well-being and happiness of the human race is destroyed. COMMENTARY ON GENESIS 3:1-7.[2]

ADAM AND EVE WERE FIT TO BATTLE THE DEVIL. ANNA MARIA VAN SCHURMAN:
O people, consider well that
    we must all avoid this snare,
for the devil again urges us
    to war with heaven here,
as if God's justice could justly
    seem cruel or uncouth,
or as if God's truth here could
    itself conflict with Truth.
He attempts to drive mortals
    from God with cunning treason,
and instill in them his proud
    hatred through specious reasons
that unstable minds
    often imagine as needed
but nowhere should be viewed
    as wise, much less heeded.
The devil's reasons are folds of skin,
    pulled from this old serpent,
which reason itself has often
    crushed by careful argument.
They are nothing but hellish
    poison that easily infects
and casts someone among the dead
    before he even suspects.
How easy to step on a spider or snail,
    or the skin of a snake,
yet prudence will best avoid them all
    and a longer step will take.
A heart that loves God's glory
    as its greatest good
cannot but feel how such talk
    stirs its pious blood.
They lacked no strength to do
    the good nor were they weak,
before they rashly listened
    to the serpent speak.
They were not stones or plants,
    no unreasoning cow or swine;
they had an intellect and will,
    and powers of the mind;
they were able to will the good,
    and the good they could do
and, strengthened by God's promises,
    their wavering hearts renew.
PARAPHRASE OF GENESIS 1–3.[3]

THIS TEMPTATION WAS MEANT TO BE EASY. PETER MARTYR VERMIGLI: Since the devil hated human beings worst of all, he would have been glad to attack them with a harsher assault and a more unendurable onslaught. But God restrains his wicked efforts and, by his power and mercy toward us, lightened this temptation and willed it to be easier than the devil had wanted it to be. Therefore he did not allow them to be tempted except in the guise of the most repulsive serpent. By this means, they easily could have decided whether it was fitting for noble human beings to be advised by such a brute creature and to take counsel from it. You should also see here how the human mind at that time possessed such eminence that the devil could not invade it. He was permitted to attack humans only through an external action, by the body of serpent, I mean, which was a symbol perfectly suited for his cunning, his evil wiles, his jealousy and the trickery he would manifest against us. COMMENTARY ON GENESIS 3:1.[4]

THE SERPENT'S TREACHEROUS FRIENDSHIP. WOLFGANG MUSCULUS: Behold the

---

[2]*In Mosis Genesim* (1554), 89. [3]*Uitbreiding*, 11.5–12.1. [4]*In Primum Librum Mosis* (1569), 13r.

serpentile cunning! "Why did God command you," he asks, "not to eat from any tree of paradise?" Thus, he cites the word of God not in good faith but deceitfully and treacherously. Indeed, by no means did God say it like this, "You may not eat from any tree of paradise," but quite the contrary: "Of any tree of paradise," he said, "you may eat." But Satan, in order to provoke a response from the mind of the woman and hunt out a chance to lead her astray, confronts her with a simulation of friendship and benevolence, as if he greatly sympathized with their situation, so very unfair, and therefore he frames the question so that it might seem as if God were a bit displeased, that he should be unwilling to let them enjoy all the fruits of paradise. So, with this simulation of benevolence, he put her off guard and at the same time treated the word of God as not quite the truth. By the trickery of his perverse interpretation, he elicited from this precept a response that could devastate her. . . . By this example we are warned to detest such fraudulent and phony benevolence as we would a vicious dog or a snake, because by it God's grace, so lavishly supplied to the human race, is dishonored; our benefactor is himself provoked to jealousy; and if anything should seem disagreeable, it is impiously wielded against God, allegedly in the name of sympathy. COMMENTARY ON GENESIS 3:1-7.[5]

THE FOOLISHNESS OF LISTENING TO A SERPENT. JOHN CALVIN: The disgrace of human ingratitude is more clearly perceived from the fact that while Adam and Eve would have known that all animals were placed in subjection to them by the hand of God, they nonetheless allowed themselves to be led away by one of their own slaves into rebellion against God. As often as they beheld any of the animals that were in the world, God's supreme authority as well as his singular goodness ought to have come to their minds. On the contrary, when they see that the

serpent has become an apostate from his creator, not only do they fail to exact punishment, they subject themselves and devote themselves to it against all lawful order, as participants in the same apostasy. What can be imagined to be more dishonorable than this extreme depravity? Thus, I take the name *serpent* not allegorically, as some foolishly do, but in its genuine sense. COMMENTARY ON GENESIS 3:1.[6]

SATAN, SERPENTS AND SUBTLETY. ANDREW WILLET: It was a true serpent that talked with Eve, as may appear by the punishment inflicted upon this kind; the devil used the serpent, a subtle beast, as his instrument and spoke through him. This our Savior confirms in the gospel, that it was Satan who was a murderer from the beginning and caused the death and fall of our parents (Jn 8:44). And Saint Paul affirms that the serpent beguiled Eve through his subtlety: but the woman was not deceived by the serpent, but by the craft of the devil, speaking and working through the serpent. . . . *The serpent was more subtle than any beast of the field*: these words cannot be understood, as Cajetan thinks, of the devil, who is metaphorically called a serpent here: for there is no comparison between the beasts of the field and the devil, who in subtlety far exceeds humans and who is wiser than any brutish nature. Neither was the serpent more subtle only for this time, as Augustine seems to think, for Satan could not infuse more subtlety into the serpent than it had by nature; and the text itself seems to insinuate that the serpent by nature was more subtle than other beasts. So the truth is that because the serpent *is* a most subtle beast, it was not by chance that Satan used him as his instrument. . . . Our Savior witnesses to the natural wisdom of the serpent, saying to his disciples, "Be as wise as serpents, innocent as doves" (Mt 10:16). Some

---

[5]*In Mosis Genesim* (1554), 90-91. [6]CTS 1:141-42* (CO 23:54).

think this is set forth as a praise and commendation of the serpent, that he had such a gift of wisdom and subtlety given him in the creation. On the contrary, although this natural gift in the serpent was good, here the term is related to Satan's craft, whereby he seduced Eve. Adam and Eve are said before to be *gnarumim*—naked or simple—but here the serpent is said to be *gnarum* in the opposite sense—crafty or covert, not simple. COMMENTARY ON GENESIS 3:1.[7]

WHY IS SATAN NOT MENTIONED IN THIS CHAPTER? JOHN CALVIN: It hardly seems consonant with reason that only the serpent should be introduced here, with all mention of Satan suppressed. I acknowledge, indeed, that from this place alone nothing more can be concluded than that human beings were deceived by a serpent. But there are sufficiently numerous testimonies of Scripture in which it is openly and clearly asserted that the serpent was merely the mouthpiece of the devil: for it is not the serpent but the devil who is declared to be the father of lies, a perpetrator of fraud and the author of death. But the question is still unanswered as to why Moses has passed over the name of Satan in silence. I myself freely subscribe to the opinion of those who maintain that the Holy Spirit deliberately used obscure figures at that time, because it was fitting that the full and clear light should be reserved for the kingdom of Christ. In the meantime, the prophets attest that they were well acquainted with Moses' intention when, in various places, they cast the blame for our ruin upon the devil. COMMENTARY ON GENESIS 3:1.[8]

THE SERPENT IS, IN FACT, THE DEVIL. PETER MARTYR VERMIGLI: In John 8[:44], Christ shows us that [the first] humans were deceived by a demon: "He was a murderer from the beginning." Death was brought in by his suggestion; therefore *he* is the one who led

them astray. But the curse pronounced on him later on is to be understood allegorically, and the things that seem to fit the serpent are to be applied to the devil. COMMENTARY ON GENESIS 3:1.[9]

SATAN'S RHETORIC. ANDREW WILLET: Some take this to be ironic speech, as though Satan in the serpent should scoffingly say, "[As if] it is likely that God cares what you eat!" Some make it an interrogation, as though Satan should ask the reason why God had so said, etc., as in the Latin and Septuagint. Some make it a naked question: "Is it true that God has said?" Rashi expounds it as "perhaps," and would have it doubtfully spoken. Some put the emphasis or force of the sentence on this word *God*: "It is not likely that God would give you any such precept." Ibn Ezra interprets [the opening] as "how much more," in that after Satan had showed many reasons to persuade the woman that God loved them not, he urged this above the rest, that God had given them this prohibition. But the best interpretation is this, that after a long conversation with the woman, the serpent comes at last to that which he intended—to draw from the woman some answer on which he might work further; and therefore, with some admiration he says, in effect, "It seems very strange," or "I much wonder, that God would give any such prohibition to you." COMMENTARY ON GENESIS 3:1.[10]

SATAN DISTRACTS US FROM WHAT WE KNOW. JOHANNES OECOLAMPADIUS: Satan with remarkable cleverness diverted her from the simplicity of her senses. This is Satan's way, so that he can ambush as many of the

---

[7]*Hexapla* (1608), 46, invoking "most of the ancient fathers, Basil, Chrysostom, Augustine, Damascene, etc.," citing Augustine, *The Literal Meaning of Genesis* 11.29 (ACW 42:161), and crediting Mercerus. [8]CTS 1:140-41* (CO 23:53). [9]*In Primum Librum Mosis* (1569), 13v. [10]*Hexapla* (1608), 47, also crediting the Chaldee Interpreter (usually = Targum Jonathan); Rashi (cited as R. Sel.); and Mercerus.

faithful as possible. First he wants to create in us the suspicion that God does not want the best for us. He suggests that God is somehow jealous of us, or [he tries] at least to make us less certain of those things that have been said by him. . . . Thus Satan wants to persuade by saying, "Those things aren't as sure as you say. Do you think that God would prohibit you from *any* of the trees of paradise? What is that to God? What is food to God? What goes into the mouth does not contaminate a man. Do you think that God would prohibit you from such a thing?" This is the cunning of the devil, that he makes our hearts doubt concerning the word of the Lord. Wherever he shakes loose fear and faith, so that we think that God's word has not been spoken soundly, there he conquers easily, because he finds us weak and in doubt concerning the word of the Lord. COMMENTARY ON GENESIS 3:1.[11]

THE SERPENT TWISTS GOD'S MOTIVES.

CARDINAL CAJETAN: It is also to be noticed that in this suggestion, the serpent always speaks in the plural by saying "*You* shall not die, *you* shall eat," and things like this. In fact, he is exerting himself not so that the woman would eat alone but that he might induce the man as well to eat the forbidden fruit. Nor should you miss that in this suggestion, the devil twists the prohibition against eating the fruit of this tree back into God's desire not to want human beings to possess the great good of knowing good and evil. For by saying that "God knows this great good will result from eating of that tree," he is saying nothing other than that he has therefore forbidden humans from having such a great good. To be sure, he was clever in not wishing to explain this, lest he be openly seen provoking the woman against God. Truly, he was cloaking his suggestions under the appearance of good, so that he would not be recognized as an enemy but as one suggesting something good to the woman and her husband. COMMENTARY ON GENESIS 3:4-5.[12]

THE DEVIL'S LIKENESS. PETER RIEDEMANN:

Just as God is the Spirit of truth, so the devil is the spirit of lying and the father of lies. The lie, sin, injustice, or the spirit of lying are in the image of the devil. With such things, the devil clothes his children, whereas God adorns his children with truth. Thus one can be distinguished from the other. . . . Adam bore the true likeness of God. Therefore, God made him lord and ruler over all other created things, and made them all subject to Adam's will. The one exception was the tree of knowledge and the recognition of good and evil. Using that tree, God the Lord wished to test Adam to see if he wanted to be firm in his obedience. Through this prohibition God wished to show Adam, and to impress upon his inner being, that just as God made him lord over all created things, so God is Lord over him. Adam was to cling to God and serve and obey God as his Lord, Father, and Creator. But Adam, deceived and beguiled by the counsel of the serpent, spurned such obedience and cast aside God's image, that is, God's righteousness, purity, and holiness. Adam stained himself with sin, with the image of the devil, whom he obeyed. CONFESSION OF FAITH.[13]

SATAN GAVE KNOWLEDGE TO ADAM AND EVE IN THE WORST WAY. WOLFGANG

MUSCULUS: Notice how unsuccessfully divine honors are sought by Satan's plan and proposal. Compare these words of the serpent, "You will be as gods, knowing good and evil," with the calamity and most miserable ruin into which Adam fell by transgressing the divine precept. Satan promised divinity if they would eat of the forbidden tree's fruit. They ate, and they were so far from acquiring the glory of divinity that they became more like vile and subhuman beasts than like God. He promised knowledge of good and evil, by which they

---

[11]*In Genesim* (1536), 43r-v. [12]*Commentarii illustres* (1539), 29-30. [13]CRR 9:90-91, alluding to Jn 8:39-47.

would have an understanding of all things. And behold, they became more demented than brute animals. True, they did obtain knowledge of good, but they lost it through sin. They did obtain knowledge of evil, but an evil that they brought on themselves and came to know by experience, through their own great evil. They became fully acquainted not with one but with every kind of evil. . . . While we are weighing these things, we must declaim against the wickedness of Satan's impostor, by which he makes such "gods" even as he seduces these careless wretches by deceitful persuasion. But by no means let us merely declaim it, but let us also avoid him with the most careful vigilance on the part of all. We must make ourselves familiar with God's word here, so that whenever we run into someone who has been seduced by an impostor like Satan we should say, "Behold, this man has become like God on the earth, there is nothing he does not know, there is nothing he cannot do!" But we should say this not by way of sarcasm, by which we would laugh at these wretches, but out of righteous indignation, on account of which we should detest and condemn Satan's malice and deceit. COMMENTARY ON GENESIS 3:22.[14]

THE DEVIL TEMPTS US WITH THINGS WE ALREADY POSSESS. PETER MARTYR VERMIGLI: See what he promises to the woman! What did he mean, "Your eyes will be opened"? Were they blind, perchance? Not at all—neither the eyes of her body nor those of her mind. She was not physically blind, else how would she have seen the serpent? How would she have eaten from any of the trees that were in paradise? But if you say this is to be understood of the eyes of her mind, she saw with those, too—she wasn't a fool! She was able to recall the Lord's command from memory, and she knew that death was evil and something to flee from, for she remembered that it had been set up as a punishment. Nor is it to be supposed that God had denied to the

humans those things that he had granted to the rest of the animals, who know both what to avoid and what to seek that contributes to their well-being. So the things that would be harmful or useful to humans did not escape their notice. Later, he promises that they would be like God, but hadn't that been imparted to them when they were made, given that they had been created in God's image? When the devil tempts us, he promises us things we already have from God and things better than he could possibly deliver. So far, he doesn't propose anything to her that was necessary to sustain life, for fruit was supplied them in abundance for the eating. COMMENTARY ON GENESIS 3:4-5.[15]

SATAN'S LIES AND TRICKS. ANDREW WILLET: In his reply, Satan heaps up many lies together: that they shall not die; that God envied their happiness; that knowledge might be had by eating the fruit; that they should thereby be made like unto God. In addition, Rupert's idea here is excellent, that the devil in every one of these points speaks doubtfully (as he gave the oracles of Apollo), so that every word he spoke might have a double meaning: "You shall not die"—that is, not the death of the body right away, though immediately made subject to mortality. "Your eyes shall be opened," and so they were, to their confusion: knowing good and evil not by a more excellent knowledge but by miserable experience after their transgression. "You shall be as gods," either as angels, or like unto us—as sinful and wicked spirits. COMMENTARY ON GENESIS 3:1.[16]

SATAN'S FALSE COMFORT AND EMPTY PROMISES. JOHANNES OECOLAMPADIUS: Satan does two things. He dissolves fear, lest they fear for themselves on account of death, and he promises good things to transgressors,

[14]*In Mosis Genesim* (1554), 118. [15]*In Primum Librum Mosis* (1569), 14r. [16]*Hexapla* (1608), 48.

as if God were jealous. He is a liar, and from the beginning. Their eyes are certainly opened but to their own great calamity. And they are not made gods but, more correctly, living beings. Didn't Adam previously know good and evil? Otherwise he would not have known about the command. God wanted us to do according to his word. Satan carried us off from obedience to God and abandoned us merely to ourselves. By those promises poor Eve was seduced immediately, and she saw what beforehand she had not seen. Now, as we read or hear these things, we can recognize the various schemes of Satan by which he troubles the human race. COMMENTARY ON GENESIS 3:2-5.[17]

WHY DOES THE SERPENT CALL GOD ELOHIM? ANDREW WILLET: Ibn Ezra notes that the serpent uses the name *Elohim* [when] speaking of God—not *Jehovah*, because he knew it not. But that is not the reason, for the woman, who was not ignorant of *Jehovah*, also uses the name *Elohim*. Rather, Satan deliberately avoids using that name *Jehovah*, which is a name of mercy, and urges in the name *Elohim* the severity of God. COMMENTARY ON GENESIS 3:3.[18]

NO RICHES ARE BETTER THAN GOD'S FAVOR. JOHN CALVIN: We must keep in mind the nature of the pretense by which they were led into this delusion so fatal to themselves and to all their descendants. The flattery of Satan was plausible, "You shall know good and evil," but that knowledge was accursed precisely because it was sought in preference to God's favor. For this reason, unless we deliberately want to get tangled in the same snares, let us learn to depend wholly upon the will of God alone, whom we acknowledge as the author of all good. And since Scripture everywhere admonishes us of our nakedness and poverty, and declares that what we have lost in Adam is to be restored in Christ, let us

renounce all self-confidence and offer ourselves empty to Christ, that he may fill us with his riches. COMMENTARY ON GENESIS 3:6.[19]

3:2-3 Eve's Doubts

EVE ILLUSTRATES OUR OWN PATTERN OF SIN AND TEMPTATION. HULDRYCH ZWINGLI: The woman, having neglected the voice of the most holy Father, listens to his foe. She not only listens, but she considered closely and turned over in her mind (for she is a curious animal) just what the demon had suggested. She sees that the fruit is lovely and pleasing, she extends her hand, she plucks and tastes it. Even today, this happens in every sin: we are tempted and tickled by desire, as James says. If we give in and eat the fatal fruit, we meet with death, "for the wages of sin is death." If, however, we do not eat from our desire, no temptation will harm us but it will be for our testing. And this will happen, if we listen to God our admonisher; he alone watches over us and we ought to give thanks to this one alone. ANNOTATIONS ON GENESIS 3:6.[20]

EVE DESIRED TO KNOW MORE THAN GOD ALLOWED. JOHN CALVIN: I have no doubt but that Satan promises them divinity, as if he had said, "The only reason God defrauds you of the tree of knowledge is that he's afraid to have you as colleagues." Moreover, while his account of the divine glory or equality with God as consisting in the perfect knowledge of good and evil has a semblance of the truth, it is a mere sham, meant to ensnare the unfortunate woman. Because a desire for knowledge is naturally implanted in everyone, it is supposed that knowledge is the seat of happiness. Eve erred, however, by not conforming the manner of her knowing to the

---

[17]*In Genesim* (1536), 44r-v. [18]*Hexapla* (1608), 49, crediting Mercerus. [19]CTS 1:157* (CO 23:63). [20]ZSW 13:23; cf. Jas 1:14; Rom 6:23.

will of God. And we all suffer every day with the same disease, because we desire to know more than is right and more than God allows. Yet the principal point of wisdom is well-regulated sobriety in obedience to God. COMMENTARY ON GENESIS 3:5.[21]

THE TEMPTATION OF A DIVIDED HEART.
ANNA MARIA VAN SCHURMAN:
> Look, now, are they faithful?
>   Do they their Creator acclaim,
> directing all honor to God?
>   Is that their highest aim?
> Is their light, their love,
>   their highest good, in God alone?
> Is he their life, their greatest joy,
>   their heart's rest and home?
> No, alas! Not long with their God
>   did humankind remain;
> they turned to things created,
>   where they gave their eyes free rein.
> They found things wonderfully good,
>   yet they were never sated
> by all there was to gather from
>   among those things created.
> The lord of darkness then began
>   to spread his hellish vapors, quite
> intending through them to draw
>   first of all the woman from the light.
> With guile he makes her see her
>   current luster (so clear and bright),
> compared with what she could have,
>   as merely dim and dark as night.
> When the serpent speaks to her,
>   she begins to hesitate:
> Was her greatest good
>   actually missing from her state?
> And since she did not depend
>   on God in every part,
> lust then arose within
>   and seized her divided heart.
> The devil said, "Such a command
>   was God pleased to give,
> that you too could be as God:
>   you could eat and yet live."
> She sees a lovely tree,
>   its fruit so pleasing to the eye;
> she seeks knowledge in it—
>   and does not notice that he lied.
> However much the evil spirit
>   with his godless talk does show
> that he had fallen far from God
>   and of truth was now the foe
> (and that his own firstborn
>   son was just this lie,
> reward enough for his
>   hatred, spite and pride),
> yet that she must trust in God
>   alone, she remains unsure
> and stakes her greatest welfare
>   on the devil's word and lure.
> She takes a bite and thus she eats
>   what God had set apart;
> she shares it with her husband,
>   and God's blessing then departs.

PARAPHRASE OF GENESIS 1–3.[22]

SATAN ATTACKED THE WEAKER OF THE TWO. MARTIN LUTHER: Satan's cleverness is perceived also in this, that he attacks the weak part of the human nature, Eve the woman, not Adam the man. Although both were created equally righteous, nevertheless Adam had some advantage over Eve. Just as in all the rest of nature the strength of the male surpasses that of the other sex, so also in the perfect nature the male somewhat excelled the female. Because Satan sees that Adam is the more excellent, he does not dare assail him; for he fears that his attempt may turn out to be useless. And I, too, believe that if he had tempted Adam first, the victory would have been Adam's. He would have crushed the serpent with his foot and would have said: "Shut up! The Lord's command was different." Satan, therefore, directs his attack on Eve as the weaker part and puts her valor to the test, for he sees that she is so dependent on her

---

[21]CTS 1:151* (CO 23:59). [22]*Uitbreiding*, 8.9–9.11.

husband that she thinks she cannot sin. LECTURES ON GENESIS 3:1.[23]

SIN IS ALWAYS FUELED BY IGNORANCE.

PETER MARTYR VERMIGLI: In our temptations, it goes like this: We already know God's precept and what the Lord's will ought to be, just as Eve recited God's command from memory. But as soon as an object is set before us by the tempter, we are seized by a desire to think about that thing attentively, turning it over in our minds. From doing that, concupiscence bursts into flame. But if we were to run back to meditate fixedly on God's word and commandment, we would not be defeated in this way. Thus, sin is always accompanied either by ignorance or by careless reflection, which comes close to ignorance. COMMENTARY ON GENESIS 3:4-5.[24]

THE REAL OBJECT OF EVERY SIN IS GOD.

DAVID CHYTRAEUS: Every sin is a violation of the divine law and constitutes contempt of God. Therefore, whatever the external objects [of sin] may be (and they can be dissimilar), the first and principal object of sin is God and God's law, which requires the conformity of the heart and every external action with the will of God. For sin is nothing other than contempt for God, departure from God's Word and a turning of the will from God that follows one's turning toward an unlawful and prohibited external object. Accordingly, when the fall of our first parents is spoken of, one should regard not merely the childish eating of an apple, but first of all contemplate the defection of the mind and the turning of the will from God, and the neglect of and contempt for the divine word and command; then, the choosing of an external act or the turning toward an unlawful object, namely, the apple to which Eve clung, having wandered beyond the order prescribed by the word. COMMENTARY ON GENESIS 3:1-6.[25]

EVE WAS AMBITIOUS, NOT IGNORANT.

ANDREW WILLET: Though she well knew that God had created angelical powers, Eve was carried away with the voice and goodly promises delivered by the serpent and paid attention not so much to from whom they came as to what was spoken. Ravished by an ambitious desire to better her estate, she did not consider whether a good or a bad angel might thus speak out of the serpent. But to claim that [Adam and Eve] were ignorant either of the creation of angels or of the power and faculty of beasts—that is too great a defect of knowledge to be allowed in their perfect state. COMMENTARY ON GENESIS 3:1.[26]

EVE'S DEFENSE WAS SINCERE BUT WEAK.

JOHN CALVIN: What the woman seized upon, that only one tree was forbidden, she means to be a defense of the command, as if she would deny that it ought to seem harsh or burdensome, since God had singled out only one from the great abundance and variety of trees he had granted them. . . . It was impossible for Eve to have repelled Satan's assault more prudently or more sensibly than by objecting that she and her husband had been so bountifully dealt with by the Lord that the provisions granted to them ought to suffice abundantly. Indeed, she indicates that they would be most ungrateful if, instead of being content with such affluence, they should desire more than was lawful. When she says that God had forbidden them to eat or to touch [the tree], some think the second word was added as if she were accusing God of excessive severity, that he should prohibit them from even touching it. But I take the view, instead, that to this point she still persisted in obedience and demonstrated her pious disposition toward God by carefully keeping his precept—except that she wavers in her account of the punishment, inserting the

[23]LW 1:151 (WA 42:114). [24]*In Primum Librum Mosis* (1569), 14r. [25]*In Genesin* (1576), 123-24. [26]*Hexapla* (1608), 47.

adverb "perhaps," when God had stated with certainty, "By death you shall die." For while the Hebrew [word] does not always express doubt, it is more often taken in this sense, and I therefore willingly embrace that the woman was beginning to hesitate. Certainly, she did not keep death before her eyes as she should have, that is, as the consequence, were she to disobey God. In truth, she shows that she regarded the danger of death as something far off and unimportant. COMMENTARY ON GENESIS 3:2.[27]

EVE'S "PERHAPS." MARTIN LUTHER: She does not mention the punishment as God had stated it. He had simply stated (Gen 2:17): "On whatever day you will eat from it, you will surely die." Out of this absolute statement she herself makes one that is not absolute when she adds: "Lest perchance we shall die." This is a striking flaw, and one that must not be overlooked; for it shows that she has turned from faith to unbelief. For just as a promise demands faith, so a threat also demands faith. Eve should have maintained: "If I eat, I shall surely die." On this faith Satan makes such inroads with his crafty speech that Eve adds the little word "perchance." She had been persuaded by the devil that God was not so cruel as to kill them for eating the fruit. To this extent Eve's heart was now poisoned with Satan's venom. LECTURES ON GENESIS 3:3.[28]

EVE'S DANGEROUS ADDITION TO THE WORD OF GOD. PETER MARTYR VERMIGLI: She is properly mindful of the command, so that she should be condemned all the more because she *didn't* sin from forgetfulness. But she adds this, "nor shall you touch it," which certainly is by no means allowed to do to God's law. Whoever adds to it deserves to be diminished! . . . Often, an opening for transgression is obtained from the things we add: Human traditions and additions are the source of the transgression of the divine law. COMMENTARY ON GENESIS 3:2.[29]

EVE'S WRETCHED EXAMPLE. KONRAD PELLIKAN: The woman should have remained silent and pointed right away to her husband. It is dangerous to converse with those who are experts, to lend an ear and yield to the persuasions of demons. More than anything, the woman should have hurled back what the Lord had said. . . . But in the end, she added "and neither should you touch it" to God's word and even recalled God's declaration with doubt, "lest *perhaps* you should die," when God had said, "By death you will die," that is, *without a doubt* you will die. She showed herself not so much grateful for the many great enjoyments permitted in the world, as impatient and querulous; denied a single thing, she betrayed herself. From the example of their first mother, the more insolent among women here learn to gab with strangers, disobedience, lying, ingratitude, treachery, gluttony, pride, to strive for things forbidden and to desire what has been denied. COMMENTARY ON GENESIS 3:3.[30]

OBEDIENCE SHOULD NOT WAIT FOR UNDERSTANDING. JOHN CALVIN: I have no doubt but that the serpent incites the woman to inquire about the reason [for the tree's prohibition] because otherwise he would not have been able to draw her mind away from God. There is an exceedingly dangerous temptation whenever it is suggested to us that God is to be obeyed only so far as the reason for his command is apparent. The true rule of obedience, however, is for us to be content with a bare command and to persuade ourselves that whatever he enjoins is just and right. COMMENTARY ON GENESIS 3:1.[31]

---

[27]CTS 1:148-49* (CO 23:58). [28]LW 1:155 (WA 42:116-17). [29]*In Primum Librum Mosis* (1569), 14r. [30]*Commentaria Bibliorum* (1532) 1:6r. [31]CTS 1:147-48* (CO 23:57).

THE ALLEGORY OF TEMPTATION'S PROG-
RESS. PETER MARTYR VERMIGLI: One should
not neglect the insight from Augustine and
Ambrose, that *Eve* allegorically corresponds to
the weaker part of our soul, which is affected
by confusion and desires. *Adam*, however,
corresponds to the mind or spirit, the part that
was made for governing things. Therefore, as
they say, the serpent that was going to tempt
us attacks us by that part by which we are
weaker: for the powers of desire and confusion
often work with the devil in situations where
they lure the mind to themselves and cause the
stronger part of the soul to waver. COMMEN-
TARY ON GENESIS 3:15.[32]

AGAINST ALLEGORIZING ADAM AND EVE AS
HIGHER AND LOWER REASON. MARTIN
LUTHER: I ask you, dear reader, what need is
there of those obscure and most foolish
allegories when this light is so very clear? For
all I care, let us concede the division of reason
into two parts: the higher and the lower. It
would be much more correct to use the term
"lower" for that which has the ability to
administer the affairs of the household and of
the state, and not for that brutish lust; but call
that the "higher" by which we look upon or
observe the things beyond state and home, the
knowledge of God pointed out in the Word,
where we effect nothing by our endeavor but
merely learn and observe. But even though we
were to make these statements, what have they
to do with this passage? Do they not utterly
smother the true meaning and replace it with
an idea which is not merely useless but disastrous? For what ability or insight has reason in
religious matters? Then there is also something absurd in making Eve the lower part of
reason, although it is sure that in no part, that
is, neither in body nor in soul, was Eve inferior
to her husband Adam. This ridiculous interpretation is the source of the familiar secular
discussions about free will and about reason's
striving toward the supreme good, which

finally turn the whole of theology into philosophy and into specious prattle. LECTURES ON
GENESIS 3:14.[33]

3:6 Adam's Complicity

ADAM SHOULD NOT HAVE LISTENED TO
EVE. PETER MARTYR VERMIGLI: He descends
from the woman's sin to the man's crime.
There was no need for the serpent here, now
that the woman is on hand to take its place,
and the poison it devised seeps into the man. It
is to be supposed that she would have recounted everything the serpent explained to
her and that to this she would have added
flattery and pleadings: wherefore the man, too,
ate. And he sinned gravely, because he made
more of his wife's voice than God's commandment. God reproaches his sin here, for he
should not have taken advice from her, given
that she was inferior to him. Instead, he should
have ruled over her. And here you see how
those who forsake God consult those who are
of lower rank than themselves: they obey those
who were their own subordinates and beg
favors of them. The woman obeyed the
serpent, and the man obeyed the woman.
COMMENTARY ON GENESIS 3:6.[34]

ADAM DISOBEYED ONLY TO PLEASE EVE.
WOLFGANG MUSCULUS: There are some who
have thought that Adam was moved to eat for
this reason, that he saw that nothing bad
happened to the woman after this fruit was
eaten—as if he, too, then began to doubt the
word of God. But this view does not fit very
well with the words of the apostle, who clearly
says that the woman was deceived and led
astray, but by no means the man. Wherefore it
is more believable that he wished to gratify the
woman at her urging and shameless insistence
by eating this fruit. For he was driven to ruin

---

[32]*In Primum Librum Mosis* (1569), 16r-v. [33]LW 1:184-85 (WA
42:138). [34]*In Primum Librum Mosis* (1569), 14r.

wholly by the words of Eve, as God himself testifies below: "Because you have listened to the voice of your wife," etc. COMMENTARY ON GENESIS 3:6.[35]

ADAM'S MOTIVE WAS AMBITION, NOT LOVE FOR HIS WIFE. JOHN CALVIN: The opinion has been commonly received that Adam was more captivated by his wife's allure than persuaded by Satan's fraudulent claims. For this purpose, Paul's statement is cited, "Adam was not deceived, but the woman" (1 Tim 2:14). But in that text, Paul is only speaking comparatively, because he is teaching that the starting point of evil derived from the woman. It was not, therefore, merely to indulge his wife's wishes that he transgressed the law laid down for him; rather, being drawn by her into a fatal ambition, he became a partner in the same defection. And it's a fact that Paul elsewhere relates that sin came not by the woman, but by Adam himself (Rom 5:12). In addition, the assessment that follows shortly after this, "Behold, Adam is as one of us," clearly proves that he, too, foolishly coveted more than was lawful and put more trust in the devil's flatteries than in God's holy word. COMMENTARY ON GENESIS 3:6.[36]

ADAM WORRIED MORE ABOUT STAYING ALIVE THAN STAYING PURE. WOLFGANG MUSCULUS: To *extend the hand and take* is to grab something not suddenly, through ignorance or by happenstance, but deliberately, through planning and concentrated effort. In just this way is expressed our human nature, which normally inclines more toward preserving its life than to its purification or justification. Indeed, Adam was well aware of his guilty conscience and of the corruption and change within his mind; but he was thinking as much about how he might assuage that evil as about how he might escape his fear of death, . . . which is sufficiently declared by the fact that he called his wife "Life." We who are also

his offspring are all endowed with that very same character, which is what everyone experiences in one's very own self—unless you're a toadstool or a stick of wood! COMMENTARY ON GENESIS 3:22.[37]

ADAM WAS AND WAS NOT DECEIVED. MARTIN LUTHER: Here we must give consideration to Paul's statement in 1 Timothy 2:13-14: "Adam was first formed, then Eve. And Adam was not seduced; but the woman, since she had been seduced, was in the transgression." Almost everybody understands this statement to mean that Adam was not seduced but sinned knowingly. For he did not yield to the persuasion of the devil as Eve did; but he was unwilling to cause sadness for his delight, that is, for his wife, and so he preferred his wife's love to God. They try to make this interpretation likely by saying that the serpent was afraid of the male, as the master, and approached the woman; for although she herself was also holy, nevertheless, as the weaker creature, she was more likely to yield to persuasion. And thus Eve was seduced by the serpent, but Adam was not. He was seduced either by himself or by the woman: by the woman, because she handed him the apple; by himself, because, since he had seen that Eve did not die immediately after eating the fruit, he did not believe that the punishment which the Lord had threatened would follow. . . . I do not disapprove of this opinion. It indicates that both statements are true: that Adam was deceived, and that he was not deceived. He was not deceived by the serpent, as Eve was. Nevertheless, he was deceived by his wife and by himself when he persuaded himself that his deed would not result in the punishment concerning which the Lord had said that it would follow. LECTURES ON GENESIS 3:13.[38]

---

[35]*In Mosis Genesim* (1554), 85. [36]CTS 1:152* (CO 23:60). [37]*In Mosis Genesim* (1554), 118. [38]LW 1:182 (WA 42:136).

ADAM WAS NOT DECEIVED, BUT HE STILL ERRED. PETER MARTYR VERMIGLI: In the epistle to Timothy, Adam is not described by Paul as having been deceived. That is to say, he wasn't deceived by that external conversation with the serpent or by Eve's words. . . . Not that the apostle's account entirely acquits him of all error, but the apostle is trying to explain that he was not beguiled by external persuasion. Accordingly, he wishes men to speak in church—not women, who (unlike the man) were exposed to deception through conversation. Indeed, Adam didn't believe that he would become more like God than he already was, or that wisdom or an "opening of his eyes" would follow, because he knew that he had been made in God's image and he saw that the woman's vision hadn't improved at all. So perhaps he ate because he did not wish to antagonize her. Or, when he saw that she hadn't died, he began to have doubts about that threat God had uttered. He inferred that it wasn't genuine but had been made as a sign of something else, sort of like a scarecrow, a sham by which they would be kept in line. These considerations would not have found a home in him if he had not already become too much taken with himself. COMMENTARY ON GENESIS 3:6.[39]

ADAM WAS DECEIVED, BUT NOT LIKE EVE. ANDREW WILLET: Satan first assails the woman, both being as the weaker and more easily seduced and as a fit instrument also to entice Adam. Adam not only inclined unto her out of a loving intent (and was thereby enticed as Sampson was by Delilah, and Solomon by his wives), but it is likely that he was seduced by the same flattering and false persuasions whereby the woman was first beguiled, being carried away with ambitious desire not to be made equal but to be made like unto God in knowledge. . . . Nor is this opinion contradicted by 1 Timothy 2:14, that "Adam was not deceived. . . ." For whether we expound it with

Epiphanius and Calvin, that the apostle's meaning is that the woman was *first* deceived, not the man; or with Mercerus, that the man was not deceived but *enticed* by the woman; or with Jerome, that Adam was not deceived by the *serpent* but by the woman; or that Eve did not *wittingly* deceive Adam, as the serpent beguiled Eve (of which views, the first two are one in effect and most agreeable to the apostle's mind), by this text Adam is not wholly exempted from being deceived, but only in that manner as Eve was perverted and seduced. COMMENTARY ON GENESIS 3:1.[40]

ADAM WAS LIABLE TO THE SAME DECEPTION AS EVE. JOHN CALVIN: From these words, some conjecture that Adam was present when his wife was tempted and persuaded by the serpent, which is by no means believable. Yet it could have happened that he soon joined the woman, even before she tasted the fruit of the tree, and that she related the conversation she'd had with the serpent and entangled him in the same fallacies by which she herself had been deceived. COMMENTARY ON GENESIS 3:6.[41]

3:6 *Their Mutual and Respective Sins*

CAPTURED BY PRIDE. ANNA MARIA VAN SCHURMAN:

> They left their first duty when
>   their proper Lord they disowned,
> turned God into their enemy,
>   and stood upon their own.
> Yet when without their God
>   they tried alone to live,
> God could not equip them—
>   no new powers could he give.
> Not for this did God give strength,
>   nor for this did they arise;
> wanting so to be the first,

---

[39]*In Primum Librum Mosis* (1569), 14r-v. [40]*Hexapla* (1608), 48-49. [41]CTS 1:151* (CO 23:60).

they fashioned their own demise.
To be nothing and to do nothing,
    in the truth not to abide,
these alone are the attributes
    to the creature justly ascribed.
It was not doing, doing nothing,
    when they needed most to fight:
truly, that was what they undertook
    to land themselves in this plight.
The sound of God's command
    thereafter vanished from their ears,
they took no thought of how God
    once in voice to them appeared
as one who passes by;
    perhaps it was that they surmised
they heard not the Creator,
    but some creature they despised.
Reckoning themselves too burdened
    by that heavenly threat,
their conceited hearts were captured
    in pride's insidious net.
PARAPHRASE OF GENESIS 1–3.[42]

A RASH BUT VICIOUS ACT. JOHANNES
BRENZ: It could have happened, perhaps, that
our first parents did not think about their
disobedience with precision or sophistication
but rashly, so that they ate with no great
deliberation and without any careful plan. If
Satan had plainly said, "You ought to conclude
that God is stupid and you are wise," they
certainly would have driven him away. But no
matter how they regarded him, surely they
should have discussed these things more
carefully together before they obeyed the
promptings of Satan. Indeed, their heavenly
gifts sufficiently enabled them to consider
these matters more properly. So even if maybe
they didn't see what lurked within their
disobedience and hid in the recesses of their
hearts, God still saw and understood that in
their secret thoughts they regarded themselves
as wise and God as the fool who gave such a
command. COMMENTARY ON GENESIS 3:6.[43]

UNBELIEF THE SOURCE OF ALL SINS.
MARTIN LUTHER: Satan here attacks Adam
and Eve in this way to deprive them of the
Word and to make them believe his lie after
they have lost the Word and their trust in
God. Is it a wonder that when this happens,
man later on becomes proud, that he is a
scorner of God and of men, that he becomes an
adulterer or a murderer? Truly, therefore, this
temptation is the sum of all temptations; it
brings with it the overthrow or the violation of
the entire Decalog. Unbelief is the source of all
sins; when Satan brought about this unbelief
by driving out or corrupting the Word, the rest
was easy for him. LECTURES ON GENESIS 3:1.[44]

WHAT WAS THE FIRST SIN? JOHN CALVIN:
What was the sin of these two? That they were
enticed by *gluttony*, as some of the ancients say,
is childish. For when there was such an
abundance of the choicest fruits, what dainti-
ness could there be about one particular kind?
Augustine is more correct to say that *pride* was
the beginning of all evils, and that by pride the
human race was ruined. Yet a fuller definition
of the sin may be drawn from the kind of
temptation that Moses describes. For first of
all, by the wiles of Satan, the woman is led
away from the word of God by her *unbelief*.
Thus, the beginning of the catastrophe by
which the human race was overthrown was the
desertion of God's command. But notice that
human beings deserted God at a time when,
having forsaken his word, they lent their ears
to Satan's lies. From this we deduce, then, that
God wishes to be respected and honored in his
word, and that all reverence for him is shaken
off, therefore, when his word is despised. . . .
However, just as God does not make himself
known to human beings otherwise than
through the word, so also does his majesty not
abide in our midst nor his worship remain

---

[42]*Uitbreiding*, 12.2-17. [43]*Opera* 1:45. [44]LW 1:147 (WA
42:110-11).

sound any longer than while we obey his word. Hence, unbelief was the root of defection, just as faith alone unites us with God. From here flowed forth ambition and pride, so that first the woman and then her husband desired to exalt themselves against God. Commentary on Genesis 3:6.[45]

Was the First Sin Really the Worst Ever? Peter Martyr Vermigli:
The sin of the first man was detestable especially if we pay attention to his condition and status. What was most despicable was that he did not retain such a happy and distinguished progression of affairs, wherein he had been endowed with such great wisdom, grace and power—because considered in itself, his sort of sin does *not* surpass the wickedness of every other crime. The desperate deed of Judas and the blasphemies and contempt of God on the part of many others are far more serious than Adam's deed, except that this deed belonged to the author of our race and one who had been honored by God. On that account, it is condemned beyond all other crimes. Commentary on Genesis 2:25.[46]

The First Sin Was Many Sins. Johannes Brenz:
Sometimes people say that pride and arrogance account for why they thought so highly of themselves and aspired to be like God. "The beginning of sin," says Sirach, "is pride." At other times they say avarice, because they were inflamed by greed to desire a majesty not their own. "Avarice," says Paul, "is the root of all evils." At still other times, gluttony, in that they ate because the sweetness of the food would have captivated them. And for this reason, many take the opportunity to exhort us to fasting, because just as gluttony would have expelled us from paradise, so may we be restored to paradise by fasting. Truly, these notions are not absurd, but Paul generally calls this sin disobedience. "By the disobedience of the one man," he says, "we who are

many were made sinners." But this word *disobedience* contains both inescapable errors and serious crimes. Indeed, the first is that when the man ate the prohibited apple, he turned himself away from God's word and concluded that this word was not seriously uttered by the Lord. Therefore he turned himself from true and eternal wisdom to external foolishness. And when he desired to be made as completely wise as God, he became the most foolish of all. Commentary on Genesis 3:6.[47]

Adam and Eve Committed Not One Sin but Many. William Perkins:
Regarding the greatness of humanity's fall, some have made a small matter of it, because it was the eating of an apple or some such fruit. But we must not measure the greatness or smallness of a sin by the object or matter with which it is occupied, but by the commandment of God and by the disobedience or offence to his infinite majesty. And that this deed of Adam and Eve was no small fault but a notorious crime and apostasy, in which they withdrew themselves from under the power of God, nay, rejected and denied him, will be evident if we take a view of all the particular sins that are contained in it. The first is *unbelief*, in that they doubted and distrusted of the truth of God's word which he spoke to them. The second is *contempt of God*, in that they believed the lies of the devil rather than him. For when God said, "In the day that you eat thereof, you shall die the death," it is as nothing with Eve: but when the devil comes and says, "You shall not die at all," she takes hold of that. The third is *pride and ambition*. For they ate the forbidden fruit that they might be as gods, namely, as the Father, the Son and the Holy Ghost. The fourth is *unthankfulness*. God had made

[45]CTS 1:152-53* (CO 23:60-61). [46]*In Primum Librum Mosis* (1569), 13r. [47]*Opera* 1:44; citing Sir 10:12 [15]; 1 Tim 6:10; Rom 5:19.

them excellent creatures in his own image, [but it] is nothing with them to be like unto him unless they may be equal with him. The fifth is *curiosity*, whereby they affected greater wisdom than God had given them in creation and a greater measure of knowledge than God had revealed to them. The sixth is *reproachful blasphemy*, in that they subscribe to the saying of the devil, in which he charged God with lying and envy. The seventh is *murder*: for by this means they bereave themselves and their posterity of the fellowship and graces of God's spirit and bring upon their own heads the eternal wrath of God. The eighth is *discontent*, in that they sought for a higher condition than that in which God had placed them. In a word, in this one single deed is comprised the breach of the whole law of God. And we should often think upon this, that we may learn to wonder at the just judgments of God in punishing this fall, and his unspeakable goodness in receiving us to mercy after the same. Exposition of the Apostles' Creed.[48]

How Heinous Was Adam's Sin? Eve's?

Andrew Willet: Adam's . . . was not the greatest sin of all committed in the world: neither in respect of the kind of the sin, as adultery is greater than fornication, for we hold blasphemy and idolatry to be greater sins than Adam's was; nor in respect of the affection of the offender, for many are given over with a more ungodly, violent and sinful desire than Adam was in this temptation; neither was it the greatest in respect of the quality of the sin, for it was pardonable in Adam, whereas sin against the Holy Ghost is impardonable. But it may yet truly be said to be the greatest: in regard to the fruits and sequel of that sin, the contagion and infection of all humankind; in respect of Adam's person, who in consideration of his excellent gifts might have more easily resisted; in regard to the ease of the commandment, which required no hard or difficult thing; and also the place itself being consid-

ered, namely in paradise, where there was no provocation or allurement unto sin.

Now if Adam's sin be compared with the woman's, in some things it will be found equal, in some things superior, in some inferior to it. First, both Adam and Eve sinned in their infidelity, in not believing the word of God but giving credit to Satan's specious promises that they should not die; in their concupiscence, in coveting the forbidden fruit; in their ambition, in desiring a further state of perfection. Secondly, considering Adam's person, who was appointed to be the woman's head, and his gifts of knowledge and wisdom, the man was more faulty than the woman. Thirdly, yet simply, the woman's sin was greater, because beside other sins common unto them, seducing her husband was peculiar to her: so that, as Augustine well notes, the man sinned only against God and himself; the woman, against God, herself and her neighbor. Besides, the woman was first deceived and became the author and beginner of transgression. Therefore the opinion of them is not here to be allowed, who do either aggravate Adam's sin or extenuate the woman's. Commentary on Genesis 3:1.[49]

Ignorance of Our Corruption Is Itself Proof of Original Sin.

John Calvin: Pelagius dared to deny original sin, lest, as he falsely feared, the corruption of human nature should recoil against God. But an error so gross is plainly refuted, not only by solid testimonies from Scripture but also by experience itself. The vitiation of our nature was unknown to the philosophers, who in other respects were sufficiently (indeed, more than sufficiently) acute. Surely their stupor was clear evidence of original sin! For all who are not utterly blind perceive that no part of us is sound: the mind is smitten with blindness and

---

[48]*Works* (1608) 1:161. [49]*Hexapla* (1608), 49, citing Augustine, *The Literal Meaning of Genesis* 11.42 (ACW 42:175-76).

infected with uncountable errors; all the affections of the heart are full of stubbornness and wickedness, and base desires or other more serious diseases reign there; and all the senses swarm with many vices. Commentary on Genesis 3:6.[50]

Lessons for Our Own Weakness.

William Perkins: First, by this we learn to acknowledge and bewail our own frailty. For Adam in his innocence, being created perfectly righteous, when he was once tempted by the devil, fell away from God. What shall we do in such circumstances, then, we who are by nature sold under sin and in ourselves a thousand times weaker than Adam was? Many there are who mingle themselves with all [sorts of] companions; tell them of the danger thereof, they will presently reply that they have such a strong faith that no bad company can hurt them. But alas: silly people! Satan bewitches them and makes them believe falsehood to be truth: they know not their miserable estate. If Adam (says Bernard) had a downfall in paradise, what shall we do who are cast forth to the dunghill? Let us therefore often come to a serious consideration of our own weakness and wholly follow the practice of David, who, aware of his own corruption, prayed to God in this manner, "Knit my heart to you, O Lord, that I may fear your name" (Ps 86:11). Second, we learn here absolutely to submit ourselves to the authority of God, and simply to resolve that whatsoever he commands is right and just, though the reason of it be not known to us. For Eve condescended to listen to the speech of the serpent, and without any calling she reasoned with it about a most weighty matter—and that, in the absence of Adam her head and husband—namely, of the truth and glory of God: and hereby [she] was brought to doubt of God's word and so overturned. Third, if all people by Adam's fall be shut up under damnation, there is no cause why any of us should stand upon

our birth, riches, wisdom, learning, or any other such gifts of God: there is nothing in us that is more able to cover our vileness and nakedness than fig-tree leaves were able to cover the offense of Adam from God's eyes. We are under the wrath of God by nature and cannot attain to everlasting life of ourselves. Wherefore it behooves every one of us to abase ourselves under the mighty hand of God, in that we have become by our sin the very basest of all the creatures upon earth; yea, utterly to despair in respect of ourselves, and with bleeding hearts to bewail our own case. There is no danger in this: it is the very way to grace: none of us can be a lively member of Christ till our consciences condemn us and make us quite out of heart in respect to ourselves. And the want of this is the cause why so few perceive any sweetness or comfort in the gospel, and why it is so little loved and embraced nowadays. Exposition of the Apostles' Creed.[51]

No Tears Are Enough for This Calamity.

Christophor Pelargus: These words that follow cannot be read or contemplated without endless tears: "And she took of its fruit and ate." O misery, that she picked and took! O that lamentable calamity, never sufficiently detested, that she ate! O how utterly strange this onset of every misery, that she gave to the man: nay, that the man took the fruit from the hands of his wife and swallowed it! What can be said or imagined as sad as that such an eminent figuration of God should perish, God's image be so quickly stripped off, the happiness of paradise so speedily lost? But was the man, too, really to be led astray, while his posterity was protected? For "just as Adam and Eve were the parents of all, so too were they the destroyers of all, and more wretched still is that they were destroyers before they were parents." What can you say about the foreknowledge and foresight of the creator

---

[50]CTS 1:154-55* (CO 23:61-62). [51]Works (1608) 1:163-64.

here, except that he [merely] permitted this, for by no means would he have wished for such a horrible fall of our race. . . . COMMENTARY ON GENESIS 3:6.[52]

3:1-6 God's Involvement

WHY DID GOD PERMIT TEMPTATION? JOHN CALVIN: Why did God permit Adam to be tempted, seeing that the sad result was by no means hidden from him? That he now relaxes Satan's reins in order that he might incite us to sin, we ascribe to God's judgment and vengeance after human beings had become estranged from him; but there was not the same reason for doing so when human nature was still sound and upright. God therefore permitted human beings—who were conformed to the divine image and not yet implicated in any crime—to be tempted by Satan, on top of which he put at Satan's disposal an animal that otherwise would never have obeyed him. What else was this, than to arm an enemy for the destruction of our race? This seems to have been the occasion for Manichaeans asserting the existence of two principles. They thus imagined that Satan, because he was not subject to God, laid snares for man in opposition to the divine will and was superior not only to man but even to God himself. . . . However, anyone who thinks piously and reverently about the power of God will acknowledge that this did not take place except by his permission. For it has to be conceded, first of all, that God was not in ignorance of what was about to result; and then, that he could have prevented it, had he seen fit to do so. But when I speak of *permission*, I understand that God decreed to happen whatsoever he wished. COMMENTARY ON GENESIS 3:1.[53]

CREATURES HAD TO BE ABLE TO DEFECT. PETER MARTYR VERMIGLI: Some ask, "Why didn't God make a human being who would not be able to sin?" Such a nature cannot be appropriate for any rational creature, because a creature, considered as something created, is and continues to be weak and frail. Given that a creature would never be utterly the same as the rule by which it is to be directed (otherwise, it would be God, the very principle of goodness and justice), it follows that by its nature it can be deflected from that rule. And grace could have ensured that a creature would not be permitted to sin, as is believed to be the case now for angels and saints in their heavenly home, but that dignity or reward would not become of such great value if this shifting and inconstant human condition had not gone before. Nor does God's wisdom force him to make only the very best and most outstanding things, but in order for him to display his skill clearly, it was fitting that he make various kinds and grades of creatures. Nor can we complain about this, since in the end, we have to be carried up to that condition through Christ. Meanwhile, there is truly preserved a fitting and harmonious diversity among creatures—and it is not acceptable to argue that since eyes are more noble than ears, God should have created ears in such a way that they would be eyes. So while people who have been so confirmed that they can no longer sin are thus in a better state, we don't agree that therefore everyone should have been made like this. By this argument, the beautiful variety of all creatures would be taken away. COMMENTARY ON GENESIS 3:7.[54]

GOD DID NOT CAUSE THE FALL. HANS DENCK: When God created Adam and Eve and gave them Paradise he told them what they were to do and not to do. He laid before them life and death. By commanding them not to eat of the tree of knowledge, he told them ahead of time what to guard against. Was God then a

---

[52]*In Prophetarum Oceanum* (1612), 74, quoting Bernard of Clairvaux, *Homily 2* on Lk 1:26-27 (PL 183:62). [53]CTS 1:143-44* (CO 23:55). [54]*In Primum Librum Mosis* (1569), 14v-15r.

cause of their transgression when they fell? *God warned Adam of possible harm.* Was it not fair that he warned them of their wrong? But he did not give them this commandment that they might transgress it. Rather, they were to have an aversion to the tree, that they might live. Who then made sin? *Sin and death come from the devil.* It comes from humankind, just as death comes though sin because of the devil's envy. Adam himself indicates this, as Moses says, when God asked him how it came about that he ate of the forbidden tree, he said, "The woman whom you gave me as a companion gave the fruit to me and I ate." This is not, as some say, that Adam there sought to put the blame on God, "Had you not created the woman for me, I would not have fallen." *Adam never accused God of [causing] his fall.* Even if this had been Adam's intention, it does not follow, therefore, that God was the cause of the transgression. For God himself says a little later as he continues to talk with Adam, where it originates, "Because you listened to the voice of your wife and not to me and ate of the tree which was prohibited to you, let the earth be cursed in your work, etc." *Disobedience brought sin over all people.* [Sin] originated in disobedience thus: Had Adam not listened to his wife but to God and had the wife not listened to the serpent, but instead kept the commandment, they would not have died. Since, however, each listened to the other and wanted to know good and evil and believed the devil, it served them right when God later slapped their faces. He is absolutely blameless and did not deprive them of anything by placing them outside the garden. COMMENTARY ON MICAH 2.[55]

GOD JUSTLY PERMITTED THE FALL. WILLIAM PERKINS: Who can here complain of God? Can the devil? But God did not cause him to tempt or deceive our first parents. Can Adam and Eve? But they fell freely, without any motion or instigation from God, and their own conscience accused them for it. Can the

posterity of Adam? But the elect receive more in Christ than they lost in Adam; and the reprobate, overwhelmed with the burden of their own sins and thereupon receiving nothing but due and deserved damnation, cannot find fault. EXPOSITION OF THE APOSTLES' CREED.[56]

ADAM DID NOT FALL MERELY BY GOD'S PERMISSION. JOHN CALVIN: When I say that Adam did not fall without God's ordination and will, I do not take it as if sin had ever been pleasing to God or as if he simply willed that the precept that he had given should be violated. So far as Adam's fall subverted equity and well-constituted order, so far as it was willful defiance of the divine lawgiver and a breach of justice, it is certain that it was opposed to the will of God. Nonetheless, none of these things makes it impossible that, for a certain cause, even if unknown to us, God might have willed humankind to fall. It offends the ears of some people when it is said that God so willed. But what else, I pray, is the *permission* of the one who has the right to prevent and indeed in whose hand the whole matter is placed, but his *will?* . . . From all this, inexperienced writers wrongly conclude that the first man did not sin by his own free movement. But in fact, he himself perceived, having been convicted by the testimony of his own conscience, that he was far too free in sinning! COMMENTARY ON GENESIS 3:1.[57]

JUSTICE REQUIRES CONSISTENCY. JOHANNES BRENZ: God was not obliged by any commitment to allow this transgression to go unpunished or to turn a blind eye to it. Indeed, given that the whole human race would be propagated from Adam and Eve and was created solely to acknowledge, worship and honor God, no one would ever have been able to undertake or carry out true worship of God,

[55]*Writings,* 67-68; italics indicate original marginalia. [56]*Works* (1608) 1:160. [57]CTS 1:144-45* (CO 23:55-56).

nor could there be true knowledge of God, if this disobedience had remained unpunished. In fact, at the beginning, if God had given any precept or commanded anything just or lawful after that, no one would have thought that this was seriously required by God, no one would have judged it necessary or useful to observe, because they would have seen that the first commandment of all had not been seriously implemented, nor had punishment been exacted strictly as had been threatened. From secular laws we learn just exactly what causes the greatest part of them to be regarded with contempt and shamelessly flouted: the main reason is that he who first violates these laws is spared and no punishment is levied against him. That becomes a pretext for the second one, so that he fears nothing and sins by following the other's example. Also, a magistrate would seem to have even less of a just cause for punishing the second or third violator when he had spared the first and winked at his violation. Consequently, God was strictly obliged to turn his attention to this first disobedience, so that he might protect the authority of all the other commandments that would be given to the human race later on. COMMENTARY ON GENESIS 3:6.[58]

GOD'S JUSTICE IS TEMPERED BY GOODNESS. PETER MARTYR VERMIGLI: At this point, some say that God seems cruel, that he would condemn human beings to death and to the ultimate punishment for such a trivial matter. But those people don't really understand the issue. It was obviously necessary for there to be a place for justice, but that great strictness of God was mitigated by his goodness. For at length, God found it useful to put a limit to the distress into which human beings deservedly fell and not to leave them in these afflictions forever. Then, Christ was immediately set forth as a saving remedy, and God gave his only son for us. By this remedy, if those miserable people were willing to use it,

they would be restored not only to the pristine place they fell from, but to a better place. Is *this* cruelty? The death that was set forth as a punishment is now gain for the saints, as per Philippians 1[:21]. COMMENTARY ON GENESIS 3:1.[59]

QUESTIONS ABOUT SIN MUST BE ANSWERED BY WHAT GOD REVEALS, NOT WHAT HE HIDES. NIKOLAUS SELNECKER: It is certain, however, that God created all human beings for life, not for death or destruction; and, having given his Son, he wishes all to be saved. But whenever that does not come to pass, blame should not be ascribed to God, nor should it be said that God is the cause of human destruction, and that he simply wills that certain individuals perish but that some people in that group may not perish. No, to speak in this way, namely, that people are damned by a fatal and inevitable necessity because God wishes them to perish, is not only too paradoxical but also extremely hard on tender consciences. A message like this often cuts and wounds the conscience with despair, as experience testifies, and examples in our own day are not unknown. Therefore, we ought to hold and consider three things in this place. The *first* is that even if God's particular will is not revealed to us but remains hidden and inscrutable, . . . that inscrutable will still doesn't conflict with the will revealed in God's word, but rather fits with it in all things. So if we establish something by the truth of the divine word, we may be wholly certain about God's eternal will, which he reveals in his word, as well as his hidden will, which is the same in these matters. This is a true and unshakeable rule, so that while it remains in place, no scruple or offense can truly be maintained, regardless of what may be raised about inevitable necessity or God's omnipotence and infallible knowledge, or, likewise,

---

[58]*Opera* 1:45. [59]*In Primum Librum Mosis* (1569), 13v.

about the predestination and election of the saints to eternal life and salvation or the rejection of the lost. . . . The *second* is that those who desire to think and speak correctly about the will of God must consider the divine balance of justice and mercy for all. The justice of God is that he punishes according to his law and condemns everyone who does not obey

everything that is written in the law. . . . The *third* is that God does not wish anyone to perish, but wishes that all who believe in the Son might live and be saved. COMMENTARY ON GENESIS 3.[60]

[60]*In Genesin* (1569), 191-92.

3:7-13 FLIGHT AND INTERROGATION

⁷*Then the eyes of both were opened, and they knew that they were naked. And they sewed fig leaves together and made themselves loincloths.*
⁸*And they heard the sound of the LORD God walking in the garden in the cool*ᵃ *of the day, and the man and his wife hid themselves from the presence of the LORD God among the trees of the garden.* ⁹*But the LORD God called to the man and said to him, "Where are you?"*ᵇ ¹⁰*And he said, "I heard the sound of you in the garden, and I was afraid, because I was naked, and I hid myself."* ¹¹*He said, "Who told you that you were naked? Have you eaten of the tree of which I commanded you not to eat?"* ¹²*The man said, "The woman whom you gave to be with me, she gave me fruit of the tree, and I ate."* ¹³*Then the LORD God said to the woman, "What is this that you have done?" The woman said, "The serpent deceived me, and I ate."*

a Hebrew *wind*   b In Hebrew *you* is singular in verses 9 and 11

OVERVIEW: The aftermath of succumbing to the serpent's temptation is a new and heightened awareness on the part of Adam and Eve—an awareness that is terrifying in its mixture of fear and guilt, shame and defensiveness, blame and rationalization.

For Reformation commentators and their predecessors, these verses constituted an archetypal case study in the workings of the sinful conscience, as well as a clinic for understanding how God is likely to treat sin—and sinners. As before, these questions are pursued

with a fourfold stratification, seeking to discern and articulate some abiding and practical principles about the ways of Satan, men and women (as represented by Adam and Eve), and God. Especially on gender issues, serious disagreements were not unknown, sometimes fueled by such presuppositions as whether the woman was present to hear the prohibition in Genesis 2:18 directly from God or heard it only later, as recounted, perhaps uncertainly, by Adam.

To be sure, many peripheral questions never

went away. For example, there remained an abiding concern to understand what it meant for God to "walk in the garden in the cool of the day"—a description that long ago had offended Origen for its crass anthropomorphism and drove him to deny the historicity of such accounts and to credit only figurative readings as authentic. The reformers, of course, bristled over Origen's exegesis, yet Luther and Calvin had different takes on the ancient heresy of the Anthropomorphites, who ascribed a literal body to God. Another imponderable question wondered when Adam and Eve sinned—right away, on the sixth day? or a day or a week later, or more? Nothing much is at stake in the answer, and the question functions more like a gymnastic exercise. Yet venerable queries like these do allow commentators to muse on potential implications for larger issues—or to urge readers to renounce such curious questions as irrelevant or dangerous.

3:7 What Day Was This?

Satan Especially Resented the Sabbath Day. Martin Luther: Many scholars also believe that Adam sinned on the sixth day, and they celebrate the sixth day for its twofold fame, namely, that just as Adam sinned on the sixth day, so Christ also suffered on the sixth day. . . . What Moses clearly states is that man was created on the sixth day and that a wife was given to him. But to me, . . . it seems more likely that Adam sinned on the seventh day, that is, on the Sabbath, just as even now Satan disturbs the Sabbath of the church when the Word is being taught; but not even this can be clearly proved from Moses. Lectures on Genesis 1:27.[1]

No One Can Say When They Fell, but They Did Not Endure Long. John Calvin: A question is raised by some concerning the time of the fall, or rather ruin. The opinion has been pretty generally received that they fell on the day they were created. Accordingly, Augustine writes that they stood only for six hours. The conjecture of others, that the temptation was delayed by Satan till the Sabbath in order to profane that holy day, is far too weak. Truly, by these examples all pious persons are admonished to indulge themselves more sparingly in doubtful speculations. As for myself, while I have nothing I would assert about the time of the fall, I do think it can be deduced from Moses' narrative that they did not long retain the dignity they had received. Commentary on Genesis 3:6.[2]

The Temptation Took Place Quite Some Time after Eve Had Been Created. Wolfgang Musculus: From these words of Eve, when she says, "Of the fruit of the trees that are in paradise we eat," we may gather with some probability that when these things took place, those first human beings had eaten of the fruits of paradise and had entered into this custom and habit of eating from them for some time already. So the simple sense of these words, "We eat of the fruit of the trees that are in paradise," seems to signify that they had been dwelling in paradise for some time by then. There is therefore not enough support for what some imagine, that this temptation was placed before the woman on the second day after her creation. Commentary on Genesis 3:1-7.[3]

How Long Did They Remain in Eden? Andrew Willet: Some would have Adam continue as long in paradise as Christ lived years on earth; others, the space of forty days, because Christ fasted that long as a remedy against Adam's intemperance in paradise for the same duration. Others think that Adam fell the next day after his creation, upon the

---

[1]LW 1:70 (WA 42:52-53). [2]CTS 1:156* (CO 23:62-63). [3]*In Mosis Genesim* (1554), 91.

day of rest, as Tostatus; but it is not likely that God would execute judgment on that day, which was a time of rejoicing, nor curse on that day, which he had blessed. Some think Adam fell on the eighth day of his creation, a week after he was made, as Pererius. But the most approved opinion is that Adam fell on the same day of his creation, which seems most probable for these reasons [among others]. First, the angels who fell sinned right after their creation, . . . and our Savior says that the devil was a murderer from the beginning, not of the world, but of man's creation (Jn 8:44); therefore at the very first he set upon them. The subtlety of the devil also insinuates as much, for he wished to assault them when they were least able to resist, before they were confirmed in their obedience by experience. And it was fitting that, having sinned, they should be cast out of paradise before they had fully tasted of its pleasure, lest they afterward be tormented with the loss and attempt to return. It is further clear from the serpent's first attack ("Has God said you shall not eat of every tree, etc.") that they had not yet tasted of any fruit, but the forbidden fruit was offered them at the very first, before their appetite had been served with any other. . . . Likewise, seeing that they had been bidden to increase and multiply right away after their creation, it is only likely that the man would have known his wife in paradise if they had stayed there so long, and thus they would have begotten children without sin. And what became of the lions and bears, which live on flesh, all the while of Adam's being in paradise? They could not fast all that long, they did not eat flesh because there was no death before the fall, and they did not feed on grass, for then their nature should not so soon have been changed to devour flesh. . . . For these reasons it seems most probable that Adam did not continue one night in paradise but fell on the same day as his creation. . . .

The objection that so much business—giving of names to the creatures by Adam, the temptation of Eve by the serpent, and the seduction of Adam by the woman—could not be dispatched in so short a time as six or seven hours may be answered easily. It is evident from the text that the imposition of names was performed the day of his creation before the woman was made (Gen 2:20), and it required no long time given the singular wisdom and knowledge of Adam, who was able at the first sight of the creatures to give them appropriate names without any long search or trial of their nature. Of Satan's nimbleness in hastening the temptation and ingratiating himself to the woman there need be no doubt: the speed and agility of spirits is great. It was the cool of the day near evening when sentence was given against Adam, so that in the space of eight or nine hours from his creation to his fall, all these matters might easily be done. COMMENTARY ON GENESIS 3:23.[4]

SATAN DELUDED EVE UNTIL ADAM WAS ENSNARED. WOLFGANG MUSCULUS: The eyes of the woman are not opened in the instant when she took and ate of the forbidden fruit, but they are kept closed until Adam had also eaten at her instigation, and only then are the eyes of both opened together. You should recognize that here that restraining the eyes of the woman was the wickedness of Satan, who was keeping them closed all this time until through her he had induced Adam, too, to transgress God's commandment. Otherwise, if she had instantly realized the enormity of her sin, she would not have presented her husband with the occasion for sin. But our old enemy (*inveterator*) knew that the destruction of the human race would not follow unless Adam, too, ate of the prohibited fruit and the transgression of God's command had thus extended

---

[4]*Hexapla* (1608), 55-56, citing in support of Adam's early fall the opinions of Irenaeus, Cyril, Epiphanius, Moses Barcephas, Philoxenus, Ephrem, "and others listed by Pererius on this text, though he himself is of another opinion."

to its fullness. Here, I don't want to dispute anxiously about what might have happened to the woman if Adam had not sinned. This is but a curious question. It is rightly judged that the destruction of our race stems from this: that Adam became the slave of sin through his disobedience and spread the toxin of sin unto all his offspring by carnal propagation. COMMENTARY ON GENESIS 3:1-7.[5]

3:7a Their Eyes Were Opened

OPENED EYES BROUGHT ONLY CONFUSION. PETER MARTYR VERMIGLI: Because Scripture truly does add that their eyes were opened after sinning, it needs to be seen whether this would have abased us or made us more noble. What *is* this new excellence, that they should come to regard themselves as unworthy to be looked at and conclude that their own nakedness was shameful? As they drew back from God, concupiscence immediately sprang up in the unbridled pair, and their bodily members and affections no longer submitted to reason or the Spirit. . . . Sin did not open their eyes but immediately brought punishment, and when that came, shame began to be felt at the same time. Their nature was changed. Previously they were immortal, pure and upright in every way. They neither saw nor felt that they needed clothes for themselves, so that like rich people living at home, they experienced no lack of food or drink or clothing. But if their nature were changing and they were thrust down into our present position, they would undoubtedly have felt that those things were lacking—not because their cognition had been rendered better or more acute, but because their status and situation had been changed. . . . Nor is it the case that this embarrassment, shame or sense of nakedness ought to be ascribed to the devil, through whom (as well as through sin) there entered the law in our members that wages war with the Spirit and the law of God. Shame and dishonor are brought in, but their

awareness of these things, along with their bashfulness and embarrassment, are given by God, by which the evil that was introduced is prevented from gradually spreading further. And if, on account of our vice, our bodily members have now acquired such shame that by their very appearance they have the power to stir up perverse desires and stings of temptation, it was to our advantage that they be concealed. Nor did God, who initiated the use of clothing, disapprove. On the contrary, what they crudely sewed together—namely, fig leaves for covering themselves—God bestowed with improvements when he gave them garments of skin. The serpent, however, brought about confusion and offered no clothing of any kind as a remedy. The serpent also was unable to teach them, nor did he wish to do so. COMMENTARY ON GENESIS 3:7.[6]

THEIR OPENED EYES SAW SHAME AND DEATH. JOHANNES OECOLAMPADIUS: Through the opening of the eyes, by means of which they knew that they were naked, their innate sense of shame is indicated. For they saw in their own members the rebellion of reason, and so also in some way they understood that their own souls were mortal. For their souls were dead immediately when they had eaten, for the grace of God was lost. Nor was the Spirit of God, who had held all their members in check, as effective in them as before. This should not be understood as applying only to the genital organs, even if everyone will bring up the fact that those members ought to be covered especially for the sake of modesty. But all their senses no longer complied with the demands of reason, seeing that they were disobedient to God himself. On account therefore of this novelty, which they did not experience beforehand, now they were ashamed. Seeing good and evil, they saw at the

---

[5]*In Mosis Genesim* (1554), 95, citing Rom 5:12; 1 Cor 15:22.
[6]*In Primum Librum Mosis* (1569), 14v.

same time what they had lost. COMMENTARY ON GENESIS 3:7.[7]

A GUILTY CONSCIENCE CRIES OUT TO BE COVERED BY GOD. HULDRYCH ZWINGLI: In order for us to see how a guilty conscience follows sin in the pious (for even in the worst criminals there is a sense of sin, but they don't feel it because they are blinded by their passions), he adds, "And their eyes were opened," etc. Were they blind before this? Hardly. . . . But the eyes of their minds were strangers to indecency as long as they abstained from the forbidden tree: there was no occasion for sadness, nothing of which to be ashamed. But after they ate the fatal apple, their eyes were opened; indeed, it was plucked from the tree of the knowledge of good and evil. And what do they see now that they hadn't seen before? Their nakedness. They were naked beforehand, too, but nudity was not regarded as nudity, sin was not considered as sin, before the law came; indeed the law is knowledge of sin according to Romans 3 and 5. Nakedness was not recognized, therefore, until they noticed their lack of clothing. Yet that recognition arrived just as soon as they departed from their creator, the storehouse of all good. Even so, let us learn that whatever plans or hopes or creaturely concerns the human mind finally directs itself to, it will find nothing but afflictions, calamities and the greatest misery (for in the end, this is what nakedness is: to be exposed to every evil and destitute of God's protection), for consolation and rest are restored nowhere but in God's presence. ANNOTATIONS ON GENESIS 3:7.[8]

SPONTANEOUS SHAME IS A SURE SIGN OF GUILT. JOHN CALVIN: Truly, this opening of the eyes in the first human beings in order to see their own indecency clearly proves that they were also condemned by their own judgment. They had not yet been summoned to God's tribunal, there is no one accusing them, so is not the sense of shame that spontaneously steals over them a sure indication of their guilt? COMMENTARY ON GENESIS 3:7.[9]

3:7b *They Knew They Were Naked*

THE INADEQUACY OF FIG LEAVES. JOHANNES BRENZ: Having lost all divine wisdom on account of his sin, Adam was no longer able to look out for his true salvation. A kind of wisdom does remain to him in political matters, even as in this instance he is not acting imprudently when he covers his private parts with a loincloth of fig leaves. But he has lost true wisdom and prudence, by which he might be able to cover his sin before God. For that, fig-leaf coverings are worthless. Adam couldn't have made a tunic long enough but that the scoundrel he had become would have leapt out and appeared above his waist! Hypocrites and all those who are unworthy of the gospel of Christ follow Adam's example. Indeed, when these people feel indicted by their consciences for their sins, they try to expiate their sins. For example, they make amends for drunkenness by distributing alms; for fornication they make pilgrimage to the temple of some divinity; for blasphemy they fast for a number of days; for defrauding someone they recite a few prayers and psalms. And truly, we ought to give alms, live soberly, etc., and pray: but these works of ours do not remove our sins in God's sight: they are aprons of fig leaves, which are somewhat adequate as an external covering but are worthless for placating God's wrath and expiating sins. Only Jesus Christ the Son of God is the expiator of our sins and the true covering that perpetually covers our sins before God, if indeed we believe in him. COMMENTARY ON GENESIS 3:7.[10]

---

[7]*In Genesim* (1536), 46v-47r. [8]ZSW 13:23-24; cf. Rom 3:20; 5:13. [9]CTS 1:157* (CO 23:63). [10]*Opera* 1:48.

THE TREE OF THE KNOWLEDGE OF INDECENCY. KONRAD PELLIKAN: A wretched, sober knowledge, promised by the devil: now they regarded as evil that which had been good. . . . Now nakedness begins to displease, which not only was not indecent but was even an adornment for the innocent. Having now discerned their nakedness, they grieved to know the things they had learned, and they stitched together fig leaves in order to make loincloths and garments: they feeble-mindedly hasten to fix the work of God, as if in the human body the Lord Creator had propagated something indecent. Now they had eaten heartily, as it seems, from the tree of the knowledge of indecency: now they believed good to be evil. They who had been appointed by God as lords and rulers of all things now sought protection for their honor and integrity from fig leaves. COMMENTARY ON GENESIS 3:7.[11]

FIG LEAVES WERE MERELY HANDY. ANDREW WILLET: *They sewed fig-tree leaves*: not because its fruit, which they had tasted, was forbidden, for they would so much more have abhorred the leaves thereof; nor to betoken the desire of the flesh now procured by sin, which they say is provoked by the rubbing of the fig leaves; nor yet as the testimony of repentance, inasmuch as fig leaves prick and sting the flesh; nor need we run to allegories, that this covering with leaves or with fruit betokens the vain excuse and defense of sin. Rather, they made aprons of fig leaves, which were of suitable breadth and ready at hand, for no other reason than to hide their nakedness, of which they were now ashamed. COMMENTARY ON GENESIS 3:7.[12]

THEY SHOULD HAVE COVERED THEIR EYES AND EARS, NOT THEIR PRIVATE PARTS. JOHN CALVIN: It can be asked why, if the whole nature was infected with the filth of sin, deformity should appear only in one part of the body. Indeed, Adam and Eve cover neither the face nor the breast, but only that which we call the *pudenda* or shameful organs. In this case, I think it came about so that they would recognize how the source of life's corruption commonly lies in nothing other than sexual desire. However, they should have pondered that the cause of shame was no less in their eyes and ears than in their genitals, which had not yet been defiled by sin: for Adam and Eve were defiled by their ears and eyes, which they had offered to the devil as weapons. But for God it was enough that some shameful sign should appear in the human body to remind us of our sin. COMMENTARY ON GENESIS 3:7.[13]

3:8a *God Was Walking in the Garden*

GOD NEVER WALKS IN SILENCE! WOLFGANG MUSCULUS: God doesn't wander around paradise in silence, but declaiming and shouting. "And when they heard," it says, "the *voice* of the Lord God walking in paradise." The voice of God crying out to sinners is the word of repentance, by which those whom Satan has seduced with the allurements of this world are pursued and put back on the right path. . . . This voice was preceded by the voice of the command: "You shall not eat of the tree of the knowledge of good and evil, else you will die." It was fitting that the sound of *this* voice not be transitory to them, but perpetual, so that they might be kept safe against the temptations of Satan. But the serpent snatched it away from the woman with this temptation, just as the woman did to the man. Thus, as the sin was committed, no voice of God was heard by the wretched pair. What prevailed instead was the voice of the seductive serpent and the voice of the woman who was seduced. Thus, it is rightly written that after sinning, they again heard God's voice, by which they were brought back to their senses.

[11]*Commentaria Bibliorum* (1532) 1:6r-v. [12]*Hexapla* (1608), 50. [13]CO 23:64 (not translated at CTS 1:159n4).

Let us consider whether these things do not also happen in our experience. We too have heard God's voice: commanding, threatening and promising. But Satan turns it upside down and substitutes his own voice when his temptations subvert the course of godliness, so that when we have been cast into sin we do not hear the voice of God's word for a while. Not that God is not speaking to us, but rather that our ears have been plugged as if with the clay of earthly delights and desires. But in the end, God's grace having watched over us, our ears are opened so that we may hear the voice of the God who surrounds and pursues the wretched. COMMENTARY ON GENESIS 3:8.[14]

GOD MAY WELL HAVE TAKEN HUMAN FORM. PETER MARTYR VERMIGLI: It's believable that God spoke to Adam in human form. Indeed, he who made him in his image would not have disdained to appear to him frequently under the sign of his image. Certainly, he could have interacted with him by means of a secret and inward inspiration, but he was concerned that his presence and rebuke should not strike their minds alone. On the contrary, he wanted them to be terrified by what they perceived outwardly, to the end that they might appreciate the evil of their offense all the more. COMMENTARY ON GENESIS 3:8.[15]

SCRIPTURE DOES NOT FORBID IMAGINING GOD IN HUMAN TERMS. MARTIN LUTHER: A papal decree condemns the Anthropomorphites for speaking about God as if they were speaking about a human being, and for ascribing to Him eyes, ears, arms, etc. However, the condemnation is unjust. Indeed, how could men speak otherwise of God among men? If it is heresy to think of God in this manner, then a verdict has been rendered concerning the salvation of all children, who think and speak of God in this childlike fashion. But even apart from the children: give me the most learned doctor—how else will he

teach and speak about God? And so a wrong was done to good men. Although they believed in the omnipotent God and their Savior, they were found guilty because they said that God has eyes, with which He beholds the poor; that He has ears, with which He hears those who pray, etc. How can this nature of ours understand the spiritual essence of God? Scripture, too, here and there makes use of this very manner of speech. Therefore they were unjustly condemned. Their zeal for simplicity should rather be commended as something supremely necessary in doctrinal matters. LECTURES ON GENESIS 1:2.[16]

3:8b They Hid Themselves

SIN RUNS FROM ITS CURE. KONRAD PELLIKAN: For [their] sin, committed through weakness and directed by the devil's malice, the merciful Lord did not delay treatment: he terrifies them with the sound of a stormy wind. . . . They are well aware of their sin and that they are becoming fools when they run after prohibited knowledge, but now they attempt the impossible, desiring to hide themselves from the face of the Lord, to whom all things are manifest, and to make themselves safe among the garden's lovely trees and groves by fleeing from the Lord. This is how sin confuses and deranges the mind: in despair, it fears the Lord and tries to flee from him whose justice it hates, and it seeks consolation in creatures, having lost the good will of the Creator. COMMENTARY ON GENESIS 3:8.[17]

WHEN LEAVES COULD NOT HIDE THEM, ADAM AND EVE FLED TO THE TREES. JOHN CALVIN: This next remedy, of fleeing God's presence, now proves no better than the first one, seeing that God soon brings back the

---

[14]*In Mosis Genesim* (1554), 101-2. [15]*In Primum Librum Mosis* (1569), 15r. [16]LW 1:14-15 (WA 42:12). For Calvin's dismissal of the Anthropomorphites, see his *Commentary on Genesis 1:26* (CTS 1:94, CO 23:26). [17]*Commentaria Bibliorum* (1532) 1:6v.

fugitives with his voice alone. It is written, "Where shall I flee from your presence? If I traverse the sea, if I take wings and ascend above the clouds, if I descend into the deep abyss, you, Lord, will be everywhere." This we all confess to be true, yet in the meantime we ceaselessly hunt for contrived ways of escape, and we fancy that shadows of any kind will provide a most excellent defense for us. Nor should one disregard that those who had found a few leaves to be hardly useful to them then fled for refuge to whole trees; for it is our habit, when denied appeal to silly quibbles, to fashion new excuses to hide us as if under a denser shade. COMMENTARY ON GENESIS 3:8.[18]

ADAM AND EVE MAY HAVE HID FROM GOD ALL NIGHT LONG. JOHN CALVIN:

The opinion has prevailed that Adam, having sinned around noon, was summoned for judgment around sunset. But I incline more to a different interpretation, namely, that they passed the night quietly and in silence under their covers, with the darkness aiding their hypocrisy; then, around sunrise, freshly awakened, they again returned to their senses. . . . [Thus,] that which lay hidden under the darkness of night was revealed by the rising of the sun. Yet I do not doubt that in that cool breeze there was some notable sign of God's presence . . . to arouse the consciences of Adam and his wife. COMMENTARY ON GENESIS 3:8.[19]

FEAR DRIVES THEM TO TRY ANYTHING.

PETER MARTYR VERMIGLI: We don't suppose, do we, that they had become so foolish as to believe they could hide from God or blend into the woodwork of some secret hiding place? Hardly. They knew perfectly well that he is present everywhere, and that nothing escapes the subtle and pervasive presence of his Spirit. But they were mentally confused, and they try anything—even what they know is going to be less than successful. It's like the common servant whose master has uttered threats

against him: he immediately retreats into the corner of the hall or his bedroom, not because he thinks that there he'll be able to evade the hand of his lord now present, but his distress drives him to this even against his will, because nothing would be more upsetting to him than to endure the look of his angry lord. COMMENTARY ON GENESIS 3:8.[20]

SIN BEGETS STUPIDITY. MARTIN LUTHER:

There is nothing more grievous, nothing more wretched, than a conscience frightened by the Law of God and by the sight of its sins. This brings about what is worst: that Adam and Eve avoid their Creator and God and take refuge under the protection of the fig trees, both to cover themselves and to hide in the midst of the trees. What can be termed more horrible than to flee from God and to desire to be hidden from Him? . . . Is it not the height of stupidity, in the first place, to attempt the impossible, to try to avoid God, whom they cannot avoid? In the second place, to attempt to avoid Him in so stupid a way, that they believe themselves safe among the trees, when iron walls and huge masses of mountains could not save them? LECTURES ON GENESIS 3:8.[21]

SIN BRINGS ENDURING DEGENERATION.

WOLFGANG CAPITO: Because [Adam] ate of the forbidden fruit, on that same day he "died the death" and entirely lost the image and likeness in which he had been created. No longer did he have God and the Holy Spirit dwelling within, as he had at first; instead, Satan with his angels invaded. Immediately he sensed a corrupt nature in the place of one that was whole. Immediately he was unable to conceal that he was made in a different image—truly, that of a son of perdition and of Satan himself. For horrible crimes and shame-

---

[18]CTS 1:161* (CO 23:65-66), paraphrasing Ps 139:7-9. [19]CTS 1:160* (CO 23:65). [20]*In Primum Librum Mosis* (1569), 15r-v. [21]LW 1:172 (WA 42:128-29).

ful acts seethed forth in misery from that place, and he was tormented by the disgrace of sin, an avoidance of God and a hatred for truth. Indeed, having been shaken by those vices, he hid himself among the trees of the garden when he heard the voice of God strolling in the garden. When his wickedness was fulfilled, the just judge would bring this sequence of evil deeds to a close with punishment, for had he not quickly been recalled to grace by the voice of the Lord, every day he would have changed into something worse. Ignorance of God, blasphemies and disgraceful hostilities toward the divine would have increased; his soul would have set itself toward impiety and malice as occasion offered; and the urges of his frenzied passions would have degenerated into depraved habits. Consequently, all things were reversed once and for all, so that filthy ignorance was present in the place of knowledge; hatred, in the place of affection; rebellion, instead of obeying God; and in the place of orderliness throughout the whole person there was nothing but chaos, nothing but irreconcilable strife and outrage. In this way Adam conducted himself on account of sin.

But we who have been born into his image and according to his likeness, we are not in a better place. Indeed, on account of sin, that dead man brought forth in death, and he begot offspring for himself in the same condition: without honor, without repute—or, more correctly, without life. ON GOD'S WORK OF THE SIX DAYS.[22]

SIN CHANGED ADAM AND EVE FROM NOBLES INTO THE COARSEST OF PEASANTS.

PILGRAM MARPECK: The first unfallen, creaturely Adam was the first fleshly nobleman, . . . created in the image of God from whom all nobility and virtue derives. . . . His wife was created from his flesh and of the same lineage to help him; they were to plant the garden of God without effort and work, not as peasants but as nobles, in obedience to their Creator. Functionally, they were lord and god to the creatures, for they had been thus appointed under heaven not to work in wretchedness as a peasant does in the sweat of his brow. If Adam and his wife had not sinned against their Creator, they and all their line, their descendants of earthly lords and nobility, would be without toil and labor. Nor would there be shame, disgrace, death, sickness, toil, or labor. Nor would any suffering have come on them. Rather, all other creatures would have obeyed them as their divinely appointed lords and nobles, and they, along with their descendants, would have been accepted as such by all creatures under heaven until the appearance of the heavenly man, also of Adam's line, Jesus Christ. . . . When, however, Adam and Eve despised the noble title given them by God, fell into shame and disgrace through the deceit of sin, and trespassed the command of their Lord and Creator, all their freedom and glory and their dominion over the other creatures was taken from them, and they were expelled from the garden of pleasure. . . . Adam and his wife were made into peasants of the earth in the great village of this bleak world's wilderness in order to make his living in the sweat of his brow. . . . The noble, divine house died off through death which came from sin, and the glory of man faded. They all became wretched, coarse peasants and unfaithful workers, working the earth in falsehood and deceit, in all wickedness, shame, and licentiousness, sold under sin, and made into coarse, undisciplined slaves of sin. That is the origin of that coarse generation of peasants which knows neither discipline nor virtuous custom before God. Since the time of Adam it has grown in coarseness, licentiousness, undiscipline, and wickedness, raised up by the father of lies, the enemy of all virtue and truth, and remained till the time of Christ coarse, undisciplined

---

[22]*Hexemeron* (1539), 285r-86r.

peasants. Even though in a heathen manner they have presumed to be noble on the model of the pure nobility of creation mentioned above, it was only a theft before Christ and His noble virtue. MEN IN JUDGMENT AND THE PEASANT ARISTOCRACY.[23]

TO FLEE GOD IS TO DESIRE GOD'S DEATH. WOLFGANG MUSCULUS: What does it mean to flee from God, except to flee from life into death, from the greatest happiness into extreme misery and ruin? As the prophet says, "Those who depart from you will perish." . . . Thus, though the creature of God was raised up to be God's image, he is cast into such profound destruction by sin's wickedness that he wishes his Creator extinguished and removed from the scene. Indeed, as is commonly said, "Those whom we fear, we wish would perish." I cannot love one who makes me fear for myself, whose voice and face I cannot bear, from whom I flee with trembling and dread. . . . This is Satan's handiwork, by which the friendship and trust that had prevailed between God our creator and ourselves was at once not merely weakened in our first parents but changed into hatred and hostility, which is more detestable still. COMMENTARY ON GENESIS 3:8.[24]

ADAMIC PRIDE MAKES US HIDE. KATHARINA SCHÜTZ ZELL: Ah, God, my "pride" when I regard myself as a child of fallen Adam is this: that on account of my "wisdom" (gained by the Fall), I am not only a companion but also a member of the household, footstool, and filthy rag of the wicked, dark, damp, worthless serpent head and devil, in the lowest place of hell, on account of my inherited sins and those I have done, yes, on account of the true chief sin of unbelief. Also by nature I am a child of wrath and have a great fear of God and enmity toward Him. Therefore I hide myself in the obscurity or cover as Adam did, and like Cain I flee before God, but His countenance finds

me and He speaks to me with His angry voice. From that comes my eternal anxiety (and not my pride). However, when in faith I look on my Lord Jesus Christ, who is not merely equal to the blessed angels but a Son of God who is above all the heavens, received into the height and adored by many thousands of thousands of angels and saints; when I consider that He was sent to me by the Father, crowned through suffering, made Lord and Christ after He gave Himself as a sin offering and reconciled me with Him (God the Father) through Himself; when I consider that God raised Him, set Him at His right hand, and sent Him to His people as a glorious gift and gain from His great struggle and effective victory and triumph over the devil and eternal death; when I look on Christ in faith and consider all He has done for me—then this is my pride, that I am a daughter of Sarah who believed, one blessed of the Lord, a child of God, a bride and fellow-heir of His Son Jesus Christ, a purified shrine and temple of God the Holy Spirit, a companion who shares with all the saints the good things of heaven in eternal life. That is my glory, honor, joy, and heavenly pride, and glorying in God and Christ, not in myself. LETTER TO SCHWENCKFELD.[25]

3:9 Where Are You?

WAS GOD IGNORANT OF WHERE ADAM WAS? ANDREW WILLET: God was not ignorant where Adam was, for no place, be it ever so secret, is hidden from God. But by his question, God draws Adam to confess and acknowledge his sin, as afterward the Lord for the same reason asked Cain where his brother Abel was. We also do not reject Ambrose's insight that it was not so much an interrogation as a chiding, so that Adam should consider not in what place, but in what state he

---

[23]CRR 2:475-77. [24]*In Mosis Genesim* (1554), 103, citing Ps 73:27 and Ovid, *Amorum* 2.2.10. [25]*Church Mother*, 211-12.

was now, and from where he had fallen. COMMENTARY ON GENESIS 3:9.[26]

GOD'S QUESTIONS DO NOT PROCEED FROM UNCERTAINTY.

JOHN CALVIN: God uses the language of doubt, not as if inquiring about some disputable matter, but for the purpose of more sharply pricking the senseless man, who labors on in blind agony yet still does not perceive his calamity—just as those who are sick may complain that they are burning up, yet never imagine they have a fever. COMMENTARY ON GENESIS 3:11.[27]

WHY GOD QUESTIONED ADAM.

MARTIN LUTHER: God indeed knows that Adam sinned and that he is guilty of death. However, He questions him so that by his own witness he himself may prove himself guilty of having committed sin; for he is fleeing from God, something which in itself is a sin, just as it is a good deed to take one's refuge in God. Although Adam hopes to be able to cover his sin with a lie, he brings this witness against himself when he says that the reason for his flight was the voice of the Lord and his own nakedness. Let us learn, therefore, that this is the nature of sin: unless God immediately provides a cure and calls the sinner back, he flees endlessly from God and, by excusing his sin with lies, heaps sin upon sin until he arrives at blasphemy and despair. LECTURES ON GENESIS 3:10.[28]

GOD DOES NOT FORSAKE THE DESERTER.

HULDRYCH ZWINGLI: Here we see in a clearer light that true religion and piety, as well as the conversion and salvation of humankind, took root when God called back this fugitive, who otherwise was going to remain forever a deserter. Indeed, he saw his nakedness, namely, his guilt, which was so great and so extensive that he despaired of returning to God's favor. But God, ever merciful, took pity on the obstinate and stupefied soul in his flight, no

differently than a dutiful father (who indeed hates the folly or recklessness of his son but cannot hate the son) entreats the lost and hopeless boy and even inquires about his state of affairs. . . . The heavenly father asks Adam where in the world he is so that he would forever be mindful of just where he was, and in what condition, when God gently called him. . . . This, therefore, is what religion or piety is: God exposes a person to himself, so that he might acknowledge his disobedience, disloyalty and misery no less than did Adam. This happens so that he might despair of himself, deeply; but at the same time God exposes the tenderness and breadth of his generosity, so that the one who had come to despair of himself might see how, in the presence of his creator and parent, a grace abounds that is so sure and full that nothing can ever tear this grace from the one who relies on it. ANNOTATIONS ON GENESIS 3:9.[29]

GOD CALLED TO ADAM OUT OF MERCY AND CARING.

KONRAD PELLIKAN: We are shown the kindness of God, who takes back in grace someone who has betrayed him and is not yet a suppliant but is still fleeing headlong. Out of mercy, God first calls to repentance, rebukes with a zeal for righteousness and watches out for the one who, in the midst of afflictions, has no idea how fortunate he is. . . . God interrogates him, showing his indignation more by brevity of speech than by outward expression. Asking "Where are you?" is less harsh, as if he were to say, "What were you like when you were simply obedient? And what are you like now, when you have colluded with the enemy?" COMMENTARY ON GENESIS 3:9.[30]

GOD GIVES THEM A FAIR HEARING.

PETER MARTYR VERMIGLI: Our judges wouldn't act

---

[26]*Hexapla* (1608), 51. [27]CTS 1:163* (CO 23:67). [28]LW 1:175 (WA 42:130-31). [29]ZSW 13:25-26. [30]*Commentaria Bibliorum* (1532) 1:6v.

this way. They use all their power to see that criminals and evildoers are dragged before them, though they did not regard them as worth looking for themselves. The Lord wishes to act rightly, not to punish them without a hearing. Not once do the Scriptures speak as if God were unwilling to search for human merit. When he was going to condemn the proud builders of the tower, or the detestable citizens of Sodom, he himself went down (it says) to investigate whether they rightfully deserved it. If he who knows all things makes this [effort], how much more is it to our advantage not to pass judgment in a matter that has been neither heard nor discussed? COMMENTARY ON GENESIS 3:9.[31]

GOD'S REBUKE IS BETTER THAN SATAN'S. JOHANNES OECOLAMPADIUS: It was said emphatically: "Where, oh where?" The Lord does not speak through ignorance, as if he did not know what had been done or where he was, but in order to provoke him to confess his own sin and to acknowledge what misery he had brought upon himself. It was as if to say: "Oh, Adam, how have you been cast down? thrown into so deep a pit? fallen from such a blessed state? Fleeing from the light, you are no longer the Adam I made, you who were lord of the whole world." These are the words of God spoken to Adam, by which God addressed his conscience. There is no need for us to understand this divine address as an external voice, although the Lord, to whom nothing is impossible, was easily able to form such a voice through the angels. But we don't wish to argue with anyone about this matter. For we daily experience in ourselves what Adam felt when we transgress the command of the Lord, and also when we recognize how evilly we have acted whenever a sin comes to completion. For God admonishes us for our sins in a different way than Satan. God admonishes so that through repentance we should cease from sin. Satan admonishes and mocks us, so that those who have already been seduced into sin are

struck down and perish altogether through despair. Here, however, you see that our inner selves have been most beautifully described, how we are crushed within ourselves and seek everywhere a way of escape, although none appears until we are converted to God. COMMENTARY ON GENESIS 3:9.[32]

GOD ACTS AS A MODEL JUDGE. CARDINAL CAJETAN: Direct your attention here to the fact that while an awareness of nakedness could have been caused by a variety of sins, God did not interrogate them about any sort of weighty sin at all, but about the very least. Indeed, paying no heed to sins against the law of nature and against articles of faith, he inquired merely about a sin against the single positive law that had been given at that time. From this text, then, criminal judges should learn to abstain from the vice of making leading questions when interrogating defendants. COMMENTARY ON GENESIS 3:11.[33]

3:10-12 Adam's Defense

ADAM'S GREAT CONFUSION. PETER MARTYR VERMIGLI: These words—"Where are you?"—bear great emphasis. "I created you to be so upright that you would not be ashamed of yourself, nor would you flee from my sight. But where have you hurled yourself now?" He's looking for a confession of the crime. But Adam is so agitated that he does not yet exhibit a full awareness of his guilt. Instead, he has his eyes fixed on the punishment for his sin. "I heard your voice," he says, "but I was afraid because I was naked." He doesn't confess *because I sinned*, but *because I was naked*. "But *why* are you naked? You ought to think carefully about what you *didn't* experience before this!" COMMENTARY ON GENESIS 3:9.[34]

---

[31] *In Primum Librum Mosis* (1569), 15v, citing Gen 11:5; 18:21.
[32] *In Genesim* (1536), 48r-v. [33] *Commentarii illustres* (1539), 31.
[34] *In Primum Librum Mosis* (1569), 15v.

**CONFRONTED BY GOD, ADAM STILL RE-
FUSED TO REPENT.** JOHN CALVIN: Although
this seems to be the confession of a dejected
and humbled man, it will in fact soon appear
that he was not yet properly subdued, nor led
to repentance. He ascribes his fear to the voice
of God and to his own nakedness, as if he had
never before heard God speaking without
being alarmed, or rather as if he had expected
to be pleasantly cheered by God's speech. His
excessive stupidity appears in this, that he fails
to recognize the cause of his shame in his sin,
and he thereby shows that he does not yet so
feel his punishment as to confess his guilt.
COMMENTARY ON GENESIS 3:10.[35]

ADAM'S MISPLACED SHAME. ANDREW
WILLET: He was more ashamed of his nakedness than of his sin. Thus do many fear rather
to offend because of public shame than for any
consciousness of sin, just as Cain grieved more
because he was made a vagabond than because
he had killed his brother. COMMENTARY ON
GENESIS 3:10.[36]

ADAM HAS DEFACED HIS OWN BEAUTY.
ANNA MARIA VAN SCHURMAN:
  Hell enters their souls and
    stirs up those alien passions:
  of fear, envy and hate—
    monstrosities hell has fashioned.
  Conscience is their tyrant and
    drives them from God's clearing;
  they cover their shame, while
    the devil stands there jeering.
  They hear the voice of God,
    who walks upon the wind,
  they fear God's vengeance
    will devour them both for sin.
  Yet Adam then is asked, aloud,
    whither does he flee:
  no tree or leaf gives him cover,
    for God his heart can see.
  He'd hoped, it seems, to attain
    an even greater renown

  and with his own glory
    (yet without God) himself to crown,
  and to become God's own equal,
    at least in his own opinion:
  greater not in holiness,
    but in majesty and dominion.
  God wants the man's own mouth
    to speak and not dissemble
  why he has fled from God
    and now before Him trembles.
  How far the foolish man has fallen!
    He does not find it odd
  to suppose that by deception
    he can also blind his God.
  He hardly knows of any guilt,
    he rather calls it *shame*,
  and tries to cloak his flight as fear
    of God's own holy name.
  His nakedness alone it is
    that fears God's voice right now,
  and he argues here no better
    than would a pig or cow.
  Was he not naked before? Did he
    not then hear God speak about
  blessing and warn of the curse
    before he wanted his law to flout?
  Seeing God was his happiness,
    the voice of God his joy,
  as long as he clung to God
    and true virtue did employ.
  But now that he has cast away
    his Lord's favor and his duty
  and absorbed a hellish poison
    that has ruined his former beauty,
  he fears to show his God
    the devil's image on his visage
  and feels that death and hell
    have become his lot and lineage.
PARAPHRASE OF GENESIS 1–3.[37]

HIDDEN GUILT ONLY FESTERS. WOLFGANG
MUSCULUS: Adam does not say, "And I was

---

[35]CTS 1:162* (CO 23:66). [36]*Hexapla* (1608), 59. [37]*Uitbreiding*,
9.12–10.13.

afraid because I am guilty and a transgressor of your command," but "because I was naked." We see here that the disposition of the flesh is not only that of a sinner but also a liar: and that, not only before other people but also before God, who is the knower of our hearts and of all secrets. He does not have the courage to strip off his disgrace and guilt at once, but instead he utterly disguises it for as long as he can. Yet he doesn't know that it is impossible for him to be freed from the disturbance and commotion in his miserable conscience so long as he continues to disguise and cover up his sin. Indeed, just as a wound one has received cannot be healed as long as the pus hidden inside has not been expelled, so the mind of a sinner cannot be rendered tranquil and at peace unless the guilt that bites and gnaws from within is taken away by a full confession of sin. COMMENTARY ON GENESIS 3:10.[38]

ADAM'S LIES AND DISLOYALTY. JOHANNES

BRENZ: He was not content with one lie but piled lie upon lie. Indeed, when God was charging him with blatant vanity and sin, . . . he immediately added another lie and accused God in order to excuse himself: "The woman whom you gave me as a companion gave to me and I ate"—that is, "It's your fault, for you gave me a companion like this who drove me to eat." Hear, I beg you, how impious Adam is, as much toward God as toward his own wife! Indeed, first he makes God the author of sin, because he gave him such a companion. This is deceitful impiety and an impious lie. Then he also acted impiously and cruelly against his wife, whom he ought to have defended from danger even with his own life. By redirecting the blame from himself back onto his wife, what does he do but betray the miserable woman and expose her to a ghastly death, delivering her (as far as he was able) to a butcher's shop to be slaughtered. He puts his own wife on the butcher's block! Alas, how unlike

himself Adam has become! Before, when he was endowed with the Holy Spirit, he said of the woman, "This is now bone of my bones and flesh of my flesh," . . . etc. But now he has become the betrayer of the woman, that is, of his own flesh and blood. See how sin is the cause of all these things! Indeed, after Adam lost the Holy Spirit through sin, what followed was the spirit of Satan, who drives a person into all foolishness and folly, impiety, mendacity, brutality, and thus into every kind of crime. COMMENTARY ON GENESIS 3:12.[39]

ADAM BLAMES GOD FOR HIS WIFE. JOHN

CALVIN: Adam's insolence now more clearly betrays itself; indeed, he is so far from being subdued that he breaks forth into coarser blasphemy. Previously, he was complaining to God in silence, but now he begins to contend with him openly and even insults him, as if all restraints were now lifted. From this we can see how fierce and fractious an animal the man began to be after he is estranged from God, for a lively picture of corrupt nature is presented to us in Adam from the moment of his revolt. Each of us is tempted by our own desire, says James, and even Adam did not take on the role of a rebel against God without doing so knowingly and willingly. Nonetheless, just as if he were unaware of any evil, he substitutes his wife as the guilty party in his place. "I ate," he says, "because she gave." Nor was he content with this, for at the same time he charges God with a crime, objecting that the wife who brought this ruin had been given to him by God. We, too, trained in the same school of original sin, are far too ready to resort to evasions just like this one, but all to no good: for regardless of how we may be driven by outside urges and impulses, the unbelief that draws us away from obeying God remains within us; the pride that begets

---

[38]*In Mosis Genesim* (1554), 104; his comment goes on to cite David's confession in Ps 32. [39]*Opera* 1:50.

contempt lurks within. Commentary on Genesis 3:12.[40]

Satan's Poison Leads Us to Blame Others.

Wolfgang Musculus: Then let us consider the peculiar kind of malice in this excuse, wherein you may discern one who has recently imbibed the poison of Satan. In no way whatsoever does he excuse his deed, but he clearly employs a deceitful transfer of blame. Indeed, he transfers it both to his wife and to God himself. He once considered no one more deserving of his loyalty and kindness than God first, then his wife, but he spares neither one nor the other. He could have confessed his sin without any mention of his wife. He should have thought to himself, "Even if she sinned and offered you the forbidden fruit to eat, she sinned only because she was deceived, and you were made not to consent, but to correct her." But he preferred to saddle his wife with this blame rather than take full responsibility for the crime by sparing her. And this sickness, namely, denying one's own confusion, grew from its beginning to such strength that it now attributes blame for the deed more quickly to God than to itself, and it simultaneously blames both gift and giver. Would that this impiety had been extinguished in Adam and not also spread to his posterity! Yet do we not hear today of many such Adams who say, "The flesh that God gave me seduces and destroys me"? Likewise, "If I had been made by God differently, I would behave otherwise. But I didn't make myself!" The mouths of the impious utter these and many similar things against God. Where they should have given thanks to their Creator, there these impious ingrates accuse him. This impiety hides in our flesh, and so its promptings are to be diligently watched for and severely repressed. Commentary on Genesis 3:12.[41]

Adam Does Not Really Blame God or Eve.

Peter Martyr Vermigli: Adam confesses the motive for his sin: that he wished to gratify his wife, whose voice he preferred to God's commandment. Some people want this to be an excuse, as if Adam cast the blame for the crime he committed back onto God—as if he were to say, "You, O God, are not beyond blame, you who gave me such a wife." But this excuse doesn't seem worthy of the man, who knew he had been created to be the head of the woman, from whom he was not to take advice, so his duty would be to rule her. It seems to me, therefore, that he doesn't cast the blame onto God, yet he does excuse his kind of sin, implying that it didn't arise from contempt of God and that he wasn't moved to this act in order not to be subject to God or obedient to him. He wanted to show that he fell from weakness and that he was therefore not wholly unworthy of pardon. It's also worthy of attention that he does not say that he had been deceived by the woman, but asserts only that she had been given to him. She, however, confesses that she was deceived, according to the words of the apostle, by the serpent. . . . Nevertheless, neither of them pleads as an excuse here that they were forced to this deed, because they had been endowed with sufficient grace to be able to resist. Commentary on Genesis 3:12.[42]

Adam Is Treated Gently.

Martin Luther: Just as the end of this affair shows the very great kindness and mercy of God toward man (inasmuch as He calls him back for the remission of his sins and for eternal life through the Seed who was to come), so also the beginnings of this affair, if we evaluate them properly, are more lenient than what Adam deserved. There is not that terrible sight as on Mt. Sinai, where trumpet blasts were mingled with flashes of lightning and peals of thunder. But God comes in a very soft breeze

---

[40]CTS 1:163-64* (CO 23:67), citing Jas 1:14. [41]In Mosis Genesim (1554), 106. [42]In Primum Librum Mosis (1569), 15v.

to indicate that the reprimand will be fatherly. He does not drive Adam away from Himself because of his sin, but He calls him and calls him back from his sin. Yet Adam does not understand or see this fatherly concern, since he is overwhelmed by his sin and terror. He does not notice that God deals far differently with the serpent. He does not call the serpent. Nor—in order in this way to call it to repentance—does he ask the serpent about the sin that has been committed. But He condemns it immediately. This shows that even then Christ, our Deliverer, had placed Himself between God and man as a Mediator. Lectures on Genesis 3:13.[43]

3:13 Eve's Defense

Blaming the Serpent Is a Lie. Johannes Brenz: In the same way, Eve too casts the blame back onto the serpent, by which she plainly indicates that she has been deserted by the Holy Spirit and is in thrall to the spirit of falsehood and folly. Indeed, she thinks she is excused of sin by blaming another. But she lies in saying she was not to blame, for certainly the serpent could not have led her astray if she herself had not put her trust in him, that is, if the main portion of blame were not stuck to her. Commentary on Genesis 3:13.[44]

Only Adam Heard the Command Directly. Martin Luther: Just as [Adam] alone heard the commandment, so he alone is first called to trial. But because Eve also sinned and fell away from God, she hears the verdict at the same time and shares in the punishment. Lectures on Genesis 3:9.[45]

The Woman Had Received the Prohibition Directly from God. Cardinal Cajetan: But as to the originator of the precept, the woman responds firmly, asserting that God had announced this sort of prohibition both to her husband and to her and

stating that "*Elohim* said 'you shall not eat.'" Two things are deduced from this text. The first is that God delivered this precept to the woman through himself and not through Adam. For in fact the woman herself discloses this by saying "God said *you* may not eat," in the plural number. This argument is also persuasive: for if the woman had possessed her awareness of this precept only from her husband's reportage, she would easily have been shaken loose from the assertion that "God said," and she would have responded, "My husband reported that God prohibited us lest we eat," and this would have been the easiest way to lead the woman into transgression. Thus, the woman's own constancy in her assertion that "God said" is evidence that God spoke to both of them. The second is that the woman had [already] been created when God said to humanity, "In whatever day you eat of the tree of the knowledge of good and evil, by death you shall die." Commentary on Genesis 3:2.[46]

Eve's Weakness Was Not that She Received the Command Indirectly. Wolfgang Musculus: Ambrose notes here that the serpent preferred to tempt the woman more than Adam because it knew that Adam had heard the command about the tree of the knowledge of good and evil from the very mouth of God; but the woman, because she had not yet been created at the time when God gave that command, was constrained to learn of these things as best she could, not from the mouth of God but from Adam. . . . Nonetheless, it is also not impossible that those who have heard the truth from the mouth of God can be led away from him by Satan's deceptions, which they encounter not in any simple form but in amazement and even in a kind of stupor. The clearest possible example of this is

---

[43]LW 1:180-81 (WA 42:135). [44]*Opera* 1:50-51. [45]LW 1:173 (WA 42:129). [46]*Commentarii illustres* (1539), 28.

found in the Israelites, who did not persist in the word that was brought forth with great marvels on Mt. Sinai from the mouth of God. Thus Ambrose's conjecture, which is also followed by some recent writers, is not supportable. COMMENTARY ON GENESIS 3:1-7.[47]

EVE WAS NOT FORCED TO LISTEN TO THE SERPENT. JOHN CALVIN: Eve should have been astounded at the monstrosity of the crime for which she was rebuked. Yet she is not struck dumb. Instead, following her husband's example, she redirects the accusation to another, and by laying blame on the serpent, she foolishly and shamelessly thinks herself absolved. Indeed, her plea finally comes down to this: "I received what you had forbidden from the serpent, so the serpent was the impostor." But who forced Eve to lend an ear to his fallacies? Nay, to put her trust in them more readily than in God's word? In fact, why did she let them in at all, unless she had already opened and abandoned watch over an entryway that God had sufficiently strengthened? However, the fruit of original sin makes itself known everywhere, and because it is blind in its hypocrisy, it would happily render God mute and speechless. COMMENTARY ON GENESIS 3:13.[48]

GOD ALWAYS LEAVES ROOM FOR REPENTANCE. JOHANNES OECOLAMPADIUS: You see

that the woman also brings out a foolish excuse. The snake did not take her by force, so she ought to have ascribed that sin to her own foolishness, not to the snake. Indeed, she condemns herself with her own words, since she ought freely to have confessed her own sin. All through the whole of Scripture one can see that as often as God administers justice and wishes to threaten some punishment, he first makes well known the sin on account of which he is considering to punish humankind. So also in this place, before he has found fault with Adam and Eve. But once matters had been found out, he passed the sentence which their facts merited. However much these things may seem too harsh or severe, in reality, if considered rightly, they are ripe with the mercy of God. Once again it is right to acknowledge the divine benevolence, for God does not do with humankind what was merited by the magnitude of the sin. Adam together with all his posterity deserved to be completely rejected and wholly condemned. Nevertheless, God gave both to him and to his posterity room for repentance, and he did so through the Redeemer, out of pure kindness, and without provocation. These facts must therefore be held up alongside those punishments. COMMENTARY ON GENESIS 3:13.[49]

---

[47]*In Mosis Genesim* (1554), 90. [48]CTS 1:165* (CO 23:68). [49]*In Genesim* (1536), 50r-v.

3:14-19 VERDICT AND PUNISHMENT

¹⁴*The* LORD *God said to the serpent,*

"Because you have done this,
 cursed are you above all livestock
 and above all beasts of the field;
on your belly you shall go,
 and dust you shall eat
 all the days of your life.
¹⁵*I will put enmity between you and*
  the woman,
 and between your offspring^a and her
  offspring;
he shall bruise your head,
 and you shall bruise his heel."

¹⁶*To the woman he said,*

"I will surely multiply your pain in
  childbearing;
 in pain you shall bring forth children.
Your desire shall be for^b your husband,
 and he shall rule over you."

¹⁷*And to Adam he said,*

"Because you have listened to the voice
  of your wife
 and have eaten of the tree
of which I commanded you,
'You shall not eat of it,'
cursed is the ground because of you;
 in pain you shall eat of it all the
  days of your life;
¹⁸*thorns and thistles it shall bring*
  forth for you;
 and you shall eat the plants of the
  field.
¹⁹*By the sweat of your face*
 you shall eat bread,
till you return to the ground,
 for out of it you were taken;
for you are dust,
 and to dust you shall return."

a Hebrew *seed*; so throughout Genesis   b Or *against*

OVERVIEW: God's interrogation abruptly ends with the unsatisfying replies of Adam and Eve. God then moves directly to issue the divine judgments. Each of these declarations forecasted and explained the way things are, now that sin has entered the world, with respect to serpents, women and men—but each also raised anew some traditional problems.

In the case of the serpent, commentators wondered what the point was at all. Why curse a snake, when it was really Satan (all agreed) who was the real perpetrator of this evil?

Especially of interest here, then, is the way Reformation commentators explain how a literal reading implicates someone—the devil—whom the text never actually names.

The woman's punishment clearly looks to her lot today: pain in childbirth and subjection to men. Given that nearly all commentators of this era and before would have already found women's subjection implied in Genesis 2, where she is described as created to be man's helper, it is no surprise that most Reformation commentators see her punishment as a matter of going from easy submission to an oppressive servitude—though it is also possible, rarely, to find an assertion of the equality of the sexes before the fall. More generally, it may be a sign of the times that so many Protestant writers try to ameliorate Eve's punishment by urging husbands and wives to a degree of mutuality and reciprocity within the context of a still-hierarchical household.

The penalties levied upon Adam are those commonly experienced by all men—or at least by most men, for commentators usually worry that the rich and powerful have found ways to avoid labor and sweat. The same question leads them to important hermeneutical reflections on whether Adam's punishment is a mandate or just a description, as when Calvin wonders if these verses mean that God wills all to be farmers. Reformation interpreters found diverse ways to remain with a literal reading of Genesis that retained the plenary scope of the sentence on Adam and his descendants, particularly by considering the severest aspect of that sentence: namely, death, when Adam and Eve would return to dust.

One of the liveliest discussions emerged from Genesis 3:15, which describes the enduring enmity between the woman's "seed" and that of the serpent and enigmatically speaks of how the serpent's head will be crushed and another's heel bruised. This grammatically difficult text was popularly known as the *protoevangelion*—the first announcement of the gospel of Christ, in that Christ was seen as the seed or offspring promised to Eve who was destined to destroy Satan while also being wounded in the process. Protestants agreed here against Roman Catholics that it was Christ, not Mary, who defeated the devil, but Reformation commentators disagreed on major details: some took the verse allegorically; others read it christologically and noted Christ's identity as the second Adam; still others preferred to see the verse as looking to the general strife between Satan and the human race.

3:14 The Serpent's Punishment

WHY DIDN'T GOD QUESTION THE SERPENT? JOHN CALVIN: He does not interrogate the serpent as he had the man and the woman, because in the animal itself there was no sense of sin, and to the devil he would extend no scrap of hope for pardon. COMMENTARY ON GENESIS 3:14.[1]

THERE WAS NO NEED TO INTERROGATE THE SERPENT. PETER MARTYR VERMIGLI: Adam and Eve are interrogated by the Lord, but not so the serpent. They are asked so that, compelled to reply, they might better recall their sin sincerely and with thoughtful reflection. But the serpent, who proved to be the source and head of all this evil, is not interrogated. Because his evil intentions against God had already been apprehended, no other cause for his action was to be sought. Moreover, because his sin was irremediable, a confession of his evil would have gained him nothing. COMMENTARY ON GENESIS 3:14.[2]

THE "SERPENT" WAS EXAMINED PREVIOUSLY. JOHANNES BRENZ: In passing judgment, God doesn't listen to the serpent as he had listened to Adam and his wife—yet he is not thereby an unjust judge. For although the serpent was the tool of Satan and a sentence pronounced against Satan would pertain chiefly to Satan, there was naturally no need to interrogate Satan, who had previously been judged and condemned when he sinned in heaven. So it is not necessary for him to be heard also in these proceedings. Let us also note that the things said against the serpent would pertain to the external and bodily serpent . . . in such a manner that they would look above all to Satan, who was using the serpent as his tool. Accordingly, the Lord

---

[1]CTS 1:165* (CO 23:68). [2]*In Primum Librum Mosis* (1569), 15v.

spoke to that *bodily* serpent so as always to look to the *spiritual* serpent, who is Satan. Commentary on Genesis 3:14.[3]

Why Would God Curse an Unwitting Reptile? Wolfgang Musculus: It might seem that this curse's decree would have been better restricted to Satan himself than to the serpent, which is admittedly a sly animal but still devoid of either human or angelic sense and understanding. But if anyone looks more deeply into God's judgments, according to which not only the authors of crimes but also the instruments they employ—including brute beasts and even inanimate objects that are devoid of all sense—are to be subjected to punishment and destruction, one will easily conclude that condemnations of this kind are levied to amplify the execration not only of the crime committed but also its author. So far as concerns Satan himself, he was already condemned long before this and cast from his heavenly habitation. But in order to rightly curse his malice, fraud and wickedness, every one of his instruments is also subjected to punishment. Commentary on Genesis 3:14.[4]

Why the Snake Needed to Be Punished. Andrew Willet: God curses the serpent because he was Satan's organ and instrument, and this manifests God's justice, to punish the instrument with the [one who uses it]: "and he that lay with a beast, they were both to be burned" (Lev 20:15). And though the serpent had no understanding, God yet curses him for man's instruction, that they might see how much their action in seducing him was displeasing to God. . . . Some wonder why the serpent is not made mute and dumb, seeing that Satan abused his tongue and mouth to tempt the woman. The Hebrews think that the punishment is included, in that dust is appointed to be his food: for those whose mouths are filled with earth cannot speak. And to this

day we see that the punishment remains upon the serpent, who makes no perfect sound, as other animals, but only hisses. Satan had been previously accursed before God, nor did any hope of recovery remain, but now the sentence is declared to the comfort of humanity and Satan's state declared to be irreparable, for his punishment shall endure all the days of his life, that is, forever. Commentary on Genesis 3:14.[5]

The Curse on the Serpent Is Our Consolation. Martin Luther: These words are not spoken by God for the devil's sake. God does not regard him worthy of His condemnation, but it is enough that his own conscience condemns Satan. These words are spoken for the sake of Adam and Eve that they may hear this judgment and be comforted by the realization that God is the enemy of that being which inflicted so severe a wound on man. Here grace and mercy begin to shine forth from the midst of the wrath which sin and disobedience aroused. Here in the midst of most serious threats the Father reveals His heart; this is not a father who is so angry that he would turn out his son because of his sin, but one who points to a deliverance, indeed one who promises victory against the enemy that deceived and conquered human nature. Lectures on Genesis 3:15.[6]

Lessons from the Curse on the Serpent. Peter Martyr Vermigli: It's disputed why the serpent was cursed. Wasn't that animal merely the instrument of deception, not its original author? Chrysostom says that God delivered here an image of an extremely tender-hearted father, who if his beloved son were killed, not only wants the murderer himself put to death, but also

---

[3]*Opera* 1:51. [4]*In Mosis Genesim* (1554), 99. [5]*Hexapla* (1608), 52, crediting Mercerus. [6]LW 1:189 (WA 42:141).

destroys his sword, his spear and all his other weaponry. At the same time, Chrysostom supposes that the serpent was previously of erect stature, but for this misdeed he was cast down to the ground.

For our part, we can discern three useful insights from this verse. First, from this we can have proof of how great the punishment was with which God condemned the devil, when in this way his instrument was so severely punished. The argument runs from the lesser to the greater: If the serpent, who is less blameworthy, is punished like this, how much more will the devil receive? Another useful point is that when we see a serpent thus cast down and flat against the ground, the sight of it ought to remind us of the destruction of this first serpent. Third, if the instrument or occasion of our fall was devoted by God to such punishments and detestation, in a similar way we ought to be opposed to the occasions and instruments of our sins. COMMENTARY ON GENESIS 3:14.[7]

WHY GOD PUNISHED THE SERPENT. JOHN

CALVIN: If it seems absurd to anyone that the punishment of another's fraud should be exacted from a brute animal, the solution is at hand. Since the serpent was created for human benefit, there was nothing improper in its being accursed from the moment that it was turned toward human destruction. And by this act of vengeance God wished to prove how highly he esteems human salvation, just as if a father should hold in execration the sword by which his son had been slain.[†] And here we must consider not only the kind of authority God has over his creatures, but also the end for which he created them. . . . For the equity of divine judgment depends on the order of nature that he has ordained, lest it have any affinity whatsoever with blind revenge. In this manner the reprobate will be delivered over into eternal fire with their bodies, which are not self-moved but are

nonetheless instruments that perpetrate evil. Likewise, whatever crime a person commits is ascribed to his or her hands, so that they are therefore deemed polluted. For even though hands do not move themselves, except as impelled by a depraved affection of the heart, they still carry out what the heart has conceived. According to this reasoning, the serpent is said to have done what the devil did through it. But if God so severely punishes a brute animal for the ruin of the human race, he spared Satan even less. COMMENTARY ON GENESIS 3:14.[8]

GOD'S PUNISHMENTS FIT THE CRIME.

JOHANNES OECOLAMPADIUS: God most powerfully punished in the case of sinful humankind chiefly what is accustomed to turn them away from God. The snake walked erect. Therefore God punished and humbled him that he should crawl along on the ground, because in walking upright he seemed familiar to humankind, and thus deceived them. In the snake we find that overweening pride which is Lucifer's own, but in the woman only the pleasure of illicit delight. So the two are punished in contrary ways, though certainly with sufferings. In Adam we find laziness, from which he is released through hard labors. COMMENTARY ON GENESIS 3:14.[9]

THE SERPENT'S PUNISHMENT EXACER-BATED ITS ORIGINAL NATURE. ANDREW

WILLET: It is not to be thought that the serpent previously went upon its feet as other beasts, for God would not alter the nature and shape of his creature, having already given power to every creature to multiply its own kind, and this would be to despise the work of his own hands. Nor is it to be supposed that the serpent was

---

[7]*In Primum Librum Mosis* (1569), 15v. [8]CTS 1:166* (CO 23:68-69). [†]Like Vermigli, Calvin admires Chrysostom's analogy of the "sword of execration." [9]*In Genesim* (1536), 51v.

caused by the spirit to stand upright only during this time of temptation, for it would then be no punishment for the serpent to return to its first nature. Neither do we approve the views of those fathers who allegorically apply these words to the devil, that he goes upon his belly when he tempts us to gluttony and lechery (of which the belly is the instrument), and he eats earth by having power over earthly-minded people—for after this manner, the whole story may likewise be allegorized. Neither do we approve both a historical sense of this malediction in the serpent and an allegorical in the devil, but the whole is historical: the first part concerns the serpent as the instrument; the other, Satan the principal, that his head and power should be broken by this means, and where he had thought to have gained, he should sustain a greater loss. Our opinion, then, is that the curse denounced against the serpent consists not in the thing itself but in its manner: the serpent did from its creation creep upon its breast and feed on the earth, but now this is made ignominious and a curse unto him, which it was not before. Just as weeds and thistles were created before man's fall but after it began to be a curse to the earth; and humans were naked before their transgression but were not ashamed of it till afterwards. So, too, the rainbow existed before the flood but only afterwards was ordained to be a sign of the covenant, that God would no more destroy the world with water. COMMENTARY ON GENESIS 3:1.[10]

3:15 The Serpent, the Woman and Their Seed

WHY SUCH HOSTILITY BETWEEN THE WOMAN AND THE SERPENT—OR WAS IT REALLY JUST A SERPENT? WOLFGANG MUSCULUS: Those who refer the terms of this condemnation not to the serpent but to Satan ask what it means here, that God said he would put enmity between the woman and Satan, when Satan is the enemy not only of the

woman but also of the man? Augustine responded along these lines: ". . . Here it is shown that we cannot be tempted by the devil except through that animal part [of our minds], of which the woman is an image or example of what is found in every person. . . ." For Augustine, then, the woman is not a woman but *our animal intellect*, the lower part of the human [mind]; and the serpent is not a serpent but *Satan*; and the woman's seed is not the human race but *the fruit of good works* . . . and the seed of the serpent is not the serpent's offspring but *evil suggestions*. Thus he thinks the condemnation of this serpent is to be understood not historically but mystically. . . . But in my judgment, the historical sense is not to be compromised. Indeed, we should pay no attention to what is absurd. The simple and proper meaning of words is to be retained, so that the woman is still Eve; the woman's seed is her offspring, the human race; it should be a genuine and natural serpent that misled the woman; the serpent's seed is its offspring as well. The enmity between the serpent and the woman and between the seed of them both may be recognized as the enmity that even now endures between mortals and that cursed beast.

At the same time, following Chrysostom, one may see in these things a certain image of Satan, the enemy of the human race, who used this serpent as an instrument of his evil. Between him also and the woman's seed, the human race, irreconcilable enmities prevail. Certainly, he is permitted to lie in wait for our heels, that is, to tempt us to a certain extent; but he is not permitted to carry out what he truly desires. In turn, his head—that is, the very height of his power—is crushed by the woman's seed. This was done by Christ, who, because he is the true man, is rightly called the seed of the woman and thus related to Eve.

---

[10]*Hexapla* (1608), 47-48, dissenting in turn from Moses Barcephas; Didymus the Blind; Augustine, Gregory and other Fathers; and Pererius.

Indeed, if Luke rightly refers Christ's generation to Adam, what would hinder it from also
being referred to Eve as well, given that she
was the mother of all living? COMMENTARY ON
GENESIS 3:15.[11]

ADAM AND EVE ARE NOT CURSED LIKE
THE SERPENT. MARTIN LUTHER: For Adam
and Eve not only do not hear themselves
cursed like the serpent; but they even hear
themselves drawn up, as it were, in battle line
against their condemned enemy, and this with
the hope of help from the Son of God, the
Seed of the woman. Forgiveness of sins and
full reception into grace are here pointed out
to Adam and Eve. Their guilt has been
forgiven; they have been won back from death
and have already been set free from hell and
from those fears by which they were all but
slain when God appeared. LECTURES ON
GENESIS 3:15.[12]

EVE FORESHADOWS THE CHURCH. PETER
MARTYR VERMIGLI: The church is that which
was foreshadowed in Eve, but it is between the
church and the devil that exceedingly severe
and everlasting hostilities arise. The nature of
the hostility itself suggests that the verse is to
be understood in this way, because serpents are
despised no less by men than by women. [In
this hatred] there is truly a most pleasing
allusion to what happened: the woman perished through an instant of too unguarded a
friendliness toward the serpent, so God
introduces the exact opposite—eternal
hostility. And this curse upon the serpent
carries with it a law from God that is extremely useful for us, that we should regard
the devil as the most dangerous of enemies.
COMMENTARY ON GENESIS 3:15.[13]

GOD PROMISED THE SEED AND THE SPIRIT,
BUT ALSO THE CROSS. PILGRAM MARPECK:
The man who, through genuine works of
repentance (that is, through faith in Jesus

Christ), submits to the fellowship of suffering
under God's hand and discipline will also
participate in the suffering and expiation of
Christ, and upon him God's Spirit will be
poured by faith; he will receive the rich spirit of
transformation, the knowledge of Christ in his
heart, indeed, the Spirit of the New Testament,
which He promised in these days to pour over
all flesh. Wherever He has promised the Spirit
and grace of the new covenant, we are to
understand that it is this Spirit, even as He
promised to Abraham: *In his seed*, that is, the
seed of this Spirit, *all the nations will be blessed.*
This Spirit was promised as soon as Adam
transgressed the commandment. To whomever
this seed or Spirit is given, in him the Spirit
crushes the head of the serpent, that is, he
resists his advice, deception, and lust. For the
fastest way to kill a serpent is to step on its
head. Therefore, it refers to the head. While
the head is being stepped on, it bites Christ in
the heel; without suffering and the cross, it
cannot be crushed or killed. It lies under
Christ's feet and bites, not His toes, but His
heel. Why? Because Christ's countenance is too
sharp, and therefore, the serpent attacks from
behind, for he is a murderer. Murderers do not
attack honorably. So, too, the serpent does
everything in a crafty way, seeking to deceive
and to kill and lead men spiritually and
physically astray. A CLEAR REFUTATION.[14]

THE IDENTITY OF THE WOMAN'S SEED.
JOHN CALVIN: Other interpreters understand
seed as an indisputable reference to Christ, as
if it were saying that someone was going to
arise from the seed of the woman who would
wound the serpent's head. I would happily
endorse their opinion with my support, except
that I regard the word *seed* as too violently
distorted by them—for who will concede that

---

[11]*In Mosis Genesim* (1554), 100, citing Augustine's *Commentary on Genesis against the Manichees* 2.18. [12]LW 1:190 (WA 42:142). [13]*In Primum Librum Mosis* (1569), 16r. [14]CRR 2:61-62.

a collective noun is to be understood of one individual only? Further, just as the conflict is marked as perpetual, so also is victory promised to the human race through a continuous succession of ages. I therefore interpret *seed* to mean the woman's offspring in general. But since experience teaches that many of Adam's sons fall short of rising up to conquer the devil, we must necessarily come to one head in order to discover to whom the victory belongs. Paul thus leads us from the seed of Abraham to Christ. For many were degenerate sons, and a considerable part of them were adulterous on account of their infidelity. It follows, then, that the unity of the body flows from the head. COMMENTARY ON GENESIS 3:15.[15]

THE SERPENT'S ENMITY TAKES MANY FORMS. ANDREW WILLET: Where the Lord says, "I will put enmity between your seed and her seed," this first is truly understood of Christ, who was thus the seed of the woman as he was not of the man, and the greatest enmity was between Christ and Satan, who consented to him in nothing. We may also understand by the seed of the woman, all the elect, and by the seed of the serpent, all the wicked, who are the sons of the devil, . . . between whom (the elect and the wicked) there shall be perpetual enmity. . . . By the *heel*, some understand the end or extremity, that in the end the devil as a serpent shall bite the heel. Some [understand] the inferior part of the soul; some, the humanity of Christ, which Satan pinched at when Christ was put to death, but Christ gave him a deadly blow upon the head. But generally it signifies the weaker parts of Christ's body, which is the church: that Satan shall be nibbling and biting at the heel, as a serpent does when he is overwhelmed and turned upon his back. That is, he shall touch the members of Christ and try them with many temptations, but he shall not be able to hurt them. COMMENTARY ON GENESIS 3:14.[16]

NO PEACE BETWEEN THE WOMAN AND THE SERPENT'S SEED. ANNA MARIA VAN SCHURMAN:

God wants to snatch from the devil's
      jaws that weak and hapless prey,
and turn the Serpent's guile and
      power into shame and dismay.
God pronounces over him
      a curse filled with hell's own fire
and gives a sign to that animal
      of his wrath and ire:
God wants no peace between the
      woman and the Serpent or its seed,
but the seed of this woman will,
      at the last, crush its head indeed.
Behold, from the mouth of God now
      comes that promise, that great word
in which the new covenant
      between God and mortals is heard!
How earth and hell and heaven
      did then stand here astounded
while God's voice rumbled and
      curses from heaven resounded!
Here a wonderful light shines forth
      from God's gracious throne:
the devil's highest punishment
      yields our highest crown.
Satan is condemned,
      God lifts up the human race
to live now without end
      in God's almighty grace
through that wonderful covenant
      that the Lord did provide
by the Son of man's death—
      the Son of God at God's own side!
No greater work of love
      could God's grace anoint,
wherein God's virtues meet
      in a single point.

PARAPHRASE OF GENESIS 1–3.[17]

THE WOMAN'S HATRED FOR THE DEVIL IS

---

[15]CTS 1:170-71* (CO 23:71). [16]*Hexapla* (1608), 52, crediting Targum Onkelos and Mercerus. [17]*Uitbreiding*, 16.16–17.8.

TO BE COMPREHENSIVE. CARDINAL CAJETAN: According to the Hebrew it reads, *And I will put hostilities between you and the woman, and between your seed and between her seed:* "You shouldn't conclude from the fact that you've bested the woman that you're going to have dominion over all women. For while woman may be weak in herself, I will nonetheless put a deadly hatred between woman and you, so that she will regard you not as her lord but as her foe; so that she will not yield to you but perceive you as her enemy; so that she will avoid her enemy; so that she will pursue you with hatred." And we see this fulfilled in countless women who lead holy lives—not by these women's own strength but by the divine gift by which he has placed in their minds not just any sort of hatred but a hatred comprising every kind of hostility (indeed, this is why he says *hostilities*, in the plural number) between them and the diabolical serpent. But it's not enough for hostility toward the devil to be directed toward those things that pertain to faith or hope. Rather, it is necessary that hostility be present in all its parts: in those things that pertain to chastity, abstinence, generosity, works of mercy, and the other duties of the saints. COMMENTARY ON GENESIS 3:15.[18]

THE FIRST SERMON OF THE GOSPEL OF CHRIST. JOHANNES BRENZ: This verse is the first sermon about the gospel of our Lord Jesus Christ. . . . The heel of the virgin's son, whom the serpent bites, is the Son of God's human nature, which he was going to receive from the virgin. . . . "His heel" has this meaning: that the son of the virgin, who is our Lord Jesus Christ, was going to blast with venom—that is, depose and destroy—all of Satan's power, majesty and dominion; but in turn, Satan was going to infect with venom—that is, afflict—Christ with every kind of adversity in his humanity, as much in his own person as in his members who are believers in him. . . . This is

the first sermon, and the first gospel in all the world about the Christian religion and our Lord Jesus Christ. You see, therefore, how after sin Adam and his wife were justified and saved, and were the first Christians. COMMENTARY ON GENESIS 3:15.[19]

THE PROMISED SEED MAKES SATAN AFRAID OF ALL WOMEN. MARTIN LUTHER: He says "her Seed." It is as if He were saying: "Through the woman you, Satan, set upon and seduced the man, so that through sin you might be their head and master. But I, in turn, shall lie in wait for you by means of the same instrument. I shall snatch away the woman, and from her I shall produce a Seed, and that Seed will crush your head. You have corrupted the flesh through sin and have made it subject to death, but from that very flesh I shall bring forth a Man who will crush and prostrate you and all your powers." Thus this promise and this threat are very clear, and yet they are also very indefinite. They leave the devil in such a state that he suspects all mothers of giving birth to this Seed, although only one woman was to be the mother of this blessed Seed. Thus because God is threatening in general when He says "her Seed," He is mocking Satan and making him afraid of all women. LECTURES ON GENESIS 3:15.[20]

THE SERPENT IS FITTINGLY OVERTHROWN BY THE WOMAN'S SEED. HULDRYCH ZWINGLI: The serpent's head was not crushed by the woman but rather by her seed, namely, Christ. . . . The mystery here lies deeply hidden. For what was so great if there was hostility or treachery between the woman and the serpent? Here, already from the beginning, deliverance is promised, as well as that blessed seed through whom all the nations would be blessed. The sense of God's word is, "through a

---

[18]*Commentarii illustres* (1539), 32-33. [19]*Opera* 1:53. [20]LW 1:193 (WA 42:144).

woman you seduced, through a woman you will succumb. Indeed, since you saw woman (speaking by extension of the whole sex) as a suitable means for carrying out your tricks and plotting, however weak she may be, however foolish and susceptible to your tricks, she will nonetheless bring forth the seed that will crush your head." . . . For the devil is the prince of this world, under whose tyranny and power we were all taken captive, until that blessed seed should be born from the woman, Christ Jesus our Lord. ANNOTATIONS ON GENESIS 3:15.[21]

HERE GOD ANNOUNCES A NEW COVENANT. WILLIAM PERKINS: Now we come to the covenant of grace, which is nothing else than a compact made between God and humankind touching reconciliation and life everlasting by Christ. This covenant was first of all revealed and delivered to our first parents in the garden of Eden, immediately after their fall, by God himself in these words: "The seed of the woman shall bruise the serpent's head," and afterward it was continued and renewed with a part of Adam's posterity, as with Abraham, Isaac, Jacob, David, but it was most fully revealed and accomplished at the coming of Christ. EXPOSITION OF THE APOSTLES' CREED.[22]

THE VICTORY OF THE WOMAN'S SEED IN US. KONRAD PELLIKAN: "I do not permit you to tyrannize," says the Lord, "but I will impose hostilities," namely, a natural and perpetual dread of snakes among humans, so that they will desire to trample the head of the serpent; and where there is vigor of life, truly, you are going to lie in ambush, even as you will . . . strike the foot of a human being wherever you can. However, it is a sure and certain mystery celebrated in every age that these things signify the enmity between Satan and the woman's seed, Christ the Lord, who was promised to the woman in this text. Indeed, what was so

notable about hostilities between a woman and a serpent, or that they were described as seeking to bruise the other's head or heel? Truly, here, right from the very beginning, is promised a *liberation* from the recently-committed sin of the first human, through that blessed seed by which all peoples were also to be blessed, in this sense: "You deceived by means of the woman; you will fall by the woman's seed. Indeed, that weak sex was tricked by your wiles, but through her offspring your head, power, strength and tyranny are destined to be crushed. But you will bruise his heel, the humanity of Christ, who was afflicted for our sins." In short, there is great enmity between the flesh and the spirit, between the wisdom of this world and the word of God, between sensuality and the cross, between the impious and the faithful. Indeed, the head of the serpent is the reign of sin within us, the power of darkness and the tyrannical authority of Satan that Christ has defeated. And he has made the faithful to conquer through him. [Satan] lies in wait, assails, disturbs: but the victory of Christ stands firm for us. COMMENTARY ON GENESIS 3:15.[23]

CHRIST, NOT MARY, CONQUERS THE DEVIL. PETER MARTYR VERMIGLI: One should note that "he" (*ipsum*) is what the Hebrew uses, so that attention is thereby drawn to the seed of the woman, that is, Christ, who has truly crushed the powers of the devil. It is not to be translated "she" (*ipsa*), in the feminine gender, as the Vulgate has it. Let the glorious virgin keep her place of honor, but Christ's triumph over the devil is not to be attributed to her. . . . Here, the gospel is promised to us, that is, victory over the devil through Christ. COMMENTARY ON GENESIS 3:15.[24]

---

[21]ZSW 13:28-29. [22]*Works* (1608) 1:164. [23]*Commentaria Bibliorum* (1532) 1:7r. [24]*In Primum Librum Mosis* (1569), 16r.

CHRIST IS THE SEED, BUT NOT EXCLUSIVELY. JOHANNES OECOLAMPADIUS: I am not unaware that more recent expositors say that this "seed" is to be understood as pertaining to Christ. This may be true, but nowhere do we see this testimony cited by the Apostle, although he brings in other texts about Christ the Son of God. If we should cite this text to dispute against the Jews, I fear we would more likely be ridiculed than accomplish anything. Among the pious, however, this testimony avails much, because they know that through Christ the "seed," the devil has been stripped of his power, indeed, inwardly defeated as well. Similarly they also suggest that the "heel," for which Satan lies in ambush, means that Christ would suffer and be nailed to the cross. For it was Judas who betrayed Christ, and he was incited to do this by the devil; likewise also the Jews. However, if we attend also to the specific meaning of the word *seed*, the blessing in Christ is applicable not to one person but to the coming generations. COMMENTARY ON GENESIS 3:15.[25]

GOD WAS DETERMINED TO HAVE HIS IMAGE ON EARTH. MENNO SIMONS: Here the counsel, purpose, will and conclusion of the Almighty, eternal God were unchanged: He would make manifest his glory and have a man after his own image and likeness. Inasmuch as this was resolved upon, . . . the unchangeable, will, counsel and resolution of the unchangeable God would therefore be executed, [that] there must be another who was like the corrupted Adam before his fall: for upon such a man, God's will had resolved, and with Adam all was lost. Therefore the ineffable eternal Word by which Adam and Eve were created [and] by which all things are and must forever remain—the Almighty power and wisdom of God—must become man, that he might bruise the head of the deceiving serpent, for the salvation of the condemned Adam and all his descendants; that temptation might be

overcome; that the holy and unchangeable will of the Father might be fulfilled; that the dominion and power of the devil might be destroyed; and that he might, by his willing obedience and spotless offering, discharge and put away the guilt and deserved death of Adam, by his innocent death. Behold, this joyous gospel, and these glad tidings of the divine grace, which God declared to the poor, afflicted and fugitive, Adam, [who] accepted them through faith, consoled himself therewith, and sincerely rejoiced in his grace. ON THE INCARNATION III (CONFUTATION).[26]

APOSTASY AND RESTORATION THROUGH THE WOMAN'S SEED. DIRK PHILIPS: *The congregation of God* was first begun with the angels in heaven. Afterward the congregation of God was also begun in paradise with Adam and Eve. They were created after the image of God and were made in his likeness, upright, good, and pure creatures of God, incorruptible and immortal. They had an upright, pious nature and divine character, a true knowledge, fear, and love of God existed, as long as they remained in the first creation and ordering of God and had borne that image of God. Therefore the congregation of God is a congregation of saints, namely, the angels in heaven and believing born-again people on earth who are renewed according to the image of God. . . . But *the first apostasy* from God in his congregation occurred among the angels in heaven who had sinned, and were untrue to their Creator. Therefore they were cast out of heaven, bound with the chains of darkness, that they could no more do anything except what God permitted them to do. . . . *The second falling away* from God in the congregation happened in paradise through Adam and Eve who were led astray through the cunning of the snake, destroyed through the corrupting

---

[25]*In Genesim* (1536), 53r. [26]*Works*, 2:165 (cf. *Writings*, 817; *Opera*, 373a).

sin, and thus have lost the image of God, the pure, created, natural holiness, and highly excellent reason, full of all wisdom and knowledge of God and all creatures. This image, which was zealous in love and obedience to God, was lost. Yes, they passed out of righteousness into unrighteousness, out of immortal being into corruption and damnation, out of eternal life into eternal death. *The first restoration* of the corrupted persons, the renewal of the divine image in them, and the new upbuilding of the fallen church of God occurred through the promise of that future seed of the woman, which would trample the head of the snake. This seed is principally Jesus Christ, and was therefore called the woman's seed, because he was promised from God to Adam and Eve, and was born according to the flesh out of a woman. . . . And this Jesus Christ is the true trampler and conqueror of the old crooked snake, who with his death has released the human race from all the tyrannical violence of Satan, sin, and eternal death. This was the first preaching of the gospel of Jesus Christ, the only Deliverer and Savior of the world, through whom Adam and Eve were again established and have again received that lost image of God. ENCHIRIDION.[27]

THE FAITH OF ADAM AND EVE FALTERED BUT WAS NOT WHOLLY EXTINGUISHED. ANDREW WILLET: Whereas we say that all sins are venial to the faithful and elect, Bellarmine replies that Adam committed a mortal and damnable sin, because it was said unto him, "in the day you eat of it, you shall die the death." But we say that though this sin was damnable in it own nature, yet by God's grace through Christ it was made venial and pardonable to Adam—unless Bellarmine would say, with the heretic Tatian, that Adam was damned. By this text he would also prove that Adam and Eve lost their faith, because they did not believe the sentence of God that they should die if they transgressed the

commandment. However, this proves that they failed in faith, but not that their faith was utterly lost and extinguished: for if Adam had no faith remaining, to what purpose should God have propounded the promise of the Messiah to a faithless man? COMMENTARY ON GENESIS 2.[28]

3:16 The Woman's Punishment

EVE'S LOST EQUALITY. MARTIN LUTHER: If she had not sinned, Eve would have carried her child in her womb without any inconvenience and with great joy. Now there is also added to those sorrows of gestation and birth that Eve has been placed under the power of her husband, she who previously was very free and, as the sharer of all the gifts of God, was in no respect inferior to her husband. This punishment, too, springs from original sin; and the woman bears it just as unwillingly as she bears those pains and inconveniences that have been placed upon her flesh. The rule remains with the husband, and the wife is compelled to obey him by God's command. He rules the home and the state, wages wars, defends his possessions, tills the soil, builds, plants, etc. The woman, on the other hand, is like a nail driven into the wall. She sits at home, . . . [to] look after the affairs of the household, as one who has been deprived of the ability of administering those affairs that are outside and that concern the state. . . . If Eve had persisted in the truth, she would not only not have been subjected to the rule of her husband, but she herself would also have been a partner in the rule which is now entirely the concern of males. LECTURES ON GENESIS 3:16.[29]

"YOU COULD HAVE BEEN HIS EQUAL."
KONRAD PELLIKAN: "Having forsaken the man, you stuck with the serpent and sought

---

[27]CRR 6:352-53*. [28]*Hexapla* (1608), 43, citing Bellarmine, *De amissione gratiae* 1.7; 3.6. [29]LW 1:202-203 (WA 42:151).

delights against my precept; you desired to be like God, and you deceived the man. Therefore I will increase your afflictions and impose sorrowful conceptions upon you. Your delights will be to be subject to your husband, to look always to him and to pay attention mindfully. Formed from his side, you were able to be his equal and his companion. You did not know how to govern: now learn to be a subject." Women are to be admonished so that they may submit themselves to God and their husbands, bearing their afflictions patiently and humbly, and they should not be despised by their husbands on account of their weakness of body and mind. COMMENTARY ON GENESIS 3:16.[30]

GENTLE SUBJECTION BECOMES SERVITUDE. JOHN CALVIN: The second punishment he imposes is subjection. For this form of speech, "Your desire shall be for your husband," is of the same force as if he had said that she would not be free and at her own command, but subject to her husband's authority and dependent upon his will—as if he had said, "You shall desire nothing but what your husband wishes," even as Genesis 4:7 reads, "Its desire shall be for you." Thus the woman, who had recklessly exceeded her proper bounds, is brought back into line. To be sure, she was previously subject to her husband, but that was a gentle and honorable subjection; now, however, she is cast into servitude. COMMENTARY ON GENESIS 3:16.[31]

THE WORSENING OF WOMAN'S LOT. ANDREW WILLET: Herein are signified the many sorrows that women endure in the conception of their children: as faintings, loathing of food, longing for strange things, grief, ache, diffidence, peril of miscarriage, and such like. Moreover, whereas women should have brought forth without pain, now their travail is full of labor, inasmuch as many have miscarried in the birth of their children, as Rachel did, and it is well observed by Aristo-

tle that no other creature brings forth her young with such difficulty as women do, which is an evident demonstration of this punishment laid upon them. Also, where it is said that "the woman's desire shall be to her husband, and he shall rule over her," this is not understood of the natural desire the woman regularly has of her husband's company, notwithstanding her painful travail, which is no punishment but a delight unto them. Rather, this is that subjection whereby by the law of nature, practiced [even] among pagans, women depend upon their husbands. The woman should have been obedient to man before, but out of a loving society, so as to be made partaker of all his counsels, not of an urging necessity as now: whereby the woman, in respect of her weakness, depends on her husband not only with her will for her direction and for the provision of things necessary, but she also often endures against her will the hard yoke of an unequal commander. COMMENTARY ON GENESIS 3:16.[32]

THE CHURCH, LIKE EVE, SHOULD LOOK TO HER HEAD. PETER MARTYR VERMIGLI: Because a woman may be taken captive by diverse appetites and desires, she should not be a law unto herself but should always look to her husband, listening to see whether what she wants to undertake would be approved by him. Accordingly, as often as she desires something, she looks to her husband to see whether it will win his approval. Sometimes she looks to him so that she might secure his help for what she desires, because she herself is weak and unable to attain what she wants. This is the situation of the church. Whenever something is to be done or planned, it always looks to Christ, to his words and Spirit, and it attempts nothing except what it has first tested as to whether it

---

[30]*Commentaria Bibliorum* (1532) 1:7r, in all likelihood paraphrasing John Chrysostom's *Homily 17 on Genesis* 3:16 (FC 74:240-41). [31]CTS 1:172* (CO 23:72). [32]*Hexapla* (1608), 53.

is approved by Christ or not. COMMENTARY ON GENESIS 3:16.[33]

EVE'S PUNISHMENT BROUGHT HER HOPE.
MARTIN LUTHER: Truly happy and joyful is this punishment if we correctly appraise the matter. Although these burdens are troublesome for the flesh, yet the hope for a better life is strengthened together with those very burdens or punishments, because Eve hears that she is not being repudiated by God. Furthermore, she also hears that in this punishment she is not being deprived of the blessing of procreation, which was promised and granted before sin. She sees that she is keeping her sex and that she remains a woman. She sees that she is not being separated from Adam to remain alone and apart from her husband. She sees that she may keep the glory of motherhood, if I may use the phrase. All these things are in addition to the eternal hope, and without a doubt they greatly encouraged Eve. Above all, there remains also a greater and more genuine glory. Not only does she keep the blessing of fruitfulness and remain united with her husband, but she has the sure promise that from her will come the Seed who will crush the head of Satan. Without a doubt, therefore, Eve had a heart full of joy even in an apparently sad situation. Perhaps she gave comfort to Adam by saying: "I have sinned. But see what a merciful God we have. . . ." LECTURES ON GENESIS 3:16.[34]

EVE'S PUNISHMENTS ARE REALLY MORE CURATIVE. PETER MARTYR VERMIGLI: This passage is to be understood in the following manner. The plan for the conjunction of male and female was instituted by God in such a way that the man should have taken charge of the woman, but with a gentle governance. Yet because she has fallen, the man is obliged to act more severely toward her and in such a way that he may be said to dominate her. But it is to be noticed above all that by God's mercy,

these punishments constitute declarations of their duties, extremely useful laws for the conduct of life, healthful advice, enhancements to the human condition, remedies against vice and helps in the time of temptation. COMMENTARY ON GENESIS 3:16.[35]

WOMAN'S CURSE IS COUNTERACTED BY HER OBEDIENCE. HULDRYCH ZWINGLI: These [afflictions] are the curse of women and a punishment for disobedience, which they counteract and expiate if they are submissive and obliging to their husbands, bear children and raise them in piety. . . . The sense is this: "You will be weak and defenseless, so destitute of power and aid and so beset by calamities and afflictions, that you will always flee to your husband and implore him for aid." Or: "You will look up to your husband as your head and superior, for the head of a woman is her husband." ANNOTATIONS ON GENESIS 3:16.[36]

WOMAN'S "CORRECTIONS." JOHANNES BRENZ: Now let us attend to the cross—or what they call the "corrections" (for so they call the works of satisfaction that are customarily imposed on sinners for the sake of correcting their lives)—that God imposes on the woman. . . . There are two parts to a woman's cross. One concerns conception and childbirth. This includes all the sorrow, all the labor, all the worry and anxiety of bearing and raising children. Women have varied hardships when they conceive. Their sorrows are many and grievous during birth, which the prophets have often mentioned. There is great worry in raising offspring. And not even a barren woman or a virgin is without her troubles, of course, because both the barren woman and the virgin are equally liable to sin. The other

[33]*In Primum Librum Mosis* (1569), 17r. [34]LW 1:199 (WA 42:148). [35]*In Primum Librum Mosis* (1569), 17r. [36]ZSW 13:29; cf. 1 Tim 2:15; 1 Cor 11:3.

part of a woman's cross is subjection to the man's authority. This is a great cross. Just as the woman, if she hadn't sinned, would have given birth not only without pain but even with great joy and delight, so also she would have been equal to the man in the administration of things, though the man would always have remained the head of the woman. But now, having sinned, she is subjected to the will and authority and domination of the man. Accordingly, God not only imposes this cross on the woman . . . but also establishes this order in the public administration of things, so that the man may be the ruler and the woman should be under the man's authority. COMMENTARY ON GENESIS 3:16.[37]

GOD CURES BY CONTRARIES. PETER MARTYR VERMIGLI: The church, too, does not regenerate unless the sorrows of repentance have gone before, and when any lost soul converts to Christ, the part born to lust is crucified, for the flesh must be put to death along with all its appetites. The very model of a wise physician, God cures maladies with their exact opposites. The woman wanted to be delighted more than was proper, for she began to muse that the tree seemed good, sweet to taste and attractive for acquiring understanding. Here, in turn, she is punished with sorrow and sadness. God wants her to have troubles and toil, to care for her family and to labor over household concerns. If she should strive to avoid or mitigate these things by using maids or servants, nonetheless by these means she cannot, in any case, escape the hardships of childbearing. But this punishment seems rightly to have been fulfilled when she is captivated by the desire for children. COMMENTARY ON GENESIS 3:16.[38]

EXCEPTIONS TO THE RULE? JOHANNES BRENZ: What is to be made of the fact that, even though it was carefully stipulated and ordained that a husband should rule, it still

often happens that wives dominate? In Judges 4, Deborah became a prophetess and a judge of the whole people of God. Writers recount the wondrous deeds of the Amazons, and even though some regard them as fables, the stories told seem likely when so many writers agree about them. These Amazons are said to have arisen in Scythia, and when their husbands were killed in battle, they took up arms and defended their borders. . . . What shall we say about the everyday domestic examples, which clearly teach that women rule the household more than men? How do these things come to pass? Deborah, one may say, is a one-of-a-kind example, raised up by God to signify that the female sex is not cast aside by God (as it seems to be by the world) and that God is not a respecter of persons. But of the Amazons one may say that it was more a monstrosity and portent of nature than a divine ordination, which is why these women's reign was short-lived, abolished and extinguished after some years. But when women aspire to dominate their husbands in running the household, this is sedition, and it arises from sin. To be sure, a man commonly shifts blame to his wife, and a wife to her husband: the man accuses his wife of unreasonable demands, she in turn accuses him of unfairness and cruelty. But it is not for us to follow the example of our first parents by hurling blame against one another. It could never come to pass that a husband repays his wife with evil, nor would a wife repay her husband with evil, if that evil hadn't previously been born in us. COMMENTARY ON GENESIS 3:16.[39]

THAT ALL WOMEN SHARE EVE'S PUNISHMENT PROVES THEY SHARE HER CHARACTER . . . WOLFGANG MUSCULUS: These hardships were inflicted not just on Eve but

---

[37]*Opera* 1:56. [38]*In Primum Librum Mosis* (1569), 16v. [39]*Opera* 1:57, citing the ancient historians Diodorus of Sicily and Justinus on the Amazons.

also on all the poor ladies of her line who came after her, which clearly proves that the corruption of character with which the serpent's persuasion infected Eve afterwards spread unto all women. Otherwise, there would seem to be too little equity of punishment in this affair, if all women had to share in Eve's punishment when they had no share at all in her sin—the cause of this punishment, so to speak. Unless a woman is transformed by a special gift from God, then, it is not to be hoped that she will possess a character any different than Eve had when she was misled and infected by the serpent's conversation. As for what Eve's character was like, that is sufficiently declared by the preceding narrative of her transgression, and everyday experience teaches how womanly character does not differ from it. I note these things not to disgrace the womanly sex but to justify God's just judgment [on her]. COMMENTARY ON GENESIS 3:16.[40]

... BUT THE FAULTS OF WOMEN MAY ALSO BE FOUND IN MEN. WOLFGANG MUSCULUS: Here is something about which husbands should be warned. Most of them are accustomed to boast excessively that they have acquired power and dominion over their wives. But if they rightly reflect on the reason, they would see that God was not furnishing an opportunity for boasting and insolence against women, but rather entrusting men with care and responsibility for prudent oversight, by which women might direct and control their desires with knowledge and prudence. Whence Paul, too, imposes this office on men, to teach their wives at home and instruct them in matters of faith. Wherefore just as parents should not boast that they have authority over their children, but rather provide care and instruction to bring order to their children's ignorance, redirect their foolish or harmful desires and at the same time make provision for their children's needs as well as for their greater weakness, so also should husbands take

care never to forget why God granted them authority over their wives, lest their care and prudence come to be regarded more as the stuff of tyranny and insolence. But how will those men exercise authority who themselves are no less susceptible to foolish and vain longings than are women, whose desires they have taken on when they should have governed them by their skill, seriousness and prudence? You may find husbands of whom it can more rightly be said, "your desire and your longing will be for your wife," than "your wife's desire will be for you." Many parents sin in this matter, who regard it as the best plan for their daughters when they give them to husbands who are totally sluggish and stupid, solely for the reason that they have great earthly riches. And thus is God's order perverted, so that an Abigail is joined to a foolish Nabal. COMMENTARY ON GENESIS 3:16.[41]

YET NOT ALL WOMEN ARE LIKE EVE!
WOLFGANG MUSCULUS: One should beware lest we stretch this example of Adam and Eve further than the apostle's proposition would require—that is, lest we take a specific proposition and make it into something general and perpetual. True, Adam was not misled by the lie of the serpent, but the same cannot be reliably said of just any man whatsoever. Moreover, what happened to Eve does not automatically happen without exception to every woman, many of whom have stoutly resisted the lies and temptations of Satan. In each sex, then, many can be exempted: some, though they be men, nonetheless let themselves be led astray; and others, though they be women, by no means believe Satan's lies. We

---

[40]In Mosis Genesim (1554), 108. Note that this is the first of three excerpts from Musculus, which as a series show a remarkable progression from the expected patriarchal stereotype to a striking resistance to the same stereotype in a later commentary. His comments on Genesis date from 1554; on 1 Timothy, from 1563, the year of his death. [41]In Mosis Genesim (1554), 109; cf. 1 Sam 25.

should therefore draw something more from this verse than that it behooves everyone, men as well as women, to be prudent and cautious, always abiding in the fear of the Lord: namely, that men should not presume upon the privileges of their sex, and that women should not despair that Eve's fall and the infirmity of their sex render them incapable of resisting Satan. Nor is it implausible that when the apostle said in 2 Corinthians 11:3, "But I fear lest it should happen, that even as the serpent deceived Eve by his wiles," he did not append ". . . so might your *women's* minds be corrupted," but rather ". . . so might *your* minds be corrupted from the simplicity which was in Christ," in order to indicate that *all* should fear the wiles of Satan—men as well as women. Indeed, he did not write these things only to women, but to men and women alike, who are joined to the Lord Christ through faith in the gospel. COMMENTARY ON 1 TIMOTHY 2:14.[42]

3:17-19 Adam's Punishment

GOD'S REBUKE TO ADAM. KONRAD PELLIKAN: "Because your wife's love was more important to you than mine, you regarded her voice more than my precept." From which it is clear that Eve did not simply give [to Adam] but repeatedly persuaded him with many words and urged him on by example. COMMENTARY ON GENESIS 3:17.[43]

"AS IF HE WERE CONDEMNED TO THE MINES." JOHN CALVIN: In this text we find the antithesis of that which Adam was previously engaged in, namely, a labor so pleasant that in a way he was playing. Indeed, he wasn't made for idleness, but for doing something. That is why the Lord had put him in charge of cultivating the garden. But while there was a sweet delight in his previous work, servile labor is now imposed on him, no differently than as if he were condemned to the mines. COMMENTARY ON GENESIS 3:17.[44]

THORNS PREACH TO US OF OUR SIN. MARTIN LUTHER: Whenever we see thorns and thistles, weeds and other plants of that kind in a field and in the garden, we are reminded of sin and of the wrath of God as though by special signs. Not only in the churches, therefore, do we hear ourselves charged with sin. All the fields, yes, almost the entire creation is full of such sermons, reminding us of our sin and of God's wrath, which has been aroused by our sin. LECTURES ON GENESIS 3:17-19.[45]

SWEATING MORE A BLESSING THAN A CURSE. WOLFGANG MUSCULUS: The terms of this divine reprimand smack more of God's good providence than of the honor of an irascible God. Indeed, as daily experience teaches, who can count how many kinds of diseases lazy people are prey to, from which those who sweat by laboring and eat their bread by the sweat of their face are wonderfully free? People run to doctors and buy unknown drugs, at great expense and not without danger, in order to expel noxious humors. But by working and sweating, laborers preserve bodily strength by the fastest and best route. Physicians teach that it is good to sweat, and they devise ways to induce sweating. Potions are prepared, baths are drawn, fiery bricks are applied to the feet, and I know not what other things are employed at bodily risk in pursuit of even a modicum of sweat. How much better would it have been to embrace the plan for sweating that God himself imposed on us, from which there is this benefit, that the body's health is protected and its powers remain robust? COMMENTARY ON GENESIS 3:19.[46]

THESE PUNISHMENTS DRAW US TO CHRIST. PETER MARTYR VERMIGLI: By his

---

[42]*In . . . primam ad Timotheum* (1565), 392. [43]*Commentaria Bibliorum* (1532) 1:7r. [44]CTS 1:174* (CO 23:73). [45]LW 1:209 (WA 42:156). [46]*In Mosis Genesim* (1554), 112.

first coming, Christ did not take these things away from the faithful, but he made them lighter. For that reason, among the faithful they should no longer occupy the place that punishments do for one who is hostile. Rather, they should be exercises that conform us to our head, who has labored much on our behalf. Yet this curse still threatens the impious: it hounds them, it daily becomes more burdensome, and then, in the next life, it overtakes and wholly overwhelms them. COMMENTARY ON GENESIS 3:19.[47]

WORK IS A PUNISHMENT TO WHICH ALL ARE BORN. HULDRYCH ZWINGLI: The decree is a general one: leisure, which is the mother of all vices, is prohibited, for we are all born to labor, and the one who does not labor should not eat. No one is excused from this law, at least if they fear God; indeed, it is a punishment for sin. ANNOTATIONS ON GENESIS 3:19.[48]

THIS IS A GENERAL SENTENCE. ANDREW WILLET: Only the serpent is pronounced accursed, because his state is remediless and desperate, but neither the man nor the woman is accursed, for whom there is hope. The earth is accursed not in itself but with respect to humanity's use of it: Saint Paul says, "the creatures do yet groan with us together." Some Hebrews note that some men are exempted from the punishment of eating their bread in the sweat of their brows, as kings and princes, but no women are exempted from their punishment because the woman not only sinned herself but also enticed the man, which Adam did not do. But this is a general sentence against all men, so that although only one particular is expressed—labor and toil in tilling the ground—yet therein are contained all the other cares and troubles of this life, from which none are free. COMMENTARY ON GENESIS 3:17.[49]

GOD IS PASSING JUDGMENT, NOT LEGISLATION. JOHN CALVIN: Certain writers who lack discernment mistakenly wish to consign everyone to manual labor, using this passage as a pretext. However, God is not giving orders here as a commander or legislator, but imposing a penalty, just as a judge would do. And if a rule had been prescribed here, of course, it would be necessary for all to become farmers! There would be no place given to the mechanical arts, so that clothing and other necessities of life would have to be sought outside this world. What, then, does the passage mean? Truly, God declares as from the judge's bench that from now on human life shall be miserable, because Adam proved himself unworthy of that tranquil, happy, and joyful state for which he had been created. If someone should object that many people are inactive and indolent, that doesn't mean that this curse has not spread itself over the whole human race. COMMENTARY ON GENESIS 3:19.[50]

GREATER TOIL IN LEADING CHURCH OR STATE THAN IN FARMING. MARTIN LUTHER: The sweat of the face is of many kinds: the first is that of the farmers or householders; the second is that of the officers of the state; and the third is that of the teachers in the church. Among these classes the best-situated are the farmers. . . . Although they are plagued with hard labor, that labor is seasoned with matchless pleasure, as daily the new and wonderful sight of the creatures impresses itself upon their eyes. In both state and church, on the other hand, there are daily dangers and countless burdens, if you desire to perform your duty faithfully. LECTURES ON GENESIS 3:19.[51]

EVEN THE RICH CANNOT ESCAPE THE CURSE. JOHANNES BRENZ: "By the sweat of

---

[47]*In Primum Librum Mosis* (1569), 17v. [48]ZSW 13:30; cf. 2 Thess 3:10. [49]*Hexapla* (1608), 53, crediting Mercerus. [50]CTS 1:175-76* (CO 23:74). [51]LW 1:212 (WA 42:158).

your brow you will eat your bread" should not be understood as if God ordains everyone to be farmers or that they are not following God's calling unless they practice agriculture. There are various kinds of divine calling. One is called to administer the magistracy; another, to be an artisan; another, to be a merchant; another, to lead the church. Each of these is divinely ordained and attested by the Holy Spirit. So when it says, "By the sweat of your brow," you should understand it not only of agriculture but of every station in this bodily life. Indeed, whatever your station or class in this earthly life, you necessarily have to obtain and consume food with much sweat and labor. Even if fortune has blessed you so that you possess many riches and leisure, your wealth still has its annoyances and your leisure has its troubles and misfortunes. Indeed, wherever there is flesh and blood in us, there is also sin; and where there is sin, there is also the curse, unhappiness and troubles. So wherever you take your flesh and blood, there you will always find, even at the height of leisure and tranquility, that which tortures and afflicts you with evil. Just as someone who walks around with a thorn in the foot is unable to step anywhere without being pricked, even if walking on silk, because they bear and carry with them a spine that punctures them, so too whoever bears sin-infected flesh and blood finds, wherever one may go, the curse and its troubles. So, if we want to obtain a soft pathway, we must pull the thorn from our foot. And if we want to obtain the blessing, we must be healed from sin. COMMENTARY ON GENESIS 3:17-19.[52]

SOME AVOID SWEATING BY PURSUING FAR WORSE THINGS. WOLFGANG MUSCULUS: *In the sweat of your face you shall eat your bread.* There are two kinds of people who subvert this clause. One of these consists of those who sweat not by working but by devouring and gorging, which the lazy and idle are accus-tomed to do. They work like this to be ready when winter draws near, stuffing themselves like this so that they can barely wipe the sweat off their faces. Where something needs to be done, they loiter and are last in line; where there is food to be eaten, they arrive first and panting. These people are fit for nothing useful but were born only to swallow up the harvest. The other kind is those who are worse than the first, who do indeed eat from the sweat of the face—but the sweat of others, not their own, and they eat not their own bread but that of others. This class of people is twofold. Some by their cunning cleverly embezzle the sweat of others either by stealing it through fraud or treachery, or through lying or usury, or by negotiating with insincere language under a contrived pretense of law and legal process. . . . The dregs of these people have filled and oppressed the church of Christ at the highest levels. Others are robbers and thieves, despots and their henchmen, who live through coercion and violence and are lured by the sweat of others. But the seriousness of this sin, by which the sweat of the poor is embez-zled by fraud or force, is seen in Ecclesiasticus 34, where the Latin version reads, "Whoever steals hard-earned bread is as one who kills his neighbor." COMMENTARY ON GENESIS 3:19.[53]

GOD'S ANGER AGAINST SIN IS EVERY-WHERE, BUT SO ARE TOKENS OF HIS GOODNESS. JOHN CALVIN: The Lord deter-mined that his anger would overflow all parts of the earth like a flood, that wherever human beings might look, the atrocity of sin should meet their eyes. Before the fall, the world's condition was a beautiful and especially delightful mirror of God's favor and fatherly indulgence towards humankind. Now, in all the elements of the earth, we perceive that we are cursed. And though the earth is still "full

---

[52]*Opera* 1:58-59. [53]*In Mosis Genesim* (1554), 112, citing Sir 34:26; the passage also quotes 2 Pet 2:3.

of God's mercy" (as David says in Ps 33:5), at the same time, clear signs of his dreadful alienation from us still appear, and we betray our blindness and insensibility if we are unmoved by them. And so, lest sadness and horror should overwhelm us, the Lord everywhere sprinkles tokens of his goodness. COMMENTARY ON GENESIS 3:17.[54]

3:19 "To Dust You Shall Return"

WASN'T THE PENALTY TOO HARSH? JOHANNES BRENZ: Isn't the eating of an apple a childish crime? Indeed, if opportunity arises, boys are quite likely to snitch apples and eat them. So how is it fitting that for such a childish sin, as it seems, such a horrible punishment is inflicted? How would this agree with divine justice? Doesn't the Law, which is the norm of justice, say that "the number of lashes will be proportionate to the crime"? And how is it appropriate that an eternal penalty be levied on a transitory sin that was done sporadically and only for a moment? I would answer that it does seem like a light and childish sin to eat a forbidden apple. Yet if we consider not only who it was who prohibited it and was offended by this prevarication, but also with what intention the sin was committed, then it is neither unjust nor unfair that a light, transitory and momentary deed be punished with a weighty and everlasting penalty. In the first place, even if the deed seems light and childish, it remains that he who prohibited it is not childish but the eternal God. So when a sin is committed against the eternal God and his eternal word, it is fitting to punish the crime with an eternal penalty. Then, those who sin against God turn themselves by that sin away from an eternal good, which is God himself. But what should those who have turned from eternal good suppose is owed them, except eternal evil? Finally, those who sin and remain unrepentant, even if they don't constantly perpetuate

the external act of sinning, nonetheless, because they don't repent, their will to sin endures. So they rightly deserve an enduring penalty, and God remains just when he delivers up unjust people by afflicting them with eternal torments. COMMENTARY ON GENESIS 2:16-17.[55]

DEATH IS UNNATURAL AND DREADFUL. JOHN CALVIN: Now, after he had been stripped of his divine and heavenly excellence, what remains in the face of his life's exit but that he should realize that he himself is earth? This is why we dread death: because the dissolution [of body and soul] is contrary to nature, it cannot naturally be desired. Truly, the first man would have passed over to a better life if had he remained upright, but in that case the soul would not have departed from the body, and there would have been no corruption, no form of destruction—in short, no violent change. COMMENTARY ON GENESIS 3:19.[56]

ALL DECAY FORESHADOWS OUR DEATHS. ANNA MARIA VAN SCHURMAN.
But before God is willing
　　His love to espouse,
He shows them the fearful
　　wrath their fall has aroused.
A death sentence is pronounced,
　　indeed, already it begins
the very moment the first
　　covenant is broken by sin.
God adds a punishment
　　for the woman to sustain,
a curse to follow marriage:
　　misfortune and pain.
Adam is deprived of a
　　blessing sweet, rich and grand
that God had intended
　　for him in tilling the land.

---

[54]CTS 1:173* (CO 23:73).　[55]Opera 1:36, citing Deut 25:2.
[56]CTS 1:180* (CO 23:77).

In all that he sees,
    a silent curse sleeps:
he sows with sweat
    and with sorrow he reaps.
A hidden decay is
    revealed through his toil;
his death is foreshadowed
    when things rot and spoil.
All is in vain,
    heaven has been provoked:
he plows the fields but
    with thorns they are choked.
Yet these curses the foolish
    man tries to blunt,
to seek in his offspring
    what he lacks but wants.
He looks to the mother
    whom he names *Eve*,
because through her,
    his seed its life receives.
God was pleased still more
    to check their prideful sin,
to cover their shame
    with dead animals' skin
as a sign that those who
    do not fear their God's name
are more filthy than beasts
    and persist in their shame.
PARAPHRASE OF GENESIS 1–3.[57]

ADAM'S LONG LAST BREATH. JOHANNES BRENZ: "In the day that you eat of it . . ." should not be interpreted according to external appearances, as if Adam were destined to be buried by a sudden death right away (though he did deserve such a death), but rather that he became liable to death in the very moment of his disobedience and thereafter began to die and, as they say, to breathe his last. Indeed, even though Adam lived 930 years after committing this sin, he always remained exposed during those years to a temporal death, and his bodily existence was nothing more than a continual exhaling of his last breath. So too is our life in this world no more than a meditation on death or a training exercise for death, to which we hasten with as many steps as the days, hours and minutes of the life we lead. All the things that now follow in Adam's life are nothing but preludes, overtures and steps toward death. COMMENTARY ON GENESIS 3:7.[58]

WHY ONLY ADAM SEEMS SENTENCED TO DIE. WOLFGANG MUSCULUS: The corruption that accompanies death is predicated of Adam even though not only Adam but also Eve became liable to it. We are reminded that Adam's transgression unleashed this sin, so that if he had not eaten of the forbidden apple, there would have been no place for death or corruption—neither in him nor in the woman. Then, because he was the head of the human race and through his sin death would pass to all his posterity, the sentence is rightly imposed that condemns him to death, even though it was going to overtake not him alone but also Eve. COMMENTARY ON GENESIS 3:19.[59]

HOW DEATH COMES TO THE CHILDREN OF ADAM AND EVE. BALTHASAR HUBMAIER: After our first father Adam transgressed the commandment of God by his disobedience, he lost this freedom for himself and all his descendants. Likewise, if a nobleman receives a fief from a king and if he acts against the king, the king will take this fief from the nobleman and all his heirs, for they must all carry the guilt of their forefather. Thus the flesh has irretrievably lost its goodness and freedom through the Fall of Adam and has become entirely and wholly worthless and hopeless unto death. It is not able or capable of anything other than sin, striving against God and being the enemy of his commandments. . . . When Eve, who is a figure of our flesh, desired

---

[57]*Uitbreiding*, 17.9–18.4. [58]*Opera* 1:47. [59]*In Mosis Genesim* (1554), 112.

to eat and did eat of the forbidden fruit, she thereby lost the knowledge of good and evil, indeed of wanting and doing the good, and had to pay for this loss with death, so that as soon as a person is conceived and born, he is conceived and born in sin. From the first moment already he is up to his ears in sin and from that moment on when he receives life he begins to die and become earth again. FREEDOM OF THE WILL, Book 1.[60]

WHY THE PUNISHMENTS ENDURE. JOHANNES BRENZ:

If Adam and his wife are now justified by faith from hearing the gospel and absolved of their sins, why are they still punished? Why doesn't God suspend the punishment he imposed on Adam as much as on the woman? There is no doubt but that if Adam and his wife had died immediately after having believed the gospel about the virgin's son, they would have reached the heavenly kingdom. Why therefore are they afflicted?

There are the weightiest of reasons for this. It should not be thought that the punishments that follow and are divinely imposed on them are inflicted so that by them their sins would find atonement before God. In God's sight, there is no other expiation of sin than the passion and death of the son of the virgin: an expiation that Adam had already accepted by faith. But there are other reasons. First, after they received the remission of sin, God imposed on them a cross or affliction, so that it would be a memorial of the sin committed in paradise, and of the sermon that he promptly spoke to Satan about how he was perpetually cursed and how his head would be crushed by the virgin's son. Indeed, even as we are ungrateful, so also are we forgetful, so that even if great blessings are bestowed on us, we do not easily remember. So it seemed good to God to afflict humans after they had been forgiven for their sin, so that in just that way they would be admonished and reminded of what happened in paradise, and they would naturally show their thanks to God that while they deserved to be perpetually damned, they were nonetheless freed by God's mercy through the virgin's son. Second, he imposes a corporal punishment, the eternal one having been remitted, so that it would be an example to posterity, lest they suppose that God is pleased by disobedience and sin, and so be warned against sinning. . . . In addition, also after the remission of sins had been received, God imposes adversities on them to bear in order to restrain the remnants of the flesh that still inhere in them. Just as by doing nothing, so also by suffering nothing do people learn to conduct themselves wickedly. Therefore a person bears the cross in order to remain dutiful amidst adversities, for in prosperity we are inclined to neglect our duty. Finally, the Lord imposes a cross on them in this world so that he might train them to desire the happiness of the world to come and the heavenly kingdom. COMMENTARY ON GENESIS 3:16.[61]

---

[60]CRR 5:433-34. [61]Opera 1:55.

3:20-24 EXPULSION FROM THE GARDEN

²⁰The man called his wife's name Eve, because she was the mother of all living.ᵃ ²¹And the LORD God made for Adam and for his wife garments of skins and clothed them.

²²Then the LORD God said, "Behold, the man has become like one of us in knowing good and evil. Now, lest he reach out his hand and take also of the tree of life and eat, and live forever—" ²³therefore the LORD God sent him out from the garden of Eden to work the ground from which he was taken. ²⁴He drove out the man, and at the east of the garden of Eden he placed the cherubim and a flaming sword that turned every way to guard the way to the tree of life.

a *Eve sounds like the Hebrew for* life-giver *and resembles the word for* living

OVERVIEW: Genesis 3 ends with a quick movement from consolation, to irony, to loss. Reformation commentators routinely found hope and consolation, even on the threshold of our first parents' eviction, based on the guardedly optimistic name that Adam gave his wife: Eve, "mother of all living." That the Lord God made garments of skins for Adam and Eve also provided these commentators with grounds to speak of God's compassion—as well as grounds for revisiting more than resisting some traditional allegorical readings of the animal skins God used.

Yet the chapter ends not only with the definitive banishment of the first man and woman, but also with God's puzzling dialogue with himself (it would seem), in which the specter of an insurrection on the part of Adam and Eve is raised and then summarily dismissed. Reformation exegetes mostly revived old questions and answers in these verses, finding God's speech to be largely ironic but deriving other lessons, too, such as the benefits of losing paradise and the implicit promises of grace to come.

3:20 Eve, the Mother of All Living

"EVE" IS A SIGN OF ADAM'S HOPE. MARTIN LUTHER: If Adam had not been aware of the future life, he would not have been able to cheer his heart; nor would he have assigned so pleasing a name to his wife. But by assigning this name to his wife he gives clear indication that the Holy Spirit had cheered his heart through his trust in the forgiveness of sins by the Seed of Eve. He calls her Eve to remind himself of the promise through which he himself also received new life, and to pass on the hope of eternal life to his descendants. This hope and faith he writes on his wife's forehead by means of this name as with colors, just as those who are freed from their enemies set up trophies and other marks of their joy. LECTURES ON GENESIS 3:20.[1]

"MOTHER OF ALL LIVING" IS A SIGN OF ADAM'S CONSOLATION. JOHN CALVIN: I have no doubt but that he would have taken a breath and recovered his courage when he heard God saying that their lives would be prolonged, and that then, as one revived, he gave his wife a name derived from "life." But it does not follow that he triumphed over death as he

[1]LW 1:220 (WA 42:164).

should have, by a faith that accorded with God's word. Hence, I interpret it like this: upon escaping the immediate threat of death, he was heartened by this bit of consolation and, in the name he gave his wife, he celebrated that God had been kind to him beyond all hoping. Commentary on Genesis 3:20.[2]

The Name Eve Was Adam's Sermon.
Johannes Brenz: That the imposition of the name Eve is described in this place signifies that Adam said something like this to his wife: "Come, my dearest wife! Even if you were first to begin to pluck the fruit forbidden to us and to extend it to me to eat, still, I do not put the blame on you for the misery into which we two have been thrown, but most of all upon myself, who did not stand firm with a mind set more steadfastly on the words of our Lord God. So let us not argue about this matter nor reproach one another in anything, but let us obediently bear the cross that God has placed on us and comfort each other with the promise about your seed, of which it was said, 'The seed of the woman will crush the head of the serpent.' Let us take comfort in all our calamity from this most encouraging gospel, and let us find peace of mind so that we may know that, whatever adversity befalls us, our God favors us and will save us in our death unto eternal life, by the seed that will be born of your sex. As a reminder of this, I impose on you the name Eve, . . . that is, 'life' or 'life-bearing,' so that whether I call you this name or you hear it, we'll be reminded not only that you will be the mother of the human race, but also that there will be a woman born from our offspring who while still a virgin will be the mother of all life, that is, of Christ the Son of God, and he is the only son who is our life and salvation. By this son we will be consoled. Of this son we will be reminded every day when the name Eve sounds in our ears, so that not only may we endure the calamities that befall us with a steady mind, but also diligently follow God's

calling from then on, and eventually also conquer even death itself." This was more or less the oration of Adam to his wife when he imposed the name Eve on her. Commentary on Genesis 3:20.[3]

"Eve" Looks to Mercy, Not Woe. Peter Martyr Vermigli: Some Christian commentators trifle when they say that Eve (Eva) was named from the woe (Vaeh) that she brought into the world— whence, on the other hand, "Hail" (Ave) was said to Mary, because she took away the woe (Vaeh). The Septuagint has the name Zōē, that is, "life," which doesn't fit here. . . . Yet Mother Church truly is said to be the mother of the living. After learning that her seed was going to crush the devil and death, Adam rightly and deservedly wished her to be called by that name, so that this salutary promise of God would always come to his mind. . . . Adam had already conceived the hope of life through Christ, and once he knew that his wife would be the mother of all of those (including himself) who were to be made alive through Christ, he called her Eve, because she was the mother of the living. Now, you may say that even the impious are descended from her according to the flesh, and we indeed confess as much, but in his naming of her, Adam was looking to the mercy that God had bestowed on him. If he had looked only at her condition, he would have seen her as both dead herself and the mother of the dead: truly, those who have sinned, even if they still seem to be alive, . . . are given over to death. Commentary on Genesis 3:20.[4]

"Eve" May Have Been a Backhanded Compliment. Huldrych Zwingli: "Eve" signifies life or living. "Of all living things" is figurative, for she was not the mother of wolves but of the living, namely, human beings. Some

---

[2]CTS 1:181* (CO 23:77). [3]*Opera* 1:63. [4]*In Primum Librum Mosis* (1569), 17v.

say calling Eve *life* carries a deeper meaning, because just as life consists of nothing but affliction and change, so woman is full of afflictions and fickle, liable to change with every breeze, just like life and the moon. ANNOTATIONS ON GENESIS 3:20.[5]

EVE AND THE RESURRECTION. DAVID CHYTRAEUS: To this discourse about the death of the body, one should append the whole doctrine of the resurrection and eternal life, of which Adam had conceived for himself a certain hope, as the very name *Eve* shows. Indeed, this is why he named her *life-giver*: he was declaring his conviction that he would conquer by faith in the promised seed, by whom death would be abolished. And there is another pious explanation for her name, too, in that Adam hoped Eve herself would become the mother of this promised seed. COMMENTARY ON GENESIS 3:19-20.[6]

3:21 Garments of Skins

SKINS TOLD OF GOD'S CARE AND HUMAN MORTALITY. KONRAD PELLIKAN: God's mercy did not desist from doing kindness, even clothing the sinners with garments of skins, which I think is to be understood simply, as a kindness not unworthy of the Creator, no more than his production of other things. It is as if he were to say, "You provided imprudently for yourselves. I will show you a more suitable means of clothing from the hides of certain animals, whence you may be reminded of your own mortality. These are prepared without much trouble, unlike linen, wool or silk." COMMENTARY ON GENESIS 3:21.[7]

GARMENTS OF SKIN REMINDED ADAM AND EVE OF THEIR SIN. JOHN CALVIN: It seems to me that the Lord clothed them with garments of skin ... because garments made from this material have more of a beastly quality about them than those made of linen or wool.

Therefore, just as God previously wished the first human beings to be naked, he now wanted them dressed like this, so that they might behold their own vileness and thus be reminded of their sin. COMMENTARY ON GENESIS 3:21.[8]

SKINS AS REMINDERS OF THE FALL. MARTIN LUTHER: Whenever they looked at their garments, these were to serve as a reminder to them to give thought to their wretched fall from supreme happiness into the utmost misfortune and trouble. Thus they were to be constantly afraid of sinning, to repent continually, and to sigh for the forgiveness of sins through the promised Seed. This is also why He clothed them, not in foliage or in cotton but in the skins of slain animals, for a sign that they are mortal and that they are living in certain death. Therefore just as the name Eve is a joyous omen of life, so these skins are a reminder not only of past and future sin, but also of their present misfortunes, which their sins deserve. LECTURES ON GENESIS 3:21.[9]

SKINS WERE GOD'S SACRAMENTAL GIFT TO HIS CHILDREN. JOHANNES BRENZ: God does not leave them without a sign of his favor. Indeed, after he sees that Adam and Eve had listened with all diligence to the proclamation of the gospel about the seed of the woman, and that faith had been begotten from it along with peace of conscience, he added something like a sacrament—garments made from animal skins. . . . God clothed them so that by this sign or sacrament he might attest that he had received them in grace and would care for their salvation, guarding and preserving them. It's just like when parents declare their favor toward their children by promising and procuring new and different garments to clothe them. How

---

[5]ZSW 13:30. [6]*In Genesin* (1576), 148. [7]*Commentaria Bibliorum* (1532) 1:7r. [8]CTS 1:181-82* (CO 23:78). [9]LW 1:221 (WA 42:165).

wonderfully the children jump about, how they wave their hands and clap for their parents, even if the garments be made from common cloth! Likewise, when Adam and Eve were clothed by God with new garments, they too would have shown remarkable delight, for by this sign they would have realized the immense charity of God the Father toward them and would have strengthened their faith against every misfortune that might happen to them. Our sacraments are established for this same purpose, so that by them we too might strengthen our faith. COMMENTARY ON GENESIS 3:21.[10]

CLOTHING SIGNALS GOD'S COMPASSION FOR SINNERS. PETER MARTYR VERMIGLI:

Clothes are a symbol of our sin and God's mercy. If God bestows clothing on those whom he condemns and keeps them warm, it behooves judges to encourage those whom they condemn by showing some human kindness, by which they may endure their punishment more easily. God lavishes upon us not only his goods but also their use—and so he does not merely provide the clothing but he actually clothes them. From this you ought to deduce, allegorically, that the clothing given to us by God can cover our nakedness, that is, strengthen our conscience so it does not shrink from the sight of God. Even though this clothing calls to mind a dead animal, bear in mind that Christ, having suffered on our behalf, truly covers our sins. This clothing is given by God, because by faith we obtain that which is God's gift and not from ourselves. But our works, like fig leaves, strengthen us not the least bit in order to withstand the sight of God. Someday, this clothing given to us by God will be changed, because at present, as long as we live under the cross and share in the death of Christ, it has a vile appearance. But when we come to be sharers in Christ's resurrection in reality and no longer merely in hope, the clothing which now seems filthy will be made so glorious as to be called a wedding garment. COMMENTARY ON GENESIS 3:21.[11]

COATS OF SKINS PROMISED A FUTURE COVERING WITH CHRIST'S RIGHTEOUS-

NESS. DIRK PHILIPS: Humanity has become wretched, poor, and naked through Adam and is thus born out of him. Over against this Christ Jesus is the garment of righteousness, yes, the innocent and unblemished Lamb of God with which every believing and baptized Christian is clothed. But how this comes to pass is portrayed for us in Adam and Eve. That is, that Adam and Eve before the fall in Paradise were innocent, upright, and naked, and needed no garment, for they were of a good nature, without falsehood, and knew no evil. Yes, they were made after the image and likeness of God and were created for eternal life. The pious nature which was imaged in them by God was the garment with which they were gloriously clothed. But as soon as they had eaten of the tree of the knowledge of good and evil, against the command of God, they recognized their nakedness, felt shame, and made a cover of fig leaves. However, they could not find cover nor hide from God but had to stand red with shame before the Lord on account of their transgression, and therefore suffer and bear his punishment. Nevertheless, he did not leave them comfortless but comforted them overall with his boundless mercy, inwardly with the promise of Christ, outwardly with bodily attire. For God had promised Christ Jesus to them as a Redeemer and conqueror of the serpent. As a true sign of this, he gave them coats of skin with which to clothe themselves as a witness that Christ Jesus, the Lamb of God, would cover and take away the sin of Adam and of the whole world, and that all believers should be clothed with him. ENCHIRIDION.[12]

---

[10]*Opera* 1:63. [11]*In Primum Librum Mosis* (1569), 18r. [12]CRR 6:76.

The Skins Have a Moral, but They Don't Harbor Fantasies. Andrew Willet:

These coats of skins were not their *bodies*, as Origen and some of the other fathers seem to think, for God had already made man of the dust of the earth. Neither were these coats made of *the bark of trees*, as Barcephas and Gregory of Nazianzus, for the Hebrew word *gnorh* is nowhere found in that sense. Neither is Theodoret's argument sound, that they could not be the skins of beasts because they were created but two and two, and so if any of them had been slain, the generation of that kind would have been hindered; for that there were created no more than two of each sort is not to be found in Scripture. Neither need we imagine with Hugh that these skins might be made of *the elements*, or some other matter: we are not to run to miracles where an ordinary course is offered. Some would have these skins made of *sheep's wool*, but that is not skins. [Targum] Jonathan suggests *the serpent's skin*, but this is too curious. Neither did the Lord merely teach them how to make garments for their necessary use afterward, for the text says that he clothed them, that is, actually, presently. So there is nothing unfitting in saying that God caused skins—whether of slain beasts or otherwise, by the ministry of his angels or however else it pleased him—to be brought to Adam, from which he made them coats.

It pleased God to clothe them, then, not for any typological signification, as either to betoken the incarnation of Christ that was clothed with our flesh, or the clothing of the nakedness of the soul by repentance. Rather, [he did so] for these reasons: to show them how their mortal bodies might be defended from cold and other injuries, for this use of skin or leather clothing was the first used in the world; to cover their nakedness for the sake of modesty (and therefore the Chaldee paraphrast calls them "garments of honor"); to teach them that it was lawful to use the beasts as much for meat as for clothing; to give them the rule that modest and decent, not costly or sumptuous, apparel should be used; so that they might know the difference between God's works and man's invention, between coats of leather and fig leaves; and to put them in mind of mortality by their clothing of dead beasts' skins, as Origen well notes. Commentary on Genesis 3:21.[13]

3:22 The Man Has Become Like One of Us

God Derides Their Folly. Andrew Willet:

By transgressing God's commandment and eating the forbidden fruit, they [now] had an experiential knowledge (previously they had a speculative knowledge of good and evil, as the rich have of poverty) of what good they had lost and what evil they were fallen into: and this is the opinion of most of the Fathers. Nor is this interpretation contradicted by Genesis 3:22, where the Lord says "the man has become like one of us, knowing good and evil," [as if] man in knowledge had now become like unto God (and this experiential knowledge is not in God). . . . But here the Lord speaks ironically: not that they had now become truly like God in knowledge—for it is not to be thought that their knowledge was increased by their sin, and if it were so, Satan would not have lied in promising them to be like unto God—but the Lord derides their folly, which led them to such a foolish notion that they would be made like God by breaking his commandment. Commentary on Genesis 2:9.[14]

The Irony of This New Likeness to God. Peter Martyr Vermigli:

"Like one of *us*" is spoken in the plural either on account of

---

[13]*Hexapla* (1608), 54-55, citing Theodoret, *Question 35 on Genesis*, and Origen, *Homilies on Leviticus*. [14]*Hexapla* (1608), 28-29.

the mystery of the Trinity or from the dignity of the divine nature. But I like the simple and common explanation, that "the man has now become *like one of us*" is ironic—because, superficially, Adam does understand sin better. In this irony, God also expresses compassion and grief at our misfortune. But God especially targets his knowledge of sin, as if to say, "Already the fruit of sin now shows the man how much he has sinned. This is that likeness of God that the devil promised him! This is that splendid knowledge of good and evil that he sought by sinning! By sinning, he first of all discovered embarrassment: he realized that he needs to clothe himself. Later on, when he is laden with all the curses that have been uttered, he will recognize good and evil in abundance." COMMENTARY ON GENESIS 3:22.[15]

ADAM'S DOUBLY IRONIC NEW LIKENESS.

PHILIPP MELANCHTHON: Some wish to take [God's words] as a manifestation of irony, that Adam should have believed the *serpent*, who promised that he would become like God, as if God were saying here, "Watch whose word you believe, Adam! I ordered you not to eat from the tree of the knowledge of good and evil; the serpent, on the other hand, promised that by eating you become like God. You have not believed my word, which is truth and life, therefore it is fitting that, having believed a lie, you should die. See how you *haven't* been made like us—you've become liable to death and sin! So where are those attributes of God—wisdom, righteousness, life—that the serpent promised?" But besides these things, I think [irony] is also manifested in that Adam was promised that he would be *like God*, as if God were saying, "Look what you're like now! Obviously, your flesh is guilty and impure, and it won't be saved—and yet it will, when you become just like one of us: not by the way the serpent wanted but by this way, which I now set before you, truly, the way of the cross and of death: you will indeed be like God in

Christ, clothed with the glory of God," [as in] 1 John 3:2, "When he appears we will be like him." COMMENTARY ON GENESIS 3:22-23.[16]

GOD'S IRONY MASKS COMPASSION.

KONRAD PELLIKAN: This seems ironic: he upbraids him for his folly and rashness, as if to say, "See how much Adam has accomplished, for he already sees evil and good. Now, then, so he will at least not live in that misery forever, let us prohibit access to the tree of life, lest he presume to take from it as well and live always in everlasting torment." COMMENTARY ON GENESIS 3:22.[17]

GOD'S REPROACH WAS NOT ENVIOUS OR BITTER BUT STRATEGIC AND COMPASSIONATE.

DAVID CHYTRAEUS: The reproach is indirect but nonetheless sorrowful and emphatic. Accordingly, it was uttered by God not only for that time, when he was about to expel them from paradise, so that it would be a penitential sermon about admitting that enormous ingratitude by which they had desired to be equal to God; but mainly so that it would be an admonition to later generations about avoiding the devil's snares and lies. Indeed, it was God's strategy to repeat the very words of that liar and murderer in this reproach, so that the cause and occasion for Adam's incurring so many and such great calamities would remain fixed in his mind—namely, that they allowed themselves to be led away from God's word, yielded to the devil's lies and sought equality with God. Therefore, not only from this rebuke but also from the mass of punishments that followed, Adam and all his offspring ought to learn that this is the height of wisdom: to adhere and rely constantly on God's word.

Nor are God's words born of envy or cruelly meant to insult Adam in his wretchedness. Rather, they are the impassioned words of the

---

[15]*In Primum Librum Mosis* (1569), 18v. [16]MO 13:782. [17]*Commentaria Bibliorum* (1532) 1:7r.

Son of God, who shows that he is moved with feeling and sympathy for Adam's immense distress, as if he were to say, "Oh, Adam, how miserably you have been deceived by the devil, who promised you equality with God and the highest degree of God's image and wisdom! Now you are cast out of paradise and have lost not only your previous gifts but also eternal life, which you could have retained by eating from the tree of life. And yet you *will* be like God, eventually, when your body, purged by the cross and by death, will be renewed, just as 1 John 3 says, "When he appears, we will be like him." COMMENTARY ON GENESIS 3:22.[18]

CREATURES CANNOT BECOME GODS. ANNA MARIA VAN SCHURMAN:

> Alas, our parents wanted God
>   to make them God too, whereby
> God would have fashioned a lie:
>   yet God could not himself deny.
> They wanted to be the highest good
>   (they who were all but naught)—
> a wicked desire not from God
>   but of hellish vermin wrought.
> God alone is so good that
>   goodness is his constant nature;
> one who unites with him
>   rises high enough for a creature.
> He who is the first cannot be
>   the second in a race,
> and only Satan's poison
>   drives us to our God displace.

PARAPHRASE OF GENESIS 1–3.[19]

THE TREE OF LIFE HAD NO INTRINSIC POWER. WOLFGANG MUSCULUS: If Adam had eaten of the tree of life, even after having sinned and having been sentenced to mortality by God, would he have lived forever on that account? At first glance, if the words are overanalyzed, it might seem possible to conclude from their appearance that if Adam had eaten from the tree of life after having sinned, he might have freed himself from the condemnation of death, and that by devouring what he had snatched away, he might have recovered the immortality that he lost by sinning. But this view cannot be approved by those who understand that God's unshakeable oracles can in no way be flouted by his creatures: for they know that no fruit of any tree whatsoever, even one designed to be beneficial for life, can, against God's will, produce an effect that for which it was not ordained by God. The tree of life was not made for this, that—contrary to God's will and decree—it should confer eternal life on those who deal falsely. So even if Adam had eaten of it after his innocence had been lost and the sentence of his condemnation had been levied against him, clearly, it would have had no effect. COMMENTARY ON GENESIS 3:22.[20]

GOD CANNOT ENVY CREATURES. ANNA MARIA VAN SCHURMAN:

> The Greatest Good envies naught
>   nor covets for renown,
> but shares with all his creatures
>   his riches so profound.
> Had it not been for God's goodness,
>   dust we would remain,
> and neither being nor reason
>   would we have attained;
> and had God's gracious will not brought
>   us forth to see the light of day,
> his glorious image would not be
>   stamped upon our worthless clay.
> But once humankind chose
>   to desert God so willingly,
> cannot the great God justly judge
>   and render this decree—
> "Be your own god now,
>   your greatest good and all!"—
> and, speaking thus, justly
>   leave them in their fall?

PARAPHRASE OF GENESIS 1–3.[21]

---

[18]*In Genesin* (1576), 151-52. [19]*Uitbreiding*, 13.6-13. [20]*In Mosis Genesim* (1554), 116. [21]*Uitbreiding*, 13.16-25.

The third chapter contains sin's origin, manifestation, punishment, and remedy. We will therefore see these four [theological] topics:

I. On the fall of humankind and the origin of sin:

1. With crafty speech, the serpent said to the woman: "Did God really say 'You shouldn't eat from any tree in the garden?'"

2. The woman responded: "We eat every fruit, etc. But of the fruit of the tree in the middle of the garden, etc."

3. And the serpent, again: "By no means will you die. But God knows, etc."

4. The woman
   - saw that the tree was good,
   - desired it,
   - took from it,
   - ate,
   - gave it to her husband.

5. Their eyes were opened. They saw that they were naked.

6. They stitched together loincoverings for themselves from fig leaves.

Whereby we are taught that

Satan uses amazing ploys and tangled questions so as to make God's Word seem doubtful.

disputations with Satan are dangerous, and for that reason his suggestions are best rejected altogether.

in leading human beings astray, the devil's lie is both bald-faced and subtle.

looking at something is often an opportunity for sin.

a desire that goes against God's restraints is vicious.

agreement leads to action.

we are often led astray by our neighbors.

Therefore let us be on guard

for ourselves against Satan. Indeed, just as the weaker part of the human race is attacked here, so also today: wherever he finds us weaker, there he stretches forth his powers, taking full account of those vices to which we might be most inclined by our corrupted nature.

lest our teachings be rendered doubtful in our own minds, and lest we allow darkness to spread over God's word.

Let us learn what original sin is: truly, the absence of original righteousness that followed Adam's fall. In particular, among the things that arise from its mature seed are the loss of light, an avoidance of God's will, [and] hardness of heart (lest they be able to obey God's law properly), etc.

See Philipp [Melanchthon] in his Loci.

the perception of one's transgression immediately follows sin, and Satan spurs this on in order to inflict hopelessness.

our first parents were stripped of all their original righteousness.

human nature tries to cover up its errors.

they had not sufficiently relied on God alone.

[II.] On the manifestation of sin,

Doctrine:

1. They heard the voice of God.

   The preaching of the Law terrifies sinners.

   preaching the Law ought to be moderated in such a way that you can hear it, but not endure it.

2. They fled.

   The perversity of human beings.

   it is the nature of sin that the further from God [sinners] are, the further still do they desire to be far from God. These are the futile efforts of those who are aware of their own disgrace.

3. God called Adam.

   A good shepherd (pastor) seeks the lost sheep.

   he does not interrogate Adam in order to learn, but to lead him to the shame of his crime and to repentance.

4. Adam excuses his flight.

   The foolishness of human beings.

Whence we may observe that

   Adam betrays himself, and yet he transfers blame to the voice of God. Thus do transgressors slip from one sin into another: from security into doubt, unbelief, defiance, etc.

5. Adam is reprimanded.

   The Law's terrifying sermon.

   God knows all things.

6. Another excuse from Adam.

   The custom of transferring blame to others.

   Adam provokes God with an enormous blasphemy, as if to say, "If you hadn't given me a wife, I would not have been led astray."

7. Eve is reprimanded.

   The Law pricks the conscience.

   the woman is accused of a twofold crime: that she ate, and that she gave to the man.

8. Eve's excuse.

   We who are unrighteous wish to seem righteous.

   Eve maliciously transfers blame for her sin onto God, because he created the serpent.

See following page. †

Sin and the Fall of the Human Race. Cyriacus Spangenberg,
Table 3a on Genesis 3 (*In Pentateuchum*, sig. A3ʳ).

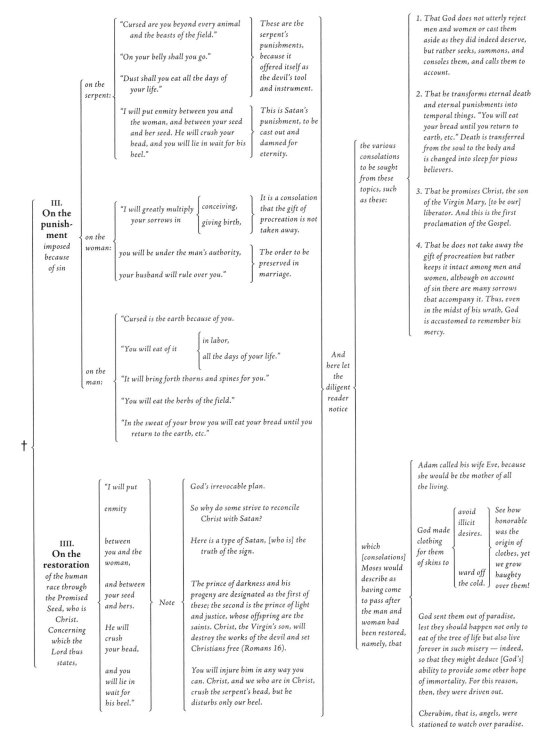

III.
On the punishment
imposed because of sin

on the serpent:

"Cursed are you beyond every animal and the beasts of the field."

"On your belly shall you go."

"Dust shall you eat all the days of your life."

These are the serpent's punishments, because it offered itself as the devil's tool and instrument.

"I will put enmity between you and the woman, and between your seed and her seed. He will crush your head, and you will lie in wait for his heel."

This is Satan's punishment, to be cast out and damned for eternity.

on the woman:

"I will greatly multiply your sorrows in" { conceiving, giving birth,

It is a consolation that the gift of procreation is not taken away.

you will be under the man's authority,

your husband will rule over you."

The order to be preserved in marriage.

on the man:

"Cursed is the earth because of you.

"You will eat of it" { in labor, all the days of your life."

"It will bring forth thorns and spines for you."

"You will eat the herbs of the field."

"In the sweat of your brow you will eat your bread until you return to the earth, etc."

the various consolations to be sought from these topics, such as these:

1. That God does not utterly reject men and women or cast them aside as they did indeed deserve, but rather seeks, summons, and consoles them, and calls them to account.

2. That he transforms eternal death and eternal punishments into temporal things. "You will eat your bread until you return to earth, etc." Death is transferred from the soul to the body and is changed into sleep for pious believers.

3. That he promises Christ, the son of the Virgin Mary, [to be our] liberator. And this is the first proclamation of the Gospel.

4. That he does not take away the gift of procreation but rather keeps it intact among men and women, although on account of sin there are many sorrows that accompany it. Thus, even in the midst of his wrath, God is accustomed to remember his mercy.

And here let the diligent reader notice

IIII.
On the restoration
of the human race through the Promised Seed, who is Christ. Concerning which the Lord thus states,

"I will put enmity between you and the woman, and between your seed and hers. He will crush your head, and you will lie in wait for his heel."

Note

God's irrevocable plan.

So why do some strive to reconcile Christ with Satan?

Here is a type of Satan, [who is] the truth of the sign.

The prince of darkness and his progeny are designated as the first of these; the second is the prince of light and justice, whose offspring are the saints. Christ, the Virgin's son, will destroy the works of the devil and set Christians free (Romans 16).

You will injure him in any way you can. Christ, and we who are in Christ, crush the serpent's head, but he disturbs only our heel.

which [consolations] Moses would describe as having come to pass after the man and woman had been restored, namely, that

Adam called his wife Eve, because she would be the mother of all the living.

God made clothing for them of skins to { avoid illicit desires. ward off the cold. }

See how honorable was the origin of clothes, yet we grow haughty over them!

God sent them out of paradise, lest they should happen not only to eat of the tree of life but also live forever in such misery — indeed, so that they might deduce [God's] ability to provide some other hope of immortality. For this reason, then, they were driven out.

Cherubim, that is, angels, were stationed to watch over paradise.

The Punishment of Transgression and the Remedy for Sin.
Cyriacus Spangenberg, Table 3b on Genesis 3 (*In Pentateuchum*, sig. A3ᵛ).

3:23-24 *The Lord God Sent Him Out*

God Knows, Humans Can Be Nervy!
Wolfgang Musculus: Human audacity was
not unknown to God, and that is why he was
not content with evicting Adam but also
blocked up the way to the tree of life. Commentary on Genesis 3:24.[22]

**Perpetual Life Now Would Be Perpet-
ual Sin.** Peter Martyr Vermigli: It was
equitable that one who had abandoned the true
life of the soul by sinning should be kept away
from even the symbol of life, that is, from the
tree of life. "He showed that he lacks self-control, so now if I command him not to eat from
the tree of life, he will not obey. But it would
be ruinous for him to live forever. Indeed,
because he subjected himself to sin, he will
continue in sin forever, always, and nothing
could happen to him that would be worse than
that. In addition, because I have already
inflicted many punishments on him for his evil
accomplishments, he will be subject to them in
perpetuity; yet it is preferable that they be
ended by death, once and for all. Moreover,
given that my verdict does need to be carried
out, it will be obstructed if he makes use of the
tree of life, because he won't die but live
forever. So, he needs to be driven out." See
here the special character of divine justice,
which may well have a good bit of mercy mixed
in with it. Commentary on Genesis 3:22.[23]

**The Pleasures of Paradise Must Be
Withdrawn.** Johannes Brenz: Adam and
Eve are not expelled from paradise without the
Father, Son and Holy Spirit having discussed
the plan among themselves. This signifies that
God's decree is precise, reliable and final, to
the effect that after having sinned, human
beings should no longer enjoy the pleasures of
paradise while they remain in this life, but
must instead cultivate the earth "by the sweat
of one's brow," that is, afflicted by various

calamities in this earth and bodily existence.
Truly, there are many people who push ahead
with zeal in this matter so that they might prepare for themselves in this world and in this
land a paradise, or a life free from all cares. For
this they labor, they endure cold and hunger,
all so that they might at last attain a life of
tranquility in this world, free from all hardships. But these people are refuted by the
present description of the ejection of Adam
from paradise. Indeed, God the Father, Son
and Holy Spirit have laid it down as a firm and
fixed rule that in this life we ought to be
evicted from paradise and afflicted with
hardships on earth until we return to the
earth. Commentary on Genesis 3:22-24.[24]

**Christ Is Now the Door and the Way
to Paradise.** Huldrych Zwingli: God
expels them as degenerates, just as an imposter
is thrust out of the nest, and he posts a sentry
at the entrance of paradise to block anyone
wishing to return. In this way he closed off life
and salvation, lest anyone ever be able to return
there except through him who became the way
and the door, through whose blood we are
heirs of freedom in holy living, namely, on the
"new and living way" he proclaimed in Hebrews 10. Annotations on Genesis 3:24.[25]

**Expulsion from the Garden Forced
Adam and Eve to Seek a New Life.** John
Calvin: By depriving them of the symbol,
God also takes away the thing signified. We
know how sacraments are meant to work, and
that (as stated earlier) the tree was given as a
pledge of life. Accordingly, a solemn excommunication is added, in order that they might
realize that their former life had been taken
away. Not that the Lord intended to cut off all
hope of salvation, but rather, by taking away

---

[22]*In Mosis Genesim* (1554), 115. [23]*In Primum Librum Mosis*
(1569), 18v. [24]*Opera* 1:64. [25]ZSW 13:31; cf. Jn 10:7; Heb
10:20.

merely what he had given, to cause them to seek new assistance elsewhere. Moreover, there yet remained expiation through sacrifices, which might restore them to the life they had lost. Previously, communion with God was life-giving for them, but once they became estranged from God, it was necessary to recover life through the death of Christ and to live by his life from then on. COMMENTARY ON GENESIS 3:22.[26]

APPROACHING THE GIVER OF LIFE RE-QUIRES REPENTANCE. PETER MARTYR VERMIGLI: Here you may say to me, "If you first assert that Christ signifies the tree of life, yet Christ is the cure for sin, how is it that Adam is forbidden to use that tree?" I would answer that those to whom Christ is proposed as a remedy are often rightly forbidden to feed on Christ, so that they first display the requisite signs of repentance. The lapsed are excluded and commanded to fast—and that, for their own salvation. The excommunicated are prohibited from the sacraments for their own benefit, so that they might take more responsibility for themselves, bewail their guilt and eventually come to desire to take more delight in those very things that they realize have been withheld from them. By so doing, they're rendered more fit for God's blessing. COMMENTARY ON GENESIS 3:22-24.[27]

EARTHLY PLEASURES DISTRACT US FROM THE TRUE PARADISE. JOHANNES BRENZ: It's not that God does not favor the church or that he would begrudge it the fruit of the tree of life. Rather, it's because he favors more (and thus cares more) that the pious *not* eat the fruit of the tree of life, that is, that they not give themselves to the delights and pleasures of this *bodily* life only to lose *eternal* life. Indeed, God does not expel Adam and Eve from paradise because he wouldn't want to return them to the true paradise, but rather so that they would be trained for some time by earth's

hardships and be led back to the heavenly paradise, which was opened later on by the Son of God on the cross, when he said to the thief, "Today you will be with me in paradise." COMMENTARY ON GENESIS 3:22-24.[28]

A "HISTORICAL" ALLEGORY OF THE FALL. MARTIN LUTHER: The historical account is like logic in that it teaches what is certainly true; the allegory, on the other hand, is like rhetoric in that it ought to illustrate the historical account but has no value at all for giving proof. . . . Let those who want to devise allegories follow this lead and look for their basis in the historical account itself. . . . Dealt with in this manner, what else can the closed Paradise and the cherubim with their swords, stationed to guard Paradise, signify than that without faith in Christ man can endure neither the Law nor the Gospel? Paul speaks this way when he says that the Jews were unable to look at Moses' shining face and that Moses was compelled to place a veil before his face (2 Cor 3:7). The tree of death is the Law, and the tree of life is the Gospel, or Christ. Those who do not believe in Christ cannot draw near to these trees. They are prevented by the sword of the angel, who cannot put up with hypocrisy and corrupt righteousness. But for him who acknowledges his sin and believes in Christ, Paradise remains open. He brings with him not his own righteousness but Christ's, which the Gospel announces to all so that we all may place our reliance on it and be saved. LECTURES ON GENESIS 3:23-24.[29]

THE EXPULSION FROM EDEN. ANNA MARIA VAN SCHURMAN:
> Now they know good and evil,
>   and now they can discern
> whether they compare with God,
>   for which they once had yearned.

---

[26]CTS 1:184* (CO 23:79). [27]*In Primum Librum Mosis* (1569), 18v. [28]*Opera* 1:65. [29]LW 1:233-34 (WA 42:173-74).

God drives them from the garden
  so they will understand
that they are unworthy
  before their Lord to stand.
No more to view its lovely streams,
  nor its noble fruit to taste,
nor in the tree of life itself
  to apprehend God's grace.
The hopes they set upon that tree
  now were gone and grim,
the way unto the tree of life
  now blocked by cherubim:
turning in every direction,
  a flaming sword stood there,
barring access to the garden
  by the unfaithful pair.
When God's vengeance drove them
  fully out, Eden was denied
and heaven itself seemed to close—
  leaving them shut outside.
 Behold, with the way closed off,
  they must either die forever,
or else obtain again God's favor
  by some new endeavor.
Sin thus leaves a gaping chasm,
  a detestable maw,
between God and everyone
  who dares to flout his law.
For God is a holy God,
  himself he cannot deny;
those who would draw near to God
  his justice must satisfy.
A holy, shining garment
  must adorn one's soul,
like that first radiance
  in which they pleased God whole.
But when they owe their Creditor
  for all they have each day,
how shall this unhappy pair
  ever that first debt repay?
And now that they have nothing
  (yet have everything to do),
heaping debt upon their debts,
  how can God receive his due?
Where now is the white garment

that was formerly their boast,
  a robe of pure virtue
to delight the heavenly host?
How shall they go to God,
  they who gaze only down
and place the world's honors
  before heaven's renown?
The human soul does, to be sure,
  retain some heavenly light:
it discovers them in guilt
  and disqualifies them from life.
Standing in as law and
  judge, it has this aim:
God's righteousness in
  humankind to maintain.
Alas, that light can only condemn;
  the law it does not fulfill,
yet it forces them to sing the praise
  of God's laws against their will.
For it is the highest justice
  that God should forsake
those who do not rest in him
  and view his laws with hate.
How could the wicked ever set
  their hearts more at odds
than by seeking to separate
  their welfare from God?
Creatures do become a hell
  and the devil's very own,
whenever they depart from God
  to try to stand alone.
And how could mortals ever
  chart a more foolish course
than 'twixt holiness and glory
  to make a divorce?
One who separates light
  from lamp, I say, errs less
than one who divides
  holiness from blessedness.
And how could God as the Judge
  of all the earth be revealed
if his perfect love for justice
  be forever concealed?
His justice and truth demand obedience,
  else punishment—as well

of the body as of the soul:
  a destiny of death, grave and hell.
Our bottomless misery
  exhausts its breath
crying for comfort
  from God's merciful depths.
Yet had there been no misdeed,
  we would never have known
the pity on misery
  that God's virtue has shown.
Now God's wisdom has
  found us such a Remedy
into whose depths mortals
  and angels long to see.
A Guarantor is given
  who pays the full debt,
one who passed through hell
  to restore our lives from death;
a Champion whose great power
  surpasses all in wonder,
who managed to steal back what
  that hellish dragon had plundered.
By his own flawless virtue,
  life eternal he gains
and to whomever he wishes
  he gives them the same.
This one is that long-promised Seed
  whose heels were pierced,
with one step he crushed the head
  of that serpent fierce.
Happy are those who choose
  this Lord—happy and blessed!
All things are theirs, though
  they seem wholly dispossessed.
PARAPHRASE OF GENESIS 1–3.[30]

HAVING LOST GOD'S IMAGE, OUR TASK IS TO REGAIN IT. WILLIAM PERKINS: Humans, by creation, were made goodly creatures in the blessed image of God: but by Adam's fall we lost it and have now become the deformed children of wrath. Our duty therefore is to labor to get again our first image and endeavor to become new creatures. If a nobleman should stain his blood by treason, after his death his

posterity will never be at rest till they have got away the spot. Everyone, by Adam's fall, has become a limb of the devil, a rebel and a traitor against God's majesty. And this is the state of every one of us: by nature we are at enmity with God and therefore we ought to labor above all things in the world to be restored in Christ to our first estate and perfection, so that we may become bone of his bone, flesh of his flesh, being justified and sanctified by his obedience, death, and passion. EXPOSITION OF THE APOSTLES' CREED.[31]

EXPELLED FROM PARADISE, WE ARE BROUGHT BACK TO THE FATHER BY CHRIST'S MOTHERLY LABORS. KATHARINA SCHÜTZ ZELL: No lord with his servant and no woman with her maid is so quick and kindly to listen and attend as the father and the mother do with their child. . . . A woman who has never had a child, never experienced or felt the pain of birth and the love of feeding a nursling, cannot understand. Who would love, treat kindly, and have compassion for helpless children as the true mother can and does? So also God: with His former folk He did not want to be called a "Father" but a God and Lord, because He created us in His image intending for us to obey and serve Him and be of like mind with Himself. But we fell away, we disobeyed Him but obeyed the serpent. So all God could show us was wrath and punishment as a Lord and zealous God. For He did not experience the bitter and hard labor of a mother, He created us by His word without work, created us pure, in obedience to Him, to honor Him, and therefore He could have no pity on us. For after Adam's fall, He was no longer so kindly toward us, but He was a God who punished transgressions, for He is not like us: He is God without any imperfection. That is why He could not accept Adam's excuse but cast him out of paradise as punishment.

---

[30]*Uitbreiding*, 18.5–20.16. [31]*Works* (1608) 1:153.

But the grace of God through Jesus Christ is the true mother, that Christ who is in God and God in Him. Christ became a human being like us, and therefore He is also called Emmanuel, God with us, for He has come to us in our flesh. With great anguish He bore us in grace or brought us back to grace, such anguish that He also poured out bloody sweat over the effort.... And He gives the analogy of bitter labor and says, "A woman when she bears a child has anguish and sorrow," and He applies all of this to His suffering, in which He bore us with such effort and pain, nourished us and made us alive, gave us to drink from His breast and side with water and blood, as a mother nurses her child.... Therefore the apostle also says, "We do not have a high priest who cannot have compassion for our weakness but one who has been tempted in every way like us but without sin. Therefore let us approach with confidence the throne of grace," that is, Christ Jesus, who is the true throne of grace and mediator and the only Son born of God whom the Father loves, and God loves us in Him. For through the Beloved we are all beloved, for through the Son God has given us birth again and given the Son birth from eternity. On the Lord's Prayer.[32]

The Son Restores the Father's Image and Honor. Anna Maria van Schurman:

God now wants a better image
   of himself to raise
in those who lovingly desire
   God's honor and praise:
in it the divine pattern
   will never fail nor be undone
and through it God the Father
   will be glorified in the Son.
Adam was too far from
   the divine life, it seems indeed,
God's endless good within himself,
   alas, he could not read.
The bond between God and Adam
   had to be in one person,

so that he might remain faithful to God
   and one with God's Son.
Thus is revealed the deep
   secret of our God above
in the new covenant, which
   imparts these bonds of love:
a love by which God's enemies
   turn to their Creator anew
so as to honor the Father himself
   as their own Father true.
Paraphrase of Genesis 1–3.[33]

True Self-Knowledge Is to Know God's Image in Ourselves as Created, Lost and Restored. John Calvin: Knowledge of ourselves lies first in considering what we were given at creation and how generously God continues his favor toward us, in order to know how great our natural excellence would be if only it had remained unblemished; yet at the same time to bear in mind that there is in us nothing of our own, but that we hold on sufferance whatever God has bestowed upon us. Hence we are ever dependent on him. Secondly, to call to mind our miserable condition after Adam's fall; the awareness of which, when all our boasting and self-assurance are laid low, should truly humble us and overwhelm us with shame. In the beginning God fashioned us after his image that he might arouse our minds both to zeal for virtue and to meditation upon eternal life. Thus, in order that the great nobility of our race (which distinguishes us from brute beasts) may not be buried beneath our own dullness of wit, it behooves us to recognize that we have been endowed with reason and understanding so that, by leading a holy and upright life, we may press on to the appointed goal of blessed immortality. But that primal worthiness cannot come to mind without the sorry spectacle of our foulness and dishonor present-

---

[32]*Church Mother*, 152-54; this meditation on the Lord's Prayer is part of her exposition of Ps 51. [33]*Uitbreiding*, 16.4-15.

ing itself by way of contrast, since in the person of the first man we have fallen from our original condition. From this source arise abhorrence and displeasure with ourselves, as well as true humility; and thence is kindled a new zeal to seek God, in whom each of us may

recover those good things which we have utterly and completely lost. INSTITUTES 2.1.1.[34]

---

[34]LCC 20:242 (OS 3:228.20–229.8).

4:1-7 CAIN AND ABEL BRING OFFERINGS TO THE LORD

¹Now Adam knew Eve his wife, and she conceived and bore Cain, saying, "I have gotten*a* a man with the help of the LORD." ²And again, she bore his brother Abel. Now Abel was a keeper of sheep, and Cain a worker of the ground. ³In the course of time Cain brought to the LORD an offering of the fruit of the ground, ⁴and Abel also brought of the firstborn of his flock and of their fat portions. And the LORD had regard for Abel and his offering, ⁵but for Cain and his offering he had no regard. So Cain was very angry, and his face fell. ⁶The LORD said to Cain, "Why are you angry, and why has your face fallen? ⁷If you do well, will you not be accepted?*b* And if you do not do well, sin is crouching at the door. Its desire is for*c* you, but you must rule over it."

a *Cain sounds like the Hebrew for* gotten   b Hebrew *will there not be a lifting up* [of your face]?   c Or *against*

OVERVIEW: Genesis 4 is dominated by the story of the brothers Cain and Abel, even though Abel is mostly just background for the enigmatic rejection of Cain's offering and the volatile reaction that led Cain to murder Abel. The chapter focuses largely on two conversations between Cain and the Lord, both before and after his fratricidal act, then traces the lineage of Cain through a number of generations (and miscellaneous observations) to Lamech, whose notoriety apparently surpassed that of Cain by virtue of combining homicide with polygamy. The chapter ends by turning to a more praiseworthy son of Adam and Eve, Seth, through whose line

the patriarchs will be traced in the chapters to come.

The opening verses of the chapter traditionally drew attention due to the unsettled argument about what it was that God preferred in Abel's sacrificial offering, as opposed to Cain's. Some commentators found clues elsewhere in the Bible, as in Hebrews 11:4, where "faith" is credited for Abel's "more acceptable sacrifice." But additional reasons were also often cited—arguments that drew more on speculation about what life was like in the household of Adam and Eve, somewhere east of Eden. These speculations frequently tried to account for the origins of the practice of presenting sacrificial offerings as an act of worship, given the obvious fact that no such instructions are to be found in the preceding three chapters.

In the absence of other exegetical puzzles to solve, commentators took great interest in the mechanism, so to speak, of moral success or failure—as seen earlier with respect to Adam and Eve. Hence, considerable attention is paid to what the Lord says to Cain by way of exhortation before Cain killed his brother. However, these moral issues seem to have sparked few controversies or even contrasts between Reformation-era commentators and their predecessors, nor among Reformation commentators—except, perhaps, for a sharp disagreement as to whether or not God's exhortation to Cain implied or presupposed that Cain possessed sufficient freedom of will to change his course and avoid sinning.

Most Reformation commentators, Anabaptists included, will also tend to favor a trajectory of exegesis implied by Hebrews 11 but hugely and influentially developed by Augustine in *The City of God*. In brief, it was exceedingly common to use Augustine, often tacitly, to describe the course of salvation history as defined by two cities—one heavenly and destined for righteousness (as in Heb 13:14), the other earthly and destined for destruction—each of which could be traced to one of Adam's sons as the founder of each respective city. Accordingly, beginning here in Genesis 4, we will see commentators regularly calling attention to the conflict between these two lines of descent—between the godly and those who persecute them. This theme emerges particularly in Genesis 4:17, where Cain is described as the first to establish a city, but traditional commentators are quite prepared to recognize this theme as soon as the conflict between Cain and Abel is introduced and to pick it up again in the contrast between Cain and Seth at the chapter's end.

4:1-2 *The Births of Cain and Abel*

Procreation Still an Honorable Work. Martin Luther: No one should take offense at the mention of the fact that Adam knew his Eve. Although original sin has made this work of procreation, which owes its origin to God, something shameful, at which we see pure ears taking offense, nevertheless spiritually minded men should make a distinction between original sin and the product of creation. The work of procreation is something good and holy that God has created; for it comes from God, who bestows His blessing on it. Moreover, if man had not fallen, it would have been a very pure and very honorable work. Just as no one has misgivings about conversing, eating, or drinking with his wife—for all these are honorable actions—so also the act of begetting would have been something most highly regarded. Lectures on Genesis 4:1.[1]

God's Blessing Seen in Cain's Birth, but Adam's Sin in Abel's Death. John Calvin: This benediction of God, "Increase and multiply," was not abolished by sin. Not only that, but Adam's heart was divinely strengthened so that he did not shrink back from having children. However, just as the truly fatherly moderation of God's anger was recognized by Adam when he began to have children, so also was he compelled later on to taste the bitter fruits of his sin a second time, when Cain slew Abel. Commentary on Genesis 4:1.[2]

Only Three Examples from Adam's Many Children. Johannes Oecolampadius: Now he continues on to the fourth and following chapter, in which we will learn from the example of two brothers . . . what the character is of those who are good and those who are evil, as well as who are the true sons of

---

[1]LW 1:237-38 (WA 42: 176-77). [2]CTS 1:189* (CO 23:82).

God and who are not. For Abel, the first righteous man, will beautifully sketch for us how the good have it in this age. Then Cain, who was more fortunate in this age, will declare what the evil are like. Moses could have written other genealogies, and it is sure that Adam in the beginning procreated many children. However, only these three—Cain, Abel, and Seth—are here mentioned. These alone are set forth for our good, because all things have been written down for our instruction so that we might be corrected. COMMENTARY ON GENESIS 3:24.[3]

EVE MISTOOK GOD'S PLANS FOR HER SONS.

HULDRYCH ZWINGLI: In Hebrew, *Abel* means "empty, vacant, unnecessary." . . . We learn here how human reason and prudence is often deceived in its counsels. Eve thought Cain was the one from whom salvation was to be expected. So, exulting, she said, "I have gotten a man by God," just as in scorn she named her other son Abel. Thus we see that God rejects those whom we extol, while those whom we condemn are not infrequently exalted on high, such as Joseph, David and Gideon. ANNOTATIONS ON GENESIS 4:2.[4]

EVE'S COMMENDABLE FAITH IN THE GOSPEL. JOHANNES BRENZ: The poor woman

thought that she had just given birth to that man, or to the son of the virgin who was promised earlier and whom she knew through the Holy Spirit to be not only human but also our true Lord and God. So, having forgotten all the sorrow that befell her during childbirth, she exults with exceedingly great joy and imposes on him the name *Cain*, that is, "treasure." Granted, the honorable woman is wrong about her hope, as were many other matriarchs: truly, she had not given birth to Christ, the repairer of the human race, but to Cain, a destroyer and murderer of the human race, for it was not the time for Christ to be born, and the mother appointed for Christ was

not one known by a man but a virgin. Nonetheless, she clearly shows that she had accepted the gospel about the woman's seed with great faith, having received every consolation from this gospel, and that she credited her eternal salvation to the unique seed of the woman, that is, to Christ the Son of God. Surely this honorable woman will rise up in the last judgment against all who disbelieve along with their disobedient children. For although she herself was once the only one to heed Christ's gospel, which was completely obscure at that time, she exercised her faith all the same and guarded it with all diligence. But though they may hear the gospel all the time with utter clarity, they still do not believe it or guard it, nor will they obey it. COMMENTARY ON GENESIS 4:1.[5]

ABEL WAS CONCEIVED IN SIN JUST AS MUCH AS CAIN. WOLFGANG MUSCULUS:

When David says in Psalm 51, "Behold, I was conceived in iniquity and in sin my mother conceived me," it should not be understood that the work of generation in a legitimate marriage is immoderate or illicit, but that the malice of sin that is in our flesh is transmitted along with the seed of the man. . . . So when it is written here that Adam, already a sinner with a corrupt nature, knew his wife Eve, who also was infected with sin, and she conceived and gave birth to Cain—it should be no surprise to anyone that their firstborn proved to have so corrupt and depraved a character, when he was conceived and born from the seed of the flesh of sinners. Nor should one think that Abel was just and pious, that is, that he would have had [these qualities] from his parents, as if he had not been conceived in sin just as much as Cain! Rather, by the singular grace of God, he received a better disposition than Cain, and in him was fulfilled what Job said: "Who can make a clean thing from

---

[3]*In Genesim* (1536), 58v-59r. [4]ZSW 13:32. [5]*Opera* 1:66.

something conceived from unclean seed, except You alone?" COMMENTARY ON GENESIS 4:3-5.[6]

"ABEL" RECALLS THE SORROW OF SIN. JOHN CALVIN: While in naming her firstborn, Eve bore witness to the joy that had suddenly shone upon her and celebrated the grace of God, later on, in naming her other son, she fell back on her recollection of the miseries of the human race. To be sure, this new benediction of God was an occasion for uncommon joy, and yet she could not turn her thoughts to the coming generations, devoted to so many evils that she herself had caused, without the most bitter grief. That is why she wanted there to be a conspicuous reminder of her sorrow in the name she gave her second son—a mirror held up for all, by which she might warn all her descendants against human race's vanity. COMMENTARY ON GENESIS 4:2.[7]

WE ARE ALL PARTLY LIKE CAIN, PARTLY LIKE ABEL. NIKOLAUS SELNECKER: Allegorically, "Adam" receives both "Cain" and "Abel." Cain stands for *possession*; Abel, for *vanity*. We are all born like this: we are Cain, that is, we seem to ourselves to be much; but we are Abel when we perceive and reflect on everything within us as we act and use things throughout the course of our lives. Cain, however, is the old nature without Christ; Abel is the new nature, justified by faith. The latter is killed by Cain—by the old nature, or by sin. Indeed, our sins have scattered us like the wind, and death is sin's wages. But the blood of the Son of God cries out to God the Father, and sin sleeps at the doors of the tomb, until perfection is brought about at the advent of the Son of God, when rewards are bestowed upon believers and punishments on the ungodly. COMMENTARY ON GENESIS 4:8.[8]

4:3-5a *The Offerings of Cain and Abel*

THE FIRST SACRIFICES WERE NOT CON-

DUCTED WITHOUT GOD'S WORD. MARTIN LUTHER: Although in this passage mention is made only of the sacrifice and not of the preaching, it must nevertheless be maintained that they did not offer a sacrifice without the preaching of the Word. For God is not worshiped by means of a speechless work; the work must be accompanied by the Word which rings in the hearts of men and in the ears of God. Thus calling upon the name of God also accompanied this sacrifice. But at this point the question is raised whether they had a word or command to sacrifice. I answer yes. For all the sacred accounts give proof that by His superabundant grace our merciful God always placed some outward and visible sign of His grace alongside the Word, so that men, reminded by the outward sign and work or Sacrament, would believe with greater assurance that God is kind and merciful. LECTURES ON GENESIS 4:3.[9]

THE LESSONS OF SACRIFICES. DAVID CHYTRAEUS: A sacrifice is a kind of ceremony or work offered to God in order to ascribe honor to him. But all ceremonial sacrifices had their principles and true purposes. First, to preserve the assemblies of the people. Indeed, God wished there to be public gatherings in which the voice of the promise about Christ might sound forth and the entire teaching of true religion could be passed on to posterity. He therefore instituted sacrifices and rites so that they might be the sinews and bonds of such assemblies. Second, they were pictures to warn people's minds of the coming sacrifice of Christ that would placate God's wrath and merit the forgiveness of sins. When Abel saw that the lamb had been consumed—indeed, by a fire divinely kindled—he understood that it signified a different lamb, namely, the coming

---

[6]*In Mosis Genesim* (1554), 123, citing Job 14:4. [7]CTS 1:191* (CO 23:83). [8]*In Genesin* (1569), 248. [9]LW 1:247-48 (WA 42:184).

Seed. . . . Third, for those who were godly and born again, sacrifices were sacraments, that is, testimonies of the promise that excited and confirmed faith. When Abel offered the lamb that was consumed by heavenly flames, he was admonished by this spectacle so that by faith he applied the promised benefits of the messiah to himself. He thus nourished and strengthened his faith. COMMENTARY ON GENESIS 4:3-4.[10]

SACRIFICE AND THE GOSPEL. JOHANNES BRENZ: Who taught them to sacrifice to God, whether the fruit of the soil or flocks and their fatty parts? Here again it is shown to us that the proclamation about Christ or the Messiah was common among our first parents from the world's beginning. In fact, no human mind could contrive the reason for sacrifices. On the contrary, some peoples have declared it a capital offense to sacrifice a cow. So how would they have concluded that the sacrifice of a cow constitutes worship pleasing to God? And how is the sacrifice and immolation of a cow congruent with the divine majesty? Who among mortals would think it would be a favor to anyone if, in their presence, one should slit the throat of a cow and cast it into the fire? How, then, could human reason imagine that this service would please God? So the fact remains that the custom of sacrificing to God cows, sheep, fruits of the soil, and other things was divinely invented and revealed to Adam. . . . There can be no doubt that God showed Adam what would happen regarding the virgin's son, namely, that his blood would be shed for our sins, and afterward commanded him to teach his family and his descendants according to this example, and to hand on the custom of slaughtering and sacrificing sheep and cows, so that a reminder of the coming sacrifice of Christ for sins would always be retained until the very thing was fulfilled. Therefore Cain and Abel make sacrifices and offer their gifts to God out of a tradition

divinely disclosed to their parents. COMMENTARY ON GENESIS 4:3-4.[11]

BOTH CAIN AND ABEL HAD BEEN RAISED WELL. JOHN CALVIN: Each brother followed a manner of life that was in itself holy and worthy of praise. Indeed, the cultivation of the earth was commanded by God, but the labor of pasturing sheep was no less honorable than it was useful. In fact, everything about rustic life was innocent and simple, perfectly suited to the true order of nature. It is first of all to be held, then, that both exercised themselves in occupations that were approved by God and needed by human beings to supply necessities of everyday life. It can also be inferred here that they had been well instructed by their father, as the rite of sacrificing more fully confirms, because it proves that they had been trained to worship God. In appearance, then, Cain's life was very well regulated, seeing that he cultivated the duties of piety towards God and sought to make a living for himself and his family by honest and just labor, as was fitting for the provident and sober father of a household. COMMENTARY ON GENESIS 4:2.[12]

WHAT ABEL KNEW ABOUT SACRIFICES. WOLFGANG MUSCULUS: We should not imagine that God desires the offerings of mortals, for all things are his and he himself supplies all things for our benefit. But he does seek from us that we be grateful for his gifts. A grateful heart is thus the means by which one may set forth proof to someone else. This arrangement was taught in an elementary way by external sacrifices, by which the faithful might declare that they acknowledged God's blessing, through which they received all things from his hand. The logic of such

---

[10]*In Genesin* (1568), 165-66; these pages were missing from my digital copy of the 1576 edition. [11]*Opera* 1:67. [12]CTS 1:192* (CO 23:83-84).

gratitude dictated, consequently, that God should be presented with the first and best of his gifts. . . . It is the nature of things that the firstfruits of good things are regarded as more precious than the rest. Thus the firstborn of humans as well as of sheep, the firstfruits of wine, oil, grain, and the rest of the crops are more esteemed and regarded as more desirable. In the same way, things that are fat and rich are more acceptable than things meager and thin. So we rightly praise those who sanctify to the Lord the first and richest of their things. The same logic also pertains to time, whereby the first of the year or the first of the month is consecrated to God. We ought to ponder, then, how such matters remind us that we ought to be grateful to God in all things. Let us consecrate the first and best parts of our life, our spirit, our actions and efforts to God's glory. Let us give of the firstfruits of our wealth to paupers. Let us give from the richness of our pantries to the poor and destitute. Those who do otherwise make their offerings to God not with Abel but with Cain, and neither their persons nor their gifts are accepted. COMMENTARY ON GENESIS 4:3-5.[13]

GOD MUST HAVE GIVEN FIRE AS A SIGN OF APPROVAL. JOHANNES BRENZ: God acknowledged and approved Abel's offering but repudiated the offering of Cain. But by what proof was God's will known in this offering? To be sure, in this passage Scripture does not deliver this information to us with words to that effect, but our ancient writers cited certain proofs—especially Hebrews 11[:4], where it is said that "God spoke well of Abel's offerings"—and concluded that Cain and Abel did not set their offerings on fire but waited for fire from heaven, so that that sacrifice might be judged as pleasing to God which was ignited by fire sent down from heaven. . . . Accordingly, one might easily conclude that in these offerings of Cain and Abel, fire sent from heaven devoured Abel's sacrifice and

neglected that of Cain. COMMENTARY ON GENESIS 4:3-5.[14]

DETAILS BEHIND THE STORY OF ABEL'S SACRIFICE. ANDREW WILLET: Though no mention is made of Adam having sacrificed, [it is] because nothing remarkable happened as it did in his son's sacrifices. But it is not to be doubted that he was accustomed to sacrifice and that his sons learned to do the same from him. Abel's sacrifice was preferred before Cain's in three respects. First, as the apostle says, it was more plentiful, "a greater sacrifice." Cain brought sparingly of the fruit—not fruits—of the earth; Abel brought plentifully. Secondly, Abel brought of the fat and the best; and, thirdly, he offered in faith (Heb 11:4). It seems that God by some outward testimony approved Abel's sacrifice, whether by igniting it with fire from heaven, as he did to Moses' sacrifice (Lev 9:24) and Elijah's (1 Kings 18); or by the flames of Cain's sacrifice rebounding upon himself, as the fire of the furnace into which the three children were cast slew those who made it (Dan 3:22). It is likely that by some visible sign God delivered his acceptance, as the apostle says, "God giving testimony to his gifts" (Heb 11:4). COMMENTARY ON GENESIS 4:4.[15]

GOD PREFERS THE HUMBLE TO THE FIRSTBORN. MARTIN LUTHER: Abel is the shepherd; Cain, as the first-born son, is king and priest, who was born into the glorious hope of the restoration of all things (Acts 3:21). But consider at this point God's wonderful design. From the beginning of the world primogeniture was a matter of the utmost importance, not only among the people where the right of primogeniture was established by God Himself and was given honor but also among the

---

[13]*In Mosis Genesim* (1554), 125. [14]*Opera* 1:67, citing support also from Lev 9:24; 2 Chron 7:1; 1 Kings 18:38. [15]*Hexapla* (1608), 60-61, crediting Jerome and Theodotion.

heathen. And yet, particularly among the holy people, actual experience proves that first-born sons disappointed the hope of their parents and that those who were born later assumed their place, rank, and prestige. How bitterly Cain, the murderer, thus disappointed the hope of our first parents! Abraham, too, was not the first-born son; Haran was. Esau is the first-born son, but the blessing passes on to his brother Jacob. David was the youngest among his brothers, and yet he is anointed king. So it was also in the case of others. Although by divine right the first-born enjoyed the prerogative of rule and priesthood, nevertheless they lost it, and those who were born later were given preference over them. How did this abnormal situation arise? It was unquestionably due both to the fault of the parents and to the personal haughtiness of the first-born son. The parents regarded their first-born sons as something distinguished. Then the first-born sons themselves were spoiled in this way by the indulgence of their parents. Relying on their right, they despised and lorded it over their brothers. But God is the God of the humble; He gives grace to the humble and resists the proud (1 Pet 5:5). Because they are proud, the first-born sons are deprived of their right, not because they did not have the right of primogeniture but because they begin to be proud of their gifts and become conceited. This God cannot bear. LECTURES ON GENESIS 4:2.[16]

CAIN'S MISTAKES: PRIDE AND UNBELIEF. JOHANNES BRENZ: Why did God regard Abel's sacrifice and not that of Cain, when Cain was, after all, the firstborn and his parents harbored the greatest expectation for him? Some think that Abel's sacrifice was more costly according to its external appearance and thus more acceptable to God, but . . . God does not care about the external cost of an offering. Instead, he cares about the greatest, true and spiritual value that is in the offering, namely, Christ himself, God's Son.

Truly, wherever God finds this, there he cannot be kept from regarding offerings with mercy. Why Abel offered a sacrifice more pleasing to God and better than Cain's is thus plainly expounded by Hebrews 11[:4]: "By faith," it says. . . . Therefore let us see what it is to offer sacrifices by faith and what it is to do good works entirely by faith. . . . First, to sacrifice or to do good works "by faith" is to obey the word of God, by which God's will is revealed, that requires such a work. . . . Then, to sacrifice by faith is to believe that this external sacrifice does not in itself atone for sins but merely foreshadows Christ, who alone is the expiator of sins. Likewise, to do good works by faith is to believe that not our works but only the work of Christ, only the sufferings of Christ, can placate the wrath of heaven. But our good works are only the fruits of faith; they are not perfect, and so they should not be thrust before God as an expiation of sin. We may now see how Cain and Abel offered their sacrifices. For Cain did not sin in the external work itself, but he sinned in his internal affection. Indeed, he made his offering not by faith but from unbelief. For while God's word about making sacrifices was not obscure, Cain nonetheless made his offering not because God so instructed him but because it was pleasing to Cain to humor his parents, who had prescribed his sacrifice. Moreover, he did not believe that this sacrifice foreshadowed the sacrifice of the virgin's son, our Lord Jesus Christ. Instead, Cain thought that he himself was the savior of the world and that the merit of his sacrifice would please God. This was the greatest impiety! But Abel offered by faith. First, because he acknowledged God's word, by which sacrifice had been instituted. Then, he acknowledged the seed of the woman, the virgin's son, as his Savior and the expiator of his sin, and he wished by this sacrifice merely to confirm his faith in the virgin's son—but

---

[16]LW 1:243-44 (WA 42:181).

not to atone for his sins by the merit of his work. And so, faith and unbelief constitute the difference between the sacrifices of Cain and Abel. COMMENTARY ON GENESIS 4:3-5.[17]

GOD ACCEPTS PERSONS BEFORE HE ACCEPTS THEIR WORKS. JOHN CALVIN: Here, the order observed by Moses must be noted, for he does not simply state that the *worship* Abel presented to God was pleasing to him, but he begins with Abel's *person*. This signifies that no works will find favor with God unless the doer of those works has already found favor and been approved by him. COMMENTARY ON GENESIS 4:4.[18]

HYPOCRISY IN WORSHIP IS HARD TO DETECT. WOLFGANG MUSCULUS: Of the two brothers, Cain and Abel, one is an image of the godly, while the other is an image of the ungodly. Cain the impious made an offering: yet he did not offer it to false gods but to the true God; nor to many gods but to the One. Abel was pious and also brought an offering, yet he brought it not to a different God but to the same God as Cain did. Nor did Abel merely bring a spiritual sacrifice, but he brought a physical victim and worshiped God with visible and external rites just as Cain did. But Cain did not make his offering from faith and heartfelt gratitude as Abel did. Rather, his worship was merely a custom he had learned from his father or else was done just for show. . . . But it is difficult to detect on the basis of external worship who worships God truly or falsely. COMMENTARY ON GENESIS 4:3-5.[19]

CAIN EXCELLED IN ALL WAYS BUT ONE. KONRAD PELLIKAN: Cain offers a work of obedience and conducts himself in a more holy manner if one considers his work—but not, however, if one considers his election. He offers the work that was required, he acts more blamelessly, he labors harder, and he bears more diligently the punishment laid upon the

human race: but he was the lesser in faith and devotion, things regarded by God. . . . All things depend on the election of God, who gives faith and works to whom he pleases: he receives whomever he wills, and he hardens whomever he wills. COMMENTARY ON GENESIS 4:2, 5.[20]

4:5b-7 Cain's Anger

GOD REBUKED CAIN THROUGH ADAM. MARTIN LUTHER: When Cain clearly showed his disaffection for his brother, his parent Adam reproved him. I believe that these words were spoken by Adam himself. Moses says that these words were spoken by the Lord, because Adam had now been accounted just and had been endowed with the Holy Spirit. What he now says in accordance with the Word of God and through the Holy Spirit is correctly declared to have been said by God. Similarly today, those who preach the Gospel are not themselves directly the preachers, but Christ speaks and preaches through them. LECTURES ON GENESIS 4:6.[21]

CAIN ENVIED ABEL AS THE UNGODLY ALWAYS ENVY THE RIGHTEOUS. MENNO SIMONS: The Lord regarded Abel and his sacrifice but he looked not upon Cain and his gift. Therefore, Cain was very wroth, and his countenance fell through great wrath, even as the ungodly always are envious of the pious, because the Lord regards the pious and loves their sacrifices. Cain spoke deceitfully to his pious, humble brother Abel, who knew not the malicious, bloody heart of his brother, saying, "Let us go out," and when they were in the field, Cain's hot, envious spirit could no longer be restrained and his blood-thirsty, revengeful

---

[17]*Opera* 1:68. [18]CTS 1:194* (CO 23:85), illustrating Calvin's doctrine of *double justification*, that faith alone is the basis for God's acceptance not only of one's person but also of one's works. [19]*In Mosis Genesim* (1554), 124-25. [20]*Commentaria Bibliorum* (1532) 1:7v. [21]LW 1:262 (WA 42:194).

spirit could not be hid. That which [lies] concealed in the heart must break out in the actions; he arose against his innocent brother and in his fierce wrath slew him. Why did he do this? Because Cain was of the evil one and his works were evil, and his brother's works were righteous. It seems to me, dear brethren, that this is a fair example and a good reference; for the righteous always have been offscourings and a prey to the unrighteous, and so will they continue to be as the Scriptures sufficiently testify, and as daily experience plainly teaches. THE CROSS OF THE SAINTS.[22]

CAIN'S SELF-SERVING VIEW OF JUSTICE. JOHANNES BRENZ: On what pretext would Cain have assaulted Abel? Even if Scripture says nothing explicit on this question, it is likely . . . that, along the lines of the Jerusalem Targum, Cain began to dispute with Abel about religion, saying, "There is no judgment, nor judge, nor other world; nor is there a good reward for the righteous or punishment for the ungodly. The world was not created by God's mercy, nor is the world governed by God's mercy," etc. Indeed, when Cain saw that Abel was preferred to him, he concluded . . . that something utterly unjust had come to pass, that the younger should be preferred to the older, and he therefore thought that either there is no God, or if there is a God, he does not watch over human affairs but does everything capriciously. It's likely that Cain undertook this disputation about religion with Abel, and when Abel contradicted his brother's impiety, he was cruelly killed by him. Let us understand, then, that this story of Cain and Abel is not to be regarded as a private deed with no bearing on others. Rather, because these two brothers were the first men in the world after Adam, we should realize that the description of this story signifies for us that, with this incident involving the first two brothers, the brutality of ungodly hypocrites against the pious begins, and it goes on

continuously until the last day of this age. Truly, Cain persecuted Abel in just this way on account of religion and religious disputes, for the sake of domination. Thus the church of the wicked always persecutes the church of the pious, because while the latter glory in God's favor and the heavenly kingdom, the former fear lest they be deprived of even their earthly kingdom. So they rise up against the church of the pious and march against it like a tyrant wherever they can. For this reason one should take great care to understand that whoever pursues godliness must know to expect his own "Cain" and not to trust the flattering words of hypocrites. Instead, one should be prepared to bear whatever the Lord may send, fully trusting that God will repay every affliction with a heavenly blessing. Then, whenever quarrels and persecutions arise on account of religion, we should not suppose that God has forsaken the earth and that he does not require our actions, but we should rather think that this is the same old pattern of things in this age, that the ungodly persecute the godly. Let us not forsake our duty but continue in our calling and await our heavenly liberation. COMMENTARY ON GENESIS 4:8.[23]

THE FIRSTBORN SHOULD HAVE MODELED GRATITUDE. JOHN CALVIN: [What God says here] seems to me to be more of a rebuke, by which God accuses the impious man of ingratitude for regarding the honor of being the firstborn as if it were nothing. The greater the divine benefits with which any one of us is adorned, the more we betray our impiety if we do not earnestly strive to honor those blessings' author, to whom we are obliged. When Abel was regarded as his brother's subordinate, he was still a diligent worshiper of God. But he

---

[22]*Works*, 1:186 (cf. *Writings*, 588; *Opera*, 140a). [23]*Opera* 1:71-72; the Targum excerpt probably derives from Paul Fagius, *Thargvm, hoc est, Paraphrasis Onkeli Chaldaica in Sacra Biblia* (Strasbourg, 1546), sig. b1r; for English, see *The Aramaic Bible* (Collegeville, MN: Liturgical Press, 1992), 1A:66-67 and 1B:32-33.

who was born first worshiped God negligently and as a mere formality, even though he had arrived at such a rank by God's own kindness. God therefore makes much of his sin, because he had not at least imitated his brother, whom he ought to have surpassed in piety as far as he did in the degree of honor. COMMENTARY ON GENESIS 4:7.[24]

GOD'S SUBTLE AND MERCIFUL WARNING. HULDRYCH ZWINGLI: "Sin lies at the door." . . . God uses this maxim to chide Cain, wishing to forestall matters, lest he carry out the homicide that he had devised in his mind. It is as if he had said, "You both are mine. Why does it displease you that your brother has made the best offering to me?" This is God's inestimable compassion: when he sees that we have devised evil things, he forewarns us lest we rush out and do them. ANNOTATIONS ON GENESIS 4:7.[25]

IF CAIN COULD HAVE MASTERED HIS SIN, HOW MUCH MORE CAN WE? BALTHASAR HUBMAIER: If now Cain was a lord and master over his sin, yes, over all his anger and rage, then, as God himself says, he would have been able to master, suppress, and knock it to the ground. So that the sin, if he had wanted otherwise, would have had to be subject to him and bow before him. It follows that we also can be lords and masters of our sins, which lordship and mastery comes to us out of the new grace of the sending of the divine Word by which God breathes on us newness, awakens us, gives us birth anew, and gives us the choice and the power to become his children. For Cain was born only after the Fall, like us, coming from Adam and Eve. That is the simple and right understanding of this Scripture. FREEDOM OF THE WILL, BOOK 2.[26]

WE CANNOT STAND AGAINST SIN WITHOUT THE SPIRIT'S HELP. MARTIN LUTHER: If any man ever possessed either adequate strength or a free will by which he could protect himself against the assaults of Satan, these gifts would surely have existed in Cain, who was in possession of the primogeniture and of the promise of the blessed Seed. But the state of all men is the same: If this nature is not assisted by God's Holy Spirit, it cannot stand. Why, then, do we engage in unprofitable boasting about our free will? LECTURES ON GENESIS 4:8.[27]

CAIN WRONGLY PRESUMED TO BE ABEL'S LORD. HULDRYCH ZWINGLI: It's as if God were to say, "Surely Abel's desire is not also obliged to entail respect for you, unlike a wife's desire for her husband? You're not his lord or head, are you?" . . . Those who seek a defense of free will from this text prove nothing about how human beings become liable to condemnation. For if we cannot be saved except we master our sin and our inborn desires, then all flesh stands condemned. Rather, the sense is this: "Abel didn't temper his desire, that is, his faith in God and his love, to your authority, did he? He honors me greatly and nothing is more important to him than I am. That is why he presented an offering of the highest excellence. You, on the other hand, are a hypocrite, a worshiper of me who wishes to seem not inferior to Abel, when you should not be so. Hence your hatred and rashness. Should he therefore be no more pious and respectful of me than you would direct him to be?" ANNOTATIONS ON GENESIS 4:7.[28]

CAIN OVERREACHED HIS AUTHORITY. KONRAD PELLIKAN: It's as if God had said, "You both are mine, so why are you displeased

---

[24]CTS 1:203-4* (CO 23:90). [25]ZSW 13:33. [26]CRR 5:457. [27]LW 1:273 (WA 42:202). [28]ZSW 13:33-34. Zwingli refers the pronouns in Gen 4:7b not to *sin* but to *Abel* and translates these two clauses as questions, in parallel with Gen 4:6-7a, along lines like these: "Should [Abel's] desire be for *you*? Ought *you* to be his master?" The sin "crouching at the door," then, is Cain's presumption that he has the right to dominate Abel.

by your brother's integrity in his offering? Why do you hate your brother? If you continue as you have begun, the punishment of your sin is ready to hand and you will openly confirm your impiety. Should Abel look up to you, his brother, as a wife to her husband? You aren't his lord, are you? Should he accommodate his faith in God to your authority? He worships me assiduously and regards me as great above all; therefore he brings me the very best he has. You wish to be seen as my worshiper but without incurring any loss, so you bring me an inferior offering." Precepts from both tables are taught here, namely, that God is to be worshiped, and that one should not be angry with a brother. COMMENTARY ON GENESIS 4:7.[29]

CAIN EXEMPLIFIES SO MANY BAD THINGS. NIKOLAUS SELNECKER: First, [he is] an example of how divine judgment brings secrets to light and removes the bar from the doors where sin sleeps. Second, Cain is an example of insolence, indignation and defiance in refusing to honor God or his parents, in not offering them any respect and in not wishing to confess his sin. Third, an example of the world's perversity in neglecting and despising one's

neighbor. "What is my brother to me? I am a neighbor to myself! 'What is it to us if Greeks are dying?'[†]" Fourth, an example of those who, when they wish to excuse themselves, actually accuse themselves, and they stain more than they make clean. Indeed, when Cain says the word *brother*, he surely accuses himself for not exercising care for him. When he says the care of his brother does not pertain to him, surely he is a liar and a criminal. And by answering in this way, he himself makes public his obstinacy toward God and his parents, his lovelessness toward his brother, and his crime. This is what Hilary said: stupidity is always annexed to impiety. . . . Fifth, an example of what is often said, that one sin begets another, just as Cain's presumption and unbelief gives birth to envy and hatred against his brother. Envy begets hypocrisy and false or simulated benevolence. Hypocrisy eventually begets blindness, excusing one's sin comes after blindness, and despair follows that. COMMENTARY ON GENESIS 4:8.[30]

---

[29]*Commentaria Bibliorum* (1532) 1:7v-8r. [30]*In Genesin* (1569), 248; [†]the reference to Greeks dying is described by Luther as a "common proverb," even as the reference to Hilary (*On the Trinity* 6.15) is also derived from Luther (LW 1:276, 278n38).

4:8-15 CAIN KILLS HIS BROTHER, ABEL

[8]*Cain spoke to Abel his brother.[a] And when they were in the field, Cain rose up against his brother Abel and killed him. [9]Then the LORD said to Cain, "Where is Abel your brother?" He said, "I do not know; am I my brother's keeper?" [10]And the LORD said, "What have you done? The voice of your brother's blood is crying to me from the ground. [11]And now you are cursed from the ground, which has opened its mouth to receive your brother's blood from your hand. [12]When you work the ground, it shall no longer yield to*

you its strength. You shall be a fugitive and a wanderer on the earth." ¹³Cain said to the LORD, *"My punishment is greater than I can bear.^b ¹⁴Behold, you have driven me today away from the ground, and from your face I shall be hidden. I shall be a fugitive and a wanderer on the earth, and whoever finds me will kill me." ¹⁵Then the* LORD *said to him, "Not so! If anyone kills Cain, vengeance shall be taken on him sevenfold." And the* LORD *put a mark on Cain, lest any who found him should attack him.*

a Hebrew; Samaritan, Septuagint, Syriac, Vulgate add *Let us go out to the field*   b Or *My guilt is too great to bear*

OVERVIEW: Not surprisingly, this account of the world's first murder elicits a kind of stark fascination. Of particular interest is what one might call the psychology of Cain, in which commentators asked about his varied motives, the workings of conscience and his dramatic shift from aggressor to supplicant. At the same time, the innocent blood of the martyred Abel raises issues of divine providence, justice and retribution, even as these two sons serve as a type of the two cities and the two great families of the earth: the righteous and the ungodly. Eventually, of course, the company of those who were godly but persecuted would lead to Christ himself, and even the literal exegesis of Reformation commentators did not pass by this connection with Abel.

This passage, like most passages, also raised questions marked less by weighty theological or ethical implications than for their attempt to fill in the Bible's silences about secondary or background details. For example, the punishment levied on Cain is described as a *curse*, but there is enough similarity between his curse (that the earth would be barren to him) and the penalty declared to Adam that readers understandably wanted to know how Cain suffered any significant or additional punishment. Of even less theological weight, but just as interesting to inquiring minds, was the so-called *mark* of Cain. What was it? How did it work? Again, nothing much depended on the answer, but once asked, the question took on a life of its own.

4:8-9 Where Is Abel Your Brother?

NATURE TEACHES US TO BE OUR BROTHER'S KEEPER. KONRAD PELLIKAN: By the law of nature, a brother ought to guard the well-being of his brother by birth, but if he did not wish to guard him, at the very least he should not have killed him. COMMENTARY ON GENESIS 4:9.[1]

CAIN KNEW HE SHOULD HAVE BEEN HIS BROTHER'S KEEPER. MARTIN LUTHER: Cain believes that he has eloquently disclaimed any guilt when he refuses to be his brother's keeper. But the moment he calls him his brother, does he not confess that he ought to be his keeper? Does he not also accuse himself of being unfriendly to his brother, and does he not at the same time raise the suspicion in his parents that the murder has been committed, since Abel nowhere puts in an appearance? In Paradise, Adam, too, disclaims any guilt and passes the blame on to Eve. But Cain's excuse is much more foolish; for truly when sin is disclaimed, sin is doubled, while a free confession of sin obtains mercy and overcomes wrath. LECTURES ON GENESIS 4:9.[2]

GOD DELIVERS ORACLES EVEN TO THE REPROBATE. JOHN CALVIN: Those who imagine that the father had questioned Cain about his son Abel vitiate the whole force of

[1]*Commentaria Bibliorum* (1532) 1:8r.   [2]LW 1:274-75 (WA 42:203).

the instruction that Moses intended to deliver here, namely, that by his secret inspiration as well as by some unusual means, *God* summoned the murderer to his tribunal, as if he had thundered from heaven. . . . Just as God now speaks with us through the Scriptures, so he formerly manifested himself to the patriarchs through oracles, and he revealed his judgments also to the saints' reprobate offspring in the same manner. An angel challenges Hagar in this way, in the forest, after she had abandoned the church. . . . To be sure, it's possible that God may have interrogated Cain by a silent examination of his conscience, and that he in turn may have responded by inwardly fretting and murmuring. Nonetheless, it is not to be thought that he was examined merely by the audible voice of a human being, but rather by a divine voice, so that he would feel that he was dealing with God himself. As often, then, as the hidden pangs of conscience invite us to reflect upon our sins, let us remember that God himself is speaking with us. COMMENTARY ON GENESIS 4:9.[3]

GOD INTERROGATES CAIN WITH THE UTMOST KINDNESS. CHRISTOPHOR PELARGUS:
This is an emphatic *elenchus* or refutation, for by showing him the way of kindness and salvation, God is eager to turn aside Cain's wrathful resolve and lure him from his impious proposition. "For in fact, if you repent" (God seems to say), "your offering, too, will be accepted. If you don't repent, sin, which is lying at the doors of your heart, will rise against you more violently and will easily bring you under its control. So resist these vicious feelings, beware of the devil's snares!" Rhetorically, however, you should see how each element here is adorned by the Holy Spirit. He uses interrogation at the beginning, not because he doesn't know the cause for that wrath but in order to call that wrath to Cain's awareness and show him that his hatred and malice has been found out and has been

recognized as such. By this gradual and gentle approach, God calls him to mercy; he invites him into his own conscience, into his heart, so that he himself might see what he is thinking. COMMENTARY ON GENESIS 4:6-7.[4]

CAIN'S FOURFOLD SIN AND THREEFOLD PUNISHMENT. ANDREW WILLET:
Concerning Cain's sin, he shows himself to be a liar, in saying, "I know not"; wicked and profane, in thinking that he could hide his sin from God; unjust, in denying that he was his brother's keeper or that he ought to have any care of him; obstinate and desperate, in not confessing his sin but stubbornly complaining of the greatness of his punishment. He [also] sustains a threefold punishment: he is cursed in his soul, a vagabond in his body, and unprosperous in his labors so that the earth should not yield its fruit. Thus, just as the devil was cursed, so is Cain, the devil's minister. To Adam, God said not "cursed are you," but "cursed is the earth for your sake." COMMENTARY ON GENESIS 4:9.[5]

4:10 Abel's Blood Cries from the Ground

GOD SPEAKS FOR THE DEAD. WOLFGANG MUSCULUS:
It is not to Adam, nor to Eve, nor to his sisters, nor to the brothers of Abel (if there were any then), but to Cain, the murderer himself, that he says, "Where is Abel your brother?" From the hand of the killer he seeks the one who was killed. Cain was thinking that he would be free from the trouble that his brother's presence was causing him if he killed him and took him away. However, he learned that God is one who seeks after those who have been killed. He realized that God is a ready judge against all those who are oppressors of brothers and innocents. Who

[3]CTS 1:205* (CO 23:91), citing Gen 16:8. [4]*In prophetarum oceanum* (1612), 106, with unspecified credit given to Rupert in this passage. [5]*Hexapla* (1608), 61-62.

can sufficiently gauge how much distress, quaking and dread there will be for tyrants and all those who oppress their brothers and other harmless people when they hear this from the voice of God, "Where are those whom they have oppressed?" Clearly, they are all as blind as Cain when they think they will go unpunished or that they can do violence to their brothers and other innocents as if, on account of their own reputation, they would never be summoned to judgment. "The dead," they say, "do not wage war." That may be true, but there is a Lord in heaven who seeks the blood of those killed from the hands of tyrants and who speaks for the dead. COMMENTARY ON GENESIS 4:9-10.[6]

GOD VINDICATES ALL INNOCENT BLOOD. KONRAD PELLIKAN: God vindicates not only the blood of Abel but also of all the righteous who have been slain, from Abel until the very last innocent one. From this passage we learn of God's care for the pious, whether they live or die, for we see that even when the pious die, they are sought by the Lord. Those who trust in God do not have family patrons, [yet] they are not slain except the Lord knows and wills; they lack scarcely a thing when they seem wholly bereft. . . . When human help fails, the divine rushes in. COMMENTARY ON GENESIS 4:10.[7]

GOD'S CARE FOR ABEL TESTIFIES TO THE RESURRECTION. MARTIN LUTHER: God inquires about Abel, who has been removed from this life. He does not want to forget him; He keeps him in mind and asks where he is. Therefore God is the God of the dead (Mt 22:32); that is, therefore, the dead, too, live and have a God who cares for them and preserves them in a life that is different from this physical one in which the saints are afflicted. This passage is noteworthy, since God takes care of Abel, who is dead, and so, because of Abel, who is dead, excommunicates

and destroys the first-born Cain while he is alive. This is truly an important matter. Abel, though dead, lives; and in another life he is canonized by God Himself in a better and truer manner than all whom the pope has ever canonized. But Cain, though alive, is excommunicated and dies an everlasting death. Abel's death is indeed frightful, for he suffered death with great torment and with many tears. But it is a truly salutary death, inasmuch as he now lives a better life than before. We live this physical life in sins, and it is subject to death; but that other life is eternal and without any afflictions, physical or spiritual. God does not inquire after sheep and cattle that have been slaughtered, but He does inquire after men that have been killed. Therefore men have the hope of resurrection and a God who leads them out of bodily death to eternal life, who inquires after their blood as after something precious, just as the psalm also says (Ps 116:15): "Precious is the death of His saints in His sight." This is the glory of the human race, which was won by the Seed when He crushed the serpent's head. LECTURES ON GENESIS 4:9.[8]

ABEL WAS DEAD TO CAIN, BUT NOT TO GOD. DESIDERIUS ERASMUS: Abel was the first of all to deserve to be called righteous. Truly, he is all the more to be praised because he showed himself innocent and faithful toward God, but without anyone else's example to inspire him. But what was it that made him more beloved by God than was his brother Cain? Without a doubt, *faith*, by which he wholly depended on God. Cain, however, was more or less distrustful and, not content with those things that the soil freely sent forth for food as an innocent means of livelihood, he plowed up the ground. They both offered God sacrifices from their means, but the sacrifice of

[6]*In Mosis Genesim* (1554), 139. [7]*Commentaria Bibliorum* (1532) 1:8r. [8]LW 1:285 (WA 42:210-11).

Abel alone was accepted by God, because with a pure heart the innocent man trusted in God's goodness and was not intent on the goods of this world but waited for his piety's reward in heaven. Therefore not by his sacrifice but through his faith did he deserve that God, embracing his offerings, should testify that he was righteous with fire sent down from heaven. By reason of this most beautiful testimony, he is still the talk of everyone even after so many thousand years, so that even while dead he seems to live and speak. To his brother, the blameless man was dead the moment he was killed; but he was not dead to God, to whom his blood was still crying from the earth. PARAPHRASE OF HEBREWS 11:4.[9]

WHY DID GOD FORSAKE ABEL . . . AND CHRIST? JOHANNES BRENZ: It seems quite foolish that God attends to Abel only now, when he has been slain. Why didn't he show some concern for him earlier, before he was killed? Why didn't he miraculously rescue him from Cain's hands earlier? As the proverb says of those who are foolish and imprudent, "they close the barn door after the cow is gone." But though this seems foolish, it is the greatest wisdom. Indeed, after God wholly determined that his Son would atone for our sin by his suffering and death, right away, from the beginning of the human race, the suffering and death of Christ his Son seemed to be foreshadowed and proclaimed not only by the sacrifice of animals but also by the example of Abel. Just as Abel was killed by his own brother, so was Christ the Son of God killed by members of his own people, who were his brothers according to the flesh. And just as Abel seemed abandoned by God into the hands of his brethren, despite having prayed for God's help, so Christ the Son of God seemed so abandoned by God that he even cried out, "My God, why have you forsaken me?" And just as the blood of Abel cried for vengeance against his brother, so does the blood of Christ cry for

vengeance against all the ungodly and impenitent. In fact, God deliberately turned a blind eye not only to Abel's death but also to that of his Son, and abandoned them into the hands of the ungodly even until they were slaughtered. For if he had miraculously defended Abel (and, later on, Christ his Son) from the cruelty of their brothers and preserved them in this bodily life, other godly people would draw upon their example and, unless they too were physically defended by some unusual miracle, they would conclude that they were forsaken by God. But now, after they see the examples of Abel and of Christ the Son of God, whom they know to have been completely in God's care, they do not lose heart or despair of their salvation, even if they should be abandoned to the hands of their enemies and be cruelly put to death. COMMENTARY ON GENESIS 4.[10]

CHRIST KILLED BY CAIN YET VICTORIOUS IN ABEL. PILGRAM MARPECK: Whatever of pain and torment the serpent (as the source of all agony) inflicts on the flesh and blood of believers, and thus bites the heel of Christ, his head is nevertheless crushed, overcome, and executed by the heel. The heel is all the weakness of the flesh and blood of Christ in all patience in His saints. This holy cross of Christ is the occasion of the enmity between the seed of the serpent and [the seed of] the woman, . . . [which] hates and opposes the wickedness, deviousness, deceit, and cunning of the serpent and his seed and resists it with all power by the word of truth, and carries out the strife and battle against all pain, death, sin, and hell . . . with true and proper patience, and thus will overcome eternally with Christ (the Lamb of patience) and achieve the victory. Thus the lamb was killed by Cain in Abel according to the flesh (meaning not the physical killing but because of patience), but it

---

[9]*Paraphraseon* (1541), 2:373; cf. CWE 44:244-45 and *Seconde Tome* (1549), 18v-19r. [10]*Opera* 1:75.

was victorious in the spirit according to creaturely love and faithfulness through patience which he showed to his brother. CONCERNING THE LOVE OF GOD IN CHRIST.[11]

4:11-12 God's Curse on Cain

CAIN'S CURSE WAS HARSHER THAN ADAM'S. MARTIN LUTHER: When punishment is inflicted on Adam because of his sin, the person of Adam is not cursed, but only the earth. . . . Here, in regard to Cain, the Holy Spirit uses a different language; for He curses the person. Why does He do this? Is it because Cain, the murderer, sinned more grievously than Adam and Eve? No, but because Adam was the root from whose flesh and loins Christ, the blessed Seed, would be born. This seed is spared, and for the sake of this blessed fruit the curse is transferred from Adam's person to the earth. Hence Adam bears the curse placed on the earth, but not a curse placed on his person. For from his descendants Christ was to be born. Because Cain forfeited this glory through his sin, his person is cursed, and he is told: "Cursed are you," to have us understand that he has been cut off from the glory of the promised Seed and that he would not have among his descendants a seed through which the blessing would come. LECTURES ON GENESIS 4:11.[12]

A HARSHER CURSE FOR A WORSE CRIME. CARDINAL CAJETAN: To Adam he had said, "Cursed is the earth on your account," but to Cain he says, "Cursed are you from the earth." Far greater is this latter punishment than the former one, because this crime was also greater than that one. There, the earth is cursed with respect to humankind; here, Cain is himself cursed by the very earth. And this curse is manifested not by words, but by effects, . . . namely, that the earth will not respond according to its power to bring forth fruits when Cain cultivates it. This is no small

punishment for a farmer. COMMENTARY ON GENESIS 4:11.[13]

CAIN'S SUCCESSES ARE ILLUSORY. JOHANNES BRENZ: What? Does God inflict upon Cain no other punishment than this external and mundane unhappiness? He marked Cain as a cruel fratricide, and yet he seems to be punished with no other penalty than sterile fields, exile and no assurance of a home. How much more tolerable does his condition seem than that of his brother, Abel! After all, the latter is deprived of life while the former remains alive. Even if some unhappiness in life befalls Cain, that unhappiness is nonetheless compensated by the blessing of life, which virtually all people regard as nobler and more precious: "Skin for skin!" [Satan] said. "People will give all they have to save their lives." As an additional point, we should notice how that external curse or punishment befalls the godly much more than the ungodly. Cain himself builds cities, establishes governments and seems incredibly fortunate. But the patriarchs wander around with no fixed home. What is the meaning of this inversion of things? Let me say that the punishment would indeed be more tolerable if, for committing fratricide, only a certain external unhappiness were inflicted in this bodily life. But what is said about the curse and exile in this place addresses only the literal external punishment: the prophetic and apostolic writings, however, understand that the curses that God's law pronounces against sin are more than corporal punishments and pertain chiefly to spiritual and eternal matters. Indeed, even if sin as an action seems temporary and transitory, it still merits an eternal and never-ending punishment: because not only do those who are addicted to sinning have an eternal desire to sin, as far as it lies in their power, but by

---

[11]CRR 2:546. [12]LW 1:290-91 (WA 42:214). [13]*Commentarii illustres* (1539), 39.

sinning they also turn themselves away from eternal good, and they are therefore most justly afflicted with eternal evil or punishment. . . . And so the condition of Abel is far better than that of Cain, because while Cain achieves a measure of external happiness in life but remains under an eternal curse, Abel loses the blessing of his bodily life yet remains in eternal happiness. Truly, God has thoroughly just reasons for why he should bless the ungodly in this life yet afflict the pious. COMMENTARY ON GENESIS 4.[14]

CAIN'S CRIME CONTAMINATED THE EARTH.
JOHN CALVIN: After Cain has been convicted of his crime, his sentence is now pronounced. And first of all, God appoints the earth as the minister of his vengeance, because it was polluted by Cain's impious and abominable parricide, as if he had said, "You just now denied before me the murder that you committed, but the senseless earth will itself demand your punishment." He does this, however, to emphasize the enormity of the crime, as if a kind of contagion flowed from it even to the earth, for which it was required that punishment be enforced. COMMENTARY ON GENESIS 4:11.[15]

WHY NOT EXECUTE CAIN? JOHANNES BRENZ: This is the punishment for murderers: that they always think a sword is about to fall on their necks, just as history and daily examples attest. What then? The Lord recites the penalty he imposed on Cain, which is a curse on the earth, sterility of the land and exile. God intends to be content with this penalty for the present, nor does he mean for Cain to be killed in turn by someone else. So he gives him what is, in effect, a safe-conduct. He imposes a mark on him, though Scripture does not tell us what it was. Some, however, have thought it was a trembling of the head or a ferocious appearance. This mark was on Cain as a public safe-conduct, so that no one

would dare to kill Cain, even though he was a murderer. "Whoever should kill Cain," he says, "will be punished sevenfold," that is, most severely. But is it to be wondered why God would give safe passage to a murderer? We should take note of some reasons in particular. One is that, because at that time the right to execute hadn't yet been instituted, God did not wish for murderers to be killed privately, by private individuals acting on their own rash impulse. For the right to execute was first instituted after the flood in Genesis 9. . . . Instead, everyone should observe their proper callings and leave others to the judgment of God. Another reason is that he wished to indicate by this example that, even in the midst of severity, mercy is pleasing to God. COMMENTARY ON GENESIS 4.[16]

4:13-14 Cain's Lament

UNBELIEF LEADS CAIN TO DESPAIR.
KONRAD PELLIKAN: Cain's words here could be explained as desperation, because he recognized that his sin was beyond expiation. . . . Perhaps he realized that the magnitude of his crime was so great that it would be impossible to be punished sufficiently in this world. He feared human beings more than God, the death of the body more than offending God. He did not trust sufficiently in God's words; he was desperate and deeply disturbed in his conscience, and that is why he spoke like this. COMMENTARY ON GENESIS 4:13.[17]

CAIN'S COMPLAINT IS A FALSE REPENTANCE. HULDRYCH ZWINGLI: He who moments earlier had impudently made excuses, nay, obstinately denied his sin, now clearly loses heart and despairs. Such is the way of all the impious. First they say, "There is no God." Then they are dissuaded from their impiety by

---

[14]Opera 1:76-77, citing Job 2:4. [15]CTS 1:208* (CO 23:93-94). [16]Opera 1:78. [17]Commentaria Bibliorum (1532) 1:8r.

the exhortations of no one, nor are they terrified by threats. But after an angry God puts their sin right before their eyes and they see there is no way out, then they shamelessly lose heart, tremble and moan, and at last despair, and those who had scorned God's mercy are unable to bear his justice. Annotations on Genesis 4:13.[18]

How Does Cain's Curse Differ from the Lot of the Pious throughout the Ages?

Wolfgang Musculus: How does it amount to a curse on an impious and murderous man that he should become a wanderer and fugitive on the earth, given that such trouble and misfortune in life frequently—indeed, usually—occurs more to the godly than to the ungodly? . . . My response is that this curse is not to be considered in terms of his external homelessness or the hardship of exile, but (first) more in the fact that Cain was banished not only from his homeland but also from the face of God, deprived of God's grace and protection on account of his monstrous and lethal crime. In addition, he was so prodded by the pricking of his conscience that he just wandered and floated along: anxious of heart, devoid of counsel, torn by fear of death and uncertain of his life, trusting no one, without faith or hope in God, most miserable and unhappy, even though persecuted by no one. So it is not without reason that this kind of life of total unhappiness be regarded as a curse. Far different are the comparable wanderings of the saints, . . . who are not abandoned by the grace and presence of God, under whose wings they are kept calm and safe, however much they are driven out by the ungodly. Commentary on Genesis 4:11-14.[19]

The Wanderings of the Faithful Differ from Those of the Wicked.

John Calvin: The faithful are sojourners upon the earth, yet they nevertheless enjoy tranquil lodgings. Difficulties often constrain them to move to some new place, yet wherever storms may carry them, they bring an untroubled mind. In brief, they dash about, constantly changing their place, and pass through the world in such a way that they find a home everywhere with the hand of God constantly supporting them. Such security is denied to the wicked. They find all creatures menacing, and even if those creatures were kindly disposed to them, the mind of the wicked is so disturbed that it would not allow them any rest. Consequently, even if Cain had not moved to a new place, he could not have shaken off the trepidation that God had implanted in his mind, nor did the fact that he was the first person to build a city prevent him from always being restless even in his own nest. Commentary on Genesis 4:12.[20]

4:15 Cain Is Spared to Be a Fugitive

The Mark of Cain. Andrew Willet: "God set a mark upon Cain," but not, as some read, that God made Cain to *be* a sign or mark. Rather, God set some visible mark upon Cain, whether it was a horrible trembling and shaking of his whole body (as in the Septuagint, which instead of "you shall be a vagabond and renegade" reads "you shall sigh and tremble"); or an exceeding shame and confusion, in that he ran from place to place to hide himself; or some visible mark set upon his face, as Lyra thinks. (Some Hebrews think it was a horn on his forehead; some, a letter; some, that a dog led him about; but these are human imaginings.) Certainly, whatever it was, it was a sign of God's wrath and not, as Josephus thinks, a token that God was appeased by Cain's sacrifice and forgave the punishment of his fratricide: for if God did not accept his sacrifice before, how much less would he after? Neither was this mark placed on Cain to

---

[18]ZSW 13:35. [19]*In Mosis Genesim* (1554), 137-38. [20]CTS 1:211* (CO 23:95).

exempt him from the assault of beasts, as though there were no one else alive on the earth but his parents. Given that this murder occurred, as is supposed, when Adam was in his hundred-and-thirtieth year, the world by this time was much replenished. And where the Lord says "Whoever slays Cain, etc.," he speaks of human beings, not of beasts. Wherefore God set this visible and fearful mark upon Cain both so that other men, seeing apparent signs of God's wrath upon him, might fear to commit the like, and so that he might have the greater punishment by having so wicked and miserable a life prolonged. Commentary on Genesis 4:15.[21]

It Was God's Perfect Justice That Protected Cain. Cardinal Cajetan: God says that for this very reason—namely, because *I* have punished you—it will not be lawful for just anyone to kill you, but anyone who kills you will undergo vengeance seven times. The term translated as *seven times* is not a relative term of the sort that *sevenfold* is (and as double and triple and quadruple are), but is rather a numerical term and an adverb of the number seven that signifies seven times. Nor is the meaning that he will be punished on seven successive occasions (because God would not judge the same thing twice), but that he will be punished perfectly and completely—just as what is said in the psalm, "silver tested by fire, purified seven times," doesn't mean seven occasions, but "perfectly." And so two things are stated here about the killing of Cain: that he will be punished, and that it will be done perfectly. Indeed, he *will* be punished, lest it be supposed that it is lawful for anyone at all to kill a person who has committed fratricide; but *perfectly*, lest it be supposed that a lesser punishment ought to be imposed as punishment for [such] a homicide because such a wicked person had been killed. To be sure, though a fratricide may deserve to be killed, he still cannot be lawfully killed by just anyone,

but only by the public authority whose right it is to declare and to execute in situations of this kind. For this reason, God didn't restrain Adam (who was the ruler at that time) from killing Cain, but he did restrain any private person in general when he said "*whoever* kills Cain." Commentary on Genesis 4:15.[22]

Cain's Survival Warns against Revenge. Konrad Pellikan: God permitted him to live either for his correction or his punishment—or rather, he was not to be killed as an example. Here the Lord decrees a law of gentleness: he detests revenge between people and reserves to himself the judgment of oppressors. Commentary on Genesis 4:15.[23]

We Should Pity Those Like Cain, Not Harm Them. Desiderius Erasmus: Hatred of one's neighbor is a step toward murder, and envy is diametrically opposed to love. Cain was not a child of God but was descended from the devil. Why? Because he fell away from his good creator and reverted to the devil, who, himself stung by jealousy, was the first to kill a human being by his deadly promptings. Cain called to mind his father's character in slaying Abel his brother. But what was the cause of his hate? Evidently, their dissimilar ways of life, wherefore they were also of different stock, even though by bodily descent they were full brothers. Each did resemble his father: Abel was an innocent man who warmed to the pursuit of doing well; Cain, by contrast, having conceived hatred for his brother, thought not about how to amend himself but about how to slaughter his brother. Just as in this case the wicked could not abide the godly, nor the devil's child abide the child of God, even so it shouldn't seem surprising . . . if those who have surrendered to the world should turn against you. They hate those who are blameless, but

---

[21]*Hexapla* (1608), 62. [22]*Commentarii illustres* (1539), 39-40, citing Ps 11:7. [23]*Commentaria Bibliorum* (1532) 1:8r.

no one should hate them in return. Because they are destined for death and serve the author of death, they devise death for others. It is our part to pity them, not to strike them back. PARAPHRASE OF 1 JOHN 3:10-13.[24]

CAIN DID NOT RETURN TO HIS SENSES. CARDINAL CAJETAN: His mind was moved more by his fear of the punishment of death than by the offense he committed against God, his parents and his brother. Someone banished from the face of God should therefore have begged for pardon, but he makes it clear that he did not return to his senses by this very fact: that he went away from the face of God, that is, from the special divine care that God exercises on behalf of the righteous. COMMENTARY ON GENESIS 4:16.[25]

---

[24]*Paraphraseon* (1541), 2:341; cf. CWE 44:189-90 and *Seconde Tome* (1549), 48v-49r. [25]*Commentarii illustres* (1539), 40.

4:16-24 CAIN AND HIS DESCENDANTS

[16]*Then Cain went away from the presence of the LORD and settled in the land of Nod,[a] east of Eden.*

[17]*Cain knew his wife, and she conceived and bore Enoch. When he built a city, he called the name of the city after the name of his son, Enoch.* [18]*To Enoch was born Irad, and Irad fathered Mehujael, and Mehujael fathered Methushael, and Methushael fathered Lamech.* [19]*And Lamech took two wives. The name of the one was Adah, and the name of the other Zillah.* [20]*Adah bore Jabal; he was the father of those who dwell in tents and have livestock.* [21]*His brother's name was Jubal; he was the father of all those who play the lyre and pipe.* [22]*Zillah also bore Tubal-cain; he was the forger of all instruments of bronze and iron. The sister of Tubal-cain was Naamah.*

[23]*Lamech said to his wives:*

"Adah and Zillah, hear my voice;
    you wives of Lamech, listen to what I say:
I have killed a man for wounding me,
    a young man for striking me.
[24]*If Cain's revenge is sevenfold,*
    then Lamech's is seventy-sevenfold."

a *Nod means* wandering

OVERVIEW: God did not put Cain to death for his crime. Instead, the text goes on to tell of his notable roles as the founder of a city—presumably the first city ever—and as the progenitor of a line of descendants that included those credited as the discoverers of important human arts, such as animal husbandry, music and the invention of tools and metalwork. Commentators then had to wonder why the line of Cain should be so favored with such worldly success.

One venerable question pertained to Cain's wife, namely, whom could he have married except his sister? Remarkably, the commentators of the Reformation era do not, as a rule, worry about the question of incest here, nor about the failure of this chapter to mention the births of daughters; instead, their working assumption is that there are many details that the text leaves unstated—and that laws of incest that came later obviously did not and could not apply to the children of Adam and Eve.

Cain's line also led, less admirably, to the figure of Lamech—a man of violence like Cain, but also evidently the world's first polygamist. Significantly, Lamech is the last of Cain's descendants to be named, even though there were presumably many others born during the ensuing centuries prior to the destruction of nearly all of humanity in Noah's day. However, as Luther notes, Lamech is a fitting representative of the entire line of "worldly" people—those who proved to be enemies of Seth and the godly who "began to call on the name of the Lord" in the verses that will conclude the chapter.

In many ways, commentators had an easy and obvious task in Genesis 4, for if there were some exegetical obscurities to puzzle over, there were no moral ambiguities—at least, if the narrative were read in light of the rest of the Bible, as all did. Consequently, Reformation exegesis here is rarely at odds with what has gone before, except in the matter of restraining allegorical excesses.

4:16-17 Cain's Wife and City

WHOM DID CAIN MARRY? KONRAD PELLIKAN: *Cain knew his wife.* Not his mother, not his sister, but some other relative. Indeed, there were many women whom Scripture does not catalogue, just as [it lists] not all men, but only those whose succession led to Abraham, then to Judah, whence Christ was born. COMMENTARY ON GENESIS 4:17.[1]

CAIN'S PRAISEWORTHY WIFE. MARTIN LUTHER: If Cain was not married at that time, it is surely a far more remarkable fact that later on he obtained a wife. Furthermore, the girl who married him must be lavishly praised. How could she be glad at the marriage of her brother, who was a murderer, accursed, and excommunicated? Moreover, she undoubtedly asked her father humbly why he was joining her, an innocent person, with the accursed man and was forcing her into exile. Cain's conduct, too, justifiably filled her with fear that he would dare to do to his sister and wife what he had dared to do to his brother. When Adam was bringing this marriage about, he, therefore, had to be extremely eloquent in order to persuade his daughter that she should not reject her father's command, and that, although Cain was cursed and was bearing the punishment for his sin, God would nevertheless preserve her, who was innocent, and would bless her. I have no doubt whatever that because of his wife, who married her bloodthirsty brother in holy trust in God and out of obedience to her parents, God bestowed many personal blessings on Cain through all his descendants. LECTURES ON GENESIS 4:17.[2]

THE INCONGRUITY OF CAIN WANTING CHILDREN. JOHN CALVIN: In fact, it is

---

[1]*Commentaria Bibliorum* (1532) 1:8v. [2]LW 1:313 (WA 42:230-31). Luther goes on to conclude that Cain was probably married already.

reported as a marvel that Cain, having shaken off the terror he had mentioned, should have turned his thoughts to having children. Indeed, it's a wonder that someone who was imagining that he had as many enemies as there were people in the world did not instead hide himself in some wilderness far away. It is also contrary to nature that he could receive any pleasure, dazed by fear as he was, and sensing God's hostility. Commentary on Genesis 4:17.[3]

Cain's Successes Mask His Futility.
Johannes Brenz: Cain aspires to world domination and to the highest glory and honor on earth, but the final outcome teaches that the flood would take away not only his dominion but also all his posterity, and replace his glory with utter disgrace. So what is the reason for everything falling the other way round for Cain? Surely this isn't the cause, that dominion over the earth is an evil thing and that glory should be shunned? Hardly! These things are gifts that God meant to create: God himself decided to make humankind lord over the earth [in Gen 1:28]. . . . And to Solomon it is said, "I will give you wealth, riches and glory," etc. Glory is thus a gift from God. Therefore Cain is deprived of dominion and glory not because these things are evil in themselves, but because he contends for them by evil means. He wanted to gain dominion and glory by murdering his brother. Hence, he is so far from acquiring what he is pursuing that instead he loses what he once possessed. The same should be said regarding other things. There is no dishonor in seeking provisions for your family: Christ commands us to ask for our daily bread. But it is, ultimately, dishonorable and unjust to seek such provisions through evil schemes. Commentary on Genesis 4.[4]

Cain Built a City Because of Fear and Pride. John Calvin: The exile Cain, whom

God had commanded to wander as a fugitive, not content with a private house, builds himself a city. But it is likely that, knowing himself to be an evil man, he would have been unsure of his safety within the walls of his own house and therefore devised a new kind of fortification. Truly, Adam and the others have homes that are dispersed among the fields for no other reason than that they are less afraid. Hence, it is a sign of an agitated and guilty mind, that Cain is overtaken by the urge to build a city in order to separate himself from the rest of humanity. But it also seems that pride was mixed in with his mistrust and anxiety, for he named the city after his son. Commentary on Genesis 4:17.[5]

Cain, Cornerstone of the Devil's City.
Konrad Pellikan: Cain is the patriarch of all the impious, the first stone in the edifice of the city of the devil, the archetype of the sons of this world who do not believe in God, who blaspheme his judgments, persecute their neighbors, envy their brethren's good fortune and despair of the mercy of God. But Abel, according to the testimony of Christ, is the first righteous one, the ancient church's first martyr for the sake of righteousness, chosen by God through faith and charity, and his works were accepted on that account. Commentary on Genesis 4:8.[6]

Cain Represents the False Church That Persecutes the True. Martin Luther: Here the church begins to be divided into two churches: the one which is the church in name but in reality is nothing but a hypocritical and bloodthirsty church; and the other one, which is without influence, forsaken, and exposed to suffering and the cross, and which before the world and in the sight of that hypocritical church is truly Abel,

---

[3]CTS 1:215* (CO 23:98). [4]Opera 1:80, citing 2 Chron 1:12. [5]CTS 1:216* (CO 23:98). [6]Commentaria Bibliorum (1532) 1:8r.

that is, vanity and nothing. For Christ also calls Abel righteous and makes him the beginning of the church of the godly, which will continue until the end (Matt 23:35). Similarly, Cain is the beginning of the church of the wicked and of the bloodthirsty until the end of the world. . . . Even then the divine promise began to work itself out, in that the serpent's seed bit the heel of the blessed Seed (Gen 3:15), just as we experience today. Therefore this lot should not frighten us. It should rather be a source of comfort for us to learn from experience that we are being dealt with by our adversaries in the way bloodthirsty Cain dealt with righteous Abel. We today are not the first to whom it happens that we are deprived of the name "church," that we are called heretics, and that those who kill us pride themselves on being the true and only church and maintain their claim to this name with the sword and with every sort of cruelty. . . . The true church is hidden; it is banned; it is regarded as heretical; it is slain. LECTURES ON GENESIS 4:4.[7]

CAIN AND ABEL REPRESENT TWO CONGRE-GATIONS. DIRK PHILIPS: From this Adam and his wife, Eve, have come two brothers, Abel and Cain, the one upright and the other godless. Abel was a child of GOD and a member of the Christian church; but Cain was a child of the devil and captured in his fellowship. The pious and righteous one was hated by the evil and murderous Cain, and was murdered out of the envy of his evil heart. And this is a clear symbol and witness that from that time on two kinds of people, two kinds of children, two kinds of congregations have existed on earth. They are, namely, God's people and the devil's people, God's children and the devil's children, God's congregation and the synagogue or assembly of Satan, and that God's children must suffer persecution from the devil's children. ENCHIRIDION.[8]

4:18-22 Cain's Clever Descendants

SOME BLESSING STILL REMAINS FOR CAIN'S OFFSPRING. JOHN CALVIN: Moses expressly celebrates the divine benediction that remained on that clan, which otherwise would have been deemed devoid and barren of all good. Let us know, then, that though they were deprived of the spirit of regeneration, the sons of Cain were nonetheless endowed with gifts that were not to be despised—even as the experience of all ages teaches us that, so far as concerns the cultivation of the present life, the rays of divine light have always shone upon the unbelieving nations, and we also see today how the Spirit's distinguished gifts are distributed throughout the whole human race. Moreover, the liberal arts and sciences have descended to us from people who were irreligious, and we are forced to consider that from them we have also received astronomy and the other parts of philosophy, along with the art of medicine and theories of political order. Nor is there any doubt but that the Lord has so generously enriched them with such excellent favors in order that their impiety might have less excuse. However, let us admire the riches of his favor that God has poured out on them in such a manner that we value far more highly the grace of regeneration, by which he specially sanctifies his elect unto himself. COMMENTARY ON GENESIS 4:20.[9]

ONLY THE RIGHTEOUS DESERVE TO BE REMEMBERED. WOLFGANG MUSCULUS: In his listing of Cain's descendants, Moses does not assign the number of years that each individual lived, nor does he commemorate the deaths of any of them. Neither does he mention that they bore any other sons, as he would do later, in the next chapter, in the catalog of Seth's

---

[7]LW 1:252-53 (WA 42:187). Luther credits Augustine's *City of God* in this context. [8]CRR 6:353-54, omitting many Scripture references. [9]CTS 1:218* (CO 23:99-100).

descendants. Instead, having touched the chief points in passing, he hastens on to the histories of the godly generations from whom Christ was to come. Thus we see that the godless offspring of the ungodly do not deserve to have their lives hallowed by perpetual remembrance. It belongs to the righteous to be remembered in perpetuity. Consequently, it always amazes me greatly to see how some men, who are otherwise not evil, can take such delight in the images of the godless—Julius, Nero, Domitian, Herod, Julian, and other tyrants like them—when they deserve that their memory should have faded away a long time ago with a hollow sound. COMMENTARY ON GENESIS 4:17-22.[10]

THE CHILDREN OF THIS WORLD SUCCEED AND RUIN THE CHILDREN OF GOD. MARTIN LUTHER: So far Moses has told the story of the generation of the children of this world. And when he has finished with this enumeration, he buries them as though there were no promise left for them either of the future life or of the present. For they had nothing besides that accidental blessing which granted them children and a livelihood. Nevertheless, they so increased in power and numbers that they filled the entire world. In the end they also brought about the downfall of the holy generation of the children of God, who had the promise of the future life; they worked havoc among them and plunged them into such a deep hell of ungodliness that only eight persons remained spiritually alive. LECTURES ON GENESIS 4:23.[11]

4:23-24 Lamech's Polygamy and Savagery

POLYGAMY WAS NOT INVENTED BY GOD. WOLFGANG MUSCULUS: Here we see the origins of polygamy. Marriage, by which two are conjoined in one flesh, is commended as instituted by God at the very beginning of the

world itself. Polygamy, however, was introduced by human fancy later on, in the seventh generation, by this man Lamech. Granted, even some of the godly made use of polygamy, but with a good intention, for the sake of increasing their offspring; but most polygamists served the desires and lusts of the flesh with an evil resolve. Now the world is such that there is great cause to hope that monogamous partners will use marriage to raise offspring to be not so much numerous as godly and upright. COMMENTARY ON GENESIS 4:19.[12]

LAMECH'S POLYGAMY. MARTIN LUTHER: I myself do not think that he became a polygamist solely because of his lust, but because of his desire to increase his family and because of his desire for rule, especially if, as his name indicates, the Lord at that time punished the descendants of Cain either with the plague or with some other disaster. LECTURES ON GENESIS 4:19.[13]

POLYGAMY WAS AN EXCEPTION, NOT THE NORM. KONRAD PELLIKAN: The sacred history announces that Lamech had two wives as if it were some rare event, not the custom of the men of that time. COMMENTARY ON GENESIS 4:20.[14]

LAMECH'S EMPTY BOAST. MARTIN LUTHER: These words are not to be taken in the same way as those addressed above to Cain; for those were God's words. These, however, are the words of an ungodly man and a murderer. They are not true; they are rash, fabricated after the pattern of the words Adam addressed to Cain. Why does Lamech make this announcement in his home and only in the presence of his wives, rather than before his church? Moreover, it is possible that the good

---

[10]*In Mosis Genesim* (1554), 151. [11]LW 1:318-19 (WA 42:234-35). [12]*In Mosis Genesim* (1554), 151. [13]LW 1:316-17 (WA 42:233). [14]*Commentaria Bibliorum* (1532) 1:8v.

and godly wives were perturbed by the murder their husband had committed. Therefore the ungodly murderer, in order to appear to be in a similar situation with his father Cain, desires to reassure his wives, so that they might not think that he ought to be killed. This is the custom of the wicked church: it wants to utter prophecies which have their origin in its own head. But such prophecies are futile. LECTURES ON GENESIS 4:23.[15]

LAMECH MOCKED GOD'S JUDGMENT ON CAIN. JOHN CALVIN: God had intended Cain to be a horrifying example to others that murder should be avoided at all costs, and to this end he marked him with a shameful stigma. Moreover, lest anyone imitate Cain's crime, God declared that anyone who killed him would be punished seven times more severely. But Lamech mocks the severity of God's declaration, impiously inverting it: for he seizes upon it as a greater license to sin, as if God had granted murderers some special privilege. Not that he would seriously think so, but being destitute of all sense of piety, he promises himself impunity and at the same time, in jest, invokes God's name as an excuse. COMMENTARY ON GENESIS 4:24.[16]

SAVAGERY WAS CAIN'S LEGACY. WOLFGANG MUSCULUS: Lamech was a violent and godless man, and the things he said to his wives here about his homicides were said not as if they concerned some hidden crime but one done openly, and he was moved not by repentance but by arrogance. And what he added about Cain, he added in order to set them forth as a threat to punish seventy-sevenfold, lest someone off in the future plan *his* murder on account of the slaughters he had perpetrated. Indeed, I think Moses wanted to relate these things about Lamech, namely, that he took two wives and that he killed both a man and a boy, in order to record the godlessness, malice and tyranny of Cain's posterity. COMMENTARY ON GENESIS 4:23-24.[17]

LAMECH AS A TYPE OF THE WORLD AND THE SERPENT'S SEED. MARTIN LUTHER: Lamech is a type of the world, by which Moses wishes to show what sort of a heart, will, and wisdom the world has. It is as if he were saying: "This is the way the seed of the serpent conducts itself. This is the way the children of this world conduct themselves. They amass riches; they pursue pleasures; they strive after power, and by their tyranny they misuse it against the true church, which they pursue and kill. But while they commit such great sins, they have no feeling of alarm; but they are proud and smug." LECTURES ON GENESIS 4:24.[18]

---

[15]LW 1:320 (WA 42:236). [16]CTS 1:222* (CO 23:102). [17]*In Mosis Genesim* (1554), 149-50. [18]LW 1:322 (WA 42:237).

4:25-26 ADAM AND EVE BEGET SETH

²⁵*And Adam knew his wife again, and she bore a son and called his name Seth, for she said, "God has appointed^a for me another offspring instead of Abel, for Cain killed him."* ²⁶*To Seth also a son was born, and he called his name Enosh. At that time people began to call upon the name of the LORD.*

a *Seth sounds like the Hebrew for he appointed*

OVERVIEW: From the violent and immoral Lamech, the narrative turns to the birth of Seth, who is presented as a replacement for the godly Abel. The whole of the chapter to follow will make clear that it is from Seth that the line of godly worshipers descended to Noah, who was prophesied at birth to be destined to deliver his people in some way. The children of Adam and Eve were thus split into two contrasting lines of descent: Cain and Seth. But even the "Sethites" would prove to be unsteady in their allegiance to godliness.

Reformation commentators make two characteristic moves in this passage. First, they attend to the implications for marriage and family by emphasizing how it is an act of faith and courage that Adam and Eve did not despair but, instead, ventured to conceive another child. These commentators' pastoral instincts emerge especially in reflections on what Adam and Eve must have felt in the wake of losing one son to murder and the other to such a heinous defection. Second, the cryptic closing verse, that "people *began* to call upon the name of the Lord," piques intense interest. What world of disarray must lie behind this unexplained passing remark? Reformation commentators, so actively engaged in restoring purity of worship to the church of their own day, have their answers ready at hand.

4:25 *The Birth of Seth*

EVE'S DEVOTION TO GOD'S PROMISE.
WOLFGANG MUSCULUS: Eve was endowed with a singular hatred for the serpent and its seed, so that she fiercely desired the blessed seed through whom the head of the serpent would be crushed, and she depended on God's promise with unwavering faith. She had been deceived earlier in the case of Cain, but now with firm faith she believes she has a son from whom would come the serpent's vanquisher and victor. If only those of us who are Christians were endowed with a similar hatred for that old serpent and with an equal desire for our blessed and promised seed and Savior! But now, who can keep from mentioning how dull we are at hating Satan and seeking Christ with zeal? COMMENTARY ON GENESIS 4:25.[1]

"SAINT EVE" AND THE BIRTH OF SETH.
MARTIN LUTHER: Eve, the mother of us all, is deservedly praised as a most holy woman, full of faith and love, because she so gloriously extols the true church in the person of Seth without paying any attention to the Cainites. She does not say: "I have another son in Cain's place." She prefers the slain Abel to Cain, although Cain was the first-born. It is, there-

[1] *In Mosis Genesim* (1554), 154.

fore, the outstanding glory not only of her faith but also of her obedience that she is not provoked at the judgment of God but herself changes her own judgment. . . . She does not give way to her motherly affection. She does not excuse or minimize her son's sin. But she herself also excommunicates the excommunicated Cain and sends him away with all his descendants into the jumble of nations which live without any sure mercy, except insofar as they have obtained accidental mercy as beggars, not as heirs. Since the pope's church has invented such a vast swarm of saints, it is indeed amazing that it did not give a place in the list to Eve, who was full of faith, love, and endless crosses. Lectures on Genesis 4:25.[2]

Seth Was Named by His Mother.
Konrad Pellikan: His mother imposed a name on Seth . . . by which it was signified that children of God are not born naturally but are bestowed by him. Commentary on Genesis 4:25.[3]

Adam and Eve Continued to Grieve over Their Children. Johannes Brenz: So how do you think the parents would have felt after they discovered that their son Cain, of whom they had expected the very best, had killed his brother with such enormous savagery? In the face of such sadness, it would be no wonder if they were engulfed in mental anguish and were wasting away—especially Eve, given that womanly nature is usually weaker and less able to bear adversity. There are some who think Adam and Eve were so seized by stupor that they mourned this calamity and abstained from embracing one another for a hundred years. They infer this from Genesis 5[:3], below, "Adam lived 130 years and begot a son in his own image," etc., but the point should be proved from the sources. Indeed, this passage can be understood so that during those hundred years he assuredly begot sons and daughters, but among

them Seth was the special one. But however one may regard this hundred years of mourning, it certainly cannot be denied that both of them were stricken with the deepest of sorrows. They called to mind their own sin that they committed in paradise, they reopened the wound that they had received by sinning, and they imagined that they themselves were to blame for one brother killing another so savagely. In fact, if they had not sinned in paradise, this savagery of their son would not have ensued—and a hellish fire thereby ignited within them once again. So, what should the miserable parents have done? Should they have killed Cain, too? But the right to execute murderers was not yet established (as in Gen 9). Surely they shouldn't have killed themselves as well, but should they have raged against themselves? Should they have despaired of their salvation and wholly abandoned their duties? Nothing could be worse, for that would not heal the evil but rather add one evil to another. What should they have done, then? They should have acknowledged the sin that they had long ago committed. They also should have believed that their sin was forgiven on account of the virgin's son. Finally, they should have called on God to help, borne this cross patiently and persevered in their calling. Commentary on Genesis 4.[4]

4:26 Calling on the Name of the Lord

Worship Did Not Begin with Seth, but the Church Took Firmer Shape. John Calvin: It is a foolish contrivance to say that God then began to be called by *other* names, because Moses isn't censuring wrongheaded superstitions here. Rather, he is commending the piety of a single family that worshiped God

---

[2]LW 1:325 (WA 42:239-40). [3]*Commentaria Bibliorum* (1532) 1:8v. [4]*Opera* 1:72-73; *the text goes on to offer the faithful grieving of Adam and Eve as a consolation to those who have inadvertently caused the death of their child or whose children have become degenerate.*

in purity and holiness at a time when, among other families, religion had become vitiated or extinct. To be sure, there is no doubt but that Adam and Eve and a few others from among their children were themselves true worshipers of God. But Moses means that the flood of impiety in the world at that time was already so great that religion was hastening to the brink of destruction, because it remained only among a few individuals and did not flourish in any one group. It is easy to deduce that Seth was an upright and faithful servant of God. However, after he had begotten a son like himself and had a properly constituted family, the face of the church begins to be distinctly visible and the worship of God is set on a course that would remain for the coming generations. Such a restoration of religion has been effected also in our time. COMMENTARY ON GENESIS 4:26.[5]

SETH THE REFORMER. JOHANNES BRENZ: Wasn't the name of the Lord called on before this? Weren't Adam and Eve, or Abel, true worshipers who called on God? Certainly they were, but when Moses writes, "Then the Lord's name began to be invoked," he indicates without obscurity that when Abel was killed and Cain excommunicated, the public worship of God declined among the people. In fact, those who were then from the families of Adam's other sons, as well as from Cain's family, were not especially attentive to the teachings of religion, especially concerning the seed of the woman. Because of Cain, each of them feared to preach the true doctrine about the woman's seed, that is, Christ, lest they be killed by Cain just as Abel had been killed. So even if Cain had not, perhaps, put a stop to all sacrifices, the public proclamation about the seed of the woman and his worship, that is, the faith and prayer that are typically nurtured by sacrifices, had completely died out. But God raised up Seth, together with his son, so that they restored this doctrine and reformed (as we are accustomed to say) God's

church, even though they saw themselves threatened with great danger in this matter. We have an example of this in our own times, that the restoration of the true doctrine of piety in the church corresponds with danger to all life and prosperity. Nonetheless, Seth and his son Enosh were undisturbed by these dangers. They also were an encouragement to their father Adam, who by that time, owing to the deep wound he suffered from Cain's bloodshed, had possibly grown weary of life, consumed by grief, and had ceased to care properly about providing religious instruction. As a consequence, the offspring of Seth and Enosh were preserved from the flood, and their seed now sits at God's right hand. COMMENTARY ON GENESIS 4:26.[6]

WHAT WAS SO NEW ABOUT CALLING ON THE NAME OF THE LORD? WOLFGANG MUSCULUS: It is not unreasonable to ask here why Moses says that the name of the Lord began to be invoked at the time of Seth and Enosh. What should we say about Abel? While he was alive, did he not also worship God and call on his name? And Cain, too, when he offered a sacrifice to the Lord from the fruits of the earth, did he not worship the same God with Abel? Should we then suppose that Adam and Eve had abstained from worshiping God until this point in time? By no means! What, then, does Moses mean . . . ? I could argue that the name of God as YHWH was manifested only at that time by the teachings of Seth and Enosh, and therefore God began to be known, worshiped and invoked not merely as *Elohim* but as YHWH, that is, *He Who Is*. Moses himself seems to support this view when he doesn't simply say "Then God began to be called upon," but "Then the name YHWH began to be called upon." That is, then at last the true knowledge of God as *He Who Is* became known in the church of the godly and God began to be

---

[5]CTS 1:224* (CO 23:103). [6]*Opera* 1:82.

invoked by that name YHWH. But I by no means support this view. I think a surer response lies along these lines: First, Moses speaks not of just any sort of worship of God and invocation of his name, but worship of such a kind that wholly differed from that of Cain and all the impious. I don't mean that every external rite for worshiping God was totally excluded, but rather that even external worship could not be performed by the impious with a sincere heart and upright faith. So even if Cain worshiped God with external sacrifices just as Abel did, he still lacked sincerity of faith, which is more or less the defining mark of true worship of God. Second, Moses does not deny that the Lord was invoked also by Adam and Abel from the very beginning. But since the line of godly people who rightly called on the Lord stemmed neither from Cain nor Abel but from Seth, he added this phrase on account of the beginnings of that church and its fuller knowledge, adoration and invocation of the divine name, in order to remind us that [the sort of worship] that began with Abel grew somewhat cool for a while after his death, but with Seth and Enosh it sent forth new shoots and acquired greater strength. COMMENTARY ON GENESIS 4:26.[7]

HOW DID THEY "BEGIN" TO CALL ON GOD'S NAME? ANDREW WILLET: Now, when the worship of God began to be corrupted and profaned in the wicked posterity of Cain, Adam, Seth, and others of the righteous seed began publicly to exercise religion and to have their holy meetings and assemblies for the service of God. Some read it as if then God's *name* began to be profaned when called upon, as by giving the name of God to beasts, trees and plants. But "invocation" here is taken in the better sense, and Moses is describing the practice of the church and righteous seed in those days. We likewise reject the notion that the name *Jehovah* began now to be called upon, whereas previously he was invoked by the name *Elohim*, for Cain and Abel offered sacrifice to Jehovah (Gen 4:3, 6). Wherefore the true meaning is . . . that now the church of God, having increased to a full number, made a public separation in their worship from the generation of the wicked and began to worship God in a solemn manner, apart from the others. COMMENTARY ON GENESIS 4:26.[8]

---

[7]*In Mosis Genesim* (1554), 153. [8]*Hexapla* (1608), 64, crediting Mercerus.

5:1-5 THE BOOK OF THE GENERATIONS OF ADAM

[1]This is the book of the generations of Adam. When God created man, he made him in the likeness of God. [2]Male and female he created them, and he blessed them and named them Man[a] when they were created. [3]When Adam had lived 130 years, he fathered a son in his own likeness, after his image, and named him Seth. [4]The days of Adam after he fathered Seth were 800 years; and he had other sons and daughters. [5]Thus all the days that Adam lived were 930 years, and he died.

a Hebrew *adam*

OVERVIEW: Nearly all of Genesis 5 is comprised by a list of the descendants of Adam through Seth; similar lists will appear also in Genesis 10 and 11, eventually tracing a line of descent to Abraham. In all three cases, commentators were regularly hard pressed to find suitably edifying material for readers and found themselves forced to make the most of any extra word or phrase. So it is here: there is essentially nothing to say about most names in this list. Hence, commentators focused exclusively on three—Enoch, Methuselah and Noah—for the obvious reason that these three are the only figures adorned with any details at all.

The opening sentence that announces this as Adam's genealogy, however, is itself interrupted by a curious flashback to Genesis 1:26-27, to the creation of Adam and Eve in the likeness of God, and by the further statement that their son Seth was fathered by Adam "in his own likeness, after his image." What is meant by Adam's image? Origen had taken the phrase as figuring the unity of the divine Son with God the Father; Augustine saw a contrast implied between Seth and Cain that also signaled the conflict between the "two cities."[1]

Reformation commentators had their own preferred readings. As a rule, they are friendly to Augustine's long narrative of conflict between the people of God and their enemies and, thus, to identifying Seth as standing in the line of the righteous. But Protestant exegesis is perhaps even more concerned here to stress that while the line of descent running from Adam through Seth may be the line that God will favor, it remains also a line of sinners who have inherited above all their parents' depravity.

5:1b-3 Adam's Image and Likeness

OUR CREATION IS A LESSON THAT BEARS REPEATING. KONRAD PELLIKAN: The creation of humans by God is again commended and inculcated, as it were, so that we might know for whom we exist and that we ought to live so as to remember what was taught: how to acknowledge and worship the Lord and love him with complete confidence, and how to emulate the image of God, namely, in mercy, prudence and beneficence. COMMENTARY ON GENESIS 5:1.[2]

THE IMAGE OF GOD VERSUS THE IMAGE OF ADAM. MARTIN LUTHER: Adam was created after the image and similitude of God, or the image was created by God and not begotten; for he did not have parents. He did not remain in this image but fell away from it through sin. And so Seth, who is born later on, is not born after the image of God but after that of his father Adam. That is, he is like Adam; he is the image of his father Adam, not only in the shape of his face but also in likeness. He not only has fingers, nose, eyes, bearing, voice, and speech like his father but is also like him in the remaining qualities both of mind and of body, in manners, character, will, etc. In respect to these Seth does not reflect the likeness of God, which Adam had and lost, but the likeness of his father Adam. But this is a likeness and image which was not created by God but was begotten from Adam. This image includes original sin and the punishment of eternal death, which was inflicted on Adam on account of his sin. But just as Adam recovered the lost image through faith in the future Seed, so Seth did also after he had grown up; for through His Word God stamped His likeness upon him. LECTURES ON GENESIS 5:3.[3]

WHAT ADAM LOST COULD NOT BE PASSED TO SETH. JOHN CALVIN: In saying that Adam begot a son after his own image, he refers in part to the first origin of our nature; but at the same time one should note its corruption and vitiation, which was contracted by Adam through his defection and has been passed

---

[1]See ACCS 1:116-17 for these motifs. [2]*Commentaria Bibliorum* (1532) 1:9r. [3]LW 1:339-40 (WA 42:249-50).

down to all his posterity. If he had remained upright, he would have imparted to all his children what he had received. Now, however, we read that Seth was corrupted along with all the others: because Adam, who had fallen away from his original state, could beget none but such as were like himself. COMMENTARY ON GENESIS 5:3.[4]

WAS ADAM HIMSELF UNSAVED? WOLFGANG MUSCULUS: We can easily imagine at least some reasons for conjecturing what would move some to this opinion, given that Adam was a sinner—indeed, the first one, from whom sin, death and condemnation was passed on to the whole human race—in addition to which, we do not read that he repented of his sin. . . . It's also true that, on account of his transgression of the divine command and the corruption that stems from sin, he deserved condemnation: nor would he have been able to extricate himself from these things. Nonetheless, one cannot conclude from this that he was less capable of salvation, which comes through Christ, than other mortals. Christ came into this world to save sinners. Adam was a sinner. Therefore, did not Christ come also on account of this, that the first man sinned? . . . Who would say that a doctor had cured his whole family if he did not cure the head of the household? The whole of it was diseased; who would not remove the head and root of the illness? If Christ was unwilling to save Adam, why did he himself descend to partake of his flesh? If Adam alone has been excluded from the grace of Christ, what was Luke's reason for tracing the origins of Christ's incarnation back to him? Who does not see that Luke did this to admonish us that Christ came in our flesh to save not merely a certain portion of it but the whole, from our head and first parent down to the last? COMMENTARY ON GENESIS 5:5.[5]

WEREN'T CAIN AND ABEL IN GOD'S LIKE-NESS? PETER MARTYR VERMIGLI: Here, the

Scriptures wanted to indicate to us that we all derive our likeness to God from Adam. . . . But some ask why this isn't said also about Abel and Cain. The question is answered in this way: This likeness of God was placed in him so that a human being might rule and be in charge. This was not granted to Abel because he died a premature death. It was taken away from Cain as from one cursed by God and, more to the point, the earth was commanded not to bear for him. It was handed over to Seth, for he was a good man and he governed things well and justly. COMMENTARY ON GENESIS 5:1.[6]

ADAM'S LIKENESS WAS AN IMAGE OF CORRUPTION. ANDREW WILLET: "Adam begot a son in his own likeness" is not to be understood of the shape and image of his body, for Cain too was in outward shape like to Adam. Neither is it to be taken for the image of virtue and piety in his soul, for Adam had lost that image, and virtue is not engendered by nature. Besides, Abel had the image of his father's virtue before Seth. Neither is this said here because the image of mankind was continued and preserved in Seth, in that not only did Abel die without issue but Cain's posterity was extinguished in the flood: for, the flood notwithstanding, Cain still might be said to be after Adam's image, seeing that the world was increased by him. Instead, *likeness* here signifies that original corruption that descends unto Adam's posterity by natural propagation, which is expressed in the birth of Seth—not of Abel, because he had no offspring; nor of Cain, so that it might appear that even the righteous seed by nature are subject to this original depravation. And yet Seth bore the image of Adam differently than did Cain, because Seth's seed was sanctified of God, who determined in Seth and his seed to make good

---

[4]CTS 1:228-29* (CO 23:106). [5]*In Mosis Genesim* (1554), 158; the question stems from an excerpt from Irenaeus that Musculus finds in Eusebius, *Ecclesiastical History* 4.28. [6]*In Primum Librum Mosis* (1569), 25r.

217

the promise made to Adam regarding the woman's seed, that it should break the serpent's head. Commentary on Genesis 5:3.[7]

Adam's Likeness Was Nothing Like the Image of God.

David Chytraeus: A brilliant witness to the doctrine of original sin may be observed . . . [where] it says that "Adam begot a son in his image and likeness." . . . The emphasis on the pronoun *his* ought to be carefully weighed. In the beginning, Adam was formed in God's image, adorned with light and wisdom, rightly acknowledging God; in next place, his will was turned toward God; and finally, the obedience of all his powers conformed with the dictates of God's law, which had been implanted in his mind. Now, after the fall, the divine image has become horribly deformed, and [Adam] begets a son according to *his* image and likeness, that is, one similar to himself not only in the features of his body and the arrangement of his members, but also in all the conditions of his soul, namely, the darkness of his intellect, his abhorrence of God, the absence of reverence, faith and love for God in his will and the obstinacy of his heart—on account of which he is liable to the wrath of God and to bodily and eternal death, unless he should seek the remission of his sins through the coming Seed. Commentary on Genesis 5:3.[8]

Seth Was in Adam's Image, Infected with Self-love and Original Sin.

Huldrych Zwingli: In the end, what else should we suspect as the cause of such a foolish achievement, other than love of self? Adam regarded himself with wonder and reckoned that he was not unworthy to have a greater authority than that which he possessed, namely, over the beasts. . . . Here we have the source of our double dealing, namely, *selfishness*,[†] that is, loving one's own self. From this has poured forth everywhere whatever is evil among mortals. This is why humans are already as good as dead; by no means were they

meant to beget degenerate offspring, no more than a wolf should give birth to a sheep, or a raven to a swan. The children of our first parents were therefore in no better condition than they were, nor than their entire posterity. . . . In our first parents, our nature was vitiated; it sins by doing nothing but loving itself in all things, and if God leaves it to itself it thinks of nothing noble or honorable, just like a runaway servant. That is the propensity toward original sin, then, to sin by love of oneself. This propensity is not sin per se, but it certainly is its source and character. . . . What is really monstrous is that while God made humans to *his* image, Adam after sinning begot children like himself: sinners, of course. Annotations on Genesis 5:3.[9]

Seth's Complete Solidarity with Adam.

Wolfgang Musculus: How is it to be understood that when Seth was born, it is written that Adam begot a son after his image and likeness, when nothing of this was said about Cain nor even of Abel, neither of whom can we deny were true sons of Adam? There are various opinions. . . . In my view, it is wholly fitting that the image and likeness of Adam, in which it is written that Seth was begotten, be referred to those things that were found in Adam as a prototype when he begot this son. Regarding Adam's nature, he was a man, endowed with reason; regarding his dignity, he was created from the earth according to the image of God; regarding his corruption, into which he fell by sinning, he was liable to sin, to multiple calamities and to death and decay. So, that Seth is said to be begotten according to the image and likeness of Adam should be referred to nothing else than those things I've just listed, which are also detected in Seth, namely, that by nature he was a man, born from a human being; as to

---

[7]*Hexapla* (1608), 67, crediting Junius. [8]*In Genesin* (1576), 203-4. [9]ZSW 13:37, 38, 40; [†]*philautian*.

his dignity, he succeeded to the place of Cain, who was excommunicated by God, so that he was the lord and head of the descendants who would follow after; regarding his corruption, he was a sinner, wretched, mortal and corruptible, just as Adam was, too. Nonetheless, the fact that these things could also be set forth from Cain and Abel, who were themselves also like this, does not hinder them from doing more to confirm my view. Indeed, when these things were written, the Holy Spirit did not wish to propose anything specially to be looked for in Seth that would differ from the usual simplicity or be more abstruse, but simply to teach about that conformity of nature, condition and corruption that obtains between Adam as the head of our race and all of his offspring. COMMENTARY ON GENESIS 5:3.[10]

----

[10]*In Mosis Genesim* (1554), 156-57.

5:6-20 SETH AND HIS DESCENDANTS

[6]*When Seth had lived 105 years, he fathered Enosh.* [7]*Seth lived after he fathered Enosh 807 years and had other sons and daughters.* [8]*Thus all the days of Seth were 912 years, and he died.*

[9]*When Enosh had lived 90 years, he fathered Kenan.* [10]*Enosh lived after he fathered Kenan 815 years and had other sons and daughters.* [11]*Thus all the days of Enosh were 905 years, and he died.*

[12]*When Kenan had lived 70 years, he fathered Mahalalel.* [13]*Kenan lived after he fathered Mahalalel 840 years and had other sons and daughters.* [14]*Thus all the days of Kenan were 910 years, and he died.*

[15]*When Mahalalel had lived 65 years, he fathered Jared.* [16]*Mahalalel lived after he fathered Jared 830 years and had other sons and daughters.* [17]*Thus all the days of Mahalalel were 895 years, and he died.*

[18]*When Jared had lived 162 years he fathered Enoch.* [19]*Jared lived after he fathered Enoch 800 years and had other sons and daughters.* [20]*Thus all the days of Jared were 962 years, and he died.*

OVERVIEW: Faced with an unadorned list of fathers, sons and daughters as part of a divinely inspired Bible, Calvin surely spoke for many when he wondered why the Holy Spirit seems to have left so many details in silence—details that surely would have been of interest or benefit to us now. Brenz agreed: the entire chapter might easily *seem* superfluous! However, like most of their colleagues, both quickly cautioned readers not to judge too quickly, for there are often lessons in dry details, and for those who read with care, even the silences speak.

5:6-20 *From Seth to Enoch*

EVEN ARID GENEALOGIES HAVE THINGS TO TEACH US. JOHN CALVIN: Although we do not comprehend the design of the Spirit as to why great and truly memorable events should go unrecorded, it is our business all the same to reflect on many things that are passed over in silence. . . . Even from a bare and seemingly dry narrative, one can deduce what the state of affairs was in those times, just as we'll see in the proper places. . . . Moreover, the purpose for which this catalogue of generations was woven together was to inform us that among the large—or rather, enormous!—multitude of human beings, there was always a number, admittedly small, who worshiped God; and that this number was wonderfully preserved by heavenly protection, lest the name of God be entirely obliterated and the seed of the church fail. Commentary on Genesis 5:1.[1]

This Genealogy Is a Tale of Endurance.

Martin Luther: This is the greatest glory of the primitive world, that it had so many good, wise, and holy men at the same time. We must not think that these are ordinary names of plain people; but, next to Christ and John the Baptist, they were the most outstanding heroes this world has ever produced. And on the Last Day we shall behold and admire their grandeur. Likewise, we shall also see their deeds. For then it will be made manifest what Adam, Seth, Methuselah, and the others did; what they endured from the old serpent; how they comforted and maintained themselves by means of the hope of the Seed against the outrages of the world or of the Cainites; how they experienced various kinds of treachery; how much envy, hatred, and contempt they endured on account of the glory of the blessed Seed who would be born from their descendants. No one must think that they lived without the severest afflictions and endless crosses. These facts will be made manifest on the Last Day. Lectures on Genesis 5:1.[2]

This Chapter Leads to Noah . . . and to Christ.

Johannes Brenz: This fifth chapter seems largely superfluous and useless because, as you see, it contains only the lineage of certain patriarchs and their lifespans, which do not seem to pertain to us at all but rather do more to provoke us to impatience when we hear of how long were the lives of the patriarchs, some of whom exceeded nine hundred years while we scarcely reach ninety! But surely, if we carefully examine what is set forth for us in this chapter, we cannot fail to receive great benefit from it. At the outset, the genealogy of Adam through his son Seth is listed, up to Noah and the flood, making no mention in this chapter of Cain and his descendants or of the other sons of Adam, but only of Seth and the other direct ancestors of Noah. It is evident that this was done mainly on account of Noah, who was saved in the flood. However, because it was said at the end of the previous chapter that Seth and Enosh had restored godly teaching about the seed of the woman, and because Luke attests that these patriarchs were ancestors of Christ our Lord, for these reasons we should conclude that when the Holy Spirit describes the line of these patriarchs, the focus was on Christ above, so this reference would remind readers about Christ. Indeed, even if Cain and his posterity were mentioned earlier, they are then covered in darkness and more or less excluded from the book of life. Mention is made only of Seth and the other patriarchs from whom Christ was to be born, by which the Holy Spirit indicated that God takes great pleasure in that family from which Christ his Son would descend and in which Christ is found through faith. To be sure, God watches over other people with his general governance, but he looks out for the family of Christ his son above all, and for their sake he also blesses others who are their kin and neighbors. For the sake of Christ his Son, he saves the patriarch Noah from the flood, and afterward

---

[1]CTS 1:227* (CO 23:105).   [2]LW 1:334-35 (WA 42:245-46).

saves his descendants in Egypt, gives them the realm of Canaan, defends them in the midst of enemies, protects them in Babylon, restores them to their land and preserves them through the cruelest persecutions of Antiocus Epiphanes until Christ should be born. But if God took such great care to defend the ancestors of Christ according to the flesh, so that for their sake he sometimes overthrew kingdoms and destroyed monarchies, with how much more care will he defend and save believers in Christ, who by faith become true members of Christ and his kin, not only in the flesh but in the spirit? COMMENTARY ON GENESIS 5.[3]

CAIN'S DESCENDANTS ARE ONLY FOILS FOR SETH. PETER MARTYR VERMIGLI: These two generations of Cain and Seth lived at the same time. The latter was good; the former, wicked. Indeed, God would not allow the world to persist unless among the evil he had mixed in certain ones of his own, who in a way are the pillars and the mainstay of the world. And you should note this, that in Cain's genealogy the narrative was *not* so meticulous or exact, with the description of each one divided into three parts and the years meticulously computed [as is done for Seth's genealogy], because Cain's generation was bloodthirsty and violent. There is no other reason to mention them, except to commend God's longsuffering and the truth of his threats, so that they all finally perished in the seventh generation as they deserved. COMMENTARY ON GENESIS 5:3.[4]

SETH'S FAME LAY IN HIS DESCENDANTS. KONRAD PELLIKAN: Having passed over the descendants of the impious and left them to be forgotten, Scripture describes the lineage of those through whom the world was renewed a second time, namely, Noah. It is not to be understood that Adam had begotten no other sons prior to that time, after Cain and Abel, but it is written that Seth was begotten after

these others. His descendants would be saved in the flood to come, and from his seed Abraham would be begotten after Noah. COMMENTARY ON GENESIS 5:3.[5]

5:8, 11, 14, 17, 20: *"And He Died"*

STRANGE WORDING IN THIS GENEALOGY. JOHANNES BRENZ: It is puzzling in this account that Moses, when he lists the ages of the patriarchs, adds for each of them (except Enoch), "and he died." It sounds a bit unusual if, when so many years of life have been enumerated (say, seventy or ninety), it is added, "he died." What does Moses mean by this addition? First of all, he calls to mind God's law in paradise, as well as human sin and the wrath of God. Indeed, God's severity is so great that even if Adam and the rest of the patriarchs were reborn in Christ and received forgiveness for their sins, it still remains necessary for them to undergo the punishment of death according to the law of the Lord. So when God forbids us to sin, we shouldn't regard it as a joke but as something delivered with utter seriousness, and we should treat it with all diligence. COMMENTARY ON GENESIS 5:5.[6]

THESE PATRIARCHS WERE NOT AMONG THE WICKED KILLED IN THE FLOOD. PETER MARTYR VERMIGLI: The Hebrews allege a twofold reason for this saying. First, so that the wound of death recently introduced through Adam would be rubbed open, and he would be shown to have had so many descendants who were just as he had become: *mortal*, without a doubt. Second, because in the genealogy braided together here, there were many good and holy men of whom it is written that they died, and you shouldn't conclude that

---

[3]*Opera* 1:82-83. [4]*In Primum Librum Mosis* (1569), 25r. [5]*Commentaria Bibliorum* (1532) 1:9r, echoing Augustine, *City of God* 15.15. [6]*Opera* 1:84.

they were buried together with the rest of the mob of evil people in the waters of the flood, thus dying a violent and unnatural death. The first of these reasons is by far the more likely one, for the second could be known by adding up the years. COMMENTARY ON GENESIS 5:1.[7]

[7]*In primum librum Mosis* (1569), 24v.

5:21-27 ENOCH AND HIS SON METHUSELAH

[21]*When Enoch had lived 65 years, he fathered Methuselah.* [22]*Enoch walked with God[a] after he fathered Methuselah 300 years and had other sons and daughters.* [23]*Thus all the days of Enoch were 365 years.* [24]*Enoch walked with God, and he was not,[b] for God took him.*

[25]*When Methuselah had lived 187 years, he fathered Lamech.* [26]*Methuselah lived after he fathered Lamech 782 years and had other sons and daughters.* [27]*Thus all the days of Methuselah were 969 years, and he died.*

a Septuagint *pleased God* b Septuagint *was not found*

OVERVIEW: Nothing in this genealogy was more fascinating than its concise, cryptic reference to Enoch, who "walked with God, and he was not, for God took him." In this one-sentence narrative, exegetes could find a host of questions—and more than a few answers. First of all, there was the only relatively mundane matter of what it meant to "walk with God." Beyond the expected attributes of personal holiness or righteousness, Reformation commentators saw other ingredients that were especially pertinent in their own day. Luther extolled Enoch as a model for ministry, including the aggressive proclamation of the gospel; others observed with interest that Enoch was a married man with children, which surely argued that celibacy was not a prerequisite for either godliness or fruitful ministry.

Naturally, commentators also pondered just exactly where Enoch was taken, and what his removal was supposed to teach us. For many, Enoch was a testimony to the resurrection, but there still remained some question as to whether he was fully in heaven or whether he was waiting for the final blessed state. Just barely discernible in the excerpts below one may hear echoes of the controversy over "soul sleep" that was to provoke Calvin and others against views they attributed to certain Anabaptist writers.

The typological resemblance of Enoch to Christ was not missed, nor a similar resemblance to Elijah, who was taken up to heaven in a chariot. The connection to Elijah proved troublesome, however, on account of canonical and extracanonical references to both Elijah and Enoch as end-time figures. By and large, Protestant writers are concerned to reign in such speculations—sometimes by means of a positive use of allegory or typology.

Enoch's son Methuselah stands deep within his father's shadow, but the longest-lived figure in the Bible cannot but elicit comments in his own right. While details of his life draw little interest (there being no such details), his advanced age is commonly the springboard for general remarks on the long lives of these patriarchs. Such remarks seem to serve no particular agenda, except nostalgia for a purer age.

5:24 Enoch Walked with God

ENOCH WAS MEANT TO GIVE HOPE TO THE PATRIARCHS. MARTIN LUTHER: The inference is universal: Adam died; therefore he was a sinner. Seth died; therefore he was a sinner. Infants die; therefore infants have sinned and are sinners. This is what Moses wants to point out when he states of the entire series of patriarchs that they died even though they were sanctified and renewed through faith. But in this series there shines forth like a star the most charming light of immortality, when Moses relates about Enoch that he was no longer among men and yet had not died but had been taken away by the Lord. Moses is indicating that the human race has indeed been condemned to death because of sin, but that there has still been left the hope of life and immortality, and that we shall not remain in death. It was for this reason that the original world not only had to be given the promise of life but also had to have immortality demonstrated to it by an example. Therefore it is stated about the individual patriarchs: "So many years he completed and died," that is, he bore the punishment of sin, or he was a sinner. But about Enoch Moses does not make this statement, not because he was not a sinner but because even for sinners there is left the hope of eternal life through the blessed Seed. LECTURES ON GENESIS 5:1.[1]

ADAM NEVER SAW THE RESURRECTION FORESHADOWED BY ENOCH. JOHN CALVIN: It is strange that Adam was deprived of this support for his faith and consolation. Given that God's terrible verdict—that "by death you shall die"—would have been constantly ringing in his ears, he was greatly in need of some source of comfort, so that he would have something else to call to mind on his deathbed besides the curse and his own extinction. However, it was a hundred and fifty years or so after Adam's death when God took Enoch, who was to be like a visible mirror of the blessed resurrection. Had Adam been enlightened about Enoch, he might have girded himself for his own departure with equanimity. COMMENTARY ON GENESIS 5:24.[2]

WALKING WITH GOD MEANT RESISTING SATAN AND PREACHING THE GOSPEL. MARTIN LUTHER: [Moses] exalts godly Enoch like a sun above all the teachers or patriarchs of the primitive world. From this we gather that Enoch had an unusual fullness of the Holy Spirit and outstanding courage, because he was bolder than the other patriarchs in offering resistance to Satan and the Cainite church. For, as we said above, to walk with God does not mean to flee into the desert or to hide in a nook but to go out according to one's calling and to offer resistance to the iniquity and malice of Satan and the world; moreover, to confess the Seed of the woman, to condemn the religion and the endeavors of the world, through Christ to preach another life after this life, etc. This kind of life godly Enoch lived for three hundred years, like a chief prophet and priest who had six patriarchs as his teachers. LECTURES ON GENESIS 5:21-24.[3]

ENOCH TRUSTED THE INVISIBLE GOD. DESIDERIUS ERASMUS: It was no impediment

---

[1]LW 1:332-33 (WA 42:244). [2]CTS 1:231* (CO 23:107-8).
[3]LW 1:344 (WA 42:252-53).

to the godly Enoch that he descended from an ungodly father.† For Holy Scripture bears witness to him, that he spent his time with God even while he lived on earth, namely, pursuing by faith not those things that are seen but those that are not seen, that is, those that are eternal and heavenly. For this reason he was taken up while still alive to those things that he loved, and delivered from death. For before he was removed from human fellowship, he lived in such a way that he seemed to live more in heaven than on earth, and as one who had committed nothing worthy of death, he also seemed unworthy to die. People should learn from his example, first of all, that the way to immortality is opened by faith and innocent living. He was taken away, therefore, because he was pleasing to God. But he pleased him chiefly by faith, without which no one can please God, however much one may otherwise abound with good deeds. For anyone who desires to be commended by God must first of all believe that a God exists who can do all things and who wills what is best. Then, that God exercises care over human affairs so as to ensure that the godly, who neglect the visible goods of this world and seek after the invisible God, will not be cheated out of their reward, however much they may be afflicted in this life; and that neither will the ungodly lack their punishments, even if in this age they seem to enjoy favorable breezes. It is to his faith, then, that Enoch owes this outcome (whether described as his glory or his happiness), that he was removed from human companionship and lives with God. PARAPHRASE OF HEBREWS 11:5-6.[4]

ENOCH IS NOT THE ONLY ONE EVER TO PLEASE GOD. WOLFGANG MUSCULUS: That Enoch was taken by God is clearly stated here, but *where* he was taken and *why*—beyond the fact that "he walked with the Lord"—is not to be read here. Accordingly, what the godly reader finds written should be accepted as beyond question, but what one does not see written should be judged not to pertain to oneself. Instead, one may say with Cyprian, "*Where* Enoch was taken, God only knows." . . . *Why* God took this Enoch seems to be expressed by what the text says, . . . and we can assign no other cause than that which is put here. Nonetheless, it's not meant to be a perpetual and necessary cause, as if it were always the case that anyone who walks with God ought to be taken by God in the way that Enoch and Elijah were. Otherwise, the rest of the patriarchs, who all agree were godly, would stand convicted of not having walked with God, since they were not taken in this way but rather just died. It is rightly surmised from their being taken that Enoch and Elijah pleased God. But it is not right to surmise that the rest of them, who were not so taken but were subjected to the common law of death, displeased God. Indeed, this is not the only proof or basis for God's good pleasure, that one be taken to heaven without having tasted death, for otherwise all those godly people who have died and we ourselves will be punished— along with Christ himself. But there are countless other proofs as well for the grace of God, from which assurance of his good pleasure can be drawn. COMMENTARY ON GENESIS 5:25.[5]

MARRIAGE AND FAMILY DO NOT IMPEDE WALKING WITH GOD. KONRAD PELLIKAN: To walk with God is to please God by one's innocence of life, to exhibit toward others a nearly heroic way of life, to attend to God as his servant and to experience his special grace. Nonetheless, just as with Noah and others, marriage and the proliferation of a family were not obstacles but did more to add to the example of these holy ones. Indeed, holy Enoch

---

[4]*Paraphaseon* (1541), 2:373; cf. CWE 44:245 and *Seconde Tome* (1549), 19r. †Erasmus has probably conflated the Enoch of Gen 5:18 with that of Gen 4:17.   [5]*In Mosis Genesim* (1554), 165-66.

begot Methuselah himself. But at the age of 365, Enoch was taken, and for reasons unknown: for the judgments of God are not to be fathomed. COMMENTARY ON GENESIS 5:23.[6]

BOTH ABEL AND ENOCH WERE SAINTS, DESPITE THEIR DIFFERENT ENDS. PETER MARTYR VERMIGLI: It is the opinion of the Fathers concerning Enoch that he was taken up by God and now lives—the same thing they assert about Elijah, who (as 2 Kings 2[:11] has it) was taken away to heaven in a fiery chariot. And they diligently record that the same blessing befell these two, who entered into diverse ways of life: one, Elijah of course, was unmarried and his wife and children are not mentioned; but the other, Enoch, begot sons, and among them was Methuselah. This demonstrates that marital status has little or no effect on who will cling to God, who will please him and who will be carried off to heavenly places. They also want to show us God's fairness and justice in taking this man. Having fallen by sinning, Adam was expelled by God, the same thing that we saw happen to Cain, above, but by his faith and piety Enoch was received by God. According to Hebrews 11[:5], "by faith" he "was taken up so that he should not see death." From this, the saints in the church knew how they might strengthen themselves and be comforted with hope for something better. For, having first seen Abel, a righteous man, killed by Cain, they could be shaken by some temptation. But later on, when they saw Enoch taken up like this on account of his faith and piety, they were right to conclude at once that the saints would have both the cross and joys, given that these examples exhibited both. COMMENTARY ON GENESIS 5:24.[7]

ENOCH TEACHES ABOUT THE SABBATH REST THAT AWAITS. HULDRYCH ZWINGLI: Note here that Enoch was the seventh generation from Adam! But on the seventh day the Lord rested from every work. Therefore in Enoch the Sabbath is renewed and restored. For Moses does not say that he died, as he says of everyone else, but that he was taken away, namely, from all labor into the repose of the saints, that is, those who have worshiped God in true faith. By Christ this place was then called the bosom of Abraham, on account of his remarkable faith and uprightness; Elijah also was received here, as well as however many have walked innocently before God. Everything here is filled with lessons and mysteries. First, we learn that the Sabbath is nothing other than innocence of life and conduct before God. Second, that we who now live in the seventh age are ourselves "Enochs," so we ought to walk innocently with God. Third, a kind of everlasting Sabbath is signified here (which Isaiah calls "from one Sabbath to another"), namely, the saints' rest, into which God will receive us, if with Enoch we have lived innocently before him, having endured our labors to the end. ANNOTATIONS ON GENESIS 5:22.[8]

ENOCH AND THE RESURRECTION. JOHANNES BRENZ: When Moses writes that Enoch did not die but was taken by God, he shows that God wanted to attest to the other patriarchs by this miracle that there remains a life to come and that there is a resurrection of the dead. Indeed, it was explicitly being proclaimed that there is another life after this one, because by seeing one patriarch die after another and no one returning from another world who could explain the future state, they were coming to regard statements about the other world as vain. For this reason, God raised up the patriarch Enoch, who led a most godly life for many years and then, while the patriarchs looked on, was taken up on high by the Lord so that there would be clear proof that he

---

[6]*Commentaria Bibliorum* (1532) 1:9v. [7]*In Primum Librum Mosis* (1569), 25v. [8]ZSW 13:40; cf. Lk 16:22; 2 Kings 2:11; Is 66:23.

had been taken by God and that there is another life to come in which Enoch would live with God in utter happiness. COMMENTARY ON GENESIS 5:24.[9]

ENOCH'S DEATHLESS TRANSITION TO HEAVEN. MARTIN LUTHER: The flesh indeed cannot be without pain; but since the conscience has been quieted, death is like a fainting spell through which we pass into rest. That pain of the flesh would have been absent in the innocent nature; for we would have been taken away as if by a sleep, and, awaking shortly, we would have been in heaven and would have lived the angelic life. But now, when the flesh has been corrupted by sin, it must first be destroyed by death. So Enoch, perhaps when he was lying in some place covered with grass and was praying, fell asleep; and as he slept, he was taken away by God without pain and without death. LECTURES ON GENESIS 5:21-24.[10]

ENOCH STILL AWAITS THE GENERAL RESURRECTION. JOHN CALVIN: Being taken in this way was a gentle and joyful departure from this world. Yet he was not received into celestial glory but was freed only from the miseries of the present life, until Christ should come, the firstfruits of those who will rise again. And since he was one of the members of the church, it was necessary for him to wait until they all go forth together to meet Christ, that the whole body may be united to its Head. COMMENTARY ON GENESIS 5:24.[11]

ENOCH DID NOT FULLY ENTER HEAVEN UNTIL CHRIST DID. ANDREW WILLET: Because it is said that God took away or translated Enoch, popish writers imagine that Enoch is yet alive in his flesh, together with Elijah. On the contrary: given that Elijah is said to be taken up into heaven, or that he went into heaven (2 Kings 2:11), where Enoch also "walked with God," we cannot believe that

they entered heaven in their whole humanity. That prerogative was to be reserved for Christ, for the apostle says that he has prepared "a new and living way into the holy place for us by his veil, that is, his flesh" (Heb 10:20). Therefore, Christ's flesh must make a way into heaven before any one else's flesh can enter. COMMENTARY ON GENESIS 5:24.[12]

WILL ENOCH RETURN? JOHANNES BRENZ: According to the epistle of Jude, it appears that as the time of the flood was drawing near, Enoch harshly attacked the corrupt behavior of his age and urgently prophesied of the coming flood, using the opportunity to provoke people with these threats so they might repent. From this, stories arose even among Christians that before the last judgment Enoch would come, along with Elijah, to preach repentance. What is said of Elijah's coming is taken from Malachi and fulfilled in John the Baptist, as is abundantly shown elsewhere, but what is said about Enoch's coming is taken from this passage in Genesis, where it is written that he did not die, and from the epistle of [Jude†]. But one should regard it as the truth of the matter that Enoch prophesied before the flood of the coming wrath of God and exhorted the people to repent. Elijah, on the other hand, who is John the Baptist, predicted that one day the Jews would be driven out, and he warned them to come to their senses. So also will it occur in the last days, before the whole world is destroyed, that God will raise up certain ones who will call people to repent, so that if not all, at least some may be saved. I suspect, then, that either an apostle or some other pious person in the early church uttered allegories to the effect that Enoch and Elijah (that is, preachers of repentance) were going to come prior to the last judgment and the world's

---

[9]*Opera* 1:85. [10]LW 1:349 (WA 42:256). [11]CTS 1:232* (CO 23:108). [12]*Hexapla* (1608), 70.

consummation through fire. The [apostle] himself interpreted these preachers allegorically, in order to urge people to repent, but others referred this to these patriarchs' own persons. But let us imagine that Enoch and Elijah are sent to us every single day, as often as we are called to our senses, so that we may escape the coming judgment. COMMENTARY ON GENESIS 5:5.[13]

THE REAL ENOCH MUST BE DISTINGUISHED FROM FABLES. ANDREW WILLET:
Concerning the end and reasons for Enoch's translation [to heaven], we first admit that God thereby wished to comfort the righteous that, notwithstanding the sentence pronounced against Adam, there was a way of righteousness whereby Adam's lost state might be recovered. Also, to minister comfort to the afflicted members of Christ, so that they should not doubt but that their reward is with God, just as Abel, though he had an untimely end, yet lived with God as Enoch did (so Theodoret). We also do not reject the inference here of Thomas Aquinas, that God wished to nourish the hope of life in his church: both by Enoch's translation before the law [was given] and by Elijah's, under the law. They were types representing the ascension of Christ, in whom the promise of salvation should be accomplished.

These causes of Enoch's translation may safely be received. But we do not agree with the book of Wisdom (which is not canonical scripture and we may therefore safely dissent from it) that he was taken away lest wickedness alter his understanding. For just as he walked with God before and God kept him in fear and preserved him from evil, so could God have guided him still, . . . even as Methuselah, Enoch's son and the longest lived of all the patriarchs, continued righteous to the end. Nor is the notion fit to be received that Enoch is kept alive to preach repentance at the end of the world and to maintain the gospel against

Antichrist, which is the common opinion of the papal professors. For there is no mention in Scripture of Enoch preaching at the end of the world, but only of the sending of Elijah, which is not to be understood of Elijah's person but of his spirit and zeal. COMMENTARY ON GENESIS 5:24.[14]

5:27 Methuselah's Long Life

METHUSELAH'S GREAT AGE REMINDS US THAT WE ALL FALL SHORT OF PERFECTION.
WOLFGANG MUSCULUS: It is not read that any mortal lived in this flesh longer than Methuselah, who nonetheless did not make it to a thousand years. But it is not without spiritual significance that none of the patriarchs, however long a life he was granted, lived a thousand years in this world. The number 1000 symbolizes perfection. . . . Yet none of the patriarchs reached this number of perfection while living in this life but died, all of them, before they had reached this summit—a fact that beautifully depicts for us how our present life cannot reach the perfection of piety and happiness as long as we remain in the flesh, however much we endure its many worldly cares. This is why it is finally necessary to die, that we might acquire by dying, then, what we could not attain while we lived. COMMENTARY ON GENESIS 5:27.[15]

WHY THESE PATRIARCHS WERE LONG-LIVED. KONRAD PELLIKAN: The extremely long lives of those fathers is to be ascribed more to the miracle of God than to the favorable climate, the perfection of human nature at that time or the healthful food. Nor does it seem to have been the common lot of many, but perhaps only of those of whom

---

[13]*Opera* 1:85, †reading Jude for *Iacobi* (James), which mentions not Enoch but Elijah (Jas 5:17). [14]*Hexapla* (1608), 71. Wisdom does not mention Enoch, but cf. *Midrash Rabbah* §25.1 (Soncino ed., 1:205) for the account of Enoch here. [15]*In Mosis Genesim* (1554), 169-70.

Scripture bears witness. Commentary on Genesis 5:24-27.[16]

On the Long Lives of the Patriarchs.

Andrew Willet: The causes of the long life of the patriarchs [are] four. The *natural* cause was the sound constitution of their bodies, which had not yet decayed, and the wholesome air, not yet corrupted with terrestrial vapors as after the flood. The *moral* cause was for the invention and discovery of arts and sciences. As Josephus writes, they caused [their findings] to be inscribed on two great pillars, one of brick and another of stone, so that if the world were destroyed with water, the second pillar might remain, and if with fire, the first would remain (for they had learned from Adam that the world would twice be destroyed). Josephus further states that the pillar of stone was to be seen in Syria in his time. The *civil* or *political* cause for the long life of the patriarchs was for procreation and for populating the world. The *theological* cause was so that God, by giving them such long life, might make trial of their obedience to see if they would use this benefit of long

life to the glory of God—which they did not, and therefore he shortened the human lifespan. Yet while they enjoyed this long term, the Lord would not allow any of them to attain unto a thousand years: not for the reason the Hebrews suppose, that God granted seventy of Adam's thousand years to David; nor for the reason Irenaeus mentions (which seems too curious), namely, to make good on what he said to Adam, "in whatever day you eat of it, you shall die," and because a thousand years with God is as yesterday (Ps 90:4), Adam died during that first "day," before he came to a thousand. Rather, God hereby wished to put the fathers in mind of their mortality, that although they lived many hundred years, yet none of them filled up a thousand, lest they have flattered themselves for their long lives. Seeing that a thousand is a number of perfection, God would let none of them attain to a thousand so that we might know that nothing is perfect here. Commentary on Genesis 5:5.[17]

---

[16]*Commentaria Bibliorum* (1532) 1:9v. [17]*Hexapla* (1608), 68, crediting Mercerus.

5:28-32 NOAH

[28]*When Lamech had lived 182 years, he fathered a son* [29]*and called his name Noah, saying, "Out of the ground that the Lord has cursed this one shall bring us relief[a] from our work and from the painful toil of our hands." *[30]*Lamech lived after he fathered Noah 595 years and had other sons and daughters. *[31]*Thus all the days of Lamech were 777 years, and he died.*

[32]*After Noah was 500 years old, Noah fathered Shem, Ham, and Japheth.*

a *Noah* sounds like the Hebrew for *rest*

OVERVIEW: Noah's appearance here at the end of Genesis 5 is in effect no more than a cameo, for he will be alone in the spotlight for nearly all of Genesis 6 through 9—after yet one more curious interruption at the outset of chapter 6. Here, however, he is of interest for two reasons.

First, his father's prophetic benediction struck many Reformation commentators as excessive: Noah was surely virtuous and his deliverance in the ark was itself wonderful, but Noah should not be confused with Christ, who alone has truly fulfilled Lamech's prophecy. This was by no means a Protestant discovery, for Origen had made the same observation long before.[1]

Second, some attention is paid to the advanced age, even relative to these other long-lived patriarchs, at which Noah began to father children. Reformation commentators are quite sure that his delayed start, along with the small number of his sons, is due to the design of providence—but they are in no particular agreement as to what that design was meant to be.

5:29 Noah as the Deliverer of His People

NOAH WAS NOT THE MESSIAH, BUT CHRIST IS THE TRUE NOAH. HULDRYCH ZWINGLI: When Noah was born to him, Lamech said, "This one will bring to us rest from the works and labors of our hands." . . . But the time had not arrived, nor was he the one who was promised—only the type of that one, as Peter testifies. Thus, the promise that God made to the first mortals was guarded by them, even though it had been explained in but a few words. And the faith, or rather hope, that they held toward that Seed did not disappoint them. These most holy men were sometimes mistaken about the person or time, to be sure, but never about the promise itself. Nor was their faith false, even if Noah was not the one. Indeed, they always hoped in another

one, truly, in the blessed Seed that was Christ. Therefore this is a prediction and figure of Christ the coming liberator, who was one day going to bring rest to the human race from their works. Indeed, works cannot save. The "earth" of our bodies is cursed, it brings forth nothing but spines and thorns as long as we live; however much it is tilled, it always fights and opposes the spirit. Therefore we long "to depart and be with Christ." He truly brings us rest, he truly brings solace, he is the true Noah, father of the age to come. ANNOTATIONS ON GENESIS 5:29.[2]

LAMECH THOUGHT NOAH WAS THE PROMISED SEED. MARTIN LUTHER: It was a unique manifestation of divine mercy that Enoch was taken away to the Lord alive. . . . Thus after Lamech has seen that his grandfather has been taken away to Paradise without pain, sickness, and death, he assumes that Paradise with all its glory will follow at once. It is his opinion that Noah is the promised Seed and that he will bring about the restoration of the world. LECTURES ON GENESIS 5:28-29.[3]

MISTAKING NOAH FOR CHRIST. JOHANNES BRENZ: From the very moment of his birth, the patriarchs conceived a great hope concerning this Noah, and they supposed they would be freed from their miseries by him. Hence, they imposed the name Noah on him, which signifies *paraclete* or *comforter*. . . . I think an angel of the Lord foretold his birth and indicated that Noah would carry out great works on earth and renew the human race. Although the angel intended this of the renewal of the human race after the flood, the good fathers understood it of the true and spiritual renewal that was promised through the woman's seed, or through Christ. Thus,

---

[1]See ACCS 1:122-23; none of the Reformation writers examined seem aware of Origen on this point. [2]ZSW 13:41-42; cf. 1 Pet 3:20; Phil 1:23. [3]LW 1:352 (WA 42:259).

they hoped Noah was that coming Savior or Christ who had been promised from the beginning of the world. But even if these poor fathers were wrong in their opinion, . . . it still appears from this, first, just how much evil they endured in that age and how they were afflicted in this bodily existence, not only by the various hardships they themselves bore but also in seeing that the customs of the age were thoroughly corrupt; and, second, with how much desire they sighed for the coming of Christ. COMMENTARY ON GENESIS 5:29.[4]

LAMECH'S HOPES FOR NOAH WENT BEYOND WHAT GOD TOLD HIM. JOHN CALVIN: There is no doubt in my mind, then, but that Lamech hoped for something rare and unusual from his son—and that, too, by the prompting of the Spirit. Some think he was deceived, in that he believed Noah was the Christ, but they furnish no reasoning that suits their case. It is more probable that because something great was promised concerning his son, he did not refrain from mixing his own imaginings with the oracle. Even saints are sometimes prone to exceed the bounds of revelation, and it thereby comes to pass that they are in touch with neither heaven nor earth. COMMENTARY ON GENESIS 5:29.[5]

5:32 Noah: Late Marriage, Small Family

NOAH'S RELUCTANCE TO MARRY. MARTIN LUTHER: Why shall we suppose that he refrained from marriage, unless it was because he saw all his cousins degenerating into giants or tyrants and filling the world with violence? Accordingly, he thought that he would rather do without children than have that kind. Therefore I think that he would never have married unless he had been urged and commanded either by the patriarchs or by some angel. LECTURES ON GENESIS 5:32.[6]

NO OBVIOUS REASON WHY NOAH WAITED

TO HAVE CHILDREN. PETER MARTYR VERMIGLI: Why would Noah (considering him on his own) have begotten children so late in his life? Rabbi Solomon says this happened because sons received by him any earlier would have easily been corrupted by the vices of others, but God wanted them to be still at a young age at the time of the flood so that they would not be able to be infected by the abominable crimes of the others. In brief, he argues like this: if these sons had been born a long time before the flood, they would have been either righteous or wicked. If wicked, they would perish with the others on that account. Sorrow would thereby have been added to their righteous father, which God did not want to happen. If good, and if they too had begotten children, and if Noah himself had had still others as well, all of whom God wanted to save for Noah's sake, the ark would have needed to be much larger and Noah would have been unfairly wearied in building it. This is an amusing interpretation, but it will seem sufficient for Christian readers . . . either that these were not the first of his sons or that Noah was denied offspring for as long a time as it pleased God, for it is not right to rely on fables so curiously contrived. COMMENTARY ON GENESIS 5:32.[7]

GOD WANTED NOAH'S FAMILY TO BE SMALL. ANDREW WILLET: Although the patriarchs began to beget children at diverse ages—Mahalaleel and Enoch at 56 years, Jered at 162, Lamech at 282, Noah at 500—it is not to be imputed to Noah's holiness that he so long abstained from marriage, seeing that Enoch who was translated [to heaven] on account of his godly life had children at age 65. Neither (as Pererius conjectures) is it likely that Noah had other, older sons who were dead before the flood came: for whereas it is said of

---

[4]*Opera* 1:86. [5]CTS 1:234* (CO 23:109). [6]LW 1:356 (WA 42:261). [7]*In Primum Librum Mosis* (1569), 26v.

all the other patriarchs that they begot sons and daughters besides those expressly mentioned, no such thing is said of Noah, that he begot sons and daughters besides these three. The Septuagint reads, "Noah begot three sons, etc.," insinuating that these were all their sons. . . . I do not think that Noah deferred his marriage until he was 500 years old, nor that, though married, he abstained from the company of his wife all that time. Rather, seeing that God intended to save Noah and all his sons from the flood, God arranged that Noah would not abound with offspring as his fathers before him, lest they too should have followed the wickedness of that age and so have perished with the rest. The Lord ensured that there might be enough to replenish the world again, and it was more to God's glory to increase the world afterward by so small a number. COMMENTARY ON GENESIS 5:32.[8]

---

[8] *Hexapla* (1608), 69.

6:1-7 GOD GRIEVES OVER INCREASING WICKEDNESS

[1] *When man began to multiply on the face of the land and daughters were born to them,* [2] *the sons of God saw that the daughters of man were attractive. And they took as their wives any they chose.* [3] *Then the LORD said, "My Spirit shall not abide in[a] man forever, for he is flesh: his days shall be 120 years."* [4] *The Nephilim[b] were on the earth in those days, and also afterward, when the sons of God came in to the daughters of man and they bore children to them. These were the mighty men who were of old, the men of renown.*

[5] *The LORD saw that the wickedness of man was great in the earth, and that every intention of the thoughts of his heart was only evil continually.* [6] *And the LORD was sorry that he had made man on the earth, and it grieved him to his heart.* [7] *So the LORD said, "I will blot out man whom I have created from the face of the land, man and animals and creeping things and birds of the heavens, for I am sorry that I have made them."*

a Or *My Spirit shall not contend with*   b Or *giants*

OVERVIEW: Although Noah was briefly introduced in the previous chapter, the biblical narrative pauses to set the stage for the impending judgment of the flood by calling attention to the increasing wickedness of the human race. Clearly, human behavior did not improve in the generations that followed Cain and his vengeful descendant Lamech in Genesis 4, and the opening paragraph in Genesis 6 only ratifies that decline. Yet this exasperated account of human depravity is at risk of being upstaged by the overwhelming obscurity of the actors here. Traditional commentators all wanted to know: Who were these "sons of God"? Who were the daughters after whom those sons apparently lusted? And then, who were the *Nephilim* (a word often translated as "giants," perhaps in agreement with their description as "mighty men")?

Reformation views here were fairly traditional, ranging among the common patristic opinions that these sons of God were either fallen angels of some sort, or sons of Seth who were now perversely favoring beautiful Cainite women over the godly women of their own line, or maybe just powerful but ungodly men who valued beauty over purity. There is a bit more certainty that the *Nephilim* are just giants, but some also want to stress that they may have been gigantic only with respect to the power or tyranny or even arrogance they exercised with respect to others, especially the godly.

Despite exegetical uncertainty on these lexical details, no one doubted that wickedness of several kinds must have been abundant at this time. The point is driven home especially by the report that God had seen the evil of the human heart and grieved—indeed, repented!—of having made them, and that he would destroy not only people but the earth's animals and birds as well. Protestant exegetes, very much like their forebears, use the text to decry the world's lack of piety and moral rectitude here. But they are exercised perhaps more than their forebears to give a good account of how it is that the Lord "was sorry" or repented of making humankind—a topic that surely drew special attention in light of the Reformation's revival of an Augustinian understanding of God's utter prevenience, omniscience and changeless constancy. Not surprisingly, most are quick to invoke the doctrine of divine accommodation here.

6:1-2 *The Sons of God . . . Took Any They Chose*

Sins against the Second Table Were Now Added to Those against the First. Martin Luther: The original world

. . . had wisdom, godliness, worship, and religion superb in appearance but adulterated and false. Therefore since wickedness contrary to the First Table was aboil, there followed the depravity of which Moses is going to speak in this chapter, namely, that men first polluted themselves with their lusts and then filled the world with tyranny, bloodshed, and injustice. Accordingly, when the ungodly world has scorned both tables in this way, God, who is a consuming fire and jealous (Deut 4:24), comes to inflict judgment. He punishes ungodliness in such a way that everything turns to ruin and neither king nor subject remains. Therefore we may assume that the closer the world was to Adam's Fall, the better it was; but it has deteriorated from day to day until our times, in which live the dregs and, as it were, the ultimate dung of the human race. Lectures on Genesis 6.[1]

Dissipation Was Possible Even without Wine. Johannes Brenz: Compare what Scripture says here with what Christ relates later on in Matthew 24[:38] and Luke 17[:27]: "For in the days before the flood," says Christ, "people were eating and drinking, up to the day Noah entered the ark." What then? Is it a sin to eat and drink? And at that time, before the flood, how could they have had raucous dinner parties when wine was not yet in use, nor eating flesh or fish? My reply is that eating and drinking are not only not sinful in themselves, but they are even ordained by God for sustaining the life of the body. However, to eat and drink so that you become a glutton, pursuing idleness, neglecting your responsibilities and holding God's word in contempt, well, this is nothing but impiety. And even if wine was not in use prior to the flood, nor flesh or fish, still, the fruits people enjoyed were extremely tasty and sweet, and the water

---

[1]LW 2:6-7 (WA 42:266).

was delightful to drink, because, obviously, it was not yet tainted from the flood. And although the earth had been cursed on account of sin, people were not yet forced to exert so much labor in cultivating the land as they had to do after the flood. So people were conducting themselves then in idleness and were preoccupied with conviviality. From these arose their contempt of God's word and neglect of their calling. Observe, therefore, how complacent feasting leads in those regions to destruction at the hands of foreigners, as in Isaiah 5 and Daniel 5. COMMENTARY ON GENESIS 6:1.[2]

WHO WERE THESE "SONS OF GOD"? WOLF-GANG MUSCULUS: Here Moses documents a specimen, as it were, of that corruption which began to increase as mortals multiplied on the earth. But these [beings] are variously explained. Some read it of fallen angels, that is, evil spirits that took visible forms and had relations with women, which the ancients called *incubi* and *succubi*. They think they are called either angels of God or sons of God here on account of their spiritual nature, but their opinion fully deserves to be rejected in this place. Others, including some recent writers, identify them as Seth's offspring, whom they wish to have called "sons of God" because they were from the nation of the godly. . . . Others, whose opinion seems more likely to me, explain it neither of Seth's offspring nor of the nation of Cain in particular, but more generally of the sons of great and powerful leaders, who began to abuse the power of their elders, to the point that their lusts made them arrogant. Thus, having violated every law of purity and honor, they violently took from among the daughters of common everyday folk, and each would choose women for himself, whether married or virgin, relatives or strangers, all for no other reason than to abuse them to satisfy their lust. COMMENTARY ON GENESIS 6:1-4.[3]

GOD'S LAW WAS VIOLATED BY LOOKING FOR BEAUTY, NOT PURITY. DIRK PHILIPS: The ordinance is the divine uniting of two persons who are born pure and holy out of God the Father, through faith in Jesus Christ in the Holy Spirit. . . . That is then a true Christian marriage which may stand before the LORD in his congregation. For thus it was instituted in the beginning by God himself in paradise, but that after time this good divine ordinance has come into great misuse, . . . [for] "the children of God looked upon the daughters of humanity, that they were beautiful and fair, and took as wives those whom they wanted" and did not observe the first ordinance God made with Adam and Eve in Paradise, but looked much more on the beauty of the daughters, for they were all spoiled and became flesh. Therefore, they followed the desires of their evil flesh. Now when God saw that he said: "My spirit will not always be judge among people, for they are fleshly. . . ." From this it is clear what an abomination it is before the Lord to break his ordinance and to act against it. ABOUT THE MARRIAGE OF CHRISTIANS.[4]

EVEN THE GODLY CAN BE DERAILED BY THE POWER OF THE FLESH. HULDRYCH ZWINGLI: Moses does not say merely that they had taken wives for themselves, . . . but he magnifies the guilt of those who seized wives and daughters sheerly from lust. Indeed, he explains why such shameful deeds inundated the earth, so that even pious people clung to carnal affections. For this is the power of the flesh, this its character, that even the pious and "the sons of God" are captivated by concupiscence. The sons of God were thus knocked off course: they were guided more by the affections of the flesh than by the fear of God; they gave more consideration to what concupiscence de-

---

[2]*Opera* 1:88. [3]*In Mosis Genesim* (1554), 171-72. [4]CRR 6:558*.

manded than what rectitude requests. Annotations on Genesis 6:2.[5]

The Roots of Two Families and Two Worlds.

Peter Martyr Vermigli: There
are some, with whom all usually agree, who
think *sons of God* here rather signifies men
from the family of Seth. They are spoken of in
this way because they had privately given up
divine worship and pure religion and they are
described here as even having fallen into
disgrace by this time. These sorts of men are
called sons of God in a special sense, because
as many as received that [name] would have the
power to be made God's sons, and after a
fashion they would be one sort of angel,
namely, God's messengers, for it belonged to
them not only to offer sacrifices but also to
preach and teach people. So now, according to
this explanation, you see the world of human
beings divided into two congregations: one
descended through Cain, an earthly people,
carnal, impious and wholly estranged from
God; the other derived from Seth, in which
piety and divine worship flourished. Commentary on Genesis 6:2.[6]

Seth's Sons Married the Daughters of Cain.

John Calvin: At that time, it was as if
the world was divided into two parts, because
the household of Seth cherished the pure and
lawful worship of God that the rest had
abandoned. To be sure, the entire human race
had been made for the purpose of calling upon
God, so that pure religion should have reigned
everywhere. However, because the greater part
of them had prostituted themselves either to
contempt of God or to depraved superstitions,
it was fitting that the small portion that God
had adopted to himself for special privilege
should remain separated from the others. It
was base ingratitude, therefore, that Seth's
offspring mingled themselves with the
Cainites and other godless people, because
they wantonly deprived themselves of the

inestimable grace of God. Commentary on
Genesis 6:1.[7]

The Flood Stemmed from the Degeneration of the Righteous, Not the Ungodly.

Martin Luther: Moses desig-
nates as sons of God those people who had the
promise of the blessed Seed. It is a term of the
New Testament and designates the believers,
who call God Father and whom God, in turn,
calls sons. The Flood came, not because the
Cainite race had become corrupt, but because
the race of the righteous who had believed
God, obeyed His Word, and observed true
worship had fallen into idolatry, disobedience
of parents, sensual pleasures, and the practice
of oppression. Similarly, the coming of the
Last Day will be hastened, not because the
heathen, the Turks, and the Jews are ungodly,
but because through the pope and the fanatics
the church itself has become filled with error
and because even those who occupy the leading
positions in the church are licentious, lustful,
and tyrannical. This is intended to produce
dread in all of us, because even those who were
born of the most excellent patriarchs began to
be conceited and depart from the Word.
Lectures on Genesis 6:1-2.[8]

These Sons of God Abused Authority.

Peter Martyr Vermigli: *Sons of God* can
also refer to the sons of rulers or judges, who
are themselves called "gods," because they carry
out God's office and they should be distinguished by God's authority, seeing that they
are his ministers, as you find in Romans [13].
Thus, these men, who especially ought to have
fostered justice, violated it—carrying off the
daughters of humble families, perhaps forcibly
snatching them away, because they were
abusing their position. Already, then, the
reasons are splendidly clear as to why God

---

[5]ZSW 13:42-43. [6]*In Primum Librum Mosis* (1569), 27r. [7]CTS
1:238-39* (CO 23:111). [8]LW 2:12 (WA 42:270).

justly determined to send the flood. COMMEN-
TARY ON GENESIS 6:2.[9]

6:3 *"My Spirit Shall Not Abide Forever"*

EVEN GOD'S WARNING REMINDS US OF HIS
PATIENCE. WOLFGANG MUSCULUS: Note the
anthropopathism that is attributed to God here:
interior monologues, such as occur in humans, do
not apply to God. Nonetheless, by this expression
we are meanwhile directed to God's patience, by
which he is accustomed to show forbearance to
sinners for quite a long time; to God's mercy, by
which the severity of his justice is broken, lest he
rush to punish those who offend; and, once again,
to God's justice, which he employs in order to
exact the punishments deserved on a daily basis
by our impenitence. Let us consider that God is
disposed more to watch over us than to destroy
us; more to do good to us who submit to him
than to exact a penalty from those who resist. Let
us consider that it is due to our malice and
obstinacy when we are visited and corrected by
his justice, for he is slow to anger and quick to
show mercy. COMMENTARY ON GENESIS 6:3.[10]

GOD'S ANGER WAS NOT HASTY. JOHN
CALVIN: Since this would have been a horrifying example of God's anger, such that its bare
mention makes us grow fearful even now, it
needed to be explained that God was not
driven to haste by the heat of his anger nor did
he vent his rage more vehemently than was
appropriate. Rather, he was almost forced by
necessity to demolish the whole world down to
the ground, except for one single household.
Truly, most people do not restrain themselves
from accusing God of excessive haste when
human sins are punished, or else they picture
him to themselves as cruel. Therefore, lest
anyone should murmur, Moses here declares
(speaking in the person of God) that the
world's depravity was intolerable and more
obstinate than any remedy could hope to cure.
COMMENTARY ON GENESIS 6:3.[11]

GOD'S REBUKE SET AN AGENDA FOR
PREACHING. PETER MARTYR VERMIGLI:
When the Lord said, "My spirit will not
remain in human beings forever, . . ." to
whom did God say this? Some say to himself,
but I think it would have been spoken to
Noah and to the preachers of that time, so
that by these words they might admonish the
people and exhort them to come to their
senses, because now the evils of that age
would no longer be tolerated by God. COM-
MENTARY ON GENESIS 6:3.[12]

GOD'S EXASPERATION WAS VOICED BY
LAMECH OR NOAH. MARTIN LUTHER: These
words were spoken either by Lamech himself
or by Noah as a new discourse addressed to
the entire world. It was a public discourse or a
declaration put forward in a public convoca-
tion. After Methuselah, Lamech, and Noah
saw that by its sins the world was hastening
straight to its destruction, they came to a close
with this declaration: "My Spirit will no longer
judge among men. That is, we are teaching in
vain; we are warning in vain; the world does
not want to be improved." LECTURES ON
GENESIS 6:3.[13]

"FLESH" IMPLIES A DIVINE REBUKE. JOHN
CALVIN: It is in vain for the Spirit of God to
dispute with the flesh, which is incapable of
reason. Indeed, God calls human beings by the
name *flesh* as a mark of disgrace, even though
he had originally formed them in his own
image. Scripture's way of speaking here is
well-known, and those who restrict this name
to the inferior part of the soul are greatly
deceived. For since the human soul is vitiated
in every part, and our reason is no less blind
than our affections are perverse, the whole is
properly called *fleshly*. We should understand,

[9]*In Primum Librum Mosis* (1569), 27r. [10]*In Mosis Genesim*
(1554), 175-76. [11]CTS 1:240* (CO 23:113). [12]*In Primum
Librum Mosis* (1569), 27v. [13]LW 2:16 (WA 42:273).

therefore, that the whole person is flesh by nature, until by the grace of regeneration one begins to be spiritual. Now regarding Moses' words, there is no doubt but that they represent God's sorrowful expression of grievance together with a divine rebuke. Human beings ought to have excelled all other creatures on account of the mind with which they were endowed; but now, alienated from right reason, they are almost like cattle. Commentary on Genesis 6:3.[14]

Awaiting Repentance. Konrad Pellikan: The Lord said, willed and decreed that such human evil would not be tolerated for long, much less forever. Indeed, he saw that such defiance and incorrigibility was disinclined to obey either reason or human admonitions. "I created the beasts of flesh, but because humans too are flesh, I made them to be more than wild animals—with reason, understanding, and a sense of law. Yet so far, these human beings degenerate even unto bestiality, so that they abandon themselves to nothing but the flesh. Nonetheless, I will extend a time of repentance to them, up to 120 years, during which, if they pay no heed to changing their ways, I will suffocate them with a flood." Commentary on Genesis 6:3.[15]

120 Years Represented Time to Repent, Not Lifespan. Andrew Willet: Although it is true that man's life was shortened after the flood and thrice halved—from 900-odd to 400-odd (as with Arphaxad who lived 425 years), and then halved again from 400-odd to 200-odd (as with Serug who lived 230 years), and then almost halved to 100-odd (as with Abraham who lived 175 years)—yet we see that many of these [patriarchs] exceeded 120 years. With Jerome, Chrysostom, and others, we rather take this time set [by God] to be that space of years which God gave unto the old world for their repentance. [But this figure of 120] was not shortened by twenty years

because of their wickedness, as Jerome thinks, for the flood came 100 years after, when Noah was 600 years old (Gen 7:6). Neither need we say with Augustine that Noah was said to be 500 years old when he was but 480 because he had lived the most part of it: for Shem was but 100 years old two years after the flood (Gen 11:10), but now he should be 120 if Noah were then but 480 when he began to have his sons. Therefore this doubt is more easily reconciled, to say that this time was set before Noah was 500 years of age; but by way of anticipation, mention is made of Noah's sons before, because of the continuing of the story—just as we see in Genesis 2, where the creation of the woman is recorded after the seventh day, [even though] it was done previously. Commentary on Genesis 6:3.[16]

6:4 Giants, and Mighty Men of Renown

These Giants Were Notable for Their Arrogance, Not Their Stature. Martin Luther: Now he adds that wickedness had increased to such an extent that there were giants on the earth. Moreover, he explicitly states that from the cohabitation of the sons of God with the daughters of men there were born, not sons of God but giants, that is, arrogant men who usurped both the government and the priesthood. . . . Moses calls such men "giants," who usurp powers, both of the state and that of the church, and sin without the least restraint. . . . Giants were such men as boldly opposed the Holy Spirit when He warned, entreated, taught, and reproved through Lamech, Noah, and the sons of Noah. Lectures on Genesis 6:4.[17]

The "Mighty Men" Were Tyrants. John Calvin: Those who were the first to exercise

---

[14]CTS 1:242* (CO 23:114). [15]*Commentaria Bibliorum* (1532) 1:10r. [16]*Hexapla* (1608), 77, citing Mercerus and Pererius. [17]LW 2:32-33 (WA 42:285).

tyranny or power in this world, as well as excessive licentiousness and an unbridled lust for domination, began from these people. . . . These were men on an uncontrolled rampage, who exempted themselves from the common rank and file. Their first fault was pride, for they relied on their own strength and arrogated to themselves more than was lawful. Pride begot contempt of God, because, puffed up with disdain, they began to shake off every yoke. At the same time, they were also abusive and cruel towards others, for it can never happen that those who do not tolerate submitting to God will display self-restraint toward their fellow humans. Moses adds that they were "men of renown," by which he indicates that they boasted of their wickedness and were what are called "honorable thieves." In fact, there is no reason to doubt that they did have some quality that distinguished them from the crowd and procured for them favor and glory in the world. Nevertheless, under the magnificent title of *heroes*, they cruelly exercised dominion and acquired power and fame for themselves by injuring and oppressing their brethren. This, then, was the world's first nobility. And, lest anyone derive excessive pleasure from a long and dingy ancestral line, I repeat: this was the nobility, which raised itself on high only by pouring contempt and abuse on others. COMMENTARY ON GENESIS 6:4.[18]

6:5 His Every Intention Was Only Evil

JUSTIFYING THE FLOOD. PETER MARTYR VERMIGLI: The prophet now reviews the causes of the flood so that human beings would be seen to have been punished by God justly and not rashly. But he is also opposed to those who think that these floods and the world's other disasters are caused by fate or because the stars are in certain positions. Moses doesn't agree, but he first gives a diligent account of how our race had been corrupted at that time. First, he said that the

sons of God had gone in to the daughters of men, because that kind of crime besets men when they are not alone but in a considerable throng. Then, he described human beings as "mere flesh," because they did not think about anything that was spiritual or heavenly but paid heed only to their stubbornness, just like those who think they have quite a long time to come to their senses and won't be changed. Finally, he asserts that whatever they set out to do throughout their whole life, the thoughts of all were nothing but evil. To this point, he has related these things by means of a general statement, by which he speaks unfavorably of everyone insofar as they are human beings. But these conclusions are not to be read as exaggerations, for they truly characterize all people who had descended from Adam. COMMENTARY ON GENESIS 6:11.[19]

WILLFUL MALICE IS THE WORST SIN OF ALL. CARDINAL CAJETAN: The judgment of the flood takes its beginning from the divine gaze, and [Moses] rightly introduces God not as hearing but as seeing, so that every sort of certitude might be put down in writing. And the first thing recorded as having been seen was the malice in the human will. Not weakness, not passion, but that which is the worst thing in the will: *malice*. And it was not small or isolated, but immense, so that we might thereby understand that people had sunk into evil to such a degree that they were sinning from malice, and that they were incapable of correction. COMMENTARY ON GENESIS 6:5.[20]

THE FLOOD DID NOT END THE CONFLICT OF SPIRIT AND FLESH. KONRAD PELLIKAN: God saw that the malice of people had increased in the earth, and that every thought and imagining of the human heart was always and only evil. Above, God said that human

---

[18]CTS 1:246* (CO 23:116). [19]*In Primum Librum Mosis* (1569), 29r. [20]*Commentarii illustres* (1539), 46.

beings are flesh: let us therefore understand—and it is fitting for us to ponder—that those who are human are consistently of the flesh. What do *we* do that is any different from what God's *enemies* do? Indeed, the spirit lusts against the flesh and the flesh against the spirit: truly, these are mutually opposed to one another. Therefore the entirety of human thought is not only prone to evil but *is* wholly evil, from which the worst fruits also spring forth. And this is attested by God as true of human beings not only before the flood but also afterwards, as the prophets boldly declare. . . .† Therefore God looks down from heaven (speaking in a human fashion), and when he has understood that no spark of uprightness remains among people, he decides to destroy them once and for all. COMMENTARY ON GENESIS 6:5.[21]

REJECTING GOD'S DIAGNOSIS AND CURE. JOHANNES BRENZ: Among so many crimes, was the state of preaching God's word intact? It's no secret that the patriarchs diligently preached God's word about the true religion regarding the virgin's son and would have urged people to piety and modesty, as is clear in the cases of Seth and Enoch. But contempt for God's word was the worst of all: for they regarded those who called them to repent and warned them of God's punishment as fools and lunatics. This is the worst crime of all. It's just like a sick person on the very edge of death, who not only is afflicted with pain but is also so insane as to refuse treatment. So then, their crimes were so utterly severe that not only did they sin, but they also rejected and even condemned the teaching by which they were called from sin to righteousness. So, when the human race had come to such a pitch of evil that they even rejected the medicine of God's word, God arises up to avenge their iniquity. COMMENTARY ON GENESIS 6:5-7.[22]

THE HUMAN HEART WAS UNIVERSALLY

EVIL. ANDREW WILLET: From this text, we conclude (against Bellarmine) that original concupiscence is properly sin, because the imagination of the human heart is only evil. By nature, people have no free will to do any good, seeing that their thoughts are only evil. There is thus no good work so perfect but that it is blemished by our natural corruption, because it is said, "their thoughts are continually evil, etc." All these conclusions are denied by the papists, who therefore have devised two answers to this place: First, that Moses uses hyperbole here, because people's thoughts were for the most part evil, not altogether and only evil. Secondly, he is speaking only of the wicked, not the righteous, for Noah is here excepted, who is said to be just and upright (Gen 6:9). To answer Bellarmine and Pererius, first, this general speech admits no exception, for by nature the thoughts of mortals are only evil. For our Savior says "that which is born of the flesh is flesh" (Jn 3:6), and in this chapter they are said to be flesh (Gen 6:3); so by nature, then, all their thoughts were carnal and fleshly. Secondly, even Noah and other righteous people are altogether corrupt by nature: as Saint Paul says, "We were by nature the children of wrath, as were others" (Eph 2:3). Noah's righteousness was by grace, not by nature. COMMENTARY ON GENESIS 6:5.[23]

6:6-7 God Grieved—and Repented

HOW GOD REPENTS, OR NOT. JOHANNES BRENZ: What is said here seems amazing: "The Lord's heart was touched with sorrow," and (he says) "I repent that I made humankind." What could be more unchanging or more constant than God? What could be wiser than God? Yet it is not a mark of wisdom to say, "I hadn't thought." Didn't God see long

---

[21]*Commentaria Bibliorum* (1532) 1:10r., †omitting citations of the classic accounts of human sin in Jer 17:9; Pss 14/53 (Rom 3:23, 12); Ps 142:2; Is 64:6. [22]*Opera* 1:89. [23]*Hexapla* (1608), 84.

before that humans would fall into sin and later on sin gravely? What novelty can befall him? Doesn't 1 Samuel 15[:29] say, ". . . [God] is not a mortal, that he should repent"? Let us consider, then, that Scripture often speaks of God in human fashion, just as this text attributes sorrow and repentance to him, and in other places it attributes to him eyes, hands, feet, and other body parts. However, these things are rightly understood as a divine way of speaking. Whatever pertains to the nature or essence of God is eternally immutable and unchanging and is free from all sorrow or affliction. By his nature, moreover, God is the wisest intellect, and when he once decides something, it persists always and forever and is never softened by repentance, as Samuel calls it. Thus, in his own nature, he has neither hands nor feet, but his *power* is called his "hands." Yet if we ponder God further, as he exists in the hearts and words of pious people, and in their works, then he could properly be said to grieve when the pious grieve, and they bear witness to his sorrow in their words. And he is said to repent when he destroys something he previously had made. So, when he now decides to destroy humankind, which in the beginning he had created, he is said to be led to *repentance*—not in his essence, but in the changing of his works. Finally, when human feelings and members are attributed to God by the Holy Spirit, it secretly shows that . . . there would one day be a time when God would be made human and take up everything that pertains to human existence, except for sin. COMMENTARY ON GENESIS 6:6.[24]

GOD'S "REPENTANCE" ACCOMMODATES OUR LIMITED UNDERSTANDING. JOHN CALVIN: That repentance does not apply to God is easily established by this one fact: that nothing comes to pass that is not expected or foreseen by him. The same reasoning and recognition applies to what follows, that God was moved with sadness. Certainly, God does not grieve or grow sad, but remains forever like himself in his celestial and happy repose; but because it could not otherwise be known how greatly God hates and detests sin, the Spirit accommodates himself to our capacity. COMMENTARY ON GENESIS 6:6.[25]

THE DESTRUCTION OF ANIMALS SHOULD MAKE US DREAD SIN ALL THE MORE. JOHN CALVIN: It is no surprise that the things that were created for the sake of human beings and that lived to be used by them should be entangled in their ruin. Cows and donkeys deserved nothing of this, nor did the other animals; but because they had been placed under human authority, once those humans fell, the animals were drawn into the same destruction. The earth was like a wealthy house, well supplied with every kind of provision in abundance and variety. But now, because the people had stained even the earth itself with their crimes and had shamefully corrupted all the riches with which it had been filled, the Lord likewise wanted a reminder of this punishment to be visible in that very place—just as if a judge, in punishing a most heinous and abominable criminal, should command his house to be razed to the foundation in order to heighten the criminal's disgrace. All this is meant to instill us with a dread of sin, for we may easily deduce how very atrocious sin is when its punishment is extended even to brute creatures. COMMENTARY ON GENESIS 6:7.[26]

ON GOD'S REGRET. PETER MARTYR VERMIGLI: Because we are not accustomed to defend ourselves unless we are angered, the same thing induces God, when angered, either to exact vengeance or to plan to do so. Husbands are not diligent guardians of a wife's chastity unless they are repeatedly touched by jealousy.

---

[24]*Opera* 1:92. [25]CTS 1:249* (CO 23:118). [26]CTS 1:250* (CO 23:119).

For that reason, Scripture shows us that God especially watches over the souls that have already been betrothed to him, lest they mix themselves with the profane worship of alien gods, which provokes him to jealousy. And because *we* change what we have begun or transform it into something else only with reluctance unless we regret what was done, when the sacred letters want to show that *God* does not wish to rule or protect things made by him, they say he regrets them. Thus, by these emotions, when they are attributed to God, we understand those things that come to pass because human beings themselves provoked them. . . .

But the will of God is itself efficacious and certain and immutable, so that change is to be attributed not to it but to things. Augustine says the same thing in *The City of God* 15.25, that God's "regret" is his unchangeable plan as applied to things liable to change: for it is fixed in God's plan that some things that are regarded as thus-and-so are to be changed, while other things that exist in such-and-such a state are to be left alone. Holy Scripture has pointed out this constant and unchangeable nature of God to us more than once, especially in 1 Samuel 15, where Samuel himself prophesies that the kingdom is to be taken from Saul and given to David, saying, "God does not change his mind as human beings do." And David himself said, "The Lord has sworn and will not change his mind." Thus, this apparent conflict may be reconciled: for in the Scriptures these emotions are initially attributed to God so that you may understand that he most capably produces those emotions' *effects*, which are found in us. COMMENTARY ON GENESIS 6:6.[27]

THE CHURCH FATHERS UNDERSTOOD GOD'S REPENTANCE WELL. ANDREW WILLET: The ancient writers have diverse opinions about [the Lord's "repentance"], but all to good purpose. Chrysostom says it is "a word applied

to our weakness" to express the greatness of their sins, "which compelled the merciful God to be angry." Theodoret reads *I repent* as "I have decided to destroy humankind," just as the Lord says *I repent that I have made Saul king*, that is, "I have decreed to depose him." So, as Augustine well says, "this repentance is no disturbance within God but an imposition of punishment." For Rupert, [the phrase] "shows his pity," how reluctant the Lord is to punish; but in that the Lord intends to destroy them, "it shows his just severity." But more to the purpose, Augustine says "repentance in God is his unchangeable disposition of changeable things." God is not changed, but the things are altered. Justin Martyr has most plainly exposed this point: God is immutable, "but when those for whom God cares are changed, then God changes the course of things as he sees expedient for them." For God "unchangeably forgives" those who repent, as the Ninevites, and "unchangeably does not forgive" those who do not amend, as Saul. So here the Lord maintains his unchangeable course of judgment in punishing sin, yet seems to repent in undoing his work by destroying the human beings whom he had made. COMMENTARY ON GENESIS 6:6.[28]

THE CHURCH'S PRAYERS ARE A WALL AGAINST GOD'S WRATH. MARTIN LUTHER: It is impossible for the ungodly to pray. Let no one, therefore, hope for any prayer from our adversaries, the papists. We are praying for them and setting ourselves up like a wall against the wrath of God; and if by any chance they were to come to repentance, they would, without a doubt, be saved through our tears and groaning. It is an awful example that God did not spare the first world when Noah, Lamech, and Methuselah set themselves up

[27]*In Primum Librum Mosis* (1569), 28r-v, citing 1 Sam 15:29; Ps 110:4. [28]*Hexapla* (1608), 78, citing 1 Sam 15:11 and crediting Pererius overall.

like a wall. What shall we suppose will happen when there are no such walls, that is, when there is no church at all? The church is always a wall against the wrath of God. It grieves, it agonizes, it prays, it pleads, it teaches, it preaches, it admonishes, as long as the hour of judgment has not yet arrived but is impending. When it sees that these activities are of no avail, what else can it do than grieve deeply over the destruction of impenitent people? . . . This grief Moses was unable to portray in a better and clearer manner than to state that the Lord was sorry that He had made man. Lectures on Genesis 6:6.[29]

6:8-22 NOAH BUILDS AN ARK FOR THE FLOOD TO COME

[8]*But Noah found favor in the eyes of the Lord.*

[9]*These are the generations of Noah. Noah was a righteous man, blameless in his generation. Noah walked with God.* [10]*And Noah had three sons, Shem, Ham, and Japheth.*

[11]*Now the earth was corrupt in God's sight, and the earth was filled with violence.* [12]*And God saw the earth, and behold, it was corrupt, for all flesh had corrupted their way on the earth.* [13]*And God said to Noah, "I have determined to make an end of all flesh,ᵃ for the earth is filled with violence through them. Behold, I will destroy them with the earth.* [14]*Make yourself an ark of gopher wood.ᵇ Make rooms in the ark, and cover it inside and out with pitch.* [15]*This is how you are to make it: the length of the ark 300 cubits,ᶜ its breadth 50 cubits, and its height 30 cubits.* [16]*Make a roofᵈ for the ark, and finish it to a cubit above, and set the door of the ark in its side. Make it with lower, second, and third decks.* [17]*For behold, I will bring a flood of waters upon the earth to destroy all flesh in which is the breath of life under heaven. Everything that is on the earth shall die.* [18]*But I will establish my covenant with you, and you shall come into the ark, you, your sons, your wife, and your sons' wives with you.* [19]*And of every living thing of all flesh, you shall bring two of every sort into the ark to keep them alive with you. They shall be male and female.* [20]*Of the birds according to their kinds, and of the animals according to their kinds, of every creeping thing of the ground, according to its kind, two of every sort shall come in to you to keep them alive.* [21]*Also take with you every sort of food that is eaten, and store it up. It shall serve as food for you and for them."* [22]*Noah did this; he did all that God commanded him.*

a Hebrew *The end of all flesh has come before me*   b An unknown kind of tree; transliterated from Hebrew   c A *cubit* was about 18 inches or 45 centimeters   d Or *skylight*

OVERVIEW: The second half of the chapter reintroduces the central figure of Noah (from Gen 5) and reiterates God's earlier declamation against human evil. Then follow the arresting details: Noah is to build an enormous boat—large enough to house not only his wife and sons with their wives, but also mated pairs of every animal and bird, *and* food for all as well—in order to prepare for an unprecedented and devastating flood. Thus will God's judgment be visited upon all flesh. Only Noah's family will survive, for God here promises to establish his covenant with them.

Most commentators have already mused extensively on human evil by this point in the chapter, but they are happy to return for more. At the outset, however, Reformation writers were naturally suspicious of the description of Noah in Genesis 6:9 not only as righteous but even as "blameless" or "perfect." Not surprisingly, they find ways to account for the wording of Scripture here, but we may be surprised to discover the dimensions of their sensitivity to this global destruction. While granting the divine prerogative to exercise judgment, commentators take pains to justify God's wrath by calling attention to the effects of human corruption in terms that remain apt today. Some also wonder about Noah's role as an intercessor for his immoral contemporaries: did he pray for them? And the argument is also made that to be drowned in the flood is not proof that one was also damned, for some may have belatedly repented. Some of these same elements will be revisited in Genesis 6:17, when God announces and describes the flood.

The ark's construction introduced some difficult problems that in turn elicited some solutions regarded by many as all too clever—including Origen's account of the ark's size in terms of so-called geometric cubits. The question of the ark's size and design had traditionally been raised by pagan objectors to Christianity as grounds for dismissing the Bible, and Christianity along with it. The

question was thus intrinsically two-edged: it could be raised to elicit the praise of God for this miracle, or it could fuel the scorn of unbelievers. Later in the sixteenth century and throughout the seventeenth, the believability of the blueprints for the ark in Genesis 6 will become intensely discussed and contested in treatises variously informed by pious conjecture and the best science of the day.[1] However, that discussion is only occasionally overheard in these earlier Reformation commentaries, which tended to resist speculation (in theory, at least) and to remain content to recognize the ark as first and foremost a miracle.

The ark itself was also traditionally fodder for complicated allegories. Many Reformation exegetes resisted this move; some did not. Here, in the context of Genesis 6, some invoked the analogy drawn in 1 Peter 3 between the church and Noah's ark as grounds for a figural reading—a mild form of allegory, relatively speaking. More attention was paid to the pastoral implications and analogies of Noah's great labors here, although in Genesis 8 and 9 we will see some truly extensive Reformation allegories that draw on many details of the flood.

The covenant mentioned in Genesis 6:18 will also receive more attention later on, in 9:9-17, when the terms of the covenant—and its sign, the rainbow—feature more prominently in the biblical text. Here, it is mostly God's providential care and beneficence toward Noah that is highlighted. Likewise, in addressing the logistics of gathering the animals and providing for them, a few commentators will address some of the traditional puzzles of storage and animal behavior, but

---

[1]For a fairly concise account of the sixteenth- and seventeenth-century revival of this and other questions related to Noah, the ark and the flood, see Don Cameron Allen, *The Legend of Noah: Renaissance Rationalism in Art, Science and Letters* (Urbana: University of Illinois Press, 1963), 66-91; and Norman Cohn, *Noah's Flood: The Genesis Story in Western Thought* (New Haven: Yale University Press, 1996), 38-42.

Reformation writers seem more concerned to note (once again) pastoral analogies and implications. This theme is further ratified by the closing verse, which signals Noah's integrity and faithfulness: "He did all that God commanded him."

6:9 Noah Was Righteous and Blameless

NOAH WAS FAVORED BY GOD, THE FOUNT OF BEING. CARDINAL CAJETAN: According to the Hebrew it reads, "And Noah found favor in the eyes of YHWH." It is rightly said that he found favor, not righteousness; and that, not in the eyes of *Elohim* (that is, God the Judge) but in the eyes of YHWH (that is, God the Fount of Being†); since [God's] favor was there to save the *being* of humankind and the rest of the animals. Consider the progression of divine kindness: in the first place, he gave space for repentance; but in the second, he received Noah into his favor so that the human race might be preserved in him. And by saying "he found," Noah's zeal for seeking divine favor is commended. COMMENTARY ON GENESIS 6:8.[2]

NOAH WAS A LIVING MARTYR IN HIS DAY. MARTIN LUTHER: Just as we stated above that Noah is a virgin above all virgins, so here we also observe that he was a martyr above all martyrs. The situation of our so-called martyrs is most fortunate; for, strengthened by the Holy Spirit, they overcome death in one hour and surmount all perils and temptations. Noah, however, lived among the ungodly a full six hundred years, amid many serious temptations and dangers, just as Lot did in Sodom. LECTURES ON GENESIS 6:1-2.[3]

CHOSEN BY GOD, NOAH WAS BETTER THAN HIS PEERS. HULDRYCH ZWINGLI: Someone will ask, "If earlier it was said that every human being is flesh, but that flesh is God's enemy, how was Noah able to find favor before God if he too was flesh?" To this we will reply

. . . that Noah had been chosen by God to be the seed of the age to come, through whom God wished to preserve a remnant of the human race. Indeed, even if Noah was also flesh, he nonetheless remained untainted by the worst of those scoundrels, such as the *Nephilim*. We say that among the blind, a person with one eye is king. So, compared with other mortals who lived at that time, Noah was more righteous, and that, by the grace and protection of God. Wherefore, if someone should surpass others in uprightness, lest anyone boast, it is truly from God. ANNOTATIONS ON GENESIS 6:8.[4]

NOAH WAS RIGHTEOUS BUT STILL FALLIBLE. WOLFGANG MUSCULUS: Those who follow [the Latin] reading here on account of their ignorance of Hebrew raise the question of how Noah was said to be *righteous* at the same time that he was declared to be *perfect*. After all, it is written in 2 Chronicles 6[:36] and 1 Kings 8[:46], "There is no one who does not sin," and in Proverbs 20[:9], "Who can say, 'My heart is clean, I am pure from sin'?" Indeed, just as anyone who carries around some bodily defect is not perfect in loveliness, . . . and just as someone who retains a streak of folly cannot be perfect in wisdom, so one cannot be said to be perfectly righteous if something of unrighteousness remains and prevents him from putting the finishing touch on all the parts of perfect righteousness. . . . But if they had consulted the Hebrew, the response would be easy, because the Hebrew does not read, "Noah was a righteous and perfect man," but "Noah was a righteous man and unimpaired." Someone endowed with a heart that is pure, unaffected and sincere could be called unimpaired even if he still should fail in many things on account of the weakness of

---

[2]*Commentarii illustres* (1539), 47. †Cardinal Cajetan is not unique in mining the divine names for theological content in this way. Note that "favor" here is the Latin *gratia*, which can also be translated as "grace." [3]LW 2:7 (WA 42:267). [4]ZSW 13:46.

the flesh and therefore cannot be called perfectly righteous. When he denied Christ, Peter still retained a kind of wholeness and purity toward Christ in his heart, for his act of denial did not stem from an insincere or malevolent heart but from a weak one. Yet since he was said to be false and thus he failed, he cannot be said to be perfectly righteous. So those who read the sacred Scriptures should take care, when they run across passages of this sort that attribute perfection to human beings, to investigate the Hebrew context and distinguish between integrity of the heart and the perfection of righteousness. COMMENTARY ON GENESIS 6:9.[5]

NOAH WAS STILL FLESH AND STILL A SINNER. KONRAD PELLIKAN: *Noah found favor before the Lord*, not because he was righteous, but so that he *might be* righteous. Certainly, he was not without sin, since he too was flesh, but he was not as evil as the rest. But he was chosen so that he might preserve the seed of the age that would come after him: and that, not by his merits but by the grace of God, and because his sins were not imputed to him. COMMENTARY ON GENESIS 6:8.[6]

WAS NOAH REALLY PERFECT? ANDREW WILLET: Neither Noah nor yet anyone living can be said to be perfect in respect of God's justice or in the sight of God; as the psalmist says: "If you, O Lord, should mark what is done amiss, who shall be able to abide?" (Ps 130:3). Nor [did he possess] that perfection that the saints shall attain in the kingdom of God, as the apostle shows: "Not as though I had already attained or were already perfect" (Phil 3:12). Neither is anyone yet so perfect that he can be found without sin in this life, which was the heresy of the Pelagians; for the Preacher says "there is not one just person upon the earth who does good and sins not" (Eccles 7:20). Nor is anyone said to be perfect because they can keep the commandments and

even do more than commanded by observing the counsels of the gospel (as Pererius and other popish writers say). Rather, Noah is said to be perfect in comparison with others, and therefore it adds *in his generation*, or in regard to the perfection that may be attained in this life, which is more in the will and desire to be perfect and in increasing and going still forward than in any actual accomplishment of the desire. In this sense, the apostle, having a little before denied himself to be perfect, yet says to the Philippians, "Let as many as are perfect be thus minded" (Phil 3:15), and so our Savior bids us be perfect, "as our heavenly Father is perfect" [Mt 5:48], that is, that we should more and more labor for perfection. . . . How Noah is said to be perfect is expounded in verse 8: "Noah found grace in the sight of God." It was the perfection of faith, then, whereby Noah was accepted as just and perfect in the sight of God, being clothed with the perfection and justice of Christ by faith. COMMENTARY ON GENESIS 6:10.[7]

NOAH, TOO, WAS CORRUPT. JOHANNES BRENZ: "All people had become corrupt." Noah, too, was corrupt in his nature, and therefore he too deserved to be buried by the waters. "But Noah found favor (*gratia*) before God." Notice what is said about Noah. It doesn't say he finds *merit* in his own nature, but he finds *grace* in the Lord his God. From where, or on what basis? He was a just man, walking rightly with God. Did he therefore merit God's grace by his own righteousness and integrity? Not in the least. He didn't find favor before God because he pursued righteousness and integrity. Rather, because he was accepted by God, he was on that account given the Holy Spirit so that he might walk in righteousness and in a life of integrity. COMMENTARY ON GENESIS 6:5-12.[8]

---

[5]*In Mosis Genesim* (1554), 182. [6]*Commentaria Bibliorum* (1532) 1:10r. [7]*Hexapla* (1608), 78-79. [8]*Opera* 1:92.

NOAH'S FAITH WAS FOCUSED BY FEAR.
JOHN CALVIN: When the apostle commends Noah's faith (in Heb 11:7), he links Noah's trust also to fear and obedience. Indeed, it is certain that Noah was deliberately warned of the horrible vengeance at hand, not only so that he might be confirmed in his holy resolve, but also so that fear would compel him to desire more ardently the favor God had bestowed on him. We know that when evildoers go unpunished, it sometimes entices even good people to sin. Thus, an announcement that punishment is coming ought to be enough to restrain the minds of the godly, lest they slip bit by bit, to be swept at last into the same wantonness. Yet God was especially concerned for something else, namely, that by keeping the terrible destruction of the world constantly before his eyes, Noah's fear and concern might be roused more and more. Truly, it was necessary that Noah be bewildered by the hopelessness everywhere else so that, in faith, he might lodge his safety within the ark. For as long as he continued to promise himself life on earth, he would never be as intent as he ought to be on building the ark; but after God's judgment has startled him, he eagerly embraces the promise of life that was given to him. He no longer relies on natural causes or means of staying alive but rests solely on God's covenant, by which he was to be miraculously preserved. No toil or trouble is difficult; no weariness disheartens him. For the spur of God's anger pierces him too sharply to allow him to continue asleep in carnal delights, or to weaken under these trials, or to be delayed by vain hopes: instead, he stirs himself up both to flee from sin and to seek a remedy. And the apostle teaches that it was not the least part of his faith that Noah built the ark, fearing (obviously) "things that were not yet seen." When faith is discussed in simple terms, mercy and the gratuitous promise come into the account; but when we wish to express all its parts and to examine its entire force and nature, it is necessary that fear be added as well. And truly, no one will ever seriously flee to God's mercy for refuge except those who, having been stung by God's threats, come to dread the sentence of eternal death that they denounce, so that they are sick of themselves on account of their sins and neither carelessly indulge their vices nor lie in the torpor of their filth. Rather, they anxiously sigh for a cure for their evils. . . . If we consider God's purpose, he deemed his servant worthy of an inestimable benefit when he warned him to avoid this danger. COMMENTARY ON GENESIS 6:13.[9]

6:11-13 The Earth Was Filled with Violence

JUDGMENT BRINGS HOPE TO THE GODLY.
KONRAD PELLIKAN: This is certainly to be feared by us in our own day as well—or, far to the contrary, more to be *hoped for* by the godly—that an end may finally be assigned to the ferocity and shameful deeds of human beings. COMMENTARY ON GENESIS 6:13.[10]

GOD "SAW" ALL ALONG. MARTIN LUTHER: Moses wanted to indicate in this passage by the verb "He saw," . . . that at last God saw the afflictions of the godly and heard their cries, which finally filled the heavens, so that God, who thus far had paid no attention to anything and had appeared to support the efforts of the ungodly by giving them success, is awakened as though from sleep. Indeed, He saw everything far more quickly than Noah, for He is the searcher of hearts and cannot be deceived by a pretense of godliness as we can; but only when he is thinking of the punishment does Noah realize that He sees. LECTURES ON GENESIS 6:12.[11]

---

[9]CTS 1:254-55* (CO 23:121-22). [10]*Commentaria Bibliorum* (1532) 1:10v. [11]LW 2:62 (WA 42:305).

DEFENDING THE VULNERABLE. PETER MARTYR VERMIGLI: "And the earth was filled with *ḥāmās*," that is, with iniquity, fraud, and deceptions, to which violence would have nonetheless been joined. Indeed, in Hebrew it is called *ḥāmās*, for the word is broadly used to signify blood feuds, plundering and the abduction of women, but it mainly refers to the oppression of the poor. COMMENTARY ON GENESIS 6:11.[12]

THEY VIOLATED GOD'S IMAGE AS WELL AS THE LAWS OF NATURE. PETER MARTYR VERMIGLI: The law of nature, as we have explained elsewhere, is derived from God's image, according to which we have been created. Those actions that are opposed to God's attributes are also scarcely appropriate for the nature that was prepared for us. Hence, those who do such things are racing toward self-destruction and are not to be reckoned as living happily, because we ought to live our lives in accordance with our nature, not in opposition to it. COMMENTARY ON GENESIS 6:11.[13]

GOD JUDGES PLACES AS WELL AS PEOPLE. WOLFGANG MUSCULUS: He does not simply say, "And I will destroy them," but adds, "with the earth." We are reminded that not only are the *ungodly* made liable to God's judgment by their iniquity, so too are the *places* that they corrupt before God's face, filling them with iniquity in his presence, also subject to destruction on their account. Thus the great cities contaminated and filled with the evils of humankind are destined to be overthrown. The very temple in Jerusalem had become a robbers' den, filled with the greed and profiteering of its priests; and so, when those who defiled it were destroyed, it too was plundered and pulled down, so that no stone remained attached to any other, as Christ predicted. COMMENTARY ON GENESIS 6:13.[14]

IT IS FOOLISH TO DENY GOD'S WRATH BY APPEAL TO GOD'S COMPASSION. MARTIN LUTHER: Undoubtedly the descendants of the patriarchs who perished in the Flood vastly overstated their argument about the prestige of the church. They charged Noah himself with blasphemy and lies. "Stating that God is about to destroy the whole world by the Flood," they maintained, "is the same as saying that God is not compassionate and not a father, but a cruel tyrant. Noah, you are preaching the wrath of God! Has not God promised deliverance from sin and death through the Seed of the woman? God's wrath will not swallow up the entire earth. We are God's people, and we have outstanding gifts of God. God would never have granted us these gifts if He had decided to proceed against us in such a hostile manner." In this manner the ungodly are wont to apply the promises to themselves, and because of their reliance on them they disregard and laugh at all threats. The careful consideration of all this is profitable to fortify us against being offended by the smugness of the ungodly. For the same things that happened to Noah happen to us. LECTURES ON GENESIS 6:6.[15]

IT IS NEVER IMPIOUS TO PRAY FOR THE WICKED (EVEN IF NOAH DID NOT). WOLFGANG MUSCULUS: Here it could be asked why Noah did not intercede before the Lord on behalf of the world that was about to perish, even though he had found favor before him. Below, in Genesis 18, we read that Abraham did so on behalf of the inhabitants of Sodom. When he heard God's plan to destroy the men of Sodom, Abraham zealously resisted it, so that he might turn God's wrath away from them: and he succeeded to a large extent, so that if ten just men had been found in the

---

[12]*In Primum Librum Mosis* (1569), 29r. [13]*In Primum Librum Mosis* (1569), 29v. [14]*In Mosis Genesim* (1554), 190. [15]LW 2:53 (WA 42:299).

city, for their sake God would have spared the whole multitude. It seems strange that Noah did not make similar use of intercession, especially in such a serious case where not just one city or another but the whole human race was endangered by an extreme crisis. Can it be that Noah was less moved by the destruction of the whole world than Abraham was by the loss of several townsmen? My first response is that Abraham knew that his [nephew] Lot, living in Sodom with his family, was a righteous man; but Noah knew no one like this in the whole world. In addition, Noah had heard from the mouth of God the sure and fixed decree that all flesh would be wiped from the face of the earth. He had also heard the eminently just reason why. . . . But Abraham had not heard from God what the end of that region and its citizens would be, or that the iniquity of Sodom had ascended on high, or that God wished to exterminate them with fire from heaven. . . . Yet even if one prays for people like them, it is not an impious undertaking. For though one may act in vain, as happened to Abraham as well as to Samuel and Jeremiah, no one can be faulted for being moved to this kind of compassion. COMMENTARY ON GENESIS 6:14-21.[16]

NOAH'S PRAYERS, TOO, "DISCERNED THE SPIRITS." PETER MARTYR VERMIGLI: It seems amazing to the Hebrews here as to why Noah, though he was a righteous person and would have heard of the coming destruction, would not have prayed for those people just as Abraham did for Sodom and Gomorrah. It's not a bad question, but the response of those who insist on asking it is not very plausible. They say Noah hardly would have done this, because he would have known that no nation would be rescued if the number of persons were less than ten, for they assert that when Abraham heard that ten righteous persons could not be found in Sodom, he ceased to

pray to God any further on behalf of that people. So when Noah saw that such persons did not exist in his own day (which he would have already known by divine revelation), he would by no means have dared to bother God on behalf of their salvation. A godly and sensible Christian does not speak like this but admits that both outcomes could be granted, namely, that he prayed or that he didn't pray. If he did pray, it's not surprising why it wasn't recorded, for the sacred history does not relate everything whatsoever that he did or all the things that happened to him. Indeed, it suffices that what doesn't appear in this account of Noah's deeds can be read by us later on, among the affairs of Abraham, for it is better recounted there than here. Described there is that well-known dialogue between Abraham and God, in which we are taught about the divine mercy by which God showed himself ready to forgive that people if ten righteous persons could have been found there. Because it didn't turn out that way in Noah's prayers, sacred Scripture was not concerned to pass it in review. Even if maybe he did not pray for them, he should not be described as cruel or inhumane. Rather, God revealed to him by the Holy Spirit that their salvation was beyond hope and that they had sinned unto death, and for this kind of person God does not want us to pray. Jeremiah, as you know, was forbidden to pray "for that people," and if such a thing should happen to any of our people, we ought to obey. Nonetheless, we should not be moved by our own opinion to desist from praying for our brothers or sisters unless we have a sure oracle from the Spirit on this matter. For if anywhere, this is especially the place where there is a need for that gift that Paul calls the discernment of spirits. COMMENTARY ON GENESIS 6:17.[17]

---

[16]*In Mosis Genesim* (1554), 189. [17]*In Primum Librum Mosis* (1569), 30v, citing Jer 11:14 and probably 1 Jn 4:1.

Not All Who Drowned Were Damned.
Andrew Willet: Did all those who were
destroyed in the flood perish everlastingly, that
is, both in body and soul? For our answer, we
neither think that most of the old world were
only temporally punished (Jerome). . . .
Neither do we approve the opinion that many
of the old world, though previously disbeliev-
ing, yet, when they saw the flood coming,
repented even at the end of their lives (Lyra,
Bellarmine). For Saint Peter calls them "the
world of the wicked" (2 Pet 2:5), so that those
who were wicked, then, continued as such to
the end. Neither is the opinion to be received
that "they were not simply incredulous, that is,
without true faith in God" (Cajetan), but they
only disbelieved Noah in this [particular], that
the flood should come; trusting in God's
longsuffering, they hoped that it would not be
so. For it is evident from Genesis 6 that
besides this special point of disbelief, the old
world was outrageous in many other sins: "the
earth was filled with cruelty" (Gen 6:11).
Moreover, by giving no credit to Noah, God's
prophet, they were thereby also incredulous
against God. . . . Also to be rejected is the
opinion that though the wicked of the old
world were condemned to hell, yet they might
be redeemed from there by the descent of
Christ, who is said by Saint Peter to have
preached to the spirits in prison who were
formerly disobedient—at which time some
have also fabled that Plato, at the preaching of
Christ in hell, believed. . . . But these imagina-
tions are contrary to Scripture, for there is no
redemption out of hell. . . . Nor is there any
value to the idea that some of those who
perished in the flood repented before they died
and so went not to hell but to purgatory,
whence they were delivered by Christ when he
descended there. . . .

Wherefore our opinion is that all those who
were disobedient and incredulous in the days
of Noah were first destroyed bodily in the
flood, and afterwards perished everlastingly in

their souls. But from this number one must
exempt not only infants (such as were of the
children of God), who are not capable of faith
and obedience and therefore were neither
unfaithful nor disobedient, but also such as
were ignorant of the preaching of Noah and
the framing of the ark. On these, God might
have mercy. Commentary on Genesis 6:13.[18]

6:14-16 Make Yourself an Ark

**God's Attention to Detail Was a
Pastoral Matter.** Johannes Brenz: One
may wonder why God would descend to such
humility and common service that he would
prescribe even the smallest details about the
ark that was to be built. Wasn't Noah able to
use his own wits to design a suitable plan?
Couldn't God, with a single word, have created
a ship that would have been much more
suitable for keeping Noah and the animals safe
than what is dictated in these words, just as in
the beginning he created heaven and earth by
his word? Yet there are very serious reasons
why God would have wanted to dictate to
Noah the plan for assembling the ship and to
safeguard him in a boat rather than any other
way. First, by these instructions he wanted to
indicate that we should undertake nothing
concerning the worship of God without the
word of God. God well knew the curiosity and
superstition of human beings, who are accustomed to cast aside God's glory and on their
own whim dream up other ways of worshiping
God that nonetheless worship more the idols
of their hearts than the true God. . . . Second,
God wanted to dictate the plan for building
the ship so that Noah would be able to endure
the mockery of others, who would deride him
for building the ship and urge him to quit.
Truly, the day was coming when Noah, while
carrying out the plans for a boat designed as a

---

[18]*Hexapla* (1608), 79-80, also citing Theophylact, Theodoret,
Rupert and Augustine.

refuge against the flood's destruction, would himself be mocked and reviled by his contemporaries. They'd say to him, "What's this foolish little man attempting? What idiot put him up to this? Surely he doesn't think it will ever happen that the world and its people will be destroyed by God, who created it according to his own counsel? Does he think God has regretted his creation, when God is by far the wisest of all? Does he believe God has changed? So what *are* you doing, Noah? Seriously, if you don't stop preaching about a flood and building this boat, you'll qualify as a heretic in our eyes. If we imagine what a flood would really be like, why, I ask you, were you pleased with such a fragile ship? How easily it could be dashed by the waves against the rocks or the mountains and smashed to pieces! You couldn't have attempted anything more foolish or insane!" Such were the voices and the mockery that Noah would have to endure. So God did not want to allow him to build a ship of his own design but wanted to dictate the plan to him, so that when Noah heard the mocking of others, he would dismiss them and carry on. COMMENTARY ON GENESIS 6:14-16.[19]

BUILDING THE ARK AS AN ACT OF PRUDENCE. KONRAD PELLIKAN: A miracle is not to be asked of God when dangers can be met with natural means alongside human craft and diligence. COMMENTARY ON GENESIS 6:18.[20]

THE ARK WAS LARGE, BUT ALSO MIRACULOUS. PETER MARTYR VERMIGLI: Who doubts that [the ark's] magnitude could have proved able to contain such large and so many things? Origen solved [the problem] with his geometrical cubits, each of which comprised six common cubits. The Hebrews say that because giants inhabited the world at that time, cubits were gauged according to the height and size of those people. (In fact, according to Berosus, Noah was a giant, but not a blasphemer and wicked person like the others—on the contrary, he dissuaded the others from their crimes and wicked deeds.) But it's more pleasing to me that we believe it done by divine power, so that larger things could have been contained in a smaller space, since we ought to allow for miracles in this instance and others. Another factor is that the ark did not have only one deck but fully three, so if the same or a slightly shorter length were stacked three times, the matter is not so unbelievable to hear about. COMMENTARY ON GENESIS 6:15-16.[21]

THE SIZE OF THE ARK WAS NOT A PROBLEM. WOLFGANG MUSCULUS: Apelles, the disciple of Marcion, raised the question here of how it could be that so many kinds of animals, along with food enough for a whole year, were able to fit in the cramped and narrow space of this ark, given that a structure of this sort would scarcely have sufficed to hold four elephants. He concludes on these grounds that what Moses relates here is simply a fable, but he was an impious man who was looking for reasons to dismiss the authority of the truth of the sacred Scriptures. He thought that the cubits were no longer than ours are, something Origen denies, affirming that Moses is speaking not of regular cubits but of *geometric* cubits. A geometric cubit, he says, is equal to six regular cubits. One should consider, too, that it could have happened that the fully grown animals were left aside and their young were gathered instead—at least in most cases, if not all. Indeed, there was no necessity in the arrangements that required only adults to be gathered. In fact, it was much more convenient both to gather and to house young in the ark than bodies that were full-grown, mature and adult. I affirm none of this: what grounds

---

[19]*Opera* 1:94. [20]*Commentaria Bibliorum* (1532) 1:10v. [21]*In Primum Librum Mosis* (1569), 30r. For the forged ancient history of [pseudo-]Berosus, see chapter 3 of David M. Whitford, *The Curse of Ham in the Early Modern Era: The Bible and the Justifications for Slavery* (Burlington, VT: Ashgate, 2009), 43-76.

would I have for affirmation, when the sacred history says nothing of these things? But I do condemn the impiety of those who denigrate the sacred histories with no reverence for divine power nor consideration of circumstances. Commentary on Genesis 6:14-21.[22]

Those Who Ignore God's Power Will Regard the Ark as a Mere Fable. John Calvin: What the measure of the cubit was at that time, I do not know, for it is enough for me that God (whom, without controversy, I acknowledge to be the ark's chief builder) well knew what things the place he described to his servant was capable of holding. If you exclude the extraordinary power of God from this narrative, you will say that mere fables are recounted. But for us, who recognize that the survivors of that world were preserved by an incredible miracle, it should not seem absurd that many amazing things are recounted here, to the end that God's hidden and incomprehensible power, which far surpasses all our senses, may shine forth more brightly. Commentary on Genesis 6:14.[23]

The Foolishness of the Ark Was Wiser Than Human Wisdom. Johannes Brenz: If human wisdom had undertaken to contrive something against the force of the flood, perhaps it would have built extremely high towers that would have risen above the earth and the water by many cubits, up to the highest mountains. It would certainly not have risked trusting itself to the fragile wood of the boat—yet not even then would people have been kept safe! The sons of men in Babel built the highest of towers, but what did it gain them? So it goes: human prudence prepares its affairs with the greatest pomp and begins its songs with the loudest voice, as they say, yet a foolish outcome follows and brings shame. God, however, looks humble and abased in his works, yet he brings them to completion with evident glory and majesty.

Thus, just as in the spiritual preservation of the human race, God wished to save people through the foolishness of the cross in order to shame the wise, . . . so did it seem good to him here, in the physical preservation of the human race, to protect humans by means of the foolish ark, so that those who are wise in this world would curb their prudence and subject it to God. Commentary on Genesis 6:14-16.[24]

The Ark Is a Figure of God's Justice and Mercy. Huldrych Zwingli: Just as pious people were kept safe at that time in the ark, so now the faithful are kept safe in Christ, as Peter explains. Truly, the ark signifies the mercy of God, who in his justice does not hold back mercy yet does not allow the impious and wicked to go unpunished. At the same time, God safeguards the rest, on whom he has mercy. This is a consolation for us. Indeed, God always guards those who walk in his way or are in the midst of destruction. In addition, the deluge is a figure of the judgment to come, not only that which was impending but also of divine justice, which does not permit crimes to go unpunished, even if judgment should be delayed for a very long time. Divine vengeance is going to come wholly against the impious, and the severity of the penalty will make up for the lateness of the punishment. Annotations on Genesis 6:18.[25]

6:17 I Will Bring a Flood to Destroy All

The Flood Was Not a Natural Evil. Konrad Pellikan: God does not wish us to attribute adversities sent our way by natural causes to anyone other than to himself alone. Indeed, he wishes to be acknowledged and considered as the first cause of the influences of

---

[22]*In Mosis Genesim* (1554), 188; the account of Apelles derives from the second of Origen's *Homilies on Genesis* (FC 71:76; PG 12:161-62). [23]CTS 1:257* (CO 23:123). [24]*Opera* 1:96, citing 1 Cor 1:18-31. [25]ZSW 13:49.

the heavens and the effects of the elements. "There is no evil in a city that will not have been caused by God." COMMENTARY ON GENESIS 6:17.[26]

SUCH A FLOOD WAS UNHEARD-OF AND THUS DISBELIEVED. MARTIN LUTHER:

Because this form of punishment was unheard of in former ages, the ungodly had little faith in it. This was their thinking: "If God is angry at all, is He not able to discipline the disobedient by war and plague? The Flood would destroy the rest of the creatures too, even though they have committed no sin. God will surely not give thought to anything like this in regard to the world." To keep this sort of unbelief out of the heart of Noah and of the godly, God emphatically repeats the pronoun: "I, I will bring." Then He adds clearly that He will destroy the flesh that is under the heaven and on the earth. . . . Accordingly, this sentence serves to indicate the vastness of God's wrath, through which men lose not only their bodies and their lives but even their universal dominion throughout the world. LECTURES ON GENESIS 6:17.[27]

THE FLOOD WAS NO ACCIDENT. WOLFGANG

MUSCULUS: God doesn't just say, "Behold, a flood of waters will be upon the earth," but "Behold, I, even I, shall bring the waters of a flood upon the earth." It was not enough for the faithful Noah to be instructed about what was going to happen; rather, it was required that he know the flood was not some accident or an unusual alignment of the stars but a judgment upon the whole earth sent forth by the will and working of the Lord. The hands of the Lord who exacts punishment from all flesh had to be acknowledged. They must be seen and acknowledged in all things: not only in benefits, so that we may be grateful, but also in afflictions, so that we may fear his just judgment. COMMENTARY ON GENESIS 6:17.[28]

LIKE BAPTISM, THE FLOOD ATTESTS SALVATION AND JUDGMENT. KONRAD

PELLIKAN: But he says that *flesh* is to be destroyed, not the soul or the whole person, so that the spirit may be saved. Indeed, God does not punish twice in the same way. And therefore baptism can point to the flood, by which the body is buried and surrendered to die as if underwater, so that the soul might be renewed and live to God. It is also a figure of the judgment to come and of divine justice, which does not allow crimes to go unpunished, even if sometimes it delays for a long time. Divine vengeance will surely come upon the impious, and it will compensate the tardiness of punishment with its severity of retribution. COMMENTARY ON GENESIS 6:17.[29]

6:18 I Will Establish My Covenant with You

COVENANT SIGNALS GOD'S UNFAILING

BENEVOLENCE. WOLFGANG MUSCULUS: A covenant not only is based on friendship and mutual benevolence but also carries an obligation by which covenanting parties are mutually bound to one another. In the world, covenants are constituted for this purpose, so that each party gets something useful from it, whether peace or mutual aid. But that logic falls short here. Indeed, God does not make covenants with humans for that reason, that he might make use of their works or obtain some other advantage from their obligation to the covenant, but rather so that he might assure human beings of his will, faithfulness and beneficence by means of such a bond. The point is driven home not only by calling this a *covenant* but also by the verb *hăqîmôtî* that is, "I will establish, I will build, I will confirm." Thus he labors on behalf of the weakness of

---

[26]*Commentaria Bibliorum* (1532) 1:10v, alluding to Amos 3:6. [27]LW 2:70 (WA 42:311-12). [28]*In Mosis Genesim* (1554), 191. [29]*Commentaria Bibliorum* (1532) 1:10v.

our faith, lest we have any doubts about the firmness of his benevolence. Here, in the making of a covenant, God's benevolence comes together with his faithfulness and truth—traits in which he has never failed anyone. He could have simply blessed Noah and his family, but God wished to strengthen him in his faith and confidence in him through the firmness of his own benevolence and truth. COMMENTARY ON GENESIS 6:18.[30]

KNOWLEDGE OF GOD'S COVENANT GUARDED NOAH FROM DEATH'S TERRORS.

JOHN CALVIN: The sum of this covenant of which Moses speaks was that Noah was going to be unharmed, even though the whole world should perish in the flood. For there is an implicit antithesis that, given that the whole world had been rejected, the Lord wished to establish a special covenant with Noah alone. Consequently, it was Noah's duty to set this divine promise or covenant against all the terrors of death, like a wall of iron, even as God similarly intended to separate life from death by this word alone. COMMENTARY ON GENESIS 6:18.[31]

AN ANTICIPATION OF OUR OWN REGENERATION.

PETER MARTYR VERMIGLI: Why are these others rescued along with Noah? The first reason is that they had been given a good upbringing and so were not evil as others were. Second, God customarily gave to his saints those who were related to them by some familial bond. Third, for the sake of his posterity: thus, sometimes you may see that some are saved not just because they are righteous or on account of their elders' merit, but for the sake of the descendants who would be born from them, as with David's lineage leading to Christ. So God wanted to save these sons of Noah not only on account of their father but also so that his lineage would afterwards be propagated from them. But you may object that God could have created new

human beings, as he did in the beginning. I grant that, but I still think God was unwilling to act on that plan, because this new restoration of the world was a type of our regeneration through Christ. Those who come to the church and are regenerated are not made from nothing but are taken from their prior fleshly birth and made new. This is why God wanted to restore the world from the people of the previous age. COMMENTARY ON GENESIS 6:18.[32]

6:19-21 Gathering Animals and Food

NOAH HAD TO GATHER HIS OWN FOOD.

MARTIN LUTHER: [God] demands from us too that we do not waste the products of nature (for that would be tempting God), but that we use with thanksgiving the means He has provided and offered. It would be a sin to expect food from heaven when one is hungry and not rather to provide it in some other manner or ask for it. . . . Thus in this passage Noah receives the command to make use of the regular means of gathering food; he is not ordered to wait in the ark for some miraculous method of supplying food from heaven. LECTURES ON GENESIS 6:21.[33]

NOAH WAS LIKE A PASTOR TO THE ANIMALS.

PETER MARTYR VERMIGLI: Noah wasn't forced to search for every kind of beast. Instead, they came voluntarily, evidently drawn by God. In the same way that it happened when the animals were brought by God to the first Adam so that they might be called by their names, so now they are driven to the ark by that same impulse. And what is now taught, as you may know, is to command him to be on hand as these animals arrived in order to keep them together and lead them into the ark. Not in vain do we note that Noah, a minister of the

---

[30]*In Mosis Genesim* (1554), 192. [31]CTS 1:258-59 (CO 23:124). [32]*In Primum Librum Mosis* (1569), 30v. [33]LW 2:76 (WA 42:316).

church, does not himself lead sheep to the church, but they are impelled by God's Spirit, which stirs them up to come on their own. The minister's task, then, is to keep them together and unite them to the church by word and sacraments. COMMENTARY ON GENESIS 6:19-20.[34]

NOAH MODELED LOVE OF NEIGHBOR. KONRAD PELLIKAN: The care of all in his household who were to be saved was imposed on the righteous man, from whose duties we learn to care for the salvation of our neighbor, which is more acceptable to God than any sacrifice. COMMENTARY ON GENESIS 6:21.[35]

HEAVEN'S MINISTERS ALSO HAVE EARTHLY CARES. PETER MARTYR VERMIGLI: Here you see the man of God burdened with a load of care, so that he has to look out not only for other people but also for the animals that serve human beings—something he does out of charity, to aid our race. Ministers of the church and godly people may learn here when it is appropriate (without suspending the ministry of the word of God) to take on the care of brothers and sisters who are under duress. There are some who shamelessly boast, "I'm only concerned with spiritual things, I don't care about these things." This is no way to behave. One's wife, children and family need to be fed, even as the brethren need to be fed, and not merely with the word, but especially with those things that sustain life and health. But if this is not permitted to those who labor in God's word, let them follow the example of the apostles and see that they choose qualified deacons who will assiduously give themselves to this task, as Noah might have done here. By using the help of others, he was able to gather such a great supply of food fit for his ark. Here you see the usefulness of a righteous person: all the animals that would have perished due to the wickedness of those other people were preserved by a single holy and godly man.

Other creatures depend so much on the life and morals of human beings! When you hear that rations had to be amassed in the ark, consider that in a well-ordered church, people should be so cared for that they also do not lack the material goods that contribute to the sustenance of their bodies. COMMENTARY ON GENESIS 6:21.[36]

WHAT DID LIONS EAT ON THE ARK? WOLFGANG MUSCULUS: They also raise a question about the food that restrains the carnivorous beasts. Where, they ask, was food obtained for lions, wolves, eagles, and other beasts of this kind in the ark, given that these sorts of animals do not live except by flesh, but the animals brought into the ark were not selected to be given as food to lions, wolves and eagles, but so that they could live in the ark and be saved. First, even if it is not written that some animals were gathered into the ark so that the carnivorous beasts might live off of them, nonetheless nothing prohibits us from believing that Noah did just that. Second, it is not established as beyond dispute that certain beasts were carnivores before the flood, when flesh had not yet been allowed to humans for eating. Third, even if it were agreed that they had the same diet before the flood as that by which they now live, what prohibited a decree by which God suspended their savagery for a while and brought it about in the ark that lion and ox, eagle and dove, wolf and lamb, bear and calf not only would abide in mutual gentleness but also be fed with the same food—and in this way what Isaiah took from the kingdom of Christ and applied as a parable for his own people would be fulfilled. . . . I'm not claiming that it happened this way, but I do advise that it could have. COMMENTARY ON GENESIS 6:14-21.[37]

---

[34]*In Primum Librum Mosis* (1569), 31r. [35]*Commentaria Bibliorum* (1532) 1:11r. [36]*In Primum Librum Mosis* (1569), 31r. [37]*In Mosis Genesim* (1554), 188, omitting his quotation of Is 11:6-9.

INSECTS TOOK CARE OF THEMSELVES.
WOLFGANG MUSCULUS: People usually ask
about insects and tiny little creatures, such as
locusts, dung beetles, flies, weevils, caterpil-
lars, blister beetles, wasps, gnats, cutworms,
and all kinds of maggots and fleas. But if you
consider what God said, "They shall be male
and female," and "take them with you into the
ark by twos," it becomes clear that only those
animals were brought into the ark whose
species was preserved and multiplied by the
union of male and female. So, for those that
can arise in other ways, without intercourse,
and that are not endowed with either masculine or feminine sex, there would have been no
need to take them into the ark for the conser-
vation of their race. COMMENTARY ON GEN-
ESIS 6:14-21.[38]

6:22 Noah Did All That God Commanded

**NOAH'S FAITH WAS PROVED BY HIS OBE-
DIENCE.** MARTIN LUTHER: Noah is praised as
an example for us because he did not have a
dead faith, which is actually no faith at all, but
a living and active faith. He is obedient when
God gives him a command; and because he
believes God both when He gives a promise
and when He utters a threat, he painstakingly
carries out God's direction in regard to the ark,
the gathering of the animals, and the food. The
particular praise of Noah's faith is that he stays
on the royal road; he adds nothing, changes
nothing, and takes nothing away from God's
directive but abides completely by the command he hears. The most common and at the
same time the most pernicious plague in the
church is this: either a change is made in what
God has commanded, or something is superim-
posed upon what God has commanded. This
error is very common; for God has the habit of
commanding ordinary, unimportant, laughable,
and at times even offensive things. LECTURES
ON GENESIS 6:22.[39]

NOAH'S FAITH AND WORKS. WOLFGANG
MUSCULUS: It doesn't say, "Noah *believed*,"
but "Noah *did* everything that God commanded him." God's oracle to Noah was
twofold. First, he set before him certain
things that required not some sort of work
but faith, inasmuch as the details of the
covenant and then of the flood, too, were
being discussed. Second, he gave certain
other instructions, namely, about making the
ark, the clean and unclean animals that were
to be gathered into the ark and the foodstuffs
that needed to be amassed. Noah believed
God's oracle in those things that demanded
faith. And since he *believed* according to
God's word that a flood was going to come,
he also *obeyed* God's precepts reverently, for if
he had not obeyed, he would have perished
together with the world. COMMENTARY ON
GENESIS 6:22.[40]

**NOAH'S GREAT FAITH IN THE WORD OF
GOD.** KONRAD PELLIKAN: For a long time,
namely, a hundred years, he labored to build
such a great structure, having to cover
timbers with pitch so as to withstand the
waters, winds and rocks. It was a sign of great
obedience and the firmest faith against the
judgment and sense of the whole world. The
impious constantly derided him as if he were
sweating over a fool's errand, since God, with
a single word and a little miracle—nay, by the
conduct of nature—could have gone before
him, preserving those whom he wished in
some space of land either above or somehow
beyond the water's reach. But for him, the
word of God was far mightier than any
human opinion: against the order of nature,
he clung to his faith in the creator, fulfilling
his commands. COMMENTARY ON GENESIS
6:22.[41]

---

[38]*In Mosis Genesim* (1554), 188. [39]LW 2:77 (WA 42:317). [40]*In
Mosis Genesim* (1554), 193. [41]*Commentaria Bibliorum* (1532)
1:11r.

NOAH'S MANY TRIALS AND TEMPTATIONS.
JOHN CALVIN: It was hardly to be expected
that the people of Noah's day would tolerate
that he should promise a private deliverance
for himself—joined with disgrace for them! . . .
To be sure, there was a plausible occasion for
taking offense here, since by felling trees all
around him, Noah would have been denuding
the earth and defrauding them of various
advantages. . . . But what tended above all to
inflame their fury was this: that by building a
refuge for himself, he was dooming them to
destruction. Without a doubt, if they had not
been restrained by God's mighty hand, they
would have stoned the holy man a hundred
times. Still, it is probable that their unruliness
was not so repressed but that they constantly
assailed him with jeers and mocking, going so
far as to torment him with a multitude of
insults and chasing after him with cruel
threats. In fact, I rather think that they did
not restrain their hands from disrupting his
work. Therefore, however diligently he may
have applied himself to his assigned task, his
constancy still might have failed more than a
thousand times a year had it not developed
extremely strong roots. [Constructing the ark]
was itself an impossible task, but beyond this,
where were a year's provisions to be obtained?
Where to find fodder for so many animals? He
is commanded to store up what would suffice
for ten months' worth of food for his whole
family, for cattle, for wild beasts, and even for
birds. This is truly ridiculous, that *after* he was
transferred from farming to building the ark,
the order comes to him to gather a harvest
twice as large—and yet finding fodder for the
animals was more troublesome by far! Noah
might therefore have suspected that God was
mocking him. . . . But the most grievous
temptation of all was that, for the sake of
preserving his life, he was commanded to
descend into a tomb and willingly deprive
himself of air and the very breath of life. Truly,
the manure's odor alone, confined in a crowded
place as it was, could have stifled to death any
of the living creatures there by the end of the
third day! Let us call to mind this holy man's
struggles—so burdensome, numerous and
prolonged—so that we may understand how
heroic was his courage in pursuing to the
utmost what God had committed to his
charge. Admittedly, Moses says in a single
word that Noah did it, but we must consider
how far beyond all human power was the doing
of it: so much so, that it would have been
better to die a hundred deaths than to undertake a work so laborious, unless he had looked
to something higher than the present life.
COMMENTARY ON GENESIS 6:22.[42]

**NOAH'S FAITH TRIUMPHED OVER MOCK-
ERY.** DESIDERIUS ERASMUS: Noah displayed a
still more notable example of faith toward
God. Although warned by an oracle of what
was coming, that a flood was going to blot out
the entire stock of living creatures on earth,
there was no evidence to be found by which he
might deduce what the oracle was predicting:
for the skies were clear, people were feasting
and celebrating weddings without a care, and
they mocked the oracle's threats. Nonetheless,
Noah had no doubt that what God predicted
would come to pass would, in fact, come to
pass. He prepared an ark, by which he simultaneously saved his family and condemned the
rest, who so distrusted God's words that they
mocked him as a lunatic for carrying out his
plan against the coming flood. PARAPHRASE
OF HEBREWS 11:7.[43]

---

[42]CTS 1:260-61* (CO 23:125-26). [43]*Paraphraseon* (1541),
2:373-74; cf. CWE 44:245 and *Seconde Tome* (1549), 19r-v.

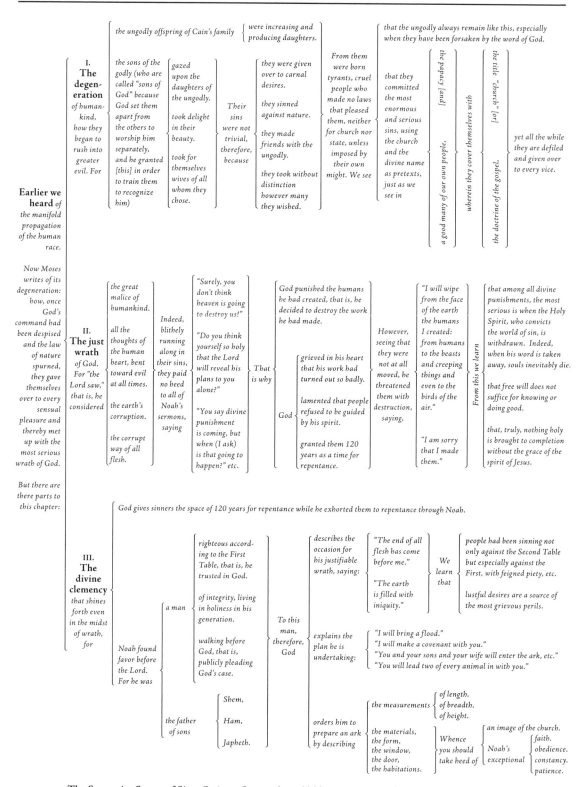

The Successive Stages of Sins. Cyriacus Spangenberg, Table 7 on Genesis 6 (*In Pentateuchum*, sig. B1ʳ).

7:1-9 ENTERING THE ARK WITH THE ANIMALS

¹Then the LORD said to Noah, "Go into the ark, you and all your household, for I have seen that you are righteous before me in this generation. ²Take with you seven pairs of all clean animals,ᵃ the male and his mate, and a pair of the animals that are not clean, the male and his mate, ³and seven pairsᵇ of the birds of the heavens also, male and female, to keep their offspring alive on the face of all the earth. ⁴For in seven days I will send rain on the earth forty days and forty nights, and every living thingᶜ that I have made I will blot out from the face of the ground." ⁵And Noah did all that the LORD had commanded him.

⁶Noah was six hundred years old when the flood of waters came upon the earth. ⁷And Noah and his sons and his wife and his sons' wives with him went into the ark to escape the waters of the flood. ⁸Of clean animals, and of animals that are not clean, and of birds, and of everything that creeps on the ground, ⁹two and two, male and female, went into the ark with Noah, as God had commanded Noah.

a Or *seven of each kind of clean animal*   b Or *seven of each kind*   c Hebrew *all existence; also verse 23*

OVERVIEW: With the ark finished and provisions presumably laid by, the narrative turns to the final preparation: assembling the passengers. It was stated in the preceding chapter that two "of every sort" of animal would need to be gathered, but here, a new detail is added. For all clean animals, not one pair but seven would need to be on board—though there was some doubt as to whether the text stipulated seven individual animals or seven pairs.

The lingering question of just how many clean animals Noah gathered did trouble traditional commentators, but rationalizations for either reading were not hard to find. Nor was anyone particularly bothered that this distinction between clean and unclean seems to have come out of nowhere. Such technical exegetical issues were dealt with, then supplemented by edifying applications.

But numbers of other kinds were also of interest. Like many passages of the Bible, this chapter is rich with details that might help one construct a calendar: 7 days, 600 years, 40 days and nights, 150 days—even the precision of a date: on the seventeenth day of the second month of the year. Many traditional commentators took an extremely specific interest in questions of chronology, eager to learn just when the flood and other biblical events occurred in the history of the world—information that would have a variety of uses, including helping to explain historical details here and elsewhere by furnishing a richer, more precise background. Luther was but one of those who tried his hand at a comprehensive chronology of biblical history, presumably as both an aid to and a byproduct of his lectures on Genesis from 1535 to 1545. Among the fruit of Luther's labor is his confidence in this chapter that Methuselah was also Noah's pastor, who died just before the flood—which he is also sure occurred, appropriately enough, in the springtime of the year.

Genesis 7 is also an excellent example of what one could charitably describe as the Bible's distinctive prose style. More to the point, it is impossible to read this chapter and not be struck by the repetition of many details: we learn multiple times about Noah's age, the duration of the rain, the pairs of animals, and so on. Reformation commentators noticed this aspect of the text as well, not least because so much repetition would make it hard to find something new to say from one paragraph to the next! Unlike modern exegetes, however, they do not look for an explanation by assigning phrases variously to separate Priestly or Yahwist authors (even though, as we have seen, they do attend to these different names for God as they are introduced in Genesis). Instead, they stay within the text, assuming that the divine author of Genesis—whether identified as an inspired Moses or as the Holy Spirit—meant to teach both Noah and us something important by what would otherwise strike the reader as a peculiar, if not tedious, element of style.

7:1 The Lord Said to Noah

METHUSELAH'S LAST TESTAMENT TO NOAH. MARTIN LUTHER: Although I do not deny that this could have been revealed by an angel or by the Holy Spirit Himself, nevertheless the ministry should be given the honor where it can be rightly maintained that God spoke through human beings. . . . Since Methuselah, Noah's grandfather, died during the very year of the Flood, it would not be improper to assume that this was the last statement of Methuselah to his nephew and, as it were, his testament—for Lamech, Noah's father, had died five years before the Flood—in which he bade his grandson farewell and added: "My son, just as you have obeyed the Lord so far, have waited in faith for this wrath, and have experienced God's protection and His faithful defense against the ungodly, so in

the future have no doubt that you will be the object of God's care. Now the end is near, not only mine, which is an end of grace, but also that of the entire human race, which is an end of wrath. . . ." Because it is sure that Methuselah died in the very year of the Flood, it can be assumed without any risk that this was his last address to his grandson, Noah, who heard his words and received them as the words of God. LECTURES ON GENESIS 7:1.[1]

NOAH'S SAD FAREWELL TO A LOVELY WORLD. JOHN CALVIN: For fully a hundred years, Noah had already sustained the greatest and most furious assaults, and the unconquered athlete had brought back memorable victories. But this was the bitterest struggle of all: to bid farewell to the world and to renounce society in order to hide himself in the ark. At that time, the face of the earth was unblemished, and Moses indicates that it was the time of year when the grasses turn green and trees begin to blossom. Gone was winter, which constricts the cheeriness of earth and sky with its bleak and bitter chill; for the world's destruction, the Lord chose a moment in the very midst of spring. COMMENTARY ON GENESIS 7:1.[2]

THE FLOOD OCCURRED IN SPRINGTIME. MARTIN LUTHER: It is my opinion, therefore, that the Flood set in at springtime, when the hearts of all men were full of the expectation of a new year. Such is the death of the ungodly that when they have said "Peace and security," then they perish. LECTURES ON GENESIS 7:11-12.[3]

LEARNING FROM REPETITION. KONRAD PELLIKAN: With often prolix and repetitive narration, he adds to and increases the general terror of all earthly creatures, so that

---

[1]LW 2:82 (WA 42:320). [2]CTS 1:264* (CO 23:127). [3]LW 2:93 (WA 42:328), citing 1 Thess 5:3.

258

the severity of the divine judgment against the impious might be impressed upon the descendants of all generations and that God's mercy unto those who believe and obey might be commended. COMMENTARY ON GENESIS 7:12.[4]

THE SCRIPTURES ARE NEVER REDUNDANT.

JOHANNES BRENZ: In this and the previous chapter, the Scriptures often repeat that God was going to destroy all flesh, and that he ordered Noah to lead pairs of every kind of animal into the ark, and that Noah obeyed God, and that everything else on earth perished except for Noah, who was preserved in the ark along with his family and the animals. This is not merely verbose, nor vain or redundant. Rather, the Holy Spirit has good reasons for this repetition. First, by that reassurance the truth of these events is also indicated. Indeed, the Holy Spirit knew that many who would be born later on, because they themselves would not have seen these things happen, would not be able by human reason to understand how so many animals could be saved in such a little boat and would conclude that these things were made up, or allegories. So the Holy Spirit constantly repeats and reiterates the story of what happened along with its circumstances in order to signify that nothing is more certain or more true than this account of events. And if these things seem amazing to us and we cannot understand how everything happened, nonetheless, because they are handed on to us with the surest proofs in the sacred Scriptures, there is no doubt but that they assuredly took place just as they are recounted. . . . Then, when the Holy Spirit drives home the same things so many times, he wishes to detain us for a longer time in considering the divine severity. Truly, human nature is so blinded by sin and prone to negligence and sluggishness that it cannot be roused to fear and obey God, but rather thinks that whatever is said about the wrath of God is

an empty threat, and that even Satan is not so horrible as he is usually depicted! And thus some who are imbued with the wisdom of this age regard anything said about God as a fable. . . . The Holy Spirit saw that these things would come to pass on earth, which is why he employed repetition in the story of the flood, in order to demonstrate that the preaching about God's wrath was not empty but quite certain. Thus, we bear in mind the fear of God so that we might flee his wrath. COMMENTARY ON GENESIS 7:11.[5]

MOSES REPEATS DETAILS BECAUSE THE EVENTS ARE INCREDIBLE. JOHN CALVIN:

Nothing is narrated here except what is difficult to be believed. This is why Moses repeatedly emphasizes the same things, so that however distant they may be from our understanding, they may still find acceptance among us. COMMENTARY ON GENESIS 7:13.[6]

GOD LIKED TALKING TO NOAH. MARTIN

LUTHER: It is obvious that God enjoys talking to Noah. It is not enough for Him to have given him orders once about what he should do, but He repeats the same orders in the same words. Reason considers this wordiness absurd, but to a heart battling desperation nothing that gives instruction about God's will can seem to be enough or too much. God sees this attitude of the heart in its trial. He repeats the same words in close succession in order that Noah, as a result of that conversation and wordiness, may realize that he is not only not forsaken even though the entire world may have forsaken him but has a friendly and kindly disposed God, who loves him so much that it seems He cannot converse enough with this pious man. LECTURES ON GENESIS 7:2-3.[7]

---

[4]*Commentaria Bibliorum* (1532) 1:11v. [5]*Opera* 1:100. [6]CTS 1:271* (CO 23:132). [7]LW 2:88 (WA 42:324-25).

7:2-3 Animals Clean and Unclean

The Seventh Animal Was Reserved for an Offering after the Flood. Huldrych Zwingli: My understanding is that there were not seven pairs but only three, plus one animal that was sacrificed after the flood, so that "seven" refers to the number of clean animals, not the pairs. Annotations on Genesis 7:2.[8]

Noah's Erudition. Konrad Pellikan: Noah possessed exceptional learning, for he could distinguish the clean animals from the unclean ones, obviously not yet having read Leviticus. Whence it is also to be understood that he excelled in many more natural gifts than Scripture makes explicit here. Commentary on Genesis 7:2.[9]

Clean and Unclean Was an Ancient Distinction. Andrew Willet: Some beasts were counted clean and others unclean not simply in respect of their nature and creation, for God saw that all things were good; nor only in regard to human use, because some were more fit for food than others; but chiefly because, by the institution of God, some were set apart for sacrifice and therefore were called clean. And this distinction of clean and unclean beasts is not inserted by Moses by way of anticipation, as though he spoke only with respect to the time of his own writing, but this difference was known to the patriarchs by revelation from God, by means of some godly tradition delivered from one to another, just as we see that sacrifice, the offering of tithes and the observation of the Sabbath were all practiced prior to the law. Commentary on Genesis 7:2.[10]

Why Some Animals Are Unclean. Wolfgang Musculus: What is the difference behind the cleanness of the clean animals and the uncleanness of the unclean ones in this context? The difference arises from various considerations. Indeed, sometimes the form of the body is such that it renders the animal unclean, as does the form of garden snakes, crocodiles, serpents, and countless others whose very appearance is repulsive to our eyes. Or else their diet is impure and detestable so as to render the animal unclean. Thus, swine are unclean, as are any animals that feed on what is unclean or obtain their food in violent and gory ways. Or an animal may be reckoned as unclean because it is not fit for human use. Such include poisonous animals and all the rest whose flesh, if eaten, is detrimental to the health of the human body. This last reason may well not have applied to the world before the flood, when (as is commonly held) humans did not eat meat. But the prior reasons sufficiently explain the difference between clean and unclean animals at that time. Commentary on Genesis 7:2.[11]

Where Did the Unclean Animals Come From? Wolfgang Musculus: How is it that some animals are called *clean* here, and others *unclean*, when there was not one of God's creatures that was not very good, just as we see in Genesis 1, where Moses says, "And God saw all that he made and they were very good"? My answer is that to be evil is not the same thing as to be unclean, which has to do not with uncleanness of soul but of bodily condition, which is itself free from evil so that for other purposes, if it is natural, it may also be good and useful. It is inaptly compared with uncleanness of soul in human beings, which is not from our first creation but from the venom of sin introduced by the serpent, and so is not good but evil. . . . In the universe that God made, even unclean animals have their use, so that they are properly numbered among the things that are "very good." If a creature of

---

[8]ZSW 13:49. [9]*Commentaria Bibliorum* (1532) 1:11r. [10]*Hexapla* (1608), 86-87. [11]*In Mosis Genesim* (1554), 196.

God is said to be good, it is only so in part and in some aspect. But if it be said of God, then *goodness* should no longer be understood as said of a part or aspect but absolutely, as referring to God in himself. The same logic holds in the case of clean and unclean animals. Whatever creature is called clean or unclean, it is said to be so not simplistically or in every way but in a restricted sense. Even clean animals have some uncleanness that makes them unclean, just as unclean animals also have a certain cleanness on account of which they could be called clean. Both kinds have no uncleanness before God, by whom they were created "very good"; but they differ in how mortals use and regard them. COMMENTARY ON GENESIS 7:2.[12]

GOD'S GOODNESS IS SHOWN IN THE ARK'S ABUNDANCE OF CLEAN ANIMALS. JOHN CALVIN: By *seven and seven*, one should understand not seven pairs of each kind, but three pairs, to which one animal is added for the sake of sacrifice. Besides, the Lord wanted to restore three times as many clean animals, because human beings were going to have a greater need for them; and in this provision we ought to contemplate God's fatherly goodness toward us, by which he is led to keep account of us in all things. COMMENTARY ON GENESIS 7:2.[13]

SOME ANIMALS DID NOT NEED TO ENTER THE ARK TO BE PRESERVED. ANDREW WILLET: Not every kind of living thing came, for some were excepted, including all that live in the water (whether wholly so, or partly in the water and partly on land), for only such creatures came as move upon the earth. [Likewise,] such creatures as arise from corruption and not by generation—as flies, [which arise] from water; worms, from dung; bees, from bullocks' flesh; hornets, from horse flesh; the scorpion, from crabs or crevices; moths, from putrefied herbs; and certain small

worms, from the corruption of wood and corn, etc. Only those creatures entered that increase by generation. Such creatures were also excepted that are of a mixed kind and are engendered by the male and female of diverse kinds, as the mule, which comes from a mare and an ass. COMMENTARY ON GENESIS 7:9.[14]

7:4 Forty Days and Forty Nights

RISING WATER MIGHT SPUR A GENUINE REPENTANCE. WOLFGANG MUSCULUS: Some ask what need there was, in order to wipe out all flesh, to send rain for forty days and nights, when it could have been accomplished not only in a single day, but even in a brief instant by the power of his word. . . . Certainly, there was no necessity for it to rain forty days and nights, nor should one conclude that . . . it couldn't have been done more quickly—only that it seems to have happened in this very manner. . . . The fact is, even if the will of God is utterly free from all constraints, it is nonetheless not irrational. How would he have done anything unreasonable who is wisdom itself and the source of all right reason? I will say what seems likely to me, then, seeing that where nothing certain is expressed in the Scriptures, one may make a sober use of plausible conjectures. Since God was going to bring about this universal flood on account of human wickedness, even though we do not read of people being saved from the billowing of the waves except for Noah alone with his family, it remains believable that during the interval of those forty days, while the waters rose, the opportunity might have been offered to many mortals to come to their senses and reflect on the things Noah had preached about—an opportunity that would have been utterly lost if they had all suddenly perished in a single moment. This is not to say that God

---

[12]*In Mosis Genesim* (1554), 196. [13]CTS 1:267* (CO 23:129).
[14]*Hexapla* (1608), 87-88, crediting Mercerus.

would have saved them from the waves if they had come around. It is a tardy repentance that is born in the midst of God's verdict and a well-earned penalty. It is too late for him to absolve them from the punishment. And yet, regarding such people, who would claim that it is utterly foolish in God's sight for them, when they see their destruction before their very eyes, to return to themselves and acknowledge the deserved judgment of God with repentant hearts? COMMENTARY ON GENESIS 7:4.[15]

STILL ROOM FOR MERCY? PETER MARTYR VERMIGLI: What shall we say about this truly severe and horrible act of vengeance? Was no room left there for mercy? I'm not speaking with respect to Noah but of those of whose truly calamitous destruction we read. And clearly, God did confer a benefit on those who were going to die. For if they repented, punishment became a guardian leading them to salvation. But those who died with their same unbelieving and wicked heart made an end and a limit to their sinning whether they wanted to or not, yet if they'd lived longer, they would have deserved harsher punishments. This is why the Lord said, "It will be more bearable for Sodom and Gomorrah" than for the children of Israel, because they paid some of their penalties by being incinerated and they made an end to their sinning more quickly than those who by living longer added to their sins and suffered no punishment in this life. COMMENTARY ON GENESIS 7:20.[16]

CONSCIENCE CAN BE MORE TERRIFYING THAN DROWNING. HULDRYCH ZWINGLI: Moses often repeats that "the waters greatly increased" and magnifies things in wondrous ways, so that we might understand the fear and horror of those whom the waters overwhelmed in punishment and who did not wish Noah's

voice to bring them to their senses. Now came the time of divine judgment: God was unwilling to spare Noah's contemporaries any longer and there was nowhere to hide. . . . Indeed, what do you suppose would have occurred to their consciences when they saw destruction at hand? Surely they were thinking nothing other than, "Oh, why didn't we believe the warnings of righteous Noah? Why didn't we come to our senses? Why did we refuse to fear God?" But this repentance is far too late, having stemmed more from desperation and fear of the evils at hand than from the love of God. Note here, too, that while destruction and devastation threaten the impious outside, a far more serious punishment lies within, namely, terror and despair of conscience, by which those who have not believed the voice of God are eventually destroyed and crushed. ANNOTATIONS ON GENESIS 7:18.[17]

NOAH'S DAY NEEDED MORE GODLY TEACHERS. MARTIN LUTHER: If at Noah's time there had been more godly teachers, a larger number of righteous people might also have been expected. Since the righteous have been reduced to such a small number that Noah alone is declared righteous, it is now sufficiently clear that the godly teachers either had been killed or had been turned to heresies and idolatry, so that there was left only Noah, the one "herald of righteousness," as Peter calls him. When the government had been turned into tyranny and the household had been ruined by adultery and fornication, how could the punishment hold off any longer? LECTURES ON GENESIS 7:1.[18]

---

[15]*In Mosis Genesim* (1554), 197. [16]*In Primum Librum Mosis* (1569), 33v. [17]ZSW 13:50, reading *interneclum* for Zwingli's *interniciem* at lines 31 and 37. [18]LW 2:84 (WA 42:321), citing 2 Pet 2:5.

7:10-24 THE FLOOD ARRIVES

^{10}*And after seven days the waters of the flood came upon the earth.*
^{11}*In the six hundredth year of Noah's life, in the second month, on the seventeenth day of the month, on that day all the fountains of the great deep burst forth, and the windows of the heavens were opened.* ^{12}*And rain fell upon the earth forty days and forty nights.* ^{13}*On the very same day Noah and his sons, Shem and Ham and Japheth, and Noah's wife and the three wives of his sons with them entered the ark,* ^{14}*they and every beast, according to its kind, and all the livestock according to their kinds, and every creeping thing that creeps on the earth, according to its kind, and every bird, according to its kind, every winged creature.* ^{15}*They went into the ark with Noah, two and two of all flesh in which there was the breath of life.* ^{16}*And those that entered, male and female of all flesh, went in as God had commanded him. And the* LORD *shut him in.*
^{17}*The flood continued forty days on the earth. The waters increased and bore up the ark, and it rose high above the earth.* ^{18}*The waters prevailed and increased greatly on the earth, and the ark floated on the face of the waters.* ^{19}*And the waters prevailed so mightily on the earth that all the high mountains under the whole heaven were covered.* ^{20}*The waters prevailed above the mountains, covering them fifteen cubits^a deep.* ^{21}*And all flesh died that moved on the earth, birds, livestock, beasts, all swarming creatures that swarm on the earth, and all mankind.* ^{22}*Everything on the dry land in whose nostrils was the breath of life died.* ^{23}*He blotted out every living thing that was on the face of the ground, man and animals and creeping things and birds of the heavens. They were blotted out from the earth. Only Noah was left, and those who were with him in the ark.* ^{24}*And the waters prevailed on the earth 150 days.*

a A *cubit* was about 18 inches or 45 centimeters

OVERVIEW: The repetitive nature of Genesis 7, noted above, removes almost all suspense in the exegesis of this chapter, because so much of what is described here has been described or predicted at least once already. So far as concerns the narrative's details, there is passing interest in explaining the "fountains" and "windows" (Gen 7:11), but most had discussed these "two waters" earlier, in Genesis 1:6-7. The greatest controversy in the text, at least from a critical standpoint, was the vexed and venerable question of the extent of the flood. From the earliest times, writers unfriendly to the biblical account or its adherents were skeptical or contemptuous of its claims. How could the waters possibly have covered even the highest mountains? Alternate solutions were sometimes sought by suggesting that the flood was not so deep, or that it was a far more local phenomenon than described here—and thus, incidentally, there may have been a few survivors after all. Like the controversy over the feasibility of the ark's design, debates over the extent of the flood were intractable. Yet not everyone felt obliged to engage. Luther and Calvin bypassed the question in their remarks on Genesis 7, as did Zwingli and Pellikan. The inundation of the mountains was defended by Vermigli, Brenz and Musculus, but their mid-century discussions are still fairly brief in comparison with Andrew Willet's recap of the debate half a century later (excerpted below).[1]

Three other topics proved more interesting to these practical theologians of the Reformation. First, they identified strongly with Noah's trials inside the ark and mused at length both on God's providence and prevenience as well as on Noah's own faith and endurance. Second, they wrote with some poignancy about the horrifying judgment visited on all flesh. This mesmerizing expression of God's wrath then led them to consider the significance of the flood as an analogue to the last judgment yet to come and, in turn, to explore with appreciation the traditional parallels drawn between the ark and the church.

7:11 The Fountains of the Deep Burst Forth and the Windows of the Heavens Opened

FLOODING FROM ABOVE AND BELOW BECAUSE OF SINS AGAINST HEAVEN AND EARTH. MARTIN LUTHER: This was not an ordinary rain, but "both the windows of the heaven and the fountains of the deep were opened" (v. 11), that is, a large quantity of rain came down from heaven, and a huge mass of water poured forth out of the earth itself. . . . This was no ordinary rain; it was a rain of the Lord's wrath, by which He intended to destroy every living thing on the earth. Because the earth was ruined, the Lord ruined it too; and because the ungodly contended against the First and the Second Table, God used heaven and earth to contend against them. LECTURES ON GENESIS 7:4.[2]

GOD PROTECTS US FROM THE WATERS OF HEAVEN AND EARTH. JOHN CALVIN: Here we must consider the wonderful counsel of God. Indeed, he might have channeled as much water as would have sufficed for all the needs of human life into designated canals or inside the veins of the earths. Instead, he has deliberately placed us between two graves, lest we presumptuously despise the kindness on which our life depends: for the element of water, which philosophers regard as one of the principles of life, threatens us with death from above and below, except so far as it is restrained by the hand of God. COMMENTARY ON GENESIS 7:11.[3]

FOUNTAINS AND WINDOWS. ANDREW WILLET: The *fountains of the deep* were the deep heads and springs of water within the earth, which were opened and enlarged to make this inundation: so that the rivers that run in the earth were cast up and the deep chasm gushed forth. (These may be the waters under the earth mentioned in Exodus 20:4.) The *windows of heaven* signify not the corruption or breaking forth of any waters in the crystal heaven (as it is called) above the starry sky, as Steuchus and Oleaster imagine, for there are no such waters above the heavens, . . . and if there were, how could they pass through the starry heaven without dissolving and corrupting it? And it would follow that the watery heaven would now be a vacant and empty place, its waters having descended from thence. Rather, the opening of the windows of heaven betokens the breaking of the clouds where the water is contained: while at other times "the Lord binds the waters in the clouds, and the cloud is not broken under them" (Job 26:8), now the Lord loosed the clouds, which, being made as if full of windows, poured forth all the water that was kept in them. COMMENTARY ON GENESIS 7:11.[4]

---

[1]Don Cameron Allen outlines both the pre- and post-Reformation course of these debates in *The Legend of Noah: Renaissance Rationalism in Art, Science and Letters* (Urbana: University of Illinois Press, 1963), 66-91. [2]LW 2:89* (WA 42:325). [3]CTS 1:270* (CO 23:131-32). [4]*Hexapla* (1608), 91, crediting Mercerus and Pererius.

7:16b *And the Lord Shut Him In*

TWO KINDS OF SHUT-IN. WOLFGANG MUSCULUS: Notice this kind of confinement. Evildoers and criminals are shut in lest they flee, but they are kept safe for punishment on the day of judgment, or at least kept from harming anyone and disturbing the public peace. On the other hand, things that are precious are also confined, lest they suffer damage from some source or another. The Lord uses both kinds of confinement. He confines angels, sinners and the ungodly until the day of judgment, when they will be condemned and punished. He confines the righteous when he safeguards them in his custody against every evil. So Noah was confined in the ark with his family, just as seed is kept hidden in a storehouse for the day of planting, lest he be lost in the violence of the flood. COMMENTARY ON GENESIS 7:16.[5]

THE DOOR WAS SECURED NOT BY NOAH'S SKILL BUT BY A MIRACLE. JOHN CALVIN: It must have been an ample door to be large enough for an elephant! Truly, no pitch could have been so firm and so tenacious, nor could any framework be so rigid, that the immense force of the water would not eventually work its way through its many seams, especially in an onrush so violent and in such severe tossing about. Therefore, in order to cut off occasion for the vain speculations that our own curiosity suggests, Moses declares with a single word that it was not by human skill but by divine miracle that the ark was made secure from the flood. There is indeed no doubt but that Noah was endowed with uncommon ability and insight, so that nothing needed for the ark's construction would be overlooked, but—lest even this favor should fail to find success—it was necessary for something greater to be added. COMMENTARY ON GENESIS 7:16.[6]

A BRIEF RESTORATION OF ORIGINAL DOMINION AND PEACE. PETER MARTYR VERMIGLI: When Noah was shut up in the ark, God wanted him to be wholly dependent on him. Once the door of the ark had been shut and the land was everywhere covered by water, he was tossed about, devoid of any assistance from nature. But he would have been consoled by this, that it was at God's command that he did this, and that he would have known that those evils came to pass not by the power of the stars or by their chance movements, but by God having willed it so. And because he remained alive in the ark, uninjured among beasts and truly ferocious and savage animals, he showed that he had in a certain sense regained that dominion of the first man, for what had been lost through sin seems to have been restored here. God is sometimes seen to grant this very thing to individual saints. Paul shook off a viper, David killed lions, and Daniel could not at all be harmed by them. But when we now see this same thing come to pass in the ark, it foreshadows the peace of those who have come to Christ. However much, back when they were still in the world and outside of Christ, they may have lived in the flesh and had barbarian habits, in Christ nonetheless all are tamed. Those who are truly related to him are peaceable and gentle toward one another, for they do not look to their own interests. COMMENTARY ON GENESIS 7:17.[7]

THE TERROR OF THOSE WHO WERE SAVED. MARTIN LUTHER: In what frame of mind do you suppose we would have been if we had been brought into the ark and had seen the waters rushing in from all sides with such force and the wretched mortals swimming in the water and wretchedly perishing without any help? . . . They sat in the ark for forty days

[5]*In Mosis Genesim* (1554), 205, citing 2 Pet 2. [6]CTS 1:272* (CO 23:132-33). [7]*In Primum Librum Mosis* (1569), 33r.

before it was lifted from the earth. During these days whatever human beings and animals lived on the earth were destroyed. This disaster they saw with their own eyes. Who would doubt that they were profoundly shocked by it? Furthermore, the ark floats on the water for one hundred and fifty days, buffeted by waves and gusts on all sides. In these circumstances no harbor could be hoped for, nor any association with other human beings. As exiles cast out of the world, they are driven hither and thither by the waves and winds. Is it not a miracle that these eight human beings did not die of grief and fear? We are indeed devoid of feeling if we can read this account with dry eyes. LECTURES ON GENESIS 7:13-16.[8]

A LONG LESSON IN FAITH AND COURAGE. PETER MARTYR VERMIGLI: Meanwhile, let us admire the strong and steadfast man shut up in the ark, to whom the care of his family and the irrational animals had been committed. No ordinary courage was needed here: danger was assured, hope hung only on God's promise. Nonetheless, however long God makes Noah wait, he does not complain. Certainly, once those wicked people had been killed, God could have immediately removed the waters from the earth and released this man from that ark and from so many hardships. He didn't do that, yet as long as God remained in hiding, so to speak, no complaints are heard from Noah here. In Exodus, Moses complained, saying, "Only a moment remains before they'll stone me!" And in Numbers he said he could no longer bear such cares and concerns by himself, asking, "Did I give birth to all these people?" Noah could have said that about the livestock, birds and beasts that he was feeding in the ark, yet he was strong and of a steady mind, so we read nothing of this kind about him. Nonetheless, this delay was not without purpose: Noah's faith grew by this exercise, for during this time he wasn't idle but was strengthened by waiting. COMMENTARY ON GENESIS 7:24.[9]

NOAH NEEDED FAITH AGAINST FEAR . . . AND BOREDOM. WOLFGANG MUSCULUS: Consider how much faith Noah needed: while the height of the waters covered everything, hiding all the mountains and persisting for so long with no hint of receding, he did not lose heart or dread that this inundation of waters would never end. Yet it is unbelievable that the heart of a man still imperfect would not have been tempted and tested by temptations, however faithful and pious he may have been. Truly, . . . it was not without boredom and longing that he waited for the land to dry up, and he busied himself by undertaking his experiment of releasing first the raven and then the dove. Still, he waited until the earth was dried by God himself. COMMENTARY ON GENESIS 7:24.[10]

NO PROCREATION DURING TIMES OF SORROW. ANDREW WILLET: Noah and his wife are not named together going into the ark, but they are joined together when they come forth in Genesis 8:16, "Come forth, you and your wife." Ambrose thus notes that "the sex is not mixed when they enter but when they exit." Wherefore he thinks that Noah and his sons refrained from the company of their wives the whole time they were in the ark. His opinion is most probable, though not on this ground but for better reasons, which he adds in the same place, saying "it was a time of sorrow not of mirth." They knew that the deluge came about because of the intemperance of the world, even as the rest of the creatures also generally abstained from the act of generation (which I prefer to think rather than what Mercerus says, that the cattle multiplied in the ark), either because the place

---

[8]LW 2:96-97 (WA 42:330-31). [9]*In Primum Librum Mosis* (1569), 33v. [10]*In Mosis Genesim* (1554), 211.

was not fit, or the seasons of the year were altered (for it was like a continual winter for the space of a year, on account of the coldness of the overflowing water), or because God so disposed their natural inclination. COMMENTARY ON GENESIS 7:7.[11]

7:19-20 All the High Mountains under the Whole Heaven Were Covered

THE FLOOD REALLY WAS THAT DEEP, UNIVERSAL AND BEYOND SURVIVING. ANDREW WILLET: [This verse] refutes those who think that some high hills were not flooded (such as Olympus, which Augustine disproves), and Cajetan, who would have the mountain of paradise to be excepted from this inundation. . . . Augustine reasons thus: "They do not consider that the earth, the heaviest of all elements, is in the top of these high hills." It need not seem strange, then, that the waters might ascend there.[†] [Next,] where does Cajetan find that paradise was situated on a hill? Nay, the contrary is gathered out of Scripture, for "out of Eden went a river to water the garden" (Gen 2:10). But rivers usually do not run up hills. And Cajetan need not have feared the drowning of paradise because of Enoch: for he was with God, taken up into heaven, where the flood could not reach him. A notion similar to Cajetan's is shared by Bellarmine, who thinks that not all the mountains were flooded, but only those where the wicked dwelt. And Josephus reports from Nicholaus of Damascus that there is a certain hill in Armenia called Baris, "where they say many who fled for refuge at the time of the flood were preserved." But these dreams and devices are overthrown by the evident words of Scripture, that "all high mountains under heaven were covered with the waters." Likewise, that fabulous dream of some Hebrews is here disproved, who imagine that besides Noah and the rest of the eight persons, Og—king of Basan, who lived till Moses' time

and one of those giants before the flood—might have been preserved. Besides the fact that no one after the flood lived so long, where should Og have been kept in the flood, seeing that the mountains were covered fifteen cubits high, which exceeded the stature of any giant. For the Hebrews are merely spinning a fable to suppose those giants to have been a hundred cubits high. Neither is that report out of Pliny much to be credited, of a giant's body found in Crete of 46 cubits. Further, Ibn Ezra refutes the opinion of some in his day who held this deluge not to have been universal: for although it may have been that not all the world was inhabited before the flood, but only the eastern parts (because they lacked the invention of ships to transport them from place to place, for Noah was the first to use a ship), yet it is without doubt that the whole earth was flooded, seeing that the highest hills were so far under the water. COMMENTARY ON GENESIS 7:19-20.[12]

7:21 All Flesh Died That Moved on Earth

NO REFUGE FROM GOD'S WRATH. WOLFGANG MUSCULUS: When waters overflow and begin to cover the surface of the earth, high and lofty mountains are regarded as a refuge. But this example declares that when God's wrath breaks forth, no place is high enough to offer safety to those against whom divine vengeance is sent. That which is illustrated by these mountains is also to be seen in high towers, in fortified cities, in the strength of the rulers of this world and in the wisdom and

---

[11]*Hexapla* (1608), 87. Ambrose's theme of abstaining from sexual relations while on the ark appears in his *De Noe et Arca* 21.76 (PL 14:397), but he was surely borrowing it from Philo, *Questions and Answers on Genesis* 2.49. [12]*Hexapla* (1608), 93, citing Mercerus. [†]Augustine's argument (in *City of God* 15.27) goes on to explain that if earth is denser and heavier than water, why should it be impossible for water to rise as high into the atmosphere as the highest mountains? The quote from Josephus that follows is from *Antiquities* 1.3.6 (95).

whatever carnal honors the mighty and powerful possess. Wherefore we should take heed not to seek refuge in this kind of honor, but only in God. The kings of Assyria, Babylon, Persia, Greece and Rome were also "great mountains," but they could not save their citizens from the flood of God's wrath. Today, too, we see great and sublime mountains rising up as impious people who think they will be kept safe by their own strength and loftiness. But the flood of God's vengeance will break forth in an instant and cover not only valleys and plains but also the highest mountains—at a time when the avenging sword of human wickedness will pass through the world, mowing down everything and overthrowing even the loftiest. COMMENTARY ON GENESIS 7:17-20.[13]

THE RAIN ANNOUNCED THAT THE TIME HAD EXPIRED. KONRAD PELLIKAN: The rain continued for forty days straight before the ark could be moved and lifted off the ground. And so, the time expired for repentance and for considering the judgment of the Lord. In great distress those people perished who had long mocked Noah for proclaiming such things to them and exhorting them to change their ways. Although people usually dread such horrifying judgments of God, they just as often despise the words of prophets and the warnings that the Lord sends through the pious. COMMENTARY ON GENESIS 7:12.[14]

THE BENEFITS OF PUNISHMENT. PETER MARTYR VERMIGLI: The punishment that God implemented was beneficial for everyone. For those who were kept safe in the ark and awaited their liberation by clinging to God's mercy, they were taught during that time to depend on God alone. For their descendants, who would hear of how God punished the wicked, they would all the more refrain from godless deeds. For those who were killed and not only made an end to their sinning in that

way, but also bore part of their punishment and would have made an end to their sinning in that they were punished now more lightly: they did not pile up sins (as did those whom God sustained longer) and they therefore bore smaller penalties. . . . Sin isn't as serious or shameful if it has been joined by punishment as it is if it goes unpunished, because when separated from the penalty it deserves, sin vents its rage more widely. COMMENTARY ON GENESIS 7:24.[15]

DO PUNISHMENTS IN THIS LIFE CANCEL FUTURE PENALTIES? WOLFGANG MUSCULUS: The question is raised here about those people who perished in the flood, as to whether they will also be punished in the future and be given everlasting penalties along with unbelievers and the impenitent. They also ask this about the people of Sodom who were consumed by fire from heaven, and of the Egyptians who were drowned in the Red Sea, and of the Israelites who expired in the wilderness, and all the rest whom God's punishments chastised and carried off in the midst of this life. To this question some respond that those who are stricken and punished by God's judgment in this life will not be punished further in the future: but since they were punished in this world, they have received the penalty for their sins and will be saved together with the faithful. They cite the saying of the prophet Nahum in chapter 1[:9], namely, that "the Lord will not bring vengeance against the same person a second time." Jerome is found to have held this view in his comments on this verse [and he concluded in all these cases] that . . . "the Lord meted out punishment in the present so that he might not punish them everlastingly. . . ." But I don't think his view is so certain or firm that it can

---

[13]*In Mosis Genesim* (1554), 209-10; the last line here credits Lactantius, *Institutes* 7.15. [14]*Commentaria Bibliorum* (1532) 1:11r-v. [15]*In Primum Librum Mosis* (1569), 33v, citing Ex 17:4; Num 11:12.

be embraced without danger. Indeed, it does not square with the grace of election, without which no one is saved, unless we're going to say that all the mortals who perished in the flood—and later on in Sodom and Gomorrah, as well as in the Red Sea, and then in the wilderness, just as much as the ungodly who were divinely stricken—were elected to [eternal] life. Nor do unequal penalties contradict God's justice, in accordance with which we believe that even if the ungodly and unrepentant were afflicted with some special punishment in this life, they will still be punished everlastingly in the future. . . . At the same time, I won't say that *no one* from the number of those who perished in the waters of the flood was saved from eternal condemnation—heaven forbid! But if any of them were saved, it was by the grace of election and the redemption which is through Christ that they were freed, not by the temporal punishments that were exacted for their sins. COMMENTARY ON GENESIS 7:21-22.[16]

SOME WHO PERISHED MAY STILL HAVE HAD A DEGREE OF FAITH. NIKOLAUS

SELNECKER: Were all those who perished in the flood also damned? By no means. Indeed, it is certain that even if many did not believe in Noah's prediction of the total destruction of the whole world, nonetheless, they were clearly not without true faith and trust in a future redemption to be brought about through the woman's promised seed, and they were clearly not godless. This too is certain, that many were converted by the inundation itself—the flood—and by their final struggle, even if they incurred bodily punishments. Peter thus seems to give a nod to this view, that Christ, in his incarnation, having made satisfaction for sins, restored those who had been detained in prison so long, from the time of the flood until Christ should have come. . . . Surely many are saved who nonetheless incur punishments in this life. Many, too, are converted in the very

instant of punishment who have until then lived recklessly. There are also many who do not easily believe that God is going to punish crimes in such a brief space of time who, for all that, do not doubt about the last day and the final judgment. We should therefore judge these things with equanimity, and we should always say, "Just are you, O Lord, and your judgment is just." COMMENTARY ON GENESIS 8:21-22.[17]

7:23c Only Noah Was Left, and Those Who Were with Him in the Ark

NOAH'S DAY WAS LIKE THE END TIMES.

MARTIN LUTHER: This verdict about the world is in agreement with Christ's statement; for because the last times will be similar to the times of Noah, Christ correctly declares (Luke 18:8): "When the Son of Man comes, will He find faith?" It is dreadful to live in such an evil and ungodly world. Since we have the light of the Word, this present time, by the grace of God, is still a golden age. The sacraments are properly administered in our churches, and godly clergymen disseminate the Word in its purity. Although the government is weak, wickedness is not yet beyond hope. LECTURES ON GENESIS 7:1.[18]

THE FLOOD AND THE LAST JUDGMENT.

PETER MARTYR VERMIGLI: This flood offers the clearest type of the last judgment. In the former, evildoers are suffocated by the waters; in the latter, the ungodly are condemned to the ultimate punishment. But if you should object, "No one is certain of that day, for the Father has placed the moments and times under his own control, which is not at all ours to know. But Noah foretold that a flood would occur at a time when it was still 120 years in the future, and then, when the hour was now imminent,

---

[16]*In Mosis Genesim* (1554), 208. [17]*In Genesin* (1569), 335, citing 1 Pet 3:19-20; Ps 119:147. [18]LW 2:83-84 (WA 42:321).

he heard that there were still seven days remaining," I don't deny it. On the other hand, I would say that if we consider the beliefs of those who heard him, people in Noah's day didn't know this. Indeed, it was *because* they did not believe that they were unexpectedly overwhelmed, as the Lord himself attests in Matthew 24. But the acute obstinacy of their minds can be made clear to us in this way, for it is not read here that anyone petitioned God or prayed to be saved, even though they would have been frightened by Noah's preaching and by his construction of the ark for a long time. Nor can people of our time plead as an excuse that they are by no means exposed to such serious threats as the ones that challenged those of Noah's day to return to their senses, because nowadays it is not the waters of a flood that are set before the ungodly, but the hell of eternal damnation that they will suffer unless they turn back. COMMENTARY ON GENESIS 7:17.[19]

THE CHURCH AND THE ARK. KONRAD PELLIKAN: Just as at that time Noah's ark rested in complete safety while the waters of the flood rose to their height, so the faithful and righteous in the church are especially lifted up and thus escape from dangers when the impious, in the midst of their infidelity, are overwhelmed by the gales of distress and perish. COMMENTARY ON GENESIS 7:19.[20]

NO SALVATION OUTSIDE THE ARK—FOR THEM OR US. JOHANNES BRENZ: First Peter 3[:21] compares baptism with Noah's ark: Just as Noah and his family were saved in the ark, lest they perish in the flood, so also we are saved by baptism, lest we perish by fire. And certainly, just as no one was saved outside the ark, so outside the baptism of Christ and faith in Christ no one is saved. But if Ham or Japheth had cast himself outside the ark, he also would have perished unless he had returned to it and been received back into it.

So, too, do we, by our various misdeeds, often cast ourselves outside the ark of baptism or faith in Christ, but the way back into this ark is well-known to us: through repentance. COMMENTARY ON GENESIS 7:6-7.[21]

THE ARK AS AN IMAGE OF DEATH AND RESURRECTION. JOHN CALVIN: The church is appropriately and deservedly compared with the ark. But we must keep in mind the point of similarity by which they mutually correspond with one other, for that in fact is derived solely from God's word. For just as Noah, acting on God's promise, gathered his wife and children together with him so that as a kind of depiction of death he might emerge from death; so is it fitting that we should renounce the world and die in order that the Lord may bring us back to life by his word. Truly, nowhere else is there a safe place for the preservation of our salvation. COMMENTARY ON GENESIS 7:17.[22]

THE ARK AS A SACRAMENT OF CHRIST'S BODY. PETER MARTYR VERMIGLI: In both *Against Faustus* and *The City of God*, Augustine asserts that the ark corresponds to the measurements of the human body, because it is six times longer than wide and ten times longer than its height, a proportion that clearly appears to have been maintained in the ark. Thus, because Christ assumed a human body, by this sacrament, he thought to denote the construction of the ark. If we admit that reading, it does not disagree at all with what we said earlier, that the church is foreshadowed in this structure, because the church itself is the mystical body of Christ. It was made from wood that was not only light but also would not decay easily—descriptions that beyond a doubt would appropriately fit those who are holy. The wooden timbers, however,

---

[19]*In Primum Librum Mosis* (1569), 33r. [20]*Commentaria Bibliorum* (1532) 1:11v. [21]*Opera* 1:101. [22]CTS 1:273* (CO 23:133-34).

remind us of the cross of Christ, because only thus, by his truly shameful death, could we who are so burdened by sin be relieved, lest we be smothered by perpetual suffering. The church tosses about amidst the waves, but it is nonetheless not submerged, because the gates of hell do not prevail against it. Individual believers, too, may be cast about a bit by mental distress and lapses, but by no means are they wholly overwhelmed unless they are cut off from their faith, which is hardly to be feared if it is true and effective. COMMENTARY ON GENESIS 7:20.[23]

---

[23]*In Primum Librum Mosis* (1569), 33v.

8:1-12 THE FLOOD SUBSIDES

[1]*But God remembered Noah and all the beasts and all the livestock that were with him in the ark. And God made a wind blow over the earth, and the waters subsided.* [2]*The fountains of the deep and the windows of the heavens were closed, the rain from the heavens was restrained,* [3]*and the waters receded from the earth continually. At the end of 150 days the waters had abated,* [4]*and in the seventh month, on the seventeenth day of the month, the ark came to rest on the mountains of Ararat.* [5]*And the waters continued to abate until the tenth month; in the tenth month, on the first day of the month, the tops of the mountains were seen.*

[6]*At the end of forty days Noah opened the window of the ark that he had made* [7]*and sent forth a raven. It went to and fro until the waters were dried up from the earth.* [8]*Then he sent forth a dove from him, to see if the waters had subsided from the face of the ground.* [9]*But the dove found no place to set her foot, and she returned to him to the ark, for the waters were still on the face of the whole earth. So he put out his hand and took her and brought her into the ark with him.* [10]*He waited another seven days, and again he sent forth the dove out of the ark.* [11]*And the dove came back to him in the evening, and behold, in her mouth was a freshly plucked olive leaf. So Noah knew that the waters had subsided from the earth.* [12]*Then he waited another seven days and sent forth the dove, and she did not return to him anymore.*

OVERVIEW: The narrative of the flood begins to come to a close in Genesis 8, signaled by the terse but potent opening sentence, "God remembered Noah." Much of the prose in this chapter repeats details and descriptions that have already been stated once or twice, but there are new things as well: the role of the wind, the location of the ark's final resting place and the picturesque narrative of the raven and the dove released by Noah.

The primary interest of Reformation commentators in the opening paragraph of Genesis 8 is pastoral. Nearly all of them pause to ponder the wondrous if anthropomorphic description of God as one who *remembers*. Most feel obliged to explain the description as an anthropomorphism, but all find it also intended as a source of encouragement to Noah and to us—along with other encouraging details to be noted.

The subsequent account of how Noah released first a raven and then a dove in order to test whether the earth had sufficiently dried was mined by traditional commentators for all sorts of reasons. Some assumed that Noah must have chosen these two particular birds on the basis of his special wisdom, revelation or insight. The Bible thus functioned for some interpreters much like a medieval bestiary here, definitively disclosing the special character of these animals for all time. For others, the story was a rich source for allegorical readings. In both cases, speculative impulses were sometimes fueled by inside information or other lore gleaned from the writings of the rabbis. Some longer excerpts are included here, in hopes of correcting the misimpression that Protestants always followed the letter and never allegorized.

However, even where commentators sought to keep to the literal sense, questions still lingered about Noah's motives for releasing these birds. Surprisingly, perhaps, not all exegetes agreed that it was proper for Noah to do so. And, to make things still more interesting, there is a small but momentous discrepancy between the Hebrew text and the Latin and Greek versions that complicated the otherwise minor issue of whether the raven did or did not return to the ark.

8:1a God Remembered Noah

GOD BREAKS HIS LONG SILENCE. MARTIN LUTHER: It is not idle chatter when the Holy Spirit says that God remembered Noah. It indicates that from the day when Noah entered the ark nothing was said to him, nothing was revealed to him, and he saw no ray of grace shining; but he clung only to the promise he had received, although meanwhile the waters and the waves were raging as though God had surely forgotten him. His children, the cattle, and the other animals of every kind experienced the same peril throughout the entire hundred and fifty days in the ark. Even though the holy seed overcame these perils, through a rich measure of the Spirit, it did not overcome them without great affliction of the flesh, without tears and great fear, which I think the dumb animals experienced too. LECTURES ON GENESIS 8:1.[1]

TEMPTATION MAKES US FEEL FORGOTTEN.
KONRAD PELLIKAN: God always regards and cares diligently for the good of all his creatures, especially humans, so that he should be believed to act (and truly does act) for the individual good of each person at the same time as he acts equally for all. Nonetheless, it seems that we are forgotten when we are overwhelmed by temptations, when we are abandoned to our own anxieties. But he "remembers" when he consoles, runs to help and sustains us. Thus he remembers Noah when he escapes from danger, when he withstands the flood waters. COMMENTARY ON GENESIS 8:1.[2]

WHY GOD SEEMS TO FORGET US. NIKOLAUS SELNECKER: In these words, "the Lord remembered," Noah's temptation in the ark is silently described, that he was deserted by God and that God clearly had forgotten him. Indeed, God is sometimes in the habit of delaying his help and suspending his grace. This suspension of grace produces the severest struggle and sadness in the saints, through which faith, having been stirred up and strengthened by the Holy Spirit, triumphs and overcomes all the temptations that the flesh could by no means

---

[1]LW 2:103-4 (WA 42:335-36). [2]*Commentaria Bibliorum* (1532) 1:11v.

conquer without the Holy Spirit. It is therefore rightly said that the highest art of the godly is †to believe in things unseen, to hope in things delayed, to love a God who presents himself to us as an enemy, and in this way to persevere to the end. And well known is the voice of Anthony in a most difficult struggle, wondering, "O good Jesus, where were you?" and receiving the reply, "I was here, so that I might see your battle." COMMENTARY ON GENESIS 8:1.[3]

GOD HAD BEEN PRESENT ALL ALONG, BUT IN HIDDEN MIRACLES. JOHANNES BRENZ: Scripture says that after 150 days, "the Lord remembered Noah and the animals in the ark." So, did he really forget about them until then? It surely seemed so to Noah and his family. After all, they were tossed about by the waves for 150 days, seeing no end to the flood. The water was looking like it would endure forever. The ark was a fragile craft. And after all that, the food began to run out, so that those who had been buried by the waters would have been judged to be happier than those still alive in the ark. Where could they then turn? And so they concluded that they had been consigned by God to oblivion. But surely God was at that time deeply concerned for their safety. To be sure, that he would keep them safe until the flood ended was not something he made known externally, by some sign of his favor. Yet he himself was securing the ark, lest it be drowned by the waters; he forbade the waves, lest they cover the ark; and in the ark itself, he confined the beasts to their proper activities. In a word, he preserved them in the ark by means of hidden miracles, while they themselves would have had no other comfort than that which they derived from the word of the Lord spoken to them earlier: "I will establish my covenant with you, and you will enter the ark," etc. Therefore Noah said to his family, "Let us have a good hope, let us be at peace in our hearts. Even if we see no end of evils or any sign of God's favor—truly, all things are full of wrath—we still have God's word, by which he commanded the ark to be built and us to enter it, and he inviolably promised he would protect us. . . ." This example should be lodged deep within our minds, so that we might know where consolation is to be sought when God seems to have forgotten us. COMMENTARY ON GENESIS 8:1.[4]

GOD KNOWS WHEN WE NEED TO BE REMEMBERED. PETER MARTYR VERMIGLI: Scripture previously said that God had seen that "Noah was righteous and upright among the people of his time." Then, when he wanted to save him and shut him up in the ark, he was seen to watch over him. But now, when Noah has been confined in the ark for so long without being delivered from it, it seems to some extent (speaking in a human way) that God, having forgotten him, could be said to remember him when he now sets him free. What I mean is that he remembered his pact and covenant and oath, which is to say that he honored all these things by leading Noah out. From this we note that our afflictions have a limit, and while God sometimes seems to have forgotten us, at the right time he does come to our aid. But we should not desire to be regarded as the deciders of when the time is right, for God knows this far better than we can grasp it. We should take comfort from this example when we seem to find ourselves afflicted for longer than is fair. COMMENTARY ON GENESIS 8:1.[5]

TRUE FAITH KNOWS HOW TO DEAL WITH A SEEMINGLY FORGETFUL GOD. MARTIN LUTHER: Moses' statement, "The Lord remem-

---

[3]*In Genesin* (1569), 324, with †an uncredited line from Luther's *Lectures on Genesis* 25:11 (LW 4:324; WA 43:370). The lines from Anthony derive from Athanasius, *Life of Anthony* 10 (NPNF[2] 4:199), but probably via the Latin version of Evagrius of Antioch (PL 73:132) or possibly from *The Golden Legend*. [4]*Opera* 1:102. [5]*In Primum Librum Mosis* (1569), 34r.

bered Noah," must not be weakened as though it were a figure of speech meaning that God acted as if He had forgotten, when actually God cannot forget His saints. A grammarian does not understand what it means to live in such a manner as to feel that God has forgotten you. The most perfect saints are those who understand these matters and who in faith can bear with a God who is, so to speak, forgetful. For this reason the psalms and the entire Bible are full of such laments in which men call upon God to arise, to open His eyes, to hear, and to awake. LECTURES ON GENESIS 8:1.[6]

GOD REMEMBERS OUR ANIMALS, AND OUR DAILY BREAD. JOHANNES BRENZ: What does it mean, that God is said to have remembered not only Noah but also all the animals in the ark? Paul asks, "Are oxen of concern to God?" Indeed they are! Oxen and the rest of the animals are not God's principal concern, but he does care for them for our sake, just as they were created for us. What should we learn from this? First of all, we should realize that our livestock are included in this line of the Lord's Prayer: "Give us this day our daily bread." Truly, we pray that God will also protect our livestock, which are necessary more for our use [than by God]. COMMENTARY ON GENESIS 8:1.[7]

GOD REMEMBERS CATTLE. ANDREW WILLET: Not that there is oblivion or forgetfulness with God, but God is said to remember when he shows by the effects that he cares for human beings. Thus, God is said to remember a person's sins when he punishes them, as the widow in 1 Kings 17:18 said to the prophet, "Have you come to call my sin to remembrance, and to slay my son?" God also remembers the cattle here, but Moses does not thereby contradict Paul in 1 Corinthians 9:9 ("Does God take care for oxen?"). There, the apostle does not deny that God's providence watches over cattle but states that his care for

us is greater and that he cares for beasts for our sake. So, then, just as cattle perished in the flood together with the wicked, so they are preserved for the sake of the righteous. COMMENTARY ON GENESIS 8:1.[8]

8:1b And God Made a Wind Blow

THE UNGODLY FAIL TO SEE GOD IN HIS INSTRUMENTS. HULDRYCH ZWINGLI: God could have flooded the whole earth with water by his word alone, but instead he opened the veins of the earth, the springs and the seas below; and he sent rain upon the earth until the waters grew strong enough to demolish everything. Likewise, he could have called the waters back with a single word, but instead he roused a wind for this, so that we might see . . . that even if he can do all things by his power alone and by a nod and a word, God nonetheless uses the instruments that he created for this. All the same, pious people recognize that all things are wrought by God and they count everything as received from God—unlike the impious, who do not recognize God but attribute things to the stars, to luck or to accidents, so that they may find an excuse for their vices. ANNOTATIONS ON GENESIS 8:1.[9]

GOD USES TANGIBLE MEANS TO DEMONSTRATE HIS POWER. JOHN CALVIN: Although God could have dried the earth by his secret power, he made use of the wind, the same method he also employed in drying the Red Sea. And thus he wished to testify that just as he then had the waters at his command, ready to execute his wrath, so did he now hold the winds in his hand to provide relief. And though a remarkable account is recorded here by Moses, we are nonetheless taught that the winds do not arise by chance

---

[6]LW 2:104 (WA 42:336). [7]*Opera* 1:103, citing 1 Cor 9:9. [8]*Hexapla* (1608), 96, crediting Mercerus. [9]ZSW 13:51.

but are stirred up by God's command. COM-
MENTARY ON GENESIS 8:1.[10]

WAS IT WIND, OR GOD'S SPIRIT? WOLF-
GANG MUSCULUS: Since the word *spirit* in the
Holy Scriptures frequently refers to the Holy
Spirit, that is, the third person of the Holy
Trinity, some would conclude that Moses
speaks of it here, just as they understand
Genesis 1, above, where we read, "And the
spirit of God was hovering over the waters."
They think that both there and here the Holy
Spirit dispersed the waters with his power and
brought them back to their place. Truly, while
it is not to be denied that not only what Moses
writes there but also here was done by the
working of the "spirit" (that is, of God's
power), it is still not at all necessary for us to
understand the word *spirit* of the spirit of God
rather than of a certain wind or instrument of
divine working and power. We read of how
this worked in Exodus 14[:21]: ". . . the Lord
drove back the sea with a strong wind . . ."—a
text where, just as here, one reads the word
ruach, which they rarely render as *spirit* if they
can translate it as either *wind* or *breath*, so that
the meaning of the narrative would be clearer
and give no one cause for questions. COMMEN-
TARY ON GENESIS 8:1.[11]

8:6-12 *The Raven and the Dove*

**GOD GUIDED THE DOVE TO PLUCK AN
OLIVE BRANCH.** MARTIN LUTHER: These
things were done by divine direction. Other
trees at that time also had leaves, especially
those that are taller and emerged more quickly
from the waters. The olive tree is low in
comparison with the rest of the trees. Therefore it was suited to this purpose; through it
Noah could become aware of the decrease of
the waters, and by a practical process of
reasoning could conclude that the wrath of
God had now ceased and that the earth had
returned to the condition in which it had been

before the Flood. This he knew with greater
certainty when the dove which was sent out
the third time did not return; for she not only
had food on the earth but could also build
nests and walk on the ground. LECTURES ON
GENESIS 8:10-12.[12]

NOAH'S CURIOSITY. WOLFGANG MUSCULUS:
To a degree, Noah suffered from his human
weakness, in that he wanted to secure evidence
that the flood had receded and the earth was
dry before the time was right and prior to
God's oracle. Indeed, why else would he have
opened the window of the ark and sent forth
the raven, and after the raven also the dove,
and at last open the very covering of the ark
and look out, except to know for sure that the
waters had ceased to cover the earth. . . ?
However, he should have waited for the mouth
of the Lord and should not have tried to
anticipate the right time not only for leaving
the ark but even for knowing the condition of
the earth. It was from curiosity that he desired
so greatly to know when the waters would
cease to cover the earth, when it was not licit
for him to leave the ark without God's command. Thus, we see in this passage how even
the saints are constantly weakened by things
that smack more of fleshly affections than of
faith. COMMENTARY ON GENESIS 8:6-13.[13]

NOAH FEARED TO OPEN THE WINDOW.
JOHN CALVIN: The degree of anxiety that
constricted the heart of the holy man can be
conjectured from this, that after he had
perceived that the ark was resting on solid
ground, he still didn't dare to open the window
before the fortieth day. Not that he was
lethargic from exhaustion, but rather because
such a terrifying example of God's vengeance
had simultaneously stricken him with such
fear and sorrow that his resolve wholly

[10]CTS 1:277* (CO 23:136). [11]*In Mosis Genesim* (1554), 213.
[12]LW 2:110-11 (WA 42:340). [13]*In Mosis Genesim* (1554), 218.

deserted him and he silently remained within the hiding-place of his ark. COMMENTARY ON GENESIS 8:6.[14]

No Rest Outside the Ark or the Church.

PETER MARTYR VERMIGLI: Although a prophet, endowed with God's spirit, Noah still used his natural diligence and resourcefulness to investigate the condition of the world. If they suffice, human means are not to be spurned. He made his first test with the raven, which went forth and returned because it could not linger outside the ark while the waters covered everything. Our Greek translation and, more surprising still, Josephus recount this by denying that the raven returned to Noah. They go on to say that like an unclean animal, it had perched upon the corpses of the dead, and for that reason the dove was sent out a bit later, so that from that, at least, Noah might be able to be more certain. Yet this error hardly injures piety, so let us take note of how this type signifies for us that those who truly belong to the church find no rest outside of it. No one who is truly a believer finds rest outside the ark of the church. But if you were to look for the true church, where is it? Where there is the spirit of Christ, the pure word of God and the sacraments administered without adulteration. Wherever you find these three marks, there too church discipline and a holy conduct of life will undoubtedly have a place. COMMENTARY ON GENESIS 8:7.[15]

The Holy Spirit Is Our Dove, Christ Is Our Ark.

HULDRYCH ZWINGLI: Noah, who . . . prefigures Christ, was assured by a dove that the waters were now dried up on earth and that divine wrath had ceased. So Christ, through the Holy Spirit who is signified by a dove, makes us sure of salvation, so that nothing is then to be feared by the godly, neither death nor hell; rather, those who believe in the Son of God have eternal life. We

may also understand Christ as the ark in which all believers are saved, "for there is no condemnation for those who are in Christ Jesus," even if everything outside the ark is destroyed. For God sees our fragility and spares us in Christ. For our sake he offered himself to God the Father as an acceptable sacrifice by which the Father was appeased and remitted his wrath. Again, just as Noah opened a window in the ark, so did Christ become for us the way and the door to life. ANNOTATIONS ON GENESIS 8:22.[16]

Peter's Baptismal Allegory of the Flood.

MARTIN LUTHER: When we condemn allegories, we are speaking of those that are fabricated by one's own intellect and ingenuity, without the authority of Scripture. The others, which are made to agree with the analogy of the faith, not only embellish doctrine but also give comfort to consciences. Thus Peter turns this very story of the Flood into a beautiful allegory when he says in 1 Peter 3:21-22: "Baptism, which corresponds to this, now saves us, not as a removal of dirt from the body, but as an appeal to God for a clear conscience, through the resurrection of Christ from the dead," who is at the right hand of God, swallowing up death in order that we may be made heirs of eternal life, and "who has gone into heaven, with angels, authorities, and powers subject to Him." This is truly a theological allegory, that is, one in agreement with the faith and full of comfort. "CONCERNING ALLEGORIES."[17]

An Allegory of the Raven and the Doves.

MARTIN LUTHER: Something must also be said about the remaining portions of the historical account: about the raven which did not return; and about the doves, the first of

---

[14]CTS 1:278-79* (CO 23:137). [15]*In Primum Librum Mosis* (1569), 34v. [16]ZSW 13:56; cf. Mt 3:16; Rom 8:1; Jn 14:6; 10:9. [17]An extensive excursus in Luther's *Lectures on Genesis* (LW 2:151; WA 42:367-68).

which returned when she did not find a place where she could set her foot, the second returned and brought back an olive branch, and the third did not return, because the earth had now been cleared of water. It is certain . . . that this miraculous action had some particular meaning, especially since the prophets also frequently mention doves in their prophecies about the kingdom of Christ. . . . Therefore the picture that this allegory presents should not be regarded with complete indifference; it should be treated with fitting skill.

The raven does not return, nor is it the bearer of a favorable omen. It remains outside the ark; and although it goes and comes, it does not let itself be caught by Noah but remains outside the ark. All this agrees most beautifully with the ministry of the Law. The black color characteristic of the raven is a symbol of sadness, and the sound of its voice is unpleasant. All the teachers of the Law who teach a righteousness of works are of the same kind: they are ministers of death and of sin. . . . And yet Moses is sent by God with this doctrine, just as Noah sends out the raven. God wants people to be instructed about morals and a holy life, and He wants His wrath and sure punishments announced to the transgressors of the Law. Nevertheless, such teachers are nothing else than ravens; they fly back and forth around the ark and bring no sure pronouncement of a reconciled God. It is characteristic of the Law that its teaching cannot make fearful consciences sure, strengthen and comfort them. Rather it frightens them, because it does nothing else than teach what God demands from us, what He wants us to do. Moreover, it bears witness against us through our conscience, because not only have we not done the will of God revealed in the Law, but we have even done the opposite.

What Moses relates about the dove is really a delightful likeness of the Gospel, especially if you carefully trace the characteristics of the dove, which are ten in number: (1) it is devoid of malice; (2) it does no harm with its mouth; (3) it inflicts no damage with its claw; (4) it picks up clean grain; (5) it feeds other young birds; (6) instead of singing, it moans; (7) it stays near water; (8) it flies in flocks; (9) it nests in a safe place; (10) it flies swiftly. . . . The New Testament relates that the Holy Spirit appeared in the form of a dove. Therefore we rightly apply the allegory to the ministry of grace.

Moses relates that the dove did not fly to and fro about the ark, like the raven; but she was sent out, and when she did not find a place to light, she returned to the ark and was caught by Noah. This [first] dove is a figure of the holy prophets, who were indeed sent to teach the people; but the Flood, that is, the era of the Law, had not yet come to an end. Thus although David, Elijah, and Isaiah did not live to see the era of grace or of the New Testament, they were nevertheless sent to be messengers of the end of the Flood, even though it had not yet ended. After they had performed their mission, they returned to the ark, that is, they were justified and saved without the Law through faith in the Blessed Seed, in whom they believed and for whom they were waiting.

After this dove another is sent out; it finds the earth dry and not only the mountains but also the trees free of water. This one alights on an olive tree and brings to Noah a branch she plucked. . . . God wanted the branch of a green olive tree brought to Noah by mouth, to make us realize that in the New Testament, when the Flood or the era of wrath comes to an end, God wants to reveal His mercy to the world through the spoken Word. . . . Hence this dove, the second one to be sent out, is a type of the New Testament, where forgiveness of sin and grace are plainly promised through the sacrifice of Christ. That is why in the New Testament the Holy Spirit wanted to appear in the form of a dove.

The third dove did not return. When the promise of the Gospel, announced to the world through the mouth of a dove, has been fulfilled, there is nothing left to do, and no new doctrine is expected. All we still expect is the revelation of the things we have believed. Hence this also serves to give us a sure testimony that this doctrine will endure until the end of the world.

The doctrine of the Gospel has been in the world ever since our first parents fell, and by various signs God confirmed this promise to the fathers. The earlier times knew nothing of the rainbow, circumcision, and other things that were ordained later on. But all ages had the knowledge of the Blessed Seed. Since this has been revealed, there is nothing left except the revelation of what we believe and our flight with the third dove into another life, never to return to this wretched and distressful life. "Concerning Allegories."[18]

An Allegorical Reading of Noah's Ark. Wolfgang Musculus: The mystical significance of this history ought to be addressed, I think, for the sake of those who take some pleasure in allegorical meanings. To be sure, I would warn them, lest they chase after allegories so excessively that all the deeds and events in the sacred histories get twisted into a mystical sense. . . .

First of all, the period when the things written in this history happened presents an image of later times, namely, of the New Testament. I'm not speaking specifically of those days when the flood occurred but of the whole sixth century of Noah's life, . . . when the malice of mortals reached a peak; God's oracles about the end of all flesh, making the ark, etc., were imparted to Noah; and the flood came, bringing the prior world to an end. In a similar way at the time of the New Testament, . . . the malice of the world grew immensely. God's oracles descended from heaven: preaching repentance, warning that God was going to

judge the world through his son, and finally, instructing the elect about how they might escape the destruction to come when, at last, the whole world here will be carried away and changed by a fiery flood. Christ himself, when he wished to call attention to the malice and carelessness of these later times, as well as their unforeseen destruction, said "Just as it was in the days of Noah, so will it be in the days of the son of man" (Lk 17:26; Mt 24:37).

Then, the ark presents an image of the house of God, insofar as it was built so that Noah and his family would be saved in it. The house of God that is the church is thus a house of salvation, made that we might be saved in it and not perish with this world.

The ark was constructed according to the instructions of the divine will by Noah, the only righteous person among the entire race of mortals. The house of God was constructed by its architect, Christ, whose voice says, "I will build my church." Thus Noah bears the figure of Christ, not only because he truly is the only righteous person whom God finds in the whole human race but also because he himself constructs the house of God as the house of salvation.

Having been coated with pitch inside and out, the ark is protected against the waters of the flood. The house of God is thus covered by the grace of Christ's blood, so that it may be secure against the universal vengeance of divine wrath, of which the waters of the flood were a figure.

The ark was divided into various living quarters. And the house of God is constructed by Christ so as to have divisions of gifts, ministries and places, according to the diversity of those who are brought into it. Indeed, in his church "he gave some to be apostles, some prophets, some teachers, some evangelists, etc." (Eph 4:11). . . .

---

[18]This excerpt abridges Luther's long excursus in his *Lectures on Genesis* (LW 2:157-64; WA 42:372-76).

However many were outside the ark, they perished in the waves, save only Noah and his family. So do all perish who are not protected with Christ in the house of God. What they say is utterly true, that no one is saved outside the church. But understand that the church is not where the Roman pontiff falsely claims for himself the role of the true Noah, but where Christ is the pilot, along with his chosen ones received from the Father. Elsewhere, in the Roman church, many perish; but no one perishes in the church where Christ is with the rest of those who are to be saved, just as in Noah's ark not even one was lost. . . .

The foot of the dove did not find any place outside the ark to rest, wherefore it returns to Noah in the ark and is peacefully received. And Christ sent his disciples from the house of God into the world, endowing them with the simplicity of doves. There, they sometimes do not find a place where they may rest, that is, where they may find some success. Therefore, when empty, they return to the church in which Christ remains with his own, and they are no less lovingly received by him. Noah, having extended his hand, receives the dove which he himself had sent forth. The hand of Christ is in the church, which sends doves forth and receives them back. Here is the true Noah, true rest, calling to all who labor and promising them rest.

The second dove sent forth in the evening returns to Noah in the ark, bearing in her mouth an olive leaf, the symbol of peace. And in the church, the symbol of peace and mercy is regularly brought by ministers of the word. Nor indeed do they offer news of salvation only to the world, but also to the servants of God's house, just as they announce to those detained in the ark the consolation of grace and restoration coming soon. The pious women who returned to the disciples in the closed room were doves like this, bringing news of the Lord's resurrection like an olive leaf in their mouth. Other olive leaves like this

are those signs predicted by the Lord that ought to precede his second coming. Of these, he said, "When you see these things happening, lift up your heads, because your redemption is drawing near" (Lk 21:28). Whatever they seem to be in the eyes of the world, for us who dwell in the house of God, they present the clearest indications of summer's impending arrival, and our own liberation. COMMENTARY ON GENESIS 8.[19]

NOAH'S ARK AND CHRIST'S CHURCH. DIRK PHILIPS: Christian baptism is signified and portrayed through the flood with which the whole world was punished, but Noah with his own was preserved in the ark through that same water. . . . That is the way it is with all the works of God. What is life to the pious is death to the godless. . . . Now to understand the figure of the flood correctly, one must observe how Noah is a figure of Christ, the household of Noah of the believing souls, the ark of the congregation, and the flood of baptism. For just as Noah in his time was a preacher of righteousness, so also Christ Jesus is the genuine Preacher of righteousness and the true Teacher who has gone forth from God. Again, just as Noah at the command of God prepared the ark for the preservation of his own and the souls of others, so also Christ Jesus has built and equipped a spiritual ark, that is, his congregation. Also through his apostles as instruments and wise carpenters, he made and erected it for the eternal preservation and salvation of all his children and household. . . . Again, just as no one outside of the ark of Noah could preserve his life, but all that was outside of the ark, that is, from the earth, perished through water, so also no one may preserve his soul nor be saved except he be in the ark of Christ Jesus. For outside of Christ and his congregation is neither salvation nor

---

[19]*In Mosis Genesim* (1554); this abridgment represents about 40 percent of his allegorical exegesis (230-32).

eternal life. . . . Again, just as the flood drowned all flesh that was outside of the ark, and the ark was preserved through the same water, so also in baptism all fleshly lusts must drown and be killed, but the soul is preserved to eternal salvation in the ark of Christ, through the power of his Word, Spirit, and blood. Enchiridion.[20]

"Look, We Were a Figure of Believer's Baptism!" Balthasar Hubmaier: Through such infant baptism people are robbed of the true baptism of Christ, imagining that they are baptized, and yet are anything less than baptized. Also Noah, along with Ham, Shem, Japheth, and their wives will testify against us and say: "Look. We were a figure of water baptism with our ark in the Flood, as Saint Peter has written to you in his epistle." Now, however, no one went into the ark unless beforehand he believed the Word of God. Thus you should properly baptize no one unless he believes beforehand. Ancient and New Teachers.[21]

A Critical Defense of the Hebrews' Text, but Not Their Fables. Andrew Willet: *He sent out a raven.* The Hebrews' text has *which went and came*; but the Septuagint and Latin have *which went and came not*, and many of the Fathers have the same. But it is in no way to be admitted here that the Hebrew text is corrupted: for the Jews could not all together conspire to corrupt the Scriptures, for their falsehood would have been discovered; nor does this text give the Jews any advantage against us, and therefore they had no cause to corrupt it; and besides, it is well known that the Jews are most careful to preserve the Scriptures, having a tally of all the words that are used in the text and how often every letter of the alphabet is found in Scripture. We also reject the conjectures of those who, in order to justify this erroneous reading, assert that the Septuagint and Latin

retain the sense if not the words: as if the crow is said not to return because he did not come again *into* the ark but only rested *upon* it; or that he returned without giving notice of that, wherefore he was sent just as the dove was (so Lyra, Tostatus). Also, the conjecture of those who say that the raven did not return but perched on some carrion or dead body cannot be allowed: it is contrary to the text and also unlikely, seeing that it was by now the eleventh month, by which time all the dead bodies were either consumed by the water or devoured by fish. Wherefore we hold the Septuagint and Latin to be corrupt, and that according to the Hebrew text, the raven went and came to the ark, because his food was there, as well as his mate or fellow, and his nest or resting place (though I think the raven was not received into the ark, as the dove was).

But the Hebrews' fables we reject: that the raven was sent forth from the ark because of his intemperance with his mate; and that two others in the ark were in the same case—Ham[†] and Canis (the dog). Likewise, they imagine that the raven argued with Noah as to why he was sent out from his mate, as though Noah should keep her for himself. Some think that this was the raven that afterward fed Elijah, but these ridiculous toys are not worth the rehearsal. The Hebrews and some Christian writers often take a stand here on allegories. Some of them, which tend to edification, we do not reject: for instance, that the dove signifies the simple-hearted, who are to be received into the church, but hypocrites and carnal people must not be admitted into the ark of the church, even as the raven did not return. Commentary on Genesis 8:7.[22]

---

[20]CRR 6:80-81. [21]CRR 5:263. [22]*Hexapla* (1608), 95*, crediting Mercerus. [†]The legend of Ham's incontinence and subsequent punishment is traceable to diverse writings of the fourth and fifth centuries—to the Talmud and to John Chrysostom, as nicely argued by David M. Whitford, *The Curse of Ham in the Early Modern Era: The Bible and the Justifications for Slavery* (Burlington, VT: Ashgate, 2009), 23-29, who also describes some later developments of the legend.

8:13-22 NOAH COMES FORTH
AND OFFERS A SACRIFICE

¹³*In the six hundred and first year, in the first month, the first day of the month, the waters were dried from off the earth. And Noah removed the covering of the ark and looked, and behold, the face of the ground was dry.* ¹⁴*In the second month, on the twenty-seventh day of the month, the earth had dried out.* ¹⁵*Then God said to Noah,* ¹⁶*"Go out from the ark, you and your wife, and your sons and your sons' wives with you.* ¹⁷*Bring out with you every living thing that is with you of all flesh—birds and animals and every creeping thing that creeps on the earth—that they may swarm on the earth, and be fruitful and multiply on the earth."* ¹⁸*So Noah went out, and his sons and his wife and his sons' wives with him.* ¹⁹*Every beast, every creeping thing, and every bird, everything that moves on the earth, went out by families from the ark.*

²⁰*Then Noah built an altar to the LORD and took some of every clean animal and some of every clean bird and offered burnt offerings on the altar.* ²¹*And when the LORD smelled the pleasing aroma, the LORD said in his heart, "I will never again curse^a the ground because of man, for the intention of man's heart is evil from his youth. Neither will I ever again strike down every living creature as I have done.* ²²*While the earth remains, seedtime and harvest, cold and heat, summer and winter, day and night, shall not cease."*

a Or *dishonor*

OVERVIEW: Many of the details introduced in the second half of Genesis 8 anticipate the fuller development of the blessing, the commandments and the covenant (with its promises and covenant sign) in the chapter that follows. Given the larger context of God's declaration of the perpetually "evil heart" of human beings and the punishment represented by the flood, it is no surprise that commentators watched Noah carefully. They certainly did not miss the fact that Noah did not venture forth from the ark until God commanded him to do so—regardless of what he may have learned from the raven and the dove.

Reformation commentators were especially eager to discuss the significance of Noah's sacrifice, which God found so pleasing. Indeed, Noah's sacrifice might be expected to be all the more intriguing to Protestants, who not only lived in a day when literal, external, material sacrifices had ceased and been replaced by sacrifices of a spiritual nature, but who might also be inclined to discount the significance of external works as a way of pleasing God.

Of equal interest, though, were the divine promises and declamations spoken in response to Noah's sacrifice. Above all, commentators tended to wonder what, really, had changed after the flood? The human heart, Scripture says here, is still evil. And despite the Lord's promise that the ground would never again be cursed, nor all living creatures be destroyed, nor the seasons disrupted, it was evident to Reformation writers that partial manifestations of such phenomena—in the form of natural disasters such as local floods and droughts—were far from uncommon. So what really changed, if not humanity? The earth? God?

8:15-19 Then God Said to Noah, "Go out from the Ark"

NOAH'S SCRUPULOUS OBEDIENCE. JOHN CALVIN: How great was his fortitude, that after a whole year of incredible tedium, when the flood has ceased and new life has shone forth, he still doesn't take a step outside of his sepulcher without God's command. We thereby see that the holy man was obedient to God with an unbroken course of faith, because at God's command he entered the ark and remained there until God opened an exit, and because he preferred to lie in the stink of the ark than to take a breath of fresh air until he should feel that his change of venue would be pleasing to God. Scripture commends such self-control to us even in minute affairs, lest we attempt anything without a conscience that is assured. COMMENTARY ON GENESIS 8:15.[1]

NOAH WAITED FOR GOD'S COMMAND. KONRAD PELLIKAN: Noah depended wholly on God; therefore he attempted nothing without his command. Just as he had entered the ark when God had commanded, so he leaves it when God ordered and not before. COMMENTARY ON GENESIS 8:15-16.[2]

A COMMISSION TO FLOURISH IN THE LAND. KONRAD PELLIKAN: The [Hebrew verb] here means *meet* or *engage one another* more than *enter*.[†] Indeed, it means to saunter, to wander around feeding oneself, to propagate oneself into a great multitude, as if he were to say, "Don't be idle or unprofitable, whether you are alone or few, but generate and propagate your kind, you who were confined in the ark and anxious for a full and disastrous year." COMMENTARY ON GENESIS 8:17.[3]

LESSONS OF AN ORDERLY EXIT. KONRAD PELLIKAN: The animals went forth in their families, grouped with whatever animals were like them in species, and they also grazed together like this in their small numbers until they multiplied. The orderly politeness even among irrational animals should thus teach humans about friendship and peaceful coexistence. COMMENTARY ON GENESIS 8:19.[4]

8:20 Then Noah Built an Altar to the Lord

NOAH'S FIRST ACT: WORSHIP. JOHANNES BRENZ: Notice what Noah undertook first of all after he left the ark with his family and animals. The animals, though they lacked reason, assigned themselves each to its own place, according to its nature: the birds to the air, the wild beasts to the wilderness, domestic animals to the company of humans. But Noah, having left the ark, does not proceed to build a tower or a house, or to plow the fields, but to build an altar on which he offers clean animals as a burnt offering. This is a description of the restoration of religion. To be sure, a burnt offering could not have been made in the ark, but there is no doubt but that Noah and his family would have prayed much in the midst of such great dangers. But because there was a good deal of confusion there, they could not have conducted public rites. Now, however, after Noah and his family have left the ark, Noah's concern is first of all to restore public rites and to establish the teaching of religion once again. He makes a burnt offering of the clean animals for several reasons: First, to attest his gratitude to God his savior, who had kept him safe with his family and animals

---

[1]CTS 1:280* (CO 23:137-38). [2]*Commentaria Bibliorum* (1532) 1:12r. [3]*Commentaria Bibliorum* (1532) 1:12r, [†]arguing that *congredimini* is closer to the Hebrew verb than *ingredimini* ("enter"), which is what the Vulgate has here, probably influenced by the Septuagint. [4]*Commentaria Bibliorum* (1532) 1:12v.

through so many dangers in such a fragile craft. Next, to declare his faith that from then on God would also protect him from the dangers of death. Finally, so that by his example he might spread the teachings of true religion as far as he was able among his offspring. COMMENTARY ON GENESIS 8:20.[5]

NOAH'S EXAMPLE OF GRATITUDE. JOHN CALVIN: Just as Noah's obedience had been attested by many proofs, so he now presents an example of his gratitude. This passage teaches us that from the beginning, sacrifices were instituted with this goal in mind, that by such exercises we should cultivate the habit of celebrating God's goodness and giving thanks to him. The bare confession of the tongue or even the silent acknowledgment of the heart, for that matter, might have sufficed for God; but we know how much by way of prodding our sluggishness requires. Previously, then, when the holy patriarchs professed their piety toward God by sacrifices, their use was by no means superfluous. Besides, it was appropriate that symbols should at all times be set before their eyes, by which they might be reminded that nothing comes to them from God but through a mediator. Now, however, the manifestation of Christ has taken away these ancient shadows, and for that reason we should use the helps that the Lord has prescribed. COMMENTARY ON GENESIS 8:20.[6]

SACRIFICE SHOULD HAVE SEEMED FOOLISH. WOLFGANG MUSCULUS: Noah made an offering of the animals that had been preserved in the ark so that they would be the seed from which the entire surface of the earth would be filled with a multitude of animals. If he had used the judgment of his reason, he would not have destroyed even one of their number. More likely, he would have thought, "The number of the animals is exceedingly small and tenuous, especially for this, that by their increase the whole earth would be filled again with animals

and restored to its original appearance. I would prefer more to add than subtract. Moreover, the Lord did not command me to take from them for sacrifice but said, 'Increase and multiply.' For the sake of increase, I will not make a sacrifice, nor reduce an otherwise exceedingly small number. We should therefore abstain from sacrifice for the present, until [we] see some significant multitude of animals." Noah considers none of this, but from all the clean animals and birds sacrificed a burnt offering on the altar. In this way a most beautiful example of faith was set forth. . . . For Noah by no means doubted that God's power, having saved a small and meager number who were consecrated to his name, could also vigorously multiply them into an immense and innumerable multitude of robust animals. COMMENTARY ON GENESIS 8:20.[7]

THE CHURCH CONTAINS BOTH CLEAN AND UNCLEAN. PETER MARTYR VERMIGLI: We will see if we can embrace a type and a foreshadowing here. Although in the ark every kind of animal was contained, both clean and unclean, nonetheless only the clean animals were sacrificed to God. In the same way, in the church, wicked people have been mixed together with the good, but only those who are truly faithful are legitimately offered up to God. COMMENTARY ON GENESIS 8:20.[8]

8:21a *The Lord Smelled the Pleasing Aroma*

GOD RECOVERS FROM THE STENCH OF SIN. MARTIN LUTHER: Thus it may be said that God, who was offended by the horrible stench of ungodliness, is now recovering. He sees this one priest [Noah] girding himself for sacrifice, in order to manifest some evidence of thankfulness and to indicate by a public act

---

[5]*Opera* 1:105. [6]CTS 1:281* (CO 23:138). [7]*In Mosis Genesim* (1554), 226. [8]*In Primum Librum Mosis* (1569), 35r.

that he is not ungodly but has a God and fears Him; for it is with these matters that sacrifices are actually concerned. Just as God thus far took pleasure in destroying the human race, so now He takes pleasure and rejoices in increasing it once more. It is for our sake, therefore, that Moses uses such an expression, in order that we may gain an understanding of God's grace and learn that He is a God who rejoices in doing good to us. Lectures on Genesis 8:21.[9]

The Sweetness of Faith and Gratitude. Konrad Pellikan: He built an altar, a raised platform of stones, earth or wood, where animals could be sacrificed in thanksgiving to God, the giver of all. He did this from faith, by which those who make the offering and the oblation itself are pleasing to the Lord. Therefore we are taught in this passage that we are daily rescued from dangers and should give thanks to God, in whom alone it is fitting to trust and hope for help. To God, such faith is the sweetest odor, not as a fragrant perfume but as the devotion and prayers of the faithful. Commentary on Genesis 8:20.[10]

The Aroma of Noah's Heart. Wolfgang Musculus: Moses attributes a sense of smell to God by way of *anthropopathy*. He does not write of Noah's sacrifice that "the Lord smelled the aroma of the burnt offering," but "the Lord smelled the pleasing aroma." God does not smell with the nostrils as humans do; and the smell of Noah's sacrifice, which the burnt offerings of animals emitted, was not that of a good fragrance but stronger and irritating. Thus we are admonished by this description that our labor, whatever sort it may be, gives off a certain smell that ascends unto God, and by it is either approved as sweet or disapproved as rank, irritating and unpleasant. That smell is not what our external deeds communicate to human

perception, but the spiritual quality that our hearts themselves emit: bad hearts breathe out an evil and rank smell; good hearts, a good and sweet smell. In Noah's sacrifice there was an external and bodily smell that the burnt flesh gave off to human nostrils, but it was a spiritual smell that the heart of Noah communicated to the nostrils of God: it was nothing other than the sincere piety of a faithful soul, acknowledging and celebrating God's blessings. Commentary on Genesis 8:21.[11]

No Odor Is Pleasing in Itself, but True Devotion Is. Cardinal Cajetan: It is called a *soothing* odor, that is, producing calmness without being wearisome, to differentiate it from [other] perceptible odors. Indeed, there is no perceptible odor that would not produce revulsion when it lingers, and for this reason no perceptible odor is in itself a soothing odor. So in order to rule out the repulsiveness of a lingering odor, it is often called a soothing odor in Holy Scripture, because, truly, the devotion of one who makes an offering is never repulsive to God. Indeed, it is evident that a "soothing odor" is described as pleasing to God not by reason of the animals offered up but rather by reason of the heartfelt devotion of the one who is making the offering. Commentary on Genesis 8:21.[12]

God Rested from His Wrath. Martin Luther: Previously Moses stated that the Lord had regard for the offering. Here he states that the Lord smelled the delightful odor, and after this Moses frequently makes use of such an expression. Actually the word does not mean "odor of pleasantness"; it means "odor of rest." . . . Moses used [this word] previously (Gen 8:4), when he stated that the ark rested on the mountains of

[9]LW 2:117 (WA 42:345). [10]*Commentaria Bibliorum* (1532) 1:12v. [11]*In Mosis Genesim* (1554), 227. [12]*Commentarii illustres* (1539), 56.

Ararat. Hence it is the odor of rest, because at that time God rested from wrath in that He gave up His wrath, was appeased, and, as we ordinarily say, was well pleased. LECTURES ON GENESIS 8:21.[13]

NOAH'S SACRIFICE HAD THE FRAGRANCE OF CHRIST. JOHANNES BRENZ: What is fragrant in the combustion of a calf, or an ox, or a goat? Especially if, along with the flesh, the bones are also burned up, which certainly produce a displeasing odor when burned! Yet it's not what we think, that God is taken with the sweetness of an external smell. Rather, there are other things in Noah's sacrifice that move God with pleasure. First, he is pleased with Noah's gratitude, even as he is pleased with his care for spreading the teachings of true religion to his offspring. Finally—and this is best of all—he is pleased with Noah's faith in the seed of the woman, in Jesus Christ, who is foreshadowed by the burnt offering. In Noah's offering, God actually sees the sacrifice of his only-begotten Son, which would one day take place for the sins of the whole world. By this sacrifice he is so delighted that he rejoices not only to favor Noah but also to promise to preserve the earth. And by that promise, the Holy Spirit shows that the sacrifice of God's only-begotten Son would have so much efficacy that on its account the earth would be preserved and all who believe in it would be freed from death and given eternal life—which Paul also shows in Ephesians 5[:2]: "Christ loved us and gave himself up for us as a fragrant offering and sacrifice to God." COMMENTARY ON GENESIS 8:21-22.[14]

8:21b *The Human Heart's Evil Intention*

GOD PRESERVES HUMANITY DESPITE ITS PERSISTENCE IN EVIL. JOHN CALVIN: As a matter of fact, having previously declared that the world must be destroyed because it was hopelessly perverse, God seems to contradict himself here. But it behooves us to look more deeply into his design, for God wanted there to be some fellowship of human beings to inhabit the earth. To be sure, if humans were treated according to their merits, there would need to be a flood every day! He thereby shows that he will exact punishment from the second world for its evil deeds, yet in such a way as to preserve the face of the earth, so to speak, and not by sweeping away the creatures with which he has adorned it. In the same way, we see how God employs such moderation in both his public and his special judgments that the world yet stands in its completeness and nature retains its course. Moreover, given that God declares here what human beings would be like even to the world's end, it is evident that the whole human race is under a sentence of condemnation for its depravity and wickedness. Nor is the sentence levied only against corrupt conduct, but viciousness is also said to be implanted in their nature, from which nothing but evil bubbles up. COMMENTARY ON GENESIS 8:21.[15]

GRACE AND CORRECTION CONTINUE IN OTHER WAYS. KONRAD PELLIKAN: God consoles people who were hitherto terrified and who fear similar things to come. Moreover, however much they may sin after this, God refuses to cover the whole earth with a general flood. Meanwhile, certain regions and cities still experience frequent flooding. In fact, the sins of human beings are punished by other misfortunes, pestilence, wars, wild animals, famine, and diseases. Satisfaction has now been made for the sin of the world, and faith and rectitude have been renewed; yet Scripture still attests that the thoughts of the human heart are prone to evil from childhood and it can do nothing but evil.

---

[13]LW 2:116-17 (WA 42:344). [14]*Opera* 1:105-6. [15]CTS 1:284* (CO 23:140).

Indeed, all works, even those holy and good in nature, fail in many ways and need God's grace and pardon. COMMENTARY ON GENESIS 8:21.[16]

ORIGINAL SIN WAS NOT PURGED IN THE FLOOD.

MARTIN LUTHER: One cannot get around this passage with the claim that such people were the ones who perished in the Flood. God uses a generic term and says that the heart of man is of that kind. But in those days there were no other people than those who had been saved in the ark, and yet He says that the imagination of the human heart is evil. Hence not even the saints are excluded here. LECTURES ON GENESIS 8:21.[17]

GOD GUARDS THE EARTH AND ITS ANIMALS AGAINST HUMAN EVIL.

WOLFGANG MUSCULUS: How is it that, prior to the flood, the very same and unchanged malice of the human heart was the cause of the destruction of all flesh; but after the flood it stands in as the reason for why God is unwilling to curse the earth again and to destroy all that lives in it as he had done before? Has God changed, so that what before the flood he judged to be just and useful, after the flood he judged to be the opposite? . . . I would reply that God does not change as humans do, nor did he bring a universal flood upon the world without extremely justifiable reasons. . . . But what is added, "for the imaginings of the human heart are evil from youth," should not be understood as if he decreed that the world would be spared *because* it is evil, or as if he is not going to punish those who continue without any repentance in their impiety and malice. . . . No security is established for sinners by these words, but he makes a pact *with the earth and with animals*, that the world and the earth as they now exist will not again be subjected to such a common destruction on account of the malice of the human heart. COMMENTARY ON GENESIS 8:21.[18]

8:22 Seedtime and Harvest Shall Not Cease

GOD PROMISES (MOSTLY) RELIABLE SEASONS.

ANDREW WILLET: The Lord does not promise that these seasons of the year shall continue forever (for after the end of the world they shall cease), but *all the days of the earth*, that is, so long as the earth continues in this state. Nor is this to be understood of every particular country, for in some times and in some places it happens by the just judgment of God that there is neither seedtime nor harvest, as it happened under Elijah (1 Kings 17:1). But this verse refers to the general condition of the whole earth, wherein there shall be a perpetual succession of these seasons. COMMENTARY ON GENESIS 8:22.[19]

THE REGULARITY OF SEASONS IS DISTURBED BY OUR SINS.

JOHN CALVIN: If anyone should object that moderate temperatures are not seen every year, an answer is easily procured, in that the order of the world is indeed disturbed by our vices, so that many of its movements are irregular: the sun often withholds its proper heat, snow or hail may follow where dew was expected, the air may be stirred up by storms of various kinds. Yet though the world is not so regulated as to produce perpetual uniformity of seasons, we still see that the order of nature prevails: winter and summer recur each year, the succession of days and nights continues, and the earth brings forth its fruits in summer and autumn. However, by "all the days of the earth," he means "as long as the earth shall last." COMMENTARY ON GENESIS 8:22.[20]

THE DAYS OF EARTH WILL YIELD TO THE DAYS OF HEAVEN.

MARTIN LUTHER: The

---

[16]*Commentaria Bibliorum* (1532) 1:12v. [17]LW 2:119-20 (WA 42:346-47). [18]*In Mosis Genesim* (1554), 223, emphasis added. [19]*Hexapla* (1608), 95 [pagination is defective], crediting Mercerus. [20]CTS 1:286* (CO 23:141).

statement of the text, "while the earth remains," is not without purpose; for it implies that at some time the days of the earth will come to an end and other days — of heaven — will follow. As long as the days of the earth endure, the earth will endure, and the changes of the seasons will endure. But when these days of the earth come to an end, everything will come to an end, and there will follow days of heaven, that is, eternal days, which will be Sabbath after Sabbath, when we shall not be engaged in physical labors for our subsistence; for we shall be like the angels of God (Mark 12:25). Our life will be to know God, to delight in the wisdom of God, and to enjoy the presence of God. We attain this life through faith in Christ. May the eternal Father, through the merit of His Son and our Deliverer, Jesus Christ, mercifully preserve us in it through the guidance and direction of the Holy Spirit. Amen. Amen. LECTURES ON GENESIS 8:22.[21]

---

[21]LW 2:129-30 (WA 42:353).

9:1-7 BLESSINGS AND MANDATES FOR NOAH AND HIS SONS

[1]And God blessed Noah and his sons and said to them, "Be fruitful and multiply and fill the earth. [2]The fear of you and the dread of you shall be upon every beast of the earth and upon every bird of the heavens, upon everything that creeps on the ground and all the fish of the sea. Into your hand they are delivered. [3]Every moving thing that lives shall be food for you. And as I gave you the green plants, I give you everything. [4]But you shall not eat flesh with its life, that is, its blood. [5]And for your lifeblood I will require a reckoning: from every beast I will require it and from man. From his fellow man I will require a reckoning for the life of man.

[6]"Whoever sheds the blood of man,
    by man shall his blood be shed,
for God made man in his own image.

[7]And you,[a] be fruitful and multiply, teem on the earth and multiply in it."

a In Hebrew you is plural

OVERVIEW: Although Genesis 9 seems to begin with the same repetition that marked previous chapters, traditional commentators were quick to notice some momentous changes. True, the blessing of procreation here closely resembles the sixth day of creation, but where Genesis 1:28-30 described a benign dominion over the beasts, fear and dread now enter into the equation. Perhaps that should be no great surprise, given that the animals are now described as lawful food for humans, alongside the plants first authorized in Genesis 1:30. But there was also great interest in the codicil that prohibits eating the blood of an animal, and in the following declaration of the special dignity of human life. This passage thus introduced readers to a new implication of what it means to bear God's image, namely, that to destroy God's image in a person is a capital offense for both animals and humans—an act that demands the forfeiture of one's own life.

Reformation commentators took their customary pastoral approach to most of these issues. God's blessing of procreation in Genesis 9:1 and 9:7 is thus a reminder that even after the great judgment of the flood, not all has been lost and God's favor still rests on human-kind—and it behooves us, as we recall the good things we retain, to ponder also the lessons of what was lost in both the fall and the flood. If procreation and fruitfulness remain for us, it is equally clear that our dominion over animals has been diminished.

The opening section of Genesis 9 also required the explanation of a few obscurities. For instance, why did God only now allow animals to be used as food for humans—or was this really anything new? Why was blood specifically forbidden to eat? Surely there was a larger lesson embedded in this detail, but what was it? Reformation commentators found pastoral replies to all these questions, but their answers were also rarely controversial. Indeed, despite occasional disagreements among themselves, Protestant exegesis here usually bore the marks of earlier exegetical traditions.

Last of all, the image or likeness of God is mentioned for the third and final time in Genesis (after 1:26-27 and 5:1-2). Commentators were less likely to argue about definitions of the image (a question usually resolved in earlier chapters) than to marvel at the sweeping implications of the attached prohibition

against human bloodshed and its stark and final punishment. Genesis 9:5-6 thus pointed not only to God's abhorrence of violence but also to the basic principles of human government as it was established after the flood, including the legitimate use of the sword to keep the peace and repress the human propensity for violence.

9:1 God Blessed Noah and His Sons

GOD'S SINCERE GOOD WISHES TOWARD US.
PETER MARTYR VERMIGLI: Now, when the world was empty and the whole order of nature had been upset, he blessed them. To *bless* is to bestow a gift on someone. Not that fertility and the power of begetting would have been given now (for they had that previously), but it was no trivial gift to know that it had been reaffirmed in them. Besides, they could have thought, "God granted this remarkable kindness to us lest we be smothered by the waters as the rest of them were, but he still harbors hatred for the human race." Indeed, he'd revealed that he regretted that he had made human beings, so perhaps they would not have dared to seek offspring for themselves—and that is why God adds others to them and commands them to enrich his creation by their number. So far, God's curses had been invoked on the earth and on Cain. But having been appeased, God now adds his blessing in turn. COMMENTARY ON GENESIS 9:1.[1]

GOD AGAIN BLESSES MARRIAGE. JOHN CALVIN: We know that brute animals do not produce offspring except by God's blessing, but Moses is making mention here of a privilege that belongs only to men and women. Therefore, lest those four men and their wives, seized with apprehension as they were, should come to doubt the purpose for which they had

---

[1]*In Primum Librum Mosis* (1569), 39r.

been rescued, the Lord outlines for them the course of their life to come, namely, that they would raise the human race up from death to life. Thus he not only renews the world by the same word by which he previously created it, but he addresses that word to human beings in order that they might recover the legitimate use of marriage—indeed, that they might know that the worry associated with bearing children is pleasing to God, and so that they might have confidence that the offspring that would arise from them would spread through all the regions of the earth. Thus would it again be inhabited, even though it may have been a wasteland and a desert. Yet promiscuous intercourse was not granted to human beings; rather, God sanctioned anew the law of marriage that he had previously established. COMMENTARY ON GENESIS 9:1.[2]

GOD'S BLESSING REPRESENTS HIS DESIRE TO NOURISH PEOPLE. KONRAD PELLIKAN: God immediately expresses what it means to *bless* here: to make fertile and to beget offspring. Otherwise, to gratify lust or to be a slave to desires is not to increase but to impede offspring. Sons are not begotten by a vow on our part but by the grace of God: from which one should not suppose that it was beside the point that Noah had sons after the flood; indeed, he was the seedbed of the new age to come. God wishes to fill the earth with people, each of whom he could nourish. . . .

He repeatedly commends and commands the multiplication of the human race, lest someone presume that it needs to be restricted for any reason whatsoever: whether by a demon or his accomplice, shaven or anointed. COMMENTARY ON GENESIS 9:1, 7.[3]

WEREN'T WOMEN PART OF THIS BLESSING? WOLFGANG MUSCULUS: Can it be that the blessing of multiplication pertained to the men alone and not also to their wives? My response is that by no means were the wives excluded.

Indeed, that he mentions only men is the custom of Scripture, as happens in lots of places. . . . Thus, just as the eating of meat was granted not to men alone but also to women, even though there is no mention of them, so also the blessing of multiplication pertained not merely to men, however much the Lord may have been addressing them, but also to their wives. Indeed, a man could not obtain the effect of this blessing without a wife, nor was the masculine sex alone meant to be multiplied, but also that of women. COMMENTARY ON GENESIS 9:1.[4]

9:2 Fear of You Shall Be on Every Beast

GOD RESTORES PRIVILEGES PREVIOUSLY FORFEITED. JOHANNES BRENZ: Dominion is restored to human beings over the rest of the animals, for the flood seemed to have collapsed and abrogated it. Indeed, just as those who are punished as criminals in a society lose the privileges of their positions and cannot enjoy them unless they be restored by law, so also was the human race punished as criminals by the flood and thereby wholly lost their original privileges. So now God restores human beings to their first dominion and commands them to be lords over all the rest of the animals. COMMENTARY ON GENESIS 9:2.[5]

DOMINION SURVIVES, BUT DIMINISHED BY SIN. JOHN CALVIN: Even if the beasts were endowed with a new ferocity after the fall of the first humans, traces of the dominion that God conferred on them in the beginning still remained. Even now, he promises that the same condition will continue. Indeed, we see that wild beasts violently attack people, mutilating many and tearing them to pieces; and if God did not wonderfully restrain their fierceness, the human race would immediately

---

[2]CTS 1:289* (CO 23:143). [3]*Commentaria Bibliorum* (1532) 1:12v, 13r. [4]*In Mosis Genesim* (1554), 234. [5]*Opera* 1:108.

be undone. Therefore, what we have said about the inclemency of the air and the irregularity of the seasons also applies here. Savage beasts do indeed prowl about and rage against humans in many ways, and no wonder: for since we ourselves shamelessly run riot against God, why shouldn't the beasts rise up against us? At the same time, God's providence is a secret bridle to restrain their fury. COMMENTARY ON GENESIS 9:2.[6]

NOT ALL THE BEASTS SEEM TO FEAR US NOW. WOLFGANG MUSCULUS: How are these things fulfilled, when many beasts may be found whose fear and trepidation is more upon human beings than that of humans is upon them? Such include lions, bears, serpents, crocodiles, and other things like them that are unknown in our regions, which surely are both feared by humans and by no means subjected to our hands. . . . This question can be answered now one way, at other times in another. On the one hand, where it says "The fear of you will be on all the animals of the earth," it could be understood as accommodated to a time when the number of people after the flood was still very small, and so the Lord would have instilled fear and trepidation into all the beasts, by which they were forcibly restrained from tearing people to pieces, lest they impede the multiplication of the human race. If we accept this explanation, these words retain their validity not perpetually but in a sort of temporary way, protecting the growth of the still fragile human race, which lost some of these powers after its multiplication. On the other hand, if that explanation doesn't please you, one could say that these words gave majesty and dominion over all the beasts to humans, so that they would have authority over animals and birds and all creatures that move on the ground or in the sea. . . . However, it is not necessary for the truth of this prerogative that absolutely *every* beast submit to human rule, serve them

and be terrified in fear of them; but it is enough, so far as the Lord is concerned, that humans have obtained right, dominion, majesty and authority over all, and may demand the use of these as needed. Servants are subjected to their lords by divine decree. . . . Can it be that this authority is rendered false if any of the servants do not fear their masters or serve them obediently? Heaven forbid! A few who disobey the law do not invalidate the prerogative's truth and integrity. . . . Things that happen commonly and in most cases are often expressed in universal terms. For example, when it is written that "all Jerusalem" went out to John the Baptist, that was by no means true unless you understand the phrase to signify the larger part of the people. So when God says in this text, "Fear of you will be upon all the animals of the earth" and "All of them are given into your hands," it is not necessary to understand this strictly, of all the beasts with absolutely no exception, when no human need or utility would require every beast—serpents, crocodiles, rhinoceroses, wild asses, tigers, harpies, eagles, lions, etc.—to be literally on hand for our service. COMMENTARY ON GENESIS 9:2.[7]

A PARTIAL RESTORATION OF OUR ORIGINAL CONDITION. ANDREW WILLET: The three privileges given to human beings in their creation—of increasing and multiplying, of rule and dominion over the creatures, of their food and sustenance—are renewed here in these three first verses, though not in [their original] integrity and perfection. For human generation takes place with much difficulty and peril; our dominion over the creatures is much impaired; our food is more gross and greater care is required to provide it. Yet humans still retain dominion and sovereignty over the creatures, though not so absolutely as Adam had it: first, we see that although savage

---

[6]CTS 1:290* (CO 23:143). [7]*In Mosis Genesim* (1554), 234.

and wild beasts have cast off our yoke, those that are more necessary for human use, as oxen, horses, sheep, still remain in subjection; secondly, even wild and unruly beasts are tamed by human wit and industry . . . ; thirdly, though God often punishes human disobedience with cruel beasts (one of the four great plagues, Ezek 14:21), they are nonetheless restrained by the power of God, in that they do not overrun the earth to destroy human beings, and they retain in part a natural fear and awe of humans, whom they are not accustomed to assault willingly, but [only if] provoked, constrained by famine, or fearing some hurt to themselves. COMMENTARY ON GENESIS 9:2.[8]

ANIMALS HAVE MORE FEAR BECAUSE THEY HAVE BECOME FOOD FOR HUMANS. MARTIN LUTHER: Here the dominion of man appears to be increased for the purpose of consoling him even more. Even though all the animals were put under the rule of man after the creatures had been called into being, we do not read that the beasts feared and shunned man to the same degree as Moses asserts in this passage. The reason is that until now the animals did not have to die in order to provide food for man, but man was a gentle master of the beasts rather than their slayer or consumer. But here the animals are subjected to man as to a tyrant who has absolute power over life and death. Because a more oppressive form of bondage has now been imposed on them and a more extensive and oppressive dominion has been assigned to man, the animals are dominated by fear and dread of man. . . . Up to that time man had used animals solely for the tasks for which they were suited and for sacrifices, but not for food and nourishment. LECTURES ON GENESIS 9:2.[9]

THE NEW DOMINION IS FAR MORE GRIM. CARDINAL CAJETAN: Notice the difference. In the beginning, when humans were created,

they were given mastery of the animals; now, they are given to constrain animals by fear. The implication is that in the state of innocence there had been a peaceful dominion, but now there is a dominion of terror. COMMENTARY ON GENESIS 9:2.[10]

9:3 Every Moving Thing Shall Be Food

THE FLOOD'S DAMAGE BROUGHT AN END TO VEGETARIAN WAYS. HULDRYCH ZWINGLI: The contrasts should be noted, as if he had said, "The soil used to bring forth all things to Adam himself without seed, without labor or sweat. There was no need to break it up with a plow, or to entrust seed to it; therefore there was no need of flesh for food. But the earth has been so devastated by the flood that it now brings forth nothing except what is wrung out of it by great labor, and even that is weak and fragile. Therefore I give to you the flesh of beasts and birds for food, just as I gave to Adam the plants of the earth for food." ANNOTATIONS ON GENESIS 9:2-3.[11]

GOD GRANTS ANIMALS AS FOOD AS A NEW CONSOLATION FOR NOAH. MARTIN LUTHER: When these words were addressed to Noah and this privilege was granted to him, there was no need for it. A small number of human beings occupied the entire earth; so there was a superabundance of the fruits of the earth, and it was unnecessary to add the flesh of the beasts. But today we could not live on the fruits of the earth alone if this great gift had not been added, which permits us to eat the flesh of beasts, birds, and fish. These words, therefore, establish the butcher shop; attach hares, chickens, and geese to the spit; and fill the tables with all sorts of foods. . . . In this passage God sets Himself up as a butcher; for with His Word He slaughters and kills the

---

[8]*Hexapla* (1608), 100-101. [9]LW 2:132 (WA 42:355).
[10]*Commentarii illustres* (1539), 57. [11]ZSW 13:57.

animals that are suited for food, in order to make up, as it were, for the great sorrow that pious Noah experienced during the Flood. For this reason God thinks Noah ought to be provided for more sumptuously now. Lectures on Genesis 9:2.[12]

God Granted Liberty in Food to Quiet Our Consciences. John Calvin: Paul says we are free to eat whatever we please, provided our consciences are assured, but that "anything is unclean for one who imagines it to be unclean." But how does this come to us, that before the eyes of God we may eat whatever we like for food with peace of mind (and with neither thoughtlessness nor unbridled license) unless we recognize that it has been divinely delivered into our hands as a just and proper gift? . . . There is no doubt but that the Lord wished to look out for our confidence, therefore, when he clearly bore witness through Moses that he had given human beings the free use of flesh, lest we eat it with a doubtful and trembling conscience. At the same time, however, he invites us to give thanks. Commentary on Genesis 9:3.[13]

May We Eat Anything? Wolfgang Musculus: Snakes and serpents also live and move, as do other beasts that are venomous. So someone may ask, "Does he thus command us to eat serpents, too, and other venomous and deadly animals? Beyond that, *humans* live and move. Does he therefore want us to eat other humans and become cruel cannibals?" My answer is that these words are to be regarded as a concession, not a command or mandate. He permits us to eat any of the animals, it would seem, but he does not command us, as if we would be sinning were we not to do so. You have a very great abundance of clean and healthful animals for eating, but if you fancy eating snakes too, you are not forbidden. . . . Indeed, those who do what is by no means prohibited do not, for all

that, do what is commanded. And when we eat clean animals, we are not doing what is commanded, nor will we have sinned even if we do not eat those things. But let us feed on vegetables and grains and the fruits of trees, remaining of sound faith, eating with thanksgiving only what is needed for maintaining our natural strength. What is to be recognized here, then, is God's generosity, whereby he gives us the freedom to eat whatever we want. At the same time, care is to be taken that we use these things soberly, for our advantage. Commentary on Genesis 9:3.[14]

Permission to Eat Meat Was Not New but Renewed. Andrew Willet: Some think that flesh was not eaten before the flood among the families of the righteous (Mercerus); others, that flesh was not at all eaten before the flood (Lyra, Tostatus, Vatablus). But freedom to eat flesh is not first granted here, it is only renewed. Neither is the opinion to be approved of those who think that eating flesh was permitted before the flood, yet not used among the faithful (so Theodoret, Thomas Aquinas), for to what end should the faithful restrain themselves from that liberty which God gave them? Nor do we think that flesh was their usual food to eat before the flood, as it is now (so Dominicus à Soto, a popish writer), for when the earth and plants were not yet corrupted by the flood but retained their natural force and vigor, they yielded more sufficient nourishment, so that eating flesh was not as necessary then. And as the more delicate use of some plants (as Noah's use of wine) was brought in later on, so did the desire for the flesh of fowls and beasts grow after the flood, which was not coveted before.

Thus, the sounder opinion is that not only was the eating of flesh permitted before the flood, but it was also used not just among the

---

[12]LW 2:133 (WA 42:355). [13]CTS 1:292* (CO 23:144-45), citing Rom 14:14. [14]*In Mosis Genesim* (1554), 235.

profane but even among the faithful, though with greater moderation. Our reasons are, first, because no new grant is made, neither in this matter nor in the rest (such as multiplying, bearing dominion, etc.), but the ancient privileges granted to humans are merely confirmed. Secondly, the distinction of clean and unclean beasts [was a distinction between those] which were lawful to eat and the unclean, which they might not eat (Lev 11:8). It is further evident from the oblation of Abel, who offered the first fruit of his sheep and their fat; but Abel would not be praised for offering the fatlings if it was not his custom to eat them. Instead, it would have been all the same to God whether he offered lean or fat, but Abel is commended here because he preferred the service of God before his own private use. . . . And the fact that eating flesh is first expressly mentioned here is not merely to describe its *use* (as one would do well to note), but rather to underscore its *necessity*: using flesh for food began to be more necessary now, because plants and herbs had lost their first natural vigor and strength. COMMENTARY ON GENESIS 9:3.[15]

9:4 You Shall Not Eat Flesh with Its Life

REGARD FOR ANIMALS IMPLIES REGARD FOR NEIGHBORS. KONRAD PELLIKAN: From this command it is seen that all human cruelty is forbidden, and so much so, that if God would not wish cruelty against an animal to go unpunished, how much less so in the case of a neighbor! COMMENTARY ON GENESIS 9:4.[16]

ANIMALS ARE TO BE KILLED AND EATEN WITHOUT CRUELTY. MARTIN LUTHER: The Lord forbids the eating of a body that still has in it a functioning, active, and living soul, the way a hawk devours chicks and a wolf sheep that have not been killed first but are alive. This cruel procedure the Lord forbids in this passage, and He restricts the permission to

kill. It may not be carried out in the inhuman fashion whereby living bodies or parts of living bodies are consumed; but a lawful manner of killing is to be followed, such as took place at the altar and at the sacrifices, where the animal was killed without any cruelty and ultimately was offered to God after its blood had been carefully washed off. LECTURES ON GENESIS 9:4.[17]

THE PROHIBITION AGAINST EATING BLOOD WAS TO TEACH US GENTLENESS. JOHN CALVIN: Because it is in the blood that the vital spirits chiefly reside, blood is like a token that symbolizes life, as far as our feeling is concerned. And this is expressly stated so that people would shrink back all the more from eating blood. For if it is a brutal and barbarous thing to devour lives or to swallow down living flesh, people betray their savagery by eating blood. Moreover, the point of this prohibition is hardly obscure, namely, that God wanted people to abstain from animal blood as a way of training them in gentleness, lest by growing overly bold and unrestrained in eating wild animals, they should at length be unsparing of even human blood. COMMENTARY ON GENESIS 9:4.[18]

GOD PROHIBITED EATING BLOOD IN ANTICIPATION OF HIS SON'S DEATH. HULDRYCH ZWINGLI: He prohibited the Jews from eating blood so that they would abstain more diligently from bloodshed and homicide. Indeed, although these rules may be externals, they nonetheless warn us against ever committing this atrocity. Yet figurative meanings are not lacking: indeed, blood is forbidden by the very one who through the blood of his own son was going to redeem the world and make all believers in his son's body and blood, so that they would always have this law before their eyes, lest they ever shed blood. . . . Thus, by

---

[15]*Hexapla* (1608), 101. [16]*Commentaria Bibliorum* (1532) 1:12v. [17]LW 2:138 (WA 42:359). [18]CTS 1:293* (CO 23:145).

means of these external things, God teaches and commands things far more profound. ANNOTATIONS ON GENESIS 9:4.[19]

BLOOD WAS FORBIDDEN FOR MANY REASONS. ANDREW WILLET: Whereas the eating of blood was forbidden both before the Law and under the Law (Lev 17), as well as after the Law in the beginning of the gospel (Acts 15), it is profitable to consider the reasons for this prohibition. First, it was forbidden before the Law not so much for decency and comeliness, nor because blood is a gross and heavy food, but either so that these ceremonial precepts might by anticipation better prepare people's minds to bear the yoke of the law that would be promulgated later on; or, rather, so that this precept of abstaining from blood might make people all the more terrified to shed human blood (so Chrysostom).

Secondly, this law was revived in Leviticus 17:11-12 for two reasons: one is civil ("because the life of the flesh is the blood"), so that they would abstain from all show of cruelty and so much the more detest the shedding of human blood; the other is religious ("because I have given the blood to offer at the altar"): the blood, the organ of life, is holy unto God the author of life, and therefore they should not pollute or profane it by devouring it.

Thirdly, the apostles forbade eating blood and things strangled not because the Gentiles regarded suffocated things as the food of evil spirits (so Origen), for it is not likely that the apostles would ground their decree upon such heathen fantasies. Nor by "blood" is homicide forbidden, neither does "things suffocated" [mean that] unclean [foods are forbidden], as some think: for the apostles would not use obscure and mystical terms in their decree, and these things were already provided for by law among the Gentiles. And the apostles did not forbid these things only to restrain intemperance, for many kinds of food are more delicate and desirable than these. But Augustine shows

the true reason for this prohibition, . . . "because the apostles wished to choose some easy thing for a while," not a burden to observe, that the Gentiles might observe in common with the Jews. The apostles did this only for a time, lest the believing Jews, who could hardly be removed from their legal rites all at once, be offended at the liberty of the Gentiles. Now, however, this reason has been removed and, there being no such fear, this decree also is expired. COMMENTARY ON GENESIS 9:4.[20]

9:5-6 For Your Lifeblood I Will Require a Reckoning

GOD CARES FOR ALL, BECAUSE ALL BEAR HIS IMAGE. JOHN CALVIN: If regarded strictly for their own sake, men and women are indeed unworthy of God's care. But because they bear God's image engraved upon them, he deems himself violated in their person. Thus, though they have nothing of their own by which they might procure his favor, God looks upon his own gifts in them and is thereby roused to love and care for them. The lesson is to be carefully observed, however, that no one can be injurious to one's brothers or sisters without wounding God himself. COMMENTARY ON GENESIS 9:6.[21]

HOPING FOR A LESS VIOLENT AGE. PETER MARTYR VERMIGLI: With these words, God gives Noah instructions about what he wants to see done, and not by him alone but, more to the point, by his sons. Truly, they do these things largely for the sake of improving the new age that is coming to pass after Noah. For one of the worst vices that provoked the flood was violence, which those who held more power inflicted upon those who were weaker. If only these things were diligently heard or carefully read by the people of our own time,

---

[19]ZSW 13:57-58. [20]*Hexapla* (1608), 102, quoting Augustine, *Against Faustus* 32.13 (PL 42:504). [21]CTS 1:295-96* (CO 23:147).

who are so prone to bloodshed and so quickly turn to it! . . . If, by his mercy, God spares people who are guilty on so many counts against them and, in a certain sense, are liable to execution at every moment, why do we withhold our compassion from our brethren and neighbors? If, for our sake, God spares even all the wild beasts, as well as livestock, birds and reptiles, why, for God's sake, do we not abstain from violence against his image? COMMENTARY ON GENESIS 9:6.[22]

INNOCENT BLOOD IS PRECIOUS TO GOD.

HULDRYCH ZWINGLI: As if he had said, "The shedding of human blood is so displeasing to me that even if it is shed by beasts, I will require a reckoning." These words express how greatly God abhors homicide. It is also possible to understand "wild animals" as those people who shed blood—everyone who is ungodly or an unbeliever—as if he had said, "If your blood is shed by the Gentiles, who are wild animals, I will vindicate, I will punish, so that there may be comfort for the oppressed, lest they grow discouraged if it ever happens that they suffer persecution." Indeed, God is the defender of innocent blood, which cries out to him. ANNOTATIONS ON GENESIS 9:5.[23]

CAPITAL PUNISHMENT IS INSTITUTED ONLY AFTER THE FLOOD.

MARTIN LUTHER: In this passage . . . the Lord establishes a new law and wants murderers to be killed by men. This was something that had not been customary in the world until now, for God had reserved all judgment for Himself. . . . Here, however, God shares His power with man and grants him power over life and death among men, provided that the person is guilty of shedding blood. . . . Therefore if such a person is killed, even though he is killed by the human sword, he is nevertheless correctly said to have been killed by God. If it were not for this command of God, it would be just as unlawful to kill a murderer now as it was before the Flood. Here we have the source from which stem all civil law and the law of nations. If God grants to man power over life and death, surely He also grants power over what is less, such as property, the home, wife, children, servants, and fields. All these God wants to be subject to the power of certain human beings, in order that they may punish the guilty. LECTURES ON GENESIS 9:6.[24]

POLITICAL AUTHORITY IS FORMALLY BEGUN.

JOHANNES BRENZ: Prior to the flood, even if the father in each household ruled over his own family, no public magistrate was yet ordained who would wield the sword to punish criminals, especially murderers. Of Cain it was said, "Whoever kills Cain will be punished sevenfold." None of the patriarchs dared to establish a precedent from this or to seize for himself the right of public punishment, because God had set aside for himself those criminals that were to be punished, whom he punished with a terrible flood when their time came. But now, having guaranteed that never again would he inflict a general punishment upon the human race until the last day, he establishes political authorities and the public use of force in order to preserve tranquility among the human race by this means. COMMENTARY ON GENESIS 9:5-6.[25]

"AN EYE FOR AN EYE" WORKS ONLY IF MAGISTRATES ARE VIGILANT.

WOLFGANG MUSCULUS: Nothing can be fairer than the law of equivalence (*lex talionis*). No one who sheds human blood can restore what has been poured out, yet one is still obliged to pay it back. Therefore it is fair that he give his own blood for that which he shed. Thus a soul is rightly demanded in turn for a soul, a hand for a hand, a foot for a foot, an eye for an eye, etc., just as it is decreed in the Law. But the logic of

[22]*In Primum Librum Mosis* (1569), 40v. [23]ZSW 13:58; cf. Gen 4:10. [24]LW 2:140 (WA 42:360). [25]*Opera* 1:109-10.

this equivalence is twofold: First, it preserves both justice and equity. Otherwise it would be unjust if the blood of a murderous and violent person were unpunished while the blood of one innocent of evil be exposed to violence and savagery. The dictates of justice and equity require something far different! Second, it curbs evil, lest a precedent be drawn from an example and every door be opened to carnage. But two things are necessary for this law to work, namely, fear of death and consistent enforcement. The fear of death is implanted in our nature by God, but the enforcement of this law has been delegated to magistrates. Those who love their lives are restrained by the fear of death, lest they commit violence against the life of another. Those who are restrained neither by love of their own lives nor by fear of death must be restrained by the sword of vengeance, lest they extend a hand against the blood of another, so that by their example, at least, others may be checked and the propensity in the human heart to shed blood may be held back by this fearsome penalty. But if the enforcement of this law wholly ceases or is weakened by collusion, what else can result

except that the blood of the innocent will become vulnerable to the violence and barbarity of evildoers, and the sheep be torn to bits while the wolves are spared? COMMENTARY ON GENESIS 9:5-6.[26]

GOD PREFERS LOVE TO RETALIATION.
KONRAD PELLIKAN: By this word of God it is established, as a law of retaliation, that anyone who sheds blood—if people can prove it and it can be known with certainty—their blood shall be shed and they shall compensate that death with their own death: not so much for the sake of retaliation as from fear of repetition, so that others might be warned. Nonetheless, love will alleviate any law in a way that no law can decide beforehand. God does not desire the death of sinners, but rather that they should turn and live. Love, I say: of God as much as of neighbor, and of the community as much as of private individuals. COMMENTARY ON GENESIS 9:6.[27]

---

[26]*In Mosis Genesim* (1554), 239. [27]*Commentaria Bibliorum* (1532) 1:13r.

9:8-17 THE COVENANT WITH NOAH

[8]*Then God said to Noah and to his sons with him,* [9]*"Behold, I establish my covenant with you and your offspring after you,* [10]*and with every living creature that is with you, the birds, the livestock, and every beast of the earth with you, as many as came out of the ark; it is for every beast of the earth.* [11]*I establish my covenant with you, that never again shall all flesh be cut off by the waters of the flood, and never again shall there be a flood to destroy the earth."* [12]*And God said, "This is the sign of the covenant that I make between me and you and every living creature that is with you, for all future generations:* [13]*I have set my bow in the cloud, and it shall be a sign of the covenant between me and*

the earth. ¹⁴*When I bring clouds over the earth and the bow is seen in the clouds,* ¹⁵*I will remember my covenant that is between me and you and every living creature of all flesh. And the waters shall never again become a flood to destroy all flesh.* ¹⁶*When the bow is in the clouds, I will see it and remember the everlasting covenant between God and every living creature of all flesh that is on the earth."* ¹⁷*God said to Noah, "This is the sign of the covenant that I have established between me and all flesh that is on the earth."*

OVERVIEW: The text comes at last to an extended consideration of the covenant that God makes with Noah. However, the actual mention of covenant in Genesis 9:9-11 generates less comment than one might expect, probably because the term had been affixed to Noah far earlier, in Genesis 6:18, and the content of the covenant itself—that there will never again be such destruction of all flesh—was fully stated in Genesis 8:21-22.

What does attract comment is the spectacular sign that God established to accompany the covenant with Noah—what we commonly call the rainbow. This sign generates questions and comments of all sorts. First, many wondered and worried about whether the rainbow was a natural sign, that is, were there rainbows before, or was the first rainbow consequent upon the divine declaration here? What, in any case, was the correspondence between this sign and the covenant to which it is attached? Reformation commentators were happy to be handed an invitation, so to speak, to muse upon such matters as the rainbow's appearance or its colors and to probe such matters for their theological significance. It was obvious to most of them that the rainbow, in its Old Testament context, was a sacrament in everything but name. They were therefore merely following patristic precedents when they expounded it as an analogue or forerunner to the sacraments of the New Testament—an exposition made only more urgent by constant controversies over the sacraments between Catholics and Protestants as well as among Protestants themselves. Once the bridge was crossed from the sacraments of the Old Testament to those of the New, many Reformation commentators discovered additional allegorical or typological insights: sometimes as a rehash of earlier writers, but sometimes with new elements of their own.

9:8-11 A Covenant with Every Living Creature

CAN GOD MAKE A PACT WITH ANIMALS?
WOLFGANG MUSCULUS: Anyone might ask here how a pact can be established, especially by God, with livestock and beasts devoid of reason, when they have no awareness of spiritual things. Indeed, it would seem that such awareness is a condition of any pact or covenant, one of the essential points by which pacts are constituted and to which not just one but each party to the covenant inviolably adheres. Now when God makes a pact with creatures, just as he himself is ready to maintain the agreements that concern him, so it is clearly fitting that those with whom he undertook the pact accommodate themselves to this divine benevolence with the faithfulness and obedience they owe in turn—something that beasts can by no means do! . . . But I would say that much depends on what kind of pact was instituted. Here it is to be considered that there are two kinds of pacts. One is conditional; the other is instituted without any condition. Those that have a condition added cannot be established with irrational beasts, for they are not capable of fulfilling the conditions, which they can neither understand nor observe or obey. Those pacts that are

struck simply and without condition do not require something to stand in for observance, acknowledgment of benefits or heartfelt gratitude, and can certainly be instituted not only with humans but also with beasts. COMMENTARY ON GENESIS 9:9-10.[1]

9:12-17 This Is the Sign of the Covenant

GOD REPEATS HIS PROMISES AS A MOTHER SOOTHES HER CHILD. MARTIN LUTHER: When the same matter is repeated so many times, this is an indication of God's extraordinary affection for mankind. He is trying to persuade them not to fear such a punishment in the future but to hope for blessing and for the utmost forbearance. Noah and his people were in great need of such comfort. A man who has been humbled by God is unable to forget his hurt and pain, for affliction makes a far deeper impression than an act of kindness. . . . It is for this reason that God shows Himself benevolent in such a variety of ways and takes such extraordinary delight in pouring forth compassion, like a mother who is caressing and petting her child in order that it may finally begin to forget its tears and smile at its mother. This comfort is expressed in many eloquent words and emphasized in various ways, to meet the need of these wretched people who had been watching the immeasurable wrath of God rage for an entire year. Therefore they could not be talked out of their fear and terror by a word or two; a great abundance of words was needed to drive back their tears and to soften their grief. Even though they were saints, they were still flesh, just as we are. LECTURES ON GENESIS 9:11, 15.[2]

THE RAINBOW COMFORTED THOSE WHO SURVIVED THE FLOOD. JOHN CALVIN: Lest the memory of the flood instill them with new terrors every time the sky should be covered with clouds, as if the earth were to be drowned again, this anxiety is banished. And certainly,

if we consider the human mind's great propensity to distrust, we will not conclude that this testimony was without its purpose even for Noah. Indeed, he was endowed with a rare and incomparable and even miraculous faith; but no constancy could be so steadfast that divine vengeance of this sort, so sad and horrible, would not overwhelm it. So whenever any great, long-lasting rainstorm would appear to threaten the earth with a flood, this reassuring sign is placed as a covering under which the holy man could find rest. COMMENTARY ON GENESIS 9:8.[3]

WHAT COULD BE SWEETER THAN TO KNOW THAT THE CHURCH SURVIVES? CHRISTOPHOR PELARGUS: There is the greatest sweetness in this text, because it clearly teaches that there is some form of church in this world and that it will continue without interruption, protected by God and strengthened by his word and sacraments. COMMENTARY ON GENESIS 9:8-17.[4]

THE RAINBOW IS A SACRAMENT OF MERCY. KONRAD PELLIKAN: God is faithful and compensates for his terrible wrath by means of manifest kindness: however much unasked, he yet promises sinners after this never to send such a punishment upon the world. And he institutes a sacramental sign of the promise, namely, a bow in the clouds, wishing it to be a sure indication of divine mercy. Therefore, whenever that arc of the rainbow shall appear in the clouds—by the command and work of God, yet no less naturally—it ought to remind the faithful of the just judgments of God, by which we may know that our crimes are to be punished. As did the people of ancient times, we too should faithfully and reverently acknowledge and honor the sacrament of divine faithfulness toward us, by which he wishes to

---

[1]*In Mosis Genesim* (1554), 241-42. [2]LW 2:145 (WA 42:363-64). [3]CTS 1:296* (CO 23:147). [4]*In prophetarum oceanum*, 205.

have such pity on our sins as to punish them less than they deserve. Commentary on Genesis 9:8-15.[5]

The Rainbow Attests God's Justice and Mercy. Andrew Willet:

The rainbow is a notable monument to God's justice, to call to our mind the sin for which the old world was destroyed, so that we fear to offend God in a similar way. But it is also a sign of God's mercy, in refusing to bring such a destruction upon the world again: and if God shows such mercy even to wicked people and to brute beasts, how great are the mercies that he lays up in store for his elect? We may also see how far the justice of God exceeds his mercy: the rigor of his justice was but for a time, in once destroying the world by water, but his mercy is perpetual in his continual preservation of the world. Commentary on Genesis 9:13.[6]

With Noah, God Renews the Covenant with Adam and Eve and Adds Signs.

Dirk Philips: It is necessary for Christians to know what that covenant of God is, namely, that God binds and unites himself with us, promises us every good, that he will be our God and Father, and we shall be his people, his sons and daughters, the sheep of his pasture, and receive from him the blessing through Jesus Christ. And this covenant has begun when God spoke to the serpent, "I will put enmity between you and the women, between your seed and the women's seed, and that the women's seed will itself tread upon and crush your head." Thereafter this covenant is thus renewed and established by God with Noah the patriarch and with his sons, to whom God spoke, "I set up my covenant with you. . . ." Hereto all the commands of God serve, which teach and command us how we should conduct ourselves toward God. Here to also belong both signs of the Lord, as baptism and the Lord's Supper, instituted to witness to this covenant and to admonish us thereto. For

although that true, genuine, and saving sign from the rich grace of the covenant is Jesus Christ, and the Holy Spirit is the sealing of all the promises of God, nevertheless, the almighty God has always witnessed to and established his covenant with external signs. For as God comforted Adam and Eve with the promise of the coming Savior and victor over the serpent, thus he gave them garments of skins and clothed them therewith (and this signifies that Jesus Christ is the cloak of righteousness and the coat of salvation, with which all believers and baptized Christians are clothed and their sins covered), because they should be assured of the grace and promises of God. For that God clothed their nakedness and shame when they had sinned was a sure and open sign that God had not turned his fatherly heart from them, but that he maintained and still cared through his bottomless mercy and love, also with bodily clothing, that they should always have a refuge in this grace of God. In the same manner, God gave Noah the rainbow and Abraham circumcision as signs of his covenant, and both of these signs image Jesus Christ for us, who is a sign of our peace in heaven at his Father's right hand. Enchiridion.[7]

Were There Rainbows Before the Flood? Wolfgang Musculus:

Curious questions are raised here, which do nothing for piety. First, they ask whether this bow arose in the clouds by means of natural causes or in some other way. Some assert that it was formed in the normal course of nature, while others attribute it not to nature but to the singular will of God, by which he determined to set it with the clouds in place of a sign. Second, they ask whether this bow was the same before the flood as it was afterwards. Here, some deny it, others affirm. Third, they

---

[5]*Commentaria Bibliorum* (1532) 1:13r. [6]*Hexapla* (1608), 111, crediting Pererius. [7]CRR 6:418-19.

also ask about the rain, whether the earth was watered by rain in the first world before the flood in the same way that we see it occur after the flood. Some assert that the rain ceased to water the earth before the flood, others deny it. . . . Again, I think it is idle curiosity for someone to inquire too energetically into these matters. Nonetheless, since many do raise these questions, I think they think best who say that this bow arose from natural causes and appeared in the clouds before the flood just as it does now, so long as they do not view it in a pagan way but consider also what would have been added to it after the flood by God's decree that it would not have had previously. Before the flood, the *nature* of the bow was no different than it is now, but now its *use* is different than it was before. Indeed, now, after the flood, it has been made into a sign of the covenant, reminding us by its very appearance that for all the days of the earth there will never be a flood like there was in the days of Noah. . . . Nor should it seem incongruous that something naturally produced should be designated for another use than it had before and become the vehicle for a sign. Commentary on Genesis 9:12-17.[8]

For the Rainbow to Be a Comfort, It Must Have Been New. Johannes Brenz: Some suppose that the heavenly arc had appeared before, indeed, seasonally, from the beginning of the world, but that after the flood it was established as a sign of the covenant. But the more likely view is that of those who affirm that this arc was divinely created only after the flood. It cannot be denied that although Noah and his family were pious, they had not yet wholly laid aside the flesh, so that at the rising of any little cloud they would have shuddered in fear of the flood coming again. . . . In such circumstances, for an arc to be seen arising quite unexpectedly in the clouds, when one had never been seen before, it is probable that they would have been not only astonished

by this miracle but also breathless with fear, because they would have inferred that nothing was more likely than that a flood was coming again. In fact, when the arc [first] appeared, clouds usually indicated more rain than at other times. That is why God immediately disclosed his plan for the arc: that he had put it there not to give notice of a coming flood but more to announce the opposite, namely, that there would never be a general flood on earth. For if they had been used to seeing it before, it would have afforded them very little comfort. Indeed, they could have said, "Didn't it also appear before, and then the flood came? So how does it now signify that a flood will *not* come again?" It is likely, then, that the arc was created not before but after the flood, in order to furnish people with greater consolation and a strengthening of faith. Commentary on Genesis 9:8-17.[9]

The Rainbow Is a Sign, Not a Miracle. Peter Martyr Vermigli: Rain, clouds and the rainbow would have been observed before the flood. Of course, if it did appear previously, it was still not a symbol of God's mercy at that time as it has been made to be now. Nor has God done this only once, that things that had been regarded as what they were by nature should be appointed by God to be symbols and signs. Accordingly, the water in baptism is a sign of the remission of sins. Bread and wine signify incorporation into Christ's flesh and blood. Even if these things have their own natural role and character prior to the action of the sacrament, by God's decree they have nevertheless gone on to be established also as symbols not only of divine promises but also of those things whose presence they reveal. The rainbow appeared as a sign, but not as a miracle, for those things happen with extreme rarity and surpass the powers of nature. Nor, on the other hand, was

---

[8]*In Mosis Genesim* (1554), 242-43.　[9]*Opera* 1:112-13.

it like the sun, moon or stars, whose rising and setting is observed every day. Nor, again, was it a symbol like our sacraments, which promise Christ to us so that they might unite him to us or us to him. Rather, the rainbow is like a kind of monument to God's good will toward us. COMMENTARY ON GENESIS 9:13.[10]

RIGHT AND WRONG WAYS TO DEAL WITH DIVINE SIGNS. WOLFGANG MUSCULUS:

When God wished to attach this pact to some sign, he did not choose something so portentous or unusual that it would move even the minds of unbelievers, but rather something of the sort that only the faithful would recognize as a sign of the covenant. Therefore, he appointed this rainbow, a common thing that had often appeared from natural causes, and to this sign he added his word, on which godly and faithful people should depend. Take someone ignorant of the word of God: even if he were to see this rainbow every day and dispute about its causes more acutely and accurately than Seneca, he would still never understand its use, namely, that it is a sign of God's covenant between God and the earth, established immediately after the flood. Wherefore we are reminded of what is especially to be observed in these kinds of signs of the divine will and favor: namely, that without the word by which the promise of God's grace is expressed and declared, the rainbow is nothing more than an image of the sun's rays stamped upon the clouds, the water of baptism is no better than any other water, and the bread of the Lord's Supper would be even less important and useful than ordinary table bread. Therefore the faithful act most rightly, because they judge signs of this sort not according to what they are by nature or appear to be externally but according to the word of God. So when they see the rainbow in the clouds, they remember God's words . . . and do not dispute about its natural causes and the variety of its colors, but they regard it as a sign of God's covenant and even more of God's manifest goodness, which they see, admire and receive more than the external figure of the sign.

They do likewise with the New Testament signs and symbols of baptism and the Lord's Supper: they do not contemplate the visible forms, matter, nature, or natural powers of the water, bread and wine. Neither do they dispute with the followers of Scotus as to whether someone is imprinted with the baptismal mark or whether that mark is indelible or not; nor, likewise, whether the form of that mark is absolute or relative, and whether it inheres in the essence of the soul as in the subject; or whether it is possible in the Eucharist that the body of Christ is really present under the appearance of the bread, and whether it is present there without any mutation or whether the body could be in many places at the same time; nor, similarly, whether the substance of the bread is changed into the body of Christ and annihilated, and [if so] what the formal result of transubstantiation would be; and finally, whether the accidents would be there without any subject, and what little creatures would eat if they were to feed on the Eucharist. The godly ignore these Scotists and simply accept the word of God with ears of faith. They make their judgments according to the infallible truth of these signs and embrace them sincerely as symbols of the grace that is imparted to us by the blood of Christ—symbols set before the world at his command by the preaching of the gospel. COMMENTARY ON GENESIS 9:12-17.[11]

ARE THE COLORS SYMBOLIC? JOHANNES

BRENZ: There is also a dispute about the colors of the rainbow, and some think that among the various colors, two predominate: one is watery, the other is fiery. The watery

---

[10]*In Primum Librum Mosis* (1569), 41r. [11]*In Mosis Genesim* (1554), 245-46.

color signifies that the earth will not again perish through water, but the fiery color signifies that the earth will perish through fire at the end. But we should understand that the rainbow is chiefly a sign of grace and preservation. So, content with this meaning, let us learn about the eventual conflagration of the world from other places in Scripture. COMMENTARY ON GENESIS 9:12-17.[12]

THE RAINBOW ALSO SIGNIFIES CHRIST.

KONRAD PELLIKAN: That bow also signifies Christ, given as a sign of our reconciliation with God the Father. Appointed to be an advocate for us, he is looked to when you seek his mercy and when we ask for his help in faith. COMMENTARY ON GENESIS 9:8-15.[13]

THE RAINBOW IS MOSTLY NOT A MYSTICAL

SIGN. ANDREW WILLET: The rainbow is not a natural sign, but a voluntary one, depending upon the will and institution of God. Nonetheless, it has some agreement with that of which it is a sign. Just as baptism in the flesh has some resemblance with the spiritual cleansing of the soul, so the rainbow is a fit and convenient sign to portend that no inundation is likely to follow, because it is ordinarily a sign either of fair weather or of no long rain. And it has been observed that a rainbow in the morning betokens showers; in the evening, fair weather. Besides, the rainbow is found to be wholesome to plants and herbs, in that where it alights, it gives them a more

pleasant and fragrant smell (as Aristotle and Pliny write), and therefore more fit in this respect to be a sign of grace and favor. . . . But there are insufficient grounds for the opinion of Rupert, who applies the covenant signified by the rainbow wholly to Christ and makes it altogether mystical. We do not deny that the rainbow, as a sign of temporal benefit, may be a type and figure of God's everlasting mercy in Christ (as in Rev 4:3, where the throne of God is described as having a rainbow round about it), yet it is evident that God covenants here with Noah for this temporal benefit, and with all other creatures and living things, to whom the spiritual covenant in Christ does not pertain. And while other mystical significations are made of the rainbow—as that the two colors of water and fire in the rainbow (blue and red) betoken the baptism of Christ by water and fire, or the two judgments of the world (the one already past by water, the other to come by fire)—these applications and others like them are more witty and pretty than wise and pithy. Furthermore, whereas other covenants are made with a condition of obedience, this covenant is absolute, in that however much the wickedness of people may deserve other particular punishments, the Lord will never again destroy the world with water. COMMENTARY ON GENESIS 9:13.[14]

---

[12]*Opera* 1:113-14. [13]*Commentaria Bibliorum* (1532) 1:13r. [14]*Hexapla* (1608), 103-4.

9:18-29 THE DRUNKENNESS OF NOAH

^{18}*The sons of Noah who went forth from the ark were Shem, Ham, and Japheth. (Ham was the father of Canaan.) ^{19}These three were the sons of Noah, and from these the people of the whole earth were dispersed.*^{a}

^{20}*Noah began to be a man of the soil, and he planted a vineyard.*^{b} ^{21}*He drank of the wine and became drunk and lay uncovered in his tent. ^{22}And Ham, the father of Canaan, saw the nakedness of his father and told his two brothers outside. ^{23}Then Shem and Japheth took a garment, laid it on both their shoulders, and walked backward and covered the nakedness of their father. Their faces were turned backward, and they did not see their father's nakedness. ^{24}When Noah awoke from his wine and knew what his youngest son had done to him, ^{25}he said,*

"Cursed be Canaan;
 a servant of servants shall he be to his brothers."

^{26}*He also said,*

"Blessed be the LORD*, the God of Shem;*
 and let Canaan be his servant.
^{27}*May God enlarge Japheth,*^{c}
 and let him dwell in the tents of Shem,
 and let Canaan be his servant."

^{28}*After the flood Noah lived 350 years. ^{29}All the days of Noah were 950 years, and he died.*

a *Or from these the whole earth was populated*   b *Or Noah, a man of the soil, was the first to plant a vineyard*   c *Japheth sounds like the Hebrew for enlarge*

OVERVIEW: Genesis 9 ends with the story of how Noah was overcome by wine and discovered, naked, by his son Ham, and how Ham's impudence led to a curse on his own son Canaan. It is a shocking and unexpected conclusion to the long story of an otherwise illustrious patriarch, and commentators of all ages sift through every detail of this scandal, looking to find explanations if not excuses wherever they can.

Modern scholars read this story backwards from its conclusion, which includes the genealogies in Genesis 10, as meant to explain the division of the peoples of the earth into three tribes: the Israelites who have descended from Shem through Abraham; the maritime peoples who derive from Japheth; and all the rest of the Gentiles who descended from Ham, including Philistines, Babylonians and Assyrians, but especially the troublesome Canaanites, who are most in focus here by virtue of Noah's curse not on Ham, but on his son

Canaan. Many today would argue that the composition of the text of Genesis dates to the time of the conquest of the promised land (or to a still later time), and that the curse on Canaan both explains and justifies that conquest—a function of the narrative that some Reformation writers, such as Musculus, were able to appreciate.

Students of the history of biblical interpretation will also know this story as the seedbed for the notorious racial exegesis that undergirded the European and American slave trade for several centuries. That line of exegesis sought to vilify Ham as Noah's dark-skinned son and Canaan as the archetypal slave—not just in his appearance or status but also in his servile character and in the divine warrant or judgment that his condition perennially represented. For the most part, however, the egregious use of Scripture as a warrant for the slave trade is not easily predicted from the exegesis of these Reformation commentators. While quick to excoriate Ham and Canaan for a variety of sins, they remain unaware of any association between these biblical villains and the pernicious stereotypes of race, color and continent that would be imposed upon the passage within a century or so.[1]

Instead, Reformation interpreters were still very much occupied with traditional questions, especially the problem of excusing Noah. As the "deliverer" of Genesis 5:29, he was supposed to be an exemplar, but in the end he disappointed badly. How should Christian readers be guided by his story, then? Naturally, this question depended on other details, including whether Noah was the inventor of wine, whether he knew what wine could do, whether his inebriation was habitual, and so forth—including whether he was especially sad or depressed after the flood. But medieval exegesis had refined other ways to excuse Noah, including a strategic invocation of allegory or typology, which even Protestant writers could find attractive.[2]

Ham's enigmatic misdeed also called for

scrutiny, though it was closely rivaled by Noah's equally enigmatic outburst not against Ham but against Canaan, Ham's son. What, exactly, did Ham do that was so evil? And why did the curse or punishment for this crime target Canaan, not Ham himself? The ambiguity of the narrative was only exacerbated by the vagueness of the accompanying blessings Noah bestowed on his other two sons, Shem and especially Japheth. While "let Canaan be his servant" seemed plain enough, far less clarity was to be found in the other phrases that called on God to "enlarge Japheth, and let him dwell in the tents of Shem." Nonetheless, with some help from their exegetical forebears, Protestant commentators were fully able to illuminate this blessing and even to draw out its implications for Reformation Europe—often with enough energy left over for some closing remarks on Noah's long life.

9:20 *Noah Planted a Vineyard*

GROWING GRAPES WAS NOTHING NEW OR SCANDALOUS. ANDREW WILLET: It is mentioned that Noah planted vines rather than that he sowed corn (with which he was also undoubtedly occupied) not because he intended to leave the invention of necessary things to God and of pleasurable things to humans (as Ambrose supposes), for there is no doubt but that wheat was in use before the flood. Rather, [the mention of vines] furnishes the occasion for the story that follows. Nor is there any ground for saying that there was no use of the

---

[1]The sinister twist in the history of exegesis regarding Ham and the slave trade develops most crucially from the end of the sixteenth century through the middle of the eighteenth; see David M. Whitford, *The Curse of Ham in the Early Modern Era: The Bible and the Justifications for Slavery* (Burlington, VT: Ashgate, 2009), esp. chapters 5 and 6. [2]One such traditional allegory taught that Christians should "cover" the sins of the clergy (represented by Noah)—an argument that some Protestants would allow but that others found suspicious, as Chytraeus and Pellikan will illustrate. See David C. Steinmetz, "Luther and the Drunkenness of Noah," in *Luther in Context* (Bloomington: Indiana University Press, 1986), esp. 104, 106.

vine before the flood, when the people were given to such sensuality and pleasure. Rather, Noah brought the grape to more perfection (and therefore it is said he planted a vineyard, not vines) in order to make drink from that which might have been used otherwise before. COMMENTARY ON GENESIS 9:20.[3]

THE VINE AND ITS MAKER ARE NOT AT FAULT. WOLFGANG MUSCULUS: Some wonder why the grapevine was produced at all among the other things born of the earth at the beginning of creation, given that countless evils arise from the use of wine. They argue that grapevines either should not have been created at the beginning or else, having been created, they should not be propagated; or, rather, given that they *are* propagated, they surely ought to be completely pulled out everywhere down to the roots. So they marvel that Noah wanted to plant a vine and tend it. But if these people would first attend to what David recited in Psalm 104—"Wine gladdens the human heart"—and ponder the wisdom of the divine goodness in this matter, they would then distinguish between a legitimate and temperate use of wine and its abuse, and not blame the creator of the vine or find fault with its cultivation. Instead, they would thankfully acknowledge the goodness of this creation and reject any vice that follows from excessive drinking. COMMENTARY ON GENESIS 9:20.[4]

NOAH WARNS US NOT AGAINST DRINKING BUT AGAINST DRUNKENNESS. JOHN CALVIN: It is commonly believed that wine was not in use before that time. And this opinion has been welcomed all the more eagerly because it would afford an honorable pretext for extenuating Noah's sin. But it doesn't seem likely to me that the fruit of the vine, which excels all others, would have lain neglected and unprofitable. Nor, indeed, does Moses say that Noah was drunk on the first day he sipped some wine. Leaving this question unresolved, then, I

rather suppose that from the drunkenness of Noah we are to learn what a filthy and detestable thing drunkenness is. The holy patriarch was an outstanding example of good character and self-control, yet he forgot himself: in a base and shameful manner, he cast himself naked on the ground so as to become a laughingstock to all. How much more, then, should we ourselves cultivate sobriety, lest something similar (or even worse) happen to us? COMMENTARY ON GENESIS 9:20.[5]

9:21 Noah Became Drunk and Lay Uncovered in His Tent

NOAH'S DRUNKENNESS WAS A ONE-TIME LAPSE. HULDRYCH ZWINGLI: Drunkards find in this verse a pretext for Noah's vice and they propose to themselves that he was faithful—but in vain. Indeed, it is one thing for someone inexperienced and ignorant and lacking an understanding of the power of wine to be overwhelmed by wine, once. But it is something else to make it one's task to gorge and abandon oneself to wine. There is no one who, ignorant about wine, would not be overwhelmed and conquered by wine once, but this is not to go so far as to be deemed a vice. The one can properly be called drunk, but the other is a drunkard; the former is troubled by wine at one time or another, but the latter is habitually guilty of the vice of drunkenness. ANNOTATIONS ON GENESIS 9:21.[6]

THE SIMPLE LESSON: MODERATION AND SOBRIETY. KONRAD PELLIKAN: In this passage we are admonished about sobriety and that wine should be used with restraint, lest we fall into a foolish state of mind, bodily disgrace and moral indecency. COMMENTARY ON GENESIS 9:8-15.[7]

---

[3]*Hexapla* (1608), 105. [4]*In Mosis Genesim* (1554), 249. [5]CTS 1:300-301* (CO 23:150). [6]ZSW 13:59-60. [7]*Commentaria Bibliorum* (1532) 1:13v.

WHY DIDN'T NOAH'S WIFE INTERVENE?

WOLFGANG MUSCULUS: Where was his wife? Why wouldn't she have watched over her husband more diligently and been mindful of his old age? For as the Hebrew text makes clear, he did not lie down to sleep in the usual place where a drunk old man could be properly laid by his wife's care and attention, but . . . in the *center* of his tent, which both the Greek and the Latin translators neglected to express. . . . Yet nothing certain can be said about Noah's wife, for there is no mention of her in the Scriptures after the flood, except that she too exited the ark with her husband and sons and daughters-in-law. So nothing can be positively adduced here, and whatever is asserted must be spoken as conjecture. If she was still among the living when Noah became drunk, I don't see what else could be said except that, following an old custom, she may have dwelt by herself, separated from the tents of her husband and sons.[†] So it easily could have happened that, unknown to her, Noah had prostrated himself in this fashion: naked, and in the middle of his tent. . . . But if this conjecture seems likely, there is nothing more to seek as to why Noah was covered not by his wife but by his sons. Someone may point out that Noah's nakedness could have been reported to his wife either by the sons or by one of the grandsons, of which by then there would have been a fair abundance. This thought leads to the conjecture that Noah may have been a widower then, his wife having died. Whatever the case, I think it is better that we hold to the first or second conjecture than conclude that Noah disgraced himself with his wife as an accessory or through her neglect. COMMENTARY ON GENESIS 9:21.[8]

NOAH CANNOT BE WHOLLY EXCUSED.

ANDREW WILLET: Though Noah's drunkenness may have some excuse, in that he was an old man and unaccustomed to this kind of drink, and being ignorant of its nature and power, he was more quickly overcome, nonetheless, he can have no just defense. For Noah was so intoxicated and under the influence that he temporarily forgot himself and all decorum, for he lay uncovered—not as Ibn Ezra thinks, by Canaan's doing, but by his own negligence and oversight—and that, in the midst of the tent, on the floor or pavement as it were. (Some Hebrews say that it was in his wife's tent, to whom he had gone in, while others think that his wife was not living, because she would have covered his nakedness; but these things are uncertain.) Accordingly, it appears how straightforward the divine story is, for it does not conceal the infirmities of the most perfect men in order that by such examples we should rather take heed: for if the strong may be overtaken like this, how much more circumspect ought the weaker sort to be? COMMENTARY ON GENESIS 9:21.[9]

WE NEED TO KNOW ABOUT NOAH'S LAPSE MORE THAN HIS LATER ACHIEVEMENTS.

MARTIN LUTHER: Even though Moses has little to say about Noah after the Flood, anyone will realize that since he lived for approximately three hundred and fifty years after the time of the Flood, such a great man could not have been inactive but was busy with the government of the church, which he alone established and ruled. In the first place, Noah filled the office of bishop; and because he had been plagued by various temptations, it was his foremost concern to oppose the devil and comfort the tempted, to restore the erring, to give confidence to the wavering, to encourage the despairing, to shut out the impenitent from his church, and to receive back the penitent with fatherly joy. . . . In the second place, Noah had his civil tasks, because he established the state and formulated laws,

---

[8]*In Mosis Genesim* (1554), 249. [†]Musculus bolsters his case for separate tents by citing Gen 24. [9]*Hexapla* (1608), 105, crediting Mercerus in part.

without which human lust cannot be kept under control. In addition to this, there was the management of his own home or care for the household.

Although reason tells us that after the Deluge Noah was occupied with so many varied tasks, Moses makes mention of none of these. To Moses it seemed necessary to record only this one item: how he began to plant a vineyard, became drunk, and lay naked in his tent. This is indeed a silly and altogether unprofitable little story if you compare it with the rest of Noah's outstanding achievements through the course of so many years. If other events were recorded, they could edify people and help them arrange their lives properly. Moreover, this story also seems to give a cause for offense and to defend people who get drunk and then sin because of their drunkenness. But the intention of the Holy Spirit is familiar from our teaching. He wanted the godly, who know their weakness and for this reason are disheartened, to take comfort in the offense that comes from the account of the lapses among the holiest and most perfect patriarchs. In such instances we should find sure proof of our own weakness and therefore bow down in humble confession, not only to ask for forgiveness but also to hope for it. LECTURES ON GENESIS 9:20-22.[10]

REAL SAINTS ARE ALSO SINNERS. JO-HANNES BRENZ: To this point, when the lawful and ordinary course of this world has been restored after the flood and the human race has been provided with instruction about divine worship, political authority and even about foods, Scripture has also commemorated the eminent virtues of the patriarch Noah. But it now recounts the disgrace of that spectacle in which, having tended grapes and imbibed their wine, he became drunk with wine and lay prostrate in his tent, stripped of everything honorable. That this spectacle is seen in such a holy patriarch, who until now had been praised

as full of the Holy Spirit, is quite abominable and even detestable. Yet Scripture is not content with this remembrance, but later on adds much about the other patriarchs that is as disgraceful as it is ridiculous. A drunken Lot despoils his two daughters. Sarah delivers her handmaid to her husband to be impregnated. Two sisters, the wives of Jacob, compete to sleep with their husband—and other things of this sort.[†] This is why they say that the Hebrew sages prohibited anyone younger than thirty (that is, before they were confirmed in the true knowledge of God) from approaching to read this book of Genesis. Some add, as a reason, that because the beginning of this book is convoluted by many difficulties, it is not to be allowed to the young and untrained, lest they rush headlong into such great mysteries. But I think that young people most of all would have been prohibited from reading this book, because so many disgraceful and ridiculous things about the holy patriarchs are contained in it. . . . For just as in political matters, people chiefly admire those things that have been powerfully used against enemies in battle, . . . so also in sacred matters, people especially welcome things that are not understood and seem to have a great appearance of heavenly wisdom.

But hypocrites in the Christian faith, if they have invented any legends of the saints, as they call them, write about these saints as if they had never perpetrated any vice or done anything foolish, but rather afflicted themselves with frequent fasting, constantly attended to prayers and vigils, and finally endured death with great bodily pleasure, wholly estranged in their minds from any feeling of pain. In brief, they praise their saints so that they would seem to have been utterly sinless.

But we should think far differently: our sacred books should not be concealed or kept

---

[10]LW 2:165-66 (WA 42:378).

secret, but rather expounded in public for everyone. Nor should anyone make sinless gods out of the saints, but their infirmities ought to be made clear, so that God alone may possess the glory of holiness. So this passage tells of the drunkenness and disgrace of the most holy patriarch Noah because it has the greatest utility to the church and thus ought to be well-known by all. But first of all, these things are not recalled for this purpose, that drunkards might seek from this example a patron for their drunkenness or gluttony. For Noah became drunk only once, but they're drunk every day, as the prophet says: "They rise early in the morning to run after their drinks and stay up late at night till they are inflamed with wine." And Noah, when he became drunk, withdrew to sleep, but they don't go to bed until they have schemed up horrible crimes. . . . So they cannot excuse their drunkenness by the example of Noah. . . . Yet neither is the story retold so we might think that Noah was not only not to be reprehended, but even to be praised—just as some are in the habit of misguidedly excusing the saints' vices, commending them as if they were virtues. And there are some who interpret Noah's drunkenness as the intoxication or greatness of Christ's love toward us, and Noah's nakedness as the humiliation, suffering and cross of Christ for us. These are indeed pious reflections, but they do not wholly fit Noah's example. Instead, there are other reasons for why this history is set forth in such a conspicuous place to be known by all, one of which is so that all pious people would be warned against placing their trust first and foremost in their own holiness and piety. COMMENTARY ON GENESIS 9:20-21.[11]

THREE WRONG WAYS TO REGARD THE SAINTS' FAILINGS. WOLFGANG MUSCULUS: At this point, three kinds of people need to be reined in. The first are those who excuse every failing in the saints, so that they are unwilling to admit anything in them by way of misdeeds. But the Holy Spirit by no means ignores the vices and infirmities of the saints, as one may see from this passage and many others like it. Nor does the Spirit act unreasonably, but rather seems to take account of our weak consciences, lest we despair of the grace of God. You'll find many unlearned and simple people who think the saints attained their salvation and heavenly bliss in no other way than by the merits of their righteousness alone, without the free remission of their sins. Indeed, they suppose that this is what it means to be holy, that in truth the saints are those in whom there is no need for sins to be remitted. . . . The second kind are those who do acknowledge that the saints failed in a great many ways and fault them for their vices, but not so that they may be reminded of God's grace, but rather to use the examples of the saints to cover their own vices and to defend themselves when *they* fail. Those who are given to wine and are frequently inebriated thus excuse the shame of their intemperance by citing Noah as an example. "So what if we're always ready to drink with gusto, even if we get drunk?" they ask. "Didn't Noah drink wine? Isn't it written that he too got drunk? But if drunkenness is so great a sin that it renders one hateful to God, how could Noah be saved?" So these wretches cite the woman overtaken in sin, the adultery of David and Peter's denial. They study the vices of the saints so that they may imitate them, but they horribly neglect their faith, piety and zeal for righteousness. Noah, having been drunk once, is hailed as the patron of these drunkards who constantly glut themselves with wine. . . . A third kind are those who

---

[11]*Opera* 1:114-15, citing Is 5:11. †The misdeeds of Old Testament saints were of perennial interest in the history of exegesis; see "Patriarchs Behaving Badly" in John L. Thompson, *Reading the Bible with the Dead* (Grand Rapids: Eerdmans, 2007), 71-92, and literature cited there.

bitterly harp upon the misdeeds of the righteous. On account of the stain of a single defect, they not only negate all of their previous piety and righteous deeds but they airily dismiss everything subsequent, too. Such people are for the most part extremely meddlesome snoops into the lives of others who act as judge and jury. For them, Noah was nothing but a drunk after he let himself become inebriated; David was nothing but an adulterer. In the eyes of these people, the saints' vices that are forgiven and cleansed by God's grace cling to them forever, and no penance, however serious and unremitting, can possibly expunge them. COMMENTARY ON GENESIS 9:21.[12]

Two Kinds of Nakedness. ANDREW WILLET: Adam and Eve were naked and uncovered in paradise yet were not ashamed, because as yet they did not feel the rebellion of their members—a just recompense of their rebellion and disobedience to their Creator. But now we are ashamed of those parts more than any other, because while other parts are not moved without the will even in the heat of our affections, "lust has subdued those members to itself," as Augustine says, "and removed them from the will's power." This is why even the barbarous nations, which have only nature to guide them, nonetheless cover and hide their secret parts. It was therefore so much the greater shame for Noah, so revered a patriarch, to lie uncovered so indecently. COMMENTARY ON GENESIS 9:21.[13]

Noah Signifies the Slandered Minister. DAVID CHYTRAEUS: Noah signifies all the godly and especially ministers of the gospel, who, even if they ought to be beyond reproach and free of offenses, nonetheless have certain infirmities, just like everyone else. But ungodly listeners and hypocrites spitefully amplify and exaggerate these infirmities, when they ought to be more inclined to rather cover

them with their own sense of fairness and correct them with virtue. COMMENTARY ON GENESIS 9:23.[14]

Should the Sins of the Clergy Be Covered Up? KONRAD PELLIKAN: A parallel case is raised of whether the sins of prelates ought to be hidden and exposed as little as possible. With brethren, the law of charity is also to be observed; indeed, for hidden sins, they are to be warned in secret. But public sins are scandalous to subordinates, contrary to sound doctrine and destructive of faith and morals. If they are persistently committed and defended for the sake of authority, it makes them appear lawful. Such [sins]—concerning which the multitude of believers cannot judge well, nor should they—certainly should be made public, censured, condemned, and in every way corrected by an ecclesiastical inquiry (if the higher authorities ignore those concerned), lest one ordained as a pastor be perceived as a destroyer. COMMENTARY ON GENESIS 9:23.[15]

Christ and the Drunkenness of Noah. PETER MARTYR VERMIGLI: Because we have alleged more than once that Noah bears an image or type of Christ, let us now see how it can be illustrated from his drunkenness. An inebriated Noah fell asleep, and Christ died, just as death is so often called "sleep" in the sacred writings that there is no need to show many examples. Moreover, it is easy to understand by what potion Christ would have been inebriated, for it was undoubtedly of that cup that he spoke in the very moment of his passion: "Let this cup pass from me." He also spoke of it to the two apostles who were asking for favor in the kingdom: "Can you drink the cup that I am going to drink?" Noah pros-

---

[12]*In Mosis Genesim* (1554), 251. [13]*Hexapla* (1608), 105, loosely quoting Augustine, *City of God* 14.19 (PL 41:427). [14]*In Genesin* (1576), 250. [15]*Commentaria Bibliorum* (1532) 1:13v.

trated himself naked, Christ too was nailed naked to the cross, and soldiers seized and divided his clothes among themselves by lot. But what seems more amazing, his human nature was visible, stripped of the protection of his divinity, for in his death no help was brought to him from that source. On the contrary, he cried out in the words of David, "My God, my God, why have you forsaken me?" Furthermore, in nothing was Christ foreshadowed by Noah more than in bearing derision. What kind of person, I ask you, did *not* mock the dying Christ? Commentary on Genesis 9:27.[16]

9:22 Ham Saw His Father's Nakedness

Ham's Many Sins. Andrew Willet: These were the degrees of Ham's sin: that he acted not ignorantly or by chance, but knowingly gazed upon his father's secrets; that he did it to his father, by whom he was not only begotten but for whose sake he was preserved in the ark (and being the youngest son and so much the more beloved of his father, his disobedience was that much greater, as was Absalom's rebellion against David); nor was he a child, but now more than a hundred years old; neither was he content with his own behavior but he tells his brothers, thinking to corrupt them also into deriding their father; and he rejoices in his father's fall . . . as the ungodly rejoice at the fall of the godly. Commentary on Genesis 9:22.[17]

Ham's Deed Was Worse Than It Seems. Wolfgang Musculus: Moses explains Ham's external act in a few words: first, he saw his father's private parts; second, he didn't cover them; third, he told his brothers who were outside the tent. These actions seem to have nothing criminal about them, so it's amazing that on their account a curse was inflicted on Canaan, Ham's son. Indeed, how can it be a crime to stumble across a naked

drunk and unexpectedly see his private parts? And then, having left him there, to go out and tell what was seen to others—not to strangers, but one's brothers, by whose efforts the naked and prostrate man would be covered? However, the seriousness of the curse leads us to suppose that Ham's deed was not only culpable but something that expressed also his son's character. First, having seen his father's nakedness from any distance, he should not have allowed his eyes to shift so easily from his father's face to his private parts. Given that the minds of those who are modest are naturally inclined to resist looking at anyone's private parts (much less their parents') unless forced to do so, it argues in favor of his vanity and shamelessness that when his father was drunk and naked, he looked not at the disgraced and downcast face but at the private parts, from which the most deeply hidden instinct of nature was accustomed to shrink. Then, when he saw his father's nudity, he ought to have covered it, lest it be exposed to the eyes of anyone else later on. But he despised and neglected this duty that he owed to his father's honor. Finally, having left his father naked, just as he was, he went out and told of his nudity to his two brothers, thereby revealing his father's disgrace when it should have been concealed with silence. Ham thus did what he should not have done, and what he should have done he did not do. Commentary on Genesis 9:22.[18]

Ham's Hypocrisy Toward His Father. Martin Luther: Ham did not laugh at his father because of some childish thoughtlessness, as children do when they stand around a drunken peasant in the street and make sport of him. He was actually offended by his

---

[16]*In Primum Librum Mosis* (1569), 43r, citing Mt 26:39; 20:22; 27:46 (Ps 22:1). Noah's prefiguration of Christ is a traditional patristic allegory. [17]*Hexapla* (1608), 106, crediting Musculus, Calvin and Ambrose. [18]*In Mosis Genesim* (1554), 252.

father's fall, because he regarded himself as more righteous, holier, and more pious than his father. We have here more than a mere appearance of offense; the very situation is an offense, because son Ham is so offended by his father's drunkenness that he passes judgment on his father and takes delight in his sin. If we want to discuss Ham's sin correctly, we must take original sin into consideration, that is, we must keep in mind the depravity of the heart. The son would never have laughed at his father, who was overcome by wine, if he had not first put out of his heart that reverence and esteem which, by God's command, children should have for their parents. Therefore just as the majority of the world regarded Noah as a fool before the Flood, condemned him as a heretic, and looked down upon him as a madman, so his son here laughs at him as a fool and condemns him as a sinner. LECTURES ON GENESIS 9:20-22.[19]

NOAH DID NOT ACT AGAINST HAM IN HASTE. JOHN CALVIN: However much Noah had just cause for lashing out in anger, it still might look as if he acts harshly here and with too little self-control. At the very least, he should have silently bewailed his sin before God, even as he should have demonstrated his shame and repentance to others; yet he now fulminates against his son with excessive severity, as if he himself had done nothing wrong. Here, however, Moses is not recording reproaches that Noah was propelled by wrath and bile to vomit forth! Rather, he introduces Noah as speaking by the spirit of prophecy. Hence, we should not doubt that the holy man had truly been humbled (as was appropriate) by his own feelings of guilt and that he had properly reflected on what he deserved. But now, having been granted pardon and with his condemnation rescinded, he appears as a herald of divine judgment. COMMENTARY ON GENESIS 9:24.[20]

9:24-25 "Cursed Be Canaan . . ."

HAM WAS CURSED IN THE PERSON OF CANAAN. KONRAD PELLIKAN: Noah did not curse his son Ham, but Canaan, who was himself the fourth son of Ham. From an impious father he made ill progress and degenerated into many criminals, on account of which they were destroyed and subjugated by the Israelites, the sons of Shem. And so the father is cursed in his impious sons; that is, he is burdened with a servile character and condition. COMMENTARY ON GENESIS 9:25.[21]

CANAAN'S SERVITUDE PUNISHES HAM'S INSUBORDINATION. PETER MARTYR VERMIGLI: The punishment by which the ungodly son was repaid fit his sin exquisitely. Because he would not submit himself to his father with the reverence and honor that befits a son, his own son was justly oppressed by wretched servitude. This is the law of equitable retaliation, concerning which no one can rightly complain. If in this case the father did not have a son like he wanted and would have deemed proper, but rather suffered indignity from him, then it was fair for Ham himself to be afflicted in *his* son, Canaan. Indeed, even as parents are adorned with honor and dignity by their children, they are also gladdened in a certain way by their happiness. Thus they are not only afflicted by their children's servitude and misery, they virtually become wretches. COMMENTARY ON GENESIS 9:27.[22]

CANAAN WAS NOT INNOCENT. JOHN CALVIN: Why does Noah, instead of pronouncing the curse upon his son, inflict the severity of the punishment that his son deserved upon his innocent grandson? And surely it is not consistent with divine justice to visit the

---

[19]LW 2:167 (WA 42:379). [20]CTS 1:304* (CO 23:152). [21]*Commentaria Bibliorum* (1532) 1:13v. [22]*In Primum Librum Mosis* (1569), 42v, alluding to the *lex talionis* or "an eye for an eye."

crimes of parents upon their children. But the answer is obvious enough, that even if God does prosecute his judgments against the children and grandchildren of the ungodly, his anger is at no time directed against the guiltless—because they too are found to be at fault. So there is nothing absurd if he avenges the evil deeds of the fathers upon their reprobate children, since all those whom God has deprived of his Spirit are of necessity subject to his wrath. COMMENTARY ON GENESIS 9:25.[23]

NOAH'S CURSE APPLIES ALL THE MORE TO HAM BECAUSE HE IS NOT NAMED. MARTIN LUTHER: The assurance with which Noah makes his pronouncement here is proof that it is full of the Holy Spirit, even though his son derided and despised him as though he had been altogether forsaken by the Holy Spirit. . . . The Holy Spirit is moved to such great wrath against the disobedient and contemptuous son that he even refuses to call him by his own name but designates him as Canaan, after his son. Some maintain that because God was willing to save Ham in the ark with the others as though he were one who was blessed, Noah wanted to curse his son Canaan, not him. Nevertheless, the curse upon the son recoils upon the father, who deserved it. Hence the name Ham disappears at this point because the Holy Spirit hates it, and this is indeed an ominous hatred. LECTURES ON GENESIS 9:23-25.[24]

ALL OF NOAH'S WORDS COME TRUE ONLY WHEN THE GOSPEL REACHES THE GENTILES. JOHANNES BRENZ: Even if some propose other reasons for why Noah would curse his grandson Canaan more than his son Ham, I think this curse was exceptional, because it didn't fall on all the descendants of Ham, but only on those who descended from Ham through his son Canaan, and who also dwelt in the land of Canaan and were de-

stroyed by the Israelites—which is also when this curse was fulfilled. You see, therefore, that God is strict and bides his time against unrepentant sinners. But the other two brothers, Shem and Japheth, are blessed. The blessing on Shem himself, however, mainly pertains to the genealogy of Christ, that Christ would come from his tribe and offspring. That is why he says, "Blessed be the Lord, the God of Shem," that is, God will send his blessed Seed from Shem's posterity. Likewise, the blessing on Japheth mainly pertains to the fact that his descendants would be called by the gospel to a knowledge of Christ. . . . This was fulfilled when the gospel of Christ was proclaimed among the Gentiles who descended from Japheth. Here you have the efficacy of the curse and blessing of a drunken and delirious old man, as Ham would have thought! So, fearing God, let us rise up in the presence of a gray head, and may we never put the vices of our elders on display out of spite. COMMENTARY ON GENESIS 9:24-27.[25]

MOSES RECOUNTS THE CURSE ON CANAAN TO AID THE CONQUEST. WOLFGANG MUSCULUS: They ask here why Noah did not curse his son Ham more than Canaan, Ham's son, given that the sin is attributed not to Canaan but to Ham. . . . Why is the curse imposed on the one who did not sin rather than on the one who deserved the curse on account of his sin? Answers here vary. Some say that this was done by the Holy Spirit, who so detested Ham's disobedience and contemptuousness that he did not wish even to mention him by name but referred to him by his son's name, calling him Canaan. According to their view, it was not Canaan but his father, Ham, who was cursed under the name of his own son— an interpretation that I cannot approve. Lyra

[23]CTS 1:305* (CO 23:153). [24]LW 2:174 (WA 42:384). [25]Opera 1:116.

says that that the father was cursed in the son to show that he was not cursed only in his own person but that the curse would extend also to his descendants. Chrysostom offers this explanation for why Ham himself was not cursed by Noah: he wished to rebuke his son for the sin and disgrace he had committed, but at the same time he did not want to undermine the blessing he had previously given. Indeed, God blessed Noah when he exited the ark, as well as his sons. Therefore lest he seem to speak ill of one whom God had once blessed, he passed over the one who committed that disgrace and levied the curse on his son. Thus, Lyra thinks both the father and the son were cursed, while for Chrysostom not the father but only the son was cursed, though he would also say the father was rebuked for having allowed the sin. There is no question about the father if we agree with Lyra and others as well that he too was stricken by this curse; but a question does remain as to why the curse was applied to the son. . . . Lyra's argument is unsatisfying because it is more general than befits this question. . . . For Canaan was not the only member of Ham's offspring, nor was he the firstborn (if we follow here the order in which Ham's sons are listed), but the last. But if Noah did this to indicate that this curse was going to spread also to Ham's offspring, there were offspring of Ham who descended not only from Canaan but also from Cush, Mizraim and Put. So there are grounds for asking why he did not say, "Cursed be Cush!" or "Cursed be Mizraim!" or "Cursed be Put!" . . . Others say that Canaan was the first to see his grandfather Noah naked and he then told his father Ham. . . . But Augustine is closer to the target, . . . that "it is a prophecy that the sons of Israel, who came from the seed of Shem, were going to possess the land of Canaan after the Canaanites had been vanquished and evicted." Therefore one should say here that Noah did not act in a spirit of vengeance or imprecation but spoke prophetically of God's coming judgment, which had been deferred to the time of Canaan's offspring. Ham is not cursed in his own person, lest this curse seem intended for all of his offspring. Canaan, however, is expressly disparaged on account of the judgment of God that would fall upon his offspring long afterwards. And Moses wanted to commemorate this present narrative for this reason, to rouse the Israelites to hope that the effects of this curse were already about to happen, so that they would occupy the land of Canaan by conquering its people. COMMENTARY ON GENESIS 9:25-27.[26]

SLAVERY IS EVIL, BUT GOD MAY YET USE IT. PETER MARTYR VERMIGLI: Truly, to be a slave is a punishment, because it is opposed to the nature and position of human beings. God established humans not to be slaves but to rule. Hence, the good fathers in ancient times did not control people by force. They were shepherds of flocks, but they governed people only by love and advice. Since humans were created in God's image, and since it belongs to God to give orders and not to follow them, it is clearly proved that it also does not belong to human nature to be a slave. Nonetheless, slavery is not to be rejected by this argument, for it may have been contrived as a bridle for iniquity and a medicine against human malice. Indeed, you may discover many things that took their beginnings from evil causes, yet they should still be retained, not utterly spurned. Hence, the apostles Peter and Paul frequently taught in their epistles that subjects and slaves were to be dutiful toward their masters and not dare to shake off the yoke of slavery. COMMENTARY ON GENESIS 9:25-27.[27]

---

[26]*In Mosis Genesim* (1554), 249; quoting Augustine, *Questions on the Heptateuch* 1.17.   [27]*In Primum Librum Mosis* (1569), 43v.

The ninth chapter has four topics especially to be observed, namely, these:

I. The blessing of Noah and his sons, which things are comprehended in these words of God:

[I.] "Increase, multiply, fill the earth."

God renews the blessing on marriage and the power for obtaining offspring. And, not long afterwards, Noah certainly had need for this sermon to be repeated, so that thereby

he might understand that God is no longer angry with the human race but rather favors it, having put aside all his anger. This consolation was quite necessary after the whole human race had perished in the flood, with only eight souls saved.

he might be rendered more certain about the multiplication of the human race, lest [he think] something could happen contrary to God's will.

II. "The fear of you and trepidation will be upon

animals, birds, reptiles, fish."

Here, all things are subordinated to human beings and authority over creatures is restored to them, so that they might be used not only for their labors and sacrifices but also for their food and nourishment. And we today could not be nourished by the earth's produce alone, had he not added this immense benefit so that it is lawful to eat the flesh of beasts, fish, etc.

III. "Every animal that moves and lives will be food for you," like living vegetables delivered over to you as food. But he adds two warnings,

"The flesh with its lifeblood you may not eat." Cruelty in the eating of an animal is prohibited,

lest a beast suffocated in its own blood be devoured.

[lest] animals be gobbled down raw, while still breathing.

This proves in two ways the abuse

of those who, when food has been granted by God for sustaining the body, use it for gluttony, luxury, and gormandizing.

lest they should suppose that because humans had been granted the right of life and death over beasts, they were also going to have that right over people.

of the papists, who nefariously teach the church that eating meat is a sin.

II. The institution of political power: by permitting punishments and the consumption of animals, God truly wished to take care lest human beings mutually kill and devour one another. For this reason

he first declares that homicide is displeasing to him, even if committed by beasts devoid of reason. Wherefore he says, "I will require

[a reckoning for] your lifeblood at the hand of every beast."

also at the hand of every human being [a reckoning for] human life."

He forbids

gratuitous, unholy, and rash killing or slaughter.

lest in the end anyone whatsoever should slay another person at will.

he lays down, secondly, the general injunction, "Whosoever shall shed human blood, by a human shall his blood be shed."

he adds, thirdly, the reasons for these sayings and counsels,

that God made human beings in God's image.

from human preeminence. "Be fruitful and multiply, bring forth offspring, etc." He wishes a great multitude of people to arise.

From this text flows forth the Law of Nations, and from it as well all the penalties with which crimes are punished. Indeed, if a magistrate holds the right of life and death over another human being, he will also have that right over all other matters — over wealth, property, etc. But the dignity of the civil magistrate is reckoned from a twofold cause:

the efficient cause is God, by whom it is instituted.

the final cause is that [the magistrate] ought to protect human beings as fashioned in God's image.

Look for the rest in the facing Table. ✳

The Restitution of Dominion over Creatures ◆ The Magistrate and the Civil Sword.
Cyriacus Spangenberg, Table 12a on Genesis 9 (*In Pentateuchum*, sig. B3ᵛ).

III. God's covenant and pact with

- Noah.
- all Noah's descendants
- every living creature

that never again would there be a flood by which he would destroy

- living things.
- the earth.

He gave them a sign of this covenant—his bow in the clouds. Indeed, God is accustomed to add external signs to his word. So whenever we see a rainbow in the clouds, we ought to be mindful of

- God's entirely just anger against sins, which he showed in the flood; and, having been warned, we should learn to fear God.
- the divine mercy toward human beings, which he exhibited in this sign of the covenant; and we ought to place our trust in him.

And here, notice that

- Scripture speaks in human fashion of God seeing and remembering, for our consolation.
- repetitions of the same thing in God's speech are a sign of his extraordinary affection for humans.
- the rainbow allegorically signifies Christ, who appears to us in the clouds of tribulations. Lest we despair of the divine goodness, he consoles us as we behold him by faith.

*

IIII. Ham's sin and curse. Indeed, Noah

- was a farmer.
- planted a vineyard.
- drank wine.
- became drunk.
- lay uncovered in his tent.

With respect to which,

- Ham, seeing this, told his two brothers, who were outside.
- Ham signifies those who even without sufficient cause expose the failings of their parents or magistrates and who take offense at the nakedness of the saints that is seen in their affliction.
- when Shem and Japheth heard, they entered with faces averted and covered their father's private parts. They signify those who respectfully shield the nakedness of the saints that appears in their afflictions.

when he awoke from the wine [and]

But Noah,

said to

found out what his younger son Ham had done to him,

Ham

- "Cursed be Canaan." You see that the wicked are cursed in their offspring in Exodus 20.
- "A servant of servants shall he be to his brothers." It is not nature, therefore, but sin that imposes servitude.

Shem

- "Blessed be the Lord God of Shem."
- "Let Canaan be his servant." Notice, however, that divine law works to give possession of the kingdom to the godly, but in faith.

Japheth

- "May God enlarge Japheth," or "God will speak gently with Japheth."
- "And he will dwell in the tents of Shem," [meaning that] the church will be gathered from the nations.
- "Canaan will be their servant" — a blessing that is to be understood spiritually.

We learn

- not to despair of God's grace on account of unforeseen lapses. This consolation is needed by the godly in their own infirmities, since they see that even the holiest people have sometimes fallen into disgrace from a similar infirmity.
- not to expose the lapses of others, but more to give them the benefit of the doubt, yet without thereby approving their open misdeeds.

God's Covenant with All Flesh • The Saints' Lapses • Ham's Sin and Curse.
Cyriacus Spangenberg, Table 12b on Genesis 9 (*In Pentateuchum*, sig. B4ʳ).

**HAM FOUND WORLDLY SUCCESS IN BABY-
LON.** MARTIN LUTHER: If Ham had considered true what he heard from his father, he
would have sought refuge in mercy and would
have begged for forgiveness of the crime of
which he was guilty. But he does neither. He
leaves his father haughtily and goes to Babylon; there, together with his descendants, he
engages in building a city and a tower, and
establishes himself as lord of all Asia. What is
the reason for this smugness? This no doubt,
that divine prophecies are trustworthy only to
faith; they are not perceptible to the senses or
subject to tests, regardless of whether they are
promises or threats. Therefore to the flesh the
opposite always appears to be true. Ham is
cursed by his father, but he takes possession of
the largest part of the world and establishes
extensive kingdoms. On the other hand, Shem
and Japheth are blessed; but if you compare
them with Ham, they and their descendants
are actually beggars. How, then, can this
prophecy be true? My answer is: this prophecy
and all others, whether they are promises or
threats, are beyond the grasp of reason and
understandable solely by faith. . . . Hence
because God delays with His promises as well
as with His threats, one must wait in faith.
LECTURES ON GENESIS 9:26.[28]

9:26-27 "Blessed Be the God of Shem, and May God Enlarge Japheth"

NOAH SAW GOD'S HAND IN SHEM'S LIFE.
WOLFGANG MUSCULUS: Noah's pious feelings
here are joined with a spirit of prophecy. First
of all he offers heartfelt praise to the Lord on
account of his son Shem. His son's probity
pleases him, but such thoughts carry him away
with praise not for his son, but for God.
Indeed, he doesn't say, "Blessed be Shem," but
"Blessed be the Lord God of Shem." He
recognized the work of God's grace in his son
as the source of all probity, and by naming
God this way he offers praises neither to

himself nor his son but to God. Much as he
was distressed by the malice of his youngest
son, he was equally revived by the probity of
the other two, so that he broke into heartfelt
praise of God for them. COMMENTARY ON
GENESIS 9:26.[29]

THE POTENT BLESSING ON SHEM. ANDREW
WILLET: Inasmuch as Shem received the chief
blessing, it would appear that he was the actor
and persuader of that reverent and dutiful
behavior toward their father. In turning
himself to God, Noah shows the excellency of
grace with which Shem was endued (which
also is implied in his name, which signifies
someone famous or of renown). Noah prophesies that the true religion and church would
remain among Shem's posterity and that he
alone would worship the true God, who is to
be blessed forever. Here too is included a
prophecy that from Shem would come Christ,
in whom all the nations of the world would be
blessed. COMMENTARY ON GENESIS 9:26.[30]

**JAPHETH'S SONS BECAME FOLLOWERS OF
GOD.** KONRAD PELLIKAN: Japheth is said to
dwell in the tents of Shem because the greatest
part of his sons, that is, the Gentiles, were
converted to faith in the one, true and only
God of heaven: whose priest, it is written, was
Shem—also known as Melchizedek. The land
and cities of the Canaanites perpetually served
and have been subjected to either the sons of
Shem, the Jews, or to those converted to the
Lord from among the Gentiles, to this present
day. COMMENTARY ON GENESIS 9:27.[31]

**JAPHETH AND SHEM ANTICIPATE THE
UNION OF CHURCH AND SYNAGOGUE.**
WOLFGANG MUSCULUS: These words, "He
will dwell in the tents of Shem," should be

---

[28]LW 2:175-76 (WA 42:385-86). [29]*In Mosis Genesim* (1554),
255. [30]*Hexapla* (1608), 108, crediting Tremellius, Pererius and
Oecolampadius. [31]*Commentaria Bibliorum* (1532) 1:13v.

considered also in another sense, in which they refer not to Japheth but to God. If someone were to conclude that the phrase refers to the descendants of Japheth—namely, the Gentiles, who embraced the religion of Christ—he will have in mind what we consider to be true of our churches. Specifically, churches are *tents*, shelters for sojourners, not enduring homes for natives. We are Japheth's offspring. We draw near to the descendants of Shem and with them we share the stage, the tents, so to speak, in Christ the son of Shem, whose kingdom is not of this world. COMMENTARY ON GENESIS 9:27.[32]

NOAH FORETOLD THE UNION OF JEW AND GENTILE IN THE CHURCH. JOHN CALVIN:

Here, a prophecy is presented about things unknown to human minds but of which the author was none other than God, as the outcome eventually shows. Two thousand years and a number of centuries elapsed before the Gentiles and the Jews would be gathered together in one faith. Then the sons of Shem, of whom the greater part had dispersed and cut themselves off from the holy family of God, were gathered together so as to dwell under one tabernacle. Likewise Japheth's progeny, the Gentiles, who had long been wanderers and fugitives, were received into the same tabernacle. For by a new adoption, God has formed a single people from those who were divided and enacted a brotherly union between those who were estranged. This was done by God's sweet and gentle voice, which he has uttered in the gospel; and every day right up until now, this prophecy is fulfilled when God invites scattered sheep to join his flock and gathers from every side those who will sit at table with Abraham, Isaac and Jacob in the kingdom of heaven. Truly, it is no ordinary support for our faith that the calling of the Gentiles is not only decreed in the eternal counsel of God but is openly attested also by the mouth of the patriarch—lest we think it a

sudden or chance occurrence that the inheritance of eternal life was offered to all in common. Moreover, the expression, "Japheth shall dwell in the tabernacles of Shem," commends to us the mutual fellowship that ought to exist and be cherished among the faithful. COMMENTARY ON GENESIS 9:27.[33]

THE GERMAN REFORMATION FULFILLS NOAH'S PROPHECY. MARTIN LUTHER: The

fact that by the mercy of God the Word of the Gospel has begun to shine for Germany is due to this prophecy about Japheth, and so what Noah foretold at that time is being fulfilled today. Even though we are not of the seed of Abraham, we nevertheless live in the tents of Shem, and we have the benefits of the fulfilled promises concerning Christ. LECTURES ON GENESIS 9:27.[34]

9:28-29 All Noah's Days Were 950 Years

WHY GOD WANTED NOAH TO LIVE SO LONG. WOLFGANG MUSCULUS: The fact that

the patriarchs lived such very long lives in the first world is not to be attributed to the efficacy of the air or the newly-formed earth by which people were then sustained, but to the singular decree of God. Otherwise, Noah would by no means have prolonged his life here so long after the flood, when everything was much more frail than before. Truly, the Lord wanted the later world at its very outset to be instructed in faith, knowledge and reverence for God's name through this patriarch and his offspring. Noah had heard about the beginnings of the first world from his father, who had learned these things from Adam himself. Afterwards, he saw and experienced the malice of the human race, received God's oracles about the coming flood, was tossed about but

---

[32]*In Mosis Genesim* (1554), 256.   [33]CTS 1:309-10* (CO 23:155).
[34]LW 2:186 (WA 42:393).

protected in the ark, witnessed the destruction of all flesh, and received the assurance of the divine will that he would not send another flood. As a faithful and qualified witness, he was able to teach his descendants about these and other things like them that contribute to a zeal for godliness. That is why the Lord appointed and arranged his lifespan, so that he might endure alive to the tenth generation of his offspring. Indeed, given that he lived 950 years, it is clear that he was alive for Abraham's fifty-eighth year. But I would think that Abraham was raised in that place where Noah himself, along with his son Shem and the rest of that chain of grandchildren and offspring that descended from Shem, lived until death. Indeed, we read that the earth was divided by Noah's sons, so that they were scattered apart from one another over the face of the whole earth; but it is believable that the seed of Noah did not remain separated but gathered to live together with his beloved son Shem on account of [Noah's] singular piety and grace, and thus, as the patriarch and bishop of the holy household from which Christ would be born, he remained among all of his descendants, teaching and instructing them all with his authority. So I would say that God wanted Noah to be like Janus,[†] facing in two directions, someone who would witness and comprehend both the old age and end of the first world as well as the beginnings and youth of the later world. This matter was so important in the eyes of God, that the course of true piety among the generations of the elect would be guided through both worlds, from Adam to Abraham, by the labors of Noah. COMMENTARY ON GENESIS 9:28-29.[35]

NOAH WAS A MARTYR'S MARTYR.[†] JOHANNES BRENZ: Noah lived six hundred years before the flood. What miseries did he not see there? During the flood, he remained in the ark for more than a year and there endured the terrors of death almost every single day. After the flood, he found some enjoyment, to be sure, in that he saw his descendants multiply and this world preserved. But at the same time he endured to the utmost many things almost more serious than death. He saw the curse that would fall on the whole family of his grandson Canaan. He saw impiety and idolatry among his offspring not only increase, but even grow openly strong and overwhelming. He saw, or at least heard about, his descendants' impious attempt to build a tower in Babylon and the confusion of tongues. He saw the Chaldaeans worship fire in the place of God. In brief, he saw his offspring stained by every kind of impiety, with almost none of them retaining the true religion of the virgin's son. What troubles could have befallen him after these? Would he not more gladly have endured death than to see such abominations among his descendants, who dismissed him as nothing but a drunk and a foolish old man? Noah's longevity thus made him a martyr among martyrs! That God should have preserved him in so many dangers, and especially through the flood, seems more a calamity than a blessing, yet surely these deliverances are immense blessings from God. COMMENTARY ON GENESIS 9:28-29.[36]

NOAH'S LATER DEEDS. ANDREW WILLET: Noah lived 350 years after the flood and died but two years before Abraham was born. . . . Although the Scriptures make no mention of the rest of Noah's acts, no doubt he was occupied in doing good and in planting religion. Berosus[†] writes that he taught the Armenians the skill of husbandry and planting of vines; that he divided the year into twelve

---

[35]*In Mosis Genesim* (1554), 257. [†]The comparison of Noah to Janus could have been found in pseudo-Berosus (n. 37, below), but Musculus does not seem to have used that recent forgery. However, he may have known of published woodcuts depicting Noah as Janus; see Whitford, *Curse of Ham*, 52-54, 62-68. [36]*Opera* 1:116-17; [†]the title of this excerpt appears as a marginal note in Brenz on p. 117.

months; instructed them in the true service of God; and from there went to Italy, where he likewise taught theology and human arts; and that he was honored by them as a god under the name of Sol and Coelus; and that there he died. This record of Noah's acts contains nothing of any improbability (except that so godly a patriarch as Noah would never allow himself to be honored as a god), so there is no necessity to receive or believe it, given that it is not expressed in Scripture. . . . But while it pleased some of the Fathers to turn this story of Noah's drunkenness to an allegory—comparing the Jews to the true vine that Noah planted; Christ to Noah, who was cast into the sleep of death by his own people; and the Jews deriding Christ's infirmities and sufferings upon the cross to Ham, scorning his father's nakedness—I regard it as unsafe to go wading without a bottom, and therefore I omit these allegorical applications as human fancies and so leave them aside. COMMENTARY ON GENESIS 9:28.[37]

---

[37]*Hexapla* (1608), 109. †This reference is to *pseudo*-Berosus, that is, to Annius of Viterbo's *Auctores vetustissimi, vel Opera diversorum auctorum de antiquitatibus loquentium* (Rome, 1498), a fabrication purporting to represent the ancient historian Berosus. The pernicious influence of pseudo-Berosus on the exegesis of this passage is carefully detailed in chapter 3 of Whitford, *Curse of Ham.*

10:1-32 THE DESCENDANTS OF NOAH'S THREE SONS

[1]*These are the generations of the sons of Noah, Shem, Ham, and Japheth. Sons were born to them after the flood.* [2]*The sons of Japheth: Gomer, Magog, Madai, Javan, Tubal, Meshech, and Tiras.* [3]*The sons of Gomer: Ashkenaz, Riphath, and Togarmah.* [4]*The sons of Javan: Elishah, Tarshish, Kittim, and Dodanim.* [5]*From these the coastland peoples spread in their lands, each with his own language, by their clans, in their nations.* [6]*The sons of Ham: Cush, Egypt, Put, and Canaan.* [7]*The sons of Cush: Seba, Havilah, Sabtah, Raamah, and Sabteca. The sons of Raamah: Sheba and Dedan.* [8]*Cush fathered Nimrod; he was the first on earth to be a mighty man.[a]* [9]*He was a mighty hunter before the LORD. Therefore it is said, "Like Nimrod a mighty hunter before the LORD."* [10]*The beginning of his kingdom was Babel, Erech, Accad, and Calneh, in the land of Shinar.* [11]*From that land he went into Assyria and built Nineveh, Rehoboth-Ir, Calah, and* [12]*Resen between Nineveh and Calah; that is the great city.* [13]*Egypt fathered Ludim, Anamim, Lehabim, Naphtuhim,* [14]*Pathrusim, Casluhim (from whom[b] the Philistines came), and Caphtorim.* [15]*Canaan fathered Sidon his firstborn and Heth,* [16]*and the Jebusites, the Amorites, the Girgashites,* [17]*the Hivites, the Arkites, the Sinites,* [18]*the Arvadites, the Zemarites, and the Hamathites. Afterward the clans of the Canaanites dispersed.* [19]*And the territory of*

the Canaanites extended from Sidon in the direction of Gerar as far as Gaza, and in the direction of Sodom, Gomorrah, Admah, and Zeboiim, as far as Lasha. ²⁰These are the sons of Ham, by their clans, their languages, their lands, and their nations.

²¹To Shem also, the father of all the children of Eber, the elder brother of Japheth, children were born. ²²The sons of Shem: Elam, Asshur, Arpachshad, Lud, and Aram. ²³The sons of Aram: Uz, Hul, Gether, and Mash. ²⁴Arpachshad fathered Shelah; and Shelah fathered Eber. ²⁵To Eber were born two sons: the name of the one was Peleg,ᵇ for in his days the earth was divided, and his brother's name was Joktan. ²⁶Joktan fathered Almodad, Sheleph, Hazarmaveth, Jerah, ²⁷Hadoram, Uzal, Diklah, ²⁸Obal, Abimael, Sheba, ²⁹Ophir, Havilah, and Jobab; all these were the sons of Joktan. ³⁰The territory in which they lived extended from Mesha in the direction of Sephar to the hill country of the east. ³¹These are the sons of Shem, by their clans, their languages, their lands, and their nations.

³²These are the clans of the sons of Noah, according to their genealogies, in their nations, and from these the nations spread abroad on the earth after the flood.

a Or *he began to be a mighty man on the earth*   **b** Or *from where*   **c** Peleg means *division*

OVERVIEW: Genesis 10 could almost be described as the endnotes for Genesis 9, insofar as it is wholly devoted to an inventory of the descendants of Noah's three sons and their respective geographic holdings. Like their predecessors, Reformation commentators tried to find something to say about what Luther bluntly described as a chapter seemingly filled with "dead words" by focusing on two main topics.

First, they continued to extol the general utility of genealogies for the faith and understanding of later generations. Second, they scoured these lists of names for any hint of a connection with later biblical events or characters. In this chapter, those connections terminate in a general way on Ham and his cursed son Canaan, who receive more of the rebukes that we have already heard; and on Japheth, who was seen as the patriarch from whom the Gentiles mainly descended.

But the chapter's most interesting character was, by overwhelming consensus, Nimrod: grandson of Ham and the first "mighty man." Nimrod drew special attention not least because he is the only figure in the chapter to be furnished with *any* biographical details, but

even more because he is credited as the founder of Babel. By implication, then, Nimrod was likely the mastermind behind the tower of Babel and ruler of the city of Babylon where it was situated—even though his name does not appear in the narrative about Babel at the beginning of the following chapter.

10:1 *The Generations of the Sons of Noah*

THE UTILITY OF GENEALOGIES. ANDREW WILLET: The reasons for mentioning these generations may be these: First, to show the effect of the blessing that the Lord gave to Noah and his sons, to multiply and increase. Second, to demonstrate God's judgment on the posterity of Ham and his blessing upon Shem, according to Noah's prophecy. Third, to acquaint the Israelites with the nations of the Gentiles, from whom they were to expect their inheritance. Fourth, to open a way to the understanding of Scripture, wherein the names of these nations often occur. COMMENTARY ON GENESIS 10:1.[1]

---

[1]*Hexapla* (1608), 113.

"Useless Names" May Contain Weighty Doctrine.

DAVID CHYTRAEUS: Though the genealogy of the sons of Noah that is recited in this tenth chapter seems to contain a useless multitude of names, it actually contains weighty doctrine and is for many reasons necessary for the church. First, so that the church might know through which men and by whose testimonies the heavenly teaching has been extended to us from the beginning of the human race. Second, the origins of nations and of the earth's regions are described in this chapter, along with the first lines of descent and the distribution of people groups. Not only do those with good hearts find these things extremely delightful to know, but they are also useful and necessary in order to locate all the narratives. Third, this description of the origin and growth of the nations is clear evidence that this unique teaching is the oldest of all those contained in the writings of Moses and the prophets and therefore is also most genuine. Truly, whatever is first is correct, but whatever is later is corrupt. Fourth, this passage also sheds light on the prophets, who are accustomed to record and distinguish the nations by the names of their lineage or their first parents, as Moses and the prophets everywhere call Egypt the land of *Mizraim*, they call Syria *Aram*, Greece is *Javan*, etc. Fifth, the etymologies of particular family names also shed some light on sacred and profane histories. But the sixth and primary utility is that the chapter makes Christ's genealogy known to the entire church. Indeed, God wanted the fathers to know from what lineage and family Christ would be born and among which people he ought to be expected—to teach, to perform miracles, to suffer and to be resurrected. For these reasons, the text of this tenth chapter deserves to be loved and extolled. COMMENTARY ON GENESIS 10:1.[2]

Noah's Provisions for Settling the World.

MARTIN LUTHER: Moses records particularly that the languages and families of these men were dispersed to definite places, and he indicates that in this manner empires were established. This was done no doubt by their own father Noah, who ordered one to sail to Asia, another to Greece, and still another to Italy, and there to establish states and churches. The obedient sons and grandsons experienced the blessing of the Lord. Hence these events are put before us as examples of their extraordinary obedience to their father Noah and of their extraordinary diligence in the establishment of churches and kingdoms, as well as of the true harmony that flourished in the churches and states until the infamous Ham troubled the world. LECTURES ON GENESIS 10:4-5.[3]

The Original Unity of the Human Race.

KONRAD PELLIKAN: Although people are now dispersed throughout the whole world, Scripture shows that the sons and later generations are from one father, so that we might love one another and not be ignorant of the ancient names of almost all the nations. With a short catalog, Scripture first sums up the generation of the sons of Japheth and Ham, from whom the Gentiles have descended, so that it might discuss more extensively the posterity of Shem, from whom the holy patriarchs and Christ were born. Before the flood, by divine providence, Noah's three sons had not begotten sons, lest they pick up the vices of a corrupt age or perish equally with the others in the flood. The first age had begun from one person, according to Scripture; the later age was to be disseminated from three. COMMENTARY ON GENESIS 10:1.[4]

Clans and Nations Are Built on a Deeper Human Unity.

WOLFGANG MUSCULUS: Just as one world is divided into three

---

[2]*In Genesin* (1576), 254-55, correcting *Arcam* to *Aram* as Chytraeus has it on 276.   [3]LW 2:193 (WA 42:398).   [4]*Commentaria Bibliorum* (1532) 1:13v.

principal parts [Asia, Africa and Europe], then each part into regions, provinces and islands, so also was the human race divided after the flood according to the three patriarchs—Shem, Ham and Japheth—then each patriarch into clans and nations. That which was in itself one of a kind is now divided into bodily members, as is required for living and interacting together in a workable way. Indeed, nations and clans under a single ruler were not divided from one another in order to mix up the clans with other clans, but so that individual clans and nations might be separated from the rest by location and by living together—like closely connected parts of the body. Meanwhile, there remains a relationship of blood, race, kinship and origin by which all the nations of the whole earth are connected by a kind of bond, so that the whole world is inhabited by nations joined in fraternal kinship. Indeed, however much Eastern peoples are separated from those in the West by great expanses, or Northern peoples from those in the South, or divided by national differences, they are still descendants from one father and are all joined as brothers by blood. So it is utterly inhuman to reject commercial dealings with regions where nations are quite familiar with other nations or, equally, to reject association with foreigners, as if one ought to make judgments about the relatedness of the human race on the basis of regional differences or national divisions. It is an evil division that separates that which was joined together so that all feeling and affection for original unity is lost. . . . But such fraternal feeling and affection does remain alive among the godly, who acknowledge and serve the creator of all and thus also harbor genuine affection for all who partake of human nature. COMMENTARY ON GENESIS 10:5.[5]

FABLES REPLACED MEMORIES OF THE FLOOD. JOHN CALVIN: This second beginning of the human race is especially worthy to be known, but the ingratitude of those who willfully forgot God's grace and salvation—even though they had heard from their fathers and grandfathers of the wonderful restoration of the world in so short a time—is detestable. The memory of the flood was buried by most people; very few cared by what means or for what end they had been preserved. Many centuries later, because their wicked forgetfulness had blinded them to God's judgment and mercy, a door was opened to Satan's lies. By his cunning, it came to pass that the pagan poets disseminated worthless and even harmful fables by which the truth about God's works was corrupted. COMMENTARY ON GENESIS 10:1.[6]

10:2-5 The Sons of Japheth

WHY NOAH'S SONS ARE LISTED IN THIS ORDER. JOHN CALVIN: The sons of Japheth are put as the first group, probably because they had moved farther from their homeland, having wandered through so many regions and even having crossed the sea; because those clans were less known to the Jews, he therefore touches on them briefly. He assigns second place to the sons of Ham, with whom the Jews were more familiar because they lived nearby. But since he had set out to weave a history of the church as one continuous narrative, he postpones the progeny of Shem, from whom the church flowed, to last place. Thus, their order does not indicate their dignity, because Moses lists first of all those whom he wished to touch on only in passing, as obscure. COMMENTARY ON GENESIS 10:1.[7]

JAPHETH'S GRANDSON AND THE GERMAN NATION. MARTIN LUTHER: We Germans throughout our entire line are descended from the first-born of Japheth. Although this is no glory before God, it does indicate that there would be some kingdom of this Ashkenaz,

---

[5]*In Mosis Genesim* (1554), 260. [6]CTS 1:313* (CO 23:157). [7]CTS 1:315* (CO 23:158).

since he is the first-born. In the second place, it is also faintly intimated that he would come to a knowledge of the Gospel; for both are the prerogatives of primogeniture. The clear meaning is this: God had merciful regard for this nation and wanted to honor it in an outstanding manner, and history bears witness that the German nation was always considered highly praiseworthy. LECTURES ON GENESIS 10:3.[8]

THE GRADUAL DECLINE OF JAPHETH'S LINE.

MARTIN LUTHER: These are the descendants of Japheth, among whom, without a doubt, were holy fathers who ruled their descendants properly in both a spiritual and a physical way, and erected altars wherever they happened to live. Because no law had yet been given about worship in a certain place, they were free to sacrifice everywhere, just as we today are free to pray everywhere. Gradually, however, the descendants degenerated into idolatry and began to worship the sun, the stars, etc. This very idolatry undoubtedly took its origin from the true worship, just as superstition always has its origin in true godliness. Godly parents taught their children to pray at sunrise and to give thanks for the beautiful light by which all things are not only illuminated but preserved; but their descendants turned this practice into idolatry. Similarly, the Chaldeans later on worshiped fire; the Turks practiced circumcision; and we ourselves, departing from the teaching of the apostles, have fallen into the abominable idolatry introduced into the church by the papal gang for its own profit. Stupid imitation by the ungodly has always followed upon the faith of the godly, and this has been the source and origin of all misfortune in the church. LECTURES ON GENESIS 10:4-5.[9]

10:6-20 The Sons of Ham

GOD STILL HOPED FOR REPENTANCE FROM CANAAN AND HIS DESCENDANTS.

JOHANNES BRENZ: The descendants of Ham's son, Canaan, occupied the region that was later handed over to the descendants of Abraham. This land was said to flow with milk and honey, so it is puzzling, however it may have come to pass, that while Ham was cursed, his descendants yet occupied the chief and finest part of the earth. But it isn't puzzling if you come to understand the character of our Lord God. First, Ham wasn't cursed in all of his descendants, but chiefly in his son Canaan. . . . So even if Ham's descendants through his other sons acquired a good deal of the blessing of this land, it remains that his descendants through Canaan were not happy or blessed for very long. Second, the Canaanites had good fortune in that region for a while, but eventually they were horribly destroyed by the descendants of Shem and Abraham. Truly, God is patient and bides his time: he does not rush to punish but waits for repentance. Just as when he promises a blessing, he seems to drag out the time so that he might test the believer's faith in the meantime, so also in his curses is he accustomed to prolong the time in order to await repentance. COMMENTARY ON GENESIS 10:15-19.[10]

CANAAN'S UNEXPECTED BUT SHORT-LIVED SUCCESS.

WOLFGANG MUSCULUS: It seems strange to say Canaan was cursed, when he grew into such a multitude of offspring (indeed, eleven sons are attributed to him, from whom eleven nations descended) and later possessed the best part of the world, including the area where many think paradise would have been. Those regions were fertile and extraordinary in every way, for they had been destined for God's people and for God's own name. Such things seem to pertain more to a blessing than to a curse, and more to dominion (or freedom, at least) than to servitude. But if you consider the

---

[8]LW 2:190 (WA 42:396). [9]LW 2:192 (WA 42:397-98).
[10]*Opera* 1:120.

fates that befell Shem and Japheth, what happened on both sides does not seem to correspond completely either to this curse or to their respective blessings. We may respond to this question from Psalm 73, that the godly people of that day would have needed to "enter the sanctuary of God" and consider not the present circumstances of godless nations but "their final destiny." . . . Accordingly, it is quite believable that Shem's godly descendants would have been put to the test when they saw the successes of Canaan, his insolence and arrogance, and it would have seemed strange to see these things as befitting a curse that Noah had inflicted on them—until the time came when at last the Canaanites were laid waste and subjected to servitude. These descendants' deeds were made clear by events, whereby it became plain that God is accustomed to dispense the curse's penalty on godless and cursed people in such a manner that they might seem to be blessed and fortunate for a while. But he exercises godly and blessed people with tribulations and adverse circumstances, so that they themselves *seem* to be cursed and ungodly in the eyes of those who *are* cursed and ungodly. In sum, questions of this sort can be answered most effectively by considering the final destiny of the godless. It is proper for the ungodly to fulfill God's measure: and when it is full, heaven will declare that their successes were not everlasting but doomed and transient, and the threats of the curse, however long they were delayed and regarded as doubtful, will prove to be the truest of all. Commentary on Genesis 10:15-19.[11]

Neither Ham Nor Canaan Seems Cursed.

Nikolaus Selnecker: Having reviewed the names of Ham's descendants, we must especially give consideration to the fact that Ham's offspring took possession of the most beautiful places and luxuries in the whole world. They were distinguished by an abundance of the best things—spices, metals, produce—and by power and authority, undoubtedly in that place where paradise used to be and where God wished his church to be later on. But how (someone may ask) does this fit with the curse on Ham and Canaan? Ham is powerful, along with his offspring. Japheth and Shem are far inferior to him. Ham, therefore, cannot be the slave of his brothers, nor be called such. In order for us to respond to this objection, the first thing to be grasped is the terms of the promise, which is primarily to be understood of eternal dominion. Japheth and Shem ought to be lords of their brother Ham; that is, to them the Son of God is promised as their eternal king, the redeemer of the human race and the savior of those who believe. Second, one must grasp the terms of the curse, which is not removed even if it is delayed: the ungodly fulfill its measure, so that they may grow more secure, but in the end they will perish. Third, it must be understood that such cases are to be adjudicated not by fate; rather, it remains to be seen how God may finally act according to the standard of his word. Indeed, God often acts amidst contradiction, and he rules and guides his saints in amazing ways while he advances them to true glory. Thus he often grants worldly happiness to the ungodly but, by promise and threat, detains his own under a fatherly cross that is yet a safe place. Indeed, at the end he shows that he is a true and just judge, and the father of mercy. So eventually Canaan is wretchedly devastated, and God's people triumph. Commentary on Genesis 10:8-12.[12]

10:8-12 Nimrod, the First "Mighty Man"

Nimrod Was the First Tyrant after the Flood.

Martin Luther: Nimrod is not listed among the rest of the sons of Cush, perhaps because he was the child of a harlot.

---

[11]*In Mosis Genesim* (1554), 263. [12]*In Genesin* (1569), 355-56.

Moses presents a careful account of him and extols him above all the other descendants of Noah. He related that Cain's son Enoch was the first before the Flood to strive for sovereignty and to build a city, which he wanted called by his own name. I believe that it was located at the place where Babel stood after the Flood; for, as the historical accounts of the heathen testify, the plain of that region was very beautiful. Similarly, Nimrod was the first after the Flood to strive for the sovereignty of the world. Not satisfied with its southern part, he extended his grasp toward the east, in the direction of the lands of Shem. Moses presents a rather careful account of him so that he might be in full view in a conspicuous place, to inspire fear in the ungodly and to give comfort to the godly. The name is indicative of the events. He is called Nimrod . . . which means "to fall away" and "to rebel," either because he went to war with his brothers, and especially with the families of the godly, in order to extend his territory, or because at that time this nation began to turn away from the sons of Shem and their religion, and sought to gain for itself the sole sovereignty over all the sons of Noah. . . . We must not suppose that he achieved this without murder and bloodshed. LECTURES ON GENESIS 10:8-9.[13]

WHAT WAS NIMROD REALLY LIKE? KONRAD PELLIKAN: Nimrod the son of Cush is called mighty, violent and a tyrant, an oppressor of others and a despiser of God. He's called a mighty hunter because he lived by plundering and piracy: a giant of a man, reckless and a robber. But Rabbi Abraham Ibn Ezra wishes him to have been a tracker and exterminator of wild animals who would also have sacrificed to the Lord, giving thanks to God for the strength of mind and body he had received—as if he had been one of those heroes called Hercules. Rabbi Solomon[†] says he was the author of a rebellion of men against God. . . . The source of his first kingdom was *Babel*, that is, perpetual

confusion and an unresting opposition to the faithful. COMMENTARY ON GENESIS 10:8, 10.[14]

THIS WICKED HUNTER PREYED ON HUMANS. CARDINAL CAJETAN: Everyone understands this as pertaining to hunting *people*, in order to signify that he used his might to capture human beings after the fashion of a hunter. But "before the face of God" can be taken in two ways. Either it is *contemptuous*, that is, he behaved in God's presence with contempt, so that this is said to magnify his sin, just as a crime is magnified if committed with a magistrate watching. Or it is *simulative*, to signify that Nimrod was pretending that he was a God-worshiper, but as a pretext for exercising tyranny. COMMENTARY ON GENESIS 10:9.[15]

NIMROD DEPARTED FROM THE MODERATION OF THE AGE. JOHN CALVIN: Moses tells the particular story of Cush's son Nimrod because he began to emerge from obscurity in an unusual manner. Moreover, I take the passage as indicating that people at that time conducted themselves with such moderation that even if some were in charge of others, they did not lord it over them or arrogate royal rule to themselves. Instead, content with a degree of dignity, they governed others in an unassuming way and had more authority than power. . . . But now, says Moses, Nimrod seized a higher position, as if forgetting he was a human being. Noah was still alive at that time and was certainly great and venerable in the eyes of all, and there were also other excellent men. But such was their moderation that they cultivated equality with their inferiors, who honored them voluntarily rather than by force of command. Nimrod's ambition disturbed and destroyed what this moderation had achieved. Moreover, since it is clear enough from Moses' indictment that the

[13]LW 2:196-97 (WA 42:400-401). [14]*Commentaria Bibliorum* (1532) 1:14r; [†]aka Rashi. [15]*Commentarii illustres* (1539), 62.

tyrant is branded with an eternal mark of shame, it is right to think it greatly pleasing to God when people are governed with moderation. And truly, all those who remember that they too are human will gladly cultivate their association with others. COMMENTARY ON GENESIS 10:8.[16]

TYRANTS BEGET PROVERBS . . . AND MORE TYRANTS. WOLFGANG MUSCULUS: If Nimrod had remained as the only tyrant ever in the land and had had no imitators, there would have been no occasion for this proverb. . . . But there were base men who followed Nimrod's footsteps and practiced tyranny in the land, and it was of them that it was said, "Like Nimrod, a mighty hunter before the Lord." The proverb thus warns us of how tyrants follow one another. Whatever was done by the first tyrant was not neglected by those who followed his footsteps. Where public morals are corrupt and true religion has declined, ten tyrants emerge more quickly than one legitimate prince or magistrate. We also see in this proverb that not only do tyrants sprout up in abundance, so that even though the first one should be struck by lightning from heaven or die a cruel death (and they are truly unworthy even to die of thirst), nonetheless another will immediately arise; but also that tyrants are so like one another that, for the sake of custom, a later one will take a name similar to that of his predecessor as an obvious proverb, just as if his predecessor were brought back to life in him. COMMENTARY ON GENESIS 10:9.[17]

EVIL LINGERS IN THE MEMORY MORE THAN GOODNESS. WOLFGANG MUSCULUS: This text pictures the misery and unhappiness of human affairs. Among all his descendants, Noah alone was so righteous and godly that he could have given rise to a proverb, so as to say, "Like Noah, a righteous man before the Lord." I'm not saying that no one among

Noah's offspring was righteous; what I'm saying is that his righteousness will *not* pass on into a proverb, either because no equal will be chosen from among [Noah's] descendants or else because the principle of righteousness would not have mattered to the multitude. However, so little did the godless tyrant Nimrod lack for followers, that on account of a succession of imitators, his name *will* pass on to his descendants as a proverb. COMMENTARY ON GENESIS 10:9.[18]

10:21-31 *The Sons of Shem*

EBER'S DIGNITY ANTICIPATED ABRAHAM. JOHN CALVIN: The benediction of Shem did not descend to all his grandchildren indiscriminately but remained in one family. However, even though Eber's grandchildren themselves also fell away from the true worship of God, so that the Lord could have justly disinherited them, the benediction was not utterly extinguished for all that. Rather, it was only buried for a season, until Abraham was called, and it is in his honor that this remarkable dignity was ascribed to the race and name of Eber. COMMENTARY ON GENESIS 10:21.[19]

ASSHUR, NINEVEH'S GODLY FOUNDER. MARTIN LUTHER: I . . . would assume that Asshur, Shem's son, went out from the land of Babylon, just as Abram later on departed from the land of the Chaldeans. . . . It was the wickedness and the violence of the ungodly generation of Ham that forced Asshur to depart. He was unable to put up with the ungodly forms of worship and the idolatry of Ham's descendants. He yielded before their madness and joined our ancestors, the descendants of Japheth, to be somewhat closer to them; and he built Nineveh. For this reason

---

[16]CTS 1:316-17* (CO 23:158-59). [17]*In Mosis Genesim* (1554), 264. [18]*In Mosis Genesim* (1554), 264-65. [19]CTS 1:320* (CO 23:161).

the Lord was fond of Nineveh, as appears from Ezekiel and Jonah, and bestowed on it the honor of becoming a monarchy. Ezekiel (31:9), therefore, compares it to a beautiful tree with wide-spreading branches. Finally Jonah was sent to these remnants of Shem; and after Nineveh was converted, it repented, acknowledged the Lord, and was saved. It is not without reason that Jonah calls it a great city of God (Jonah 3:3). LECTURES ON GENESIS 10:11-12.[20]

GENESIS 10 DRAWS ALL HISTORY TOGETHER WITH THE THREAD OF CHRIST.

MARTIN LUTHER: This very chapter, even though it is considered full of dead words, has in it the thread that is drawn from the first world to the middle and to the end of all

things. From Adam the promise concerning Christ is passed on to Seth; from Seth to Noah; from Noah to Shem; and from Shem to this Eber, from whom the Hebrew nation received its name as the heir for whom the promise about the Christ was intended in preference to all other peoples of the whole world. This knowledge the Holy Scriptures reveal to us. Those who are without them live in error, uncertainty, and boundless ungodliness; for they have no knowledge about who they are and whence they came. LECTURES ON GENESIS 10:26-32.[21]

---

[20]LW 2:201 (WA 42:404). In Hebrew, *Asshur* and *Assyria* are identical, as the King James Version illustrates. Luther is by no means alone in wondering why one of Seth's sons (Gen 10:22) shows up in Nimrod's kingdom (Gen 10:11). [21]LW 2:208-9 (WA 42:409).

11:1-9 THE TOWER OF BABEL

[1]Now the whole earth had one language and the same words. [2]And as people migrated from the east, they found a plain in the land of Shinar and settled there. [3]And they said to one another, "Come, let us make bricks, and burn them thoroughly." And they had brick for stone, and bitumen for mortar. [4]Then they said, "Come, let us build ourselves a city and a tower with its top in the heavens, and let us make a name for ourselves, lest we be dispersed over the face of the whole earth." [5]And the LORD came down to see the city and the tower, which the children of man had built. [6]And the LORD said, "Behold, they are one people, and they have all one language, and this is only the beginning of what they will do. And nothing that they propose to do will now be impossible for them. [7]Come, let us go down and there confuse their language, so that they may not understand one another's speech." [8]So the LORD dispersed them from there over the face of all the earth, and they left off building the city. [9]Therefore its name was called Babel, because there the LORD confused[a] the language of all the earth. And from there the LORD dispersed them over the face of all the earth.

a *Babel* sounds like the Hebrew for *confused*

OVERVIEW: Ham's disgrace in Genesis 9 led
to the curse on his son Canaan, and now this
chapter begins with an account of a disaster
precipitated by another of Ham's descendants—presumably Nimrod, son of Cush and
thus Noah's great-grandson. The audacious
attempt to build a tower in Babel that would
reach the heavens provoked God to confuse the
speech of human beings and to scatter them all
over the earth. It was, without a doubt, a story
to fuel the imagination.

For Reformation commentators, as for
their predecessors, the center of the story is a
simple account of crime and punishment, but
one that recalls earlier details, such as God's
deliberation prior to evicting Adam and Eve
from the garden. As might be expected, there
is great interest in probing the motives behind
the actions of both the human perpetrators
and the divine judge. But other descriptions
also elicited attention, including some speculation about what the earth's original "one
language" may have been. More poignantly,
these Christian commentators were moved to
muse about the disastrous, widespread and
enduring effects of the confusion of tongues—
and about how this confusion has been
affected for the better by the advent of Christ.

11:1 The Whole Earth Had One Language

**THE LATER TRIALS OF NOAH'S DESCEN-
DANTS.** MARTIN LUTHER: This chapter . . .
deals with the extraordinary example of the
holy patriarch Noah and of his family, especially those who were godly. It is intended to
show us how much faith and godliness there
was in these holy men despite the incredible
wickedness, envy, and tyranny that were
widespread and dominant among the children
of men. For some time after the Flood the
entire earth was in a blessed state; for all
people had one language, no small bond for
maintaining harmony and a particular asset for
maintaining the teaching of religion. The fresh
memory of the immeasurable wrath of God in
the Flood kept their hearts in the fear of God
and in reverence for their ancestors. LECTURES
ON GENESIS 11.[1]

A BRIEF UTOPIA AFTER THE FLOOD.
KONRAD PELLIKAN: I imagine that for a
considerable time among people after the
flood, there flourished a candor in business
dealings, similar moral values, a mutuality
born of love, cordial and free discourse, and
integrity in all of life. COMMENTARY ON
GENESIS 11:1.[2]

**A COMMON LANGUAGE OUGHT TO HAVE
PROMOTED PURITY OF WORSHIP.** JOHN
CALVIN: When Moses says, "the earth was of
one lip," he commends God's exquisite kindness in desiring to maintain the sacred bond
of society even among people widely scattered
by their possessing a common language among
themselves. And truly, diversity of tongues
ought to be regarded as a marvel: for since
language is the stamp or imprint of the mind,
how does it come to pass that all people—partakers of the same reason and born for social
life—do not communicate with each other in
the same language? Moses therefore teaches
that this defect was a mishap, because it is
repugnant to nature, and that the dispersion
of tongues is a punishment divinely inflicted
upon humans because they impiously con-
spired against God. Unity of language ought
to have nurtured their agreement in piety, but
this mob of whom Moses speaks, after they
had alienated themselves from the pure
worship of God and the sacred assembly of the
faithful, come together in order to stir up war
with God. Consequently, their tongues were
divided by God's rightful vengeance. COMMEN-
TARY ON GENESIS 11:1.[3]

---

[1]LW 2:210 (WA 42:409). [2]*Commentaria Bibliorum* (1532)
1:14v. [3]CTS 1:325-26* (CO 23:164).

HEBREW WAS ONCE THE UNIVERSAL LANGUAGE. WOLFGANG MUSCULUS: What was this "one language" that people used until the time when the variety of languages was introduced? Does that ancient and original idiom of the human race still remain, or has it been changed into something new? If so, among which people does it remain? While nothing certain can be deduced from Holy Scripture to address the first question, it is commonly thought that the language of the first age was nothing other than Hebrew . . . and in my judgment this view does not lack probable support, which we can gather from things written about the first world. Thus, the first man taken from the earth was called *Adam*, that is, "reddish" and "earthy." His wife was *Eve*, because she was the mother of all the "living." Their firstborn was *Cain* or "acquired," so to speak; their second was *Abel*, as if he were "superfluous"; and their third was *Seth*, or "established." Finally, the son of Lamech was called *Noah*, under whom there would be a "rest" from evil. I think this is adequate proof that Hebrew would have been the language of the first humans back then, and of the first age through the Babylonian confusion [of tongues]. . . . Truly, these are nothing other than [originally] Hebrew terms. Nor is it likely that these words were contrived by Moses, introduced in place of other words that were in use in the first world. Even though languages may change, the proper names of famous people remain the same, so that the names of Adam, Eve, Cain, Abel, Seth and Noah are still in use not just among the Hebrews, but also among Greeks, Latins, and other nations. COMMENTARY ON GENESIS 11:1.[4]

11:3-4a *"Let Us Make Bricks. . . . Let Us Build a City and a Tower"*

WHICH CAME FIRST, THE CITY OF BABEL OR ITS TOWER? MARTIN LUTHER: Nimrod built that structure in order to make an everlasting name for himself in the world and among his descendants. When he saw that this building project was brought to naught and was interrupted by God through the confusion of tongues, then he began to build the city of Babel. LECTURES ON GENESIS 10:10.[5]

BABEL'S SIN IS MORE IMPORTANT THAN ITS TOWER. MARTIN LUTHER: Opinions vary both about the structure or tower itself and about the sin of its builders. The more daring a man is in answering each of these two questions, the more outspokenly he expresses himself. And the common people, too, did not refrain from inventing stories. Thus they say that the height of the tower was nine miles, but that when the languages were confused, a third of it was destroyed by the force of wind and weather and the rest sank into the earth, so that now only one third of it is still in existence. Moreover, they claim that it was so high that from it one could hear the voices of the angels singing in heaven. But we disregard these foolish tales. It is worthier of our inquiry to give thought to the sin of the builders, something that cannot be clearly understood from the text. LECTURES ON GENESIS 11.[6]

BETTER A SCHOOL THAN A TOWER! JOHANNES BRENZ: If they had been pious men, they would first of all have done nothing in pursuit of such a difficult undertaking without the advice of the patriarch Noah, who was then still alive. Then, because they saw that they would eventually have to disperse on account of their growing numbers, they would have consulted together about preserving the teaching of religion and writing a confession or creed, and they would have built a temple— partly as a monument to the divine blessings by which they were preserved through the

---

[4]*In Mosis Genesim* (1554), 271. [5]LW 2:200 (WA 42:403). [6]LW 2:210-11 (WA 42:410).

flood, and partly as a school in which they would preserve and teach the doctrine about the coming of Christ, the woman's seed and the virgin's son. However, having neglected and scorned all these things, they now slide toward ruin on account of their impiety and ingratitude, so that they applaud their own wisdom and regard Noah and their other ancestors as fools and idiots, and they busy themselves solely with the majesty of their own name. Surely this is to make war on God, and it is not unlike that sin that was perpetrated in the beginning by Satan and then by Adam, who also were contemptuous of God and aspired to make a name for themselves. COMMENTARY ON GENESIS 11:3-4.[7]

BABEL AND THE RESTLESSNESS OF THE FLESH. WOLFGANG MUSCULUS: Consider here the pursuits to which the counsels of the flesh lead when the flesh begins to tire of its former simplicity, plainness and frugality. The fathers of these sons dwelt with Noah in tents as sojourners in this world and as lifelong farmers. But when these sons stumbled upon a fertile plain, they were already tired of their fathers' and grandfather's diet, and they took hold of the plan to build a city and tower. . . . Thus, boredom with their original rural life ran together with their skill in making bricks and the endowments of the land. The flesh, of course, is ingenious at abandoning the simplicity and frugality of its ancestors for a life that is vainly splendid and splendidly vain. And while examples of this defection are visible throughout every age, they are manifested above all in our own, in which there is no end of splendid buildings. COMMENTARY ON GENESIS 11:3-4.[8]

INSURANCE AGAINST ANOTHER FLOOD. KONRAD PELLIKAN: They encouraged one another to construct a city and a tower, to be raised for the sake of a name among their posterity, [and to do so] before they were

scattered here and there into many lands and forced into settlements in a vast and untamed territory on account of their continued multiplication. Therefore they were trying to erect a memorial of their unity and concord, possibly with the presumptuous plan that if flood waters happened to return in force, they would prepare a refuge for themselves to which they would flee to save their lives. COMMENTARY ON GENESIS 11:4.[9]

CARNAL PRUDENCE BRINGS NO SAFETY. WOLFGANG MUSCULUS: If you were to understand that they wanted to raise a tower that would extend up to heaven for this reason, so that afterwards they would be safe and secure against the waters of a flood if the lands should be covered again as before, . . . then you have an example of the impious advice that proceeds from the flesh's own prudence. The flesh argues like this: "Water destroyed the world. They lacked towers and fortified citadels then. 'Come, therefore, let us build for ourselves a city and a tower whose top will rise to heaven' and whose roof the waters will not reach." The impious, unbelieving and stupid flesh deliberates in just this way. It does not see whence comes destruction, of whose roots and sources it is ignorant. Better should they have said, "The evil and impenitence of the corrupt world destroyed all flesh in a flood, but God's grace and a zeal for righteousness saved our father Noah. So let us be grateful to God, by whose mercy it happened, lest we ourselves also perish; and let us remain zealous for true piety and righteousness, lest we stir his wrath against us and we perish in the end." But they were carnal, and strangers to such thoughts of this faith and true wisdom. They are like all those who are destitute of the spirit of faith and who rely solely on the judgment of the flesh to think about either their safety or

---

[7]*Opera* 1:121. [8]*In Mosis Genesim* (1554), 275. [9]*Commentaria Bibliorum* (1532) 1:15r.

the causes of their destruction. COMMENTARY ON GENESIS 11:4.[10]

THE TOWER'S BUILDERS SOUGHT AN ARTIFICIAL IMMORTALITY. JOHN CALVIN: "Whose top may reach unto heaven" is a hyperbolical expression, fine words by which they boastfully extol the loftiness of the structure they are laboring to build. What they immediately tack on—"Let us make a name for ourselves"—pertains as well, for they thereby indicate that it was going to be the sort of work that would not only attract the attention of bystanders as a kind of miracle, but also win renown everywhere, even to the utter ends of the earth. This is the world's perpetual folly: having neglected heaven, to seek immortality on earth, where everything is perishable and passing away. COMMENTARY ON GENESIS 11:4.[11]

INNOCENCE MAKES THE BEST FORTRESS. HULDRYCH ZWINGLI: For the sake of gaining a name, . . . they erected this high tower and a fortified city, no doubt relying on their plan so that if the waters were once again to increase, they would be safe from destruction—indeed, they attributed the previous destruction to the waters, not to God. Their impiety is manifested in this, too, for if they had been pious and faithful, they certainly would have known this: we are to live according to God's plan and his word, lest he also punish and destroy us as he did our fathers. Our life is to be protected with innocence, not with watchtowers and citadels. ANNOTATIONS ON GENESIS 11:4.[12]

THE BUILDERS WERE VAIN BUT NOT STUPID. KONRAD PELLIKAN: Human feelings induced the Lord to descend to see what was happening among the people. But God, who always is everywhere in his entirety, is not moved according to place; but he is said to descend when he does something on earth that happens as a marvel, beyond the usual course

of nature. Thus he shows his presence, in a fashion, to the people who were building the city and the tower whose top was going to touch heaven (a hyperbole for the tallest and highest buildings). They were not so stupid, of course, that they would try to build to heaven or to attack the Lord. Indeed, they are called "sons of men," that is, vain and feeble-minded, able to do nothing without God's help and empowerment or against his will. COMMENTARY ON GENESIS 11:5.[13]

THE SIN LAY NOT IN THE TOWER BUT IN FALSE RELIGIOSITY. MARTIN LUTHER: It was no sin in itself to erect a tower and to build a city, for the saints did the same; and Asshur, whom I believe to have been altogether a saint, built Nineveh because he could no longer live with the ungodly (Gen 10:11). This, however, is their sin: they attach their own name to this structure; having despised Noah and the true church, they are intent on sovereignty; they maintain that they are the people who are very close to God, to whom God listens, and to whom He grants success; and they conclude that Noah, in turn, has been abandoned and cast aside by God. LECTURES ON GENESIS 11.[14]

11:4b "Let Us Make a Name for Ourselves, Lest We Be Dispersed"

UNITY MAY WORK FOR EVIL AS WELL AS FOR GOOD. PETER MARTYR VERMIGLI: Their wicked goal is further expressed here. They did not want to be scattered, despite the fact that when God blessed Noah's sons, he would have proposed to them that they should fill the earth. This plan of theirs was to obtain fame and renown for themselves, lest they be scattered, but they were thinking that a fortress would be the key to a kingdom, a

---

[10]*In Mosis Genesim* (1554), 276. [11]CTS 1:327* (CO 23:165). [12]ZSW 13:63. [13]*Commentaria Bibliorum* (1532) 1:15r. [14]LW 2:214 (WA 42:412).

monarchy and some sort of mighty government. Truly, people do have great power where they agree and join together. But if the grace of God does not intervene, their efforts always erupt in evil deeds, just as is manifestly clear here. COMMENTARY ON GENESIS 11:4.[15]

A REPUGNANT UNITY. WOLFGANG MUSCULUS: Truly, this unity was repugnant to the divine will, and that is why it was torn apart by the confusion of tongues. We should heed this example, that an evil concord is worthy of being divided. The Lord himself is the dissolver and disturber of such unity, which is not of itself evil, yet it is seized for evil ends and rendered perverse. The unity of Noah's descendants was not evil, in that they were one people and spoke with one tongue. But that unity of blood, cohabitation and language was nourishing a concord of perverse zeal, to which they were so enslaved that they obstinately continued in ungodly labors. For this reason they were handed over as worthy of destruction, so that they would no longer be one people, nor would they speak one and the same language, but many, diverse and discordant. . . . If all concord is good and it doesn't matter what kind it is, then that of which Moses writes here was also good, that the people were one and built the city and the tower of Babel with harmonious zeal—and so God is to be blamed for disturbing and dissolving it! Yet if it is not just any concord of any kind that would be good and unlawful to disrupt, but instead matters greatly who and what sort be joined in unity, then it unquestionably follows that not just any concord is good and pleasing to God, even if it be clearly a "catholic" unity. Nor should people so quickly be blamed and condemned as schismatics and disturbers of catholic unity . . . if they have heeded the warning of the Holy Spirit and left Babylon, dissolving its unity while attempting to take others with them, lest they find themselves sharing in its crimes

and, at the same time, its destruction. COMMENTARY ON GENESIS 11:6.[16]

HUBRIS DEFILES OUR PACTS AND PROJECTS. NIKOLAUS SELNECKER: Truly, raising up a structure is a good thing in itself, and it shows that there were excellent architects and craftsmen at that time. And today, too, the fortifications of a city and confederations of the just and godly, along with other things like this, are not condemned, nor do they violate godliness. But when reckless self-confidence is added, just as these people thought they would be safe in their tower, then the experience of all times shows that God overthrows chariots and horses, walls and men, towers and ramparts, reducing them to ashes and annihilating them. Indeed, God can tolerate nothing less than confidence in human defenses—a confidence that is really nothing other than apostasy from the true God, as well as complacency and arrogance joined with contempt for God. COMMENTARY ON GENESIS 11:4.[17]

THOSE IN BABEL FORETELL THEIR OWN DEMISE. MARTIN LUTHER: What is the meaning of this? Who put these words into their mouth, to cause them to foretell their future dispersion over the entire world? They are not prophesying like Caiaphas (John 11:49-51), are they, and saying something of which they have no knowledge? It is a common occurrence . . . that the ungodly foretell evil for themselves, and that what they dread happens to them. . . . Nevertheless, the foreknowledge in the instance before us is not a prophecy like that of Caiaphas; it has a different cause. . . . [Instead,] the words reveal a conscience that is troubled and yet smugly keeps on disregarding the punishment. LECTURES ON GENESIS 11:4.[18]

---

[15]*In Primum Librum Mosis* (1569), 46r. [16]*In Mosis Genesim* (1554), 278-79. [17]*In Genesin* (1569), 362. [18]LW 2:218, 219 (WA 42:415, 416).

11:5-6 The Lord Came Down to See . . . "Nothing Will Be Impossible for Them"

GOD'S ALARM IS IRONIC. KONRAD PEL-LIKAN: [This passage] is better read as irony, as if he were to say, "These people ought to use their accord to do something good and useful, to exert themselves on behalf of what I have promised, and to attempt nothing without my counsel or command. So, now, let them try! They will see how the ventures of those who promise themselves the utmost, even to invade heaven (so to speak), avail for nothing." COMMENTARY ON GENESIS 11:6.[19]

GOD FORBEARS BUT DOES NOT IGNORE. JOHN CALVIN: God frequently bears with the wicked to such an extent that he not only allows them to plan many vile deeds, just as if he were unconcerned or idling about, but he even furthers their wicked and perverse efforts with favorable results, so that he may in the end cast them down to a lower depth. Indeed, the "descent" that Moses mentions here looks more to the human perspective than that of God, who we know does not move from place to place. Rather, he is indicating that God appeared as an avenger gradually and (so to speak) at a languid pace. Therefore "the Lord came down to see," that is, he revealed that the heart of what the Babylonians were attempting to do was not unknown to him. COMMENTARY ON GENESIS 11:5.[20]

11:7 "Let Us Confuse Their Language"

GOD IS NOT SPEAKING TO THE ANGELS. ANDREW WILLET: The Lord is not speaking here to the angels or to the persons of the Trinity and the angels together. Rather, this is a consultation of the whole Trinity, as it is said in verse 8, "Jehovah scattered them," and this speech corresponds to that in Genesis 1:26 in the creation of humankind: "Come, let us make humankind." Those to whom God speaks here

he makes as equal [to him] in the same degree: "Come, let us go down." God indeed uses the ministry of angels sometimes, not that he needs their help; but, as Philo says, "God sees what is fitting for himself and what is fitting for the creatures," for God is more honored in such ministers, and the infirmity of human beings is thereby helped. But at this time and in this case, God did not need the ministry of angels. This confusion of tongues was his immediate work, as was the gift of tongues (Acts 2:4). COMMENTARY ON GENESIS 11:7.[21]

CONFUSION OF LANGUAGES IS LIKE A SECOND FLOOD. HULDRYCH ZWINGLI: The confusion of tongues and variety of idioms is the punishment for sin and is like another flood: indeed, it makes confusion and discord. The same thing happens in the world even today. Truly, it is a huge inconvenience that there is not a single language for all people. For it is common for translators (a task that remains extremely valuable today) to wander off the path due to the ignorance of some of them, while others introduce errors born of their own faithlessness. Indeed, there are some who learn to misuse languages either for vainglory or for profit or fraud. But if people use languages for God's glory, for education, for the benefit of the Christian common-wealth, this certainly is no ordinary gift of God, who knows how to "misuse" our sins and the punishment of our sins for his own glory. ANNOTATIONS ON GENESIS 11:7.[22]

AFTER DEATH, THE NEXT WORST PUNISH-MENT. JOHANNES BRENZ: This is the gravest punishment upon the human race. First, it is a kind of muteness. Indeed, were a Spaniard not to understand a German, and a German not

[19]*Commentaria Bibliorum* (1532) 1:15r. [20]CTS 1:329* (CO 23:166). [21]*Hexapla* (1608), 128, criticizing Augustine, Gregory, Philo, Cardinal Cajetan and Mercerus; crediting Rabanus, Rupert and Calvin; and quoting Philo, *On the Confusion of Tongues* 34.175. [22]ZSW 13:64.

understand the Italians' language, and an Italian not understand the language of the Greeks, what else is a Spaniard toward a German or an Italian toward a Greek, except a mute? Then, this punishment sets the nations at odds with one another, so that they cannot engage in commercial trade. Finally, even though languages can be learned by foreigners, it still requires great labor and expense. After the imposition of mortality upon the human race, the next most serious punishment is the diversity of languages. COMMENTARY ON GENESIS 11:3-4.[23]

DIVERSITY OF LANGUAGE RECALLS HUMAN ARROGANCE. PETER MARTYR VERMIGLI: These words, "Come, let us go down and confuse them," are a reply to the earlier statement, for they were saying, "Come, let us make bricks and build," and the allusion is made in a genial tone of voice. By the union and agreement of their languages and words they sinned, having misused so great a gift, so now they are deservedly punished in their speech. Because the world was to be filled with inhabitants, they were given diverse languages. But because the church was likewise to extend in every direction, gifts of tongues were bestowed on Christ's faithful by the Holy Spirit in such a way that all nations could hear the apostles when they were preaching and all the apostles in turn would understand and be able to speak with those with whom trade was conducted. Thus, as often as we hear people in the world around us speaking in diverse dialects, let us regard it as a symbol of that human arrogance. COMMENTARY ON GENESIS 11:7.[24]

THE LANGUAGES WERE NOT CONFUSED— THE SPEAKERS WERE. ANDREW WILLET: This division of tongues is called a *confusion*, but not with respect to the diverse speech, which was indeed divided, not united or confounded. Rather, it is so called with respect to the speakers, who were confounded in their

affection by being astonished at so sudden an alteration; in their *memory* by forgetting their accustomed speech; and in their *understanding*, because they could not understand one another in their work, which was confused, so that a server would bring one thing when the builder had called for another. COMMENTARY ON GENESIS 11:7.[25]

BABEL VERSUS PENTECOST. JOHANNES BRENZ: In a way, the Son of God restored to us the blessing of a single language, when on the day of Pentecost he poured out upon the apostles the miracle of speaking in diverse languages, so that the one true religion might be proclaimed among all nations. In these days, that one gospel of Christ has been poured into various languages, so that all nations might be able to know the one Christ. COMMENTARY ON GENESIS 11:3-4.[26]

CHRIST BRINGS A COMMON LANGUAGE. JOHN CALVIN: Although the world bears this curse to the present day, even in the midst of punishment and the most dreadful evidence of divine anger against human pride, God's amazing goodness yet shines forth: because the nations do communicate with one another, despite their different languages; but especially because God has proclaimed the one gospel in all languages throughout the whole world and equipped the apostles with the gift of tongues. Thus it has come to pass that those who once were pitifully divided are now growing together in the unity of the faith. In this sense Isaiah says that the language of Canaan would be shared by everyone under the reign of Christ, because even though they may differ in the sound of their words, they nonetheless say one and the same thing when they cry, "Abba, Father!" COMMENTARY ON GENESIS 11:7.[27]

---

[23]*Opera* 1:122. [24]*In Primum Librum Mosis* (1569), 46v. [25]*Hexapla* (1608), 136. [26]*Opera* 1:123. [27]CTS 1:331-32* (CO 23:167), alluding to Is 19:18.

THE CHURCH, TOO, IS A TOWER OF SORTS.
CHRISTOPHOR PELARGUS: An antithesis may
be observed between the Babylonian project
and the miraculous work of the apostles. A
brutish and impious multitude of people
raised the tower of Babel. By the proclamation of the word, Christ builds the church—a
lofty tower whose top strikes heaven itself—
from living stones, equipping the apostles
with gifts of the Holy Spirit. In Babel, their
efforts are dissipated and the people are
bewildered by a kind of insatiable spirit, so
that the various languages confused the
hearing and understanding of each one. In the
New Testament, by the inspiration of the
Holy Spirit, the apostles gathered dispersed
peoples to the true unity of faith, and they
were helpfully informed by the various
languages that each one heard and understood. The Babylonians' outcome is an
unhappy one, for their every exertion notwithstanding, God scattered them with
thunder and lightning. The apostles' outcome
is extremely happy, with the Lord working
everywhere and confirming his word. COM-
MENTARY ON GENESIS 11:5-9.[28]

11:8 The Lord Dispersed Them

THE BLESSINGS OF DISPERSION. ANDREW
WILLET: Although the division of tongues was
imposed upon them as a judgment, God turns
it to the benefit of the world by dispersing
them, which was profitable in many ways. For
if they had continued in once place, many
goodly countries in the world should have
remained as desert, wasteland and untilled.
Also, sufficient food could not have been
provided in one place for such a multitude.
And further, if they had continued together
they might have been in greater hazard due to
war or pestilence, because wicked people
dwelling together would have had greater
strength to do mischief. COMMENTARY ON
GENESIS 11:8.[29]

11:9 Therefore the City Was Called Babel

FAME TURNED TO INFAMY. JOHN CALVIN:
Just see what they accomplished by their
foolish desire to acquire a name! They were
hoping that the tower would be inscribed with
an everlasting tribute to its creators. However,
not only does God frustrate their false confidence, he also brands them with everlasting
disgrace so that they would be detested by all
their descendants on account of their responsibility for the great calamity inflicted on the
human race. Truly, they do have a name, but
not of the sort they'd wished for! Thus does
God reduce to shame the pride of those who
seize for themselves more than is lawfully
theirs. COMMENTARY ON GENESIS 11:9.[30]

IMPIETY WILL DARE ANYTHING. HULD-
RYCH ZWINGLI: The lessons of this story are
to be considered with diligence. First, what
will impiety not dare to do, even against God
himself, whom they try to dislodge from
heaven, as did the giants of old? Those who
strive against his might and powers, against his
wisdom and counsels, who covet wealth and
are eager for profits, who wheel and deal in the
marketplace, who protect themselves by
cunning and by raising cities—these people
undertake a great and arduous task. They
begin to weave a web, but not from God, nay,
they do not think there is a God nor do they
believe that God is concerned for the affairs of
mortals. These are our buildings, which a
wretched creature raises against the Creator.
Indeed, what are bricks, which are made from
clay, except our intentions? What is tar or
pitch, which seeps up spontaneously, except
what signifies sham piety? Truly, with this
plaster we smear over adultery, homicide,

---

[28]*In prophetarum oceanum*, 235; some words are conjectural here,
owing to defacement of the page. [29]*Hexapla* (1608), 128-29.
[30]CTS 1:332* (CO 23:167-68).

usury, and everything indecent and abominable. ANNOTATIONS ON GENESIS 11:8-9.[31]

WE ARE STILL PRONE TO BUILD OUR OWN BABEL. KONRAD PELLIKAN: Babel is the commonest name for the city and region divided by disorder and confusion, because there the Lord showed those who rely on their own counsels and prudence, those who undertake great and arduous but vain tasks, how they accomplish nothing and there is no counsel against the Lord. What else are bricks that are made from clay, except the plans of mortals? What else is tar, except a cloak of piety with which we plaster over our impieties? COMMENTARY ON GENESIS 11:9.[32]

BABEL'S PUNISHMENT ALSO AFFLICTS THE CHURCH. MARTIN LUTHER: This is a description of the awful punishment from which wars, murders, and evils of every kind throughout the entire world have resulted. One should not think that this punishment has come to an end. It continues until now, and especially the church is conscious of this severe affliction. How often has it happened that churches were at variance with one another because of one little, inconsequential ceremony! LECTURES ON GENESIS 11:7-9.[33]

---

[31]ZSW 13:65. [32]*Commentaria Bibliorum* (1532) 1:15r. [33]LW 2:226 (WA 42:421-22).

11:10-26 SHEM'S DESCENDANTS

[10]*These are the generations of Shem. When Shem was 100 years old, he fathered Arpachshad two years after the flood.* [11]*And Shem lived after he fathered Arpachshad 500 years and had other sons and daughters.*

[12]*When Arpachshad had lived 35 years, he fathered Shelah.* [13]*And Arpachshad lived after he fathered Shelah 403 years and had other sons and daughters.*

[14]*When Shelah had lived 30 years, he fathered Eber.* [15]*And Shelah lived after he fathered Eber 403 years and had other sons and daughters.*

[16]*When Eber had lived 34 years, he fathered Peleg.* [17]*And Eber lived after he fathered Peleg 430 years and had other sons and daughters.*

[18]*When Peleg had lived 30 years, he fathered Reu.* [19]*And Peleg lived after he fathered Reu 209 years and had other sons and daughters.*

[20]*When Reu had lived 32 years, he fathered Serug.* [21]*And Reu lived after he fathered Serug 207 years and had other sons and daughters.*

[22]*When Serug had lived 30 years, he fathered Nahor.* [23]*And Serug lived after he fathered Nahor 200 years and had other sons and daughters.*

[24]*When Nahor had lived 29 years, he fathered Terah.* [25]*And Nahor lived after he fathered Terah 119 years and had other sons and daughters.*

[26]*When Terah had lived 70 years, he fathered Abram, Nahor, and Haran.*

OVERVIEW: The genealogy of the Hebrew nation that broke off in Genesis 10:25 with Peleg, great-great-grandson of Shem, is now taken up again, tracing the line from Peleg another four generations to Terah, father of Abram. Despite the many names listed earlier, in Genesis 10, this genealogy would seem to be the important one—a fact attested by the inclusion of precise lifespans and the year each patriarch was born.

The inclusion of these numbers is therefore of some interest to Reformation commentators, but principally for the sake of observations about the decline of human vitality after the flood and after Babel. In addition, while by no means a new theme, God's constant providential care for his people, however diminished they may be in numbers, renown or faith, continues to be a lesson that the Reformers prized in the ongoing saga that would lead to Abraham.

11:10-26 The Generations of Shem

A NEW BOOK BEGINS WITH SHEM. JoHANNES BRENZ: It would be proper, from this place on, not only for a new chapter to be started, but even for a whole new book. Indeed, now Scripture turns its attention to that for which it was chiefly established. For Holy Scripture is not concerned with commemorating the history of all the nations, or only with morality, or with the political concerns of one nation or another, nor was it given to teach the arts, whether grammar or mathematics. Rather, it is concerned to describe true religion and the true knowledge of our Lord Jesus Christ, so that we may thereby pursue true righteousness and eternal salvation. . . . Therefore it leaves off the description of the other nations that descend from Japheth and Ham and takes up only the account of Shem's genealogy, which also leads to Abraham . . . from whose family our Lord Christ would descend. So the things that have preceded so far in this first book of Moses are

like a prelude or a preface of all the histories of all the nations of the earth. But what now follows, not in this book alone but also in all the remaining books of the Old Testament, is an exposition of the things done by that nation from which Christ descended. And even if mention is sometimes made of other nations and kingdoms, it is done only in passing. For the primary goal of the sacred Scriptures of the Old Testament pertains to this, aims at this: to describe the offspring of Abraham, who were a people divinely chosen, first, so that Christ would be born from them, and second, so that they might be the custodians of God's promise regarding Christ until he should come. COMMENTARY ON GENESIS 11:10.[1]

NOAH AND ABRAHAM AS RESTORERS OF THE FAITH. WOLFGANG MUSCULUS: Note how these two groups of ten patriarchs were adorned as much at their outset as at the end by men who were like shining lights, distinguished and famous for their piety. The first group had Adam at its beginning and Noah at the end; the second followed with the extremely righteous Shem at its beginning and, at its foot, the extremely godly Abraham, celebrated as the friend of God. I don't disparage the piety of those fathers who came in between, but I do consider the divine providence that, amid mortals such as these, constantly looks after the luminaries and exemplars of the faith, so that no excuse may remain for any ignorance or impiety. At the same time, I would also observe how the descendants of the godly persevered with too little constancy in the faith and piety of their forebears, so that by the tenth generation they had by no means retained the course of true and ancestral piety without weakening or breaking it. So it is not beyond reason that Noah was provided after Adam had completed his course. It's obvious from what has gone

---

[1]*Opera* 1:123.

before how much desertion and corruption had grown among the race of mortals at that time. So also here, it is not unreasonable to suppose that at the end of the second group of ten, Abraham was provided, in whom the ancient faith and godliness might be renewed, as it were, and transmitted to posterity. Commentary on Genesis 11:10-26.[2]

Lists of the Patriarchs Assure Us That God Does Not Abandon the Church.

Martin Luther: This latter part of the eleventh chapter seems to be of little importance, because it contains nothing except the generations of the fathers. In reality, however, there is need of this account, especially as an example for our time. For we hear that after the division of languages not only governments and the affairs of the home but also the church was thrown into disorder in various ways. And so, lest we suppose that Satan had been allowed to remove the sunlight of the Word utterly from the world and to suppress the church, the generation of the holy fathers is set before us, to show us that by the mercy of God the remnants were preserved and the church was not completely wiped out. . . . This list of the fathers teaches us the basic doctrine that God has never altogether abandoned His church, even though on some occasions it was larger and on others smaller, just as also on some occasions its teaching was purer and on others less clear. Let us sustain ourselves with this hope against the great wickedness of the world and of the opponents of the Word. Lectures on Genesis 11:10.[3]

The Honor of Shem's Progeny Derives from Grace, Not Merit.

John Calvin: As a mark of honor, God numbers the years of the world by the descendants of Shem, just as historians date their annals by the names of kings or consuls. Nevertheless, he has granted this honor not so much on account of the family's dignity and merits as on account of his

own gratuitous adoption, for (as we shall immediately see) a great part of Shem's line abandoned the true worship of God. Accordingly, they deserved not only that God should expunge them from his chronicle but also that he should utterly remove them from the world! However, the election by which God separated that family from all people is too important to him to allow it to perish on account of human sin. Commentary on Genesis 11:10.[4]

11:10-26 The Lifespans of Shem's Line

Shorter Lifespan Was Not a Universal Punishment.

Konrad Pellikan: Arpachshad lived 438 years; Shelah, 433; similarly, Eber, 464. From this it is clear that the period of 120 years had not been set for the lifespan of these people, but as punishment of those who had lived with Noah and sinned. Commentary on Genesis 11:13-15.[5]

Life Declines after the Flood.

Wolfgang Musculus: Notice in this genealogy of the holy fathers how the long lifespan of these ancestors, by which before the flood they lived to be 800 or 900, with some drawing close almost to 1000, after the flood begins to diminish and weaken. Shem did not equal the age of his father Noah, but fell 348 years short of him. Arpachshad, Shem's son, lived little more than half of his father's years. Peleg died much sooner than his forefather Shem by almost 400 years, and equaled barely half the age of his father Eber. Likewise, Reu, Serug and Terah lived barely a few years beyond 200. Finally, in Abraham human life waned so much that neither he, nor Isaac, nor Jacob lived to reach 200. Clearly, such diminution of life happened in the ten generations after the flood, so that within the

---

[2]*In Mosis Genesim* (1554), 285. [3]LW 2:228-29 (WA 42:423). [4]CTS 1:333* (CO 23:168). [5]*Commentaria Bibliorum* (1532) 1:15v; cf. Gen 6:3.

space of 292 years a lifespan declined from 600 to barely a century. The ten patriarchs who preceded the flood, from the beginning of the world up to the flood itself, are together reckoned at 1656 years. The ten in this chapter, who followed the flood up to the birth of Abraham, did not fill even three centuries and thus fell short of the first ten by 1364 years. This consideration reminds us of the great weakness of human life, so that though the succession of ages it is constantly worn down more and more, and the law of mortality is experienced more quickly than before. It happens, then, just as it was posed by the prophet in Psalm 90: the days of our lives scarcely reach seventy years, or at most, eighty. With our lives diminished and curtailed in this way, what are they like but a kind of wind or shadow that is briefly glimpsed as it passes and disappears? COMMENTARY ON GENESIS 11:10-26.[6]

GENEALOGIES TEACH US THE AGE OF THE WORLD. JOHN CALVIN: Moses now connects the names of these individuals with the years of their lifespan, lest we be ignorant of the age of the world. Indeed, if this brief description had not survived, people today would not know how much time intervened between the flood and the day when God made his covenant with Abraham. COMMENTARY ON GENESIS 11:10.[7]

AS CARNIVORES AND GLUTTONS, OUR LIVES ARE SHORTER. MARTIN LUTHER: This chapter points out that after men were permitted to eat meat, they became weaker, and that they began to beget children as well as to die at an earlier age. Having originally brought on our death by eating the fruit, we hasten our death by the variety of our food and by our gluttony. If we used plain foods, without foreign spices, which stimulate the appetite, we would undoubtedly enjoy a longer life. LECTURES ON GENESIS 11:10.[8]

DIDN'T THE LATER PATRIARCHS DIE? JOHANNES BRENZ: Although these patriarchs who are listed in the genealogy of Shem did not live as many years as the patriarchs before the flood, it remains the case that that usual phrase, "and he died," is not added as it was above. It is certainly the case that they did die, but Scripture does not add the phrase because it rushes on to Abraham, to whom Christ was promised—just like when you are in the midst of doing something and fail to see what is right before your eyes. And because the Holy Spirit, when he dictated these things, chiefly had Christ in view, who is our true and eternal life, he refrained from adding this little phrase . . . to the account of these patriarchs in order to signify that even if they died in the body, nonetheless—because wherever Christ is, there isn't death but life—they were said (one may infer) to be more alive than dead because they were so close to the promise of Christ, which was soon to be announced to Abraham. COMMENTARY ON GENESIS 11:10-26.[9]

SMALL GENEALOGICAL DISCREPANCIES ARE NOT IMPORTANT. PETER MARTYR VERMIGLI: In the Septuagint translation, you'll find an error in the reckoning of the numbers of those years, owing to a mistake on the part of the copyists. From this, different totals arise between the Hebrews and us, but . . . the Hebrews' computation is not to be disputed. The Septuagint also has one generation that is not listed here, in that it records that Arpachshad became the father of Cainan, when Shelah is nonetheless listed under him here by the Hebrew account. And when Luke 3 reverses the order of Christ's genealogy, ascending through these generations to Adam and God, he follows the Septuagint version and inserts that same Cainan. This is not to be regarded as a defect, for he would have

---

[6]*In Mosis Genesim* (1554), 284. [7]CTS 1:332-33* (CO 23:168).
[8]LW 2:231 (WA 42:425). [9]*Opera* 1:125.

been writing to Gentiles, and the Septuagint was the common version that would have been in everyone's hands. Besides, in genealogies it is not so important a matter that Luke should have been excessively worried about this detail. It was enough for him to faithfully

deliver those things that bring about our salvation through Christ. COMMENTARY ON GENESIS 11:27.[10]

---

[10]*In Primum Librum Mosis* (1569), 47r.

11:27-32 FROM TERAH TO ABRAM

²⁷*Now these are the generations of Terah. Terah fathered Abram, Nahor, and Haran; and Haran fathered Lot.* ²⁸*Haran died in the presence of his father Terah in the land of his kindred, in Ur of the Chaldeans.* ²⁹*And Abram and Nahor took wives. The name of Abram's wife was Sarai, and the name of Nahor's wife, Milcah, the daughter of Haran the father of Milcah and Iscah.* ³⁰*Now Sarai was barren; she had no child.*

³¹*Terah took Abram his son and Lot the son of Haran, his grandson, and Sarai his daughter-in-law, his son Abram's wife, and they went forth together from Ur of the Chaldeans to go into the land of Canaan, but when they came to Haran, they settled there.* ³²*The days of Terah were 205 years, and Terah died in Haran.*

OVERVIEW: In the wake of so many dismal turns in the history of the human race that Genesis 3–11 has chronicled, nothing could generate as much excitement as the gradual emergence of Abraham and Sarah from the gloomy shadows and judgments of the fall, the flood and the tower. For Paul, Abraham was "the father of all who believe without being circumcised so that righteousness would be counted to them as well" (Rom 4:11)—a message about justification by faith alone that was of paramount importance to Protestant Reformers.

But the origins of Abraham (here, still Abram) were by no means unclouded. Like their predecessors, Reformation commentators knew that Abram's father was tainted by idolatry: as Joshua 24:2 reported, Terah lived

"beyond the Euphrates" and "served other gods." What about Abram? Protestant exegetes proved to have no interest in sanitizing Abraham's past, especially since he was destined to be justified by faith and not by his works—much less, then, by his family tree.

Abraham's story is thus rooted foremost in the mercy of God, and that same mercy is manifested by the unlikely qualifications brought also by his wife Sarah (here, still Sarai), who for the moment is ingloriously characterized only by what she lacks: "Now Sarai was barren; she had no child." This is the sort of scenario relished by commentators of the Reformation era, for here the narrative tells of how the people of God begins with Abram as virtually a creation out of nothing:

An idolatrous father takes his son and a barren daughter-in-law into exile to live, essentially, as refugees. And then the father dies, leaving the unlikely couple dispossessed of everything—everything except a call and a promise. How could what God will do for Abraham offer anything but the greatest hope to the distressed churches of the Reformation?

11:27-28 Terah and Abram

A NEW WORLD AND A NEW CHURCH BEGIN WITH ABRAHAM. MARTIN LUTHER: It is true that at the time of Abraham many patriarchs were still alive; for Abraham was fifty-eight years old when Noah died, while Shem survived Abraham by thirty-one years, and some of his ancestors were alive after him. Nevertheless, it is correct for us to say that with Abraham a new world and a new church began; for with Abraham God begins once more to separate His church from all nations, and He adds a very clear promise concerning Christ, who was to bless all nations. Therefore it is also proper that we begin a new book at this point, where a new light comes from heaven. This light reveals that Christ will be born from the descendants of Abraham; and it makes the very sweet announcement concerning His ministry that He will bring a blessing for the world, that is, that He will atone for the sins of the world and thus reconcile us to God and give us eternal life. Added to this is the designation of the place where Christ is to be born. Because the land of Canaan is promised to the descendants of Abraham and Christ was to be born of the descendants of Abraham, it is sure that Christ will be born in the land of Canaan and from the Jews. This light the church did not have before Abraham. Therefore there now arises almost a new church, because a new Word is beginning to shed its light. LECTURES ON GENESIS 11:27-32.[1]

ABRAHAM, HOLIEST OF THE PATRIARCHS. JOHANNES BRENZ: Certainly, Abraham was by far the holiest of all the patriarchs. Even if he lingered among his idolatrous ancestors, as is written in Joshua 24, and was also (as it seems) somewhat soiled by his father's mania for idols, nonetheless, once he turned to the Lord and to knowledge of the true God, so great was his righteousness and piety through faith that he has been set forth as an example to all the nations of following after righteousness before God, just as Paul attests in Romans 4. Nor is there any patriarch in all of Scripture who surpasses Abraham in the dignity of his name. This is why even God calls himself by Abraham's name, saying, "I am the God of Abraham." But it is not to be supposed that Abraham was divinely commended either for his own sanctity or on account of the dignity of his descendants according to the flesh, but rather on account of Jesus Christ, who descended from the seed of Abraham. COMMENTARY ON GENESIS 11:27-32.[2]

MOSES IS INTERESTED LESS IN THE STORY'S ORDER THAN ITS MEANING. JOHN CALVIN: Here, Abram is placed first among his brothers, not because he was the firstborn (as far as I can tell), but because Moses, intent on his narrative's main point, was not very careful in the ordering of Terah's sons. Moreover, it could have happened that he begot other sons as well. But it is obvious why Moses made mention of these three in particular, namely, on account of Lot and the wives of Isaac and Jacob. COMMENTARY ON GENESIS 11:27.[3]

ABRAHAM'S FORMER IDOLATRY. ANDREW WILLET: As for whether Abraham was at any time infected with the superstition of the Chaldees, there are diverse opinions (as cited

---

[1]LW 2:236-37 (WA 42:430). [2]*Opera* 1:125. [3]CTS 1:335* (CO 23:169).

by Pererius). First, Suidas thinks that at age fourteen Abraham reproved his father for his idolatry. But it is not likely that Abraham, having been brought up under superstitious parents and not yet acquainted with God's voice, was so soon called in the absence of other means. Neither do I think (with Philo) that Abraham did not know God until "after he had changed" his country, when he was nearly seventy years old, or that Abraham nestled in superstition for so long. Nor do I agree with Josephus, that "by the observation of the stars," the earth and sea, Abraham first began to acknowledge the true God. For Abraham's first calling was from God, as the Lord says: "I took your father Abraham from beyond the flood" (Josh 24:3). God called him not only from that country but also from its idolatry. The opinion of some Hebrews is more probable, that Abraham at age forty-eight began to acknowledge the true God. But at what time of his life Abraham was called remains uncertain, although it *is* certain that at the first, before God called him, he was tainted with superstition. Joshua 24:2 seems to prove it directly: "Your fathers dwelt beyond the flood in old times, Terah, the father of Abraham and father of Nachor, and served strange gods." All those who dwelt beyond the river were idolaters at first, even the whole family of Terah (so Luther). God's mercy more notably appears in his having called Abraham first, before he knew God, in that the beginning of Abraham's calling was not his own sincerity but God's love. . . . Also, it is only likely that Abraham, having been brought up in a superstitious family, did likewise at his first taste of their superstition, and he is therefore bid to come out of his father's house (Gen 12:1). And seeing that Terah, Abraham's father, . . . was addicted to idolatry until he obeyed God's calling to go out of that country, it is more likely that Abraham too slept in the same sin until God roused him and called him away, than that he was never inclined to

idolatry (as Pererius thinks). COMMENTARY ON GENESIS 11:31.[4]

TERAH'S TEMPORARY DECEPTION. MARTIN LUTHER: Terah was deceived by the Nimrodic faction, departed from the faith with his household, and became an idolater. Yet when he was rebuked by the holy patriarch Shem, he decided that he had to give up the Nimrodic fellowship. LECTURES ON GENESIS 11:31-32.[5]

IF TERAH AND NAHOR WERE APOSTATES, ALL OTHERS MUST HAVE BEEN WORSE. JOHN CALVIN: When God brings it up as a reproach against the Jews that their fathers Terah and Nahor served strange gods, we should also be aware that the household of Shem, in which they were born, was God's special sanctuary, where pure religion should especially have flourished. What do we then suppose happened to the others, who could be seen as having been emancipated [from God's authority] from the very beginning? COMMENTARY ON GENESIS 11:10.[6]

11:29-30 Now Sarai Was Barren

WHY THE MATRIARCHS WERE SO OFTEN BARREN. KONRAD PELLIKAN: Almost all the mothers of holy offspring are described as naturally barren, in order to signify that nature produces nothing holy, but holy things proceed from God alone: namely, at a time when physical infirmity has clearly been made known and not before, lest they come to boast of their natural abilities. COMMENTARY ON GENESIS 11:30.[7]

AN UNLIKELY BLESSING ON AN UNLIKELY COUPLE. WOLFGANG MUSCULUS: External

---

[4]*Hexapla* (1608), 134-[35], quoting Philo, *On Abraham* 17.78, and Josephus, *Antiquities* 1.7.1 §156, and citing Chrysostom, *Homily 31.7 on Genesis* 11:31 (corrected; cf. FC 82:242). [5]LW 2:242 (WA 42:434). [6]CTS 1:333* (CO 23:168), citing Josh 24:2. [7]*Commentaria Bibliorum* (1532) 1:15v.

appearances may bear little resemblance to God's plans, in which he miraculously governs the things that concern his saints. Abram is called "exalted father." He had accepted this name, but not without the leading of the Holy Spirit, which afterwards was also increased within him by way of some assistance. Sarah is called "lady" and "princess." Those names called for the very thing that was divinely destined, namely, a great multitude of descendants. Yet their external fortune and position in life displayed nothing of all this. Indeed, Sarah was sterile, neither having nor expecting the sons by which there would be some proof of offspring. Similarly, without sons but with a sterile and barren wife, Abraham was an exalted father. Truly, in this way God wished to declare that the seed that Abraham was awaiting and of which he was going to be the father did not depend on an ability of the flesh but on the freedom and power of divine grace. Ishmael and Esau, sons of the flesh, did not belong to this seed; but the sons of grace and election, Isaac and Jacob, did. Hence, according to the truth of the apostolic teaching, no one is a son of Abraham except those who are of Abraham's faith, so that he might be the father of those who believe not only among the Hebrews but also among the Gentiles. COMMENTARY ON GENESIS 11:30.[8]

SARAI'S BARRENNESS WAS TO SHOW GOD'S POWER. ANDREW WILLET: Sarai's barrenness is noted not, as some Hebrews imagine, so that she should be reserved for the birth of Isaac and not be polluted with other births, for birth is no pollution of the womb; and if this were the reason, Isaac might have been the first-born. Neither was Sarai barren so that by this means Ishmael should be born of Hagar, to be a plague afterwards to the Israelites, as some Hebrews think. Rather, the reason was so that God's power might afterwards appear, in giving her a son in her old age. COMMENTARY ON GENESIS 11:30.[9]

11:31 Terah, Abram and Sarai Leave Ur

EXILE IS BETTER THAN LIFE WITH THE GODLESS. WOLFGANG MUSCULUS: It would seem to be a token of earthly happiness, to depart this life while still in the land of your birth, in your parental home with your father present, especially if some upheaval were going to transpire after your death. Such were the circumstances that befell the household of Terah after Haran's death, so that Terah and his family became exiles. But if what happened to Haran is rightly considered, it should be seen more as a matter of unhappiness than happiness: for in reality it is an unhappy thing to die in a land of impiety among the godless and idolators prior to the time of grace, and to be prevented from following the call of heavenly grace. I don't want to rush to judgment about the faith and salvation of Haran, but I do affirm that Abraham's exile would have been far happier, however distressing, than Haran's death, even though he died and was buried in his parents' land where he was born. COMMENTARY ON GENESIS 11:28.[10]

THOUGH THE CALL WAS HIS ALONE, ABRAHAM DEFERRED TO HIS FATHER. JOHN CALVIN: Terah was not so much the leader or author of the journey as the companion of his son. Nor is it an obstacle to this inference that Moses assigns first place to him, as if Abram had departed at his leading and direction rather than at God's command, for this is an honor conferred upon the father's name. Neither do I doubt that when Abram saw his father willingly obey God's calling, he himself offered compliance to his father in turn. For this reason, it is ascribed to the father's authority that he took his son with him. Indeed, that Abram had been called by God before he moved a foot from his native

---

[8]*In Mosis Genesim* (1554), 289. [9]*Hexapla* (1608), 133. [10]*In Mosis Genesim* (1554), 288.

soil will soon become more than clear, but we do not read that his father was called. It may be conjectured, therefore, that the divine oracle was disclosed to Terah by his son's report. Truly, God's command to depart did not prohibit Abram from bearing witness to his father that he was leaving him for no other reason than that he preferred God's authority more than all human obligations. COMMENTARY ON GENESIS 11:31.[11]

11:32 The Death of Terah

TERAH'S PROVIDENTIAL DEATH. WOLFGANG

MUSCULUS: It was not without God's special planning that Abraham's father Terah died in Haran, before they had come into Canaan. The land of Canaan was promised to Abraham and his seed, not to his father Terah. Wherefore, lest Abraham's special prerogative seem to derive not from God's special command but as an inheritance from his father, it rightly came to pass that Terah would not at all enter this promised land but would die in Arabia. COMMENTARY ON GENESIS 11:32.[12]

---

[11]CTS 1:338* (CO 23:171). [12]In Mosis Genesim (1554), 289.

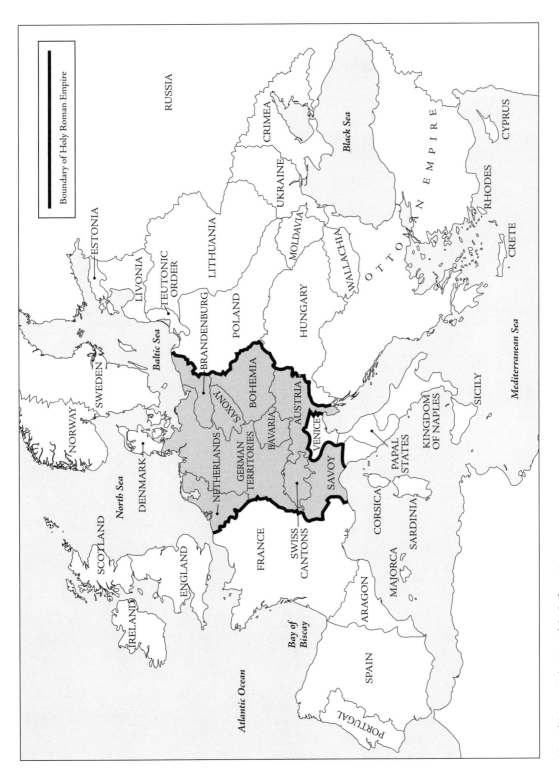

Map of Europe at the time of the Reformation

Timeline of the Reformation

	German Territories	France	Spain	Italy	Switzerland	Netherlands	British Isles
1337-1453		Hundred Years' War					Hundred Years' War
1378-1415		Western Schism (Avignon Papacy)		Western Schism			
1384							d. John Wycliffe
1414-1418							
1415				Council of Constance; d. Jan Huss			
1450	Invention of printing press						
1452				b. Leonardo da Vinci (d. 1519)			
1453				Fall of Constantinople			
1455-1485							War of Roses; Rise of House of Tudor
1456	Gutenberg Bible						
1460							
1466		b. Jacques Lafèvres d'Étaples (d. 1536)					
1467						b. Desiderius Erasmus (d. 1536)	b. John Colet (d. 1519)
1475				b. Michelangelo (d. 1564)			
1478	b. Wolfgang Capito (d. 1541)		Ferdinand and Isabella				b. Thomas More (d. 1535)
1480	b. Balthasar Hubmaier (d. 1528); b. Andreas Bodenstein von Karlstadt (d. 1541)						
1481-1530			Spanish Inquisition				
1482					b. Johannes Oecolampadius (d. 1531)		
1483	b. Martin Luther (d. 1546)						
1484					b. Huldrych Zwingli (d. 1531)		
1485	b. Johannes Bugenhagen (d. 1554)						b. Hugh Latimer (d. 1555)

	German Territories	France	Spain	Italy	Switzerland	Netherlands	British Isles
1486	r. Frederick the Wise, Elector (d. 1525); b. Johann Eck (d. 1543)						
1488							b. Miles Coverdale (d. 1568)
1489	b. Thomas Müntzer (d. 1525); b. Kaspar von Schwenckfeld (d. 1561)						b. Thomas Cranmer (d. 1556)
1491	b. Martin Bucer (d. 1551)		b. Ignatius Loyola (d. 1556)				
1492			Defeat of Moors in Grenada; Columbus discovers America; Explusion of Jews from Spain				
1494							b. William Tyndale (d. 1536)
1496	b. Andreas Osiander (d. 1552)					b. Menno Simons (d. 1561)	
1497	b. Philipp Melanchthon (d. 1560); b. Wolfgang Musculus (d. 1563)						
1498				d. Girolamo Savonarola	b. Conrad Grebel (d. 1526)		
1499	b. Johannes Brenz (d. 1570)			b. Peter Martyr Vermigli (d. 1562)			
1500			b. Charles V (-1558)				
1501	b. Erasmus Sarcerius (d. 1559)						
1502	Founding of University of Wittenberg				b. Heinrich Bullinger (d. 1575)		
1504							
1505	Luther joins Augustinian Order						
1506				Restoration to St. Peter's begins			
1507				Sale of indulgences approved to fund building			
1509		b. John Calvin (d. 1564)					r. Henry VIII (-1547)

	German Territories	France	Spain	Italy	Switzerland	Netherlands	British Isles
1510	Luther moves to Rome						b. Nicholas Ridley (d. 1555)
1511	Luther moves to Wittenberg						
1512				Sistene Chapel completed			
1512-1517				Fifth Lateran Council; rejection of conciliarism			
1513	Luther lectures on Psalms			r. Pope Leo X (-1521)			b. John Knox (d. 1572)
1515	Luther lectures on Romans	r. Francis I (-1547); b. Peter Ramus (d. 1572)					
1516		Est. French National Church (via Concordat of Bologna); b. Theodore Beza (d. 1605)		Concordat of Bologna		publication of Erasmus's Greek New Testament	
1517	Tetzel sells indulgences in Saxony; Luther's Ninety-five Theses						
1518	Heidelberg Disputation; Luther examined by Eck at Diet of Augsburg			Diet of Augsburg			
1519	Leipzig Disputation		Cortés conquers Aztecs; Portuguese sailor Magellan circumnavigates the globe		Zwingli appointed pastor of Grossmünster in Zurich; b. Rudolf Gwalther (d. 1576)		
1520	Publication of Luther's "Three Treatises"; Burning of papal bull in Wittenberg		Coronation of Charles V	Papal Bull v. Luther: *Exsurge Domine*			
1521	Luther excommunicated; Diet/Edict of Worms—Luther condemned; Luther in hiding; Melanchthon's *Loci Communes*	French-Spanish War (-1526)	French-Spanish War; Loyola converts	Papal excommunication of Luther			Henry VIII publishes *Affirmation of the Seven Sacraments* against Luther; awarded title "Defender of the Faith" by Pope
1521-1522	Disorder in Wittenberg; Luther translates New Testament						

	German Territories	France	Spain	Italy	Switzerland	Netherlands	British Isles
1521-1525		First and Second Habsburg–Valois War					
1522	Luther returns to Wittenberg; Luther's NT published; criticizes Zwickau prophets; b. Martin Chemnitz (d. 1586)		Publication of Complutensian Polyglot Bible under Cisneros		Sausage Affair & reform begins in Zurich under Zwingli		
1523	Knight's Revolt	Bucer begins ministry in Strasbourg	Loyola writes Spiritual Exercises	r. Pope Clement VII (-1534)	Iconoclasm in Zurich		
1524-1526	Peasants' War						
1524	Luther criticizes peasants					Erasmus's disputation on free will	
1525	Luther marries; execution of Thomas Müntzer				Abolition of mass in Zurich; disputation on baptism; first believers' baptism performed in Zurich		
1526					Zurich council mandates capital punishment of Anabaptists	Publication of Tyndale's English translation of NT	
1527				Sack of Rome by mutinous troops of Charles V	First Anabaptists beheaded in Zurich; drafting of Schleitheim Confession		
1528	Execution of Hubmaier						
1529	Second Diet of Speyer; evangelical "protest"; publication of Luther's catechisms; Marburg Colloquy; siege of Vienna by Turkish forces	Abolition of mass in Strasbourg					Thomas More appointed chancellor to Henry VIII
1530	Diet of Augsburg; Confession of Augsburg		Charles V crowned Holy Roman Emperor				
1531	Formation of Schmalkaldic League				d. H. Zwingli; succeeded by H. Bullinger		

	German Territories	France	Spain	Italy	Switzerland	Netherlands	British Isles
1532		Publication of Calvin's commentary on Seneca; conversion of Calvin					
1533		Nicholas Cop addresses University of Paris; Cop and Calvin implicated as "Lutheran" sympathizers					Thomas Cranmer appointed as Archbishop of Canterbury; Henry VIII divorces
1534	First edition of Luther's Bible published	Affair of the Placards; Calvin flees		Jesuits founded			Act of Supremacy; English church breaks with Rome
1535	Anabaptist theocracy at Münster collapses after eighteen months under siege						d. Thomas More; d. John Fisher
1536	Wittenberg Concord; b. Kaspar Olevianus (d. 1587)				First edition of Calvin's *Institutes* published; Calvin arrives in Geneva (-1538)	Publication of Tyndale's translation of NT; d. W. Tyndale	d. A. Boleyn; Henry VIII dissolves monasteries (-1541)
1537					Calvin presents ecclesiastical ordinances to Genevan Council		
1538					Calvin exiled from Geneva; arrives in Strasbourg (-1541)		
1539		Calvin publishes second edition of *Institutes* in Strasbourg					Statute of Six Articles; publication of Coverdale's Wheat Bible
1540				Papal approval of Jesuit order			d. Thomas Cromwell
1541	Colloquy of Regensberg	French translation of Calvin's *Institutes* published			d. A. Karlstadt; Calvin returns to Geneva (-1564)		
1542				Institution of Roman Inquisition			War between England and Scotland; James V of Scotland defeated; Ireland declared sovereign kingdom

	German Territories	France	Spain	Italy	Switzerland	Netherlands	British Isles
1543	Copernicus publishes *On the Revolutions of the Heavenly Spheres*						
1545-1547	Schmalkaldic Wars; d. Martin Luther			First session of Council of Trent			
1547	Defeat of Protestants at Mühlberg	d. Francis I; r. Henri II (-1559)					d. Henry VIII; r. Edward VI (-1553)
1548	Augsburg Interim (-1552)						
1549					Consensus Tigurinus between Calvin and Bullinger		First Book of Common Prayer published
1551-1552				Second session of Council of Trent			Cranmer's Forty-Two Articles
1553							Book of Common Prayer revised; d. Edward VI; r. Mary I (1558)
1554							Richard Hooker (d. 1600)
1555	Diet of Augsburg; Peace of Augsburg; establishes legal territorial existence of Lutheranism and Catholicism	First mission of French; pastors trained in Geneva					b. Robert Rollock (d. 1599); d. Hugh Latimer; d. Nicholas Ridley
1556			Charles V resigns			b. Sibbrand Lubbert (d. 1625)	d. Thomas Cranmer
1557					Michael Servetus executed in Geneva		Alliance with Spain in war against France
1558			d. Charles V				b. William Perkins (d. 1602); d. Mary I; r. Elizabeth I (-1603)
1559		d. Henry II; r. Francis II (-1560); first national synod of French reformed churches (1559) in Paris		First index of prohibited books issued	Final edition of Calvin's *Institutes*; founding of Genevan Academy	b. Jacobus Arminius (d. 1609)	Elizabethan Settlement
1560	d. P. Melanchthon	d. Francis II; r. Charles IX (1574); Edict of Toleration created peace with Huguenots					Kirk of Scotland established

	German Territories	France	Spain	Italy	Switzerland	Netherlands	British Isles
1561-1563				Third session of Council of Trent			
1561						Belgic Confession	
1562		Massacre of Huguenots begins French Wars of Religion (-1598)					
1563	Heidelberg Catechism						
1564				b. Galileo (d. 1642)	d. J. Calvin		b. William Shakespeare (d. 1616)
1566				Roman Catechism			
1567						Spanish occupation	Abdication of Scottish throne by Mary Stuart; r. James VI (-1603)
1568						Dutch movement for liberation (-1645)	
1570				Papal Bull *Regnans in Excelsis* excommunicates Elizabeth I			Elizabeth I excommunicated
1571	b. Johannes Kepler (d. 1630)		Spain defeats Ottoman navy at Battle of Lepanto				
1572		Massacre of Huguenots on St. Bartholomew's Day		r. Pope Gregory XIII (-1583)		William of Orange invades	
1574		d. Charles IX; r. Henri III (d. 1589)					
1576		Declaration of Toleration; formation of Catholic League		b. Giovanni Diodati (d. 1649)		Sack of Antwerp; Pacification of Ghent	
1577	Lutheran Formula of Concord						England allies with Netherlands against Spain
1578			Truce with Ottomans				Sir Francis Drake circumnavigates the globe
1579			Expeditions to Ireland			Division of Dutch provinces	
1580	Lutheran Book of Concord						

	German Territories	France	Spain	Italy	Switzerland	Netherlands	British Isles
1581			d. Teresa of Avila				Anti-Catholic statutes passed
1582				Gregorian Reform of calendar			
1583							b. David Dickson (d. 1663)
1584		Treaty of Joinville with Spain	Treaty of Joinville; Spain inducted into Catholic League; defeats Dutch at Antwerp			Fall of Antwerp; d. William of Orange	
1585		Henri of Navarre excommunicated		r. Pope Sixtus V (-1590)			
1586							Sir Francis Drake's expedition to West Indies; Sir Walter Raleigh in Roanoke
1587		Henri of Navarre defeats royal army					d. Mary Stuart of Scotland
1588		Henri of Navarre drives Henri III from Paris; assassination of Catholic League Leaders	Armada destroyed				English Mary defeats Spanish Armada
1589		d. Henri III; r. Henri (of Navarre) IV (-1610)	Victory over England at Lisbon				Defeated by Spain in Lisbon
1590		Henri IV's siege of Paris					Alliance with Henri IV
1593		Henri IV converts to Catholicism					
1594		Henri grants toleration to Huguenots					
1595		Henri IV declares war on Spain; received into Catholic Church		Pope Sixtus accepts Henri IV into Church			Alliance with France
1596		b. René Descartes (d. 1650)					
1598		Edict of Nantes; toleration of Huguenots; peace with Spain	Treaty of Vervins; peace with France				
1603							d. Elizabeth I; r. James I (James VI of Scotland) (-1625)

	German Territories	France	Spain	Italy	Switzerland	Netherlands	British Isles
1605						b. Rembrandt (d. 1669)	Guy Fawkes and gunpowder plot
1606							Jamestown Settlement
1607							b. John Milton (d. 1674)
1608							
1610		d. Henri IV; r. Louis XIII (-1643)					
1611							Publication of Authorized English Translation of Bible (AV/KJV)
1616							b. John Owen (d. 1683)
1617							b. Ralph Cudworth (d. 1689)
1618-1648	Thirty Years' War						
1618/19						Synod of Dort	
1620							English Puritans land in Massachusetts
1640				Diodati's Italian translation of Bible published			
1642-1649							English civil wars; d. Charles I; r. Oliver Cromwell (1660)
1643		d. Louis XIII; r. Louis XIV (-1715)					
1648		Treaty of Westphalia ends Thirty Years' War					
1660							English Restoration; d. Oliver Cromwell; r. Charles II (-1685)
1688							Glorious Revolution; r. William and Mary (-1702)

Biographical Sketches of Reformation-Era Figures

Johannes Aepinus (1499–1553). German preacher and theologian. Aepinus studied under Martin Luther,* Philipp Melanchthon* and Johannes Bugenhagen* in Wittenberg. Because of his Lutheran beliefs, Aepinus lost his first teaching position in Brandenburg. He fled north to Stralsund and became a preacher and superintendent at Saint Peter's Church in Hamburg. In 1534, he made a diplomatic visit to England but could not convince Henry VIII to embrace the Augsburg Confession. His works include sermons and theological writings. Aepinus became best known as leader of the Infernalists, who believed that Christ underwent torment in hell after his crucifixion.

Johann Agricola (c. 1494–1566). German pastor and theologian. Agricola studied under Martin Luther* and attended the Leipzig Disputation with him in 1519; he also participated in the burning of the papal bull held in 1520, both events painting him as a loyal Luther follower. Eventually Agricola strayed from Luther's distinction between law and gospel. He saw the gospel as the reason for recognition of sin, rather than the law. Luther responded by writing anonymous pamphlets debating the subject of antinomianism. Despite his aberrant view, Agricola refused to leave the Lutheran Church. To assuage relations, in 1540 Agricola moved to Berlin and published a recantation of his views. Doing so abated the public debate, but Luther and Agricola were never personally reconciled, even though Agricola continued to revere his former teacher. Agricola served as a catechist, the head of a grammar school, a preacher, a lecturer on the faculties of the University of Leipzig and Wittenberg, and a court chaplain.

Jacobus Arminius (1559–1609). Dutch pastor and theologian. Arminius was a vocal critic of high Calvinist scholasticism, whose views were repudiated by the synod of Dort (1618–1619). Arminius was a student of Theodore Beza* at the academy of Geneva. He served as a pastor in Amsterdam and later joined the faculty of theology at the university in Leiden, where his lectures on predestination were popular and controversial. Predestination, as Arminius understood it, was the decree of God determined on the basis of divine foreknowledge of faith or rejection by humans who are the recipients of prevenient, but resistible, grace.

Richard Baxter (1615–1691). English Puritan minister. Baxter was a leading Puritan pastor, evangelist and theologian, known throughout England for his landmark ministry in Kidderminster and a prodigious literary output, producing 135 books in just over forty years. Baxter came to faith through reading William Perkins,* Richard Sibbes and other early Puritan writers and was the first cleric to decline the terms of ministry in the national English church imposed by the 1662 Act of Uniformity; Baxter wrote on behalf of the more than 1700 who shared ejection from the national church. He hoped for restoration to national church ministry, or toleration, that would allow lawful preaching and pastoring. Baxter sought unity in theological, ecclesiastical, sociopolitical and personal terms and is regarded as a forerunner of Noncomformist ecumenicity, though he was defeated in his efforts at the 1661 Savoy Conference to take seriously Puritan objections to the revision of the 1604 Prayer Book. Baxter's views on church ministry were considerably hybrid: he was a paedobaptist, Nonconformist minister who approved of synodical Episcopal government and fixed liturgy. He is most known for his classic writings on the Christian life, such as *The Saints' Everlasting Rest* and *A Christian Directory*, and pastoral ministry, such as *The Reformed Pastor*. He also produced *Catholick Theology*, a large volume squaring current Reformed, Lutheran, Arminian and Roman Catholic systems with each other.

Theodore Beza (1516–1605). French pastor and professor. Beza was compatriot and successor to John Calvin* as leader of the French Reformed ecclesial communities. He was a noteworthy New Testament scholar whose *Codex Bezae* formed the basis of the New Testament section of the English Geneva Bible (1560). A leader in the academy and the church, Beza served as rector at the Lausanne and Geneva academies. He enjoyed an international reputation through his correspondence with key European leaders. Beza developed and extended Calvin's doctrinal thought on several important themes such as the nature of predestination and the real presence of Christ in the Eucharist.

Georg Blaurock (1492–1529). Swiss Anabaptist. Blaurock (a nickname meaning "blue coat," because of his preference for this garment) was one of the first leaders of Switzerland's radical reform movement. In the first public disputations on baptism in Zurich, he argued for believer's baptism and was the first person to receive adult believers' baptism there, having been baptized by Conrad Grebel* in 1525. Blaurock was arrested several times for performing mass adult baptisms and engaging in social disobedience by disrupting worship services. He was eventually expelled from Zurich but continued preaching and baptizing in various Swiss cantons until his execution.

Thieleman Jans van Braght (1625–1664). Dutch Mennonite preacher. After demonstrating great ability with languages, this cloth merchant was made preacher in his hometown of Dordrecht in 1648. He served in this office for the next sixteen years, until his death. This celebrated preacher had a reputation for engaging in debate wherever an opportunity presented itself, particularly concerning infant baptism. The publication of his book of martyrs, *Het Bloedigh Tooneel of Martelaersspiegel* (1660; *Martyrs' Mirror*), proved to be his lasting contribution to the Mennonite tradition. *Martyrs' Mirror* is heavily indebted to the earlier martyr book *Offer des Heeren* (1562), to which Braght added many early church martyrs who rejected infant baptism, as well as over 800 contemporary martyrs.

Johannes Brenz (1499–1570). German Lutheran reformer and pastor. Brenz was converted to the reformation cause after hearing Martin Luther* speak; later, Brenz became a student of Johannes Oecolampadius.* His central achievement lay in his talent for organization. As city preacher in Schwäbisch-Hall and afterward in Württemberg and Tübingen, he oversaw the introduction of reform measures and doctrines and new governing structures for ecclesial and educational communities. Brenz also helped establish

Lutheran orthodoxy through treatises, commentaries and catechisms. He defended Luther's position on eucharistic presence against Huldrych Zwingli* and opposed the death penalty for religious dissenters.

Guillaume Briçonnet (1470–1534). French abbot and bishop. Briçonnet created a short-lived circle of reformist-minded humanists in his diocese under the sponsorship of Marguerite d'Angoulême. His desire for ecclesial reform developed throughout his prestigious career (including positions as royal chaplain to the queen, abbot at Saint-Germain-des-Prés and bishop of Meaux), influenced by Jacques Lefèvre d'Étaples.* Briçonnet encouraged reform through ministerial visitation, Scripture and preaching in the vernacular and active study of the Bible. When this triggered the ire of the theology faculty at the Sorbonne in Paris, Briçonnet quelled the activity and departed, envisioning an ecclesial reform that proceeded hierarchically.

Martin Bucer (1491–1551). German Reformed theologian and ecclesiastical leader. A Dominican friar, Bucer was influenced by Desiderius Erasmus* during his doctoral studies at the University of Heidelberg, where he began corresponding with Martin Luther.* After advocating reform in Alsace, Bucer was excommunicated and fled to Strasbourg, where he became a leader in the city's Reformed ecclesial and educational communities. Bucer sought concord between Lutherans and Zwinglians and Protestants and Catholics. He emigrated to England, becoming a professor at Cambridge. Bucer's greatest theological concern was the centrality of Christ's sacrificial death, which achieved justification and sanctification and orients Christian community.

Johannes Bugenhagen (1485–1558). German Lutheran pastor and professor. Bugenhagen, a priest and lecturer at a Premonstratensian monastery, became a city preacher in Wit-

tenberg during the reform efforts of Martin Luther* and Philipp Melanchthon.* Initially influenced by his reading of Desiderius Erasmus,* Bugenhagen grew in evangelical orientation through Luther's works; later, he studied under Melanchthon at the University of Wittenberg, eventually serving as rector and faculty member there. Bugenhagen was a versatile commentator, exegete and lecturer on Scripture. Through these roles and his development of lectionary and devotional material, Bugenhagen facilitated rapid establishment of church order throughout many German provinces.

Heinrich Bullinger (1504–1575). Swiss Reformed pastor and theologian. Bullinger succeeded Huldrych Zwingli* as minister and leader in Zurich. A primary author of the First and Second Helvetic Confessions (1536; 1566), Bullinger was drawn toward reform through the works of Martin Luther* and Philipp Melanchthon.* After Zwingli died, Bullinger was vital in maintaining adherence to the cause of reform; he oversaw the expansion of the Zurich synodal system while preaching, teaching and writing extensively. One of Bullinger's lasting legacies was the development of a federal view of the divine covenant with humanity, making baptism and the Eucharist covenantal signs.

John Bunyan (1628–1688). English Nonconformist preacher and writer. Bunyan was an English Puritan Independent, or Congregationalist, a noted preacher and beloved writer, whose *Pilgrim's Progress* is one of the best-selling English-language titles in history. Born to a working-class family, Bunyan was largely unschooled, gaining literacy (and entering the faith) through reading the Bible and such early Puritan devotional works as *The Plain Man's Pathway to Heaven* and *The Practice of Piety*. Following a short stint in Cromwell's parliamentary army, in which Bunyan narrowly escaped death in combat, he turned to a preaching ministry, succeeding John Gifford as pastor at the Congregational church in Bedford. A noted preacher, Bunyan drew large crowds in itinerant appearances and it was in the sermonic form that Bunyan developed his theological outlook, which was an Augustinian-inflected Calvinism. Bunyan's opposition to the Book of Common Prayer and refusal of official ecclesiastical licensure led to multiple imprisonments, where he wrote many of his famous allegorical works, including *Pilgrim's Progress*, *The Holy City*, *Prison Meditations* and *Holy War*.

Cardinal Cajetan (Thomas de Vio) (1469–1534). Italian Catholic cardinal, professor, theologian and biblical exegete. This Dominican monk was the leading Thomist theologian and one of the most important Catholic exegetes of the sixteenth century. Cajetan is best-known for his interview with Martin Luther* at the Diet of Augsburg (1518). Among his many works are polemical treatises, extensive biblical commentaries and most importantly a four-volume commentary (1508–1523) on the *Summa Theologiae* of Thomas Aquinas.

Georg Calixtus (1586–1656). German Lutheran theologian. Calixtus studied at the University of Helmstedt where he developed regard for Philipp Melanchthon.* Between his time as a student and later as a professor at Helmstedt, Calixtus traveled through Europe seeking a way to unite and reconcile Lutherans, Calvinists and Catholics. He attempted to fuse these denominations through use of the Scriptures, the Apostles' Creed, and the first five centuries, interpreted by the Vincentian canon. Calixtus's position was stamped as syncretist and yielded further debate even after his death.

John Calvin (1509–1564). French Reformed pastor and theologian. In his *Institutes of the Christian Religion*, Calvin provided a theological dogmatics for the Reformed churches. Calvin's gradual conversion to the cause of reform occurred through his study with chief humanist scholars in Paris, but he spent most of his career in Geneva (excepting a three-year exile in Strasbourg with Martin Bucer*). In Geneva, Calvin reorganized the structure and governance of the church and established an academy that became an international center for theological education. He was a tireless writer, producing his *Institutes*, theological treatises and Scripture commentaries.

Wolfgang Capito (1478?–1541). German humanist, reformer and theologian. Capito, a Hebrew scholar, produced a Hebrew grammar and published several Latin commentaries on books of the Hebrew Scriptures. He corresponded with Desiderius Erasmus* and fellow humanists. Capito translated Martin Luther's* early works into Latin for the printer Johann Froben. On meeting Luther, Capito was converted to Luther's vision, left Mainz and settled in Strasbourg, where he lectured on Luther's theology to the city clergy. With Martin Bucer,* Capito reformed liturgy, ecclesial life and teachings, education, welfare and government. Capito worked for the theological unification of the Swiss cantons with Strasbourg.

Martin Chemnitz (1522–1586). German Lutheran theologian. A leading figure in establishing Lutheran orthodoxy, Chemnitz studied theology and patristics at the University of Wittenburg, later becoming a defender of Philipp Melanchthon's* interpretation of the doctrine of justification. Chemnitz drafted a compendium of doctrine and reorganized the structure of the church in Wolfenbüttel; later, he led efforts to reconcile divisions within Lutheranism, culminating in the Formula of Concord (1577). One of his chief theological accomplishments was a modification of the christological doctrine of the *communicatio idiomatium*, which provided a Lutheran platform for understanding the sacramental presence of Christ's humanity in the Eucharist.

David Chytraeus (1531–1600). German Lutheran professor, theologian, and biblical exegete. At the age of eight Chytraeus was admitted to the University of Tübingen. There he studied law, philology, philosophy, and theology, finally receiving his master's degree in 1546. Chytraeus befriended Philipp Melanchthon* while sojourning in Wittenberg, where he taught the *Loci communes*. While teaching exegesis at the University of Rostock Chytraeus became acquainted with Tilemann Heshusius*, who strongly influenced Chytraeus away from Philippist theology. As a defender of Gnesio-Lutheran theology Chytraeus helped organize churches throughout Austria in accordance with the Augsburg Confession. Chytraeus coauthored the Formula of Concord (1577) with Martin Chemnitz*, Andreas Musculus*, Nikolaus Selnecker* and Jakob Andreae (1528–1590). He wrote commentaries on most of the Bible, as well as a devotional work titled *Regula vitae* (1555) that described the Christian virtues.

John Colet (1467–1519). English Catholic priest, preacher and educator. Colet, appointed dean of Saint Paul's Cathedral by Henry VII, was a friend of Desiderius Erasmus*, on whose classical ideals Colet reconstructed the curriculum of Saint Paul's school. Colet was convinced that the foundation of moral reform lay in the education of children. Though an ardent advocate of reform, Colet, like Erasmus, remained loyal to the Catholic Church throughout his life. Colet's agenda of reform was oriented around spiritual and ethical themes, demonstrated in his commentaries on select books of the New Testament and the writings of Pseudo-Dionysius the Areopagite.

Miles Coverdale (1488–1568). English reformer and bishop. Coverdale is known for his translations of the Bible into English, completing William Tyndale's* efforts and later producing the Great Bible commissioned by Henry VIII (1539). A former friar, Coverdale was among the Cambridge scholars who met at the White Horse Tavern to discuss Martin Luther's* ideas. During Coverdale's three terms of exile in Europe, he undertook various translations, including the Geneva Bible (1560). He was appointed bishop of Exeter by Thomas Cranmer* and served as chaplain to Edward VI. Coverdale contributed to Cranmer's first edition of the Book of Common Prayer (1549).

Thomas Cranmer (1489–1556). English archbishop and theologian. Cranmer supervised church reform and produced the first two editions of the Book of Common Prayer (1549; 1552). As a doctoral student at Cambridge, he was involved in the discussions at the White Horse Tavern. Cranmer contributed to a religious defense of Henry VIII's divorce; Henry then appointed him Archbishop of Canterbury. Cranmer cautiously steered the course of reform, accelerating under Edward VI. After supporting the attempted coup to prevent Mary's assuming the throne, Cranmer was convicted of treason and burned at the stake. Cranmer's legacy is the splendid English of his liturgy and prayer books.

Caspar Cruciger (1504–1548). German Lutheran theologian. Recognized for his alignment with the theological views of Philipp Melanchthon,* Cruciger was a scholar respected among both Protestants and Catholics. In 1521, Cruciger came Wittenberg to study Hebrew and remained there most of his life. He became a valuable partner for Martin Luther* in translating the Old Testament and served as teacher, delegate to major theological colloquies and rector. Cruciger was an agent of reform in his birthplace of Leipzig, where at the age of fifteen he had observed the disputation between Luther and Johann Eck.*

Hans Denck (c. 1500–1527). German Anabaptist and radical reformer. Denck, a crucial early figure of the German Anabaptist movement, combined medieval German mysticism with the radical sacramental theology of Andreas Bodenstein von Karlstadt* and Thomas Müntzer.* Denck argued that the exterior forms of Scripture and sacrament are symbolic witnesses secondary to the internally revealed truth of the Sprit in the human soul. This view led to his expulsion from Nuremberg in 1525; he spent the next two years in various centers of reform in the German territories. At the time of his death, violent persecution against Anabaptists was on the rise throughout northern Europe.

David Dickson (1583?–1663). Scottish pastor, preacher, professor and theologian. Dickson defended the Presbyterian form of ecclesial reformation in Scotland and was recognized for his iteration of Calvinist federal theology and expository biblical commentaries. Dickson served for over twenty years as professor of philosophy at the University of Glasgow before being appointed professor of divinity. He opposed the imposition of Episcopalian measures on the church in Scotland and was active in political and ecclesial venues to protest and prohibit such influences. Dickson was removed from his academic post following his refusal of the oath of supremacy during the Restoration era.

Giovanni Diodati (1576–1649). Italian reformer and translator. Diodati was from an Italian banking family who fled for religious reasons to Geneva. There he trained under Theodore Beza*; on completion of his doctoral degree, Diodati became professor of Hebrew at the academy. He was an ecclesiastical representative of the church in Geneva (for whom he was a delegate at the Synod of Dordrect in 1618) and a toiler for reform in Venice. Diodati's chief contribution to the Italian reform movement was a translation of the Bible into Italian (1640–1641), which remains the standard translation in Italian Protestantism.

Johann Eck (Johann Maier of Eck) (1486–1543). German Catholic theologian. Though Eck was not an antagonist of Martin Luther*

until the dispute over indulgences, Luther's Ninety-five Theses (1517) sealed the two as adversaries. After their debate at the Leipzig Disputation (1519), Eck participated in the writing of the papal bull that led to Luther's excommunication. Much of Eck's work was written to oppose Protestantism or to defend Catholic doctrine and the papacy; his *Enchiridion* was a manual written to counter Protestant doctrine. He participated in the assemblies at Regensburg and Augsburg and led the Catholics in their rejection of the Augsburg Confession.

Desiderius Erasmus (1466–1536). Dutch humanist and pedagogue. Erasmus, a celebrated humanist scholar, was recognized for translations of ancient texts, reform of education according to classical studies, moral and spiritual writings and the first printed edition of the Greek New Testament. A former Augustinian who never left the Catholic Church, Erasmus addressed deficiencies he saw in the church and society, challenging numerous prevailing doctrines but advocating reform. He envisioned a simple, spiritual Christian life shaped by the teachings of Jesus and ancient wisdom. He was often accused of collusion with Martin Luther* on account of some resonance of their ideas but hotly debated Luther on human will.

Paul Fagius (1504–1549). German Reformed Hebraist and pastor. After studying at the University of Heidelberg, Fagius went to Strasbourg where he perfected his Hebrew under Wolfgang Capito.* In Isny im Allgäu (Baden-Württemberg) he met the great Jewish grammarian Elias Levita (1469–1549), with whom he established a Hebrew printing press. In 1544 Fagius returned to Strasbourg, succeeding Capito as preacher and Old Testament lecturer. During the Augsburg Interim, Fagius (with Martin Bucer*) accepted Thomas Cranmer's* invitation to translate and interpret the Bible at Cambridge. However, Fagius died before he could begin any of the work. Fagius wrote commentaries on the first four chapters of Genesis and the deutero-canonical books of Sirach and Tobit.

Sebastian Franck (1499–1542). German theologian and radical reformer. Franck became a Lutheran in 1525, but by 1529 he began to develop ideas that distanced him from Protestants and Catholics. Expelled from Strasbourg and later Ulm due to his controversial writings, Franck spent the end of his life in Basel. Franck emphasized God's word as a divine internal spark that cannot be adequately expressed in outward forms. Thus he criticized religious institutions and dogmas. His work consists mostly of commentaries, compilations and translations. In his sweeping historical *Chronica* (1531), Franck supported numerous heretics condemned by the Catholic Church and criticized political and church authorities.

Johann Gerhard (1582–1637). German Lutheran theologian, professor and superintendent. Gerhard is considered one of the most eminent Lutheran theologians, after Martin Luther* and Martin Chemnitz.* After studying patristics and Hebrew at Wittenberg, Jena and Marburg, Gerhard was appointed superintendent at the age of twenty-four. In 1616 he was appointed to a post at the University of Jena, where he reintroduced Aristotelian metaphysics to theology and gained widespread fame. His most important work was the nine-volume *Loci Theologici* (1610–1625). He also expanded Chemnitz's harmony of the Gospels (*Harmonia Evangelicae*), which was finally published by Polykarp Leyser* in 1593. Gerhard was well-known for an irenic spirit and an ability to communicate clearly.

Conrad Grebel (c. 1498–1526). Swiss radical reformer. Grebel, considered the father of the Anabaptist movement, was one of the first defenders and performers of believers' baptism, for which he was eventually imprisoned in Zurich. One of Huldrych Zwingli's*

early compatriots, Grebel advocated rapid, radical reform, clashing publicly with the civil authorities and Zwingli. Grebel's views, particularly on baptism, were influenced by Andreas Bodenstein von Karlstadt* and Thomas Müntzer.* Grebel advocated elimination of magisterial involvement in governing the church; instead, he envisioned the church as lay Christians determining their own affairs with strict adherence to the biblical text, and unified in volitional baptism.

William Greenhill (1591–1671). English nonconformist clergyman. Greenhill attended and worked at Magdalen College. He ministered in the diocese of Norwich but soon left for London, where he preached at Stepney. Greenhill was a member of the Westminster Assembly of Divines and was appointed the parliament chaplain by the children of Charles I. Oliver Cromwell included him among the preachers who helped draw up the Savoy Declaration. Greenhill was evicted from his post following the Restoration, after which he pastored independently. Among Greenhill's most significant contributions to church history was his *Exposition of the Prophet of Ezekiel*.

Rudolf Gwalther (1519–1586). Swiss preacher and reformer. Gwalther was a consummate servant of the Reformed church in Zurich, its chief religious officer and preacher, a responsibility fulfilled previously by Huldrych Zwingli* and Heinrich Bullinger.* Gwalther provided sermons and commentaries and translated the works of Zwingli into Latin. He worked for many years alongside Bullinger in structuring and governing the church in Zurich. Gwalther also strove to strengthen the connections to the Reformed churches on the Continent and England: he was a participant in the Colloquy of Regensburg (1541) and an opponent of the Formula of Concord (1577).

Balthasar Hubmaier (1480/5–1528). German Anabaptist reformer. Hubmaier, a former priest who studied under Johann Eck,* is identified with his leadership in the peasants' uprising at Waldshut. Hubmaier served as the cathedral preacher in Regensberg, where he became involved in a series of anti-Semitic attacks. He was drawn to reform through the early works of Martin Luther*; his contact with Huldrych Zwingli* made Hubmaier a defender of more radical reform, including believers' baptism and a memorialist account of the Eucharist. His involvement in the Peasants' War led to his extradition and execution by the Austrians.

Hans Hut (1490–1527). German Anabaptist. Hut was an early leader of a mystical, apocalyptic strand of Anabaptist radical reform. His theological views were shaped by Andreas Bodenstein von Karlstadt,* Thomas Müntzer* and Hans Denck,* by whom Hut had been baptized. Hut rejected society and the established church and heralded the imminent end of days, which he perceived in the Peasants' War. Eventually arrested for practicing believers' baptism and participating in the Peasants' War, Hut was tortured and died accidentally in a fire in the Augsburg prison. The next day, the authorities sentenced his corpse to death and burned him.

David Joris (c. 1501–1556). Dutch radical reformer and hymnist. This former glass painter was one of the leading Dutch Anabaptist leaders after the fall of Münster (1535), although due to his increasingly radical ideas his influence waned in the early 1540s. Joris came to see himself as a "third David," a Spirit-anointed prophet ordained to proclaim the coming third kingdom of God, which would be established in the Netherlands with Dutch as its *lingua franca*. Joris's interpretation of Scripture, with his heavy emphasis on personal mystical experience, led to a very public dispute with Menno Simons* whom Joris considered a teacher of the "dead letter." In 1544 Joris and about one hundred followers moved to Basel, conforming outwardly to the teaching of the Reformed church there. Today 240 of Joris's

books are extant, the most important of which is his *Twonder Boek* (1542/43).

Andreas Bodenstein von Karlstadt (Carlstadt) (1486–1541). German reformer and theologian. Karlstadt, an early associate of Martin Luther* and Philipp Melanchthon* at the University of Wittenberg, participated alongside Luther in the dispute at Leipzig with Johann Eck.* He also influenced the configuration of the Old Testament canon in Protestantism. During Luther's captivity in Wartburg Castle in Eisenach, Karlstadt oversaw reform in Wittenberg. His acceleration of the pace of reform brought conflict with Luther, so Karlstadt left Wittenberg, eventually settling at the University of Basel as professor of Old Testament (after a sojourn in Zurich with Huldrych Zwingli*). During his time in Switzerland, Karlstadt opposed infant baptism and repudiated Luther's doctrine of Christ's real presence in the Eucharist.

John Knox (1513–1572). Scottish preacher and reformer. Knox, a fiery preacher to monarchs and zealous defender of high Calvinism, was a leading figure of reform in Scotland. Following imprisonment in the French galleys, Knox went to England, where he became a royal chaplain to Edward VI. At the accession of Mary, Knox fled to Geneva, studying under John Calvin* and serving as a pastor. Knox returned to Scotland after Mary's death and became a chief architect of the reform of the Scottish church (Presbyterian), serving as one of the authors of the Book of Discipline and writing many pamphlets and sermons.

François Lambert (Lambert of Avignon) (1487–1530). French reformer and theologian. In 1522, after becoming drawn to the writings of Martin Luther* and meeting Huldrych Zwingli,* Lambert left the Franciscan order. He spent time in Wittenberg, Strasbourg, and Hesse, where Lambert took a leading role at the Homberg Synod (1526) and in creating a biblically based plan for church reform. He served as professor of theology at Marburg University from 1527 to his death. After the Marburg Colloquy (1529), Lambert accepted Zwingli's symbolic view of the Eucharist. Lambert produced nineteen books, mostly biblical commentaries that favored spiritual interpretations; his unfinished work of comprehensive theology was published posthumously.

Hugh Latimer (c. 1485–1555). English bishop, preacher and reformer. Latimer was celebrated for his sermons critiquing the idolatrous nature of Catholic practices and the social injustices visited on the underclass by the aristocracy and the individualism of Protestant government. After his support for Henry's petition of divorce he served as a court preacher under Henry VIII and Edward VI. Latimer became a proponent of reform following his education at Cambridge University and received license as a preacher. Following Edward's death, Latimer was tried for heresy, perishing at the stake with Nicholas Ridley* and Thomas Cranmer.*

Jacques Lefèvre d'Étaples (Faber Stapulensis) (1460?–1536). French humanist, publisher and translator. Lefèvre d'Étaples studied classical literature and philosophy, as well as patristic and medieval mysticism. He advocated the principle of *ad fontes*, issuing a full-scale annotation on the corpus of Aristotle, publishing the writings of key Christian mystics, and contributing to efforts at biblical translation and commentary. Although he never broke with the Catholic Church, his views prefigured those of Martin Luther,* for which he was condemned by the University of Sorbonne in Paris. He then found refuge in the court of Marguerite d'Angoulême, where he met John Calvin* and Martin Bucer.*

Sibrandus Lubbertus (c. 1555–1625). Dutch Calvinist reformer and theologian. Lubbertis, a key figure in the establishment of orthodox Calvinism in Frisia, studied theology at Wittenburg and Geneva (under Theodore Beza*)

before his appointment as professor of theology at the University of Franeker. Throughout his career, Lubbertis advocated for high Calvinist theology, defending it in disputes with representatives of Socinianism, Arminianism and Roman Catholicism. Lubbertis criticized the Catholic theologian Robert Bellarmine and fellow Dutch reformer Jacobus Arminius*; the views of the latter he opposed as a prominent participant in the Synod of Dort (1618–1619).

Martin Luther (1483–1546). German priest, professor, reformer and theologian. While a professor in Wittenberg, Luther reinterpreted the doctrine of justification. Convinced that righteousness comes only from God's grace, he disputed the sale of indulgences with the Ninety-five Theses. Luther's positions brought conflict with Rome; his denial of papal authority led to excommunication. He also challenged the Mass, transubstantiation and communion under one kind. Though Luther was condemned by the Diet of Worms, the Elector of Saxony provided him safe haven. Luther returned to Wittenberg with public order collapsing under Andreas Bodenstein von Karlstadt*; Luther steered a more cautious path of reform. His rendering of the Bible and liturgy in the vernacular, as well as his hymns and sermons, proved extensively influential.

Georg Major (1502–1574). German Lutheran theologian. Major was on the theological faculty of the University of Wittenberg, succeeding as dean Johannes Bugenhagen* and Philipp Melanchthon.* One of the chief editors on the Wittenberg edition of Luther's works, Major is most identified with the controversy bearing his name, in which he stated that good works are necessary to salvation. Major qualified his statement, which was in reference to the totality of the Christian life. The Formula of Concord rejected the statement, ending the controversy. As a theologian, Major further refined Lutheran views of the inspiration of Scripture and the doctrine of the Trinity.

Thomas Manton (1620–1677). English Nonconformist minister. Manton, educated at Oxford, was a Nonconformist minister, serving for a time as lecturer at Westminster Abbey and rector of St. Paul's, Covent Garden, and was a strong advocate of Presbyterianism. He was known as a rigorous evangelical Calvinist who preached long expository sermons. At different times in his ecclesial career he worked side-by-side with Richard Baxter* and John Owen.* In his later life, Manton's Nonconformist position led to his ejection as a clergyman from the Church of England (1662) and eventual imprisonment (1670). Although a voluminous writer, Manton was best known for his preaching. At his funeral in 1677, he was dubbed "the king of preachers."

Pilgram Marpeck (c. 1495–1556). Austrian Anabaptist elder and theologian. During a brief sojourn in Strasbourg, Marpeck debated with Martin Bucer* before the city council; Bucer was declared the winner, and Marpeck was asked to leave Strasbourg for his views concerning paedobaptism (which he compared to a sacrifice to Moloch). After his time in Strasbourg, Marpeck travelled throughout southern Germany and western Austria, planting Anabaptist congregations. Marpeck criticized the strict use of the ban, however, particularly among the Swiss brethren. He also engaged in a Christological controversy with Kaspar Schwenckfeld.*

John Mayer (1583–1664). Anglican priest and biblical exegete. Mayer dedicated much of his life to biblical exegesis, writing a seven-volume commentary on the entire Bible (1627–1653). Styled after Philipp Melanchthon's* *locus* method, Mayer's work avoided running commentary, focusing instead on textual and theological problems. He was a parish priest for fifty-five years. In the office of priest Mayer also wrote a popular catechism, *The English Catechisme, or a Commentarie on the Short Catechisme* (1621), which went through twelve editions in his lifetime.

Joseph Mede (1586–1638). Anglican biblical scholar, Hebraist and Greek lecturer. A man of encyclopedic knowledge, Mede was interested in numerous fields, varying from philology and history to mathematics and physics, although millennial thought and apocalyptic prophesy were clearly his chief interests. Mede's most important work was his *Clavis Apocalyptica* (1627, later translated into English as *The Key of the Revelation*). This work examined the structure of Revelation as the key to its interpretation. Mede saw the visions as a connected and chronological sequence hinging around Revelation 17:18. He is remembered as an important figure in the history of millenarian theology. He was respected as a mild-mannered and generous scholar who avoided controversy and debate, but who had many original thoughts.

Philipp Melanchthon (1497–1560). German educator, reformer and theologian. Melanchthon is known as the partner and successor to Martin Luther* in reform in Germany and for his pioneering *Loci Communes*, which served as a theological textbook. Melanchthon participated with Luther in the Leipzig disputation, helped implement reform in Wittenberg and was a chief architect of the Augsburg Confession. Later, Melanchthon and Martin Bucer* worked for union between the reformed and Catholic churches. On account of Melanchthon's more ecumenical disposition and his modification of several of Luther's doctrines, he was held in suspicion by some.

Johannes Mercerus (Jean Mercier) (d. 1570). French Hebraist. Mercerus studied under the first Hebrew chair at the Collège Royal de Paris, François Vatable (d. 1547), whom he succeeded in 1546. John Calvin* tried to recruit Mercerus to the Genevan Academy as professor of Hebrew, once in 1558 and again in 1563; he refused both times. During his lifetime Mercerus published grammatical helps for Hebrew and Chaldean, an aid to the Masoretic symbols in the Hebrew text, and translated the commentaries and grammars of several medieval rabbis. He himself wrote commentaries on Genesis, the wisdom books, and most of the Minor Prophets. These commentaries—most of them only published after his death—were philologically focused and interacted with the work of Jerome, Nicholas of Lyra,* notable rabbis and Johannes Oecolampadius.*

Sebastian Münster (1489–1552). German Reformed Hebraist, exegete, printer, and geographer. After converting to the Reformation in 1524, Münster taught Hebrew at the universities of Heidelberg and Basel. During his lengthy tenure in Basel he published more than 70 books, including Hebrew dictionaries and rabbinic commentaries. He also produced an evangelistic work for Jews titled *Vikuach* (1539). Münster's *Torat ha-Maschiach* (1537), the Gospel of Matthew, was the first published Hebrew translation of any portion of the New Testament. Despite his massive contribution to contemporary understanding of the Hebrew language, Münster was criticized by many of the Reformers as a judaizer.

Thomas Müntzer (c. 1489–1525). German radical reformer. As a preacher in the town of Zwickau, Müntzer was influenced by German mysticism and, growing convinced that Martin Luther* had not carried through reform properly, sought to restore the pure apostolic church of the New Testament. Müntzer's radical ideas led to expulsions from various cities; he developed a highly apocalyptic theology, in which he heralded the last days that would establish the pure community out of suffering, prompting Müntzer's proactive role in the Peasants' War, which he perceived as a crucial apocalyptic event. Six thousand of Müntzer's followers were annihilated by magisterial troops; Müntzer was executed.

Wolfgang Musculus (1497–1563). Pastor, reformer and theologian from Lorraine. Musculus produced translations, biblical commentaries and an influential theological text, *Loci Communes Sacrae Theologiae* (*Commonplaces of Sacred Theology*), outlining a Zwinglian theology. Musculus began to study theology while at a Benedictine monastery; he departed in 1527 and became secretary to Martin Bucer* in Strasbourg. He was later installed as a pastor in Augsburg, eventually performing the first evangelical liturgy in the city's cathedral. Though Musculus was active in the pursuit of the reform agenda, he was also concerned for ecumenism, participating in the Wittenberg Concord (1536) and discussions between Lutherans and Catholics.

Nicholas of Lyra (1270–1349). French Franciscan and biblical exegete. Very little is known about this influential medieval theologian of the Sorbonne aside from the works he published, particularly the *Postilla litteralis super totam Bibliam* (1322–1333). With the advent of the printing press this work was regularly published alongside the Latin Vulgate and the *Glossa ordinaria*. In this running commentary on the Bible Nicholas promoted literal interpretation as the basis for theology. Despite his preference for literal interpretation, Nicholas also published a companion volume, the *Postilla moralis super totam Bibliam* (1339), a commentary on the spiritual meaning of the biblical text. Nicholas was a major conversation partner for many Reformers (Luther, for example), though many of them rejected his exegesis as too literal and too "Jewish" (not concerned enough with the Bible's fulfillment in Jesus Christ).

Johannes Oecolampadius (Johannes Huszgen) (1482–1531). Swiss-German humanist, reformer and theologian. Oecolampadius (an assumed name meaning "house light") assisted with Desiderius Erasmus's* Greek New Testament, lectured on biblical languages and exegesis and completed an influential Greek grammar. After joining the evangelical cause through studying patristics and the work of Martin

Luther,* Oecolampadius went to Basel, where he lectured on biblical exegesis and participated in ecclesial reform. On account of Oecolampadius's effort, the city council passed legislation restricting preaching to the gospel and releasing the city from compulsory Mass. Oecolampadius was a chief ally of Huldrych Zwingli,* whom he supported at the Marburg Colloquy (1529).

Kaspar Olevianus (1536–1587). German Calvinist reformer and theologian. Olevianus is celebrated for composing the Heidelberg Catechism and producing a critical edition of Calvin's *Institutes* in German. Olevianus studied theology with many, including John Calvin,* Theodore Beza,* Heinrich Bullinger* and Peter Martyr Vermigli.* As an advocate of Reformed doctrine, Olevianus oversaw the shift from Lutheranism to Calvinism throughout Heidelberg, organizing the city's churches after Calvin's Geneva. The Calvinist ecclesial vision of Olevianus entangled him in a dispute with another Heidelberg reformer over the rights of ecclesiastical discipline, which Olevianus felt belonged to the council of clergy and elders rather than civil magistrates.

John Owen (1616–1683). English Puritan theologian. Owen trained at Oxford University, where he was later appointed dean of Christ Church and vice chancellor of the university, following his service as chaplain to Oliver Cromwell. Although Owen began his career as a Presbyterian minister, he eventually departed to the party of Independents. Owen composed many sermons, biblical commentaries (including seven volumes on the book of Hebrews), theological treatises and controversial monographs (including disputations with Arminians, Anglicans, Catholics and Socinians).

Christoph Pelargus (1565–1633). German Lutheran pastor, theologian, professor and superintendent. Pelargus studied philosophy and theology at the University of Frankfurt an der Oder, in Brandenburg. This irenic Philippist was appointed as the superintendent of

Brandenburg and later became a pastor in Frankfurt, although the local authorities first required him to condemn Calvinist theology, because several years earlier he had been called before the consistory in Berlin under suspicion of being a crypto-Calvinist. Among his most important works were a four-volume commentary on *De orthodoxa fide* by John of Damascus (d. 749), a treatise defending the breaking of the bread during communion, and a volume of funeral sermons. He also published commentaries on the Pentateuch, the Psalms, Matthew, John and Acts.

Konrad Pellikan (1478–1556). German Reformed Hebraist and theologian. Pellikan attended the University of Heidelberg, where he mastered Hebrew under Johannes Reuchlin. In 1504 Pellikan published one of the first Hebrew grammars that was not merely a translation of the work of medieval rabbis. While living in Basel, Pellikan assisted the printer Johannes Amerbach, with whom he published some of Luther's* early writings. He also worked with Sebastian Münster* and Wolfgang Capito* on a Hebrew Psalter (1516). In 1526, after teaching theology for three years at the University of Basel, Huldrych Zwingli* brought Pellikan to Zurich to chair the faculty of Old Testament. Pellikan's magnum opus is a seven-volume commentary on the entire Bible (except Revelation) and the Apocrypha.

Benedict Pererius (1535–1610). Spanish Jesuit theologian, philosopher and exegete. Pererius entered the Society of Jesus in 1552. He taught philosophy, theology, and exegesis at the Roman College of the Jesuits. Early in his career he warned against neo-Platonism and astrology in his *De principiis* (1576). Pererius wrote a lengthy commentary on Daniel, and five volumes of exegetical theses on Exodus, Romans, Revelation and part of the Gospel of John (chs. 1–14). His four-volume commentary on Genesis (1591–1599) was lauded by Protestants and Catholics alike.

William Perkins (1558–1602). English Puritan preacher and theologian. Perkins was a highly regarded Puritan Presbyterian preacher and biblical commentator in the Elizabethan era. He studied at Cambridge University and later became a fellow of Christ's Church college as a preacher and professor, receiving acclaim for his sermons and lectures. Even more, Perkins gained an esteemed reputation for his ardent exposition of Calvinist reformed doctrine in the style of Petrus Ramus,* becoming one of the first English reformed theologians to achieve international recognition. Perkins influenced the federal Calvinist shape of Puritan theology and the vision of logical, practical expository preaching.

Dirk Philips (1504–1568). Dutch Anabaptist elder and theologian. This former Franciscan monk, known for being severe and obstinate, was a leading theologian of the sixteenth-century Anabaptist movement. Despite the fame of Menno Simons* and his own older brother Obbe, Philips wielded great influence over Anabaptists in the Netherlands and northern Germany where he ministered. As a result of Philips's understanding of the apostolic church as radically separated from the children of the world, he advocated a very strict interpretation of the ban, including formal shunning. His writings were collected and published near the end of his life as *Enchiridion oft Hantboecxken van de Christelijcke Leere* (1564).

Petrus Ramus (1515–1572). French humanist philosopher and reformer. Ramus was an influential professor of philosophy and logic at the French royal college in Paris; he converted to Protestantism and left France for Germany, where he came under the influence of Calvinist thought. Ramus was a trenchant critic of Aristotle and noted for his method of classification based on a deductive movement from universals to particulars, the latter becoming branching divisions that provided a visual chart of the parts to the whole. His system profoundly

influenced Puritan theology and preaching. After returning to Paris, Ramus died in the Saint Bartholomew's Day Massacre.

Nicholas Ridley (1502?–1555). English bishop and reformer. Ridley was a student and fellow at Cambridge University who was appointed chaplain to Archbishop Thomas Cranmer* and is thought to be partially responsible for Cranmer's shift to a symbolic view of the Eucharist. Cranmer promoted Ridley twice: as bishop of Rochester, where he openly advocated Reformed theological views, and, later, as bishop of London. Ridley assisted Cranmer in the revisions of the Book of Common Prayer. Ridley's support of Lady Jane Grey against the claims of Mary to the throne led to his arrest; he was tried for heresy and burned at the stake with Hugh Latimer.*

Peter Riedemann (1506–1556). German Hutterite elder, theologian and hymnist. While traveling as a Silesian cobbler, Riedemann came into contact with Anabaptist teachings and joined a congregation in Linz. In 1529 he was called to be a minister, only to be imprisoned soon after as part of Archduke Ferdinand's efforts to suppress heterodoxy in his realm. Once he was released, he moved to Moravia in 1532 where he was elected as a minister and missionary of the Hutterite community there. His *Account of Our Religion, Doctrine and Faith* (1542), with its more than two thousand biblical references, is Riedemann's most important work and is still used by Hutterites today.

Robert Rollock (1555?–1599). Scottish pastor, educator and theologian. Rollock was deeply influenced by Petrus Ramus's* system of logic, which he implemented as a tutor and (later) principal of Edinburgh University and in his expositions of the Bible. Rollock, as a divinity professor and theologian, was instrumental in diffusing a federalist Calvinism in the Scottish church; he lectured on theology using the texts of Theodore Beza* and articulated a highly covenantal interpretation of the biblical narratives. He was a prolific writer of sermons, expositions, commentaries, lectures and occasional treatises.

Erasmus Sarcerius (1501–1559). German Lutheran ecclesial leader, educator and pastor. Sarcerius served as educational superintendent, court preacher and pastor in Nassau and, later, in Leipzig. The hallmark of Sarcerius's reputation was his ethical emphasis as exercised through ecclesial oversight and family structure; he also drafted disciplinary codes for regional churches in Germany. Sarcerius served with Philipp Melanchthon* as Protestant delegates at the Council of Trent (1552), though both withdrew prior to the dismissal of the session; he eventually became an opponent of Melanchthon, contesting the latter's understanding of the Eucharist at a colloquy in Worms in 1557.

Anna Maria van Schurman (1607–1678). Dutch Reformed polymath. Van Schurman cultivated talents in art, poetry, botany, linguistics and theology. She mastered most contemporary European languages, in addition to Latin, Greek, Hebrew, Arabic, Farsi and Ethiopian. With the encouragement of leading Reformed theologian Gisbertus Voetius (1589–1676), van Schurman attended lectures at the University of Utrecht—although she was required to sit behind a wooden screen so that the male students could not see her. In 1638 van Schurman published her famous treatise advocating female scholarship, *Amica dissertatio . . . de capacitate ingenii muliebris ad scientias*. In addition to these more polemical works, van Schurman also wrote hymns and poems, including a paraphrase of Genesis 1–3. Later in life she became a devotee of Jean de Labadie (1610–1674), a former Jesuit who was also expelled from the Reformed church for his separatist leanings. Her *Eucleria* (1673) is the most well known defense of Labadie's theology.

Nikolaus Selnecker (1530–1592). German

Lutheran theologian, preacher, pastor and hymnist. Selnecker taught in Wittenberg, Jena and Leipzig, preached in Dresden and Wolfenbüttel, and pastored in Leipzig. He was forced out of his post at Jena because of suspicions that he was a crypto-Calvinist. He sought refuge in Wolfenbüttel, where he met Martin Chemnitz* and Jakob Andreae (1528–1590). Under their influence Selnecker was drawn away from Philippist theology. Selnecker's shift in theology can be seen in his *Institutio religionis christianae* (1573). Selnecker coauthored the Formula of Concord (1577) with Chemnitz, Andreae, Andreas Musculus,* and David Chytraeus.* Selnecker also published lectures on Genesis, the Psalms, and the New Testament epistles, as well as composing over a hundred hymn tunes and texts.

Menno Simons (c. 1496–1561). Dutch Anabaptist leader. Simons led a separatist Anabaptist group in the Netherlands that would later be called Mennonites, known for nonviolence and renunciation of the world. A former priest, Simons rejected Catholicism through the influence of Anabaptist disciples of Melchior Hoffmann and based on his study of Scripture, in which he found no support for transubstantiation or infant baptism. Following the sack of Anabaptists at Münster, Simons committed to a nonviolent way of life. Simons proclaimed a message of radical discipleship of obedience and inner purity, marked by voluntary adult baptism and communal discipline.

Cyriacus Spangenberg (1528–1604). German Lutheran pastor, preacher and theologian. Spangenberg was a staunch, often acerbic, Gnesio-Lutheran. He rejected the Formula of Concord because of concerns about the princely control of the church, as well as its rejection of Flacian language of original sin (as constituting the "substance" of human nature after the fall). He published many commentaries and sermons, most famously seventy wedding sermons (*Ehespiegel* [1561]), his sermons on Luther* (*Theander Luther* [1562–1571]) and Luther's hymns (*Cithara Lutheri* [1569–1570]). He also published an analysis of the Old Testament (though he only got as far as Job), based on a methodology that anticipated the logical bifurcations of Peter Ramus (1515–1572).

Daniel Toussain (1541–1602). Swiss Reformed pastor and professor. Toussain became pastor at Orléans after attending college in Basel. After the third War of Religion, Toussain was exiled, eventually returning to Montbéliard, his birthplace. In 1571, he faced opposition there from the strict Lutheran rulers and was eventually exiled due to his influence over the clergy. He returned to Orléans but fled following the Saint Bartholomew's Day Massacre (1572), eventually becoming pastor in Basel. He relocated to Heidelberg in 1583 as pastor to the new regent, becoming professor of theology at the university, and he remained there until his death.

William Tyndale (Hychyns) (1494–1536). English reformer, theologian and translator. Tyndale was educated at Oxford University, where he was influenced by the writings of humanist thinkers. Believing that piety is fostered through personal encounter with the Bible, he asked to translate the Bible into English; denied permission, Tyndale left for the Continent to complete the task. His New Testament was the equivalent of a modern-day bestseller in England but was banned and ordered burned. Tyndale's theology was oriented around justification, the authority of Scripture and Christian obedience; Tyndale emphasized the ethical as a concomitant reality of justification. He was martyred in Brussels before completing his English translation of the Old Testament, which Miles Coverdale* finished.

Juan de Valdés (1500/10–1541). Spanish theologian and writer. Although Valdés adopted an evangelical doctrine, had Erasmian affiliations and published works that were listed on the Index of Prohibited Books, Valdés rebuked the reformers for creating disunity and never left the Catholic Church. His writings included translations of the Hebrew Psalter and various biblical books, a work on the Spanish language and several commentaries. Valdés fled to Rome in 1531 to escape the Spanish Inquisition and worked in the court of Clement VII in Bologna until the pope's death in 1534. Valdés subsequently returned to Naples, where he led the reform- and revival-minded Valdesian circle.

Peter Martyr Vermigli (1499–1562). Italian humanist, reformer and theologian. Vermigli was one of the most influential theologians of the era, held in common regard with such figures as Martin Luther* and John Calvin.* In Italy, Vermigli was a distinguished theologian, preacher and advocate for moral reform; however, during the reinstitution of the Roman Inquisition Vermigli fled to Protestant regions in northern Europe. He was eventually appointed professor of divinity at Oxford University, where Vermigli delivered acclaimed disputations on the Eucharist. Vermigli was widely noted for his deeply integrated biblical commentaries and theological treatises.

Johann Wigand (1523–1587). German Lutheran theologian. Wigand is most noted as one of the compilers of the *Magdeburg Centuries*, a German ecclesiastical history of the first thirteen centuries of the church. He was a student of Philipp Melanchthon* at the University of Wittenburg and became a significant figure in the controversies dividing Lutheranism. Strongly opposed to Roman Catholicism, Wigand lobbied against innovations in Lutheran theology that appeared sympathetic to Catholic thought. In the later debates, Wigand's support for Gnesio-Lutheranism established his role in the development of confessional Lutheranism. Wigand was appointed bishop of Pomerania after serving academic posts at the universities in Jena and Königsburg.

Andrew Willet (1562–1621). Anglican priest, professor, and biblical expositor. Willet was a gifted biblical expositor and powerful preacher. He walked away from a promising university career in 1588 when he was ordained a priest in the Church of England. For the next thirty-three years he served as a parish priest. Willet's commentaries summarized the present state of discussion while also offering practical applications for preachers. They have been cited as some of the most technical commentaries of the early seventeenth century. His most important publication was *Synopsis Papismi, or a General View of Papistrie* (1594), in which he responded to many of Robert Bellarmine's critiques. After years of royal favor, Willet was imprisoned in 1618 for a month after presenting to King James I his opposition to the "Spanish Match" of Prince Charles to the Infanta Maria. While serving as a parish priest, he wrote forty-two works, most of which were either commentaries on books of the Bible or controversial works against Catholics.

Girolamo Zanchi (1516–1590). Italian Reformed theologian and pastor. Zanchi joined an Augustinian monastery at the age of fifteen, where he studied Greek and Latin, the church fathers and the works of Aristotle and Thomas Aquinas. Under the influence of his prior, Peter Martyr Vermigli,* Zanchi also imbibed the writings of the Swiss and German reformers. To avoid the Inquisition, Zanchi fled to Geneva where he was strongly attracted to the preaching and teaching of John Calvin.* Zanchi taught biblical theology and the *locus* method at academies in Strasbourg, Heidelberg, and Neustadt. He also served as pastor of an Italian refugee congregation. Zanchi's theological works, *De tribus Elohim* (1572) and

De natura Dei (1577), have received more attention than his commentaries. His commentaries comprise about a quarter of his literary output, however, and display a strong typological and Christological interpretation in conversation with the church fathers, medieval exegetes, and other reformers.

Katharina Schütz Zell (1497/98–1562). German Reformed writer. Zell became infamous in Strasbourg and the Empire when in 1523 she married the priest Matthias Zell,* and then published an apology defending her husband against charges of impiety and libertinism. Longing for a united church, she called for toleration of Catholics and Anabaptists, famously writing to Martin Luther* after the failed Marburg Colloquy of 1529 to exhort him to check his hostility and to be ruled instead by Christian charity. Much to the chagrin of her contemporaries, Zell published diverse works, ranging from polemical treatises on marriage to letters of consolation, as well as editing a hymnal and penning an exposition of Psalm 51.

Huldrych Zwingli (1484–1531). Swiss humanist, preacher, reformer and theologian. Zwingli, a parish priest, was influenced by the writings of Desiderius Erasmus* and taught himself Greek. While a preacher to the city cathedral in Zurich, Zwingli enacted reform through sermons, public disputations and conciliation with the town council, abolishing the Mass and images in the church. Zwingli broke with the lectionary preaching tradition, instead preaching serial expository biblical sermons. He later was embroiled in controversy with Anabaptists over infant baptism and with Martin Luther* at the Marburg Colloquy (1529) over their differing views of the Eucharist. Zwingli, serving as chaplain to Zurich's military, was killed in battle.

BIBLIOGRAPHY

Primary Sources and Translations Used

Brenz, Johannes. *Operum Reverendi et Clarissimi Theologi, D. Ioannis Brentii, Praepositi Stutgardiani Tomus Primus [- Octavus]*. 8 vols. Tübingen: George Gruppenbach, 1576-1590.

> Brenz's 1553 commentary on Genesis appears in the first volume of his eight-volume *Opera*, on pp. 1-348. Digital copy online at http://www.mdz-nbn-resolving.de/urn/resolver.pl?urn=urn:nbn:de:bvb:12-bsb 10142717-2.

Cajetan, Cardinal (Thomas de Vio). *Commentarii illustres planeque insignes in Quinque Mosaicos libros*. Paris: Guillaume de Bossozel, 1539.

> Digital copy online at Google Books. First printed in 1531 as *Omnes Authenticos Veteris Testamenti historiales libros, & Iob, Commentarii* (Rome); also incorporated into Cajetan's *Opera Omnia qvotqvot in Sacrae Scripturae Expositionem Reperiuntur*, 5 vols. (Lyons: Jean and Pierre Prost, 1639).

Calvin, John. *In Primum Mosis Librum, qui Genesis vulgo dicitur*. Geneva, 1554.

> Modern edition in CO 23 (1882); digital copy online at http://archive-ouverte.unige.ch/Calvin/ bf_433x_51.pdf. Note that Calvin's works are being newly edited in the *Calvini Opera Denuo Recognita* (Geneva: Droz, 1992-).

——. *Commentaries on the First Book of Moses, Called Genesis*. Translated by John King. 2 vols. Edinburgh: Calvin Translation Society, 1847.

> Digital copy online at http://www.ccel.org, among other places; excerpts here represent revisions of King's ET. Calvin's commentary on Genesis was also translated into English in 1578, by Thomas Tymme (STC² 4393).

——. *Institutes of the Christian Religion* (1559). Edited by John T. McNeill. Translated by Ford Lewis Battles. Library of Christian Classics 20-21. Philadelphia: Westminster, 1960.

> Latin text available in OS 3-5 and CO 2.

Capito, Wolfgang. *Hexemeron Dei Opus*. Strasbourg: Wendelin Rihelius, 1539.

> Digital copy accessed via DLCPT.

Chytraeus, David. *In Genesin enarratio, recens recognita a Davide Chytraeo*. Wittenberg: Johannes Crato, 1557, 1561, 1568, 1576.

> The 1576 edition was used here, but the 1568 edition was consulted where pages were missing or where textual readings were problematic. Digital copy (1568) online at http://nbn-resolving.de/ urn:nbn:de:gbv:3:1-111572.

Denck, Hans. "Reflections on the Book of the Prophet Micah (1532)." In *Selected Writings of Hans Denck*, edited by E. J. Furcha, 35-181. Lewiston, NY: Edwin Mellen, 1989.

Erasmus, Desiderius. *Tomus secundus paraphraseon Des. Erasmi Roterodami in Reliquum Novi Testamenti, nempe in omnes epistolas Apostolicas.* Basel: Froben, 1541.
> Digital copy online at http://dx.doi.org/10.3931/e-rara-4004. Erasmus's *Paraphrases* first appeared between 1517 and 1524; his paraphrases of 1 Peter and the Epistle to the Hebrews, excerpted here, appeared in 1521.

———. *The seconde tome or volume of the Paraphrase of Erasmus vpon the Newe Testament conteynyng the epistles of S. Paul, and other the Apostles: wherunto is added a paraphrase vpon the reuelacion of S. John.* London: Edwarde Whitchurche, 1549. STC² 2854.7.
> Accessed digitally via EEBO; the sixteenth-century translation of Erasmus's *Paraphrases.* The excerpts I have translated here have also been translated and annotated by John J. Bateman in CWE 44 (1993): *Paraphrases on the Epistles to Timothy, Titus, and Philemon, the Epistles of Peter and Jude, the Epistle of James, the Epistles of John, the Epistle to the Hebrews.*

Hubmaier, Balthasar. *Balthasar Hubmaier: Theologian of Anabaptism.* Edited and translated by H. Wayne Pipkin and John H. Yoder. Classics of the Radical Reformation 5. Waterloo, ON: Herald Press, 1989.
> Treatises excerpted here include *The Opinion of the Ancient and New Teachers That One Should Not Baptize Young Children until They Have Been Instructed in the Faith* (1526), *A Christian Catechism* (1526) and *On the Freedom of the Will* (1527).

Joris, David. "Of the Wonderful Working of God, 1535." In *The Anabaptist Writings of David Joris, 1535-1543*, edited and translated by Gary K. Waite, 109-25. Classics of the Radical Reformation 7. Waterloo, ON: Herald Press, 1993.

Karlstadt, Andreas Bodenstein von. *The Essential Carlstadt: Fifteen Tracts by Andreas Bodenstein (Carlstadt) from Karlstadt.* Classics of the Radical Reformation 8. Edited and translated by E. J. Furcha. Waterloo, ON: Herald Press, 1995.
> Treatises excerpted here include his *Regarding Vows* (1522) and *Regarding the Sabbath and Statutory Holy Days* (1524).

Luther, Martin. *In Primum Librum Mose Enarrationes, Reverendi Patris D. D. Martini Lutheri, plenae salutaris & Christianae eruditionis, bona fide & diligenter collectae.* Wittenberg: Peter Seitz, 1544.
> Luther lectured on Genesis from 1535 until late in 1545; this, the first volume of his lectures to appear in print, covered Genesis 1–11. The best modern edition of the Latin text, used here, is WA 42.

———. *Lectures on Genesis.* Edited by Jaroslav Pelikan. Translated by George V. Schick et al. Luther's Works 1-8. St. Louis: Concordia, 1958-1966.
> Excerpts here on Genesis 1–11 are from LW 1-2 and used by special arrangement with Concordia Publishing House. An older ET, covering only chapters 1–9, is that of John Nicholas Lenker, *Luther on the Creation: A Critical and Devotional Commentary on Genesis* [1–3] (Minneapolis: Lutherans in All Lands, 1904), and *Luther on Sin and the Flood: Commentary on Genesis* [4–9] (Minneapolis: The Luther Press, 1910); digital copies available at http://www.archive.org.

Marpeck, Pilgram. *The Writings of Pilgram Marpeck.* Edited and translated by William Klassen and Walter Klaassen. Classics of the Radical Reformation 2. Kitchener, ON: Herald Press, 1978.
> Treatises excerpted here include his *Clear Refutation, Confession* (1532), *Letter: "Judgment and Decision," Men in Judgment and the Peasant Aristocracy* and *Concerning the Love of God in Christ.*

Melanchthon, Philipp. *In obscuriora aliquot capita Geneseos Phil. Melanchth. Annotationes.* Hagenau: Johann Setzer, 1523.
> These notes cover only Genesis 1–6. Modern edition in MO 13 (1846); digital copy available at http://www.archive.org.

Musculus, Wolfgang. *In Mosis Genesim plenissimi Commentarii, in quibus veterum & recentiorum sententiae diligenter expenduntur.* Basel: Johann Herwagen, 1554.
> The 1554 edition is cited here (IDC microfiche). The 1565 edition was accessed via DLCPT, also online at Google Books.

———. *In Divi Pauli Epistolas ad Philippenses, Colossenses, Thessalonicenses ambas, & primam ad Timotheum, Commentarii.* Basel: Johann Herwagen, 1565.
> Complete through 1 Timothy 3. The 1565 edition is cited here (IDC microfiche). Digital copy of 1578 edition accessed via DLCPT, also online at Google Books.

———. *Loci communes in usus S. Theologiae Candidatorum parati.* Basel: Johann Herwagen, 1560.
> Digital copy online at http://www.mdz-nbn-resolving.de/urn/resolver.pl?urn=urn:nbn:de:bvb:12-bsb10144108-2; the 1599 edition was also consulted via DLCPT.

———. *Common Places of Christian Religion.* Translated by John Man. London: Henry Bynneman, 1578. STC[2] 18309.
> Accessed digitally via EEBO; the sixteenth-century translation of Musculus's *Loci Communes* (above). This translation was first published in 1563 (STC[2] 18308).

Oecolampadius, Johannes. *D. Io. Oecolampadii in Genesim Enarratio.* Basel: [Johann Bebel], 1536.
> Accessed by IDC microfiche. ET of chapters 1–3 by Mickey L. Mattox is forthcoming from Marquette University Press.

Pelargus, Christophor. *In Prophetarum omnium Oceanum, sive Genesin Sacram Mosaicam ex antiquitate puriore magna parte erutus Commentarius.* Leipzig: Nicolaus Nerlingus, 1598.
> The second edition is cited here (Leipzig: [Abraham Lamberg], 1612), accessed by a digital copy of the exemplar in the Pitts Theology Library at Emory University (Atlanta).

Pellikan, Konrad. *Commentaria Bibliorum et illa brevia quidem ac Catholica.* 5 vols. Zürich: Christoph Froschauer, 1532-1535.
> Vol. 1 (1532) accessed by IDC microfiche. Digital copies of some volumes are online at Google Books.

Perkins, William. *An Exposition of the Symbole, or Creed of the Apostles.* In *The workes of that famous and vvorthie minister of Christ, in the Vniuersitie of Cambridge, M. W. Perkins.* 3 vols. [Cambridge:] John Legate, 1608-1609. STC[2] 19649.
> Digital copy accessed at EEBO; Perkins's *Exposition of the Creed* comprises pp. 119-329 of vol. 1.

Philips, Dirk. *The Writings of Dirk Philips, 1504-1568.* Edited and translated by Cornelius J. Dyck, William E. Keeney and Alvin J. Beachy. Classics of the Radical Reformation 6. Waterloo, ON: Herald Press, 1992.
> Treatises excerpted here include his *Enchiridion* and *About the Marriage of Christians.*

Riedemann, Peter. *Peter Riedemann's Hutterite Confession of Faith: Translation of the 1565 German Edition of "Confession of Our Religion, Teaching, and Faith, by the Brothers Who Are Known as the Hutterites."* Edited and translated by John J. Friesen. Classics of the Radical Reformation 9. Waterloo, ON: Herald Press, 1999.
> Riedemann's confession was originally written in the early 1540s while in prison.

Schurman, Anna Maria van. *Uitbreiding over de drie eerste capittels van Genesis*. Gronigen: Jacob Sipkes, 1732.
> Translated from IDC microfiche by Albert Gootjes and John L. Thompson; original poem dates to c. 1660.

Selnecker, Nikolaus. *In Genesin, primum librum Moysi, commentarius*. Leipzig: [Johannes Rhamba], 1569.
> Digital copy online at http://www.mdz-nbn-resolving.de/urn/resolver.pl?urn=urn:nbn:de:bvb:12-bsb10142973-0; also at Google Books.

Simons, Menno. *The Complete Works of Menno Simon*. 2 vols. bound as 1. Elkhart, IN: John F. Funk & Brother, 1871.
> Digital copy available at http://www.archive.org. The 1871 edition, used here, undergirds much of the 1956 edition, which often merely repunctuates the earlier edition; see *The Complete Writings of Menno Simons, c.1496-1561*, edited by J. C. Wenger. Scottdale, PA: Herald Press, 1956. Treatises excerpted here include his *Confession* [against John a Lasco], *Confession of the Poor and Distressed Christians*, *The Cross of the Saints*. Note that titles of Menno's treatises are often inconsistently rendered in English.

———. *Opera Omnia Theologica, of Alle de Godtgeleerde Wercken*. 1681. Reprint ed. Amsterdam: Joannes van Veen, 1989.
> Digital copy available at Google Books.

Spangenberg, Cyriacus. *In Sacri Mosis Pentatevchvm, Sive quinque Libros, Genesim, Exodum, Leuiticum, Numeros, Deuteronomium, Tabvlae CCVI*. Basel: Johannes Oporinus, 1563.
> Digital copy online at http://diglib.hab.de/drucke/b-41-2f-helmst-1/start.htm.

Vermigli, Peter Martyr. *In Primum Librum Mosis, qui vulgo genesis dicitur commentarii doctissimi*. Zürich: Froschauer, 1569.
> Accessed by IDC microfiche; digital copy available at DLCPT, also at http://dx.doi.org/10.3931/e-rara-5004. Vermigli's Genesis commentary derives from lectures given in Strasbourg in the early 1540s. ET by Daniel Shute and John Patrick Donnelly is forthcoming as part of the Peter Martyr Library.

———. *In selectissimam S. Pauli priorem ad Corinth. epistolam . . . commentarii doctissimi*. Zurich: Froschauer, 1551.
> Accessed by IDC microfiche; digital copy of 1578 edition available at DLCPT.

Willet, Andrew. *Hexapla in Genesin, that is, A Sixfold Commentary upon Genesis*. London: Thomas Creede, for John Norton, 1605. STC² 25682.
> A digital copy of the second edition is cited here (1608, STC² 25683), accessed by EEBO and DLCPT.

Zell, Katharina Schütz. *Church Mother: The Writings of a Protestant Reformer in Sixteenth-Century Germany*. Edited and translated by Elsie McKee. The Other Voice in Early Modern Europe. Chicago: University of Chicago Press, 2006.
> Treatises excerpted here include her meditation on the Lord's Prayer (a subsection of "The Miserere Psalm . . ." [1558], 123-73) and her 1553 letter, "To Sir Caspar Schwenckfeld," 180-215.

———. *Katharina Schütz Zell*, vol. 1: *The Life and Thought of a Sixteenth-Century Reformer* and vol. 2: *The Writings: A Critical Edition*. Edited by Elsie Anne McKee. Leiden: Brill, 1999.

Zwingli, Huldrych. *Farrago Annotationum in Genesin*. Zurich: Christoph Froschauer, 1527.
> Digital copy (1527) online at http://dx.doi.org/10.3931/e-rara-1788. Modern edition (1944), used here, in ZSW 13.

Other Reformation-era Works Cited or Consulted

Fagius, Paul. *Thargum, Hoc Est, Paraphrasis Onkeli Chaldaica In Sacra Biblia*. Strasbourg: Machaeropoeus, 1546.

Digital copy online at http://diglib.hab.de/drucke/b-92-2f-helmst-1/start.htm. For ET, see *Targum Neofiti 1: Genesis* and *Targum Pseudo-Jonathan: Genesis.* The Aramaic Bible, vols. 1A and 1B. Collegeville, MN: Liturgical Press, 1992.

Lyra, Nicholas. *Biblia Sacra cvm Glossis, Interlineari & Ordinaria, Nicolai Lyrani Postilla & Moralitatibus, Burgensis Additionibus, & Thoringi Replicis.* 5 vols. Lyons: [Gaspard Trechsel], 1545. Digital copy online at http://www.mdz-nbn-resolving.de/urn/resolver.pl?urn=urn:nbn:de:bvb:12-bsb10141268-3.

Marlorat, Augustin. *Genesis cum Catholica Expositione Ecclesiastica.* Morges: Jean Le Preux and Eustache Vignon, 1584.
Digital copy online at http://dx.doi.org/10.3931/e-rara-2581.

Mercier, Jean [Johannes Mercerus]. *In Genesin, Primum Mosis Librum sic a Graecis Appellatum, Commentarius.* Geneva: Matthaeus Berjon, 1598.
Digital copy online at http://www.mdz-nbn-resolving.de/urn/resolver.pl?urn=urn:nbn:de:bvb:12-bsb10142891-3.

Münster, Sebastian. *En Tibi Lector Hebraica Biblia Latina planeque noua Sebast. Mvnsteri tralatione.* Basel: Johann Bebel, 1534.
Digital copy online at http://www.mdz-nbn-resolving.de/urn/resolver.pl?urn=urn:nbn:de:bvb:12-bsb10141282-1.

Pererius, Benedict. *Prior tomus Commentariorum et Disputationum in Genesim: continens historiam Mosis ab exordio mundi vsq[ue] ad Noëticum diluuium.* Lyons: Officina Iuntarum, 1594[-1600].
The first volume of Pererius's four-volume commentary. Digital copy online at Google Books.

Zanchi, Jerome. *De operibus Dei intra spacium sex dierum creatis opus.* Neustadt: Matthaeus Harnisius, 1591.
Digital copy online at http://www.mdz-nbn-resolving.de/urn/resolver.pl?urn=urn:nbn:de:bvb:12-bsb10142564-2.

For Further Reading

Other English-Language Exegetical Literature of the Reformation Era, to 1700
It would require a lengthy inventory to list not only the fifty or so commentaries on Genesis that appeared in the sixteenth century but also the numerous sermons; lengthier still would be a list of all the exegetical works produced in the century that followed. The following bibliography is restricted to works now available in English, and it therefore naturally favors Anglican and Puritan writers. Nonetheless, continental writers continue to find their way into English, as the recent translations of Calvin and Herberger (below) attest. For a regularly updated account of English-language commentary literature before 1700, see http://purl.oclc.org/net/jlt/exegesis.

Ainsworth, Henry. *Annotations upon the first book of Moses, called Genesis.* [Amsterdam], 1616. STC[2] 210.

Babington, Gervase. *Certain Plaine, Brief, and Comfortable Notes, upon Every Chapter of Genesis.* London, 1592. STC[2] 1086-88.

Brewer, Thomas. *A discovery of Adam's three-fold estate in paradise, viz. moral, legal, and evangelical.* London, 1656. In Wing A4429.

Calvin, John. *Sermons on Genesis: Chapters 1:1–11:4.* Translated by Rob Roy McGregor. Edinburgh: Banner of Truth, 2009.

Donne, John. *Two sermons preached before King Charles, upon the xxvi verse of the first chapter of Genesis.* Cambridge, 1634. STC² 7058.

Herberger, Valerius (d. 1627). *The Great Works of God or Jesus, Parts One and Two: The Mysteries of Christ in The Book of Genesis, Chapters 1–15.* Translated by Matthew Carver. St. Louis: Concordia, 2010.

Hooker, Thomas. *The saints guide in three treatises: I. the mirror of mercie, on Gen. 6.13. . . .* London, 1645. Wing H2655.

Hughes, George. *An analytical exposition of the whole first book of Moses, called Genesis, and of XXIII chap. of his second book, called Exodus.* [N.p.], 1672. Wing H3305.

Hunnis, William. *Hunnies recreations: conteining . . . discourses, intituled Adams Banishment: Christ his crib. The lost sheepe. The complaint of old age. . . . The creation or first weeke. The life and death of Ioseph.* Cambridge, 1595. STC² 13973.

Kidder, Richard. *A commentary on the five books of Moses.* London, 1694. Wing K399.

Lightfoot, John. *A few and new observations upon the booke of Genesis.* London, 1642. Wing L2054.

Needler, Benjamin. *Expository notes, with practical observations; towards the opening of the five first chapters of the first book of Moses called Genesis.* London, 1654. Wing N412.

Patrick, Simon. *A commentary upon the first book of Moses, called Genesis.* London, 1695. Wing P772.

Pettus, John. *Volatiles from the history of Adam and Eve containing many unquestioned truths and allowable notions of several natures.* London, 1674. Wing P1912.

Poole, Matthew. *Annotations upon the Holy Bible.* London: John Richardson, 1683. Wing P2820.

Richardson, John. *Observations . . . upon the whole book of Genesis.* London, 1655. Wing R1385.

Trapp, John. *A clavis to the Bible: Or, A new comment upon the Pentateuch: or five books of Moses.* London, 1649. Wing T2038.

Whately, William. *Prototypes, or, The primarie precedent presidents out of the booke of Genesis.* London, 1640. STC² 25317.

Wright, Abraham. *A practical commentary or exposition upon the Pentateuch.* London, 1662. Wing W3688.

General Studies of Genesis in the Era of the Reformation

The abundance of Reformation-era exegetical literature is paralleled by an ever-growing number of historical and theological studies of the history of biblical interpretation in this era. The following selection of titles is restricted to English works that focus on Genesis or some aspect of Genesis 1–11.

Kolb, Robert. "Sixteenth-Century Lutheran Commentary on Genesis and the Genesis Commentary of Martin Luther." In *Théorie et pratique de l'exégèse,* ed. Irena Backus and Francis Higman, 243-58. Geneva: Droz, 1990.

Lane, Anthony N. S. "The Sources of the Citations in Calvin's Genesis Commentary." In idem, *John Calvin: Student of the Church Fathers,* 205-59. Edinburgh: T&T Clark, 1999.

Maxfield, John A. *Luther's Lectures on Genesis and the Formation of Evangelical Identity.* Kirksville, MO: Truman State University Press, 2008.

Puckett, David L. *John Calvin's Exegesis of the Old Testament.* Louisville: Westminster John Knox, 1995.

Robbins, Frank Egleston. *The Hexaemeral Literature: A Study of the Greek and Latin Commentaries on Genesis.* Chicago: University of Chicago Press, 1912.

Williams, Arnold. *The Common Expositor: An Account of the Commentaries on Genesis, 1527–1633.* Chapel Hill: University of North Carolina Press, 1948.

Zachman, Randall C. "Calvin as Commentator on Genesis." In *Calvin and the Bible,* edited by Donald C. McKim, 1-29. New York: Cambridge University Press, 2006.

Special Studies of Adam and Eve (Genesis 1–3)

Crowther, Kathleen M. *Adam and Eve in the Protestant Reformation.* New York: Cambridge University Press, 2010.

Mattox, Mickey Leland. *"Defender of the Most Holy Matriarchs": Martin Luther's Interpretation of the Women of Genesis in the "Enarrationes in Genesin," 1535-1545.* Leiden: Brill, 2003. [Chapters 1, 2]

Thompson, John L. *John Calvin and the Daughters of Sarah: Women in Regular and Exceptional Roles in the Exegesis of Calvin, His Predecessors, and His Contemporaries.* Geneva: Droz, 1992. [Chapters 2, 3]

———. *Reading the Bible with the Dead: What You Can Learn from the History of Exegesis That You Can't Learn from Exegesis Alone.* Grand Rapids: Eerdmans, 2007. [Chapters 4, 8]

Special Studies of Noah and the Flood (Genesis 6–9)

Allen, Don Cameron. *The Legend of Noah: Renaissance Rationalism in Art, Science and Letters.* Urbana: University of Illinois Press, 1963.

Cohn, Norman. *Noah's Flood: The Genesis Story in Western Thought.* New Haven: Yale University Press, 1996.

Pleins, J. David. *When the Great Abyss Opened: Classic and Contemporary Readings of Noah's Flood.* New York: Oxford University Press, 2003.

Special Studies of Noah's Drunkenness and the Curse on Ham (Genesis 9)

Haynes, Stephen R. *Noah's Curse: The Biblical Justification of American Slavery.* New York: Oxford University Press, 2002.

Steinmetz, David C. "Luther and the Drunkenness of Noah." In *Luther in Context,* pp. 98-111. Bloomington: Indiana University Press, 1986.

Whitford, David M. *The Curse of Ham in the Early Modern Era: The Bible and the Justifications for Slavery.* Burlington, VT: Ashgate, 2009.

Author Index

Subject Index

Scripture Index